The Marble House in Second Street

The Marble House in Second Street

BIOGRAPHY OF A TOWN HOUSE

AND ITS OCCUPANTS

1825–2000

A HISTORIC STRUCTURE REPORT

Prepared by

JOHN G. WAITE ASSOCIATES,

ARCHITECTS, PLLC

ALBANY, NY

With essays by

DOUGLAS G. BUCHER,

STACY POMEROY DRAPER, AND

WALTER RICHARD WHEELER

RENSSELAER COUNTY HISTORICAL SOCIETY

TROY · NEW YORK

2000

We acknowledge the assistance of the New York State Office of Parks, Recreation and Historic Preservation and the Natural Heritage Trust in the preparation and funding of this publication.

The publication of this book would not have been possible without the generous support of FURTHERMORE, the publication program of The J. M. Kaplan Fund

RENSSELAER COUNTY HISTORICAL SOCIETY
59 Second Street, Troy, New York 12180

Donna J. Hassler, *Director*
Stacy Pomeroy Draper, *Curator*
Kathryn T. Sheehan, *Registrar*

JOHN G. WAITE ASSOCIATES, ARCHITECTS, PLLC
384 Broadway, Albany, New York 12207

John G. Waite, *Senior Principal*
Douglas G. Bucher, *Project Manager*
William P. Palmer
Lee Pinckney
Donna S. Spriggs
Grace Jukes
Frederick D. Cawley, *Editor*
Walter Richard Wheeler, *Consultant*

FRONTISPIECE 59 Second Street Front Door, pen and ink, Sanford Cluett, c. 1925.

FRONT COVER PHOTO 59 Second Street, c. 1900.
BACKGROUND Detail, HABS Sheet 4

BACK COVER PHOTOS
TOP ROW Richard P. and Betsey Howard Hart, first owners of 59 Second Street.
MIDDLE ROW George B. and Amanda R. Cluett, second owners of 59 Second Street.
BOTTOM ROW Albert E. and Caroline I. Cluett, third owners of 59 Second Street.

Dedicated to the

HART & CLUETT FAMILIES

*who lived at 59 Second Street for 135 years,
and to their descendants, who continue to support the
Rensselaer County Historical Society
in its efforts to preserve the house and its history.*

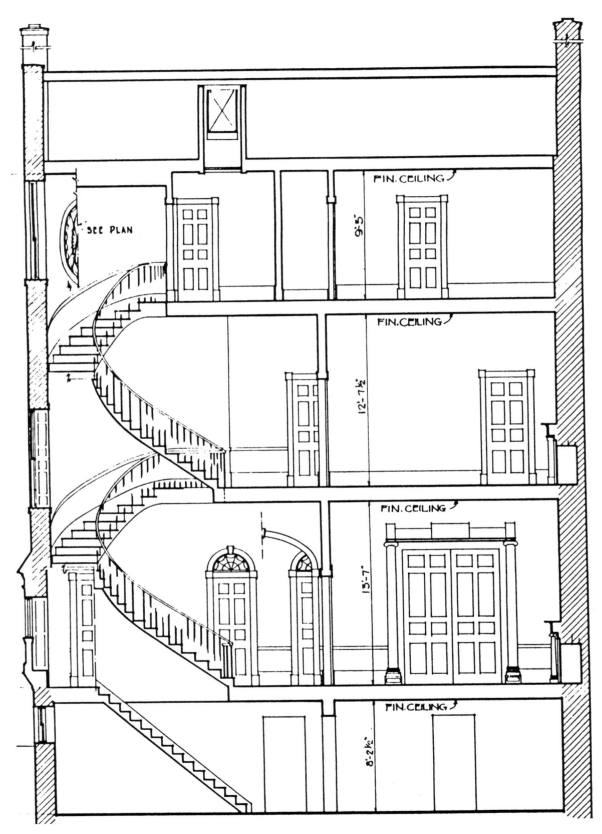

FIN. CEILING

SEE PLAN

9'-5"

FIN. CEILING

12'-7½"

FIN. CEILING

15'-7"

FIN. CEILING

8'-2½"

Detail, HABS Sheet 3.

Contents

Preface

IT RARELY HAPPENS that one of a city's supremely fine buildings is also an architectural pioneer in a much larger geographical context, and is amply and illuminatingly documented. It is rarer still to find such a landmark in the permanent, enlightened stewardship of an owner devoted to its preservation in the public interest. To the extraordinary good fortune of the people of Troy and Rensselaer County, New York, and indeed of all who respond to excellence in art and design as an amenity of urban life, such is the case at 59 Second Street, Troy.

Since 1953 the Hart-Cluett Mansion has been the sumptuous white marble flagship of the Rensselaer County Historical Society. It is now the subject of this eloquent, lucid and comforting book—one that deserves a wide and appreciative audience. The volume is part biography of a city seen through the lens of one building, its origins, furnishings and its occupants; part detective story, persuasively distilling the results of prodigious research and weighing circumstantial evidence when the documentary evidence is absent; and part a lost chapter in the annals of New York City's rise to preeminence. Just as we are lucky to have the "marble house in Second Street" come down to us essentially intact after 175 years, so we are lucky to have this scholarly but readable and splendidly illustrated account, to encourage interest in our built heritage and in the magnificent chronicle of people and places of the Hudson River Valley from the foot of Manhattan to the head of the great estuary at Troy.

That is what the Rensselaer County Historical Society and their research/writing team have given us. Like the house itself as of yore, this book's contents gleam and sparkle in one's mind, and brighten the street that leads us onward to a more enlightened age. The recent munificent grant by the state of New York toward the restoration of the house lifts the hearts and speeds us on our way.

John Winthrop Aldrich
Deputy Commissioner for Historic Preservation
New York State Office of Parks, Recreation
and Historic Preservation

The Hart-Cluett Mansion: A Unique Museum Story

Donna J. Hassler

HISTORIC HOUSE MUSEUMS have unique stories to tell about the people who created buildings for domestic use as well as the people who lived and worked within their walls. The story of the Hart-Cluett Mansion, opened to the public by the Rensselaer County Historical Society in 1953, is being told for the first time in printed form in this comprehensive publication. *The Marble House in Second Street: Biography of a Town House and Its Occupants, 1825–2000,* contains new and exciting information recently discovered about the architect of the Mansion and estate matters of the Hart family, which has greatly illuminated the rich material collected on the building and its occupants over the years. Through a wealth of illustrations, many of which have never been published before, a detailed picture of nearly two centuries of life in Troy as it relates to the history of the Hart-Cluett Mansion is clearly discernible. The story reaches beyond the confines of Troy, however, and reveals a previously unrecognized and fascinating connection with established New York City patrons, architects, and artisans. Indeed, a convincing argument is made in this publication that certain nineteenth century architectural design elements of the American Federal-style are found for the first time in the *Marble House in Second Street*, before they appear in later buildings in New York and Albany. On the National Register of Historic Places since 1973, and within the Central Troy Historic District, the Hart-Cluett Mansion's important place in the history of American architecture and the socio-economic development of this country will be reconfirmed through the pages of this book.

The authors of *The Marble House in Second Street*—Douglas G. Bucher with John G. Waite Associates, Architects, PLLC; Stacy Pomeroy Draper, Curator, Rensselaer County Historical Society; and Walter Richard Wheeler, independent architectural historian—have spent close to two decades gathering information that has brought a new understanding and appreciation for the significance of the building and its occupants. Frederick D. Cawley, the book's editor, had the enormous task of bringing all the written material together in a cohesive manner; while Christopher Kuntze, the book's designer, skillfully arranged the text and photographs as well as coordinated the details of production.

The Marble House in Second Street: Biography of a Town House and Its Occupants, 1825–2000, was generously funded with grants from the State of New York through the support of Senate Majority Leader, Joseph L. Bruno; from Furthermore, the publication program of the J. M. Kaplan Fund; and from Mrs. Catherine J. Bell. It is the Rensselaer County Historic Society's vision that this groundbreaking publication will be the first of many such educational endeavors that promote broad public participation and interest in the history of Rensselaer County and its place in the region, state and nation.

59 Second Street, ca. 1892

The Marble House in Second Street:
Biography of a Town House and its Occupants, 1825–2000

FROM ITS COMPLETION in 1827, the house at 59 Second Street was recognized as something unique for Troy and the surrounding area. Referred to as the "marble house in Second Street" in the obituary of its builder John Colegrove, the initial impression of the elegantly detailed white marble façade reveals a house unlike any other in the region. An account of the sale of the house in 1893 referred to it as the most valuable property in the city. In the twentieth century, the building's significance was recognized by the Historic American Buildings Survey in 1934 when it was included in that ambitious project to document American architecture. Recognizing the importance of the house, Albert and Caroline Cluett made a gift of the building to the Rensselaer County Historical Society and in 1953 it became accessible to a wider public. Not until recently, however, has it become clear that the Hart-Cluett House (this name recognizes the original private owners) has an even greater significance in American architectural history.

This study originated in the mid-1970s through the encouragement of Breffny A. Walsh, then director of the Rensselaer County Historical Society (RCHS) and the architectural interests of Douglas Bucher, one of the authors of this monograph. At that time the intent was to produce a guidebook to the house and some of the more significant collections. The author's ongoing research into the work of Albany architect Philip Hooker proved useful since a tradition traced back to the 1920s indicated that Hooker was the designer of the house. While living in the building for two and a half years and studying its details, Bucher determined that the involvement of Hooker was unlikely since the architectural character of the exterior did not coincide with the architect's work in the 1820s. A more probable scenario pointed to the involvement of an unidentified architect in New York City where many of the same architectural details were found. Ironically more recent research has revealed a connection to Hooker via the woodcarver

Henry Farnham; a complex tale that will be revealed in this monograph.

With the discovery by John Polnak, then education director for RCHS, of Richard P. Hart's inventory and the subsequent finding of John Colegrove's obituary and a newspaper article referring to the delivery of marble in Troy for William Howard, father of Betsey Howard Hart, it became increasingly clear that more research was needed to fully comprehend the history and significance of the Hart-Cluett House and its place in the history of American domestic architecture.

What follows in this study is the biography of a house and the many significant people who were involved in its construction and who lived within its walls over the past one hundred and seventy-five years. The cast of characters includes a New York merchant and banker and his wife, an architect whose significance has been overlooked, an entrepreneur responsible for the early growth and significance of Troy, a woman said to be one of the wealthiest in America in the mid-nineteenth century, men involved in the growth of the collar and shirt industry in Troy as well as a husband and wife who insured the preservation of the house for future generations.

The Hart-Cluett House was well documented with several sets of interior and exterior photographs taken at various periods, a colorful reminiscence written by one of the Hart grandchildren which included a detailed description of the house and grounds in 1855, and a Hart family history entitled *Furnace Grove, 1858–1958, The Story of a Family Home* that included important information concerning family members. In the early 1980s gifts of Amanda Cluett's Diary (1900–1917) and other documentation, received as part of an oral history project with Cluett family members, provided information on the twentieth century history of the house.

Clearly the most fortuitous event was the discovery of ten trunks full of papers relating to the house and family during the years of Betsey Hart's widowhood, uncovered in the mid-1980s in storage at the Troy Savings Bank building. One of the very first items to come to light was a detailed room-by-room estate inventory done at Betsey Hart's death in 1886. This hand-written document immediately brought to life the Hart era photographs in the Society's collection. What are now called the Hart Papers were deposited at RCHS in 1987. For several months, thanks in part to a grant (originally intended for the production of the guidebook) from the New York State Council on the Arts, RCHS curator Stacy Pomeroy Draper, one of the authors of this monograph, was able to organize the thousands of bills and other documents which detailed the expenditures at the house from 1844 to 1892.

This material revealed the wide range of goods and services Betsey Hart purchased in Troy and in New York City as well as her other involvements in the two cities. She patronized all of the best shops and cabinetmakers in Troy and New York over a period of more than forty years and was extensively involved in real estate in both cities. It rapidly became clear that the perspective on the house and its importance needed to be broadened to include this strong connection to New York City and the ramifications of these patterns of consumption and taste. Also included in the papers were documents on the earlier business dealings of Richard Hart, providing evidence for the setting in which the house was built in 1826–27. Together, these documents supplied the information needed to better understand the evolution of the house, its furnishings and its decoration. Subsequent research in New York City by Walter Richard Wheeler, the third author of this monograph, has shown new connections and helped to identify Martin E. Thompson as the likely architect of the Hart-Cluett House. Through his research a more complete picture of Thompson's professional career than has heretofore been possible is revealed.

Particularly timely have been the visits of several scholars from the Metropolitan Museum of Art who have been examining the influence of New York City artisans for the exhibit *Art and the Empire City: New York, 1825–1861* at The Metropolitan Museum Art on New York City from 1825 to 1861. Clearly the Hart Papers, the surviving artifacts and the Hart-Cluett House itself help with this reappraisal of New York City's evolving role as arbiter of culture in the early years of the Republic.

With this wealth of material at hand a more intensive study of the building began in the mid-1990s, with many evenings spent probing each room and every surface, assembling the descriptive material needed for a full historic structure report. This document would include a complete history of the house, its construction, evolution and physical condition as well as the story of its occupants and the Rensselaer County Historical Society. The historic structure report would serve as the first step in the preparation and implementation of a comprehensive program for the restoration and long-term preservation of the house. The resulting document is essentially a biography of the house and site.

RCHS had occupied 59 Second Street since 1953, but beginning in the early 1980s much of the Society's energy was focused on the much needed repair and restoration of the adjacent Carr Building acquired in 1978 to house a meeting room, exhibit galleries, and a research library. During this period the Hart-Cluett House began to show serious signs of deterioration. The House Committee and subsequently the Board of the Rensselaer County Historical Society were alerted to the need to care for and restore the Hart-Cluett House before further problems surfaced. The necessity for a historic structure report as a planning and fundraising tool became clear to one and all. John G. Waite Associates, Architects, were engaged to coordinate the completion of the historic structure report which included an assessment of the condition of the house and recommendations for conservation and restoration. All of these resources have come together to produce this complex document which is the story of a remarkable house in Troy, New York, that ultimately provided the basis for an important aesthetic trend that flourished in New York City. With this monograph the "marble house in Second Street," with its rich architectural and social history and wealth of documentation, is revealed to a national audience, achieving the recognition it deserves.

DOUGLAS G. BUCHER
JOHN G. WAITE ASSOCIATES,
ARCHITECTS

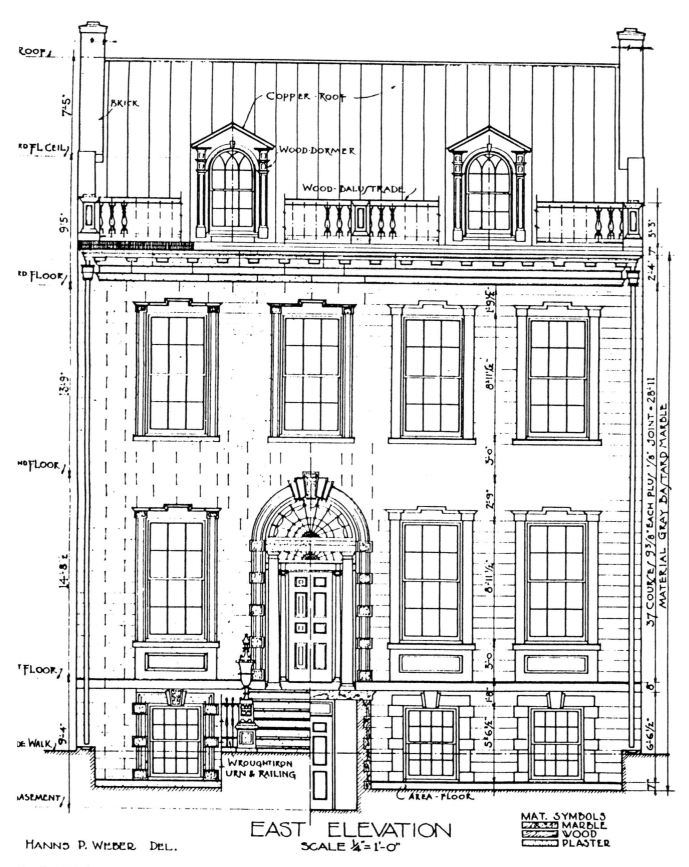

ROOF

7'5"

RD FL CEIL

9'5"

RD FLOOR

13'9"

ND FLOOR

14'8½"

T FLOOR

9'4"

DE WALK

ASEMENT

BRICK

COPPER ROOF

WOOD DORMER

WOOD BALUSTRADE

1'9½"

8'11½"

5'0"

2'9"

8'11½"

5'0"

5'6½"

2'4' 7' 5'5"

37 COURSE 9⅝" EACH PLUS ⅛" JOINT = 28'11"

MATERIAL GRAY BASTARD MARBLE

WROUGHT IRON
URN & RAILING

AREA FLOOR

EAST ELEVATION
SCALE ¼" = 1'-0"

HANNS P. WEBER DEL.

MAT. SYMBOLS

MARBLE
WOOD
PLASTER

Detail, HABS Sheet 2.

59 Second Street as recorded in a detail of Fig. 119, c. 1890

History of 59 Second Street and Its Surroundings

Stacy Pomeroy Draper

Troy—From Its Founding to 1830

AFTER THE American Revolution, the community that became the City of Troy began expanding along the flood plain on the east side of the Hudson River about five miles above Albany, New York. Division of farm lands along the Hudson River known as the Middle Farm, owned by Jacob D. Vanderheyden, took place in 1787 dividing the property into a grid of town lots 50 feet wide by 130 feet deep and subdivided by service alleys.[1] By the fall of 1787, the village was known as "Vanderheyden" in honor of the original owner of the land. In 1789, the name was changed to "Troy," influenced by the many New England settlers coming west and the current taste for things classical (see Fig. 1). These New Englanders "of restless spirit and even roving mind, had, in 1790 . . . in search of wealth, braved the dangers of the wilderness, left the homes of their fathers on the bleak hills of New England, boldly pursued their fortunes into the 'west,' as the valley of the Hudson was then called, and had built some dozen dwellings and a half a dozen small store houses along the margin of the river."[2] Building first near Ashley's Ferry, the community rapidly expanded to the east, north, and south. Competition with New City (Lansingburgh), the community to the north of Troy proper which had been established in 1771, ended with establishment of the county seat in Troy in 1793 by act of the New York State Legislature and removal of a number of businessmen, like George Tibbits, from Lansingburgh to Troy during the first decade of the nineteenth century. In 1794, the residents of Troy incorporated as a village through an act of the New York State Legislature with seven trustees elected on the second Tuesday in May each year. At the same time, a president was elected for the year from among the trustees.

The key to Troy's rapid growth and economic success was its location at the head of navigable waters on the Hudson River and its access to water power (the Wynantskill, Poestenkill, and Piscawenkill creeks) which had been harnessed by the late seventeenth century to operate mills. Grain products and lumber were the two main commodities at the beginning of the nineteenth century. These raw materials were received in warehouses on River Street and transported down river (see Fig. 2). Pot and pearl ashes were also brought to Troy in large quantities from Vermont and northern New York as were dairy products like butter and cheese.[3] Trade was carried on by a system of barter during these early years. There was little or no capital, no banks, and produce brought to market was "received in store to be shipped to New York (City), and sold for the account of the owners."[4] By the end of 1800, according

To the Public.

THIS evening the Freeholders of the place lately known by VANDER HEYDEN'S or ASHLEY'S-FERRY, situate on the east bank of Hudson's-river, about seven miles above Albany, met for the purpose of establishing a name for the said place; when, by a majority of voices, IT WAS CONFIRMED, that in future, it should be called and known by the name of

TROY.

From its present improved state, and the more pleasing prospect of its popularity, arising from the natural advantages in the Mercantile Line, it may not be too sanguine to expect, at no very distant period, to see TROY, as famous for her Trade and Navigation as many of our first towns.
Troy, 5th January, 1789.   3w

1 Notice of name change to Troy, 1789, from *Troy's One Hundred Years*, Arthur J. Weise, 1890.

2 View of Troy from Mt. Ida (*Mt. Olympus*), print, c. 1825.

to the *Northern Budget*, the village of Troy contained over 1,800 inhabitants.[5] Troy's first financial institution, the Farmers' Bank, was established in 1801. Construction of the first road to help farmers west of the Hudson bring their produce to Troy took place in 1802 with the establishment of the Troy & Schenectady Turnpike. "The expense of first opening the road west was then quite an onerous one, and drew heavily upon their spare resources. The whole expenditure for the first three miles out was raised and paid for by the subscriptions of those interested in trade at the village, but this improvement amply repaid them for the outlay and returned its cost in a few years, while great subsequent remuneration came with the increased trade diverted from Albany to this point."[6]

This was the situation when Richard P. Hart (1780–1843) permanently settled in Troy, circa 1806 (see Fig. 3). He made use of the economic system as it existed to trade grain and lumber, investing his profits in land and manufacturing. By 1806, Troy's population had grown to almost 3,000. Only seven years later, the *Gazeteer of New York State* (1813) noted that

the village (of Troy), is laid out into streets and squares, and contains 660 houses and stores (540 dwellings, 120 stores), 5 houses of worship, 2 banks, the court-house and prison for the county, a market-house, and many other buildings. A large proportion of the houses are wood, but many of them are large and elegant, as are also those built of brick, which form a considerable number of the whole. . . . In wealth and trade, Troy takes the third rank in the state among its populous towns.[7]

Among other ventures that grew out of the expansion of the community, Richard Hart was a partner in the Conduit Company of Troy (established 1814) to lay cast-iron pipes made in Salisbury, Connecticut, for conducting water to the village from the small reservoir on the stream created by the spring on Hollow Road (now Spring Avenue). Water had been piped with earthen aqueducts as early as 1806 and sold to Troy residents for domestic use.[8]

The impact of the War of 1812 was felt throughout the region. Beginning almost immediately after the Revolution, Britain continually annoyed the new United States at sea by disrupting trade and impressing American sailors into the British navy. After 1803 when France, under Napoleon, and England went to war, the United

3 Richard P. Hart, watercolor on ivory, signed "Blanchet," c. 1815.

1810 with Napoleon's repeal of the "Decrees," but conflict with Britain finally became full-fledged war in 1812. "The industry and enterprise of the country was forced into new channels, and developed new resources."[10] Initial resistance to the war with Britain can be seen in a letter circulated and signed by many key Troy residents, including Richard Hart.[11] This resistance soon faded as much of the early action of the war caused troops to come through Troy and Albany on their way north and west (see Fig. 4). In addition to providing troops for the Army of the North, Troy merchants supplied the Army with provisions.[12] Business responded creatively and expanded in some areas, but manufacturing, textile manufacturing in particular, was dealt a blow after the war ended by resumption of trade with Britain. This resulted in an economic downturn in 1816–1817.[13] At the same time, Troy was doing well enough to incorporate as a city in 1816, having grown to a population of 5,000[14] (see Fig. 5).

Beginning in 1815 with a public meeting in New York City which resulted in the appointment of a committee to obtain the passage of an act of the New York State Legislature for the construction of two canals from the Hudson River, one to Lake Champlain and one to Lake Erie, citizens of Troy worked to get the canals built.[15] The Erie Canal opened on October 8, 1823. While Albany was celebrating the opening of the canal that day, the first boat to go west, much to the chagrin of Albany and Lansingburgh merchants, was the "Trojan Trader,"

States tried to maintain a position of neutrality. Both England and France issued orders that effectively blockaded the other country's commerce with outsiders. By 1807, the United States had issued its own embargo on France and England, causing further damage to American businesses.[9] Commerce with France resumed in

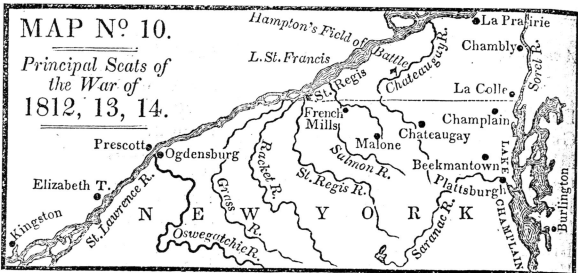

4 Map 10, The Principal Seats of the War of 1812, 13, 14, woodcut, *Abridged History of the United States*, Emma Willard, 1846. This map shows the northern theater of the War of 1812. Troy was a staging area for troops and supplies heading north and west into the area shown here.

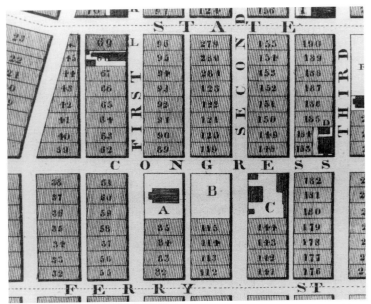

5 Detail, *Map of the City of Troy from Actual Survey of John Klein*, engraved by C. Wright, Albany, 1818. The grid of the original 1789 plan had been expanded to accomodate the rapid development of the city in the early nineteenth century. Seen is the area immediately around what would become 59 Second Street, located next to the top of the "S" on Second (Street).

loaded with goods from Troy. This was considered typical of the get-ahead style of Troy in general.[16] The 1824 *Gazeteer of New York State* noted that "as a manufacturing town Troy has very commanding advantages compared with most others enjoying the like commercial facilities. The Poesten Kill and Wynants Kill . . . are tolerable-sized millstreams, on each of which there are near 200 feet fall. . . . Among the manufacturing establishments of this town, the Troy Iron and Nail Factory claims distinguished notice. . . . There is another nail factory, and rolling and slitting works a little below this. . . . [T]hese two establishments will soon use 1,300 tons of iron a year."[17] The *Gazeteer* goes on to notice textile mills, stoneware manufacturing, tanning and currying of leather, millstone manufactories, and two furnaces making patent ploughs.

The second quarter of the nineteenth century saw the rise of industry over commercial activity as the basis of Troy's economy.[18] This was furthered by the establishment in 1824 of the Rensselaer School (later the Rensselaer Polytechnic Institute) which Stephen Van Rensselaer and others founded "for teaching the physical sciences with their application to the arts of life."[19] Transportation of goods was a major issue at this time

with a great deal of attention given to the new technology of steam power. Steamboat travel became possible after 1820. As soon as Chief Justice Marshall declared the monopoly of the North River Steamboat Company illegal in 1824, the Troy Steamboat Company was formed with its steamboat, *Chief Justice Marshall* named in honor of the Chief Justice who had opened up river transportation with his ruling[20] (see Fig. 6). The opening of the Erie Canal, and subsequently the Champlain Canal, positioned Troy for greater expansion. By 1825 the population of Troy had grown to almost 8,000.[21] In 1827, the same year that Richard and Betsey Hart occupied their new house, "the growth of the city was advanced by the erection of 330 buildings. The business of the year exceeded that of all previous years. The flouring mills ground 94,385 barrels of flour and one provision-house packed 3,800 barrels of pork." The year 1827 also saw George M. Tibbits, Alsop Weed, Nathan Warren and others petition the New York State Legislature to incorporate the Troy & Bennington Turnpike Company. The turnpike (now Route 7) which they proposed did not become feasible until passage of an act in the New York State Legislature in 1831 authorized the Troy & Bennington Turnpike and Railroad Company to construct a turnpike and also, eventually, a railroad between the two communities.[22] This period saw intense competition between Albany and Troy for land and water transportation routes. In 1832, to prevent a monopoly by the Mohawk & Hudson Railroad that ran from Albany to Schenectady, a group of Trojans got together and petitioned the Legislature to establish the Rensselaer & Saratoga Railroad Company.

6 Detail, Staffordshire dish with scene of the *Chief Justice Marshall* steamboat operated by the Troy Steamboat Company, c. 1825.

Construction began in the same year and in October, 1835, the first passenger train ran on the line.[23] After several years, directors of the Rensselaer & Saratoga Railroad Company managed to gain control of the rival Schenectady & Saratoga Railroad Company and soon had through lines to Saratoga for both freight and passengers.

A brief setback in Troy's growth occurred on the afternoon of June 20, 1820. A stable in the rear of Col. John Davis' residence, on the west side of First Street, north of Congress Street, caught fire. By the time the rapidly spreading fire was put out ninety buildings on First, State and River streets were destroyed, including a six-story wooden warehouse building owned by Richard Hart at 205 River Street which housed his business office.[24] Losses were estimated at $700,000. Contributions from other towns and cities of over $14,000 helped to start the rebuilding of the devastated area. One of the lasting results of the fire was changes in the laws of the city regarding use of brick instead of wood for buildings. The prospering city saw many improvements. The first use of lamps to light the city streets at night was in December 1826 when River Street was lit from Washington Street to Hoosick Street.[25] In 1829 the first city directory was published when the population was 10,840. This also necessitated the numbering of houses.[26] A fine, new classically inspired court house began construction in 1827. A public market at the northwest corner of Third and State streets was established in 1828.

The Harts and Howards at 59 Second Street

Richard P. Hart (1780–1843) was raised in a large Quaker family from Hart's Village in Dutchess County near Millbrook, about twenty miles east of Poughkeepsie. The family arrived there around 1760 from New England, following what is now a well-documented Quaker migration west from the coastal cities. Richard's father, Philip Hart, had many agricultural interests, primarily as a farmer and grist mill owner. Through the marriage of Richard Hart's sister, Mary, Richard was related to Jacob Merritt, and the Merritt family who had a role to play in Troy's commercial development and Richard Hart's business career.[27] Richard Hart came to Troy around 1802 and worked for Daniel and Isaac Merritt who had one of the earliest commercial houses in the village.[28] In 1803, he became a partner of Benjamin

Merritt at White Creek, New York, in Washington County, where he stayed for about three years. He returned to Troy in 1806 where he joined another commercial house and soon became its head.[29] Despite his initial reluctance to join the war effort, during the War of 1812 he was a contractor for supplying the Northern Department of the Army and the naval force on Lake Champlain.[30] After the war he became involved in textile manufacturing in addition to his commercial activities. He owned extensive textile mill property in Hart's Falls, now Schaghticoke, New York.[31] He was a member of the New York State Assembly (1821) and Mayor of Troy in 1836–1837. Richard Hart owned extensive property in Troy and on the western side of the Hudson River, some of which was sold to the Erie Canal.[32] He was a founder of several Troy banks including the Bank of Troy (founded 1811) and Troy Savings Bank (founded 1823), Troy's second and third banks respectively[33] (see Fig. 7). He invested in the Erie Canal, steam boats and the early railroad system and actively supported the educational institutions in the city, including Emma Willard's Troy Female Seminary where he was a member of the building committee, the Rensselaer School (later Rensselaer Polytechnic Institute) and the Troy Orphan Asylum, of which he was a founding member (see Fig. 8). One of his obituaries noted that he "was self-educated . . . [and] as an accountant and financier . . . was highly gifted. . . . His education among the Friends (Quakers) probably influenced his taste for simplicity in dress and appearance; and his ample fortune never produced in him anything like ostentation."[34]

Richard P. Hart married three times; first in 1800 to Phebe Bloom of Clinton, Dutchess County, New York (with whom he had a daughter, Phebe, who died in 1813), second in 1805 to Delia Maria Dole of Hudson, New York, who died the same year, and finally in 1816 to Betsey Amelia Howard of New York City (1798–1886), with whom he had 14 children (see Genealogy chart, Appendix IA). Betsey's father William Howard was Richard P. Hart's first cousin.[35] While none of Richard Hart's personal papers or diaries have come to light to date, some sense of his home life after 1835 can be seen in the letter books that are part of the Hart Papers. Although these documents generally deal with his business affairs, occasionally there are glimpses of daily life and the ups and downs of such a large family.[36]

John Woodworth noted in his *Reminiscences of Troy* (1860) that "Troy had in three of its Citizens an

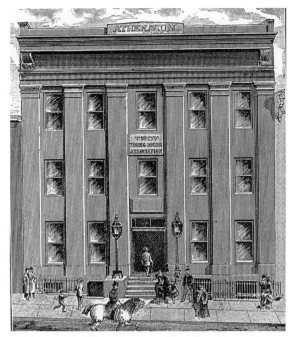

7 Atheneum Building, First Street, Troy, from *Troy and Vicinity,* Arthur J. Weise, 1876. This was the second building of the Troy Savings Bank. No image of the first building has survived.

Influence and Efficiency in great Emergencies, such as no other City could boast. . . . They were Richard P. Hart, Stephen Warren, George Tibbits; each great in a particular Sphere, and neither adapted to fill the Position occupied by the other; but when acting in concert, as they generally did, they presented a Power and an Influence, the Benefits of which have left their Impress, those wise Measures that have contributed so largely to make Troy what she is."[37] Hart was involved in most of the major enterprises that laid the groundwork for Troy's rise, first as a commercial power and then as an industrial center to be contended with in the mid- and later nineteenth century. It appears that he was generally content to act behind the scenes but it is also clear that his opinion was respected within the community and beyond. Although not much is known about his one term in the New York State Legislature in 1821, the political positions he took or the issues he was for or against, more is known about his term as mayor of Troy from 1836 to 1837.[38] It was during his mayoralty that a riot occurred on St. Patrick's Day, 1837, part of anti-Irish sentiment of the day.[39] From his involvement in convincing Emma Willard to come to Troy with her un-

traditional school for young women in 1821 to his support of the financial system of the community during the early 1800s to his being the largest investor in the Troy Tow Boat Company which capitalized on the demand for river transportation for goods, Hart was always in the forefront of business in Troy and the surrounding region and also put his money behind the many charitable needs of the growing community.[40]

Betsey Amelia Howard Hart (1798–1886) was raised in a very old section of New York City east of William Street and north of Maiden Lane, the only child of William Howard (1777–1845) and Rebecca White Howard[41] (1780–1870) (see Fig. 9). Educated at a young ladies seminary in New York, in 1816, at the age of 18, she married her cousin, Richard P. Hart of Troy who had already established himself as a leading citizen of that rapidly growing community.[42] The family reminiscence, *Furnace Grove, 1858–1958, The Story of a Family Home* (1958), goes into some detail of how Betsey Hart was first introduced to her husband's Quaker family. "She was not a Friend, and there was some apprehension as to how she would be received by the staid Quakers of Millbrook. Should she wear her 'worldly

8 Richard P. Hart, engraving after portrait by Abel Buel Moore. The Hart Papers include a bill from the same artist for making a copy of this posthumous portrait for use at the Troy Savings Bank where Hart had been a founding member and president.

9 Betsey Amelia Howard (Hart), oil on canvas, Leslie Emmett. This portrait is a late nineteenth century copy by Emmett of an original probably done about the time of Betsey's marriage to Richard P. Hart in 1816.

costume'—a gay dress of rose color, and a large hat trimmed with flowers? 'It would be hypocrisy to change,' said her husband, 'and besides, they love beauty.' They did and were completely won over by their daughter-in-law."[43] The first of the Hart's 14 children was born in 1817, while their last child was born in 1841. They moved into 59 Second Street with six children and eight more to come. One of the few descriptions of the house that the Harts lived in before their new home was built is found in Elizabeth Shields Eddy's reminiscence. "Whether they went at once to the house where they lived until 59 was built, I don't know, but they did live in a house which stood where Mr. Paine's now stands—a brick with brown stone trimming, owned by Mr. Pattison, a great friend of Grandfather's"[44] (see Fig. 10). The young wife found life in Troy somewhat overwhelming. "Then she came to Troy where she had no friends of her own age—all of Grandfather's friends wives being much older than she. 'I knew nothing about housekeeping' she said. 'Mother sent a woman with me who lived with us a long time. I think her name was Maria Springer. She was a good cook and manager and she certainly was needed in the influx of babies that followed.'"[45]

After her husband's death in late December 1843, Betsey took over his estate with the help of her son,

10 Detail, Second Street looking south from State Street, Troy, after the blizzard of 1888, showing the site of first house owned by the Harts. The site is the four bay building on the right side of the street above the boy standing to the left of the group of people in the right middle ground. Edward Gale photograph.

William Howard Hart (1820–1883), and parlayed his business interests into an even larger fortune.[46] Much of what we know of her activities comes from the Hart Papers, which document in detail the daily expenditures of the Hart family from 1844 to 1886 during the period of her widowhood. Records were kept of virtually every kind of expenditure for the family in part because of the need to document the costs of raising her large family charged to her husband's estate. In addition to family expenses for education of her sons and daughters, entertainment, household purchases of furnishings and art work, repairs and refurbishing 59 Second Street, servants wages, travel, food and clothing, medical expenses, and charitable donations, the Hart Papers chronicle the business activities that Betsey became involved with after 1843. It appears that she kept a firm hand on the day-to-day running of the large and varied mix of railroad and gas light company stocks, commercial and residential property holdings in Troy and elsewhere and other investments that she inherited first from her husband and then from her father when he died in 1845.[47] The papers show how she traveled to New York City for business and pleasure, purchasing clothing or furnishings for her home while attending to business related to commercial properties she owned there.[48] What the Hart Papers lack, however, is the personal correspondence or diaries which appear not to have survived.[49] The papers provide documentation of what money was spent on but not always why it was spent or what precipitated investment in certain areas.

The success of the Hart family business investments meant that there was an opportunity to support various worthy causes in Troy and beyond. Betsey Hart's charity was well-known in her day. In many instances she continued to support the interests of her husband, but she also focused on supporting a number of institutions that worked with children (see Fig. 11). She was one of the founders of the Troy Day Home (1858), a charity that provided day care for the city's indigent children and of the Troy Young Women's Association (1882). She continued her husband's interest in educational institutions, especially the Troy Female Seminary which eight of their ten daughters attended. During the Civil War she responded to relief efforts with generosity as she did numerous times to fires and other disasters.[50] Immediately following Troy's Great Fire of May 1862 which devastated a large portion of downtown Troy, she responded to the loss of institutions like

11 Betsey A. Hart, carte de visite photograph, A. Cobden, Troy, c. 1855

the Troy Orphan Asylum with a gift of $10,000 to be matched by other citizens' donations. She was also very good at getting other people involved in her charitable projects, including family members who continued her philanthropic interest in Troy to a second generation and beyond. She left sizable bequests to the Rensselaer Polytechnic Institute, the Troy Day Home, the Marshall Infirmary, one of Troy's first hospitals, and the Troy Orphan Asylum upon her death in 1886.

An important activity that Betsey Hart undertook toward the end of her life was the erection of a suitable monument to her family in Oakwood Cemetery. There are bills in the Hart Papers which document the hiring of an architect, stone supplier and various sorts of work at the Hart and Howard family plot in Oakwood Cemetery during the 1870s and 1880s. First, in December 1883, architects Gibson, Pretyman & Sherwood were paid for design work on the Howard and Hart monument in Oakwood. The $150 fee was noted as one percent of the estimated cost. Also in December 1883, a survey of the plot at Oakwood was made by L. M. Wright, a civil engineer. Then in March 1884, Clarence Cutler of New York City was paid as the "Architect of Hart Monument." Three more bills from Cutler were submitted during 1884 and 1885 amounting to $800. In November 1885, Mitchell Granite Works was paid $5,000 "on acct

12 Hart Family Plot in Oakwood Cemetery from *Picturesque Oakwood*, DeWitt Clinton, editor, 1897.

of contract price of monument in Oakwood Cemetery" indicating that the project was nearly finished.[51] Betsey Hart died in August 1886. The Hart Papers have extensive documentation for her last illness and her funeral services.[52] Today the Hart plot in Oakwood Cemetery includes many members of the Hart family as well as Betsey's parents, William and Rebecca Howard (see Fig. 12).

Betsey Amelia Hart continued the Hart family's role in the life of the city of Troy both in business and community service. She maintained many of her husband's business dealings and through her son, William Howard Hart, continued to influence a number of boards of banks and institutions where she herself could not directly participate.[53] Although it was an age when women were not generally public figures, her many generous charitable donations put her in the forefront of her community. She responded to emergencies like the Great Fire with the money to rebuild, making matching support from the community a part of the arrangement and thereby doubling the amount of money raised. However, like her husband, she seems to have kept a generally low profile in her giving. While she was often the largest donor to causes, she rarely took a leadership position as chair of a committee or president of a ladies board. She saw a number of her daughters marry and lose the money they inherited due to their husbands' lack of business sense, but she continued to support them and their children generously.[54] This was certainly true of her daughter Caroline Hart Shields, for whom there was a trust fund set up to control her money. In her will, Betsey was very specific about how

she wanted to leave her money to her daughters without control of their husbands. Although the Married Woman's Property Act had been in effect since 1848, it was still an era when men legally could have full control of any property a wife had. It would seem that this action was not only a wise but a relatively uncommon direction for her to take. From evidence in the Hart Papers it would appear that as long as she was able, Betsey maintained a direct involvement with her large and varied business affairs.[55] In this respect, the evidence forces a reevaluation of the role of wealthy women in the nineteenth century. While on the face of it, it would seem that she was unusual in her close involvement with business, further research on the lives of other women with similar histories will be necessary to determine just how unusual this was.

Among her lasting, if unintentional, contributions is the collection of documents, the Hart Papers, which she had a large hand in producing and preserving. The bills and other records in the collection provide a detailed picture of mid- and late-nineteenth-century life. The bills that relate to 59 Second Street give us an almost unique opportunity to learn what life in a household like hers was like over a long period of time. The items that relate to her other activities and interests shed new light on many aspects of nineteenth century material culture and history which will provide new information for years to come.

William Howard (1777–1845) was a businessman, investor, and banker who originally came from Pawling, New York (see Figs. 13 & 14). Almost nothing is known of his childhood or youth, although it appears that he was from a Quaker family. He married Rebecca White about 1795 and Betsey was born in 1798. By the early

13 William Howard, oil on canvas, artist unknown, c. 1815.

14 Rebecca White Howard, oil on canvas, artist unknown, c. 1815.

1800s, he had made a large fortune in New York City based on fur trade, land ownership, and banking. He and his wife and daughter lived at 39 Cliff Street prior to 1809 and at 16 Gold Street from 1809 to about 1817 and subsequently moved to 18 Dey Street where he and Rebecca lived until his death in 1845.[56] After his daughter Betsey married Richard Hart in 1816, William Howard also invested in Troy, sometimes with his son-in-law or other Troy residents.[57] He established the Howard Bank & Trust Company (1839–1843) which had an office in the Athenaeum Building in Troy, owned land that was developed as a residential row of five houses called Park Place on Congress Street, adjoining the 59 Second Street lot, as well as a number of other properties in Troy.[58] From the records included in the Hart Papers, we know that he also invested in developing transportation systems and in real estate. It is noted in *Furnace Grove, 1858–1958, The Story of a Family Home* that William Howard "was evidently a man of some literary interests, for we have a large number of his books."[59] As is noted elsewhere in this study, Howard also appears to have had an interest in architecture, most clearly seen in his involvement with the building of the house for his only daughter and her family as well as the distinguished residential row around the corner on Congress Street known as Park Place.

The story has come down to us that the Howards constructed 59 Second Street for their daughter as a wedding gift. Since the Harts had been married for ten years and had six children by the time that the house was built, the wedding gift would have been belated at best. Recent research indicates that William Howard was involved in the land transactions that consolidated title to the property. Howard was also involved in the ordering of materials for the building and the Carriage House.[60] Elizabeth Shields Eddy notes in her reminiscence that "[f]or many years Grandmother Howard had mahogany planks seasoning which made the beautiful doors on the first floor."[61] Though likely not literally true, this tradition supports the notion that the Howards constructed the house at 59 Second Street.

Rebecca White Howard (1780–1870) came to live with her daughter in 1845 after her husband William Howard's death. She and Betsey converted the Howard family home at 18 Dey Street in lower Manhattan to a commercial property which provided rental income.[62] At the time that area of New York City was being transformed from residential to commercial use.[63] From

family reminiscences, we know that Rebecca Howard was a part of the everyday life of her daughter's family after 1845. She brought a roomful of furnishings to 59 Second Street from her home in New York City, making use of one of the upstairs bedrooms. Elizabeth Shields Eddy's reminiscence provides the only extant description of Mrs. Howard.

She had always been delicate, but as grandmother told me, was always the one everybody in the family turned to in times of trouble. She was thin and seemed to me tall, but that might have been because when everybody else wore hoop skirts, she wore straight skirts, pleated at the waist, long sleeves and waists pleated on the shoulders and brought down, surplice fashion, the neck filled in with soft, plain lace. All her clothes were made alike, of silk alpaca for week days and soft, heavy silk for Sundays and holidays. I think she wore a 'false front' and over it, dainty little lace caps tied under her chin with pearl colored ribbon. The photograph I have of her is very good. She had a very sweet expression and always had something for us when we went to her room.[64]

The reminiscence goes on to note that "Grandmother Howard had the West room over the back parlor. There was the big four post bed with green moiré curtains, top and below. Then, below the window, was a beautiful little mahogany sewing table, a long sofa, between the window and the mantle piece, and at the foot of the bed, a straight backed rocking chair with a little side table in front of it where she had her meals."[65] Among other domestic arrangements, she provided the tea for the household. She also participated in the life of the community, adding her own donations to the charities that her daughter supported.[66] Mrs. Howard apparently attended the Second Street Presbyterian Church with her daughter and family (see Fig. 15). Records of this church, an offshoot congregation from the First Presbyterian Church, note that Mrs. Howard was baptized there in 1869, not an unusual occurrence as one reached the end of one's life. It is not known what church the Howards may have attended in New York City.

One of the more interesting sets of bills in the Hart Papers relate to Mrs. Howard's last illness and funeral expenses in 1870. They include bills from G. V. S. Quackenbush for "4 pr men's black lisle gloves," from William Madden, undertaker, for "broadcloth casket & case, plate & handles, outside case, white merino robe, hearse, 11 carriages, use of 8 dozen chairs, use of corpse preserver, ice, salt, saltpeter, 4 carriers, carting outside

15 Second Street Presbyterian Church, drawn by D. Herron, Jun., lithograph of G.W. Lewis, c. 1846.

case to Oakwood, services & attendance," and from Mrs. W. W. Winchester for "preserving one wreath natural flowers and furnishing frame for same." In November 1870 two additional bills from R. D. Bardwell for "flowers from Mrs. Chester Griswold, one lot of funeral flowers (½ paid by Sarah), Mrs. R. P. Hart one wreath of flowers, one cross of flowers" were submitted for $72. The wreath of flowers in the Bardwell bill was probably the same wreath framed and preserved by Mrs. Winchester as a memorial piece. This piece is no longer extant. The family apparently also used the Troy Club for dinner after the funeral, according to a bill from the Club for $15.50.[67]

The Second Street Neighborhood, 1826–1836

On May 19, 1826, at the same time that the Hart house was being built, the *Troy Sentinel* predicted "Troy will one day become a large manufacturing place. Situated near the head of navigation, and at the outlet of the great canals, her situation offers uncommon facilities for the purposes either of commerce or manufactures. Her manufacturing establishments have already become celebrated abroad, and the work, that is turned out from them, is no where, it is believed, surpassed in durability or finish. New works are every year commenced, and improvements are constantly making in such as have before been established."[68] As Troy developed during the early nineteenth century, distinct commercial and residential areas took shape. Starting at the Hudson River on Front Street were docks and warehouses which had shops and offices fronting on River Street.[69] Moving eastward, First and Second streets, starting from today's Broadway (Albany Street) and State Street, included the earliest inns and banking houses. South of State Street there were more residential properties until Congress Street was reached (see Fig. 16). Vail House on the corner of Congress and First streets, built in 1818, along with the Stephen Warren House at Third Street and Broadway and the John D. Dickinson House at 19 Second Street, were large brick structures that represent the best residences in Troy prior to the construction of the Hart House (see also Figs. 17 & 54). Along the main east-west route of Congress Street were located many groceries and dry goods shops as well as a number of "oyster cellars" or restaurants. Because of the location of the Rensselaer County Court House at the southeast corner of Second and Congress streets and the County Records Office on the

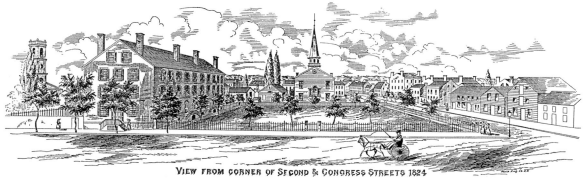

16 View of Congress Park and the Female Seminary, Troy, c. 1824, showing the site of Park Place at the right, from *History of the City of Troy*, Arthur J. Weise, 1876.

17 George Vail house (1818), First and Congress streets, Troy, c. 1890.

northeast corner of the same intersection, a number of lawyers had offices nearby as well.

From the 1829 *City Directory* it is possible to determine who was living where in the neighborhood adjacent to 59 Second Street (see Fig. 18). Richard Hart's brother-in-law, Jacob Merritt and his wife Mary, Richard Hart's sister, owned the house at 53 Second Street that included the site of 57 Second Street (now called the Carr Building and part of the Rensselaer County Historical Society [RCHS] complex) until 1825 when they sold the southern part of the lot to William Howard, most likely in preparation for the building of the 59 Second Street. Richard Hart had sold the property at 49 Second Street to John T. McCoun in December 1828 for $8,000; this was the site that the Hart's lived at prior to the building of 59 Second Street.[70] Immediately south of the property at 65 Second Street was Elijah D. Waters, listed as an innkeeper.[71] A little further north at 45 Second Street was Samuel McCoun who in 1829 was Mayor of Troy. On the opposite side of Second Street at number 50 Second Street was Richard H. Fitch, captain of the steamboat, *New London*; at 52 Second Street, Adna Treat, looking glass maker; at 58 Second Street, Samuel G. Huntington; at 60 Second Street, Elias Pattison, one time partner of Richard Hart's in several

enterprises;[72] at 62 Second Street, Richard Hart's nephew, Charles H. Merritt, son of Jacob and Mary Merritt;[73] at 64 Second Street, Philander Wells, teller at the Farmers' Bank. In 1834, the same year that he and Rebecca Howard turned over the 59 Second Street property to Betsey and Richard Hart, William Howard purchased property that provided housing on Second and Congress streets for several of Richard and Betsey's married daughters. Park Place, a row of five town houses, was built circa 1836 by William Howard.[74] Beginning in 1837, 58 Second Street was owned by Harriet Hart Doughty (1818–1870) and her husband, Ezra Thompson Doughty. It is interesting to note that 60 Second Street, virtually opposite 59 Second Street, was lived in by Mary Amelia Durkee, another Hart daughter, and was also later owned by the Cluett family (see below).

With the Rensselaer County Court House, the Troy Female Seminary, Seminary Park, the First Presbyterian Church, and the Second Street Presbyterian Church (after 1833) all immediately to the south of Congress

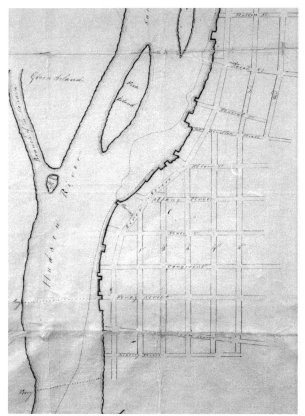

18 *Survey of the City of Troy*, ink on paper, c. 1824. The grid of streets includes the area around 59 Second Street.

19 First Presbyterian Meeting House, c. 1824, from *Troy and Vicinity*, Arthur J. Weise, 1876. This view shows First and Congress streets with the site of the Park Place row at the left background.

20 First Presbyterian Church, James Dakin, architect. Troy, 1834-36, c. 1890. The Troy Female Seminary building is on the far left side of the church.

Street and the commercial district just a couple of blocks away to the north and west, the site of the Hart's new home was conveniently situated both for Richard Hart's many business interests and his family's daily activities (see Figs. 19 & 20). Since the family was familiar with the neighborhood, having lived just a few doors north of 59 Second Street for a number of years, they apparently decided that this was where they wanted to continue to make their home.[75]

The Cluett Families at 59 Second Street

In June 1850, William Cluett and Anne Bywater Cluett left Birmingham, England with their children: John William Alfred, Mary Harris, George Bywater, Edmund, Frederick Henry, and Robert (see Fig. 21). Daughter Emily Ann stayed behind in England. A group of letters between family members provides insight into the family's arrival in Troy and decision to settle here. The letters also provide information on subsequent family activities.[76]

In 1854, William Cluett opened a book and music store at 76 Congress Street. This business was to continue well into the twentieth century. In 1857, after a brief time working for his father, George B. Cluett (1839–1912), joined the firm of Maullin and Bigelow, linen collar manufacturers—the business of which he later became the head. His brother, J. W. Alfred Cluett, worked for this firm before George, but left in 1858 to join his father's firm which became William Cluett & Son. After the Great Fire in May 1862 which damaged

the family home, the family moved from 123 Eighth Street at the corner of Fulton Street down to 170 First Street where they lived for several years.[77]

A reminiscence by Emily Cadby Henry, niece of George B. Cluett, notes that when George became the head of his collar business, he offered his brother Alfred a position as travelling salesman. "As I remember he was not a success at that, so his brother George gave him a position in the Factory as bookkeeper where he remained the rest of his life."[78] Robert, who also later joined the firm of Geo. B. Cluett, Brother and Company, "was a very active & useful member."[79]

In 1863, George married Sarah Bontecou Golden (1840–1864). She died in 1864 in childbirth within the first year of their marriage.[80] In 1867, George married Amanda Rockwell Fisher (1847–1918) (see Figs. 22 & 23). They traveled to England in 1869 to bring George's niece, Emmie Cadby to Troy to live with them. That same year Amanda Cluett wrote to her sister-in-law Emily Cluett Cadby about her concern over the strain on George due to business. She noted that "George is not as well as I could wish. He is so anxious about everything that it wears upon his brain. I hope, someday, he may leave business and join John (Emily's husband) in buying a farm."[81] In 1870, after George's sister, Emily Cluett Cadby, died in childbirth, his brother-in-law, John Cadby, brought the remaining seven Cadby children to the United States from England. They settled in Hudson, New York in 1871. Over the years the two families remained close.

In 1867, a house at 258 Eighth Street in Troy was the

21 Cluett Family Group, c. 1870. George B. Cluett is at the bottom right. Seated foreground, left to right: John William Alfred Cluett, Mrs. JWA Cluett, George B. Cluett. Seated middle ground, left to right: Mrs. Mulford (Joseph Mulford's mother), Edmund Cluett, Mrs. George B. (Amanda Rockwell) Cluett, Mary Bywater Lewis (Ann B. Cluett's sister). Standing background, left to right: Rev. Joseph N. Mulford, Mary H. Cluett Mulford, William Cluett, Ann Bywater Cluett. Seated background, looking to right: Robert Cluett.

first home of George B. and Amanda R. Cluett. William Cluett and family lived nearby at 254 Eighth Street. By 1884, George and Amanda Cluett had moved to 3 Park Place, one of the row houses originally built by William

22 George B. Cluett, from *History of Rensselaer County, New York*, Nathaniel Sylvester, 1880.

23 Amanda Cluett, c. 1917.

Howard on Congress Street. By 1886, George and Amanda Cluett's family reached its full extent and included Walter Herbert (1870–1942), Nellie Agnes (1871–1959), E. Harold (1874–1954), George Bywater, Jr. (1876–1939), Alfonzo Rockwell (1877–1900), and Beatrice (1886–1973). Two additional children died as infants—George Rockwell (1868) and Bessie Louise (c. 1873). In 1893, the family, which included the younger three children, moved to 59 Second Street.[82] The same year, George and Amanda followed his sister and brother-in-law, Mary Cluett Mulford and the Rev. Joseph B. Mulford's example and began to spend winters on the edge of Lake Worth in Palm Beach, Florida[83] (see Fig. 24). In 1905, they built "Bywater Lodge" where they spent seven winters together.[84] Among the many visitors the Cluetts entertained in Florida, as well as in Troy, was Dr. Wilfred T. Grenfell, whose mission in Labrador was world-renowned. The Cluetts supported the Grenfell Mission by providing a ship, the sloop *George B. Cluett,*

24 In addition to 59 Second Street and the property in Palm Beach, the Cluetts also owned this home in Saratoga Springs, New York. They moved from one home to another during the year, usually spending the summer months here, c. 1886.

which was used by Dr. Grenfell in his work.[85] In 1910, George and Amanda sold 59 Second Street to George's nephew, Albert E. Cluett and his wife, Caroline and their family. Unfortunately, George Cluett was never to live in the new home he and his wife were building off Pinewoods Avenue. George died at 59 Second Street in June 1912 while he was staying in his former home waiting for "Worfield Manor" to be completed.[86] He left a letter to his family which "called (their) special attention to several matters not contained in my will, and which you will, I am sure carry out as strictly as though they had been mentioned in my will."[87] In this letter he directs that "(j)ust so long as you are able to do so, I trust you will all be ready to assist in all philanthropic work, and in all the years to come, may our family reputation in this regard be fully maintained. Give generously to every good cause, help such as are needy or in distress, setting such an example in this respect as shall be emulated by others." All of the desires expressed in this letter to "My dear Wife and Children" were carried out by his family.

Amanda Rockwell Fisher (1847–1918) was born in Havana, Illinois, but came to Troy at the age of fourteen to live with her aunt and uncle and to go to school, her parents having heard of the "educational advantages of this city."[88] She graduated from Troy High School in 1866. In 1867, she married George B. Cluett. She and her husband were originally members of the State Street Methodist Church, but changed to St. John's Episcopal Church, in 1899, several years after moving to 59 Second Street.[89]

Mrs. Cluett was known for her many contributions to community organizations. As her obituary in the *Troy Times* stated, "Although very active in church work and a generous contributor to all of the funds, particularly to the mission and church extension work, Mrs. Cluett modestly refused to be honored by leadership which was time after time offered to her."[90] Perhaps her most lasting gift to the city was her support of the Troy Young Women's Association. Her husband had become interested in establishing a counterpart to the Troy Young Men's Association since "no place was provided for the young women, thousands of whom he employed." Mrs. Cluett raised funds for a new building on the corner of State and First streets in 1917 from her brother-in-law, Robert Cluett and F. F. Peabody, partner in the firm of Cluett, Peabody & Co., Inc.; she then provided the money to furnish it.[91] She also was active with the Samaritan Hospital, the Troy Times Fresh Air Fund, and the Troy Orphan Asylum. Her diary notes many meetings and projects related to these organizations.[92] Like Betsey Hart after her own husband's death, Amanda Cluett continued to support the many organizations and causes which George B. Cluett had supported after 1912.

While the newspapers and other documents do not reveal her as an obvious supporter of the Anti-Suffrage movement, she did take a box at the Anti-Suffrage mass rally held at the Troy Savings Bank Music Hall in late October 1915 just prior to the first try at getting the vote in New York State. It is interesting to note that she dealt with a number of other prominent anti-suffragists and suffragists on the boards of the charitable organizations she supported. Like many well-to-do women of her generation, she seems to have supported the status quo while she worked to make a difference in her community in more traditional ways.

One of the main documentary sources on 59 Second Street during the period that George and Amanda Cluett lived there is a diary she kept, now in the RCHS collection, between 1900 and 1917 which gives a capsulized view of life at the house during the years she and her husband lived there (see Fig. 25). One of the tragedies of this period for the family was the death on Christmas Eve, 1900 of Alfonzo B. Cluett (1877–1900) from typhoid fever. Mrs. Cluett's diary reveals that she never really recovered from the loss of her son. Her entry on

Sunday, September 2, 1900

Walter came this morning, so we are all together again except George and I have decided to telegraph him to come and spend a few days with us. It is very hot today but perfect sky.

1901

Heard a fine sermon by Bishop Walker. It poured when we came out of church and rained all the afternoon.

Sept 1st 1910

We deliver the keys of 59 Second St. and give possession to Albert today. We leave many joyous and such sad sad memories with the dear old house but we are satisfied to leave it. Dear Alfonzo spent his last days there and from there he was buried.

Sept 1st 1913 Labor Day

Walter, Mary & Geo. motored from Saranac and are to spend a few days with us. The anniversary of leaving No 59. How doubled hallowed now since dear Papa breathed his last there and from there was buried.

25 Page from Amanda Cluett's diary. The entry for Sept. 1st, 1910, notes the change of ownership of 59 Second Street.

September 1, 1910, not only notes the occasion on which she and her husband transferred the house to their nephew but also gives some idea of her thoughts at the time. "We deliver the keys of 59 Second St. and give possession to Albert today. We leave many joyous and such sad, sad memories with the dear old house but we are satisfied to leave it. Dear Alfonzo spent his last days there and from there he was buried."[93]

After George B. Cluett's death, his niece, Emily Cadby and her husband, the Rev. H. Ashton Henry and their only child, Madeleine, came to live at Worfield Manor with Amanda and her daughter Nellie.[94] Amanda died in 1918, uncannily on Christmas Eve, eighteen years to the day after her beloved son Alfonzo. Rev. Henry died in 1920. His wife died in 1943. Madeleine Henry remained to run the household for Nellie A. Cluett until the latter's death in 1959, aged 87. The Cluett house and property off Pinewoods Avenue (left to Nellie A. Cluett for life occupancy) was then sold to the Emma Willard School.

Albert Edmund Cluett (1872–1949) was born in Troy, the son of Edmund and Mary Alice Stone Cluett.

He was the nephew of George B. Cluett and the brother of Sanford L. Cluett who is particularly remembered today as the inventor of the Sanforizing process of pre-shrinking cloth.[95] Albert was educated at the Albany Academy for Boys (Class of 1889) and went to Williams College (Class of 1893) where he earned a bachelor's degree. He continued his education at the Massachusetts Institute of Technology (Class of 1896) where he received a Bachelor of Science degree (see Fig. 26). Albert worked for the Hudson River Telephone Company and the John A. Manning Paper Company before he went on to work for Cluett, Peabody & Co., Inc. for 28 years as a mechanical engineer and second vice president.[96] He was a member of the American Society of Mechanical Engineers and was a former president of the Society of Engineers of Eastern New York. During World War I, from 1917–1919, he was Fuel Administrator for northern and eastern New York. He was a director of Peterson and Packer Coal Company and became assistant treasurer and vice president of the firm in the late 1920s. In addition to being a director, secretary and vice president of Cluett, Peabody and Company, the

26 Albert E. Cluett, oil on canvas, Samantha Huntley, 1918.

27 Caroline I. Cluett and sons, oil on canvas, Samantha Huntley, c. 1916.

actively involved in the Troy community. She was a member of the Ide family of Troy, like the Cluetts early collar and shirt manufacturers. The daughter of George P. Ide and Mary Ella Savage Ide, she attended the Troy Female Seminary which later became the Emma Willard School.[98] During her lifetime she served on many local boards and took part in a number of local charities. She was one of the founders of the Women's Exchange and very active in its work during the Depression. She was also closely connected to the Samaritan Hospital, as Amanda Cluett had been before her. A lifelong member of St. Paul's Episcopal Church, she was an active member of its women's organizations as well. Both she and her husband participated in the activities of RCHS after its founding in 1927, several times hosting programs at 59 Second Street[99] (see Fig. 28).

By the late 1940s, the Cluetts were considering what to do with 59 Second Street. After offering it to Russell Sage College which would have turned the property into a dormitory, a use which the Cluetts did not approve, they developed the idea of giving it to RCHS provided that an endowment of $100,000 could be raised to support it as a museum. By the time of Albert Cluett's death in early January 1949, he and his wife had agreed to give the house to RCHS subject to a life interest of Caroline Cluett. By 1952, she had decided to move

Albany and Vermont Railroad, and the Saratoga and Schenectady Railroad, a trustee of Troy Savings Bank, (executive vice president from 1936 to 1948 and elected chairman of the Board in July 1948), his civic activities included being a trustee of the Rensselaer Polytechnic Institute, a trustee and treasurer of the Emma Willard School, trustee of the Troy Orphan Asylum and the Albany Academy for Boys, a vestryman and member of St. Paul's Episcopal Church and a member of the Troy Club, University Club of New York and a number of other organizations including the Rensselaer County Historical Society. For many years he was the chairman of the Harbor and Dock Committee of Troy.[97]

In 1904, Albert E. Cluett married Caroline R. Ide (1875–1963) of Troy. They had four sons, John Girvin (1906–1960), Edmund II (1908–1979), Albert E., Jr. (1910–1960), and Richard Ide (1914–1967; see Fig. 27). The family moved into 59 Second Street in September, 1910 with the three older boys. Caroline Ide Cluett was

Society Honors Two Great Trojans

28 Albert on the right and Caroline Cluett (second from left) hosted a meeting of the Rensselaer County Historical Society at 59 Second Street in 1940. The topic discussed was Richard P. Hart and George B. Cluett and their contributions to Troy.

29 Detail, *View of Troy, N.Y.*, lithograph, Sarony & Major, New York, 1848. Shown is the neighborhood of 59 Second Street, seen from the east. The arrow points to 59 Second Street.

and the house was turned over to the Society in early 1953. The first meeting at and tour of the building was held January 9, 1953.[100]

Life at 59 Second Street, 1827–1952

As noted above, RCHS is fortunate to have a large collection of documents that relate to the expenditures of Betsey Amelia Hart from 1844 to her death in 1886. The Hart Papers also include information on some of Richard P. Hart's business activities and for the six years after Betsey Hart's death (1886–1892) when her daughter Sarah Wool Hart was living at 59 Second Street and her expenses were being paid by her mother's estate. Equivalent archival collections for the two Cluett families do not exist. However, RCHS has conducted oral history interviews with family and staff members which, together with the physical evidence and photographic and other resources, have helped to put together an outline of what life was like at 59 Second Street during the Cluett years. What follows is a look at the way the three families who lived in the building used the spaces and lived their lives.

One of the earliest descriptions of 59 Second Street is from Elizabeth Hart Shields Eddy's reminiscence which describes her extended visit as a young girl to 59 Second Street in 1855. She notes her grandmother, Betsey Hart, telling her how she and Richard Hart had gone to a house across the street, possibly Elias Pattison's house at 60 Second Street, to look at the building when it was being built and had seen the moonlight reflected off the new white marble of the façade[101] (see Fig. 29). Elizabeth Eddy, writing many years after the fact, describes the house in detail as she figuratively walks the reader through the house and garden. Until the discovery of the Hart Papers, this document was the only descriptive information about how 59 Second Street looked during the Hart period. Because of the length of time between when the visit took place and when the memories were written down, some of the descriptions were taken with a proverbial "grain of salt." Once the Hart Papers yielded their detailed information, it was found that Elizabeth Eddy's memory was very accurate and her descriptions were confirmed by bills and receipts.[102]

The Hart Papers reveal a great deal about the daily

life of the family and servants at 59 Second Street and the community beyond. Bills for education of the youngest daughters exist—most went to the Troy Female Seminary with a year or so of "finishing" in New York City at Mrs. O'Kills' school. A number of other Troy girls attended Mrs. O'Kills' school as well. RCHS has a diary kept by Maria "Mollie" Tillman, who later married Richard P. Hart, Jr., which describes the antics and education she and Carrie (Caroline) Hart and others received at Mrs. O'Kills'[103] (see Fig. 30).

Bills exist for much of the food that was consumed by the family. Separate butcher and grocery bills were submitted on an approximate six month basis. Butter was sent in "from the country" and in at least one instance a former servant, turned farmer, provided the butter. Barrels of apples, mostly Fameuse and Spitzenburg varieties, and potatoes were sent down from the Lake George region in the fall. Other goods were sent up from New York City by steam boat or purchased at some of the shops along River Street or Congress Street. There are many catering bills, particularly from the period during the late 1840s and 1850s when a number of Hart daughters were coming out in society and getting married from the house.

With ten daughters, nine of whom married, there are many bills for wedding trousseaux, wedding cakes sent up by steam boat from New York City, and for reception food and music, which was often provided by local military bands. Bills and artifacts reflect decorative changes made to the house at this same time (see Figs. 31, 32, 33). The most extensive wedding bills exist for the wedding of Caroline Hart to Capt. Hamilton Shields in 1851. RCHS has Caroline Hart Shields' wedding veil in the collection and a piece of parlor furniture purchased for her from well-known Troy cabinetmaker, Elijah Galusha's cabinet shop.[104]

30 School Room at Mrs. O'Kills, New York City, c. 1850. This illustration was drawn by Maria Tillman who later became Mrs. Richard P. Hart, Jr. Several of the Hart daughters also attended this school.

31 Window drapery cornice, workshop of Elijah Galusha, c. 1850. This cornice and its mate matched the pair of oval looking glasses.

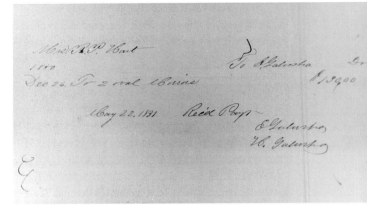

33 Elijah Galusha bill for oval looking glasses for front parlor, 1850.

Bills for clothing for Betsey's growing family, education expenses, doctor's and dentist's bills, funerals of family members and even one servant, bills for magazine subscriptions and other family entertainment like lecture series tickets can all be found in the Hart Papers. Much of the detailed information on decorative changes to rooms in the building and on plumbing, heating, and lighting systems that were installed over the years comes from bills in the Hart Papers. It is often possible to find bills for purchases made in New York City or in shops in Troy combined with shipping bills to get the goods to 59 Second Street. The Hart Papers also include many bills for installing carpeting or wallpaper from the several workmen who were used by the family over the years.

32 Oval looking glass, c. 1850. This mirror, one of a pair which flanked the front parlor mantel, was part of an order to Elijah Galusha which updated the interiors on the first floor to the new Roccoco Revival style. These changes occurred in time for a series of family weddings in the early 1850s.

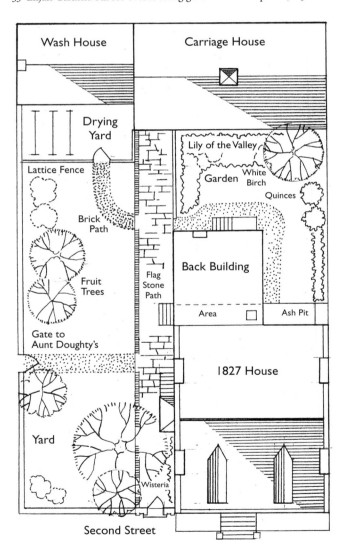

34 59 Second Street, site and garden plan, c. 1855, based on the reminisence of Elizabeth Shields Eddy. D. G. Bucher, 1999.

One space that was integral to the property was the garden lot to the south of the building (see Fig. 34). This space no longer exists due to the building which was constructed on the lot after it was subdivided in 1893. The main source of information on what the garden looked like when the Hart family lived at 59 Second Street was the reminiscence of the property by Elizabeth Shields Eddy. In a detailed description which takes the reader through the garden she notes that

in those days there was a fine yard on the south side extended to Mr. Reynold's, separated from the street by a high brick wall. This turned back at the south and ran back in the alley. There was a heavy gate on 2nd St., and in the south wall was a small gate opening into Aunt Harriet Doughty's yard so the family could exchange visits without going out into the street [see Fig. 35]. This yard gave a fine view of the south side of the house with its white brick walls and fine lines. From the 2nd St. gate a broad path of flag stones, flanked by brick, led straight to the large carriage house at the back. This took up perhaps a third of the width of the yard. The rest was grass, with a few small fruit trees here or there, and

this ended at the west in a low, white brick laundry called 'the wash house,' a three-foot brick path turning from the main path and leading to the door. There was some lattice work which came forward a little and protected the clothes lines and their drying clothes from the main walk. . . . . [Y]ou came in the big gate at 2nd St. Behind the gate was a large lilac bush that in the Spring waved its purple blossoms over the wall in a too alluring fashion for the street boys to resist and they and Aunt Sarah waged constant war upon each other. Then you walked west and on the right was a wisteria climbing. Then came the South Stoop—enclosed in blinds with steps leading down to the west. Then another space and there was what always gave an air of mystery and romance to that yard, for I never saw it in any other—a broad springing arched-way running under part of the dining room, open at both ends, and giving access by a flight of wide stone steps to what was known as the area, a wide stone paved passage. As you went down the steps, you looked through to a little green plot beyond the kitchen windows.[105]

Detailed listings of plant materials, garden furniture and walkway materials used over time can be found in the Hart Papers. From the documents we know that there was a grapevine and a variety of fruit trees (which often did not survive more than a couple of seasons). Purchases of garden tools and even a hose and sprinkler show up over the years. The Hart Papers provide documentation for virtually everything which the Eddy reminiscence records. Once the property changed hands in 1893, the garden lot was built on and a brick walkway provided access from Second Street back to the Carriage House and the courtyard area between the back wing and the adjacent building at 57 Second Street.

The Carriage House and the attached laundry building are the subject of numerous bills that reveal a great deal about the buildings themselves and their occupants and functions over time (see Fig. 36). Regular deliveries of hay and feed goods up until the 1870s seem to indicate that horses were stabled there until Betsey began to use a livery stable. Earlier, most likely when there were young children in the household, a cow was also a resident of the Carriage House.[106] The Hart Papers also include bills for the purchase and repair of carriages and other vehicles, many bought from Brewster and Company in New York City[107] (see Fig. 37). Betsey Hart purchased landaus, gigs, barouches and also maintained a sleigh. She often shipped carriage and horses down the Hudson River and on to Newport, Rhode Island, by steam boat when the family went on their summer vacations there. Purchases of horses,

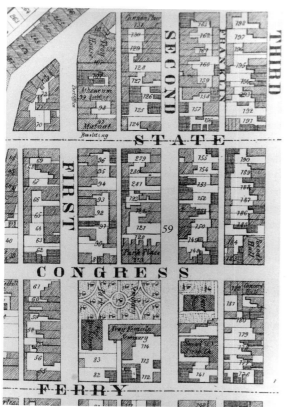

35 Detail, *Map of the City of Troy, N.Y. from Actual Surveys*, William Barton & J. Chace, Jr, 1858. The Hart property is designated as Lot 121, located above Park Place. The street address is also shown.

36 Detail, *Troy, N.Y.*, drawn and published by Messrs. H.H. Bailey & J.C. Hazen, c. 1877. The rear yard and side garden of 59 Second Street are visible in this view (look for a shadowy horse and carriage on Second Street just above the garden). Although birdseye views are generally known for accuracy, this detail does not show the carriage house, laundry buildings and alley which would have existed.

often matching pairs, take place on a regular basis. Bills for feed and the necessary harnesses and other saddlery and tack also exist in the Hart Papers. By the 1870s, it appears that a livery stable was being used more and more frequently to provide storage and service related to transportation around town. Repairs to the laundry equipment are documented as well and detail the onerous task of keeping up with the washing needed for a large household. Bills for a laundress who specialized in doing curtains, particularly lace curtains and curtains used in rooms for which there are no photographs, provide one of the few sources of information about what kinds of window treatments were used at 59 Second Street at specific dates.[108]

Some of the most exciting finds in the Hart Papers relate to Betsey Hart's purchases of furnishings for her home (see Figs. 38A & B, 39, 40, 41, 42, 43, 44). She maintained close ties with New York City, patronizing stores and shops there throughout her lifetime. The Hart Papers include bills from many of the best-known New York City cabinetmakers and purveyors of fine and decorative art objects.[109] From these bills it is clear that the

house underwent at least one major redecoration in the late 1840s and early 1850s when the social obligations of bringing out and marrying four or five daughters, changes in household technology (i.e., gas lighting, hot-air heating system with floor grates and ductwork), and a change in decorative style to the Rococo Revival required a number of large expenditures to bring the main rooms on the first floor up-to-date in the latest fashion. In addition to the related bills for family weddings at this time, it is clear that 59 Second Street received new wall and floor coverings and several large purchases of furniture also took place. About every ten years after Richard Hart's death in 1843, the bills show that wallpapers were replaced in the entrance and stair hall, the dining room and the parlors. This may have been due to the accumulated dirt and wear and tear of the increasingly industrial environment of Troy as much as to a desire to keep up with the latest styles.

Although the Hart family did spend some of the summers during the late 1840s and early 1850s in Newport, unlike the later Cluett families, Betsey Hart seems to have made 59 Second Street her primary residence.[110]

37 The early nineteenth century Howard-Hart Coach. The coach went to Bennington, Vermont after it was in Troy. It was auctioned in the 1960s and is now in the collection of The Granger Homestead, Canandaigua, New York. Photo c. 1955

Some of these trips were undoubtedly part of following the social scene when there were a number of eligible young people in the household. It is noted in *Furnace Grove, 1858–1958, The Story of a Family Home* that "Mrs. Richard P. Hart, of Troy, had taken a whole floor of the Belleview Hotel for the summer of 1850. Her family group included Mrs. Hart's mother, Mrs. William How-

ard, and nine of her children—six daughters . . . and three sons. 'It must have been an attractive party' writes Aunt Lizzie (Elizabeth Shields Eddy), 'Grandmother Hart was then about 52, fine looking with great dignity and fine carriage, always wearing a lace cap'"[111]

It is also clear from the Hart Papers that it took a number of servants to run the household smoothly.

38 Card table, one of a set of dining room chairs, and breakfast table, belonging to Richard and Betsey Hart, attributed to the workshop of Duncan Phyfe, c. 1816. Family tradition describes these and other pieces as part of Betsey Hart's wedding furnishings.

39 Girondole looking glass, c. 1820, belonging to Richard and Betsey Hart and possibly one of a pair originally used on either side of the front parlor mantle. It was later moved to the dining room. It measures 63" high x 39" wide (by sight).

40 Three-piece girondole set, marked "Messenger & Phipson" and "M&P," c. 1825.

41 Parlor suite arm chairs, rosewood, Charles Baudouine, New York City, 1849. Baudouine's bill included six chairs and two sofas, some of which can be seen in the 1892 photographs of the front parlor.

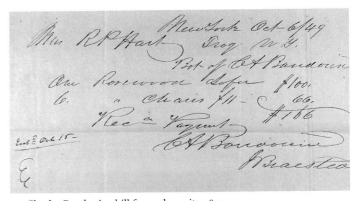

42 Charles Baudouine bill for parlor suite, 1849.

A servants' account book from the 1850s and 1860s provides a picture of the different positions that needed to be filled and of the wages paid. There was generally a cook, one or two waitresses, a laundress and a coachman on staff. There were also a series of part-time gardeners over the years who took care of the south garden lot. In addition, day labor was often hired to do odd jobs, and a nurse was eventually hired to help take care of Mrs. Howard in her later years. The only full-time

43 "Huntsmen" vases, porcelain, marked with Meissen anchor, c. 1850.

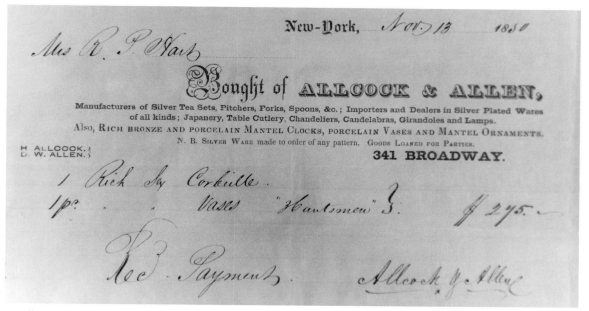

44 Allcock & Allen bill for vases and centerpiece purchased by Betsey Hart in New York City for $275, 1850 (see Fig. 43).

male servant was the coachman. Research has shown that several of the names listed for this position were people of African American descent.[112] There are also bills for livery for the coachman. Most of the remaining servants have surnames that appear to be Irish. In this,

Betsey Hart was following the usual practice of hiring Irish serving girls. The wages she paid appear to be at least average if not a bit higher than average. She also experienced the usual quick turnover in staff that was the bane of many American households at the time.

Servants were often lured away from household service by cheap western land and other, more desirable job opportunities.[113] After Betsey's death in 1886 a housekeeper, Mrs. Hastings, was hired to supervise the household staff that continued to number three or four servants.

The Hart Papers also reveal the change in household size over time. As the children grew up or went away to school and eventually married, the household by the late 1860s consisted of Betsey, her mother, Rebecca Howard, and Sarah Wool Hart, the youngest daughter. While the staff size remained about the same throughout the period, it is clear that the level of activity slowed down. It was still possible to have up to 75 direct family members pay Sunday calls on Betsey, but the general flurry of social activity seen in the late 1840s and early 1850s slowed down in the 1870s to one party usually held around New Year's Day.[114] Sarah Wool Hart, the youngest surviving Hart child, who had remained unmarried, lived on at 59 Second Street for six years following her mother's death. She, or more properly the Committee which handled her affairs and Betsey Hart's executors, continued to maintain the property, redecorating certain rooms. One bill notes the decoration of the exterior of the house with flags and bunting for the celebration of Troy's centennial on January 5, 1889.

The Hart Papers end with the death of Sarah Wool Hart on December 4, 1892. There is not the same rich documentation for the Cluett families. Instead oral histories with family members, friends and servants, Amanda Cluett's diary (1900–1917) and remaining physical evidence provide the picture of life at 59 Second Street at the end of the nineteenth century and for the first half of the twentieth century. The sale of the 59 Second Street property by the Betsey A. Hart Estate took place May 1, 1893, for $21,250 and George and Amanda Cluett and their family moved in later that year[115] (see Fig. 45). George and Amanda Cluett had acquired a house in Saratoga Springs by 1893 which they lived in during the summer months (see Fig. 24). They also had a home in Palm Beach, Florida where they generally spent the winter months after 1893. This was especially true after Alfonzo Cluett died in 1900. His mother was never able to spend the Christmas holidays in the house afterwards with any comfort.[116] Albert and Caroline Cluett also spent time in Saratoga Springs at the home of his parents, Edmund and Mary Alice Stone Cluett. They visited Palm Beach as well where the elder Cluetts had a home.

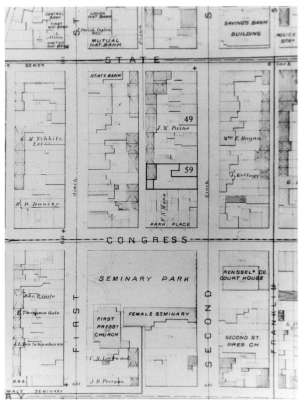

45 Detail, map of Troy, from *City Atlas of Troy, New York,* C. & M. Hopkins, C.E., 1881. Shown is the neighborhood of 59 Second Street in the early 1880s, the last map view prior to the division of the property and sale of the house to the Cluetts.

However, both Cluett families appear to have considered 59 Second Street as their main residence. A series of photographs of the main floor rooms were taken for Beatrice Cluett's 1904 coming out party held in November (see Figs. 46, 47, 151, 164, 175, 176). For the occasion much of the furniture in the parlors and dining room was removed and a veritable bower of greenery and flowers was brought in to decorate the house. These photographs show that George and Amanda Cluett had made a number of decorative changes to wall coverings.[117]

George and Amanda Cluett were probably responsible for the second addition to the building which included a kitchen on the main floor rear wing as well as additional rooms on the second and third floors of the wing.[118] This addition was undoubtedly made to accommodate the modern concept of having the kitchen on the same floor as the dining room.[119] At the same time, in 1893, the garden lot to the south of the building was being built on by the William Kemp family, effec-

46 This pair of chairs was in 59 Second Street during the residency of George and Amanda Cluett. They were returned to the house by their daughter Beatrice Cluett Black.

47 Pier table used in 59 Second Street during the residency of George and Amanda Cluett.

48 Kemp/Frear House, 65 Second Street, Troy, built circa 1893 on the original garden lot of 59 Second Street, c. 1895.

tively cutting out the southern exposure (see Fig. 48). The courtyard that was made by extending the wing westward was probably bricked over at the same time. At about this time the carriage house would have housed its first automobile. It is not known what kind of car George and Amanda Cluett had although Amanda notes they drove out on antiquing trips and family genealogy research trips as well.[120]

Albert and Caroline Cluett and their family moved into 59 Second Street in 1910. When they moved in they were aware of the architectural importance of the house.[121] Albert and Caroline Cluett made a number of decorative changes to the interior of the building which can still be seen today. They added a Zuber et Cie. scenic wallpaper in the entrance hall and added chair rail and wall panel moldings to the parlors and dining room, as well as to the main stairway. It is clear that they had a strong interest in what is recognized today as the Colonial Revival movement (see Fig. 49). This was manifested in their active collecting of American antiques to decorate their home, in their involvement in organizations related to American heritage like the Rensselaer County Historical Society, and ultimately in their gift of 59 Second Street to that organization so that it could be preserved and become an historic house museum. They participated in the Historic American Buildings Survey in 1934, allowing their home to be documented as part of that important national project. Albert Cluett also owned a copy of Edward W. Root's Philip Hooker monograph which is now in the RCHS Library.[122] It

49 Dining room looking southwest with Albert E. Cluett family, Christmas, 1934. From left to right: Richard Cluett, Albert E. Cluett, Jr., Barbara Metz Cluett, (child) Ann Martin Cluett, Edmund Cluett, Caroline Buck Cluett holding John Girvin Cluett, Jr., J. Girvin Cluett holding Jane Allen Cluett, Mrs. Albert E. (Caroline Ide) Cluett, Mary Alice Ide (Mrs. AE Cluett's mother) Sanford L. Cluett (AE Cluett's brother), Mrs. Sanford L. (Camilla Rising) Cluett, Camilla Trent Cluett (young girl), Marvin Cluett (young boy), Gregory Cluett, Sanford L. Cluett, Jr.

was during this period that the design of the house was first attributed to this well-known Albany architect.

Albert and Caroline Cluett made several major changes to the building but not to the main rooms. The third floor, which had been primarily servants' rooms and attic storage space, was renovated for the Cluett sons to use as a gymnasium and as bedrooms. This required that the back roof be raised to provide greater ceiling height. The front two rooms were refurbished and two closets added between the rooms. The front dormer windows were not changed. Great care was taken to reproduce the trim moldings and decorative elements around doors and windows in other areas of the house, although, as noted elsewhere in this report, details of the "raffle flowers" were done in cast plaster instead of carved wood. Two bathrooms were added to the third floor at the same time and the central portion of the third floor was reconfigured to include a storage room with cedar closets and two smaller closets. In 1938, apparently because of the failing health of both

Mr. and Mrs. Cluett, an elevator was installed between the first and second floors. This was placed into closet space on the main floor and second floor halls.[123]

One of the spaces at 59 Second Street that oral histories have highlighted during the residence of Albert and Caroline Cluett is the second floor southeast room. This space was used by Caroline as her "command center." It was her study and sitting room and the room to which her grandchildren remember being brought to pay a call on her. They remember family photographs lining the walls as well as her small desk and a chaise longue. In this room she wrote her correspondence, talked on the telephone, and met with household staff.

Daily life when the family was in residence included a dog, who was generally kept outside in the courtyard, and a parrot in the main floor kitchen who is remembered vividly by those who knew him. Albert Cluett and his sons hunted small game and brought home the results of their forays into the county for preparation by kitchen staff. Grandchildren often had birthday parties

50 Birthday party for a grandaughter of Albert and Caroline Cluett in the dining room, c. 1940. The bottom of the mirror shown in Fig. 39 can be seen over the sideboard.

51 Side chair from parlor suite, attributed to Joseph Meeks, New York City, used in the front parlor by Albert and Caroline Cluett. The suite was among antique furnishings collected by the Cluetts. A chair from the suite can be seen in the right background of Fig. 28.

at 59 Second Street (see Fig. 50). Other family gatherings around the holidays were held in the building as well. Daughters-in-law recalled the use of the back parlor or library for pre-dinner cocktails with the men smoking cigars.[124] Recollections are of a formal life with Albert Cluett being reserved in manner while his wife, Caroline appears to have been more outgoing (Fig. 51). Throughout their time living in the building, Albert and Caroline Cluett were conscious of its historical and architectural importance. Their plans for its ultimate preservation by giving it to the Rensselaer County Historical Society were the culmination of over forty years of living in and caring for 59 Second Street. In October 1952, Caroline I. Cluett informed the RCHS Board that by the middle of the next month she was giving up her home at 59 Second Street. The transfer was made later in 1952 and RCHS held its first meeting and tour of the house on January 9, 1953.

The Rensselaer County Historical Society, 1953 to the Present

Once the transfer was complete, the board of trustees and House Committee set about making the building into a museum and cultural center.[125] During the first few years the all-volunteer group opened the house to occasional tours and had a number of events and parties. A housekeeping couple used the second floor of the back wing for an apartment and maintained a day-to-day presence in the building. It was clear from the start that professional museum staff was needed if 59 Second Street was going to become a full-fledged historic house museum. In 1956, H. Maxson Holloway was hired as the first director of the Rensselaer County Historical Society. During the decade of his tenure, community art shows, historical exhibitions, lectures and other programs were held in the house and eventually in the renovated Carriage House meeting room. At the same time, several community groups made arrangements to use the facility as a home base. These included the Birchkill Arts and Crafts Guild, the newly formed Rensselaer County Junior Museum and several art classes. These activities were generally held in the basement level of the building as the main floor and second floor spaces were slowly renovated as period rooms displaying an increasingly refined collection of Rensselaer County art, furniture and decorative arts objects. An apartment for the director was made on the third floor main block of the building with a small kitchenette installed in what had been a bathroom.

It was during this time that Mr. Holloway was able to contact Hart and Cluett family members and acquire or get the promise of donations of a number of furnishings that had been at 59 Second Street when it was a private home. At the same time that the three dimensional museum collections were growing, so was the foundation of the RCHS collections, the research and archival materials which documented many facets of Rensselaer County history. A number of renovations were made to the building and to the Carriage House to facilitate the operations of the organization without consideration of the historic building fabric or documentation before changes were made. This was especially true of the less formal, more functional spaces like the kitchens, bathrooms, and other secondary spaces in the building. It was at this time that two service doors were removed from the dining room and the back parlor.

The second director, Archibald Stobie, began to move the organization's focus beyond Troy while at the same time continuing the slow process of renovation of 59 Second Street. The first curator, Marcia Starkey, was hired in the late 1960s. Collections continued to grow as the Civil War centennial was celebrated nationally and a number of family descendants donated objects. By the time that the Society's third director, Breffny A. Walsh, arrived in 1970, the stage was set for renovation of the basement level. Thanks to a grant from the Howard and Bush Foundation, the Cluett elevator was extended to the basement and third story to facilitate movement of collections and visitors. In 1972, RCHS became one of the first historical societies in New York State to become accredited by the American Association of Museums. With the aid of grants from the New York State Council on the Arts and other funding sources, a variety of projects were started as the public generally became more interested in local history as the nation's bicentennial celebrations began.

By the early 1970s, it was clear that with collections continuing to grow and greater demand for programs the space in 59 Second Street was not going to be adequate in the next few years. In 1975 RCHS acquired the adjacent town house at 57 Second Street.[126] This purchase focused the attention and energy of the board, staff and membership on the renovation of what was to become the programmatic space for the organization. A capital campaign was held to raise money to renovate the main floor of the Carr Building to include exhibit and meeting space so that areas in 59 Second Street and the Carriage House used for these functions could become part of the historic house museum. Staff grew to include an education director in the early 1980s.

During the tenure of fourth director, Anne W. Ackerson, in the early 1990s it became clear that 59 Second Street was in need of major rehabilitation. A major failure of the main roof of the building was the impetus for the beginning of fundraising to remedy several decades of benign neglect. Initial work to assess the existing conditions of both buildings owned by RCHS and the projected space use needs for collection storage, exhibit space and access issues was done before the fifth and present director, Donna Hassler, was hired in 1997.

Over two decades, what is now called the General Joseph B. Carr Building has increasingly taken the burden of heavy public use off the fragile 59 Second Street. The current study of the building will guide the restoration of 59 Second Street so that it will be protected from overuse and its important architectural features will be preserved. The Carr Building will become the headquarters of the Rensselaer County Historical Society taking the pressure of administrative and programmatic staff functions out of key areas of 59 Second Street and returning a number of historic spaces to public view and interpretation.

ACKNOWLEDGMENTS

In any project like this there are many people whose collective efforts help to make the finished product. While it is not possible to list everyone who has touched this report, I would like to thank several people who have played a key role. Breffny A. Walsh, RCHS Director (1970–1990), who saw the potential of the Hart Papers when they were found and arranged a leave of absence for me to work on the papers, provided me with the kind of research experience most of us only dream about. Her successor, Anne W. Ackerson helped to restart the process that led to funding of the report by Senator Bruno. Current RCHS Director Donna Hassler has allowed me the time necessary to do out-of-the-building research and the time to work uninterrupted on writing the results. Special thanks go to Kathryn Sheehan, RCHS Registrar, for her tremendous efforts to secure the reproductions of images from other institutions and collections and, as resident expert on Cluett Family information, for her close reading of that section of the text. To my other co-workers—Lorraine Weiss, Susan Fisk, Maryanne Rappaport, Sandra Harris, Abby Zoldowski, Cindy Silkworth—I extend my appreciation for their understanding when I could not participate in the day-to-day activities of the organization because my attention was focused on the nineteenth and early twentieth centuries. The same is true for library volunteers, Robert N. Andersen, Marta Andersen, Don Birkmayer, Helen Gardner, Larry Kammerer, Olive Muzicka and Betty Shaver, upon whom I called for their expertise in digging out details and retrieval of images to add to text and footnotes. Their help and understanding is greatly appreciated. The co-authors of this report—Douglas G. Bucher and Walter Richard Wheeler—have been persistent in their pursuit of historical truth and accuracy and have understood when my role in the project has included pushing all involved to meet the deadlines that always are part of this kind of effort. Editor Frederick D. Cawley has refined and improved the text and pulled the whole complex project together with his usual professional approach. Diana S. Waite and Peter D. Shaver have kindly lent their expert eyes as readers and improved the final product with their suggestions. Colleagues in the field, James Corsaro, formerly Associate Librarian for Manuscripts and Special Collections, New York State Library and Barbara Wiley, Librarian, Emma Willard School, have responded with their help in tracking down information in their collections. For all those others whose names will not fit here, without their help this project would not be a success. Finally, I would like to thank my husband

Steve and daughter Katy for letting me focus my attention on this project, take over space in our home for writing and for their reactions to my excitement about the building and its occupants with their own enthusiasm.

STACY POMEROY DRAPER
Curator

NOTES

1. Arthur James Weise, *Troy's One Hundred Years, 1789–1889* (Troy, New York: William H. Young, 1891), 24. Vanderheyden hired Flores Bancker of Lansingburgh, the community to the north of what was to become Troy, to lay out about 65 acres into "lots, streets and alleys."

2. Hon. David L. Seymour, *Address Delivered before the Friends and Patrons of the Troy Hospital . . . 1850*, Troy, New York.

3. Glass house bills from Hart Papers record payment in pot/pearl ash. See also in Abba A. Goddard, *The Trojan Sketch Book*, David Buel, Jr., "Troy for Fifty Years." Pot and pearl ash were used for fertilizer and soap making and other processes that required a caustic substance.

4. Buel, *Trojan Sketch Book*.

5. Weise, *Troy's One Hundred Years*, 54.

6. Ibid., 58.

7. Ibid., 73–74. The churches were the First Presbyterian Church (1793), the First Baptist Church (1795), St. Paul's Episcopal Church (1804), the Methodist Church (1809), the Society of Friends (1804). The two banks were the Farmers' Bank (1801) and the Bank of Troy (1811). The other two most populous towns were New York City and Albany. One of the finest houses in Troy at this time was the George Tibbits Mansion at the head of Congress Street. Built in the first decade of the nineteenth century it was a landmark on the hillside above the city. After 1861, the house was used for the Troy Day Home which provided day care for working class children. The building was torn down circa 1969 and the site is now used for a parking lot for the Rensselaer County Office Building.

8. Ibid., 54.

9. Dr. James Sullivan, Editor in Chief, *History of New York State, 1523–1927* (New York, New York, Lewis Historical Publishing Company, Inc., 1927), Vol. III, 1075. The value of American exports in 1807 was $108,000,000 prior to the Embargo taking effect. The following year the value of exports had dropped to $22,000,000. New York State in general had taken a middle road on the Embargo, but soon found that the effect was too devastating to business to support. The Embargo was repealed in 1809 although trade was still restricted with Britain and France.

10. Buel, *Trojan Sketch Book*.

11. Broadside, May 7th, 1812. Rensselaer County Historical Society (RCHS), Troy, New York. The broadside, dated about a month before the official declaration of war, was signed by a Committee of Correspondence. Committee members, in addition to Richard P. Hart, included Townsend McCoun, Daniel Merritt, John D. Dickinson, George Tibbits, Esaias Warren, William M. Bliss, Hugh Peebles, Samuel Stark, Derick Lane, Ephraim Morgan, Joseph Russell, Amasa Paine, Lewis Richards, and James Mann. They were to "communicate the proceedings of this meeting to our fellow-citizens in other parts of the country, and inviting their concurrence in the sentiments above expressed, solicit their cooperation in measures calculated to change the present gloomy aspect of our publick affairs." For a general discussion of the War of 1812 and its causes see Sullivan, *A History of New York*, Vol. III, Chapter III.

12. Alton Ketchum, *Uncle Sam: The Man and the Legend*. Troy meatpacker Samuel Wilson is perhaps the best known Troy merchant involved with the War of 1812. The story of how he sent meat to troops housed just outside Troy in barrels marked "US" and how these initials were recognized by soldiers from the Troy area as being from "Uncle

Sam" Wilson has become part of the legend of Uncle Sam, the symbol of the United States. In 1961, the United States Congress recognized Samuel Wilson as the "real" Uncle Sam. Later in his career, Samuel Wilson also operated a brickworks near the foot of Mt. Ida hill, now Prospect Park.

13. Buel, *Trojan Sketch Book*. Economic problems were worsened by weather that was cold enough to destroy crops throughout the region. See also Weise, *Troy's One Hundred Years*, 80.

14. Weise, *Troy's One Hundred Years*, 79. The Act "to incorporate the City of Troy," passed by the New York State Legislature on April 12, 1816, included the offices of mayor, recorder, six aldermen, four assistant aldermen, a clerk, marshall, chamberlain, a supervisor, one or more collectors (of taxes), six assessors, and six constables. The mayor, recorder and marshall were appointed by the governor and the Council of Appointment on an annual basis. Other positions were elected annually. The city was divided into six wards and governed by a common council made up of the mayor, recorder, aldermen, assistant aldermen. The first mayor was Col. Albert Pawling, the first recorder was William L. Marcy, the first aldermen were George Allen, Hugh Peebles, Townsend McCoun, Stephen Ross, Lemuel Hawley, and Philip Hart, Jr. (Richard Hart's brother).

15. Weise, *Troy's One Hundred Years*, 95. A public meeting was held in Troy at the court house on February 24, 1816 "at which the proposed undertakings (ie, the Champlain and Erie Canals) were ardently favored by the citizens of Troy." George Tibbits, State Senator (1815–1818), "strongly advocated these public improvements, and originated the financial measures by which the state was enabled to accomplish the construction of the two great water-ways of transportation."

16. Ibid., 96. While the move was criticized by Albany and Lansingburgh newspapers, Weise quotes the *National Democrat* as saying "The enterprise of the Trojans is worthy of all imitation. We believe that without exception they are the most enterprising people in the United States. There is among them a noble spirit of rivalship, untinctured by jealousy of each other. No man appears to envy, but every man to emulate the genius, talent, and industry of his neighbor."

17. Ibid., 102–3.

18. Seymour, *Address before Friends and Patrons of the Troy Hospital . . . 1850*. "There is a limit sooner or later reached by all inland towns in their commercial operations. This limit is prescribed mainly by the facilities offered to the surrounding country in reaching the great depots of foreign commerce. . . . In such a state of things our true policy is evident. It is to avail ourselves of the peculiar advantages of our natural position. To foster and extend our manufacturing interests. While the raw materials can be brought to our workshops by the waters of our river and canals—the manufacturing products can be with equal ease distributed throughout the length and breadth of our land. . . . When we look to the great and growing west, already teeming with its millions, and destined soon to become the richest and most populous agricultural region on earth, who can fail to see that New England, Northern New York and Pennsylvania are to become the great workshops of manufactures for the supply of the 100 millions of intelligent freemen who will yet occupy the great valley of the Mississippi."

19. Weise, *Troy's One Hundred Years*, 106–107. Van Rensselaer appointed Rev. Samuel Blatchford, pastor of the First Presbyterian Church of Lansingburgh, Elias Parmalee of Lansingburgh, John Cramer and Guert Van Schoonhoven of Waterford, Simeon DeWitt and T. Romeyn Beck of Albany and John D. Dickinson and Jedidiah Tracy of Troy as trustees of the school. Rev. Blatchford served as president and Amos Eaton of Troy and Lewis C. Beck of Albany were senior and junior professors respectively.

20. Ceramic dish, circa 1825. RCHS. A transfer printed dish with the image of this steamboat shows how deeply this image had been imbedded in the popular consciousness. Weise, *Troy's One Hundred Years*, 109. Weise lists the founding members of the Troy Steamboat Company as John D. Dickinson, George Vail, Nathan Warren, Alsop Weed, Samuel Gale, Nathan Dauchy, Philip Hart, Jr., Gurdon Grant, George Tibbits, John Paine, Townsend McCoun, James Van Brackle

and Richard P. Hart. The firm began with capital of $200,000. The actual act of the State Legislature incorporating the company was passed March 31, 1825. By early summer 1825, the company had purchased another, smaller steam boat, the *New London* which ran with the *Chief Justice Marshall* on a daily schedule between Troy and New York City. The Hart Papers, RCHS, also contain information on this company, of which Richard Hart was a major stockholder until his death in 1843.

21. Weise, *Troy's One Hundred Years*, 110, 120.

22. Ibid., 126–27

23. Ibid., 132. Richard P. Hart was among the first directors of the company. The Hart Papers, RCHS, include a great deal of material about the railroad and competition with the Albany and New York lines. The original route went from Troy across the Hudson to Green Island and then north to Mechanicville and on to Ballston and Saratoga, a distance of 24 miles. The original directors of the company in addition to Richard P. Hart, included Elisha Tibbits, George Griswold, John Cramer, John Knickerbacker, Townsend McCoun, Nathan Warren, Stephen Warren, George Vail, LeGrand Cannon, Moses Williams, John P. Cushman, and John Paine. See also David Maldwyn Ellis's discussion in "Albany and Troy . . . Commerical Rivals," reprinted from *New York History*, October, 1943.

24. A number of documents in the Hart Papers show signs of having been in this fire. The fire may also be why more business papers from Hart's early years in Troy do not survive. Weise, *Troy's One Hundred Years*, 86. Weise notes that "the immense quantities of grain, flour, provisions, etc. with which many stores, four, five and six stories high were crowded full" were still smoldering as of July 4, three weeks after the fire started. The Rensselaer & Saratoga Insurance Company of Troy, of which Richard Hart was a director, paid out $110,000 within sixty days.

25. Weise, *Troy's One Hundred Years*, 119.

26. Ibid., 121.

27. The Merritts were also Quakers. Daniel and Isaac Merritt were involved in trade in Troy by the end of the eighteenth century. They had a store on River Street near what is now Monument Square and also owned Mahlon Taylor's flouring mill with elevator, the first mill in Troy, which was on the Poestenkill Creek. In 1807 Daniel and Jacob Merritt purchased the piece of land on the southwest corner of Fourth and State streets for the building of a Quaker Meeting House. Like Richard Hart, the Merritts were involved with the early banking establishments of Troy and many of the improvements to Troy's infrastructure (water system, roads, etc.) as the community grew rapidly during the early years of the nineteenth century. Jacob Merritt was one of Richard Hart's executors, having to act as such after the death of William Howard in 1845. There appears to have been a close interfamily relationship that extended to business concerns and across several generations.

28. In nineteenth century parlance, a "commercial house" was a business which dealt in general merchandise, often holding goods for clients until the best prices might be had.

29. Much of the information we have about Richard Hart's early career comes from his obituary in the *Troy Whig* (see below). It has also been possible to piece together the names of the firms that Hart worked in during his early years in Troy from the newspaper advertisements of partnership changes that appeared in the *Troy Gazette*. It would appear that Hart first worked for Bordman & Brown, a firm established in 1805 from the previous firm of Bordman & Hillhouse. Bordman & Brown was dissolved upon the formation of the new partnership of Brown & Hart which appears to have been established within the year Hart came back to Troy. Brown & Hart was dissolved in 1807 due to the death of the senior partner, Alfred Brown. The ad announcing this event notes that Richard P. Hart would deal with all demands and collection of debts owed to the earlier firms of Bordman & Hillhouse, Bordman & Brown, and Brown & Hart. It went on to note that "The business in future will be conducted by RICHARD P. HART, in all the different branches, as usual." Two years later, Hart was still advertising that he was collecting debts owed to these earlier firms.

The 1809 ad also noted that "The subscribers having entered into co-partnership under the firm of Richard P. Hart & Co. offer for sale, A General Assortment of LIQUORS and GROCERIES, on accommodating terms . . . Richard P. Hart. Philip Hart, Jr."

30. Broadside, May 7, 1812, RCHS.

31. One of the richest resources in the Hart Papers is the group of papers, account books, and other materials which relate to Richard P. Hart's mill holdings in Schaghticoke. Several inventories exist from insurance papers, particularly a group related to an insurance claim after a fire in the 1820s. Further research into these materials would yield important information about the operation of early nineteenth century industry and textile manufacturing.

32. A partial listing of property owned by Richard P. Hart in Rensselaer County shows that he was buying and selling land in Schaghticoke, Troy, Pittstown and Brunswick with the majority of transactions in the first two communities listed. Additional title work needs to be done in Albany County and Saratoga County to develop a more complete picture of the land holdings he had in the immediate Capital District. The land in Troy was divided between commercial holdings primarily on River Street and what appears to be residential property in other parts of the city. His land holdings in Albany County included property on which work was done for the extension of the Erie Canal to Albany. Documents in the Hart Papers support the title information and add details as to how the land was worked or developed. After his death in 1843, his widow, Betsey, continued to hold and develop much of the property and added to these holdings over time. Additionally, Richard Hart, particularly in the years after the War of 1812, bought up military tract lands reserved for veterans for back taxes, particularly in western New York and Michigan. Some of this land required that he have agents who oversaw his interests. It is also clear from his papers that he traveled to see some of these properties himself. One document that seems to be typical of his business dealings is an 1826 contract between Richard Hart, Jonathan Walworth and Col. Daniel Vaughan for Hart to purchase specific lots at sales by the Comptroller of New York State. Hart was to "advance the money for the purchases charging interest thereon at seven pr cent per ann[um] and take the deeds in my name. You [Walworth] and Col. Vaughan are to sell these lands, neither party to charge any thing for personal services—but all expenses paid out one to be a charge upon the concern in which I intended to be included. Any surveys that may be nesasary [*sic*] that may be performed by Col. Vaughan. Then the profit and loss to be divided equally say one half to yourself and Col. Vaughan & half to my self. The concern to be closed within five years that is, all lands remaining on hand at the expiration of five years to be sold at Public auction to the highest bidder for cash."

33. Richard P. Hart Estate Inventory, 1844, Hart Papers, RCHS. See listing of the bank stock he held at the time of his death. Many members of both Hart family and Cluett family served on the board of the Troy Savings Bank over the years.

34. *Troy Whig*, Dec. 1843. Written by David Buel, Jr.

35. Richard P. Hart's father, Phillip Hart (1749–1837) and William Howard's mother, Phebe Hart Howard (1735–1804), were brother and sister. They were separated by 14 years, she being the elder sibling. This relationship makes Richard Hart and his third wife, Betsey Howard, first cousins once removed.

36. Richard P. Hart Letter Books, Hart Papers, RCHS. Two letter books dating from 1840 to his death in 1843, occasionally note health problems he had, where different family members were and provide some anecdotal information on how the Hart household operated.

37. *Troy Daily Budget*, July 22, 1849.

38. The same time that he was elected mayor of Troy, he was adding the back wing to the house. The enlargement of the dining room, which was one of the main effects of the addition, was probably needed due to the increased entertaining he was required to do as mayor.

39. Weise, *Troy's One Hundred Years*, 140. Weise notes that effigies had been hung mocking the Irish and a crowd of Irish citizens gath-

ered after an unsuccessful attempt to remove them. A full-scale riot ensued and Hart and other officials moved to disperse the rioters. Ultimately, Hart had to call out the Troy Citizens Corps under arms to disperse the crowd. A number of people were hurt and arrested. Violence continued that evening with shots fired, and again the Troy Citizens Corps was called out. About 20 "ring-leaders" were arrested and finally calm settled.

40. In addition to being well known and respected in Troy and the immediate vicinity, Richard Hart was also sufficiently well known to be invited to ride with former New York City Mayor, Philip Hone, during the 1842 Croton Water celebration held in New York City.

41. Tillman-Hart Genealogy, RCHS. There is an unproven story that alludes to a son of William and Rebecca Howard, John Howard, who was about eight years younger than Betsey and who was supposedly disinherited by the Howards for going west to Alabama "while in his teens." In addition, the reminiscence of Elizabeth Shields Eddy (1852–1941), one of Betsey's granddaughters, includes the following statement "Then on Mother's side there was first my great-grandmother, Rebecca (White) Howard. She came from Danbury, Connecticut. There were several sisters and brothers though, but the only one I ever saw was Uncle Moss White. He had several sons and at least two daughters, Mary and Ann. . . . His sons were brought up with Grandmother Hart like brothers, Augustus and Nelson, Granville and Alexander." The Hart Papers, RCHS, include a number of documents that refer to Augustus White.

42. RCHS has the shellwork piece Betsey Amelia Howard did as a young school girl in New York City. Known as the "Temple of Fame," it includes a wax bust of George Washington set inside a columned "temple" with shellwork roof and watercolor background. It was created both to honor the nation's first president and to show off the skills and accomplishments she had acquired at school. One of the few descriptions of Betsey's marriage to Richard occurs in the reminiscence of Elizabeth Shields Eddy. "I did not think of it when Grandmother told me, but since, I have wondered if Grandfather Howard saw a little romance budding which he did not approve of and gave his daughter's future to the keeping of a man he could trust. Grandmother said 'Richard Hart used to come to the house often, but I always thought he came to see Cousin Harriet Starr. She was very bright and a good talker. When Father [Richard Hart] told me he wished to marry me, I was quite taken by surprise.' And so she was married and went away on a trip by stage coach to Washington [Duchess County, New York] in a scarlet merino gown with a finger-deep waist, trimmed at the bottom with a Grecian border of gold and a shawl of the same and a large hat with white ostrich plumes. 'And that was what I wore to Friends wedding when I went to Harts Village to visit Richard's family. I think they likes the gay color,' said Grandmother demurely." This description can be compared with the description from *Furnace Grove* (see below).

43. Ruth Hart Eddy, William L. Shields, George Van Santvoord, *Furnace Grove, 1858–1958, The Story of a Family Home*. This reminiscence and history of Furnace Grove, the Shields family home just east of Bennington, Vermont, contains many recollections and family stories about the Harts. Betsey and Richard Hart's daughter, Caroline (1831–1899), married Capt. Hamilton Leroy Shields (1823–1889) in 59 Second Street on February 20, 1851. Many bills in the Hart Papers document this event and subsequent expenditures by Betsey Hart on her daughter and her daughter's family. It should also be noted that William Howard was apparently also from a Quaker background, although what evidence there is today points to his, and his wife and daughter's, attendance at the Presbyterian Church.

44. This building, or the one immediately prior to Pattison's, was originally owned by Richard Hart. The chain of title shows that Hart sold the property to John McCoun in 1828, just after the Harts moved into their new home down the block. The property was then sold by McCoun to Elias Pattison in the early 1830s.

45. Elizabeth Shields Eddy reminiscence, 1969, transcribed by Ruthanne Mills (Brod), RCHS. Mrs. Eddy goes on to recall "Here Grandmother entertained the dowagers of her day with much trem-

bling of heart. They were invited for the afternoon, tea was served on trays passed among the guests, first, a large tray with plates and napkins followed by a maid with another tray with teacups and sugar and cream. Then came the delicately cut bread and butter, or tiny, hot biscuits with sliced tongue or ham or chicken and then, the awful part of your ability as a housekeeper, the tray with your very best glass saucers and some of every kind of preserves you had put up during the year, quinces and plums, peaches, and pears, all subject to the inspection of the famous housekeepers of the town. Quinces must be round and even and the color of orange or ruby; plums soft yellow or deep blue, if damsons—though I think they were not 'company' sweetmeats—peaches so smoothly pared that not a ridge showed where the skin had been removed, and as for the pears, Well, I have done many of them myself and it was not easy to peel a Seckel pear, remove the blossom end, scrape the stem until it was white, the whole looking as it had come out of a mould. 'I used to sit in fear and trembling when they came,' said Grandmother, 'and watch the old ladies tasting critically and nodding their caps together as they discussed whether the preserve came up to the standard.' Poor, worried little Grandmother!"

46. Elizabeth Shields Eddy reminiscence. "Grandfather Hart died December 27, 1843. He had a cold and was taking a steam bath when the alcohol flame caught his curtains around the chair and before he could tear them away, he was badly burned. Someone rushing to his assistance, picked up a vessel which they thought was water and threw it on the flames but it was alcohol and intensified the blaze. I do not know how long he lived after this but only a day or two if as long. Grandmother was then about 45 years old. Of her 15 (actually 13) living children, four were married, the younger ones at boarding school. Uncle Jacob Merritt was appointed by Grandfather's will, guardian of the younger ones and all their bills, etc. were sent to him as guardian." Richard Hart's estate, as listed in his 1844 inventory, was valued at over $500,000. It was noted in *Furnace Grove,* 24 that "R. P. Hart on his early death left his entire fortune to his widow, and her father's estate was presently added to this. So she was for a time reputed to be one of the wealthiest women in the country." The inventory done at her death in 1886 shows that Betsey A Hart's estate was valued at over $3 million. Both inventory ledgers are in the Hart Papers. See Appendix IIb.

47. Betsey Hart's 1886 inventory lists the following stocks and bonds which she held at the time of her death: "$1000 Bond Renss & Saratoga Rail Road, $9000 Bond Citizens Gas Co., $2000 Bond Fitchburg Rail Road, $500 Bond Troy & West Troy Bridge, $38000 Bonds Troy & Bennington Rail Road, 120 Shares Union National Bank, 7 Shr Milwaukee Gas Co., 4 Shares Troy & Bennington Rail Road, 2 Shares Troy & Cohoes Rail Road, 1 Share Saratoga & Schenectady Rail Road, 2 Shares Troy & Lansingburgh Rail Road, 5 Shares Albany & Vermont Rail Road, 2 Shares Troy City National Bank, 9 Shares Troy Gas Light Co., 2 Shares Troy & West Troy Bridge Co., 2 Shares Fitchburg Rail Road, 100 (Shares) Albany & Vermont Rail Road, 100 Shares Troy & Greenbush Rail Road, 60 Shares Troy City National Bank, Troy & Bennington (Rail Road?) Bonds." Her property holdings were generally continued by her estate for a number of years. Title research is continuing to document the exact property locations. There are numerous transactions related to the mill property in Hart's Falls, now Schaghticoke. In the early 1870s there are receipts in the Hart Papers that show she was also paying tax bills on the Griswold Opera House on the east side of Third Street between Broadway and Fulton Street, implying that she had an interest in that property. That building, named in honor of her son-in-law, John A. Griswold, was one of several Troy opera houses and theaters.

48. For much of her widowhood Betsey Hart owned property at 148 Water Street, 172 Fulton Street, and 772 Broadway in New York City. The former Howard home at 18 Dey Street was also developed by Betsey as a commercial property soon after her father, William Howard, died in 1845 and her mother moved to Troy to live with her. Bills in the Hart Papers through 1886 show that she maintained ownership throughout her lifetime, modernizing and improving the buildings as needed.

49. Apparently Ruth Hart Eddy, who donated many Hart Family furnishings to RCHS in the 1960s, ordered family papers destroyed after her death. The reminiscence of her mother, Elizabeth Shields Eddy, was only made accessible to the RCHS in part. A transcription was made by Ruthanne Mills Brod, then a student at Russell Sage College and afterward (1971–1975) curator of RCHS, of a small portion of the document which describes the house and family. The complete reminiscence was also apparently destroyed after Miss Eddy's death in the early 1970s. It is also noted in *Furnace Grove,* 21 that "Cousin Ruth Eddy has a sheaf of letters our grandmother (Caroline Hart Shields) received while at Mrs. O'Kell's School in New York; Aunt Lizzie's notebook gives much intimate detail of her life and character" This "notebook" apparently refers to the reminiscence. Mrs. O'Kell's name was spelled variously O'Kell, O'Kill, Okill in various period documents.

50. Bills exist in the Hart Papers for her Civil War period donations to the Volunteer Relief Association of Troy ($1000), two donations to the U. S. Sanitary Commission whose purpose was "to protect the sanitary interest of the Volunteer Forces" ($100, $1,250), and several contributions to the Troy Soldiers' Aid. After the Civil War she made at least one donation to the South Relief Fund for $100 which may relate to Reconstruction efforts in the South.

51. Hart Papers, bills noted are from 1883 to 1885. Oakwood Cemetery was founded in 1850 as part of the rural cemetery movement that created park-like settings to be enjoyed by the living as well as to be final resting places for the deceased. Oakwood Cemetery is located on the hills above the Lansingburgh section of Troy with prominent view points and monuments, memorial sculptures and several important structures by well-known American and English architects. Betsey Hart was involved with the founding of the cemetery and the work done to make it a model rural cemetery.

52. Betsey Hart's funeral expenses were paid by her estate and include expenses for telegrams sent to family members, 22 carriages for the funeral and other related expenses from E. W. Millard listed on the bill as an undertaker.

53. During much of the nineteenth century, women were not allowed to sit on boards that dealt with business transactions. Many organizations, like the Troy Day Home, had a Board of Lady Managers who dealt with the day-to-day running of the organization while at the same time having a male board of trustees or directors who could transact any legal and financial business. An all-male committee also handled the affairs of Sarah Wool Hart (1838–1892), the last daughter in the family who never married and who stayed on in the house after her mother died. This was arranged a number of years prior to Betsey's death.

54. Elizabeth Shields Eddy's reminiscence sheds some light on this: "I do not know how Grandfather left his money; but Grandmother told me he always treated all the children alike—if he gave one a present he put the same amount to the credit of the others. Also I heard that the younger ones' share was larger when they received it on coming of age because the older ones had lost a good deal through putting theirs into their husbands business ventures." Betsey continued her husband's practice; when she gave lump sum payments to her various children and grandchildren as she did more often in her later years, the amounts were prorated depending on whether a certain child had received any additional gifts or loans in the past.

55. Many, if not most, receipts have what appear to be her initials on them indicating her approval of the expenditures requested. Occasional short notations also provide evidence that she was involved with these business dealings at least in a supervisory capacity. As time went on, her son William Howard Hart and, after his death in 1883, her grandson, William Howard Doughty, took on more responsibility for investments and management of her large estate.

56. New York City *Directories,* 1800–1845, various publishers.

57. In documents in the Hart Papers, RCHS, Howard is listed as an investor in a number of companies, almost always with Richard Hart. This is undoubtedly only be a small part of his business transactions since his own personal papers appear not to have survived.

Among the other Trojans who invested with Howard are many of the same names that are found with projects Richard Hart took on.

58. William Howard bought and sold property in Troy from 1825 to 1845 and his estate continued to make transactions as late as 1862. The first transaction was in 1825 and related to the lot line between the property he bought for 59 Second Street and Jacob and Mary Merritt's property to the north. There were also several later transactions related to property owned by or sold to his grandchildren. A total of 39 transactions are recorded in the Rensselaer County Clerk's Office.

59. Ruth Hart Eddy et al., *Furnace Grove*, 23–24.

60. A receipt dated December 7, 1826, in Richard Hart's papers indicates that William Howard was acting as agent for Richard Hart in the purchase of lumber for the "Stable" of 59 Second Street, known today as the Carriage House. The companion agreement with Richard Hart dated December 22, 1826 was for lumber sent down to Troy "immediately on the opening of the Hudson River next spring." In both bills, the lumber merchants were Thomas and John P. Laing of Saratoga.

61. Elizabeth Shields Eddy reminiscence, RCHS. This description seems to indicate that the Howards planned to build a house for their daughter for a number of years before they actually did.

62. After William Howard's death an auction of the furnishings from the Dey Street home took place. The Hart Papers contain the inventory of goods to be auctioned. Douglas G. Bucher has recreated the probable floor plan of the house and furnishings layout from this document.

63. A significant indication of this transformation was the demolition in 1851 of the south side of the street in order to widen Dey Street.

64. Elizabeth Shields Eddy reminiscence, RCHS.

65. Ibid.

66. The Hart Papers include documents for Mrs. Howard's donations to the Troy Day Home, the US Sanitary Commission during the Civil War and the Troy Orphan Asylum among others.

67. Hart Papers. The bills for Rebecca Howard's funeral expenses date from May 23 to 25, 1870, and November 11, 1870. Given the number of chairs and carriages ordered for the funeral, the number of people attending would have been too large to accommodate easily in the house. Several other family funerals are documented in the papers as a number of Betsey Hart's children and their spouses predeceased her. She also paid for the medical expenses and funeral of one of her coachmen, Robert Latour, in 1869. Bills related to Betsey Hart's funeral are noted above.

68. Page 3, column 1, *Troy Sentinel*, May 19, 1826.

69. This section is based on a study of Troy's first *City Directory* published in 1829, just two years after the Hart's moved into 59 Second Street.

70. There is some supposition about the kind of house Richard and Betsey lived in before their grand home was built. Unfortunately, the next owner after McCoun, Elias Pattison, built a new house on the property and no image of the earlier building has been found to date. Elizabeth Shields Eddy notes in her reminiscence that "they [the Harts] did live in a house which stood where Mr. Paine's now stands—a brick with brown stone trimming, owned by Mr. Pattison, a great friend of Grandfather's." It is not clear from this description whether Mrs. Eddy is describing the original house the Harts lived in between 1816 and 1827 and owned briefly by McCoun or the subsequent house built by Elias Pattison. Photos of the Pattison house during the Blizzard of 1888 show a four-bay brick structure, which supports the theory that the Hart's first house was also four-bays wide and that when they decided to build they were already comfortable with the four-bay plan.

71. Arthur J. Weise, *History of the City of Troy* (Troy, New York: William H. Young, 1876), 158. A description of a circus that stayed and performed at Water's Hotel gives an interesting picture of life at 59 Second Street. "'A grand exhibition of living animals' at Water's Hotel, 59 Second street, in 1828, included 'a sea dog, a crocodile, a Spanish lynx, a young cub, an alligator, a black coati, and a serpent.' The exhibition was 'accompanied with good music on an Italian Cymbal and other instruments.' The admittance was 1*s*. 6*d*.; and children half price. Here was also exhibited the elephant 'Columbus,' the largest animal of its kind known to showmen in the United States. Calvin Edson, the great living skeleton, was also an attraction at this well-known hotel." Note the mistake in address in the quote. The Troy *City Directories* show that in the early 1830s Mr. Waters went on to run a tavern in another part of the city and it appears that the property at 65 Second Street became residential soon after that.

72. Richard Hart had owned both 58 and 60 Second Street as early as 1822.

73. Charles H. Merritt was a son of Jacob and Mary Merritt, and so Richard P. Hart's nephew. To make family lines even more complicated, Charles H. Merritt married two of Rebecca White Howard's nieces in succession. Mary and Ann White were daughters of Rebecca Howard's brother Joseph Moss White, making them Betsey's first cousins.

74. See following section "59 Second Street: Its Design and Construction" for further discussion of a possible architect for this important row of residential buildings.

75. The other prime Troy residential area that is often thought of today, Washington Park, about five blocks to the south of 59 Second Street, was a later development during the late 1830s and early 1840s. At least one Hart daughter, Elizabeth Hart Griswold, and her family lived on Washington Park later in the nineteenth century.

76. The original letters are still in family hands. Transcriptions are in the RCHS Library.

77. George B. Cluett is first listed in the Troy *City Directories* in 1853–54 as a clerk without a business address. He boards with his parents until his first marriage in 1864. The William Cluetts move back to 115 Eighth Street and George and his new bride move to 172 First Street.

78. Emily Cadby Henry reminiscence. George B. Cluett succeeded to the head of the firm due to the retirement of one partner and death of another. The firm was listed as Maullin, Bigelow & Company in the 1862 Troy *City Directory*. It became Maullin & Cluett for one year (1863) and George B. Cluett, Brother & Company in 1864. After a number of changes within the partners of George B. Cluett, Brother & Company, in 1889 the firm became Cluett, Coon & Company which included George B. Cluett, J. W. Alfred Cluett, Robert Cluett, John H. Coon, Daniel W. Coon, Henry Statzell and Frederick F. Peabody. In 1913, the firm incorporated as Cluett, Peabody & Company and included George B., J.W. Alfred, and Robert Cluett, Frederick F. Peabody, Howard Kennedy, and George Statzell. Cluett, Peabody & Company became an international company after World War I. It was bought out by West Point Pepperell in the late 1980s and all operations ceased in the Troy factory in early 1990. Today the building on River Street has been adapted for offices and is known as Hedley Park Place.

79. Troy *City Directories*.

80. Transcriptions of Cluett Family Letters, RCHS. A letter dated April 29, 1856, from George's sister Mary to their sister, Emily Cluett Cadby, who had stayed in England reported "We often joke Alfred [J. W. A. Cluett] and George about two young ladies, of great respectability, to who they are very attentive. . . . It seems to be an understood affair by the community, who believe that Alfred is engaged to Mary, who is near my own age, and George to Sarah who is sixteen but it is nothing, it serves us to plague them about. Alfred I think has no idea of leaving home, but George is more fond of the ladies, and I guess as soon as he is old enough he will have a wife." At the time, he would have been 18 years old. A letter from George B. Cluett to Emily Cluett Cadby, Nov. 14, 1864, eight years later, poignantly details the awful death of his first wife during childbirth and the loss of their baby.

81. Letter from Amanda R. Cluett to Emily Cluett Cadby, Nov. 7, 1869. Transcription in RCHS Library. Several other letters indicate that the collar business was not always what Amanda hoped her husband would do for a living.

82. February 12, 1893, *Northern Budget*, "Buying Valuable Prop-

erty." The article notes that "The Betsey A. Hart property on Second street, one of the most valuable pieces of real-estate in the city, has been sold. William Kemp and George B. Cluett are the purchasers, and the amount paid is slightly under $40,000. . . . The property consists of a marble residence, forty feet front, and a vacant lot, thirty-five feet front. Mrs. Hart occupied the residence many years and died there. Mr. Kemp will probably occupy the residence, and there is some talk of Mr. Cluett erecting a residence on the vacant lot." In fact, just the reverse happened, William Kemp built the building at 65 Second Street and George and Amanda Cluett bought the Hart building. One of the first events that happened to the family was a November 1893 burglary which was written up in "Reminiscences of the Early '90's," *Troy Observer/Troy Budget*, November 11, 1928. The short article noted that the burglars poured syrup on a valuable rug and destroyed it.

83. By 1903 poor health had forced George Cluett to retire from most of his business affairs. Troy Savings Bank Archives include his letter of resignation from the Board. Not only did George and Amanda Cluett and the Mulfords, George's sister Mary and brother-in-law spend time in Palm Beach each winter, but another brother, Edmund Cluett and his wife and two sons, Albert E. and Sanford L Cluett, also spent time there. Amanda Cluett's diary notes many family gatherings there and in Saratoga Springs where the families also maintained summer residences. Sanford Cluett and Joseph Mulford established the first Episcopal church in Palm Beach, Bethesda-by-the-Sea, which is still very active and which includes many memorials to the Cluett families.

84. RCHS has a small watercolor of this area, including the Episcopal church, Bethesda-by-The Sea, which was generously supported by the family and at which Rev. Mulford preached. Amanda Cluett continued to spend winters there after George's death in 1912, usually with her daughter Nellie.

85. In 1892, Wilfred Thomason Grenfell was sent by the Royal National Mission to Deep Sea Fishermen to determine the health needs of Labrador's fishermen and their families. He raised funds to set up the first two hospitals in Labrador and hired two doctors and two nurses. He continued to work throughout his life to provide medical services, schools, an orphanage and cooperative "cottage industries" which provided work for the local fishermen during the eight months a year when they were locked in by ice. Today, Grenfell Mission hooked rugs, which expanded an existing craft form, are extremely collectible items of folk art. The Grenfell house in St. Anthony, Newfoundland, is now a historic site. In 1910 Amanda Cluett's diary notes several visits both in Troy and Palm Beach where Dr. Grenfell spoke about his Mission. "We invite all the families along Lake Worth to meet Dr. Grenfell and see his pictures with a magic lantern and hear his story of his Labrador work. Everybody was delighted." She also notes the 1911 launching of the sloop *George B. Cluett* on July 1 and the August 6 sailing of the sloop loaded with supplies for the Mission.

86. On July 18, 1912, Amanda Cluett's diary notes the move into the new house, now part of the Emma Willard School campus, regretting that her husband did not live long enough to live there. Worfield Manor was the name the family gave the new home.

87. This letter gives many clues to the character of the man that George B. Cluett was during his life. His wishes also included taking care of Annie Kelly, George B. Wells, and Henry Burdo, servants who had been in his employ for many years and whom he wanted to make sure were "well cared for and [their] wants supplied."

88. Amanda R. Cluett obituary, *Troy Times*, Dec. 24, 1918.

89. Ibid. William Cluett, George's father, was an active member of the Methodist Church as were all of his family. William even spent time as a lay minister, traveling around to different churches and meetings. The collection of Cluett letters to Emily Cluett Cadby in England contain many references to the family's church activities.

90. Ibid.

91. The YWCA of Troy-Cohoes has a plaque in the entry hall noting these donations. The YWCA Archives includes material related to

Amanda Cluett's, and later her daughter, Nellie Cluett's, longstanding support of this key women's organization in Troy.

92. Amanda R. Cluett Diary, RCHS.

93. Ibid.

94. Rev. Henry was at one time assistant rector at St. Paul's Episcopal Church, Troy.

95. RCHS holds the business archives of Cluett, Peabody & Company, Inc. which include the personal papers of Sanford Cluett. They provide a fascinating look at a person who was constantly inventing new processes and machinery. He also was an accomplished artist, producing among other things, a series of pen and ink drawings which he used as Christmas cards and a wonderful pen and ink drawing of the front doorway of 59 Second Street which is still used by RCHS.

96. Much of the information we have about Albert E. Cluett comes from obituary notices at his death in 1949 and oral history research done by RCHS staff over the years with members of his family and friends. The documentary record is very scarce.

97. Albert E. Cluett obituary, *Troy Record*, Jan. 4, 1949, 11.

98. The records at the Emma Willard School archives show her listed in the annual school catalogues from 1886 to 1894. It remains unclear that she graduated but it would be likely that she graduated in 1894 when she would have been 19 years old. She is last listed in the 1893–94 catalog.

99. RCHS Archives, Scrapbook, 1927–1955 includes a clipping with photograph of a meeting of the Society in 1940 at 59 Second Street when the subject was the lives of Richard P. Hart and George B. Cluett.

100. Letter from Caroline Ide Cluett to President of the Board of RCHS (October 1952), RCHS Archives.

101. Elizabeth Shields Eddy reminiscence, RCHS. "Grandmother told me that while the house was building, they used to go to one of the houses across the street and watch the effect of the moonlight on the freshly cut marble and how it sparkled in the moonlight."

102. See Ruthanne Mills' paper on the Harts which she did for a class at Russell Sage College. For the paper she was able to interview Ruth Hart Eddy, Elizabeth Eddy's daughter, and two other Hart descendants. Miss Eddy noted that her mother had not gotten on with the secretary who had been hired to type her reminiscence and so the project was halted before it was finished. As noted above, Miss Eddy instructed that all family papers be destroyed after her death and the reminiscence and many other papers were lost.

103. Maria Tillman Diary, RCHS. This diary includes lessons, clipped newspapers and drawings, including one of the interior of the schoolroom at Mrs. O'Kills' school. Maria writes extensively about her school life in New York City and her social life in Troy. One of her best descriptions is of a party held at 59 Second Street in January 1850. The party is fully documented by bills that survive in the Hart Papers.

104. The extensive bill from Elijah Galusha for the furnishings of Caroline Hart Shields' new home covers items from the parlor suite to the kitchen and bedroom furnishings. Caroline and Hamilton Shields, who met in Newport, Rhode Island, first lived at 60 Second Street for a year, then 62 Second Street for three years. Both homes were directly across from 59 Second Street. In 1854 they moved to Washington, D.C., because of Capt. Shield's duties as a member of General John E. Wool's staff. There they lived at Franklin Square and H Street. In 1858, after Capt. Shields resigned from the army, perhaps in part because of increasing tensions between North and South, the family returned to Troy to live at 22 First Street, which remained in the Shields family until 1951 when daughter, Frances Shields, who never married, died. It was the Shields family who acquired the Furnace Grove property east of Bennington, Vermont, described in Ruth Hart Eddy et al., *Furnace Grove*.

105. Elizabeth Shields Eddy reminiscence, RCHS.

106. Particularly during the first half of the nineteenth century, residents often kept cows to provide milk. These animals were pastured in a town pasture close to the eastern hillside. As the city grew,

land development pressures did away with this open land and the development of dairy farming in the surrounding towns meant that milk was available for sale. Later bills for milk and butter exist in the Hart Papers. These items were provided by a number of farmers over the years.

107. One of the few Howard family objects known to survive is an important coach which was in Bennington, Vermont, for many years at the Eddy home after it left Troy. This coach, complete with Howard family crest, is now in the carriage collection at The Granger Homestead in Canandaigua, New York

108. Maria Quinn submits a number of bills during the mid-1850s. One bill in particular outlines the different types of window coverings she is working on. The bill covered over a year of work and amounted to less than $20.

109. Bills exist from the New York City workshops of Alexander Roux, Charles Baudouine, Marcotte & Company, Tiffany & Company and its predecessors and many others.

110. Hart Papers; Bills for hotels and purchases of bathing suits, etc. occur during the 1840s and 1850s. The Hart household traveled by steam boat to New York City with horses and carriage and servants. Betsey and her family often shopped in New York before sailing by steam boat to Newport. In 1850 the family stayed at Bellevue House. In 1855, the family rented a house. At least one of Betsey's sons, Joseph M. Hart, met and married a Newport girl, Georgianna Riddel. Several of the Hart daughters also met their prospective husbands at Newport.

111. Ruth Hart Eddy et al., *Furnace Grove*, 8.

112. Troy *City Directories*. Until the late 1850s African American names are shown in *italics*.

113. James McClay, listed as coachman between 1842 and 1846, apparently left Betsey's service and became a farmer. Several times in the late 1860s and early 1870s he sends tubs of butter to 59 Second Street with brief notes appended to the bills asking after the family.

114. Ruth Hart Eddy et al., *Furnace Grove*, 28: "Grandmother Hart had 52 grandchildren.... They were on very friendly terms, and were indefatigable in their attendance at family gatherings, weddings, funerals, etc. So far as I have observed from portraits and from individuals, there was a strong family resemblance. All were blonde, blue-eyed, of medium height, often rosy-cheeked, showing very obviously their Anglo-Saxon descent."

115. Rensselaer County Clerks Office, Deeds.

116. Every year after 1900 as Amanda Cluett's diary approaches late November, her entries focus on the pending anniversary of Alfonzo's death.

117. Amanda Cluett notes in her diary that she and her husband left the house in the possession of the young people who partied well into the wee hours of the morning.

118. The Historic American Building Survey drawings of 59 Second Street include numerous errors in measurements, details, etc. The text cover sheet that accompanies the drawings includes several statements that are erroneous given current research. Of particular importance here is the statement that Albert Cluett was the builder of the last addition to the building which would date the addition to after 1910. This is not borne out by other evidence.

119. Amanda Cluett Diary, RCHS. Oral history interviews with Mrs. J. Girvin (Caroline B.) Cluett, daughter-in-law, and Becky Cluett Houston, granddaughter, of Albert and Caroline Cluett relate the information that the basement kitchen was not used as far as they recall. The rooms in the basement, except for the front northeast room which was used as a playroom, were kept closed.

120. Amanda Cluett Diary, RCHS. While she has many descriptions of automobile trips they took during the first decade of the twentieth century, the earliest clear mention of an automobile is when she notes "July 26, 1904, At 12:25 Papa [George B. Cluett] went to Troy [from Saratoga Springs] to attend the funeral of Franklin Field. On his return home Harry [E. Harold Cluett] started to bring him as far as Mechanicville in his automobile. So they entered the Waterford bridge, the steering gear became unmanageable and they ran into the bridge throwing Papa out and cutting his head and jarring and bruising him generally. It has given us a great fright but he is wonderfully preserved from death." Most other notations are less eventful. On August 4, 1906 she notes "Today Papa bought and presented to me an elegant automobile." She, her husband and daughters Nellie and Beatrice promptly took off to stay in Swampscott, Massachusetts. On August 30, 1906, Amanda notes "Nellie, Beatrice and I start from Swampscott at 8:10 in our automobile with Geo. Wells as chauffeur to ride all the way home. We took Auntie Clark and Uncle Curtis to their home in Brookline, then we proceeded to Worcester where we lunched & reached Springfield at 5 P.M., a distance of 119 miles & beautiful trip." The next day "We had a fine night's rest and at 8:30 were ready to resume our journey. The day is perfect. We lunch at Pittsfield and have a perilous ride over Potters Mtn 2000 ft. high. Reach Troy at 5:30 and arrive in Saratoga at 7:30. All well and we enjoyed our trip immensely."

121. See Fig. 25 for page from Amanda (Mrs. George B.) Cluett's diary noting this change of ownership. A *Troy Record* article of March 26, 1926 is one of a number from the period which single out 59 Second Street as a "splendid example of domestic architecture."

122. Edward W. Root, *Philip Hooker, A Contribution to the Study of the Renaissance in America* (New York: Charles Scribner's Son, 1929). This book illustrates the Rutger B. Miller house in Utica, New York which has interior woodwork similar to that in 59 Second Street. This relationship may have resulted in the assumed Hooker connection to the building. The copy in the RCHS library was owned by Albert E. Cluett.

123. In the early 1970s the elevator was extended to the basement and third floors by RCHS with a grant from the Howard & Bush Foundation.

124. Albert E. Cluett's 1918 portrait by Samantha Huntley (1865–1949), now in the RCHS collection, shows him standing casually with a cigarette in his left hand.

125. RCHS Archives, Report of the Building Committee, 1953. This report outlines the approach the Society would take to make the building open to the public.

126. RCHS Archives, "Proposal for the use of 57 Second Street as a Museum." October 1971. Breffny Walsh's "white paper" on the acquisition of the property at 57 Second Street provided the vision for the twenty years that it took to bring the building online as a programmatic space for the organization.

Bibliography

Primary Sources

Cluett, Amanda R. Diary, 1900–1917. Rensselaer County Historical Society, Troy, New York.

Cluett, Amanda R. Correspondence, Cluett Family. Transcription in Rensselaer County Historical Society, Troy, New York.

Cluett, Peabody & Co., Inc. Archives, Sanford Cluett papers, Rensselaer County Historical Society, Troy, New York.

Eddy, Elizabeth Shields. Reminiscence. Rensselaer County Historical Society, Troy, New York.

Hart, Richard P. Memorial Booklet, 1844. Privately printed. Troy, New York.

Hart Papers, Richard P. Hart Letter Books, Inventories, etc. Rensselaer County Historical Society, Troy, New York.

Historic American Buildings Survey, Report on the Hart house, 1934. Library of Congress, Washington, DC.

Laws of the State of New-York Passed at the Thirty-Fourth Session of the Legislature, S. Southwick, Albany, New York, 1811.

Mills, Ruthanne, *The Hart Family and House,* 1969, Rensselaer County Historical Society, Troy, New York.

Minutes of the Common Council of the City of New York, 1784–1831, Vol. X, New York: City of New York, 1917.

New York City *Directories,* 1800–1845, various publishers.

Broadside, May 7th, 1812. Rensselaer County Historical Society, Troy, New York.

Rensselaer County Clerks Office, Deeds. Troy, New York.

Rensselaer County Historical Society Archives. Correspondence. Rensselaer County Historical Society, Troy, New York.

Rensselaer County Historical Society Archives Scrapbook, 1927–1955, Rensselaer County Historical Society, Troy, New York.

Rensselaer County Surrogates Court, Wills & Estate Papers. Troy, New York.

Tibbits, George Papers. Account Book. Rensselaer County Historical Society, Troy, New York.

Tillman, Maria. Diary, 1846–1851. Rensselaer County Historical Society, Troy, New York.

Tillman-Hart Genealogy. Rensselaer County Historical Society, Troy, New York.

Troy *City Directories* 1829–1955, various publishers.

Troy Savings Bank. Archives. Troy, New York.

Emma Willard School Archives, Emma Willard School, Troy, New York.

Secondary Sources

Bucher, Douglas G., and W[alter] Richard Wheeler, *A Neat Plain Modern Stile: Philip Hooker & His Contemporaries, 1796–1836.* Amherst: University of Massachusetts Press, 1993.

Buel, Jr., David, "Troy for Fifty Years," Miss Abba A. Goddard, ed., *The Trojan Sketch Book.* Troy, New York: Young & Hartt, 1846.

Clinton, DeWitt, ed., *Picturesque Oakwood, Its Past and Present Associations,* Troy, New York: Frederick S. Hills, Compiler and Publisher, 1897.

Eddy, Ruth Hart, William L. Shields, George Van Santvoord, *Furnace Grove, 1858–1958, The Story of A Family Home.* Privately printed, 1958.

Ellis, David Maldwyn, "Albany and Troy . . . Commercial Rivals," Reprinted from *New York History,* October 1943.

Fairbanks, Mrs. A. W., Editor, *Emma Willard & Her Pupils, or Fifty Years of Troy Female Seminary, 1822–1872.* New York, New York: Published by Mrs. Russell Sage, 1898.

Frost, John, LLD, *Naval and Military History of the United States.* Hartford, Connecticut: William James Hammersley, D. Appleton & Co., 1842, 1845.

Hart, James M., *Genealogical History of Samuell Hartt, Nicholas Hart, Isaac Hart.* Pasadena, California: Compiled, arranged, and published by James M. Hart, 1903.

Hayner, Rutherford, *Troy and Rensselaer County, New York, A History,* Vol. I–III. New York, New York: Lewis Historical Publishing Inc., 1925.

Hinton, Harwood Perry, *The Military Career of John Wool, 1812–1863.* Ann Arbor, Michigan: University of Wisconsin, University Microfilms, Inc., 1960.

Hunt, Gilbert J., *The Late War Between the United States and Great Britain.* New-York, New York: David Longworth, 1816.

Ketchum, Alton, *Uncle Sam: The Man and the Legend.* New York, New York: Hill & Wang, 1975.

Kimball, Francis P., *The Capitol Region of New York State, Crossroads of Empire,* Vol. I–III. New York, New York: Lewis Historical Publishing Company, Inc., 1942.

O'Callaghan, E. B., MD, *The Documentary History of the State of New-York,* Vol. I–IV. Albany, New York: Weed, Parsons & Co., Public Printers, 1850.

Root, Edward W., *Philip Hooker: A Contribution to the Study of the Renaissance in America.* New York: Charles Scribner's Sons, 1929.

Seymour, David L., *Address Delivered before the Friends and Patrons of the Troy Hospital . . . 1850.* Troy, New York: 1850.

Spafford, Horatio Gates, *A Gazeteer of the State of New-York.* Albany, New York: H. C. Southwick, 1813.

Sullivan, Dr. James, Editor in Chief, *History of New York State, 1523–1927,* Vol I–VI. New York, New York. Lewis Historical Publishing Company, Inc., 1927.

Sylvester, Nathaniel B., *History of Rensselaer Co., New York.* Philadelphia, Pennsylvania: Everts & Peck, 1880.

Weise, Arthur J., *History of the City of Troy and Lansingburgh.* Troy, New York: William H. Young, 1876.

Weise, Arthur J., *The City of Troy and Its Vicinity.* Troy, New York: Edward Green, 1886.

Weise, Arthur J., *Troy's One Hundred Years, 1789–1889.* Troy, New York: William H. Young, 1891.

Wiggins, Francis S., *The Monthly Repository and Library of Entertaining Knowledge,* Vol. II, New-York, New York: G.F. Bunce, Printer, 1832.

Willard, Emma, *Abridged History of the United States, Improved Edition,* New York, New York; A. S. Barnes & Co.; 1846.

Willard, Thomas S., *Barbarities of the Enemy Exposed in a Report.* Troy, New York: Francis Adancourt, 1813.

Woodworth, John, *Reminiscences of Troy, from Its Settlement in 1790 to 1807.* Second Edition with notes by Joel Munsell. Albany, New York: J. Munsell, 1860.

Detail, 59 Second Street, c. 1892. See Fig. 121.

59 Second Street: Its Design and Construction

Walter Richard Wheeler

The city of Troy has of late become a place of considerable note. It is but a few years since the citizens of that delightfully situated city, anticipated their total destruction, on account of the advantages Albany would derive over them, on the completion of the great Western Canal. But instead of an injury it has evidently been a benefit; and with the exception of Rochester, the advances in population and wealth, have not perhaps, been so great in any place in the State of New-York as in Troy. "Its growth," says the Sentinel, "was never before so rapid and never more healthy than at the present time. Forty buildings are erecting in one ward alone."[1]

Troy altogether is a handsome place, almost wholly laid out on right angels [sic], and although not so *grand* as Albany, I think I would prefer it as a Residence but the most part of the Public Buildings are of Brick, and rather plain to please the eye of a stranger.[2]

The stores being generally confined to River-street nearly all the business is transacted there, and hence the remainder of the city exhibits the tranquil aspect and noiseless quiet, which are seldom found but in the country. Many of the buildings, particularly those recently erected, are spacious and elegant, while nearly all are remarkable for the neatness and propriety of their construction.[3]

THESE THREE ACCOUNTS bring to life a sense of the city of Troy and its prospects as perceived by visitors and natives in the late 1820s. In this spirit of optimism William Howard commissioned a New York City architect to design a home for his daughter Betsey and son-in-law, Richard P. Hart. The house that Howard presented to his only child and her spouse represented the *ne plus ultra* with regard to popular taste and the state of the art with respect to the building technology of the time. Several of the components that went into the construction of the house were mass-produced; others, with their subsequent popularization in New York and the flowering of the Industrial Revolution, would later be made widely available via the same mode of production. The technology of the time thus ultimately facilitated the propagation of an

aesthetic that otherwise would have been prohibitively expensive for all but the extremely wealthy. The Hart house occupies an important juncture in American architectural history, constructed at a point in time when the work of the manufacturer was supplanting that of the master craftsman.

This essay will present the case for attribution of the design of 59 Second Street to a particular architect, and will present new material pertinent to his biography and career, along with those of the builders thought to have been involved in the project. It will at the same time throw light on the architectural scene in New York of the 1820s—an as yet poorly understood chapter of the profession's history. Design sources for each of the component elements of the Hart house will be discussed, and their subsequent popularization will be examined.

In order to gain a clearer sense of the architectural context in which 59 Second Street was built, and to highlight just how different it was from its local predecessors, it will first be necessary to add some detail to the picture of Troy given by the above accounts, and to recall William Howard's New York.

Architecture in Troy to 1825

Troy was a small city with a population of less than 8,000 people in 1825.[4] Its first public buildings, erected in the 1790s, were uniformly constructed in the brick vernacular Georgian style popular in the New England towns where most of the people relocating to the city had their origins (see Fig. 52). Many of the earliest houses were constructed of wood and several were built of brick. Of this second group only the house at 22 Second Street (c. 1796) remains.[5] This three-bay two-story house built of brick laid in Flemish bond has its roof-ridge parallel to the street and is raised on a low ashlar brownstone basement about two and a half feet above the pavement. Its window lintels are now obscured by

52 Rensselaer County Court House and Jail, c. 1793, from *The City of Troy and Its Vicinity*, Arthur J. Weise, 1876.

Victorian-era additions but typically were of brick or brownstone with splayed ends.

Surviving masonry houses constructed in the compact part of the city during the first decade of the nineteenth century include 12 Second Street and 12 State Street, which feature splayed brick window lintels; as well as 20 and 22 First Street (c. 1803), 28 First Street (c. 1805) and 41 Second Street (c. 1803) which all share low brownstone basements and splayed brownstone lintels (see Fig. 53). The brick façades of these houses are all laid-up in Flemish bond.

The second decade of the nineteenth century saw a further increase in the scale of the city's houses and the utilization of more elaborate decorative schemes. Brownstone was used more extensively, notably in the construction of the imposts and arches of "blind arcades." Among those buildings featuring this device are the Bank of Troy at the northwest corner of First and State streets (1811), with blind arcades on its two street elevations;[6] the Wool house at 75 First Street (1812); and the Dickinson house (c. 1814) formerly at 19 Second Street, which was further ornamented with a wrought-iron balcony (see Fig. 54).

The Vail house, at 46 First Street (1818), was among the first Troy houses with a high basement, in this case approximately six feet above street level[7] (see Fig. 17). Although the building has ornate window lintels with a raised central panel and incised decoration on its street elevations, the garden façade has the older splayed brownstone type. This three-bay house continues local tradition by having a brownstone basement and brick

laid in Flemish bond. The Vail house contains sophisticated interior woodwork, marble mantels, and an elegant three-story spiral stair in its main hall. The fanlight over the entrance is a feature that first became popular in the region at the beginning of the nineteenth century.

The recession of the late 1810s deeply affected Albany-Troy area building-trades practitioners. As opportunities for employment decreased, many mechanics relocated to larger cities. While information on Troy builders for the period is sketchy, several prominent Albany builders are known to have gone south to New York City at this time.[8] Seth and Darius Geer, Asher Riley, Lewis, Rufus, Charles and Henry Farnham, and Calvin and Otis Pollard—all former Albanians—are recorded as arriving in New York in the years following 1817.[9] Some of these men returned to Albany after the opening of the Erie Canal. Others, including the Pollards and (Seth) Geer & Riley, were to become among the most successful builders in New York.

A disastrous fire had destroyed much of River and First streets in 1820, but the economic impact of the opening of the Erie Canal helped compensate for this setback. As the decade proceeded, the city expanded east and south. To the south houses as far as Liberty Street were constructed along First and Second streets; to the east the city grew as far as Fifth Avenue. These buildings were typically two- or three-story structures. Many of them survive today, frequently masked by later alterations.[10]

While marble quarried in Vermont had been in use in the Albany region from at least the turn of the nineteenth century,[11] its utilization in a Troy building is dateable only to circa 1820. A row of three extant speculative houses at 35–39 First Street (1820) has high marble basements, windowsills, and lintels. In their original form the lintels of this row appear to have had a raised central panel not dissimilar to those used at the Vail house across the street. A pair of contemporary houses at 156–58 Third Street has marble watertables, door lintels, and windowsills.[12] The marble for both of these groups of houses probably came from quarries in Vermont or Massachusetts, which were supplying area markets as early as 1802.[13]

By 1825 economic prosperity had returned to the area, bolstered by the opening of the Erie Canal. A growing number of artisans settled in the city of Troy, including cabinetmakers, artists and silversmiths; there

53 The Lane houses, 20 and 22 First Street looking south from State Street, c. 1989.

54 John D. Dickinson house, 19 Second Street, Troy, c. 1890.

were no architects active in the city until some time later.[14] While a small body of artisans provided for the needs of Troy's elite, it is clear that the citizens also relied heavily on imports from American and European sources. Wealthier families purchased furniture, china, silver, and art from New York City-based artisans or importers.[15] In this the people and merchants of Troy participated in a national trend which had been gaining force since the end of the War of 1812. By the mid-1820s a number of Troy vendors offered clothing, china, exotic foods, and beverages shipped from New York City and more distant ports.[16]

Selecting a Site

The best residential district in Troy during the first two decades of the nineteenth century extended southward from the commercial center of the city, then at the intersection of First and State streets. The favored blocks quickly filled up, however, and by the mid-1820s Second Street was the most fashionable site for elegant new residential construction. While William Howard purchased the land for the house, it is likely that his daughter and son-in-law influenced his selection. Richard P. and Betsey Hart occupied a house at 49 Second Street as early as 1816. Their motives for wanting to stay on Second Street likely included the above-quoted "noiseless quiet" of the street, and proximity to the business relations, relatives, and friends which by that time made an enclave of the block between Congress and State streets.[17]

Background to the Design of the Hart House

William Howard's own house at 18 Dey Street in New York City, as far as can be judged from the only view available, was typical of upper-middle class New York houses of the period (see Figs. 55 and 56). A three-bay, two-story structure of brick, with a high basement, dormers, and a gabled roof, it was constructed circa 1816.[18] There appears to have been nothing to distinguish it architecturally from its immediate neighbors. It was perhaps similar to the house occupied by the famous cabinetmaker, Duncan Phyfe, one block to the north at 35 Partition Street (after 1816 known as 172 Fulton Street; see Fig. 57).

Sharing Howard's New York neighborhood were Seabury Tredwell at 12 Dey Street[19] and later, William D. Phyfe, a silversmith and nephew to Duncan, who took up residence on the south side of Dey Street. Philip Hone, mayor and diarist, owned property on the street.[20] The North River Bank occupied the west end of the block while the Franklin House hotel (c. 1817) anchored the east end of the street at its intersection with Broadway. The largest building on the street, the hotel featured a blind-arcade on its second floor. Many elegant homes lined Broadway near the hotel. One

55 Detail of *New York City from the steeple of St. Paul's Church*, aquatint, Henry Papprill from a drawing by J. W. Hill, 1849. The rear of the Howard house is circled.

block to the north on Broadway was one of New York City's most prominent landmarks, St. Paul's Church.

In 1825, Howard would have been familiar with the many recent architectural improvements on Wall Street; much of his business was conducted there.[21] It was New York's showplace—prominent among the buildings then under construction or recently finished were the

Merchants' Exchange (see Fig. 58), the Branch Bank of the United States, and the Phenix Bank—all erected after designs by Martin E. Thompson. Howard also would have been familiar with the four-bay house type that was chosen for the Hart house. Several four-bay houses on lower Broadway near Bowling Green and the John Dey house on Dey Street were certainly known to

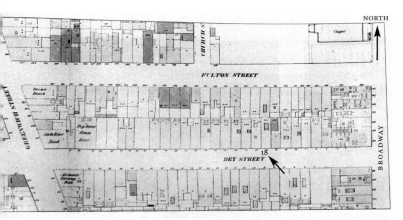

56 Detail, Plate 7 showing Dey Street, from *Maps of the City of New-York*, William Perris, 1852.

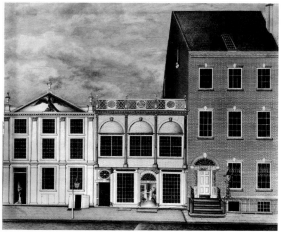

57 *The Shop and Warehouse of Duncan Phyfe*, watercolor and pen and ink, John Rubens Smith, 1816–17.

58 The Merchants' Exchange, New York City, alternate elevation design, ink and wash drawing, unidentified draughtsman after a design by Martin E. Thompson, c. 1825.

Howard (see Fig. 59). The John L. Lawrence house on East Fourteenth Street and the General Jacob Morton house on Morton Street were also of this type.

After his purchase of the Second Street property in Troy, the first decision facing William Howard was the selection of a builder or architect to execute an appropriate design.[22] Howard's sophisticated taste and social standing called for the selection of a professional architect—as opposed to one of the hundreds of builders active in the city of New York—to design the house he

contemplated for his daughter and her family. The design selected would ultimately be a product of the taste of both Howard and his architect, informed by the "campaign to beautify, one of the deepest urges within genteel culture," in the words of a modern historian.[23]

By 1825, the first professional architects[24] had begun to offer their services to the public in the nation's larger cities; many of these individuals started their careers as builders. Among this first generation of native-born professionals were John McComb, Jr., Josiah R. Brady and Martin E. Thompson in New York, Charles Bulfinch in Boston, and Philip Hooker in Albany.

The requirements of superintending the construction of 59 Second Street would have been easier had William Howard been able to select a Troy-based architect. However no architects are known to have been in practice at such an early date in Troy, and only two were active in nearby Albany during the period: Philip Hooker and Richard Allanson. Hooker's career, featuring prominent commissions from 1796 onward, is well documented. Allanson's work is less well known.[25]

Despite circumstantial connections suggesting Philip Hooker as architect of 59 Second Street, evidence points to a New York City source for the design.[26] Hart family oral tradition and an unpublished family reminiscence, *Furnace Grove, 1858–1958, The Story of a Family Home*, relates that William Howard was responsible for commissioning the house. A notice in a Troy newspaper

59 *Corner of Greenwich and Dey Streets, New York City*, watercolor by Baroness Hyde de Neuville, 1810. Note the four bay house in the center foreground which was owned by John Dey.

recording materials being accepted by Richard P. Hart and his partner Elias Pattison on behalf of William Howard adds weight to this tradition.[27] It was William Howard who assembled and purchased the lots upon which the house was constructed and he retained ownership of the property until 1834.[28]

Architects in Practice in New York City in 1825

The search to identify the New York-based architect who designed the Hart house led to the examination of the work of a number of individuals who were practicing in the years leading up to 1825. A large number of builder-architects were active in New York City at this time, and their individual careers are as yet poorly understood. Several were chosen for close examination. The lives, careers, and aesthetic preferences of John McComb, Jr., James O'Donnell, Joseph Newton, Thomas C. Taylor, Josiah R. Brady, and Minard Lafever will be briefly examined below; that of Martin E. Thompson, the probable architect of the Hart house, will be discussed in more detail.

JOHN McCOMB, JR. (1763–1853) was perhaps the most prominent architect in practice in New York at the turn of the nineteenth century. He was responsible for the design of the city's most prestigious public and private buildings, among them City Hall (1802–1810, with Francis Mangin), the Grange, home of Alexander Hamilton (1801–02),[29] and the Rotunda (1818).[30] His work encompassed many residential projects, a number of which share details with the Hart house. Unfortunately, little is known of his work through the 1820s. It has not been possible to connect him in any way with the Hart house commission.[31]

JAMES O'DONNELL (1774–1830) was born in Ireland, came to New York City about 1812 and initially worked in the Federal style. His major identified works include the Bloomingdale Asylum (1817–21), the Fulton Street Market (1821–22) and several churches and row houses, including those at 16–19 State Street (1815–17). He later designed the Gothic Revival Eglise Notre Dame in Montreal (1823–29).[32] No evidence was found to connect him to 59 Second Street.

JOSEPH NEWTON (d. c. 1826) appears as early as the 1780s in the New York Common Council minutes, most often referred to as a builder. Several of his competently executed drawings are preserved at the Avery Architectural Library, Columbia University.[33] Among these is a plan (c. 1792) for a four-bay house for Thomas Ellison, rector of St. Peter's Episcopal Church in Albany—thus indicating that his practice extended up the Hudson River Valley. Another drawing preserves his design for a

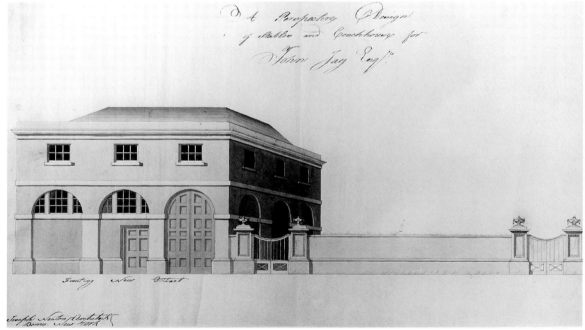

60 John Jay carriage house, New York City, ink and wash drawing, Joseph Newton, c. 1790.

carriage house for John Jay (see Fig. 60). Newton appears in the *New York City Directory* as late as 1825,[34] but it is unlikely that he survived long enough to have been involved in the design of the Hart house.

THOMAS C. TAYLOR (d. after 1843)[35] is documented as having provided designs for at least one project in the Albany area—the first design for the Albany Academy in 1815.[36] He was involved in the construction of St. John's Chapel in New York City after the designs of John McComb, Jr. in 1807.[37] By 1828, he had relocated to Westchester County, but maintained the office at 41 Robinson Street in New York that he had occupied since circa 1824.[38] Nothing is known of his later work and no evidence exists to connect him to the Hart house.

JOSIAH R. BRADY (c. 1760–1832) was a proponent of the earlier *Gothick* Revival, utilizing it in his design for Trinity Church (c. 1791), his earliest documented architectural work.[39] He was, in addition, a practitioner of the Federal style popular with that generation. Fragmentary evidence suggests that Brady and Martin E. Thompson were professionally associated in some manner, perhaps as early as 1824.[40] The exact nature and extent of the Brady and Thompson association remains unclear, but it was certainly over by December 1826, at which date Thompson is documented as in partnership with Ithiel Town. Brady may have been acquainted with Ithiel Town, as his design for St. Luke's Church, Rochester, New York (1824–28), was an adaptation of Town's design for Trinity Church, New Haven, Connecticut (1814–17). Alexander Jackson Davis became a draftsman for Brady in 1826, and left to pursue a career as an architectural illustrator the following year. Brady executed designs for the Canal Street Market in late 1827 and retired by 1829.[41]

The nature of Alexander Jackson Davis' relationship with Brady makes it unlikely that the latter was the designer of the Hart house. A. J. Davis recorded his great admiration for Brady; he also set down his equally great distaste for the "irrationality" of designs in the Hart house style. Davis, who freely offered the most vitriolic criticism of his contemporaries, fell silent only when it came to the man he considered his mentor. It is unlikely that he would write in such negative terms about a design by Brady.

MINARD LAFEVER (1798–1854) was considered as possible architect of 59 Second Street chiefly because of

61 Plate 42, *Young Builder's General Instructor*, Minard Lafever, 1829.

Plate 42 in his *Young Builder's General Instructor* of 1829, which depicts a door surround almost identical to that of the Hart house (see Fig. 61). Although frequently considered to be the designer of this surround, a close examination of the text of that book demonstrates that this is not the case. Lafever describes his plate as "similar to doors executed in houses of the first class in this city," thus indicating that the design was already in circulation. He claims for himself only the design of the "side and fan lights,"[42] which are, in themselves, unlike those at 59 Second Street.

When Lafever discusses Plate 60 (see Fig. 62) of that volume—showing the elevation of a house incorporating the same door surround—he describes the design as "very similar to Houses of three stories in New-York, excepting the Attic story." It is clear from the illustration that Lafever has added a boldly detailed tier of panels and dormers to a façade that is otherwise Federal in detail. In pointing this feature out, he apologizes for the disparity, thus distancing himself from authorship of the remainder of the façade. It is therefore probable that Lafever has only designed the attic in this elevation, merely appending it to an already extant drawing. At the very least his text suggests more than one hand contributed to the design of this plate.[43] Lafever acknowledged the assistance of Brady and Thompson in his introduction to his second published pattern book, *The Modern Builder's Guide* (1833), which suggests that he had worked for them, or at least knew them professionally.[44] Perhaps Plates 42 and 60 resulted from that association.

Martin Euclid Thompson: Architect of 59 Second Street?

Martin E. Thompson is the most likely architect of 59 Second Street. He was a pioneer in the architectural application of Westchester marble. He was arguably the most prominent among a small field of professional architects designing in the conservative style embodied in the Hart house and was described in 1828—together with Ithiel Town—as "stand[ing] at the head of their profession . . . and hav[ing] produced the best specimens of architecture."[45] It seems likely, however, given the distance involved, that Thompson merely provided plans and elevations for the project, or perhaps a bound book of drawings and specifications, like those provided by his contemporaries when rendering services

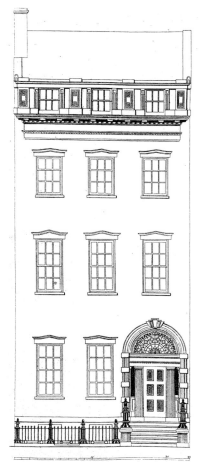

62 Detail, Plate 60, *Young Builder's General Instructor*, Minard Lafever, 1829.

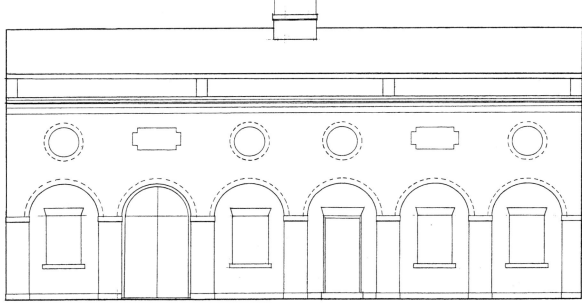

63 Reconstructed east elevation of the carriage house circa 1827, 59 Second Street, Troy, D. G. Bucher, 1999.

at long distance.[46] In addition, Thompson may have had a hand in selecting the craftsmen who executed the wood, plaster, and ironwork.

Martin Euclid Thompson was born in New Jersey during the year 1785/6.[47] He probably began his education as an apprentice to one of the number of builders with the surname Thompson, possibly relatives, known to have been active in Hudson County, New Jersey, as late as the first half of the nineteenth century.[48] Typically he would have ended his apprenticeship at age 21, and so was a practicing builder as of circa 1807. He was a resident of Elizabeth Town in 1810 when he married the former Polly Kitchell of Hanover, New Jersey, in the Presbyterian Church there.[49] Although Thompson's activities are as yet undocumented for the period 1810–1816, it is probable that he remained in the Elizabeth Town area. Thompson and his wife were living in New York City by May of 1816; he appears for the first time as a carpenter in the city *Directory* for that year.[50]

During the next several years, Thompson is recorded as a carpenter residing at 143 Lombardy Street in the city *Directory*;[51] the edition of 1823 contains the earliest known published reference to Thompson as an "architect & builder."[52] Thompson is given sole credit for the design of the Second Branch Bank of the United States (1822–24), his first major work.[53] It is likely that by 1824 he had formed a professional association with the architect Josiah R. Brady, as the latter appears to have consulted with Thompson on the design of the Merchants' Exchange (1824–27).[54] Thompson may have learned the fine points of architectural design and drafting from the elder Brady.

The importance of the Bank and Exchange commissions cannot be overstated. Although conservative in style when compared to work being done in other American cities, these two structures were highly regarded and influential in New York City.[55] The Bank and the Merchants' Exchange were the first buildings constructed in that city utilizing Westchester marble for architectural purposes.[56] Westchester (also known as American or Eastchester)[57] marble had been used for tabletops, gravestones and various utilitarian functions since its discovery, sometime before 1803.[58] Abijah Smith pioneered quarrying of the stone for building purposes in 1822;[59] this stone may have been intended for Thompson's Second Branch Bank. Brady's St. Thomas' Church, New York City (1824–26) was constructed of Westchester marble, left rough cut and trimmed with dressed brownstone.[60] Thompson and Brady together pioneered the application of this stone. For the first time, New York City builders were given the opportunity to execute classically inspired architectural detail in an archaeologically correct material.

Thompson's earliest buildings display that same mixture of Georgian and neoclassical aesthetics—in what is popularly known as "Federal" style—as that of Brady and his generation. A number of surviving drawings by Thompson from the 1820s depict details seen on the Hart house façade. Among these, one of two alternate elevations for the Merchants' Exchange is perhaps the most compelling (see Fig. 58). The drawing shows a round-topped "Venetian" window in the cupola, the transom of which appears similar to that of the Hart house door surround. The paneled treatment of the marble blocks at the base of the stairs is identical with those appearing on the Hart house. The blind-arcades of the first floor are similar in proportion and detail to those seen in the design of the carriage-house at 59 Second Street (see Figs. 63 and 216) Ironwork comprising the railing around the cupola features the Vitruvian scroll motif displayed so prominently in the ironwork at the Hart house.[61] Another drawing, an elevation of the Second Branch Bank (see Fig. 64) shows Thompson making use of paneled plinths under the second floor windows that are similar to those occupying the analogous space under the first floor fenestration of the Hart house. And finally, the Hart house and the Bank feature window architraves with the same moldings.

The Hart house was probably designed in November 1825, just after William Howard's purchase of the

64 The Second Branch Bank of the United States, New York City, ink and wash drawing, after a design by Martin E. Thompson, c. 1824.

65 The Rensselaer County Courthouse, lithograph, August Kollner, c. 1850. St. Paul's Church tower can be seen in the background to the left of the courthouse.

Troy property.[62] This would have allowed for execution of drawings for the stonecutters and delivery of the material to the site by the early spring of 1826. Thus Thompson was either working on his own, or toward the end of his speculated association with Brady, when the design was drafted.[63]

By December 1826,[64] Thompson was professionally associated with Ithiel Town, in what is known to historians as the first professional architectural office in New York City.[65] They had become acquainted as early as January of that year, when both were elected to the architectural department of the newly organized National Academy of Design.[66] Town had previously practiced architecture in New Haven, Connecticut, specializing in Greek Revival and Gothic Revival designs. Having acquired much of his design sensibility from the latest European books, Town's work did not make use of the neoclassical details that characterized Thompson's work of the period.

Alexander Jackson Davis and Thomas Rust are documented as having been draftsmen for the firm during its brief existence.[67] Ithiel Town divided his professional activities between two partnerships at this time, providing architectural designs from the office in New York he shared with Thompson, while simultaneously fielding engineering projects with Isaac Damon of Northampton, Massachusetts.[68]

Documented commissions by Town & Thompson are few. The nature of the projects from their office suggests that they frequently worked separately on commissions—Town's work retaining a bookishness, while that of Thompson retaining vestiges of eighteenth century

builder sensibilities. One structure probably designed by Ithiel Town while the two men were associated was the Rensselaer County Courthouse (demolished c. 1898) in Troy (see Fig. 65). Designed some time between March and December 1827, it featured detailing that bore direct comparison to Town's contemporary Connecticut State House, and may have been commissioned by building committee member Richard P. Hart.[69] Town & Damon were among the bidders for construction of the courthouse; builders based in New York City dominated the field of bidders proposing to construct the building.[70] John B. Colegrove, builder of the Hart house and former resident of New York City, was selected to represent the New York-based builder who won the commission.[71] The courthouse appears to have been the first building constructed utilizing stone quarried by the prisoners at Sing-Sing. This fact resulted in many delays while the commissioners of the prison, one of whom was George Tibbits, a prominent Troy businessman and mayor of the city, educated themselves in the marble quarrying business.[72] Construction extended from 1828 to 1831. Building committee member Richard P. Hart served as their representative, visiting Ossining on more than one occasion to verify the progress of the contract with the prison.[73] Town & Davis designed alterations to the Troy building in 1834, adding further weight to the attribution of the original structure to Town & Thompson.[74]

A second building may have helped introduce Town's work to a Trojan audience while he was in partnership with Thompson (see Fig. 66). St. Paul's Church was begun in April 1827. Essentially a copy of Trinity Church, New Haven, Connecticut, designed by Town and constructed in 1814–17, the similarities between the two buildings are marked. Architectural historian William H. Pierson, Jr. has suggested that Town may have been known to the residents of Troy via the rector of the church, David Butler, who had formerly resided in New Haven,[75] but it is equally probable that he was introduced to his Troy client by Thompson. Richard P. Hart's business partner, Elias Pattison, and Hart's close associate, George Tibbits, were both vestrymen of the church at this time.[76] The building may have been erected from drawings by Town; the changes one sees in the execution of the Troy version of the church may be due to the lack of Town's supervision at the site.[77] Pierson suggests that "an article published in the *Troy Sentinel* at the time of the consecration ... [is] so similar to

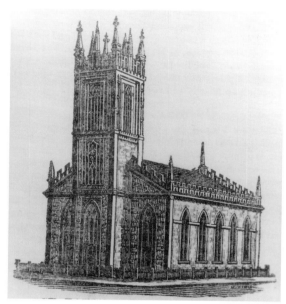

66 St. Paul's Church, woodcut engraving, Myron King, 1828.

Town's own description of Trinity that the latter must have been known in Troy and may even have been a source of vital information for the planning of the church."[78] If Town did provide the drawings and specifications for the building, he did so while in partnership with Thompson.

Subsequent to the construction of 59 Second Street, Town designed four bridges in the Troy area (between 1829 and 1832) for the Rensselaer and Saratoga Railroad Company, whose board of directors included Richard P. Hart.[79]

Town & Thompson were also responsible for the design of the Phoenix Bank in Hartford, Connecticut; the Boston Theatre, Boston, Massachusetts; the Church of the Ascension on Canal Street, New York City; and Christ Church, Hartford, Connecticut—the last in the Gothic style.[80] It is not known which man was responsible for the design of each structure, although it is probable that Town, fielding the Connecticut commissions from among his acquaintances, was principally responsible for the projects there.

It is probable that during his brief association with Town, Thompson was first exposed to the new Greek Revival style, via Town's famous library which contained many folios and engravings depicting Greek and Roman antiquities, and which Town & Thompson opened to the public by 1828.[81] Elements not featured in Thompson's designs prior to the partnership figure

prominently in the works of Town & Thompson; among the most apparent references are the archaeologically correct details from ancient Greek structures taken from Stuart and Revett's *Antiquities of Athens* (1762–1794) that begin to inform the designs emanating from the office. Town was undeniably one of the major proponents of Greek Revival architecture in the United States; while other architects in Philadelphia and Baltimore[82] had previously worked in this mode, the more conservative northeast had to wait for Town's Connecticut State House, New Haven, Connecticut (1827) for a major expression of this style. Thompson increasingly utilized the style as the 1820s drew to a close.

The partnership of Town & Thompson was over by February 1828, at which time Thompson moved from their office in the Merchants' Exchange into an office across the hall, and Davis took over as Town's new partner.[83] Town & Davis enjoyed a wide patronage in the Troy area in the years immediately after the construction of 59 Second Street.[84]

Thompson secured a number of important commissions in the years immediately following the dissolution of his partnership with Town. He was paid for a series of designs suggesting additions to the New York City Hall during 1828.[85] By 1828, Columbia College became a prominent patron of Thompson's work; he designed their College Building[86] and several row houses. Thompson's drawing for a pair of row-houses for Chapel Street in New York (c. 1829; see Fig. 67) incorporates door surrounds whose enframements are nearly identical to those of 59 Second Street, with the exception that the rusticated blocks that form such a memorable part of the Troy building's door surround are omitted there, with only the molded trim utilized.[87]

Town & Thompson had employed several draughtsmen in their office. Subsequent to the dissolution of their partnership, Thompson continued this practice, possibly retaining some employees after the end of the Town & Thompson partnership. A few of these apprentice architects can be positively identified from their contributions to the drawings that survive from the office. Among these are Robert Cary Long, Jr. (c. 1829), Charles H. Mountain, and Richard C. Harrison (c. 1840).[88] Minard Lafever and James H. Dakin (1806–1852) may have been among this group as well (see Fig. 20).[89]

Martin E. Thompson is traditionally credited with the design of The Row, a group of townhouses on the north side of Washington Square in New York City,

67 Speculative houses for Columbia College, New York City, ink and wash drawing, after a design by Martin E. Thompson, c. 1829.

68 Elevation of a house for Columbia College, New York City, ink and wash drawing, after a design by Martin E. Thompson, c. 1829.

constructed circa 1831–33 (see Fig. 70).[90] The attribution is supported by extant drawings from Thompson's office depicting row houses of a similar type designed for Columbia College (see Fig. 68). One drawing (c. 1829) depicts pointed lintels, Ionic columns and paneled bases similar to those used at The Row. Some evidence supports the proposition that Samuel Thomson was the builder.[91] While these buildings are largely Greek Revival in style, they make use of the same basement window enframements as those at the Hart house for the basement apertures (see Fig. 69). The primary spaces of these houses feature Greek Revival details, while the remainder of the rooms utilize the same carved wood corner-blocks known as "raffle flowers" featured in the Hart house.[92]

A row of five houses known as Park Place was constructed for William Howard circa 1836–37 by John B. Colegrove on Congress Street in Troy, immediately to the south of the Hart house (see Fig. 71). These dwellings shared all of their principal features with houses in The Row in New York City and can be attributed to

Martin E. Thompson on that basis (see Fig. 70). Among the features held in common were attic windows embedded in a wide entablature, molded lintels, and shallow porches featuring Doric columns supported on stoops featuring paneled plinths. Their construction ten years after the completion of 59 Second Street

69 Basement window surround, 20 Washington Square North, New York, 1999.

70 The Row, Washington Square North, New York City. The Rogers house is the seventh doorway at left from the corner, c. 1922.

71 Detail, view on Second Street looking north toward Congress Street and Park Place, Troy, c. 1885.

suggests an ongoing patronage of Thompson on the part of Howard.[93]

The 1830s witnessed Thompson's continued rise to prominence in his field; he took his place among the most influential citizens of the day. By 1833 he had become one of the Council members for the University of the City of New York (now New York University) and a director of the New York Institution of the Deaf and Dumb (see Figs. 72 and 73). He was simultaneously a director of the Tradesmen's Bank and the Traders' Insurance Company. He served as one of three vice-presidents of the American Institute of the City of New-York, organized in January 1828.[94]

Thompson is said to have been responsible for the design of a cell block at Sing-Sing Prison, probably circa 1835.[95] It is likely that he had developed a relationship, if briefly, with the institution several years previous to this date. The door surround he is thought to have designed for the Hart house had begun mass production there circa 1830–31.[96] Thomas Carmichael, who had ap-

prenticed at the office of Town & Davis, supervised all architectural stone cutting at the Sing-Sing quarries during this same period; he may have been Thompson's connection to the prison.[97]

When the Great Fire of 1835 destroyed a substantial part of the business district of New York City (including Thompson's Merchants' Exchange), Thompson and many other architects provided designs for commercial buildings to replace those lost. Thompson is documented as having designed no fewer than four of these structures in the year following the fire, and is probably responsible for many more.[98]

72 The New York Institution of the Deaf & Dumb, Fourth Avenue at Fiftieth Street, New York City, woodcut, unidentified artist, c. 1833.

73 Former Jail, as modified into the Hall of Records, City Hall Park, New York City, ink and wash drawing, unidentified draughtsman after a design by Martin E. Thompson, c. 1831.

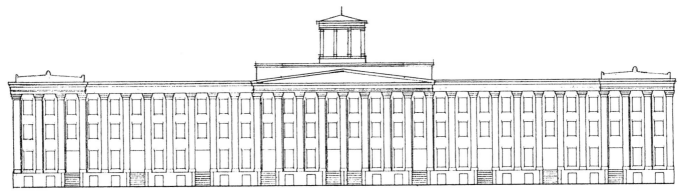

74 Washington Place, Troy, reconstruction drawing, John G. Waite, originally published in *Architecture Worth Saving in Rensselaer County, NY,* revised by D.G. Bucher, 1999.

Thompson designed several additional buildings in the upper Hudson River Valley. Among these were the First Reformed Church, in Hudson (1836),[99] and a State Arsenal (1841; probably intended for Watervliet).[100] He also may be connected to the design of Washington Place in Troy, erected 1836–42 (see Fig. 74).[101] Thompson's career ultimately encompassed commissions ranging north to Canada and south to Mississippi.[102]

Thompson readily engaged in what became known by later historians as "the battle of the styles," alternately designing buildings in the Gothic, Greek and Italian modes. Highlights of his later career include Italianate designs for the James Lenox house "Netherwood" in New Hamburg, New York (1837–38); the Gothic Revival designs for the New York Institution for the Blind, New York City (1837–42) and the State Arsenal, New York City (1847–51); and the Italianate

Hanover Bank (the present India House), New York City (1853–54) (see Fig. 75). This, Thompson's last executed work, retains the proportions and some of the detailing of his earliest projects in its interpretation of the later style.[103]

Thompson continued his architectural work until about 1855, practicing during the greater part of it in the shadow of Town & Davis.[104] Thompson's portrait, executed circa 1830 by William Sidney Mount (see Fig. 76) and now preserved in the collections of The Metropolitan Museum of Art, depicts him as a determined man, but not without a hint of mischief, expressing itself

75 The Hanover Bank, Hanover Square, New York City, now known as India House, 1999.

76 Martin Euclid Thompson, oil on canvas, William Sidney Mount, c. 1830.

about his lower lip and eyes. Mount described Thompson as "an early friend with large humanity."[105] Part of a drawing of the façade of a Doric temple occupies the lower left background of the portrait. Perhaps its presence was meant to evoke Thompson's contributions toward the spread of the Greek Revival style in America.

John Bard Colegrove: Builder of 59 Second Street

John B. Colegrove was born September 19, 1798, in Putnam County, New York[106] (see Fig. 77). One of ten children, he chose carpentry as his profession along with at least one of his younger siblings, Samuel Wheeler Colegrove (c. 1815–1862), who would later work in partnership with him.[107] Colegrove's obituary states that he "apprenticed himself to his trade and commenced business in New York City" and that he "worked there for some 10 years," suggesting his arrival there by 1816, the year of Martin E. Thompson's arrival in New York.[108] Nothing is known of Colegrove's apprenticeship, but it probably occurred in New York between 1816 and 1820, when he appeared in the New York City *Directory* for the first time, with his profession listed as carpenter.[109] Colegrove moved to Troy in 1826, expressly to oversee the construction of the Hart house.[110]

77 John Bard Colegrove, c. 1855.

The reason for Colegrove's selection as builder remains unknown, but it is possible that he was associated with Martin E. Thompson, or the firm Farnham & Pollard.[111]

Colegrove appears to have early on resolved upon remaining in Troy; soon after his arrival he joined the Apollo Masonic Lodge.[112] He was active in all lodge affairs, weathered the storm of the anti-Masonic movement of the late 1820s and early 1830s, and supported its various activities for the greater part of his life.[113] On May 27, 1828, Colegrove was one of the charter appointees to the Niagara Fire Department, serving the city of Troy. Jairus Dickerman, a prominent marble-mason who would later work at the Hart house, joined on the same day.[114] Thus it is likely they were closely acquainted from an early period in their careers.

Immediately after the completion of the Hart house, Colegrove took on responsibility for construction of the Rensselaer County Courthouse (1828–31), probably designed by Town & Thompson.[115] Only a general sense of John Colegrove's professional activities after 1830 can be assembled, chiefly through perusal of the Troy Common Council minutes and information contained in his obituary. References in the Common Council minutes are confined to small projects involving the repair of city-owned structures. The minutes also document Colegrove's early partnership with Calvin Warner, a mason and sometime partner of Jairus Dickerman. Colegrove & Warner are mentioned as in partnership during 1833, for the execution of what appears to be a contract for construction of city sewers.[116]

The next year saw Colegrove's first involvement in activities of a political nature. His motives for entry into the political arena probably included a desire to stabilize his income and expand his client base. The March 22, 1834, edition of the *Albany Evening Journal* reprinted an article from the *Daily Troy Press*, in which Colegrove is noted as having been elected as one of the vice presidents of a "Great Meeting of the Merchants, Manufacturers, Mechanics and others of the city of Troy," whose purpose was to organize protest against government actions regarding currency and banks. On May 13, 1834, he was elected city assessor of the Second District, the first of several terms in public office.[117]

Colegrove continued in public affairs during the later 1830s and into the early 1840s. In August 1839, he visited Coxsackie, New York as a delegate representing Rensselaer County at the convention of "Whig Young Men of the Third Senatorial District" of New York;[118] he had previously represented the Troy Whigs at the Rensselaer County convention in October 1835.[119] Colegrove was elected a city assessor in the elections of 1838–1841 and 1843.[120] He also continued to execute repairs to city-owned properties, including the fence of Mount Ida Cemetery and the engine house of the Phoenix Hose Company. This latter work was done in collaboration with his brother Samuel.[121]

Colegrove was at work at 59 Second Street again in 1835–37, this time in the construction of a three-story addition to the rear of the building. Involvement with the Howard-Hart family continued with Colegrove's construction of Park Place for William Howard in 1836–37[122] (see Fig. 71). As previously noted, Park Place was almost identical to The Row on Washington Square North in New York City—the design of which has traditionally been attributed to Martin E. Thompson.

The panic of 1837 caused a slowdown of construction activity across the nation, and Colegrove probably suffered along with other builders. However, at least one substantial project is known to have sustained him throughout the latter half of the decade: Washington Place, constructed 1838–42 along the south side of the newly created Washington Park in Troy, and conceived of as a unified row of ten immense, contiguous rowhouses featuring Doric pilasters (see Fig. 74). Perhaps the most striking feature of this row was a cupola in the form of a Greek temple that formerly surmounted a triangulated pediment above the central two houses. While the architect of this masterful design is unknown, the nature of patronage in Troy at this time suggests that the designer was either based or trained in New York City.[123]

Colegrove's activities during the middle of the 1840s were largely confined to Cohoes; he is noted in a city history as "then one of the principal carpenters of the place."[124] In 1844–45, he constructed the Ogden Mill No. 1 in Cohoes, New York and Ogden Mill No. 2 in that city the following year. He was also responsible for the construction of the Strong Mill in Cohoes in 1846.

During the year 1854, Colegrove was master carpenter for the construction of the castellated North Second Street Methodist Episcopal Church in Troy, erected after the designs of Jared C. Markham.[125] In 1856–58, Colegrove superintended construction of the Troy University, a large building in "the Byzantine style of architecture," to the designs of Edson & Englebert, architects of New York City[126] (see Fig. 78). He also continued

78 Troy University, Troy (1858), seen at top left of image, c. 1860.

to take on small projects including the hanging of a swing for Mrs. Nathan Warren on November 27, 1858.[127] Colegrove was active as late as April 1859, executing renovations to the Hart's store at 203 River Street in Troy.[128]

Colegrove died on April 11, 1860. His obituary depicted him as a respected citizen and builder.

Mr. Colegrove died about 8 o'clock last evening, in the sixty second year of his age. He came to this city thirty-three years ago, and in the course of his career as a carpenter and builder, erected some of the finest public and private edifices in this city and vicinity. The Court House, Washington Place, and two Cohoes Factories, we can recall as evidences of his skill and thorough workmanship.

As a man, Mr. Colegrove was correct and true—an excellent citizen, and honored in his private relations. He was a highly respected member of the Masonic Fraternity—a charter member of Mount Zion Lodge, a member of Apollo Chapter, and Treasurer of Apollo Commandery of Knight Templars—to which office he was re-elected for the 9th or 10th time last Friday evening. He will be buried with Masonic honors.[129]

The obituary published in the *Troy Daily Budget* added further details.

His life was an active one, having apprenticed himself to his trade & commenced business in the city of New York. He came to this city in the year 1827, & has resided here. . . . The marble house in Second St., the residence of Mrs. R. P. Hart, the University of Troy, the Washington Park Row, Park Place, the court house & several large factories at Cohoes are among the evidence of his talents as a builder.[130]

Francis & James Kain; Alexander Masterton & Abijah Smith: Dealers in Westchester Marble

The marble blocks used in the façade of 59 Second Street were likely fabricated by a New York City-based stone-yard. Francis and James Kain were among the first to market and quarry the Westchester stone as a building material.[131] Francis is noted as a "sculptor" and proprietor of a "marble yard" as early as 1822.[132] They provided both dressed and unfinished marble for construction purposes, and cut the stone in their shop with a steam powered saw.[133] By September 1826 (and likely as early as the beginning of 1825), the Kain brothers had formed a partnership with Alexander Masterton (1797–1859) and Abijah Smith to execute the stonework for Martin E. Thompson's Merchants' Exchange.[134] Alexander Masterton had previously joined in partnership with Smith by 1822, their shop being located on Broome Street near Thompson.[135] Both Masterton and Smith were residents of Westchester County; they operated stonecutting sheds adjacent to the quarry of the Kain brothers.[136] The Kain brothers had ended this association by May 1828, when the following advertisement appeared in an Albany paper.

Marble Factory and Chimney Piece warehouse, No. 359 Greenwich s[t]reet, New York—Francis & James Kain, keep constantly on hand, at the above factory, a general assortment of *Chimney Pieces*, of the newest and most fashionable patterns, both of foreign and domestic Marble, together with Monuments, Tomb and Grave stones, which they offer on the most reasonable terms. Also, White Marble for building, from their Quarries at East Chester, either finished or in the rough. All orders, addressed as above, will meet with prompt attention.[137]

It is probable that much of the stone for the Hart house left a shop in New York City in a rough-dressed state, with only the decorative details being finished there. The stone for the body of the façade was likely finished on site in Troy to achieve the carefully fitted work we see today. The stone for Thompson's roughly contemporary Merchants' Exchange was "brought in a rough state to the street, and worked on the spot."[138] Regardless of whether the stone was finished in New York or in Troy, the firm would have required an on-site person to supervise the placement of the stone ele-

ments. While it cannot presently be determined who provided the stone for 59 Second Street, the most likely candidate is the firm who did the stone work for the Exchange: Kain, Masterton & Smith.[139]

Henry Farnham: Woodcarver

The earliest identified structure that utilizes the distinctive corner-block and center panel designs ornamenting the interior door and window surrounds at 59 Second Street is the Albany Academy, designed by Philip Hooker and constructed 1815–17. A carver based in Albany, Henry Farnham, executed the interior work[140] (see Fig. 79). Other early structures featuring these decorative details include the renovations at the New York State Capitol in 1818—also by Hooker, also executed by Farnham[141]—and the Stephen van Rensselaer IV house of 1817—attributed to Hooker as well. All three of these projects significantly predate the Hart house, and the utilization of these design elements in New York City. Henry Farnham is connected with all of the earliest executed designs after this pattern, and as such the design of the woodwork at the Hart house can be attributed to him, or one of his followers.

79 Doorway, Albany Academy (1816), Albany, c. 1929. This image is from Edward Root's monograph on Philip Hooker.

It is not known when Henry Farnham was born, but it was probably between 1785 and 1790. His brother Lewis (1782–1842)[142] is first documented as living in Albany on April 7, 1808 when he married Betsey Albraght.[143] The census of 1810 indicates the presence of a youth aged 16–26 in Lewis' household—it is probable this was his brother Henry. Henry was likely apprenticed either to one of his three brothers, all in the building trades, or with a cabinetmaker. Contemporary rules of apprenticeship meant that Henry would have been in the service of his master until he reached his *majority*—that is, twenty-one years of age.[144]

The earliest document that details Henry Farnham's professional activities is an 1811 bill from Philip Hooker to Stephen van Rensselaer which includes costs for Farnham's carving a baluster stand for a sundial to be placed in the garden at the family's Albany Manor House.[145] Farnham's skill extended beyond that of carver—on September 5, 1818 he received a patent for a new method of "propelling boats."[146]

Bills surviving from Hooker's Albany Academy also document Farnham's early work, and the cost of the execution of the first known set of interior details of the Hart house pattern. Hooker calls the carving decorating the corner blocks "raffle flowers" in his invoices from the period.[147] He was likely referring to the then-current understanding of the word, "the subdivisions of a leaf."[148] The term is not unique to Hooker; Asher Benjamin refers to similar foliage details as "rafflelings" in a near-contemporary publication.[149]

Henry Farnham left Albany and moved to New York City about 1819 along with his brother Rufus, and was soon followed by his brothers Lewis and Charles. Otis and Calvin Pollard, related to the Farnhams by marriage,[150] arrived in New York about 1821 and circa 1826 respectively.[151] Seth Geer, superintendent of Henry Farnham's work at the Albany Academy and the New York State Capitol, moved to New York City during this same period.[152] He would later serve as master carpenter (with his partner Asher Riley, also formerly of Albany) in the construction of Thompson's Merchants' Exchange in 1824–27 and subsequently became one of the most prominent builders in New York. Geer may have introduced Farnham to Thompson and his circle. Henry Farnham's arrival in New York just precedes the earliest documented use of the raffle flower detail in that city.[153] His close connection to the Pollard family likely served him well in the professional sphere, for by

1826 Charles Farnham and Calvin Pollard formed a building firm, Farnham & Pollard, which saw much success through the 1820s and 1830s. Calvin Pollard later became a prominent architect in New York, and probably contributed to the spread of his brother-in-law's work.[154]

Farnham appears in the New York City *Directory* for most years between 1819 and 1835. It is known, however, that he maintained property in Albany during this time and was a force in promoting the rights of Albany mechanics. He was active in the Workingman's Party and ran a "Mechanic's Boarding House" in the Pastures district of that city.[155] In addition, he served on the board of directors for the Albany Journeymen House Carpenter's Architectural and Benevolent Association, formed February 8, 1831.[156]

With the popularization of the Greek Revival style, Farnham's ornate carving fell into disfavor. Bold, flat surfaces predominated, accented by equally bold carved details—owing something to the vigor of Farnham's work, to be sure, but executed on a much larger scale in keeping with the increased scale of the architecture, both public and domestic. What little evidence we have of Farnham's later career indicates that he involved himself in the execution of these early Greek Revival details, working as a carver at Stanwix Hall (1833–35, by James Dakin with Henry Rector) and the State Hall (1834–42, by Henry Rector), both in Albany. Little carved work was called for in the design of the interiors of either of these structures—Farnham instead carved the molds for casting the iron details of the interior railings, and provided a maquette for the designs of the consoles decorating the north and south porches of the State Hall, executed by another hand in marble.[157] In choosing to diversify the services he offered, Farnham was following the example of other carvers and woodworkers.[158]

Henry Farnham was likely near the end of his life when he finished the State House work. For his last documented project, renovations done at the State Capitol in Albany in 1841, payment was received by his son, Henry Farnham, Jr. on his father's behalf.[159]

It is not known when Henry Sr. died—though it is likely his passing occurred by 1856. Several Henry Farnhams are buried in the Albany Rural Cemetery—but none have vital dates that place them in the appropriate generation. His son, buried at that cemetery, died in 1901.[160]

Design and Sources: The Façade

The finest houses of the period constructed in New York City and the Albany-Troy area were most often executed in brick with brownstone basements and trim, the brownstone shipped from quarries in either Connecticut or New Jersey.[161] Marble became overwhelmingly popular soon after it became available for building purposes in New York City in 1822.[162] It was, however, rare for a private residence to have its façade executed entirely of cut and fitted stone of any variety. More likely, if this were the desired effect, "Roman cement" or "mastic" as it was also known, was applied to the brick or rubble stone surface of the wall, and scored in imitation of stone. Similar to contemporary stucco, mastic typically incorporated powdered stone of the variety being imitated, furthering the deception. Just such a treatment was utilized in the finishing of the south façade of the Hart house. The street elevation, lintels, and sills of the apertures of all elevations, and the basement of the south façade of the house were all rendered in white marble. A façade of dressed stone represented the highest standard for residential construction of the day.

A contemporary newspaper recorded that during 1826 "more than twelve hundred new houses have been built in . . . [New York City], many of them of white marble."[163] Despite this hyperbole, marble-fronted houses were never as common as the writer inferred. While many dwellings constructed in New York during the 1820s utilized marble for decorative trim, lintels and sills, no more than two dozen houses have been identified from this period that featured full fronts of marble.[164] A second contemporary source conveys the enthusiasm that met the introduction of this material.

Improvements in building.—It is not a little gratifying to an observer to witness the many recent evidences of improvement in the style shown in the erection both of public and private edifices. Since the discovery of the vast quarries of white marble in Westchester county, and the ease with which it is obtained, added to the facility and cheapness of transporting it to the city, the effect is every where manifest. Not only are there several splendid buildings, as well private as public, constructed of this rich material, but ranges of stores and dwelling houses exhibit beautiful, though partial, displays of the same article. Elegant pillars, pilasters, pediments, caps, steps, sills &c. many of them presenting the most ingenious specimens of architecture and carved work, are among the striking embellishments which adorn numbers of the newly erected houses. While these things impart an aspect of peculiar richness and beauty, they also indicate more than ordinary durability and strength. These refinements are as creditable to the taste of our citizens, as they are to the skill and ingenuity of our artists.[165]

The Hart house presents a square façade of approximately forty feet in both dimensions to Second Street. The entire front, up to the top of its cornice, is fabricated from marble quarried in Westchester County, New York, and dressed in New York City and on site. The fenestration of the basement story features rectangular windows with elaborate surrounds comprised of a molded architrave alternating with equispaced vermiculated blocks. Triple keystones convey the sense that the stone is substantial, and that it supports a great weight. This type of treatment probably has as its source the works of Renaissance architect Sebastiano Serlio, who published such a window surround in his *Tutte L'Opere D'Architettura et Prospetiva* (1619).[166] Alternately, Thompson may have been influenced by designs published in *Vitruvius Britannicus* (1715–1767)[167] or by one of the many plates featuring rusticated treatments depicted by Batty Langley in his *City & County Builder's and Workman's Treasury of Design*[168] (1750; see Figs. 80 and 81).

The basement and main façade of the house are separated by a watertable at the level of the principle floor of the house. The first floor windows sit on paneled plinths and are enframed with stone trim in imitation of typical interior woodwork of the period. Again, precedent for this type of treatment comes from publications of the Renaissance,[169] and was, like the rusticated window and door surrounds, copied extensively by British architects. The second floor windows are treated in a manner identical to those of the first floor, with the omission of the paneled bases; in their place plain sills are substituted.

The door surround at 59 Second Street features a semi-circular transom, the design of which is repeated over the front door proper, which is recessed approximately four feet from the main façade. Two unfluted Tuscan columns, executed without entasis, support a stone lintel over the outer door opening. The opening and transom are surrounded by a molded architrave alternating with vermiculated blocks, repeating the scheme employed in the basement window surrounds. A treatment similar to this arrangement is shown in Plate 10 of Swan's *Collection of Designs in Architecture*

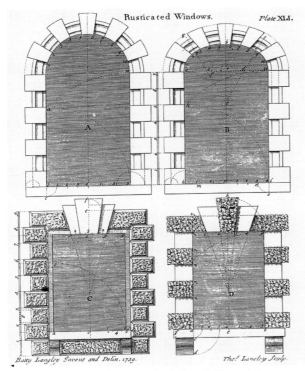

80 Detail, Plate 41, "Rusticated Windows," *City and Country Builder's and Workman's Treasury of Design*, Batty Langley, 1750.

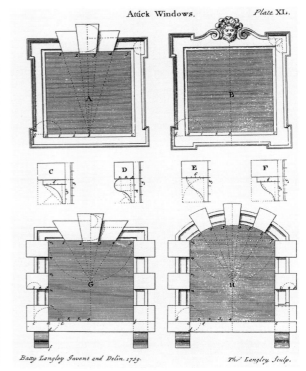

81 Detail, Plate 40, "Attick Windows," *City and Country Builder's and Workman's Treasury of Design*, Batty Langley, 1750.

(1757; see Fig. 82). Contemporary sources call this a "Venetian door."[170]

This door arrangement had a history of use in prominent London townhouses, such as those at Bedford Square, Bloomsbury, constructed c. 1775–86,[171] and a more closely related example at 29 Southenhay, West Exeter (1789). Its first appearance on an American building was probably at the William Bingham house built in Philadelphia by 1789, and recorded in a sketch elevation by Charles Bulfinch[172] (see Fig. 83). Early New York City examples were primitive in comparison to that executed in Philadelphia[173] (see Fig. 84), and were likely inspired by an English publication.

82 Detail, Plate 10, *Designs in Architecture, Vol. I*, Abraham Swan, 1757.

83 William Bingham house, Philadelphia, ink drawing, Charles Bulfinch, c. 1786.

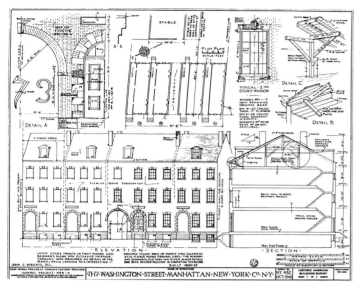

84 Fronts of four rowhouses, 71–77 Washington Street, New York City, Historic American Buildings Survey, 1940.

The entry arrangement at the Hart house differs from that typically found in a New York City town house. In New York, the front steps usually ascend to a narrow platform in front of the entrance door. At the Hart house there is no external platform; instead, that surface is held within the body of the house and the entrance door is recessed resulting in the unusual arrangement of a pair of door architraves. The outer door surround is constructed of stone while the inner doorway, complete with fanlight and sidelights, is of wood. The result is an exceptionally impressive entry. The genesis of this design may have been local regulations which restricted the distance stoops could extend onto the public sidewalk.[174] The John Paine house (c. 1825–30), formerly located at the southwest corner of State and First streets in Troy, shared this feature with the Hart house[175] (see Fig. 85).

The façade is capped with a stone entablature. Two dormers, in a style popular from the mid-eighteenth century onward, light the attic story and are partially masked behind a wooden balustrade. The balustrade hides the roof from view and enhances the monumentality of the façade.

The remaining elevations of the Hart house are constructed of brick with plain rectangular stone lintels and sills (see Fig. 86). The basement of the rear eleva-

85 Detail, First and State streets, Troy, during Blizzard of 1888 showing John Paine house (c. 1825–30) at right. Note the ironwork at the entry stairs.

86 Reconstruction of west and south façades of 59 Second Street, c. 1827, Troy, D. G. Bucher, 1999. The steps ascending to the central entrance on the west façade are not shown.

tion features rusticated window surrounds set into a random-laid bluestone wall covered with mastic. The first and second floors of this elevation were originally five bays across, with a semi-circular fanlight over a narrow centrally placed first floor door. A platform and set of steps acted as a bridge over the areaway, giving access to the back yard (see Fig. 86). On the garden elevation the brick wall was covered entirely in mastic scored in imitation of the marble blocks on the front of the house (see Fig. 121). Marble quoins extend from the front façade onto this elevation. Quarter round and arched-top windows form a prominent feature of the third story gable end of this façade.

Design and Sources: The Plan

The four-bay wide plan of 59 Second Street, while not as common as either the three-bay house typically built in urban areas or the more extravagant five-bay house with two rooms on either side of a central hall, was a viable alternative to both—particularly when it was the occupant's desire to maintain a garden plot on a double-wide urban lot. While having roots in the three- and five-bay urban house types, the plan of the four-bay house was resolved in a number of ways that diverge from them.

The reconstructed original plan of 59 Second Street can be compared to Plate 13 in Abraham Swan's *A Collection of Designs in Architecture* (1757; see Figs. 87 & 148). Both plans feature a pair of formal rooms to the right of the main circulation space, and a smaller room, with the main stair behind it on the opposite side of the hall. A minor point of difference lies in the resolution of the room to the rear left of each plan. While the room in Swan's plan is treated as a rectangular space, in the Hart house the same area is partitioned so that a rear door opens into a narrow back hallway. If one were to substitute the hall closet of the Hart house for the service stair in the Swan plan the plans would be almost identical.

Four-bay wide houses were not unknown to the Albany-Troy region before the construction of the Hart house. A number of eighteenth century dwellings constructed in Albany were of this type.[176] The Rev. Ellison house, designed by Joseph Newton in 1792;[177] the Mancius house (c. 1805);[178] the Daniel Hale house (1805–06), by Philip Hooker;[179] and the Stephen van Rensselaer IV house designed in 1817 and attributed to Philip

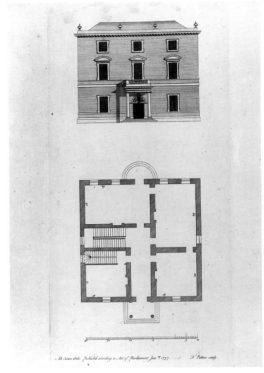

87 Detail, Plate 13, Volume I, *Designs in Architecture*, Abraham Swan, 1757.

Hooker[180]—all were constructed in Albany; all made use of the four-bay typology. Within the bounds of what would become the city of Troy, the Mathias Van Der Heyden house (c. 1752) was four bays wide, though only one-and-a-half story tall.[181] His brother Jacob constructed a similar dwelling in 1756.[182] These were both extant when the Hart house was constructed. A four-bay house once occupied the lot at 24–26 First Street; it was likely constructed circa 1805.[183] No other four-bay houses built in Troy predating the construction of 59 Second Street have been identified, and none of those known approached its level of sophistication.

Design, Sources and Influence: The Woodwork

The Hart house features highly sophisticated woodwork on both the first and second floors of the original house. The door and window architraves are composed of reeded molding finished with corner blocks featuring highly carved foliage in a bilaterally symmetrical pattern with a stylized pinecone as the central feature.[184] In the more formal rooms of the house, a rectangular reserve

88 A & B 59 Second Street, architrave details, first floor parlors.

89 A & B Detail, Plate 4, *The British Architect*, Abraham Swan, Philadelphia edition, 1775. This detail shows rosettes similar to those used in the Hart house, here proposed as part of the decor of a Doric soffit. The accompanying photograph depicts a raffle flower at the Hart house.

decorates the center of the lintel, much larger in scale than the corner blocks but utilizing the same type of foliate carving. The wide opening connecting the two parlors of the house is treated in a more elaborate manner, and includes a boldly conceived frieze and freestanding columns (see Figs. 88A & B and 125).

Corner rosettes similar to those featured at 59 Second Street were popular decorative details during the 1760s, and frequently appeared in mantels executed at that time.[185] Henry Farnham probably got some of his ideas for carvings from Philip Hooker's architectural library, including the latter's copy of Swan's *British Architect* (1775).[186] An illustration in this volume matches closely the style of carving and appearance of Farnham's corner blocks, known to him as "raffle flowers"

(see Fig. 89A & B). Similar designs can be seen in contemporary French catalogues of prefabricated architectural details,[187] and in the pattern books issued by cabinetmakers such as Thomas Sheraton.[188] Architects and builders working during this period typically used a wide range of pattern books for design sources and inspiration. Designs for mantels published by Batty Langley and Robert Adam provided precedent for the five-part arrangement adopted for the more elaborate architrave casements. It is likely that the applications of such designs as they appear in Farnham's work are the result of close collaboration with Philip Hooker. All of the earliest documented installations of Farnham's work are for buildings designed by that Albany architect.[189]

While Farnham's decorative scheme is known to

have been utilized in Albany for both public and private commissions, it seems to have been confined to residential applications in New York City and elsewhere (see Figs. 90 and 91). It is likely that while in New York City, Farnham began mass production of the carved details and sold them to builders with whom he had no other connection. This would account for the wide early dispersal of these decorative elements.[190] This theory is supported by close inspection of the extant installations of this work—in many cases the carving is clearly either too large or too small for the provided reserve. Crude techniques, such as chopping off bits of foliage to fit the carving squarely into the corner block, or allowing a carving for a central panel to swim in a dis-

proportionately large field, are evidence that the carvings were procured separately from the panels they occupy. Indeed, from their very conception the raffle flower carvings appear to have been executed separately. Farnham's invoice for work at the Albany Academy indicates that he merely provided the carved work proper and not the associated backgrounds, or the turnings for the door surrounds.[191] A reference from 1829 treats the estimation of the time required for the execution of door surrounds while specifically excluding the work on the carved elements—perhaps because they were usually purchased prefabricated by this date.[192]

The rosettes of the corner blocks are typically cut from a single piece of wood, usually white pine. The central device, most frequently a pinecone, but occasionally an acorn or similar object, was usually carved separately in the form of a plug, then secured with glue. The central panels of the more elaborate five-part lintels are sometimes carved from a single piece of wood and at other times they are composed of pieces glued or nailed together. The reeded architraves accompanying the corner-blocks at the Hart house are a common feature of neoclassical work in Europe and the Federal style in the United States, and saw widespread application between circa 1800 and the second decade of the nineteenth century. They appear in various publications, including those of Asher Benjamin.[193]

Farnham's decorative raffle flowers grew in popularity and were widely imitated. Minard Lafever published his own version, calling them "roseats," in 1829[194] (see Fig. 92). Asher Benjamin furthered the dissemination of the motif throughout the northeast via his *The Prac-*

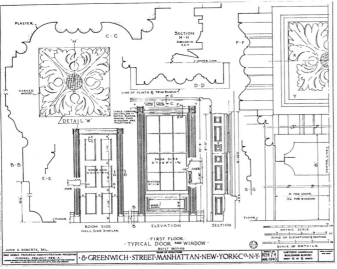

90 Sheet 6, 8 Greenwich Street, New York City, Historic American Buildings Survey, 1940.

91 Interior door architrave, Miller house, Utica, New York, photo by Frey, c. 1920.

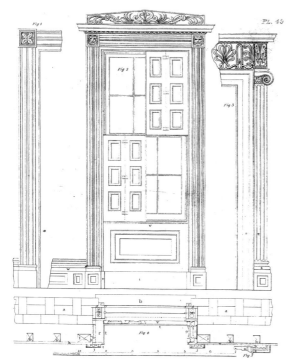

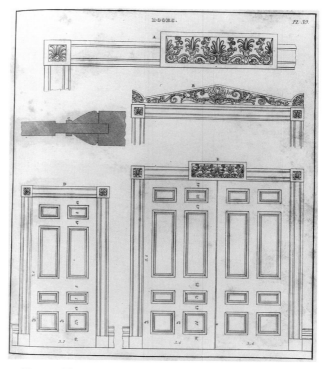

92 Plate 49, *Young Builder's General Instructor*, Minard Lafever, 1829. Figure 1 on the left side of the image shows a raffle flower corner detail.

93 Plate 39, *The Practice of Architecture*, Asher Benjamin, 1833.

tice of Architecture in 1833 (see Fig. 93). The preponderance of New York furniture from this period with details similar to the identified work of Farnham and his contemporaries suggests that some individuals executed carving for both cabinetry and architectural applications.[195] Later still, similar motifs were incorporated into cast-iron products such as stoves and window and door lintels.[196] In 1827–28, a number of houses were constructed in Albany and Troy utilizing a modified version of the five-part window lintel cast in iron to decorate their façades.[197]

The contemporary John V. Gridley house at 37 Charlton Street in New York City (1827, rebuilt in 1829) utilized the Farnham-type woodwork and shares additional details with 59 Second Street that call it out for consideration. Perhaps most significant among these is the peculiar paneled treatment found on the broad openings connecting the parlors of both the Hart and Gridley houses (see Figs. 125 and 94). In the Gridley house, the panels take up the space between Ionic pilasters which support a five-part over-door piece. The paneled treatment alternates between long and short sections, and bears no obvious relationship to the pan-

eling of the adjacent doors. At 59 Second Street the panels occupy the same space and display the same incongruous relationship to the adjacent sliding doors and additionally are not symmetrically disposed at the head of the opening. This may be due to the woodwork

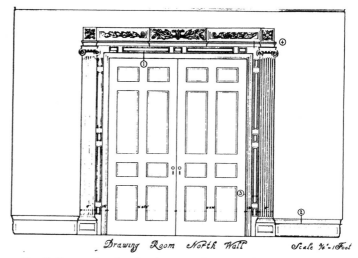

94 Detail, Sheet 4, showing drawing room doorway, John V. Gridley house, 37 Charleton Street, New York City, Historic American Buildings Survey, 1936.

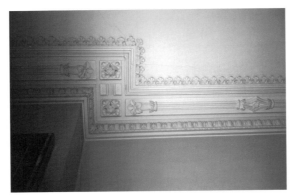

95 Detail of cornice in the parlors of 59 Second Street, Troy, 1999.

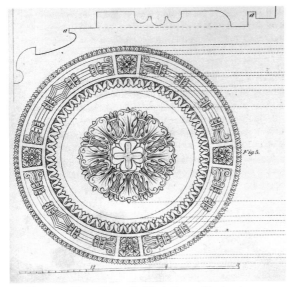

96 Plate 64a, Fig. 1, *Young Builder's General Instructor,* Lafever, 1829.

having been executed by a person who was not on site for its installation—the workmen present merely making the parts fit together as best they could. This supports the theory that the woodwork at the Hart house was largely prefabricated in New York City and shipped to Troy for installation.

Design and Sources: The Plasterwork

The Hart house was constructed at the beginning of a period in which extravagance was a feature of interior detail, encouraged by a period of national and economic confidence. Nowhere is this more apparent than in the elaborate plasterwork executed for the ceilings of houses built from the mid 1820s up to the economic

disaster of the late 1830s. Minard Lafever noted in 1829 that "[c]arved Mouldings have of late, become very fashionable . . . and thereby have excited the carvers to prodigious extravagancies, both in the quality of work and the position of the ornaments."[198]

The plaster details featured on the ceilings of the two parlors as well as the entry hall of the Hart house certainly demonstrate these "prodigious extravagancies," and are thematically related to the woodwork. The borders of the ceilings feature raffle flowers similar in design to those featured on the window and door casings (see Fig. 95). By 1829 this treatment was widespread, Lafever noting in his description of a series of designs for cornices that "these examples are calculated for the reception of roseats in the angles, and elsewhere if requisite";[199] "roseats" being Lafever's term for what Henry Farnham knew as raffle flowers. One of Lafever's designs for a cornice (see Fig. 96) bears a strong similarity to those executed for the Hart house. The related plan of a "centre flower" on the same plate shows that Lafever intended the bundled reed pattern that decorates the flat section of the cornice proper to be broken up into smaller lengths, separated by "roseats" set into rectangular reserves. The same application of these various details is seen in the plasterwork of the ceilings of the parlors at 59 Second Street (see Fig. 97).

An earlier pattern for a ceiling centerpiece and therefore a possible inspiration for the plaster centers in the parlors of the Hart house is Plate 27 of Asher Benjamin and Daniel Raynerd's *The American Builder's Companion*[200] (1806; see Fig. 98). In this engraving, Raynerd proposes a circular centerpiece bordered by a reeded ring entwined by a boldly detailed grapevine. He recommends this grape vine motif in dining rooms.[201] This very detail is used in the front and back parlors of the Hart house.

The medallions at the center of each ceiling in the parlors of the Hart house are similar to those executed for the Seabury Tredwell house (1831–32) in New York and the pair of houses constructed for Bennington Gill and Maynard French (1830–31) in Albany, and not very different from the *centre flower* shown by Lafever (see Fig. 96). All of these examples share the unusual feature of having their central sections recessed from the ceiling plane, a detail that required much more skill, time, and consequently expense, to execute.

Complex plasterwork was frequently prefabricated by a master plasterer and shipped to the site for instal-

97 View of plasterwork and gasolier in front parlor, 59 Second Street, Troy, 1976.

98 Plate 27, *American Builder's Companion*, Asher Benjamin and Daniel Raynerd, 1806.

lation. A contemporary example of this practice is the plasterwork at Hyde Hall, near Cooperstown, New York.[202] The Hart house plaster is a combination of prefabricated elements, run-in-place sections and sculpted-in-place details.[203] Lafever noted that a center flower "may be classed among the first order of Ornaments in interior finishing, and is indeed as beautiful and produces as lively an effect as any other ornament in Architecture; and none but the most experienced Stucco workmen can execute them in a manner that becomes an ornament of the first class."[204]

Design and Sources: Iron work

The most prominent feature of the iron work decorating the front of 59 Second Street are the pair of wrought and cast-iron newels that greet the pedestrian at the base of the entry stairs. These "urn newels" as they have come to be called, are composed of cages of iron worked into the form of large urns, decorated with cast and wrought elements in imitation of foliage, and sur-

mounted with pineapples. They sit on elaborate iron bases that feature a guilloche motif.

While identification of the earliest example of the urn-type cage newels has eluded scholars, it is clear that the Troy examples are among the first executed. No examples are documented as having been installed earlier than the pair that sit on the marble plinths at the base of the front stoop of the Hart house. Numerous versions of this design once graced New York City streets; a number of them survived into the twentieth century. Many examples in Greenwich Village and Chelsea are recorded.[205] Early photographs show the same type of urn-newels on the stoops of houses on St. Mark's Place, and on Varick Street (see Fig. 99). Nineteenth century engravings depict the urn newels on the stoops of the speculative rows built along Le Roy Place (1831) and on Bond Street. An intact set survives at 56 West Tenth Street (1831–32), and another at the Seabury Tredwell house on Fourth Street.[206] It is likely that the ironwork decorating the front of the Rogers house, 20 Washington Square North, New York, utilized the same motifs.

99 Ironwork at residence on Varick Street, New York City, c. 1899.

Marble plinths—identical to those at the Hart house—are still in place for these now-lost examples.[207] From this list it becomes clear that these urn-type newels most frequently appear *en suite* with marble door surrounds of the Hart House type, and almost exclusively with houses featuring Westchester marble trim. Whether this is the result of a popular aesthetic choice or the design of a specific builder or architect remains unclear.

Of the examples that we have visual documentation for, those formerly decorating a house at 34 Varick Street are the closest in design to those at the Hart house. These newels, essentially identical to the Troy examples, were installed circa 1828[208] (see Fig. 99).

A number of examples outside of the immediate New York City area are known to have existed. A house on South Ferry Street in Albany (c. 1828) once featured an interesting variant on this design. The Judge Denio house at 62 Broad Street in Utica utilized a stylized variation on this type of newel.[209] Whig Hill, the Col. James

Leslie Voorhees house (1833), near Syracuse, New York, preserves a set of urn newels very similar to those decorating the front of the Hart house.[210] The Nathan Smith house in New Haven, Connecticut, is another example.[211] Add to these the references to similar wrought-iron work in New Jersey and it becomes clear that either the work is the product of one shop, well connected to clients throughout the northeast, or that the design was widely admired and copied. This latter scenario is certainly the case with respect to the design of the Utica work. In the case of the Hart house, the sophistication of the ironwork—standing far above contemporary examples in Troy—suggests a New York City origin (see Fig. 100). It is likely that the design originated in New York, possibly provided by an architect.[212]

Prominent among the motifs featured in the design of the ironwork surrounding the areaway and the handrails to the stoop of the Hart house is what was popularly known as the "Vitruvian scroll."[213] Iron railings featuring this design were common decorative additions to the fronts of houses built in Troy and other American cities from about 1805 to 1830. The earliest extant example of its use in the Albany-Troy area is on Philip Hooker's New York State Bank in Albany of 1803. The Lane houses at 20–22 First Street in Troy (c. 1803)

100 Detail showing ironwork at 59 Second Street, Troy, Historic American Buildings Survey, 1934.

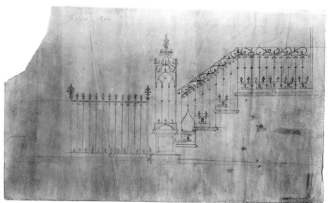

101 Elevation of a stoop and railing for the Gansevoort family, Albany, ink and wash drawing, Philip Hooker, c. 1827.

are the earliest known surviving domestic examples in the region (see Fig. 53). Extant drawings featuring this type of design for American buildings include Martin E. Thompson's alternate drafts for the Merchants' Exchange (c. 1824; see Fig. 58) and Philip Hooker's drafts for the Gansevoort family stoops and the ironwork for the First Dutch Reformed Church in Albany, both dating to circa 1827 (see Fig. 101). The nature of Hooker's drawings, in particular, suggests the contemporary participation of architects in the design of ironwork.

The fencing and rails that decorate the Hart house are largely composed of wrought and cast-iron elements, but include some pieces cast of brass as well—in particular a foliage motif in the form of a stylized bow. Identical examples of this casting are still in place on the ironwork decorating the front of the Nathan S. Hollister house at 132 First Street (c. 1831) and twin houses at 32–34 First Street (c. 1835) in Troy. Apparently identical examples of this casting were on the ironwork in front of the George Fordham house, 329 Cherry Street, in New York City.[214] A New York manufacturer probably cast this element.

Construction of 59 Second Street

Preparation for construction of the Hart house probably began in autumn 1825.[215] With design in hand, William Howard would have contracted with builders in Troy to excavate the site and construct a foundation, and with one of the New York City-based marble merchants dealing in Westchester marble,[216] to provide the facing and decorative stonework. They were probably given a deadline coinciding with the opening of the river in the spring to facilitate the commencement of construction early in 1826. A near-contemporary source describes the process of finishing the stone, and the methods of bringing it to market.

The marble chiefly used in New York for building purposes is brought from the quarries in East Chester; and as raising it in straight, or square blocks is attended with great difficulty and labor, it is generally sent off in very irregular masses; and this difficulty still increasing with the size of the blocks, a great waste of material takes place when converted into works requiring considerable lengths. A further loss also frequently arises from small cracks or veins in the blocks which are imperceptible in the rough state, but often render a block useless for an intended purpose, even after sawing or working. In estimating the price of materials, a per centage upon the prime cost, equivalent to this waste and risk, should therefore be taken into account; and also to cover the expense of landing the stone, of carriage from the wharf to the yard; and of afterwards delivering the work at the building when prepared.[217]

Some, if not all, of the stone arrived in Troy on April 11, 1826 on the sloop *Thames* and was delivered to Pattison & Hart on behalf of William Howard.[218] It is likely that some of the carved elements for the Hart house were executed in New York City—particularly the door and window surrounds, but that the majority of the blocks arrived in a rough-dressed state, requiring close fitting on site. A contemporary New York price list notes that "rusticated lintels," possibly similar to those at the Hart house, would cost $9.12 each, and rusticated blocks, approximately the size of those used at 59 Second Street, would cost $1.20 each.[219] While it is impossible to estimate how long it took to execute the masonry associated with the construction of the Hart house, Minard Lafever suggested that the construction of the type of door surround featured at the Hart house, by itself, would take a "piece workman"—a journeyman—twenty-three days to execute—not including carved work.[220]

Construction began in the spring of 1826; stonemasons and carpenters would have worked to get the building enclosed by the end of the building season, sometime in either December 1826 or January 1827. Plaster workers, likely brought from New York, would have spent February and March completing the interiors. Fireplaces would have been operational by this time, pressed into service to facilitate progress of work. Final finishing details such as the installation of doors and hardware would be accomplished before May first, the traditional moving day.[221] The painting and wall-

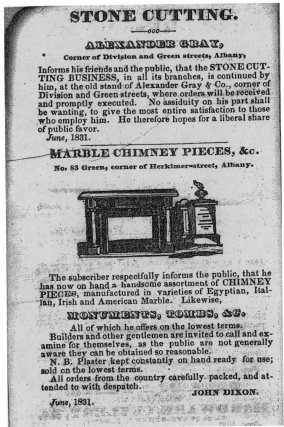

STONE CUTTING.
—ooo—

ALEXANDER GRAY,
Corner of Division and Green streets, Albany,

Informs his friends and the public, that the STONE CUT-TING BUSINESS, in all its branches, is continued by him, at the old stand of Alexander Gray & Co., corner of Division and Green streets, where orders will be received and promptly executed. No assiduity on his part shall be wanting, to give the most entire satisfaction to those who employ him. He therefore hopes for a liberal share of public favor.
June, 1831.

MARBLE CHIMNEY PIECES, &c.
No. 83 Green, corner of Herkimer street, Albany.

The subscriber respectfully informs the public, that he has now on hand a handsome assortment of CHIMNEY PIECES, manufactured in varieties of Egyptian, Italian, Irish and American Marble. Likewise,

MONUMENTS, TOMBS, &c.
All of which he offers on the lowest terms. Builders and other gentlemen are invited to call and examine for themselves, as the public are not generally aware they can be obtained so reasonable.
N. B. Plaster kept constantly on hand ready for use; sold on the lowest terms.
All orders from the country carefully packed, and attended to with despatch. **JOHN DIXON.**

June, 1831.

102 Advertisement, Stone Cutting, from *The Albany Directory and City Register for the Years 1831-32,* 1831.

papering of new plaster was typically delayed for many months to allow the material to properly cure.

The ten marble mantels ornamenting the primary rooms of the Hart house are typical of those featured in better residences of the period. They were most likely shipped from New York City, separately from the stone for the façade. The Kain brothers executed both types of work; it is known that local stonecutters worked in fancy marbles as well[222] (see Fig. 102). While "common dining-room chimney pieces, with columns" cost from $80 to $120 during this period, those selected for the Hart house, termed "Superior . . . got up in the best style, of Irish black and Egyptian" marble cost between $150 and $250 apiece.[223]

The brick utilized in the construction of the Hart house was likely of local manufacture. The earliest kiln in the vicinity of Troy was set up by Samuel and Ebenezer Wilson in 1789, and located at the base of Mount Ida.[224] As late as 1829 the Wilson family ran the only

brick kiln in the city; thus it is probable that they supplied the brick for 59 Second Street.[225]

The wood for the framing and roof structure of the Hart house was probably procured from the Adirondacks where Richard Hart had interests in wood lots and a lumber mill.[226] Local supplies of wood were running short of demand at this time. George Tibbits noted in April 1827 that "there is such a press for timber for building in this town [Troy] & New York, that the mills have more orders than they can supply."[227] But apparently this shortage had little or no affect on the construction of the Hart house.

The mahogany used for the interior doors of the Hart house is traditionally said to have been stored for ten years by "Grandmother Howard."[228] As charming as this story sounds, it is unlikely—unless the idea of constructing a house dated back to 1815, about the time of Betsey Howard's marriage to Richard P. Hart. Mahogany was the most popular hardwood in use in New York during this period, most of it being imported from Honduras. The vast quantities of that wood readily available from mahogany dealers or cabinetmakers would have obviated the need to purchase it ahead of time.[229] Many builders of the period kept such items as doors and handrails on hand, already manufactured.

The execution of the interior wood trim at 59 Second Street is probably the result of the efforts of several individuals. Complete sets of door or window architraves similar to those installed in the first and second floors of the Hart house were among the most expensive offered by builders at the time. "Moulded pilasters with blocks, plinths, and tablet, complete, per foot run" were estimated to cost $14.08 per set.[230] That the corner blocks and center panels of the door and window surrounds were probably executed in New York and shipped to Troy has already been discussed. These "carved enrichments to blocks and tablet" cost one dollar "per set" according to a near-contemporary price guide.[231] Discrepancies in the arrangement of the paneling in the archway between the two parlors on the first floor of the house suggests that these features were also prefabricated, and cut to fit the site. The reeded door and window trim could have been executed either in Troy or New York. If they were run off in New York, a qualified individual may have accompanied them to oversee their installation. The trim was likely installed during the late autumn or winter of 1826–27.[232]

While the sash for the windows could have been executed in Troy, it is more likely that they were shipped from New York along with much of the remaining finish materials. Nathaniel Challes, master carpenter and lumber inspector for the city of Troy, advertised in a contemporary newspaper that "fancy fan and side lights are filled [by him] in the first style, at short notice,"[233] likely meaning that he would provide sash frames and fill them with glass and either lead, iron or wooden cames. While it is possible that the fan and side lights ornamenting both the interior and exterior of the Hart house are the result of local efforts, their sophistication makes it more likely that they, too, were executed in New York City.

The hardware for the Hart house was procured from William Pye of New York City. Pye, who was selling locks at 12 Chambers Street in 1825,[234] provided silver-plated, polished brass and iron knobs, locks and hinges (see Fig. 103). Pye held several patents for original designs of locks.[235]

103 Brass mortice lock, marked "W. Pye, N. York," c. 1827.

Upon its completion, 59 Second Street was one of the most extravagant urban residences in Troy. While the newspapers are strangely silent regarding the completion of the house, and contemporary reaction to it, it was likely seen as additional proof of the promising future of the fledgling city of Troy.

Thomas F. Gordon in his *Gazetteer* of 1836 records a contemporary impression of Troy, suggestive of the popular reception of the Hart house. Among the structures called out for special note in the city by him were a select group of houses, "some of them of marble" which "are large, neat and commodious."[236] Certainly the Hart house figured prominently among this small group.[237] The house maintained its high status throughout the nine-

teenth century. Despite the fact that the extravagant houses built in the Washington Park neighborhood dwarfed the Hart house, as did those constructed in the city's suburbs, it was referred to as late as 1893 as "one of the most valuable pieces of real-estate in the city."[238]

Elizabeth Shields Eddy described the impact of the façade upon the Harts in 1855.

Grandmother told me that while the house was building, they [Betsey & Richard Hart] used to go to one of the houses across the street and watch the effect of the moonlight on the freshly cut marble and how it sparkled in the moonlight.[239]

The Carriage House: Design and Construction

An important document generated during the construction of the carriage house survives:

Bill of Timber for Mr. Howard's Stable 1826.

Dec 7	28 beams	27 feet 6 inches long, 3½ by 11
	8 gallows posts	10 feet long, 8 by 8
	6 Purlines	17 feet 6 inches long, 5 by 13
	10 Hammer beams	14 feet long, 4 by 9
	50 Rafters	16 feet long, 3½ by 6 & 9
	4 door posts	11 feet long, 10 by 12
	2 lintles	11 feet long, 10 by 12
	2 door posts	8 feet long, 8 by 12
	1 lintle	6 feet long, 8 by 12
	2 Trimmers	11 feet long, 6 by 11

The above of hemlock

Also
18 Beams of yellow pine clear from sap
17 feet long 4 × 10 inches @ 8/
I agree to add the above to the former
Bill annex'd of Thomas & Jno. P. Laing
The Hemlock @ 7/– yellow pine 8/–
Troy Jan'y 24, 1827

From this document it is clear that the carriage house, constructed immediately to the west of the Hart's residence, was built concurrently with the house proper. For this reason it is probable that Martin E. Thompson furnished its design as well.

The most prominent feature of this otherwise austere structure is the blind arcade on its eastern, or garden, elevation. By the end of the eighteenth century the blind arcade treatment had become immensely popular among English designers.[240] The garden elevation of the carriage house owes much to the work of these architects—particularly Robert Adam—and is more clearly derivative than the elevation of the house proper.

An early American application of this design feature as applied to a carriage house is preserved in Joseph Newton's design for John Jay (see Fig. 60).

The use of the blind arcade device had become a favorite among architects in the northeastern United States by 1800, and was published by Asher Benjamin and Daniel Raynerd in the 1806 edition of their *American Builder's Companion*.[241] Blind arcades were prominent design elements of several buildings that the Harts would have known, none being far from their new home. The Bank of Troy, north-west corner of State and First streets (c. 1811), and the Bank of Lansingburgh on Second Avenue (c. 1812) both incorporate blind arcades in the design of their façades. The General Wool house, on First Street in Troy, built c. 1812 and attributed to Philip Hooker, makes use of this feature, as did a number of additional projects by that architect. In the block immediately north of the house occupied by the Harts was the three-story Dickinson House, at 19 Second Street (c. 1814). There, blind arcades were a feature of the second story which included an elaborate wrought-iron balcony (see Fig. 54).

The overall arrangement of architectural elements on the carriage house façade—blind arches and windows including round second story recesses as well as white marble inset tablets—produced an elegant screen-like wall at the back of the site. A wood balustrade much like the one found on the front elevation of the house surmounted the façade; atop its gable roof a centrally positioned cupola vented the stable (see Fig. 63). This important component of the site was fully visible from the rear windows of the house until construction of the c. 1836 rear addition.

A single-story brick wash house was attached to the south side of the carriage house. Known only from references in Hart family documents and nineteenth century site plans, this utilitarian structure was probably contemporary with the construction of the house. The wash house and the south bay of the carriage house were demolished when the garden site was sold to William Kemp in 1893. An early twentieth century brick garage, part of the Kemp-Frear property, now occupies the site.

Influence of the Design of 59 Second Street and Its Elements

The Hart house is the first documented upper Hudson River Valley architectural application of Westchester marble. It was followed in quick succession by a number of buildings, most of them public structures, most constructed from stone quarried by the Sing-Sing convicts. Among these are the Rensselaer County Courthouse (1827–31) and the First Presbyterian Church (1834–36), both in Troy.[242] The Le Grand Cannon house at 19 Third Street (c. 1827–29), may have been constructed using that stone as well. The use of marble in Troy was largely extinguished by the economic crash of 1837.[243]

Among the first of those houses in Troy that were directly influenced by the four-bay design of the Hart house was the John A. Hall house, at 36 First Street built c. 1827–28. The house sits on a lot immediately across the alley to the west of 59 Second Street.[244] The Hall house utilizes a four-bay plan identical to that of the Hart house (flipped to orient the garden elevation to the south—as at the Hart house), with only minor dimensional adjustments (see Fig. 104). The interior decorative program was, however, executed with a more modest budget. Corner-blocks utilized in the window and door surrounds are poorly rendered cast-plaster or composition versions of the Hart house carvings (see Fig. 105). Those in the central panels over the interior doors are poorly fitted, and seem to bear no relation to the field in which they have been placed. Clearly they have been purchased by the builder, as "off-the-shelf" pieces. However, the mantels in the two major rooms are of black marble and are similar in quality to those in the Hart house.

No record exists of the original appearance of the exterior of the Hall house. What remains is—in keeping with the interior—more modest than that of the Hart house. Tripartite brownstone lintels cap each opening on the façade; an elliptical fanlight originally surmounted the main entrance. The façade featured a high brownstone basement; brick was used for the remainder of the building. The original cornice was likely made of wood.

The fact that the Hall house began construction about the time that the Hart house was approaching completion adds weight to the theory of a connection between the two. It is possible that John Colegrove, or perhaps another builder, was lent the plans of the Hart house, and executed the Hall house from them.

Another house on First Street—that of John Paine residence at No. 19—shared several details with the Hart house (see Fig. 85). Most importantly, the bases of the cage newels formerly decorating the stoop at this site appear to have been identical with those that sup-

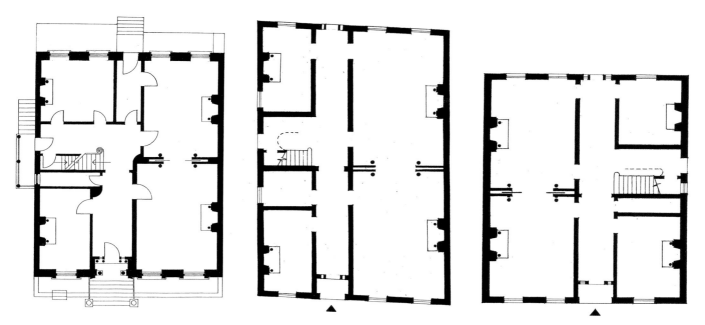

104 Reconstructed first floor plans of the Hart (1825–27), Rogers (1827–28) and Hall (1827–28) houses, W. R. Wheeler and D. G. Bucher, 1999.

port the urn newels at the Hart house. The cast and wrought iron railings utilized the same lyre motifs as those at the Hart house. The external lintels of the house featured corner blocks decorated with raffle flowers and a raised center panel. This building was razed c. 1915 to make way for construction of the YWCA building that still occupies the site.[245]

The no-longer-extant Elias Pattison house at 49 Second Street was constructed circa 1828–29, but of much more modest form. It was built on the site of the house that the Hart's formerly occupied, replacing that building. It was four bays wide, and Federal in style (see Fig.

10). The elliptical arch over its front door was modest in comparison with that featured at 59 Second Street.

The LeGrand Cannon house, cited briefly above, was completed by May 1829 and featured a façade that appears to have been executed in Westchester marble[246] (see Fig. 106). LeGrand Cannon had been a resident of Troy since at least August, 1814 when he married Esther Bouton of a prominent Troy family.[247] Cannon was a wealthy merchant, active in various local concerns. He

105 Interior door architrave, Hall house, 36 First Street, Troy, 1999.

106 View looking north on Third Street, Troy, showing the LeGrand Cannon house (c. 1827–29), center and Leopold Eidlitz's Masonic Temple, c. 1920.

107 Nathan Warren house (c. 1829), Third Street and Broadway, Troy, c. 1890.

participated in the incorporation of several early Troy organizations and sat on the boards of a number of them, including the Troy Waterworks Company (1829) and the Rensselaer & Saratoga Railroad (1832). On the latter, he served with Richard P. Hart.[248]

Cannon has previously come to the attention of scholars of Town & Davis as the client for a monumental commercial building built in 1832–35 to the designs of that firm and still extant on Broadway in Troy; known to this day as Cannon Place. The connection to Town & Davis is important; Town & Thompson may have been responsible for the design of Cannon's house five years earlier. Given that its façade incorporated the same material as that utilized in the Hart house, a connection seems likely. Cannon lived in the house at 19 Third Street until his death on May 7, 1850, at age sixty-four.[249]

Nathan Warren built his house (see Fig. 107), about 1829 at the southwest corner of Third and Albany (now Broadway) streets utilizing the four-bay model, but on a much more modest scale.[250]

Clinton Place, a row of what was six speculative houses built by 1835 on the south side of Broadway in Troy between Fourth Street and Fifth Avenue, makes use of a version of the Hart house window lintels. In this row, which survives in part, molded-paneled lintels surmount the windows, and include corner blocks that feature vermiculation. The Jesse Patrick house (1828) at 75 Fourth Street makes use of a similar type of lintel.

The General John Tayler Cooper house (1832–33),

still extant at 134 State Street in Albany, originally had rusticated basement window surrounds apparently identical to the basement windows of the Hart house. James H. Dakin, of the New York City architectural firm Town, Davis & Dakin, designed the "front door" for this house—presumably this meant the door surround and porch.[251] It is likely that Dakin was responsible for the remainder of the design, which bears striking resemblance to some of the houses of The Row, on Washington Square North in New York City.[252]

The Hart house was the precursor of a style that was soon to see wide dissemination in New York City, and ultimately resulted in the mass-production of its decorative components. The George P. Rogers house (c. 1827–28) at 20 Washington Square North in New York shares its plan and many details with the Hart house, of which it is a near contemporary.[253] The Rogers house is the only identified New York example of a four-bay, freestanding town house featuring the rusticated-vermiculated door surround seen at the Hart house, and the earliest known New York example of the type. The façade of the Rogers house was constructed of brick with Westchester marble used only for decorative details. As is the case at the Hart house, the vermiculated blocks decorating the façade of the Rogers House were individually carved, not mass-produced (see Figs. 108, 109, and 110). The interior trim, mantels, and plasterwork are of a quality equal to those used in the Hart house and share many of their features (see Figs. 111 and 112). The plan—as far as can be reconstructed—seems to be nearly identical with that of the Hart house (see Fig. 104). The exterior ironwork is now lost, but stone plinths like those at the Hart house remain and suggest that the original ironwork may have been of the urn newel type. The fact that design elements representative of four distinctly different trades—ironwork, stonework, plaster, and woodwork—were assembled here in a similar manner to their applications at 59 Second Street suggests the involvement of the same architect.

Also very similar to the Hart house were the dwellings built adjacent to St. Paul's Chapel on Varick Street, circa 1827–28 (see Fig. 113). Although these three-bay houses vary in minor details, the door surrounds, window lintels and cast and wrought iron work of two of the houses built to the south of the church are practically identical to those at the Hart house. Their architect and a definitive date of construction have not been determined.[254]

108 Typical window lintel, Rogers house, 20 Washington Square North, New York City, 1999.

109 Basement window surround, Rogers house, 20 Washington Square North, New York City, 1999.

110 Rogers house, 20 Washington Square North, New York City, 1999.

111 Interior door architrave, Rogers house, 20 Washington Square North, New York City, 1999.

112 Cornice in the parlors of the Rogers house, 20 Washington Square North, New York City, 1999.

The remainder of identified houses utilizing the set of details first used at the Hart house were all part of speculative rows, and utilized mass-produced elements in their construction (see Fig. 114). Among this latter group are the two rows of dwellings (c. 1829–33) along St. Mark's Place in New York (see Fig. 115). These speculative houses, whose construction was financed by merchant Thomas E. Davis, but whose architect and builder remain unknown, feature door surrounds, basement treatments and wrought and cast-iron work all bearing close comparison to the Hart house. The door and basement window surrounds are virtually identical with those of the Hart house with one important exception. While these details appear to have been fabricated from the same material as their Trojan predecessors, close scrutiny reveals the vermiculated

113 34 Varick Street (c. 1827–8) and St. John's Chapel, New York City, c. 1890.

Sing prison.[255] In the mass production of these details the American mechanics were perhaps unwittingly following English precedent—during the eighteenth century similar vermiculated blocks had been mass-produced in Coade stone by 1775 at Eleanor Coade's factory in Lambeth, South London.[256]

The prison at Sing-Sing (a.k.a. Ossining), New York, was founded to provide an industry whereby the convicts might earn their keep and learn a trade. It was decided early on that the skill learned should be quarrying stone—the reason given in the public literature was that the mechanic trades offered viable employment opportunities after release. In fact, half of the convicts brought to construct and occupy the prison when it opened were already experienced stonemasons.[257] Their work was largely confined to quarrying stone for use in public buildings.

The similarities between the Hart house and the two rows of houses on St. Mark's Place are limited to the exterior. The interiors of these houses feature cast-plaster or composition corner blocks with decoration in the form of Medusa heads, honeysuckle flowers, and other classical ornaments in place of the more expensive

stones on the façades of the St. Mark's rows to be of a limited number of patterns—suggesting that the work was mass-produced, possibly by making use of metal stencils to mark out the "random" pattern of vermiculation. Indeed, it has been discovered that Thomas E. Davis ordered the marble for these houses from Sing-

115 Typical door surround, 4 St. Mark's Place (c. 1829-1833), New York City, c. 1972.

114 Hudson Street at Bank Street, New York City, c. 1885.

hand-carved work, and in a material more suitable to mass production.[258] Martin E. Thompson may have been the ultimate source of the design for these rows; his documented use of Westchester marble, and subsequent connections to Sing-Sing prison, makes it likely that he participated in the introduction of the production of vermiculated stonework at the prison.[259]

A number of other New York City houses, including an extended row on Bond Street and a row on Fourth street,[260] of which the only survivor is the Seabury Tredwell house, were constructed with similar window and door enframements during the years 1830–33 (see Fig. 116). However, at the Tredwell house the rustication utilized in the earlier rows of this type has been replaced with sunken panels. This substitution of paneled blocks may be attributed to economy and ease of production. The Seabury Tredwell house also features ironwork that has much in common with that in front of the Hart house.[261] The plasterwork in the parlors on the first floor shares a number of details with that of the Hart house, most notably the recessed centerpiece, the bundled reeds terminating in floral devices and rosettes in the corners of the main cornice, and use of egg and dart moldings at the base of the cornice[262] (see Fig. 117).

The Governor William Aiken house on Elizabeth Street in Charleston, South Carolina, features a door surround with paneled blocks, virtually identical with that found on the Seabury Tredwell house.[263] It was likely executed during a remodeling dateable to about 1833.[264]

117 View of Front Parlor, Seabury Tredwell house (1832), 29 East Fourth Street, New York City, c. 1990.

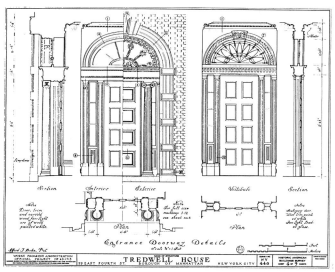

116 Sheet 4, Seabury Tredwell house, 29 East Fourth Street, New York City, Historic American Building Survey, 1936.

Minard Lafever took what were already popular designs in New York and made them accessible across the country in 1829 with his publication of *The Young Builder's General Instructor* (see Figs. 61, 62, and 92) By 1833, the Farnham-type corner block and center panel door and window surround treatment was well known enough in Boston to be featured by Asher Benjamin in several plates of his *Practice of Architecture*[265] (1833; see Fig. 93). James Gallier, an architect practicing in New York, published a Boston edition of his *Price Book* (1834 and 1836), which provided estimates for execution of such surrounds.[266]

Despite the initial wide popularity of its various design elements, the influence of the Hart house and those similar to it declined rapidly due to the popularity of the Greek Revival. Ironically, the use of Westchester stone facilitated the arrival of this style in New York, paving the way for the further economy of eliminating what was now considered fussy detail.[267] Economic collapse in 1837 insured that expensive details —so much a part of the earlier style—would be eliminated. The Hart house is the earliest known and best preserved example of a briefly popular style, and thus is an unusually important survivor of a town house from the 1820s.

Two Contemporary Critiques of a Town House Type

Professional reception of the Hart house design type was mixed. As a transitional mix of Federal and Greek Revival elements, it is perhaps not surprising that the design enjoyed only a short-lived popularity. However, during its short reign of influence (roughly c. 1827–34), the Hart house design elements came to represent the acme of urban home design, the best of what American culture had to offer. Its details were incorporated into the finest houses of the period.[268]

Alexander Jackson Davis was particularly critical of this style of row house, and credited himself (as he often did) with the progress of design away from such precedent. Not having had much if any experience in actual construction at the time, he confined his critique to observations regarding structural and material honesty. The following passages are from notes for an essay on architecture prepared by Davis between 1830 and 1837.

We will commence with the Foundation . . . here owing to three apertures, for the admission of light, of four feet each in a front of 25 ft, little space is left for embellishment, Yet that little is industriously studiously completely filled up with projecting stones, curiously tatooed or vermiculated, called rustics rustic truly! Borrowed from the barbarous and inflated architecture of modern Italy. These rustics are stuck round the windows, and upon the faces of the antaepagments, or casings architraves. The mouldings of which, are seen in the interstices, between the rustics. Should I ask a Proprietor the meaning of this, he would answer, that it contributed to impress the beholder with an exalted opinion of the *wealth* and magnificence, and he might add—*taste*, of the inhabitant.

Over one of the side apertures, right or left, are placed stone steps, leading to the principal entrance; and here, is a gorgeous display of stone work, and iron railing. Invention is exhausted in multiplying parts, moulding over moulding, and panel over panel. Is this economy?

Let us proceed to the door-way. Here, a space is left in the brick work, of about six feet in width, which is generally occupied by two diminutive columns, and as many semicolumns, Doric or Ionic, dwindled from the six and eight diameters of the antique, to 12 and 16 in height. These sticks support an entablature (so called) as "heterogeneous as the conceptions of the ARCHITECT!" and, although but six feet in length, is, most commonly broken into four or six parts. The central intercolumnation is occupied by the door, and the side spaces by lights. There is also a space left *over* the door for light, so that the columns do not assist in supporting the mass of brick work above, and are, therefore, mere ornament ostentation, for the sake of which, the whole superstructure, is weakened and in my opinion, deformed.

The stone lintel over the door, is, in many instances, circular, and in others horizontal. When circular, the pier is two [*sic*] narrow, for the curve of equilibrium would extend considerably beyond the exterior of the building, and were it not for the support the front wall receives from that of the adjoining building, it must would fall.

The horizontal lintel is, most frequently cut into a form which represents *three pieces*, thus [Davis inserts a small sketch of a tripartite lintel here]. Now, were it thus composed, it could not sustain its own weight a moment, unless the *voussoirs* were cut into a wedge like form, the sides all tending to one common centre. For the sake of variety which always commonly degenerates into inconsistency, this obvious absurdity is committed.[269]

[I have], after ten years of exertion, . . . nearly succeeded in exploding the vermiculated style of basement, for plain stone work, or a basement with horizontal sinkings between deep courses, as in Mr. Ward's house, Broadway. . . . The present style of door pieces is objectionable from the inordinate width of the intercolumnations and the frippery about the doors and glass, and especially from the ostentation of iron work, which is the more lamentable on account of the beautiful candelabra, tripods, and vases, which might be selected from the antique by a person of the least taste and which would be entirely appropriate and—far more economical.[270]

Davis appears to have had a marked dislike for Thompson, probably nurtured by professional jealousy and Davis' contempt for the builder-architects Thompson represented. This animosity coincided with the beginning of Davis' apprenticeship with Josiah Brady, and affected Thompson's decision to enter into partnership with Ithiel Town. Davis' subsequent retention as draughtsman in the Town & Thompson office, and his later replacement of Thompson as partner to Town could not have helped the relationship between the two men. His critiques of the Hart house rusticated door and window-surround type should be understood in this context.

Davis' attempts at traditionalist critique are additionally rooted in his need to defend his own ignorance of practical construction, something with which Thompson can be presumed to have had extensive experience. Davis leaned on a belief in the purity of the Greek and depravity of ancient Roman work as a support for his argument. Elsewhere Davis described Thompson's most prominent commissions as "an attempt at the Grecian amphiprostyle temple . . . a very unfortunate example of the chaste Ionic [Hall of Records] . . . ; the *semblance* of *something good*" but for "the worst examples ~~of~~ from the antique, being chosen [The Phenix Bank]"; and "one mass of deformity" in violation of "Grecian, or rational architecture [The Merchants' Exchange]."[271] Davis, who served as consultant to William Dunlap while writing the architectural content of his *History of the Rise and Progress of the Arts of Design in the United States* (1834),[272] and who, in fact, provided much of the text dealing with this subject, included a discussion of the careers of Brady and Town & Davis, but ignored the work of Thompson.[273] Although otherwise verbose and literate, Davis appears to have attempted to wish-away Thompson's very existence by omitting reference to him. Since Dunlap's work has become a chief source for our understanding of the arts in antebellum America, Davis has largely succeeded.

William Ross, an expatriate architect from England working in association with the Town & Davis office, was more evenhanded, and provided the following description of the typical New York town house for an English periodical.

In the elevations of the houses in New York there is considerable apparent variety, but it consists solely in a little difference in height, and sometimes in the size of the windows. The doorcase to the principal floor, which is always four or five feet above the street, is, in the better and middling class of houses, decorated with two columns, either triglyphed or voluted. The proportions of these columns are as various as are the builders, each having a proportion of his own; the triglyphed from seven to twelve diameters high, and the voluted from ten to eighteen: yet each are pure Greek. . . . [E]ach door has sidelights, as well as a fan-light; so that the hall is as well lighted as any room in the house. . . .the doorcase, window sills, and lintels, or supercilia, are of white marble."[274]

Alterations to 59 Second Street

There is scant evidence, but it is clear from what documents survive and an examination of the fabric of 59 Second Street, that it underwent significant alterations in the years circa 1836, 1893, and 1910. The house was also modified subsequent to its becoming the headquarters of the Rensselaer County Historical Society in January 1953.

The first significant alteration consisted of a three-story addition to the southern half of the rear of the Hart house, constructed circa 1836 and known as "the back building." Flooring structure was thrown over the existing west areaway below, and connected to a new basement, separate from that of the main house. The southwest room on the first floor of the original house, probably utilized as a family dining and sitting room, was enlarged for use as a formal dining room. A portion of the original back wall of the house was removed and the depth of the room was increased by approximately eight feet. The fireplace was relocated to a position closer to the center of the now-lengthened south wall, and two windows were cut into the same wall to compensate for the two that were lost on the west. Beyond this dining room, the first floor addition was composed of a bedroom and stair hall/pantry. The basement level comprised a hall and a single room used for the storage of coal.[275] The second floor of the addition was divided into three spaces: a hall, and two rooms. One of these was described as the "skirt room" in the 1886 inventory, the other may have been a nursery. Servants occupied the third floor. The ceilings of the addition are much lower than those of the main house, so that three levels fit into the height of two floors of the older part of the building.

The improvisational nature of the details featured in the addition suggests that a builder was responsible for its design. That John Colegrove was the builder of this addition can be surmised from reference to his being paid out of Richard Hart's domestic accounts for "1½ days labor picking out and marking timber," on February 2, 1835. Timber was typically set aside a full year before its anticipated use, so it is probable that work began on the addition in the spring of 1836. A subsequent bill from Colegrove, dated August 12, 1836 amounting to $356.88,[276] may be for construction of foundations for the proposed addition; these were usually completed the year previous to the construction of the superstructure to allow for settling. Construction of the addition likely occurred during 1836–37. The white marble lintels and sills from the removed southern half of the western façade of the house were reused in the addition. Jairus Dickerman likely executed the masonry work. Dickerman is documented as having performed various small repair and maintenance jobs on the masonry of the house in the earliest of the preserved family papers.[277] Between July 13 and September 23, 1837,

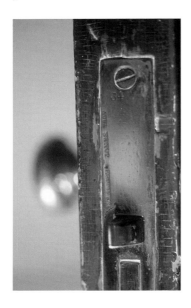

118 Dining room door hardware, marked "McKinney & Jones, Troy," c. 1836.

119 Park Place, Troy, as seen c. 1890. The Hart garden wall can be seen in this view at the right. The corner house, part of Park Place, was remodeled by Boston architect, H. Langford Warren, and was later converted into the Rinaldo Apartments.

Joseph C. Taylor billed Richard P. Hart $104.80 for various jobs relative to the roofing of the addition, including "Tin[n]ing 540½ Feet Roof," providing "15 Feet 3 in[ch] Conductor," and "Adding 2 Feet & New Spout to Cistern Pump."[278] The nature of this work suggests a completion date for the project. The original tin roof surface survives intact beneath two additional later roofs.[279]

These conjectural dates for construction of the addition are further substantiated by the door hardware, which is stamped "McKinney & Jones, Troy" (see Fig. 118). William McKinney was active as a brass founder and locksmith in Troy beginning in 1834, and was in partnership with Ebenezer Jones during 1835 and 1836.[280]

No documents survive for the circa 1893 renovations, which coincided with the occupancy of the house by George and Amanda Cluett. These seem to have involved an extension of the addition by twenty-one feet to accommodate a new first floor kitchen and the extension of the roof of this new addition over the roof of the earlier 1836 addition at a slightly higher elevation. Other significant projects included modification of the arched opening between the entrance hall (Room 101) and stair hall (Room 102), installation of hardwood flooring, and creation of two new bathrooms in Rooms 203 and 211. Although there is no record of an architect having been involved in these projects, professional advice may have been sought. The subtle changes made

to the hall archway particularly suggest an architect's hand.

The lot that the Hart house and grounds occupied was divided with the sale of the house to the Cluetts in 1893 (see Fig. 119 and 120). The garden lot was sold to William Kemp, who subsequently built a two-bay wide

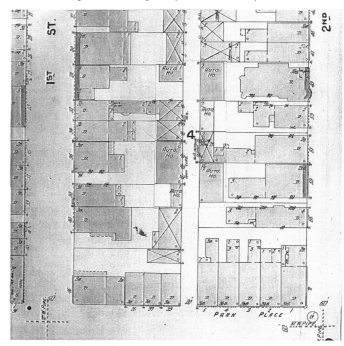

120 Detail, Plate 91, Vol. II, *Insurance Maps of Troy, Rensselaer County...*, Sanborn Map Company, New York, NY, 1903. Note that the Kemp-Frear House has been designated 65 Second Street.

row house on the site, the design of which has frequently been attributed to New York City architect Stanford White.[281]

Significant twentieth century alterations to 59 Second Street include raising of the back roof on the main house (c. 1910) to accommodate two bedrooms and one bathroom on the third floor and the installation of chair rails and trim to the primary first floor rooms for new owners Albert and Caroline Cluett. The expansion and remodeling of the third floor included the installation of woodwork that matched the elegant trim of the first and second floors. The carved wood raffle flowers —so prominent on the first and second floor door and window surrounds—were replicated in cast plaster for this location. In 1938, an elevator was installed in the hall cloak closet. It originally traveled only between the first and second floors, but a subsequent alteration for the Rensselaer County Historical Society in 1969 extended its path to the basement and third floor. The Historical Society has been responsible for a number of modifications to the house during the years of its tenancy. Some of the trim on the first floor has been altered, and doors to the back hall were closed off in both the dining room (Room 106) and back parlor (Room 104).[282]

Conclusion

Remarkably, through 173 years of occupancy, expansion and transformation, 59 Second Street has retained the architectural elements that are the hallmarks of its unique character. The elegant detailing of its exterior marble trim, the extraordinary ironwork and the exuberant interior woodwork and plasterwork remain as testaments to the talent and skill of its designer, and to the craftsmen who brought the design to fruition.

In its design the Hart house aspired to the highest cultural ideals of the time. That it was perceived as successful is made clear by the subsequent popularization of its various elements in New York City and elsewhere. As preserved, 59 Second Street is one of the most fully realized and intact examples of our rich Federal-era architectural heritage.

ACKNOWLEDGMENTS

A number of persons were instrumental to the research and writing of this essay. Regina M. Kellerman was generous with her time and knowledge of New York City architecture, and kindly read the manuscript in an early form. Wesley G. Balla, curator of history at the Albany Institute of History and Art, also read the manuscript and made a number of invaluable suggestions. Betty J. Ezequelle, principal scholar of the work of Martin E. Thompson, generously shared the fruits of her research with me. The late Jane B. Davies brought the early work of James Dakin to my attention. Michael Lynch, Vice President for Preservation Services at the Society for the Preservation of New England Antiquities, brought the 1825 New York stonecutters price book to my attention, and provided me with a formula to translate from pounds to dollars. Morrison H. Hecksher, the Anthony W. and Lulu C. Wang Curator, American Decorative Arts, Metropolitan Museum of Art, brought the Thomspon-related materials in the collections of the American Wing to my attention. Kathy Coyle, librarian at Winterthur, assisted in my search for books formerly owned by Martin E. Thompson, Henry Farnham and Philip Hooker. Michael A. Hawkins of the New York State Geological Survey gave me a crash course in the identification of Westchester marble, and a way into the dense literature on New York State geology. Paul Harmon Cole provided information on the early artisans of Troy, gathered from his study of the city's early newspapers. My co-authors, Stacy Pomeroy Draper and Douglas G. Bucher assisted at all points during the writing of this essay, providing leads, brainstorming while interpreting documents, and contributing suggestions to improve the writing. Frederick Cawley has, with much skill and patience, pushed this essay toward a point of clarity that it would have otherwise missed. Thanks go to him for assisting in telling this story.

I would also like to thank Janet Parks, curator of the Rare Prints and Drawings Department of the Avery Architectural Library, Columbia University; Jim Corsaro, formerly Associate Librarian and Billy Aul, Senior Librarian, both of the New York State Library, Manuscripts and Special Collections; Valerie Winfield of the New York Public Library, Rare Books and Manuscripts; Mary Beth Betts, former curator of Prints and Drawings at the New-York Historical Society, and the numerous staff members and volunteers at the Rensselaer County Historical Society who have assisted in many ways over the past four years.

WALTER RICHARD WHEELER

NOTES

1. *The Boston News-Letter and City Record*, 2: 6 (August 12, 1826), pp. 66–67.

2. Stewart Scott Diary (13145), September 26, 1826. New York State Library, Manuscripts and Special Collections, Albany, New York.

3. Excerpt from "A Brief Narrative of the Origin and Growth of the city of Troy," in *The Troy Directory for the Year 1829*. (Troy: John Disturnell, 1829), p. xvi.

4. Arthur James Weise. *History of the City of Troy* (Troy: William H. Young, 1876), p. 153.

5. David Buel, Jr. in his "Troy for Fifty Years" published in the *Trojan Sketch Book* (Troy: Young & Hartt, 1846), p. 16 says that among the first five houses constructed of brick were the James Spencer house (1795), and 31 First Street, 20 and 22 Second Street and the house at the corner of River and Washington streets (1796). Twenty Second Street

was razed at about the time Buel wrote. Construction dates cited throughout this essay have been determined using four basic sources: deeds, city directories, local histories, and personal assessment based on a knowledge of early nineteenth century construction techniques and technologies.

6. The Bank of Troy building was principally a residence, with two rooms on the first floor reserved for banking activity.

7. The city of Troy passed an ordinance in 1816 prohibiting the extension of stoops more than six feet from the front of a building. (*Laws and Ordinances . . . of the City of Troy* (Troy: Parker & Bliss, 1816), p. 41, cited in Diana S. Waite. *Ornamental Ironwork: Two Centuries of Craftsmanship in Albany and Troy, New York* (Albany: Mount Ida Press, 1990), p. 25. This was likely a reaction to proposals to construct houses with high basements. The first dwellings constructed with tall basements thus turned their stairs to run perpendicular with the street, or spiraled down to the sidewalk. Among these early houses are the Vail house, the houses at 35–39 First Street (1820), noted below, 42 (now razed), 45 and 54 Second Street (c. 1825–28), and 132 First Street (c. 1831). See Waite, *Ornamental Ironwork*, pp. 24–36 for more on this type of ironwork.

8. A contemporary account by Henry Bradshaw Fearon notes that "A large body of mechanics recently left here for want of employment;—the wages given to those who remain are the same as at New York," suggesting that they left for want of employment only. (Joel Munsell, comp. *Collections on the History of Albany* 2. Albany: J. Munsell, 1867, p. 334.)

9. *New York City Directories* for the years 1817–27.

10. See pages 57–58 for a discussion of these earlier structures.

11. See Peter McNab's account book. The now-lost original was photocopied and has been deposited at the Albany Institute of History and Art, McKinney Library, Albany, New York and in the Philip Hooker Research Materials Collection (sc20924), New York State Library, Manuscripts and Special Collections, Albany, New York.

12. These houses were originally two stories and built of brick laid in Flemish bond on a tall basement, and featured jack arches for window lintels.

13. Gravestones of marble dating to the eighteenth century are known in the area.

14. These included silversmiths Henry Bayeux, Abraham Fellows, Isaac Heroy, Rufus R. Smith, and James Young. See the James Young Papers (ex 11171), New York State Library, Manuscripts and Special Collections, Albany, New York. Bayeux, Smith and Young are mentioned as silversmiths practicing at Troy in the "City Register" printed in the *Northern Budget* (Troy) from January 3 to July 25, 1826. Myron King, apprenticed to Young by 1815, was at the beginning of a prominent career in copperplate engraving. See *Troy Daily Times*, February 2, 1878, for an extended obituary of King. Elijah Galusha had just moved to Troy and was apprenticed to cabinetmaker H. M. Smith. Galusha would later gain prominence as a master of elaborately carved rosewood furniture in the Rococo Revival style. See Anna T. D'Ambrosio and Stacy Pomeroy Draper. *Artistry in Rosewood: Furniture by Elijah Galusha*. Utica, New York: Munson Williams Proctor Institute, 1995, p. 1. David McKelsey operated a chair manufactory on Congress Street and A[dna] Treat and Horace Jones operated looking glass manufactories. For Jones see the *Northern Budget* (Troy), September 17, 1822. Cabinetmakers Jonathan Weeks, Robert Christie, (William) Albro & [Luke] Lockwood, and T. B & W[illiam] T. Smith were all active at this date. See the "City Register," *Northern Budget* (Troy), January 3 to July 25, 1826. Weeks' last name is also spelled "Wickes" in contemporary advertisements. He is probably the son of Jacob Weeks/Wickes, active in Troy by about 1799. (*Northern Budget* [Troy], March 12, 1799.) Charles Lemon had been creating furniture in Troy for almost twenty years by this time; see his advertisement dated May 13, 1806 in the *Northern Budget* (Troy). A bureau by Lemon has recently been purchased by the Rensselaer County Historical Society. J. Yatman was likely Troy's first cabinetmaker, arriving in the city in 1799. (*Northern*

Budget [Troy], December 25, 1799.) Itinerant portrait artists frequented the city including Edward C. Potter, "pupil of Mr. Rogers, of New-York," who spent the summer of 1823 in Troy (*Northern Budget* [Troy], July 18, 1823). Ralph E. W. Earl set up his *Lorenzo Gallery* as early as 1806 (*Northern Budget* [Troy], July 8, 1806).

15. The Hart Papers relating to purchases of furnishings do not extend as far back as the 1820s, but it is clear that they participated in this trend. The purchasing habits of a contemporary Rensselaer County family are documented in the Akin Family Papers (14723), New York State Library, Manuscripts and Special Collections, Albany, New York.

16. For example, *The Troy Sentinel* for the year 1825 carried advertisements by Southwick, Cannon & Warren, for clothing and cloth from England, France, India, and America, purchased in New York; Lockwood & Redfield for imported carpeting from Great Britain; Miss Eliza Flack and Miss C. Sheldon for the latest fabrics from New York; and French & Hart for imported teas and sherry.

17. The Elias Pattison family lived at 60 Second Street; the Jacob Merritt family at 53 Second Street (*Troy City Directory*, 1829).

18. Howard is recorded as purchasing additional property in Dey Street in January 1819 (*Minutes of the Common Council of the City of New York, 1784–1831*, 19 vols. New York: The City of New York, 1917, 10: 212 [January 25, 1819]).

19. Tredwell later occupied a still extant house on Fourth Street in New York that features a door surround similar to the Hart house type. Now a house museum, it is presently known as the "Merchant's House."

20. *Minutes of the Common Council . . . of New York*, 10: 212 (January 25, 1819).

21. Howard was a prominent merchant of the day and sat on the boards of several banking and insurance companies. See p. 25.

22. While it is possible that Howard could have procured a plan for the house before securing the lots it would be located on, this is not likely. The width of the house required the purchase of two city lots, and the orientation of the rooms required these lots to be on the west side of a street—if the garden was to be in its conventional location to the south of the house. It is unlikely that Howard could have secured a site with such particular requirements if he started with a design in hand.

23. Richard L. Bushman. *The Refinement of America: Persons, Houses, Cities* (New York: Alfred A. Knopf, 1992), p. 242.

24. In the modern sense of the term, meaning that they maintained offices and received most of their income from architectural services including execution of drawings and superintendence of construction.

25. Richard Allanson (by 1774–1827) appears to have emigrated from Ireland circa 1798 and taken up residence in Albany. His first documented activity in that city is in the form of draughts made in 1800 for St. Peter's Church, Albany, in connection with Hooker's proposal for a new building. Hooker and Allanson do not appear to have worked in partnership at any time. Allanson never achieved Hooker's fame and he was likely unknown outside of Albany. There is evidence that prejudice played a part in his failure to succeed in the profession. Among other clues to this attitude toward Allanson and other immigrants during this time is an advertisement placed by Allanson, calling for workers and noting that "It is totally immaterial whether they are *American* or *European bred* Mechanics" (*Albany Centinel*, September 14, 1802). Allanson died in 1827 (*Albany Gazette*, November 30, 1827).

26. A tradition—dating only as far back as the middle of the twentieth century—ascribes the design of the Hart house to Philip Hooker (Rensselaer County Historical Society publication dated 1952). Probably this was a result of the publication of Edward Root's monograph on the architect in 1929. (Edward W. Root. *Philip Hooker: A Contribution to the Study of the Renaissance in America* [New York: Charles Scribner's Sons, 1929].) Albert Cluett owned a copy of this book; he may be the source of the attribution. The style of the build-

ing fits neatly into Hooker's work of the period and he was one of a small group of architects who pioneered the use of the Westchester marble in Albany by the late 1820s. The interior woodwork of the Hart house, with its bold carving and corner blocks, is very similar to that in many buildings designed by Hooker from the period 1815–1827. Root himself used the presence of similar carving to attribute several structures to Hooker (Root, *Philip Hooker*, pp. 203–4).

27. *The Troy Sentinel*, April 11, 1826.

28. Deeds, Rensselaer County Courthouse, Troy, New York. Howard owned the site from 1825–1834.

29. Eric Sloan and Edward Anthony. *Mr. Daniels and the Grange.* New York: Funk & Wagnalls, 1968.

30. The Rotunda was erected to display the panoramic paintings of John Vanderlyn. It was the first purpose-built gallery in New York City.

31. A large body of McComb's architectural drawings is preserved in the New-York Historical Society. The best source for information on McComb is Damie Stillman's thesis from 1956 (see bibliography). Articles on his work published in the *Journal of the Society of Architectural Historians* include "New York City Hall: Competition and Execution," by Damie Stillman (23 [1964], pp. 129–142); "Notes for a Catalogue of the John McComb (1763–1853) Collection of Architectural Drawings at the New-York Historical Society," by Agnes Addison Gilchrist (28 [1969], pp. 201–210); and "John McComb, Sr. and Jr., in New York, 1784–1799," by Agnes Addison Gilchrist (31 [1972], pp. 10–21).

32. Franklin Toker. "James O'Donnell: An Irish Georgian in America," *Journal of the Society of Architectural Historians* 29 (1970): 132–143. See also Toker's entry on O'Donnell in the *MacMillan Encyclopedia of Architects* (Adolf K. Placzek, ed. New York: The Free Press, 1982), 3: 312.

33. The Sclater Collection, Avery Architectural Library, Columbia University, New York. A number of drawings attributable to him, but unsigned, are in the collection as well.

34. New York City *Directory*, 1825. Stokes notes that Newton was at work as master carpenter on the New York City Hall in 1803, and that an account book for that project, as well as other work by Newton extending to 1820, was located in the City Clerk's Office (Stokes, p. 1409). See also *The Arts and Crafts in New York 1777–1799* for refs. to Newton.

35. Root quotes a letter from Taylor dated February 23, 1843 (Root, *Philip Hooker*, pp. 137–38). Taylor does not appear in the Federal Census for New York State in 1850.

36. Root:, *Philip Hooker*, pp. 129–38 passim.

37. "St. John's Chapel, New-York," *New York Mirror* 6: 40 (April 11, 1829), p. 313.

38. New York City *Directory*.

39. The earlier "Gothick" revival, inspired by the mid-eighteenth century pattern books of Batty Langley and others and informed by neoclassical aesthetics, is now recognized by historians as a separate aesthetic movement from the more archeologically correct movement of the 1830s and 1840s. The earlier spelling of the word is retained to convey this. For a description and engraving by A. J. Davis of Trinity Church, see "The History of Trinity Church," in the *New-York Mirror* 5: 1, (July 14, 1827), p. 1 and frontispiece.

40. See note 54.

41. *Minutes of the Common Council . . . of New York*, 17: 147 (April 21, 1828).

42. Newark: W. Tuttle & Company, 1829, p. 103.

43. Lafever continues: "The Cornice supporting this Attic is not very appropriate to it, as well as to the front door also. Therefore it devolves upon me to give one according with my views, that will be uniform to this Elevation, which is principally of Grecian Architecture," which he includes in the plate (*Young Builder's General Instructor* [Newark: W. Tuttle & Company, 1829], Plate 60 and page 149). Although the copyright page of this book gives credit to "Minard Lafever and Lewis M. Lindsly" [*sic*], it is unlikely that Lindsley, of

which little else is known, contributed designs of the sophistication seen in these plates.

44. The passage is quoted in *The Architecture of Minard Lafever* by Jacob Landy (New York and London: Columbia University Press, 1970, pp. 12–13). The question of Lafever's apprenticeship with Thompson is explored in note 89.

45. Edmund March Blunt. *The Picture of New York, and Stranger's Guide.* (New-York: A. T. Goodrich, 1828), p. 280.

46. Philip Hooker provided bound sets of documents for his projects for the Albany Academy (1815), the William Alexander house (1816), and projects for George Hyde, Josephus Bradner Stuart, and St. Peter's Church, Sherrill, New York (all 1818). See Bucher and Wheeler. *Neat Plain Modern Stile*, pp. 136–41, 144–52, 165–74, 176–79, and 180–87.

47. Between July 25, 1785, and July 24, 1786. His obituary states that he was 91 years old at the time of his death on the latter date in 1877. Census records indicate that he was born in New Jersey. His mother was probably Letty (a.k.a. Allette) R. Thompson, who lived with Martin as late as 1860, aged 93. The 1870 Census lists him as 84, putting his birth date as circa 1786 (Federal census, 1860 and 1870).

48. See for example Samuel A. Clark. *The History of St. John's Church, Elizabeth Town, New Jersey* (Philadelphia: J. B. Lippincott & Co.; New York: Thomas N. Stanford, 1857), p. 174.

49. The date was February 10, 1810. *The Genealogical Magazine of New Jersey* 36: 3 (September 1961): 103. Polly (a.k.a. Mary) was born on October 4, 1788, daughter to Aaron Kitchel and Phebe Farrand (Family Search Database, Church of the Latter Day Saints).

50. David Longworth. *Longworth's American Almanac, New York Register and City Directory* (New-York: David Longworth, 1816), p. 416.

51. New York City *Directories* for the years 1817–20.

52. *Longworth's American Almanac, New York Register and City Directory.* New York: Thomas Longworth, June 25, 1823.

53. The building was razed in the early part of the 20th century. Its street façade has been preserved and is installed in the American Wing, Metropolitan Museum of Art, New York, New York.

54. Although this building is recognized by scholars to have been designed by Thompson and is recorded as such in contemporary literature, many researchers have overlooked clues that suggest participation by Brady in its design. Talbot F. Hamlin refers to a drawing preserved at the New-York Historical Society—an elevation of the Merchants' Exchange with a note in a contemporary hand stating that the design was by Brady and Thompson. The records of the National Academy of Design preserve A. J. Davis' description of his perspective view of the Merchants' Exchange, stating that Brady had designed the cupola in its original form. A note in Martin E. Thompson's account book, recording the receipt of $42.31 from Brady in 1825 further connects the two men during this period. While these facts do not document a professional relationship per se, they do suggest a close working relationship between the two men. Lafever mentions them together in the acknowledgments for his *The Modern Builder's Guide* (1833). Further evidence connecting the two men is the attribution to A. J. Davis of drawings descended in the Thompson family, by the late Jane Davies, the principal Davis authority (see catalogue notes accompanying the Martin E. Thompson Papers, Avery Architecture Library, Columbia University). Roger Hale Newton presumed that Brady and Thompson worked together (Roger Hale Newton. *Town & Davis Architects.* [New York: Columbia University Press, 1942], pp. 91–92). For a contemporary description of the Merchants' Exchange, see Edwin Williams, ed., *New-York As it Is, in 1833.* (New York: J. Disturnell, 1833), p. 123.

55. Numerous engravings of both structures were circulated. After the destruction of the Merchants' Exchange in the Great Fire of 1835, it was memorialized in a number of engraved views and lithographs (C. Foster. *Account of the Conflagration of the Principal Part of the First Ward of the City of New-York* [New-York: C. Foster, n.d. 1835]). In the microfiche-published version of this title (*American Directories through 1860, a Collection on microfiche . . . based on Bibliography of American*

Directories through 1860 by Dorothea N. Spear . . . 1961. [New Haven: Research Publications, 1969]), a drawing or engraving (it's not clear which) is inserted, depicting the memorial executed after the fire. It lists Lafever as its architect, but curiously notes a second fire in 1853 and attributes to Martin E. Thompson the re-erection of the memorial.

56. The Second Branch Bank is commonly described as the "second building built of marble in New York"—the first being the City Hall.

57. I will use the term 'Westchester marble' to describe this stone. Contemporary sources typically refer to it as Eastchester, Tuckahoe, Westchester, or Sing-Sing marble, depending on from which town the material was quarried. Quotes of contemporary references to the stone will reflect this.

58. New York Common Council Minutes, March 7, 1803, include the suggestion of using "Morrisania or Verplancks marble" on the end elevations of the contemplated new City Hall (quoted in "John McComb, Jr. Architect," part 2 in *The American Architect and Building News*, 94: 1704. [August 19, 1908], p. 57, by Edward S. Wilde). Curiously, this note does not appear in the published version of the Common Council Minutes. Ultimately, the front and side elevations of the building were dressed in marble from Stockbridge, Mass.

59. See page 73.

60. "St. Thomas's Church," *The New York Mirror*, 6: 50. (June 20, 1829), p. 393.

61. Its first dateable appearance is on Philip Hooker's façade for the New York State Bank in Albany of 1803.

62. Deed dated November 8, 1825, Rensselaer County Courthouse, Troy, New York.

63. The nature of the relationship between William Howard and Martin E. Thompson necessarily remains conjectural. William Howard served on the board of directors under an A. G. Thompson, president of the Union Bank, and later served as president himself (Williams, *New York . . . in 1833*, p. 98). An Alexander Thompson participated in many real estate transactions during this time with Martin E.; see *New York City and County, Index of Conveyances: Grantors*, Vol. 16 (New York: McSpedon & Baker, Printers, 1858), p. 103. The two Thompsons may have been related. Martin E. Thompson was appointed a board member and surveyor to the Fire and Inland Navigation Insurance Company by November 1825, perhaps providing another opportunity for Thompson and Howard to come in contact (*The New-York Statesman*, November 8, 1825).

64. On December 7, 1826, the "plans of Messrs Thomson & Town" for the design of the steeple for St. Mark's Church in the Bouwerie, New York City were accepted by the congregation (Aymar Embury III. *Early American Churches* [Garden City: Doubleday, Page & Company, 1914], p. 103).

65. That is to say that they were professionally associated solely for the purpose of executing drawings for buildings and superintending their erection. In this they differed from the architect-builders of the time.

66. Eliot Candee Clark. *History of the National Academy of Design, 1825–1953* (New York: Columbia University Press, 1954), pp. 13–14.

67. Newton, *Town & Davis*, pp. 54–55.

68. Isaac Damon was an engineer, sometime partner of Town's in the execution of designs after Town's patent truss bridge, and resident of Northampton, Massachusetts. For more on Damon, see Embury, *Early American Churches*, pp. 135–142.

69. The Rensselaer County Board of Supervisors were granted permission to raise funds to build a new courthouse on March 13, 1827 (Weise, *Troy's One Hundred Years*, p. 124). In a "Notice to Master Builders" published by the building committee on December 17, 1827, the "plans and specifications" are noted as "at the counting room of R. P. Hart" (*Northern Budget & City Register* [Troy], December 28, 1827, in an advertisement dated December 17th). This intriguing connection between Hart and Town & Thompson circumstantially relates these men during the year the Hart house was completed. Construction on the Courthouse was delayed so that it was not completed until 1831.

70. Thus supporting the thesis of a New York-based designer. Farnham & Pollard were also among the bidders. *The Troy Republican*, September 9, 1828.

71. Ibid.; *Troy Daily Whig*, April 12, 1860; *Troy Daily Budget*, April 12, 1860.

72. This "education" is documented in George Tibbits' letterbook, collection Rensselaer County Historical Society, Troy, New York. Letters from Elam Lynds, agent of the prison at the time, suggest that no stone had been sold on contract previous to 1827. Previous to the discovery of this letterbook it had been thought that the Hart house was one of the first structures to utilize the Sing-Sing stone in its construction, chiefly due to Hart's and Tibbits' connection to Sing-Sing and the similarity of the Sing-Sing and Westchester stone. The letterbook further suggests that quarries had previously been opened on the site, and at least during the initial years of operation, the prison shared access to these quarries with others who mined the beds.

73. George Tibbits' letterbook documents Hart's connection with the project

74. Davis Papers, Office Diary Vol. I, Prints and Drawings Department, Metropolitan Museum of Art, New York.

75. William H. Pierson, Jr. *American Buildings and Their Architects: Technology and the Picturesque, the Corporate and the Early Gothic Styles* (Garden City, New York: Doubleday & Co., 1978), pp. 140–44.

76. Weise, *History*, p. 156.

77. By way of explanation of the similarity between the two buildings, the Troy congregation has perpetuated the tradition that the builders went to New Haven to make drawings of the church there. Repeated in Pierson, *Technology and the Picturesque*, p. 142.

78. Pierson, *Technology and the Picturesque*, p. 144, citing the August 15, 1828, *Troy Sentinel*. Town's design for Trinity Church was itself adapted from Plate 26 of James Gibbs' *A Book of Architecture* (London, 1728). For a second contemporary description of St. Paul's, see the George Tibbits Papers (13253, Box 129, folder 7), New York State Library, Manuscripts and Special Collections, Albany, New York.

79. Weise, *Troy's One Hundred Years*, p. 132; Newton, *Town & Davis*, p. 74.

80. Newton, *Town & Davis*, pp. 54–56.

81. The contents of Town's library can be largely reconstructed by consulting the auction catalogues published when it was dispersed (Avery Architectural Library, Columbia University, New York).

82. For example, note the Second Bank of the United States (1818) by William Strickland, in Philadelphia, and the numerous works of Benjamin H. Latrobe in Baltimore, Washington and Philadelphia.

83. New York City *Directory*. 1828.

84. A list of these commissions (some principally by other associates of the office as noted in parentheses), reconstructed from the Davis Papers, Prints and Drawings, Metropolitan Museum of Art, New York, and contemporary published sources includes:

1829	Albany City Hall competition entry (unbuilt).
1829–32	Railroad bridge over the Mohawk at Cohoes (Ithiel Town).
1832	Cannon Place Stores (for LeGrand Cannon), Troy (Town, Davis & Dakin).
c. 1832	Four bridges over the Hudson and Mohawk rivers near Troy (Ithiel Town).
1832–33	John Tayler Cooper house, 134 State Street, Albany (James Dakin).
1833	A country seat for Mr. Van Rensselaer (James Dakin).
1833	Albany Female Academy (James Dakin with Henry Rector).
1834	Alterations to the Rensselaer County Courthouse, Troy.
1834	Beman's [First Presbyterian] Church, Troy (James Dakin).
1835	Albany Exchange competition entry (unbuilt, Ithiel Town).

1836	Albany City and Canal bank, Albany.
1837	Christ Church, Troy (attributed to Town & Davis).
1838	"Mount Ida," Nathan B. Warren house, Troy.
1838	William Patterson van Rensselaer house, Rensselaer (not built).
1840	Renovations, Trinity Church, Troy (for Stephen Warren).
1842–46	"Kenwood," Joel Rathbone house, Albany.
1843–44	Episcopal Chapel (Holy Cross Church—for Nathan B. Warren), Troy.
1845	"Nut Grove," Mrs. William Walsh house, Albany.
1847	Additions to Nathan B. Warren house, Troy.
1849	Unspecified details for Joel Rathbone (probably for enlargement of Kenwood), Albany.

85. *New York Common Council Minutes* 17: 523, December 15, 1828.

86. *New-York Mirror*, 6: 22, (December 6, 1828), Frontispiece and p. 169.

87. The terms used to describe these blocks can be confusing. Contemporary literature called the stacking of alternate long and short blocks "rustication." When the identical relationship of blocks was located at the corner of a building they were called "quoins." However, "rusticated" is a term that is also applied to blocks that are treated with a rough surface, as if left unworked. In this essay, the term "rusticated" will refer to the first definition.

88. Martin E. Thompson Papers, and Thompson Account Book. Avery Architectural Library, Columbia University, New York. Landy notes that this Harrison is likely the same as the otherwise unidentified partner of Minard Lafever during this period (Landy, *Minard Lafever*, p. 67). Landy also provides some additional information on Robert Cary Long, Jr. (Ibid., p. 77).

89. Minard Lafever is documented as having provided drafting services for Thompson, albeit at a later date (Martin E. Thompson Papers, and Thompson Account Book. Avery Architectural Library, Columbia University, New York). He is described by James Gallier as "in the employment of a builder" in 1832 (James Gallier. *Autobiography of James Gallier, Architect* [Paris: E. Briere, 1864; reprint, New York: De Capo Press, 1973].) Gallier identified almost all of New York City's self-styled architects as builders, after the habit of A. J. Davis with whom he worked. As previously discussed, Lafever's earliest work appears to owe much to both Thompson and to Brady. Lafever's acquaintance with the two men probably predates Brady's retirement in 1829.

James Dakin had been a "pupil" of A. J. Davis between June 1829 and June 1830; he probably learned the skills of the "architectural composer" from Davis (A. J. Davis Papers, Office Diary Vol. I, Prints and Drawings Department, Metropolitan Museum of Art, New York). Between the date of his departure from the office of Town & Davis, and one year later when he is first recorded as an architect, Dakin acquired further training, perhaps at Thompson's office. Certainly Dakin's earliest documented designs are remarkable for their similarity to contemporary work by Thompson.

An examination of the New York City *Directory* for 1831 and 1832 suggests that Dakin and Lafever were in professional association for at least part of this time. Dakin provided illustrations for Theodore Fay's *Views in New York* (1831) and Lafever's *The Modern Builder's Guide* (1833). Dakin and Lafever possibly knew each other from an association with Thompson dating to circa 1830–31. Lafever wrote of Dakin, "[his] talents, taste, and ideas, are of the first order, and [I hold him] in very high estimation" (Minard Lafever, *Beauties of Modern Architecture*. New York, 1835, quoted in Landy, *Minard Lafever*, p. 45).

James Gallier described Dakin in 1832 as "a young man of genius, who had been a carpenter and had studied architecture in Town's office; . . . [by April 1832], he had opened an office of his own, where he made drawings for the builders; from him I obtained the first employment I had in America" (Gallier, *Autobiography*, pp. 18–19). Dakin subsequently returned to the Town & Davis office, forming a partnership with them which lasted from May 1, 1832, to November 1, 1833 (A. J.

Davis Papers, Office Diary Vol. I, Prints and Drawings Department, Metropolitan Museum of Art, New York).

The architectural scene in New York during 1825–35 was in a constant state of flux. Associations between major architects, and among young talents, were frequently brief. For example, James Gallier worked with James Dakin, Minard Lafever, Town & Davis and James Dakin's brother Charles in the short span of three years (Gallier, *Autobiography*, pp. 18–20).

90. For example see Newton, *Town & Davis*, p. 140 (in the midst of an argument supporting attribution of some of the houses to Town & Davis). A number of additional twentieth century historians mention Thompson in connection with the project. The late Agnes Addison Gilchrist recalled seeing an elevation of these houses drawn by Isaac Green Pearson (Regina M. Kellerman to Walter Richard Wheeler, September 23, 1998). Pearson appears to have had some association with either Brady or Thompson, or both. He is credited in a period source as having drawn part of the façade for the Second Unitarian Church (1825–26) on Mercer Street in New York, attributed to Brady by Landy (*New-York Mirror* 7: 12, (September 26, 1829): 90. His name is there misspelled "J. G. Pearson"). Pearson was also responsible for the construction of LeRoy Place in New York, erected on Bleecker Street during 1827–29 (William S. Pelletreau. *Early New York Houses* [New York: Francis P. Harper, 1900], pp. 77–78). Newton mentions attribution of some of the houses to Minard Lafever and James H. Dakin.

Upon closer inspection of The Row, it becomes clear that the houses were constructed during several campaigns. This is clear not only from the variety of details featured on their façades, but also from construction joints visible throughout the row of houses. Thus it is feasible that more than one architect may have been involved in the design of the various houses.

91. Thomson constructed and occupied one of the houses of The Row. Geoffrey Carter of Barrytown, New York, is an indirect descendant of Samuel Thomson, and retains copies of his papers. These record Thomson's connection to The Row as well as a number of additional projects including the pavilions at Sailor's Snug Harbor and the United States Custom House (now Federal Hall National Memorial) on Wall Street. See Carter's article "Samuel Thomson: Prolific New York Builder," in *Newsletter/Preservation League of New York State* 17: 3, (Fall 1991), pp. 4–5.

92. The term is Philip Hooker's, used by him to describe the work to be done by Henry Farnham at the New York State Capitol in 1818. See note 147.

93. Several additional houses were constructed in Troy to this same design in subsequent years including 63–65 First Street. Only number 63 survives from this pair.

94. Williams, *New York . . . in 1833*, pp. 43, 69, 79, 97, and 109. Thompson was active as a *Manager* of the American Institute as late as 1851 (*Journal of the American Institute* 1: 5 [May 1851], n.p.).

95. Betty J. Ezequelle to Walter Richard Wheeler, December 5, 1998.

96. This is evidenced in the St. Mark's Place houses; the stonework for these dwellings is documented as having been executed by the prisoners at Sing-Sing (*Documents of the Assembly of the State of New-York, Fifty-sixth Session, 1833*. [Albany: E. Croswell, 1833], 199: 23). They have clearly been mass produced—several blocks on each façade are identical.

97. For Carmichael's activities at the prison, see *Documents of the Assembly of the State of New-York, Fifty-eighth Session, 1835* (Albany: E. Croswell, 1835), 135: 8–10.

98. Martin E. Thompson Account Book, Avery Architectural Library, Columbia University, New York.

99. William H. Gleason. *Semi-Centennial Celebration of the First Reformed Protestant Church, Hudson, N. Y., 1836–1886* (Hudson: M. Parker Williams, Register & Gazette, 1886), pp. 28–32.

100. The catalogue of the New York State Archives, Albany, New

York, lists Thompson's drawing for this structure as in the collection; it remains unlocated.

101. This project, constructed by John B. Colegrove and others, will be discussed at greater length below. See p. 72.

102. Betty J. Ezequelle to Walter Richard Wheeler, March 21, 1999.

103. For example, the window enframements of the second floor of the Hanover Bank are remarkably similar to those used by Thompson thirty years earlier in his design for the Second Branch Bank.

104. See Appendix III for a list of Martin E. Thompson's works and his life chronology.

105. From Mount's personal catalogue, quoted in John Caldwell and Oswaldo Rodriguez Roque. *American Paintings in the Metropolitan Museum of Art* (New York: Metropolitan Museum of Art, 1994), pp. 512–13.

106. William Colegrove. *The History and Genealogy of the Colegrove Family in America, With Biographical Sketches* (Chicago: Privately published, 1894), pp. 549 and 553.

107. A John "L." Colegrove was active as a carpenter in New York City during the 1820s. The New York City *Directory* gives his address as Dominick c. Varick in 1824–5, and 558 Broom in 1826–27. In 1995, Douglas G. Bucher purchased two molding planes from the Hoosick Antique Center, Hoosick, New York, that are stamped "J. L. Colegrove." It is not known what his relationship to John B. Colegrove was, but given the appearance of these tools in the Troy area, it may have been close.

108. Obituary, *Troy Daily Budget*, April 12, 1860. See above for reference to Thompson's early work.

109. New York City *Directory* for 1820 and subsequent years.

110. Obituary, *Troy Daily Budget*, April 12, 1860.

111. In 1827 Farnham & Pollard bid on the contract for the construction of the Rensselaer County Courthouse. That they were aware of the project suggests a connection to the architectural firm that may have designed the building—Town & Thompson. This firm may have been also connected to the Hart house project via partner Charles Farnham's brother, Henry, to whom the execution of the interior wood carving is attributed.

112. Jesse B. Anthony. *History of King Solomon's Primitive Lodge Troy, New York . . . Together with a Sketch of Freemasonry in the City of Troy from 1796 to 1842* (Troy: Henry Stowell Printing House, 1892), p. 13.

113. Ibid, pp. 14, 46–49, and appendix.

114. Arthur James Weise. *The Firemen and Fire Departments of Troy.* [Albany: Weed-Parsons Printing Co., 1895], p. 404. Dickerman had recently arrived in Troy.

115. For the argument for Town & Thompson's authorship of the design, see p. 66. Colegrove is mentioned as working on the Rensselaer County Courthouse in the Troy Common Council Minutes (May 21, 1833; September 24, 1835; January 27, 1837; January 18, 1838), which are preserved in the Public Safety Building and the City Hall, Troy, New York. A duplicate typescript copy of the minutes from the late 1830s is in the collection of the Rensselaer County Historical Society, Troy, New York.

116. Troy Common Council Minutes, August 15, 1833, Public Safety Building, Troy, New York.

117. Ibid., May 13, 1834.

118. *The Troy Daily Morning Mail*, August 15, 1839.

119. He represented Troy's First District at the convention and was on the "Committee to nominate officers of the Convention," *The Troy Daily Morning Mail*, October 11, 1839. Colegrove's brother Samuel W. also involved himself in politics, representing Troy's First Ward "Democratic Republican Young Men" at the First District meeting in Catskill, New York, in September 1839 (*The Troy Budget*, September 3, 1839).

120. Troy Common Council Minutes, March 3, 1840; March 2, 1841; March 9, 1843. Due to the loss of many of the minutes for this period, it has not been determined whether or not Colegrove was

elected in the intervening years, though this seems likely. Some of these election results are pulled from the city *Directory* of the period. Further research in the newspapers of the period, which frequently published Common Council minutes, may clarify this.

121. The first known mention of Samuel Colegrove occurs at this time, in the *Troy City Directory* for 1835. His middle initial is mistakenly listed as "H." Samuel's wife, Laura died April 22, 1847. See her obituary in the *Troy Budget* of April 23, 1847. It seems that he moved out of the city of Troy after her death; no references to him are found after this date.

122. Deeds, Rensselaer County Courthouse, Troy, New York. William Howard resided at 1 Park Place in 1840–41.

123. The sophistication of the design of these houses points to the likely contribution of an architect—A. J. Davis has been proposed, but this seems unlikely. Davis' work is largely well-documented, and although his London Terrace (constructed on Twenty-third Street in New York in 1845) shares many details with Washington Place, the Troy row offers a more sophisticated interpretation of the application of Doric pilasters to an extended façade. If Thompson was, in turn, responsible for the design of the Hart house, and then Park Place, perhaps it is not too much to suggest that he designed the row on Washington Park in Troy.

124. Arthur H. Masten. *The History of Cohoes* (Albany: Joel Munsell, 1877), pp. 80–81.

125. *The Troy Daily Times*, December 29, 1854. The building survived until March 1999, when it was needlessly razed. Markham appears to have come to Troy to oversee the construction of this church. It is possible that he came from New York City, to which he returned in the later 1860s. He died in 1898. Little is currently known of his career. The sophistication of the exterior of the Methodist Church suggests formal training. Markham also designed the Saratoga Battle Monument in Schuylerville, New York.

126. *Troy Daily Times*, August 31, 1858. Colegrove's contract to finish the third and fourth floors of the "South Centre" section of Troy University (dated February 19, 1858) is in the collections of the Rensselaer County Historical Society, Troy, New York (item 71.116.1). John Edson and Henry Englebert were responsible for the design of the contemporary and quite similar Convent and Academy of Mount Saint Vincent at Riverdale Avenue and West 263rd Street in New York City (1857–59).

127. Warren Family Papers (sc 17563, box 6, folder 2), Manuscripts and Special Collections, New York State Library, Albany, New York.

128. Hart Papers, Rensselaer County Historical Society, Troy, New York. Two of the daughters John Colegrove raised with Ellen Purdy Hammond attended the Troy Female Seminary—site of so many small jobs executed by Colegrove—then under the direction of the renowned Emma Willard. Susan began her education at the seminary in 1839 and graduated in 1847. She married Charles L. MacArthur, owner of the *Troy Northern Budget*, in 1849 and was living in 1898. Her sister, Caroline Bard Colegrove, is recorded as being a student at the seminary from 1842 to 1848. After that date she married Joseph Thompson, of New York, and resided there until her death in 1881. *Emma Willard and Her Pupils*, Mrs. A. W. Fairbanks, ed., (New York: Mrs. Russell Sage, 1898), p. 294.

129. *Troy Daily Whig*, April 12, 1860. On April 14, 1860, the same paper carried news of the funeral service. Colegrove was apparently a Universalist.

130. *Troy Daily Budget*, April 12, 1860.

131. William S. and John Frazee need to be mentioned as among the small group of New York-based individuals who offered various marbles for sale at this time. Their advertisement suggests that they sought a share in the business of providing architectural stonework. The larger part of the advertisement describes such products as monuments and chimney pieces, and it is likely that these supported the greatest part of their business (*The New-York Statesman*, March 31,

1823, in an ad dated September 13, 1822). John Frazee is better-known today as a sculptor working in the neoclassical style, and last architect of the United States Custom House (presently known as Federal Hall National Memorial) on Wall Street in New York.

132. New York City *Directory*, 1822.

133. *Minutes of the Common Council . . . of New York* 17: 374, (September 22, 1828).

134. Ibid., 15: 572 (September 11, 1826) ; James Hardie. *A Description of the City of New-York* (New York: Samuel Marks, 1827). Quoted in Lawrence B. Romaine, "Martin E. Thompson (c. 1786–1877) A Reconstruction of His Architectural Career from His Account Book," *Bulletin of the New York Public Library* 66: 5 (May 1962), p. 282.

135. New York City *Directory*, 1822 and subsequent years.

136. Frank E. Sanchis. *American Architecture: Westchester County, New York. Colonial to Contemporary* (New York: North River Press, 1977), pp. 54–56. Sanchis gives Masterton's partner as Robert Smith in 1819 (p. 54).

137. *Albany Daily Advertiser*, May 9, 1828.

138. Blunt, *Picture of New-York*, pp. 206–7.

139. Some evidence suggests that their Troy representative may have been Alexander Gray (1788–1864). Sources for further research into his life include Albany Rural Cemetery, Internment Records; Peter Kinnear, comp. *Historical Sketch of the St. Andrew's Society of the City of Albany 1803–1903* (Albany: Weed Parsons Printing Co., 1903), p. 94; and Corporation of the City of Albany Papers 1831–34 (MG 27), Albany Institute of History and Art, McKinney Library, Albany, New York.

140. Albany Academy Papers, SARA Collection, Albany County Hall of Records, Albany, New York.

141. Entry Documentation for Building and Maintenance of Government Facilities, 1785–1855, New York (State) Comptroller's Office (AO 825), New York State Archives, Albany, New York.

142. Joel Munsell, comp. *Annals of Albany* 10 (Albany: Munsell & Rowland, 1859), p. 334.

143. Register of Marriages, First Presbyterian Church Archives, Albany, New York.

144. Although records of their birth have not been located, it is probable that the Farnham brothers, Rufus, Charles, Lewis, and Henry, were related to the Farnhams of Boston, with whom they shared given names, if not professions. The Boston Farnhams were chiefly silversmiths.

145. Van Rensselaer Manor Papers (SC 7079), Manuscripts and Special Collections, New York State Library, Albany, New York.

146. Edmund Burke, comp. *List of Patents for Inventions and Designs Issued by the United States from 1790 to 1847* (Washington, D.C.: J. & G. S. Gideon, 1847), p. 172.

147. Entry Documentation for Building and Maintenance of Government Facilities, 1785–1855, New York (State) Comptroller's Office (AO 825), New York State Archives, Albany, New York.

148. J. Stokes. *The Complete Cabinet-Maker*, Fourth edition (London: Dean and Munday, 1841), p. 36.

149. Asher Benjamin and Daniel Raynerd. *The American Builder's Companion.* [Boston: Etheridge and Bliss, 1806], p. 45.

150. Lucien M. Underwood. *The Ancestry and Descendants of Jonathan Pollard (1759–1821) With Records of Allied Families* (Syracuse, New York: Privately printed, 1891), p. 13.

151. New York City *Directory*, 1821–27.

152. Henry is listed as a carpenter living at 47 Walker Street in the New York City *Directory* of 1819.

153. See note 190.

154. Farnham & Pollard were among the bidders for the construction of the Rensselaer County Courthouse in 1828. Because of the connection between the Farnhams and the Pollards, Calvin Pollard (1797–1850) was investigated as the possible architect of the Hart house. However his architectural career probably did not begin until after 1825. Pollard's brother-in-law Henry Farnham probably provided the carving for the door and window architraves of 59 Second Street. [Charles] Farnham & Pollard were prominent builders in New York during this period—it is possible that it was at this firm that the builder John Colegrove, the builder of record, was trained. Both Pollard and Charles Farnham had Albany connections—both had lived there immediately before relocating to New York. Their activities in Albany are documented in the Albany Academy papers, SARA Collection at the Albany County Hall of Records, Albany, New York.

155. *Farmer's, Mechanic's and Workingman's Advocate* (Albany), July 17, 1830, in an ad dated July 10.

156. Ira W. Scott. *The Albany Directory for the Years 1831–32* (Albany: J. B. Van Steenbergh, 1831), p. 194. This association appears to have had a brief existence.

157. The receipts for Farnham's work on these two projects can be found in the Gansevoort-Lansing Collection, New York Public Library, New York, and Entry Documentation for Building and Maintenance of Government Facilities, 1785–1855, New York (State) Comptroller's Office (AO 825), New York State Archives, Albany, New York, respectively.

158. For example, in 1829 Elias Disbrow of Troy, a "Carpenter & Joiner, Pattern Maker & Inspector of Lumber" advertised that he would "make Patterns for Castings of any description, at the shortest notice; having had long experience in the business" (*The Troy Directory for the Year 1829* [Troy: John Disturnell, 1829], n.p).

159. Entry Documentation for Building and Maintenance of Government Facilities, 1785–1855, New York (State) Comptroller's Office (AO 825), New York State Archives, Albany, New York.

160. March 11, 1901, he was 86 years old (Internment Records, Albany Rural Cemetery).

161. The contemporary account book of Peter McNab documents sources of this stone. See note 11.

162. According to contemporary notices. See note 131. In the upper Hudson River Valley, with its proximity to the quarries in various locations in Vermont and Stockbridge, Massachusetts, utilization of marble in architectural work became popular much ahead of New York City. The Albany City Bank (1810) and the Mechanics' and Farmers' Bank (c. 1811) both had façades of cut marble; both have been attributed to Philip Hooker.

163. *New York Mirror*, January 6, 1827.

164. None of these houses can be dated before 1829. Identified examples include the nine houses comprising Colonnade Row (a.k.a. La-Grange Terrace), twin houses at 714–16 Broadway, the rows called LeRoy Place in Bleecker Street, and a pair of houses at Broadway and Fourteenth Street. A house (c. 1830) on State Street in Albany featured a contemporary marble front; the materials comprising its façade are now part of the New York State Museum collections. The John Meads house in Albany (c. 1829) features a mastic façade imitating marble, scored to suggest blocks, while the lintels, sills, watertable, and stoop are all of marble. It is probable that the twin houses at 29–31 Elk Street in Albany (1830–31), for Bennington Gill and Maynard French (in contradiction to earlier published research) featured mastic of the same type, to accompany their marble details. One of this pair survives.

165. *New-York Mirror and Ladies' Literary Gazette*, 5: 22 (December 8, 1827), p. 174.

166. Recently published in a new translation by Vaughan Hart and Peter Hicks as *Sebastiano Serlio on Architecture Volume One* (New Haven & London: Yale University Press, 1996).

167. For example, Inigo Jones utilized similar treatments for window and door apertures in his Royal Hospital at Greenwich (*Vitruvius Britannicus* 1, [1715], plate 87), and T. Wright followed in his design for Nuthall in Nottinghamshire (*Vitruvius Britannicus* 4, [1767], plate 57). Purchase of the set of five folio volumes comprising *Vitruvius Britannicus* would have been outside of the grasp of most. Thompson would certainly have been familiar with the volumes since they were in Ithiel Town's library and in the collection of the New-York Society Library

(November 20, 1848, auction catalogue, Avery Architectural Library, Columbia University, New York).

168. London, 1750. Samuel McIntire suggested rusticated window surrounds quite similar to those seen at the Hart house in his unexecuted competition entry for the design of the United States Capitol in 1792. The White House (c. 1792) also features similar surrounds on its basement windows. There remains the possibility that the window enframements were introduced to New York at date earlier in the 1820s. The booklet, *Prices of Cut Stone and Marble, Agreed on and Established by all the Master Stone Cutters in the City of New-York, Feb. 10th, 1825* (New York: H. Sage, 1825) gives values for work that may have been similar to the type of window surround under consideration. A firm chronology of construction dates for the houses around Hudson Park in New York needs to be established before any definitive statement can be made.

169. For example, Palladio makes use of plinths under enframed windows in his reconstruction of an ancient Roman house and in his elevation design for a house for Giovanni Francesco Valmarana (Andrea Palladio. *The Four Books on Architecture*. Translated by Robert Tavernor and Richard Schofield (Cambridge, Massachusetts: The MIT Press, 1997), pp. 108 and 137).

170. See for example Lafever, *General Instructor*, p. 116. To Renaissance scholars this arrangement, more specifically a round-headed aperture accompanied by a narrow rectangular aperture to either side, separated by columns is known as *Serliana*, after Serlio who is said to have invented it. In America, it has more commonly been called *Palladian*.

171. It is of some interest to note that these door surrounds were pre-fabricated of Coade stone, thus anticipating the prefabrication of the elements at Sing-Sing for the St. Mark's Place houses (Alison Kelly. *Mrs Coade's Stone* [Upton-upon-Severn, Worcs., England: The Self Publishing Association, Ltd., 1990], p. 40).

172. Harold Kirker. *The Architecture of Charles Bulfinch* (Cambridge: Harvard University Press, 1969), pp. 119 and 121. For more on this house, see George B. Tatum. *Penn's Great Town*, revised edition. (Philadelphia: University of Pennsylvania Press, 1961), pp. 42, 49, 51, 64, 97, and 162. The door surround of this house was constructed of Coade stone, perhaps identical to that provided for the Bedford Square houses (Kelly, *Mrs Coade's Stone*, pp. 286–90).

173. Several late eighteenth and early nineteenth century structures built in New York City utilized rusticated door and window surrounds. These include St. George's Chapel (1752?), the Old North Dutch Church (1768–69), the Garden Street Dutch Reformed Church (1807), 71–77 Washington Street (likely by 1820), and Schermerhorn Row (Fulton Street, 1810–12). In Albany, St. Peter's Church (1801–03) and the South Dutch Church (1805–11), both by Philip Hooker, featured rusticated window and door surrounds. Farther afield, the church at Stone Arabia, New York (1788) used rustication.

174. See note 196.

175. See pp. 88–89 for further discussion of this house.

176. These can be seen in the watercolors executed by James Eights during the middle decades of the nineteenth century, preserved at the Albany Institute of History and Art.

177. The first floor plan of this house is in the Sclater Collection at Avery Architectural Library, Columbia University, New York. The contract for construction of the house, a parsonage for St. Peter's Episcopal Church, is in the church's archives (Box 123, SPEC 0368, St. Peter's Church Archives, Albany, New York).

178. This house was razed in June 1999. It stood on the east side of Broadway, between Livingston Avenue and Colonie Street.

179. Documents supporting the attribution to Hooker of the design of this house, formerly known as the Secretary of State's house, are in the New York State Archives, Albany, New York (Entry Documentation for Building and Maintenance of Government Facilities, 1785–1855, New York [State] Comptroller's Office [AO 825]). The house,

at the southeast corner of North Pearl and Steuben streets is extant, though modified.

180. Bucher and Wheeler, *Neat Plain Modern Stile*, pp. 304–5.

181. For an image see Weise, *History*, opp. p. 25.

182. Ibid., opp. p. 20.

183. See p. 58 for description of the houses at 20–22 and 28 First Street, which shared details with this house.

184. The example of this arrangement surrounding the southern door into the dining room on the first floor was assembled from pieces salvaged in 1964 when the southwest door in the back parlor was closed. The trim in the attic, or third floor, is an interpretation (post 1910) of the woodwork featured on the second floor, with the raffle flowers cast in plaster from one of the earlier carved pieces.

185. See Morrison H. Heckscher and Leslie Greene Bowman, *American Rococo 1750–1775: Elegance in Ornament* (New York: Harry N. Abrams, 1992), especially pp. 23, 26, and 34.

186. This volume and its use in the creation of raffle flower corner blocks is discussed at length below. It was available in Albany bookstores as early as 1797. Philip Hooker's copy of this book is said to be in the collections of Winterthur at Wilmington, Delaware, but it remains unlocated after a recent search. The late Bruce Sherwood provided this lead. Swan's book may be the source for the earlier New York examples as well. Philip Hooker owned at least one additional book by Swan, *The Carpenter's Complete Instructor* (London, 1768). That volume included rusticated surrounds in Plate 40. Hooker's copy is presently in the collection of Douglas G. Bucher.

187. For example, Joseph Beunat's *Recueil des dessins d'ornements d'architecture*, c. 1813; (Reprint, New York: Dover Publishing, Inc., 1974).

188. Influence of Sheraton is seen in furniture dating from the last decade of the eighteenth century, extending well into the second decade of the nineteenth. See J. Michael Flannagan. *American Furniture from the Kaufman Collection* (Washington: National Gallery of Art, 1986), pp. 124–5, 150–51, and 154–55.

189. Farnham also executed the woodwork for the renovations to the New York State Capitol under Philip Hooker in 1818.

190. Among buildings known from published sources, constructed utilizing the "Farnham-type" raffle flower carving and trim are included 8 Greenwich Street, New York City (originally built in 1807–09, renovated c. 1820); Edgewater in Barrytown, New York (1820); the Goodrich house, Buffalo, New York (1822); the Miller house, Utica, New York (1823–29); the Halsted house, Rye, New York (c. 1825); the David Crawford house, Newburgh, New York (1829–31); the Deshon-Allyn house in New London, Connecticut (1829); the Eames house, New Hartford, New York (c. 1830); the George Fordham house, 329 Cherry Street, New York City (c. 1830?); and the John V. Gridley house at 37 Charlton Street, New York City (1827–29). The last two mentioned houses also featured wrought-iron work that was very similar to that featured in front of the Hart house. The Roosevelt house (1833–35) and the Tristram Coffin house (c. 1832), both in Dutchess County, New York, feature raffle flowers and associated center carved panels, in this case both are thought (by Helen W. Reynolds) to have been composed of plaster. It has not been possible to investigate these examples. Nos. 10 and 18 Greenwich Street, New York City, the Cutting house at 15 Tillary Street, 115 Bleecker Street, 39 and 57–59 Morton Street, all in New York City, are additional examples for which construction dates are not currently known. Most of the New York City examples are documented in the Index of American Design, forerunner of the Historic American Buildings Survey. Its records are preserved at the Avery Architectural Library, Columbia University. Examples are known as far west as Ohio, including the Dr. John H. Mathews house on North State Street in Painesville (1829), built by Jonathan Goldsmith (I. T. Frary. *Early Homes of Ohio*. 1936; [Reprint, New York: Dover Publications, Inc., 1970], pp. 98–101).

191. Albany Academy Papers, Albany County Hall of Records, Albany, New York.

192. Lafever, *General Instructor*, p. 166.

193. *Practice of Architecture* (Boston: The Author & Carter, Hendee & Co., 1833), Plate 56; *The Builder's Guide* (Boston: Perkins & Marvin, 1839), plates 39, 51, 57 and 61.

194. Lafever, *General Instructor*, p. 114.

195. For an analogous practice in the eighteenth century, see Luke Beckerdite, "Immigrant Carvers and the Development of the Rococo Style in New York, 1750–1770," in Luke Beckerdite, ed., *American Furniture 1996* (Hanover and London: Chipstone Foundation, University Press of New England, 1996), pp. 233–65.

196. The lintels will be discussed more extensively below, when the influence the Hart house had on local architecture is examined. With respect to stoves, Tammis Kane Groft (*Cast With Style: Nineteenth Century Cast-Iron Stove from the Albany Area*, revised edition [Albany, New York: Albany Institute of History and Art, 1984], p. 47), illustrates a two-column parlor stove by Pratt & Treadwell of Albany, circa 1834–36 that incorporates many architectural details, including raffle-flowers. Franklin stoves with their front doors flanked by pilasters surmounted with blocks with raffle flower ornament are common in the Hudson River Valley and date to circa 1830.

197. These are still in place in a pair of houses at 112–114 Third Street (c. 1828), 84 King Street, 179 Fourth Street, 2164 Fifth Avenue, and a row at 1529–33 Fifth Avenue, all in Troy. The Powers Oil Cloth Factory, formerly on Second Avenue north of 109th Street in Lansingburgh, utilized a large number of these lintels. Two houses at 123–125 State Street (c. 1827) in Albany and the two houses (1828) now known as 107 Columbia Street, also in Albany, retain cast iron interpretations of the lintels. Commercial structures on lower Beaver Street and the Arch Street Brewery, both in Albany, formerly utilized the same lintels. The John Aiken house, 219 Liberty Street, Schenectady, built about 1830, continued this trend. Its lintels seem to be identical with those featured on 112–114 Third Street in Troy. Similar examples are known in Genessee Street in Utica and in Syracuse, New York.

198. Lafever, *General Instructor*, p. 159.

199. Ibid., p. 160.

200. Daniel Raynerd was responsible for the plaster designs in the publication. He was a prominent plaster worker in Boston, and executed designs for Charles Bulfinch. His own house, on Charles Street in Boston, was designed by Bulfinch. See Harold Kirker. *The Architecture of Charles Bulfinch* (Cambridge: Harvard University Press, 1969).

201. Asher Benjamin and Daniel Raynerd. *The American Builder's Companion* (Boston: Etheridge and Bliss, 1806), p. 47.

202. George Hyde Clarke Papers, Olin Library, Cornell University, Ithaca, New York.

203. The house at 9 Mulberry Street in Baltimore, constructed circa 1833, features nearly identical plaster work to that at the Hart house. It is possible that it was fabricated by the same New York City-based master plasterer.

204. Lafever, *General Instructor,* p. 159.

205. Albert H. Sonn. *Early American Wrought Iron* (New York: Charles Scribner's Sons, 1928), pp. 54–57.

206. This last set has been reconstructed from fragments found in the house.

207. A set of urn newels once graced a second residence in Troy, the Palmer C. Ricketts house, at Park Place. Ricketts likely brought them from an as-yet undetermined location. A set is in storage at Montgomery Place, Dutchess County, brought from a house in New York City. Urn newels formerly decorated the fronts of houses on Eighteenth Street and on the Lower East Side in Manhattan (*New York: A Collection from Harper's Magazine* [New York: Gallery Books, 1991], pp. 199 and 300).

208. It has not been possible to verify the exact date of construction of the Varick Street row. Trinity Church was the landowner; its

archives are currently closed to research. Contemporary documents suggest that the houses were built 1827–8.

209. Photograph Collection 347, Utica Public Library, Utica, New York.

210. *Architecture Worth Saving in Onondaga County* (Syracuse: Syracuse University School of Architecture/New York State Council on the Arts, 1964), pp. 45–9.

211. Sonn, *Wrought Iron*, p. 54, and Joseph Everett Chandler, *The Colonial House* (New York: Robert M. McBride & Company, 1924), Plates 100 and 101.

212. Philip Hooker provided designs for several different wrought iron fences and decorative elements during this period. It is highly likely that his counterparts in New York City were involved in design and production of wrought and cast iron to at least the same extent.

213. Named after the ancient Roman architect whose treatise on building is the only ancient architectural book that has come down to us, the Vitruvian scroll is composed of a repeating sequence of curves and foliage.

214. Historic American Building Survey NY-445. The large and small finials of the fence palings at the Hart house are also utilized at the Fordham house, increasing the likelihood that a New York City-based maker was responsible for both sets of ironwork.

215. William Howard had acquired the property from Jacob and Mary Merritt on November 8, 1825, and held title until November 12, 1834 (Deeds, Rensselaer County Courthouse, Troy, New York).

216. Technically, the stone is a dolomitic limestone with chondroditic inclusions. Such a composition is most frequently associated with "Franklin" marbles from Orange County and northern New Jersey or the Gouverneur marbles of St. Lawrence County. It is less common (but known) in the Westchester County deposits, those being largely of the calciferous type. The earliest marbles known to have come from the beds in Westchester County are all of the dolomitic type; it appears to have enjoyed the widest favor. The marbles from other sources, for example those quarried in Vermont and Massachusetts, are not dolomitic, but calciferous (consultation with Michael A. Hawkins, New York State Geological Survey, April 29, 1998). For extensive technical descriptions of the stone see D. H. Newland. *The Quarry Materials of New York-Granite, Gneiss, Trap and Marble. New York State Museum Bulletin*, whole no. 181 (January 1, 1916) (Albany: The University of the State of New York, 1916), pp. 179–80, 181, 195, and 200–202; and George P. Merrill. *Stones for Building and Decoration* (New York: John Wiley & Sons, 1891), pp. 96–97).

217. James Gallier. *The American Builder's General Price Book and Estimator*, second edition (Boston: M. Burns, 1836), p. 18. Also included are tables for estimating the cost of this marble delivered to the site and cut into various shapes. Because of the large number of unknowns, it proved impossible to utilize this tool to estimate the original cost of the Hart house stonework.

218. *Troy Sentinel*, April 11, 1826. The record book of freight carried on a contemporary sloop out of Sing-Sing, the *Volunteer*, captained by John Leacock in 1826–7, is preserved in the collections of the Ossining Historical Society, Ossining, New York. It may provide additional details regarding the shipping of the marble to New York City. I was unable to consult this document.

219. *Prices of Cut Stone and Marble*, pp. 6–7.

220. Lafever, *General Instructor*, pp. 165–66.

221. For documentation of the construction of a contemporary house see the history of the construction of the Elkanah Watson house in Bucher and Wheeler, *Neat Plain Modern Stile*, pp. 212–220.

222. The mantels at Hyde Hall, near Cooperstown, New York, are very similar to those at the Hart house and are documented as having been shipped from New York.

Surface collection at the site of Jairus Dickerman's marble shop during the summer of 1996 when the buildings he constructed in the late 1830s were demolished uncovered examples of various fancy marbles. While it is impossible to date the materials found, it is likely that at least some of them come from the earliest part of Dickerman's career, including as they do samples of Stockbridge marble, which is not known to have been used in Troy after 1830. Peter McNab, working in Troy about 1802, and afterwards in Albany, utilized marbles of many types in architectural applications.

223. Gallier, *Price Book*, p. 26.

224. Weise, *Troy's One Hundred Years*, p. 31.

225. Troy *Directory*, 1829.

226. Richard Hart's involvement in timber is documented in the Hart Papers, Rensselaer County Historical Society, Troy, New York. A bill of timber and a contract between Richard P. Hart and Thomas and John P. Laing of Saratoga for a large amount of timber exists, dated December 22, 1826, in the same collection. While it is unlikely that the wood for the house was procured at so late a date, it remains probable that Hart was himself responsible for contracting to procure the wood, and likely utilized the Laing's the year before when ordering the timbers for the house. The Laing's also provided the timbers utilized in the construction of the carriage house, see below.

227. George Tibbits to Elam Lynds, April 28, 1827. In George Tibbits letterbook, Rensselaer County Historical Society, Troy, New York.

228. Elizabeth Shields Eddy reminiscence, transcribed by Ruthanne Mills (Brod), 1969, Rensselaer County Historical Society, Troy, New York.

229. It is possible that the material used was part of the old stock of a cabinetmaker, such as Duncan Phyfe. Phyfe provided some of the furnishings for the Harts; dining room chairs, a card table, a breakfast table and bedstead all apparently from his shop survive and form part of the Rensselaer County Historical Society collections. At one time receipts from the Phyfe shop for the Hart furniture were in the possession of H. Maxson Holloway, former director of the Rensselaer County Historical Society (Hilda Goodwin, "Historical Society Restores 133-Year-Old Doorway," *The Record* [Troy], August 24, 1960). According to family tradition Betsey's father, William Howard, purchased the furniture at the time of her marriage to Richard P. Hart in 1816.

230. Gallier, *Price Book*, p. 92.

231. Ibid, p. 92.

232. It is probable that finishes such as the crown molding of the baseboards was fabricated on-site by John B. Colegrove. The same molding profile was used in the rear addition, constructed by Colegrove circa 1836. He apparently retained the molding planes used ten years prior.

233. *Northern Budget* (Troy), March 24, 1826. Challes was city lumber inspector during the years 1826 and 1827, and so would have had dealings with Richard P. Hart (*Northern Budget* [Troy], March 30, 1826; April 3, 1827).

234. Thomas Longworth. *Longworth's American Almanac, New-York Register, and City Directory* (New-York: Thomas Longworth, 1825), p. 348. Martin Euclid Thompson recorded some dealings with Pye in his receipt book, entries dated August 17 and October 22, 1825 (Avery Architectural Library, Columbia University, New York [IPL no. 396106]).

235. A "William Pie" held four US patents. These are for "locks," dated August 5, 1813 and April 28, 1818, and for "union locks" dated April 28, 1818 (Edmund Burke, comp. *List of Patents for Inventions and Designs Issued by the United States from 1790 to 1847* [Washington: J. & G. S. Gideon, 1847], pp. 49–50). He also held a patent for andirons, dated November 16, 1821 (ibid., p. 39).

236. Thomas F. Gordon. *Gazetteer of the State of New York* (Philadelphia: T. K and P. G. Collins, 1836), p. 648.

237. Gordon likely intended to include the Cannon house on Third Street (Fig. 106), an unidentified house on Eighth Street (c. 1830), and the row of houses at 35–39 First Street with marble basements, lintels, and sills among this group. No other marble-fronted houses in Troy are known from this period.

238. Newspaper notice of the sale of the property to William Kemp and George B. Cluett.

239. Elizabeth Shields Eddy reminiscence, transcribed by Ruthanne Mills (Brod), 1969, Rensselaer County Historical Society, Troy, New York. The house they viewed from was 58, 60, or 62 Second Street.

240. It received early promulgation in the United States through Colen Campbell's *Vitruvius Britannicus*.

241. Plate XX.

242. See Appendix III.

243. In addition, the cheap supply of marble from Sing-Sing dried up when New York State declared that no new contracts be entered into after 1835. In the meantime, trade in stone from Stockbridge, Massachusetts, had been so compromised that it is unlikely that there were any local dealers of this material by that date.

244. Hall purchased the site from Elisha Adams on April 17, 1826. Hall died on March 13, 1831, aged 42. The property was subsequently sold to John Griffith in 1835 (will no. 850 and Deeds, Rensselaer County Courthouse, Troy, New York; *Troy Sentinel*, March 14, 1831).

245. A number of the house's details are preserved in the newer building. Among these are the transom from the original doorway, now providing the central element of the current fan light. At least one of the mantels from the house is preserved, and decorates the second floor parlor of the YWCA.

246. Cannon purchased the 50 by 130-foot lot the house occupied on March 8, 1822 from Elias Lasell (Deeds, Rensselaer County Courthouse, Troy, New York). Details of the cast iron used on the front stoop suggest a construction date later than that of the Hart house. In this respect, compare with Martin E. Thompson's elevation for the Chapel Street houses, fig. 67. The Cannon house was destroyed circa 1921 in a fire that also consumed the Masonic Temple (1871–72) designed by Leopold Eidlitz, to the north.

247. *Troy Post*, August 23, 1814. The paper gives the date of their marriage as August 17, and notes that Cannon was then of Norwalk, Connecticut.

248. Weise, *Troy's One Hundred Years*, pp. 133 and 167.

249. *Troy Daily Whig*, May 8 and 10, 1850.

250. The site of this house was occupied by the Esaias Warren house as early as 1803. Some time after his death in 1824, his son Nathan moved the house a few lots south, and constructed the four-bay house under consideration (Weise, *Troy's One Hundred Years*, p. 59). The Esaias Warren house, with its new address of 47 Third Street, was razed in July 1995. The Nathan Warren house was incorporated into the building that currently houses the Troy branch of the HSBC Bank.

251. The office billed $5.00 on May 18, 1833 (A. J. Davis Papers, Journal, Prints and Drawings Department, Metropolitan Museum of Art, New York). Brought to my attention by Jane Davies. James Harrison Dakin (1806–1852) was not yet active as an architect in 1825, and so did not come under consideration as a potential designer of the Hart house. Dakin was closely connected to Minard Lafever and contributed designs to his *The Modern Builder's Guide*, published a month after the date of the Town, Davis & Dakin bill for the Cooper house. See note 89 for more on Dakin and his conjectural relationship with Thompson.

252. The design of the Cooper house likely dates to the period just before Dakin's entry into partnership with Town & Davis. The design of the door surround was possibly a last minute change, for the house was occupied that same month. For a further discussion of The Row on Washington Square, and others built in Troy sharing the same features, see pp. 88–94.

253. The Rogers family never occupied the house; it was probably a speculative venture (Regina M. Kellerman to Walter Richard Wheeler, September 23, 1996).

254. These houses were constructed on property owed by Trinity Church. Unfortunately, the archives of the congregation are presently closed to scholars.

255. *Documents of the Assembly of the State of New-York, Fifty-sixth Session, 1833* (Albany: E. Croswell, 1833), 199: 23. An interesting connection to Martin E. Thompson via the Town & Davis office is the fact that Thomas J. Carmichael, architect in charge of Sing-Sing during this time, had served his apprenticeship in the Town & Davis office. Carmichael had come from the south and worked for that office from January to March 1831 (A. J. Davis Papers, Office Diary Vol. I, Prints and Drawings Department, Metropolitan Museum of Art, New York). The nature of Carmichael's connection to Thompson is unknown, but it is curious to note that Thompson is credited with the design of the prison; it is thought that the project was for the women's dormitory, c. 1835–40 (Betty J. Ezequelle to Walter Richard Wheeler, December 5, 1998).

256. Kelly, *Mrs Coade's Stone*, p. 40.

257. These prisoners came from Auburn Prison, where they had gained experience in the construction of their prison there. The remainder of the prisoners came from the New York Penitentiary.

258. Each house had a slightly different decorative program. Martin E. Thompson's account book, preserved at the Avery Architectural Library, Columbia University, notes his payment for composition and carved materials from John Gallier. We know from A. J. Davis' *Price Book* that Gallier was providing machine-made composition ornaments in honeysuckle, rosette, and wreath designs as late as 1842 (quoted in Charles Lockwood, *Bricks and Brownstone, the New York Rowhouse, 1783–1929* [New York: Abbeville Press, 1972], p. 75). Composition ornament in New York City is discussed in Lewis Inman Sharp. *The Old Merchant's House.* Unpublished thesis, University of Delaware, 1968, pp. 59–61.

259. See p. 69.

260. Composed of at least three houses originally. The details of the houses in this row appear to have been subtly varied by the builder.

261. The Tredwells had lived at 12 Dey Street in 1820, three doors to the east of the Howard family.

262. Additional houses in New York City sharing the rusticated door surround included a pair near the corner of Greenwich and Chambers streets, three houses on Hudson Street at the corner of Bank Street, 140–142 Second Avenue, near Ninth Street, and two houses at 710–12 Broadway. Window lintels like those decorating the Hart house are known to have graced the façades of many New York row houses of the late 1820s and early 1830s. Of these, the row at 127–131 Macdougal Street (1829) is a rare survivor.

263. With the exception of the substitution of sunken panels for the rusticated blocks that are vermiculated at the Hart house.

264. Mills Lane. *Architecture of the Old South: South Carolina* (Savannah, Georgia: The Beehive Press, 1984), p. 188. This suggests the possibility of a connection between the New York and Charleston architectural scene. By 1822, the stone-cutting firm of Dick & Waterston, doing business in the metropolis, had a branch in Charleston. Thornton Niven, a stonecutter trained under Samuel Gray in New York (who, in turn was likely related to Alexander Gray), worked for them there from 1822–24. Russell Warren, a sometime associate of A. J. Davis, was also active in the Charleston area during this period (Arthur Channing Downs, Jr. *The Architecture and Life of the Hon. Thornton Macness Niven (1806–1895),* second edition [Goshen, New York: The Orange County Community of Museums & Galleries, 1972], pp. ii and 13). See also note 196.

265. Asher Benjamin. *Practice of Architecture* (Boston: the Author and Carter, Hendee & Co., 1833), especially Plates 26 and 39.

266. Cited above.

267. For a contemporary description of New York City's row houses, suggesting this attitude toward the houses of the late 1820s, see *The Evening Post* (New York), August 7, 1833.

268. These include the William Aiken house (1833) in Charleston, South Carolina.

269. "Builders Their Own Architects." First version, dated 1830 (A. J. Davis Papers [Box 2], New York Public Library, New York). Davis executed a drawing of a rusticated door surround, calling it an "old fashioned entrance" (A. J. Davis Papers, Avery Architectural Library, Columbia University, New York).

270. "Builders Their Own Architects." Second version, dated August 1837 (A. J. Davis Papers [Box 2], New York Public Library, New York).

271. "Critiques on the Public Buildings of New York written in and Before 1830 . . . with some Additions in 1838" (A. J. Davis Papers [Box 2], New York Public Library, New York).

272. New York: George P. Scott & Co., 1834.

273. Davis' manuscript for his contributions to Dunlap's work is preserved at Avery Architectural Library, Columbia University, New York.

274. William Ross. "Street Houses of the City of New York," *The Architectural Magazine* [London] 2: 490–93. The article is dated December 31, 1834.

275. Elizabeth Shields Eddy reminiscence, transcribed by Ruthanne Mills (Brod), 1969, Rensselaer County Historical Society, Troy, New York.

276. "Repairs of Flouring Mill," Hart Papers, Rensselaer County Historical Society, Troy, New York.

277. Dickerman came to Troy in 1828, and was the most prominent among the marble workers of the city. For a brief biography and portrait of Dickerman see Nathaniel Bartlett Sylvester, *History of Rensselaer Co., New York* (Philadelphia: Everts & Peck, 1880), between pp. 216 and 217.

278. Joseph C. Taylor Account Book, Rensselaer County Historical Society, Troy, New York.

279. The original roof treatment is visible today due to later alterations.

280. Troy *Directories*, 1834–37.

281. Note the similarity of this house to the King Model Houses (1891–92) constructed on West 139th Street in New York for developer David H. King, Jr. by McKim, Mead & White.

282. In addition, bath and kitchen fixtures were removed or replaced, the pantry off the Cluett-era kitchen was remodeled and the pantry hall was renovated.

Bibliography

Articles on the Hart House

"Home of Albert E. Cluett Being Studied by Architects of CWA," *The Troy Record*, February 1934.

"Rensselaer County Historical Society, Inc.," booklet produced 1952.

Goodwin, Hilda. "Historical Society Restores 133-Year-Old Doorway," *The Troy Record*, August 24, 1960.

Books

Adam, R. and J. *The Works in Architecture of Robert and James Adam Esquires.* 3 vols. London: 1773, 1779, and 1822.

Albany City Directory. Various compilers and publishers, Albany, 1813–1835.

Anthony, Jesse B. *History of King Solomon's Primitive Lodge, Troy, New York: Together with a Sketch of Freemasonry in the City of Troy from 1796 to 1842.* Troy: Henry Stowell Printing House, 1892.

Architect's Emergency Committee. *Great Georgian Houses of America.*, 2 vols. 1937. Reprint. New York: Dover Publications, 1970.

Belden, E. Porter. *New-York: Past, Present, and Future.* New-York: G. P. Putnam, 1849.

Benjamin, Asher. *The Practice of Architecture.* Boston: The author and Carter, Hendee & Co., 1833.

Benjamin, Asher and Daniel Raynerd. *The American Builder's Companion.* Boston: Etheridge and Bliss, 1806.

Beunat, Joseph. *Recueil des dessins d'ornements d'architecture.* Paris, (c. 1813). (Reprinted as *Empire Style Designs and Ornaments.* With an introduction by David Irwin. New York: Dover Publications Inc., 1974.

Biddle, Owen. *The Young Carpenter's Assistant; or, a System of Architecture, Adapted to the Style of building in the United States.* Philadelphia: Johnson and Warner, 1810.

Blunt, Edmund March. *The Picture of New York, and Stranger's Guide.* New York: A. T. Goodrich, 1828.

Bucher, Douglas G. and W[alter] Richard Wheeler. *A Neat Plain Modern Stile: Philip Hooker and his Contemporaries, 1796–1836.* Amherst: University of Massachusetts Press, 1993.

Campbell, Colen, ed., et al. *Vitruvius Britannicus.* 5 vols. London, 1715–67 (?).

Colegrove, William. *The History and Genealogy of the Colegrove Family in America, with Biographical Sketches.* Chicago: The author, 1894.

Cousins, Frank and Phil M. Riley. *The Colonial Architecture of Philadelphia.* Boston: Little, Brown and Company, 1920.

Cowdrey, Mary Bartlett, ed. *National Academy of Design Exhibition Record 1826–1860.* New York: The New-York Historical Society, 1943.

Davies, Jane, "A. J. Davis," "Ithiel Town," and "Town & Davis" in Adolf K. Placzek, ed. *Macmillan Encyclopedia of Architects.* 4 vols. New York: The Free Press, 1982. 1: 505–514; 4: 220–223; 4: 223–224.

Downs, Arthur Channing, Jr. *The Architecture and Life of the Hon. Thornton Macness Niven (1806–1895).* Second edition. Goshen, New York: The Orange County Community of Museums & Galleries, 1972.

Dunlap, William. *History of the Rise and Progress of the Arts of Design in the United States.* 2 vols. New York: George P. Scott & Co., 1834.

Dunshee, Kenneth Holcomb. *As You Pass By.* New York: Hastings House, 1952.

Eddy, Ruth Hart, William L. Shields, George Van Santvoord, *Furnace Grove, 1858–1958, The Story of A Family Home.* Privately printed, 1958.

Ezequelle, Betty J. "Martin E. Thompson," in Adolf K. Placzek, ed. *Macmillan Encyclopedia of Architects.* 4 Vols. New York: The Free Press, 1982. 4: 207–08.

Fairbanks, A. W., ed. *Emma Willard & Her Pupils.* New York: Mrs. Russell Sage, 1898.

Francis, Dennis Steadman. *Architects in Practice in New York City 1840–1900.* New York: Committee for the Preservation of Architectural Records, n.d. [1979].

Frary, I. T. *Early Homes of Ohio.* 1936. Reprint. New York: Dover Publications, 1970.

Gallier, James. *Autobiography of James Gallier, Architect.* 1864. Reprint. New York: DeCapo Press, 1973.

Gallier, James. *The American Builder's General Price Book and Estimator.* New York: Lafever & Gallier, 1833; Boston: Marsh, Capen & Lyon, 1834; second edition. Boston: M. Burns, 1836.

Gibbs, James. *A Book of Architecture.* London, 1728.

Goddard, Abba A., ed. *The Trojan Sketch Book.* Troy, New York: Young & Hartt, 1846.

Groft, Tammis Kane. *Cast With Style: Nineteenth Century Cast-Iron Stoves From the Albany Area.* Revised edition. Albany: Albany Institute of History and Art, 1984.

Hamlin, Talbot F. *Greek Revival Architecture in America.* 1944. Reprint. New York: Dover Publications, 1964.

Hamlin, Talbot F. "Martin E. Thompson," in the *Dictionary of*

American Biography 18, pp. 467–68. Edited by Dumas Malone. New York: Charles Scribner's Sons, 1936.

Hayner, Rutherford. *Troy and Rensselaer County, New York, A History*, Vol I–III. New York, New York: Lewis Historical Publishing Company, 1925.

Holley, O. L., ed. *A Description of the City of New York*. New York: J. Disturnell, 1847.

Howells, John Mead. *Lost Examples of Colonial Architecture*. 1931. Reprint. New York: Dover Publications, 1963.

Huxtable, Ada Louise. *Classic New York*. Garden City, New York: Doubleday & Company, Inc., 1964.

Jones, Newman, & J. S. Ewbank. *The Illuminated Pictorial Directory of New York*. New York: Jones, Newman & Ewbank, 1848.

Kimball, Fiske. *Domestic Architecture of the American Colonies and of the Early Republic*. 1922. Reprint. New York: Dover Publications, 1966.

Kirker, Harold. *The Architecture of Charles Bulfinch*. Cambridge, Harvard University Press, 1969.

Lafever, Minard. *The Modern Builder's Guide*. New York: Sleight, 1833.

Lafever, Minard. *The Young Builder's General Instructor*. Newark: W. Tuttle & Company, 1829.

Lancaster, Clay. *Old Brooklyn Heights*. Second edition. New York: Dover Publications, 1979.

Landy, Jacob. *The Architecture of Minard Lafever*. New York and London: Columbia University Press, 1970.

Langley, Batty. *The City and Country Builder's and Workman's Treasury of Designs*. 1750. Facsimile edition. New York: Benjamin Blom, 1967.

Langley, B[atty], and T. *The Builder's Jewel*. Charlestown, Massachusetts: S. Etheridge, 1799.

Lanier, Henry Wysham. *A Century of Banking in New York 1822–1922*. New York: The Gilliss Press, 1922.

Lockwood, Charles. *Bricks and Brownstone, the New York Rowhouse, 1783–1929*. New York: Abbeville Press, 1972.

Lockwood, Charles. *Manhattan Moves Uptown, an Illustrated History*. 1976. Reprint. New York: Barnes & Noble, 1995.

Masten, Arthur H. *The History of Cohoes, New York from its earliest Settlement to the present time*. Albany: Joel Munsell, 1877.

Merrill, George P. *Stones for Building and Decoration*. New York: John Wiley & Sons, 1891.

Minutes of the Common Council of the City of New York 1784–1831. 19 vols. New York: The City of New York, 1917.

New York City Directory. Various compilers and publishers, New York, 1810–1880.

Newland, D. H. *The Quarry Materials of New York: Granite, Gneiss, Trap and Marble*. New York State Museum Bulletin, no. 181. Albany: University of the State of New York, 1916.

Newton, Roger Hale. *Town & Davis Architects, Pioneers in American Revivalist Architecture 1812–1870*. New York: Columbia University Press, 1942.

Pain, William. *The Practical Builder, or Workman's General Assistant*. Boston: John Norman, 1792.

Peck, Amelia, ed. *Alexander Jackson Davis, American Architect 1803–1892*. New York: Rizzoli, 1992.

Pelletreau, William. *Early New York Houses*. New York: Francis P. Harper, 1900.

Perris Insurance Maps. New York, 1857–62.

Pierson, William H., Jr. *American Buildings and Their Architects: Technology and the Picturesque. Vol. 2. The Corporate and the Early Gothic Styles*. Garden City, New York: Doubleday, 1978.

Prices of Cut Stone and Marble, Agreed on and Established by All the Master Stone Cutters in the City of New-York. New-York: H. Sage, 1825.

Reynolds, Helen Wilkinson. *Dutchess County Doorways and other Examples of Period-work in Wood 1730–1830, with Accounts of Houses, Places and People*. New York: Payson, 1931.

Richmond, John Francis. *New York and its Institutions, 1609–1871*. New York: E. B. Treat, 1871.

Root, Edward W. *Philip Hooker: A Contribution to the Study of the Renaissance in America*. New York: Charles Scribner's Sons, 1929.

Scully, Arthur, Jr. *James Dakin, Architect. His Career in New York and the South*. Baton Rouge: Louisiana State University Press, 1973.

Serlio, Sebastiano. *Tutte L'Opere D'Architettura et Prospetiva*. Venetia: Giacomo de' Franceschi, 1619.

Sheraton, Thomas. *The Cabinet-Maker and Upholsterer's Drawing-Book*. 1793–1802. Reprint. New York: Dover Publications, 1972.

Small, Verna. *Nineteenth Century Dwelling Houses of Greenwich Village*. New York: 1968.

Smock, John C. *Building Stone in New York. Bulletin of the New York State Museum*, no. 2: 10. Albany: University of the State of New York, 1890.

Sohn, Albert H. *Early American Wrought Iron*. 1928. Reprint. New York: Bonanza, n.d.

Stewart, John D., ed. *The Schermerhorn Row Block: A Study in Nineteenth Century Building Technology in New York City*. Albany: New York State Office of Parks, Recreation and Historic Preservation, October 1981.

Stokes, I. N. Phelps. *The Iconography of Manhattan Island 1498–1909*. 6 vols. 1915–28. Reprint. New York: Arno Press, 1967.

Stuart, James, and Nicholas Revett. *The Antiquities of Athens*. London: J. Haberkorn, Vol. I. J. Nichols, Vols. II and III. 1762–1794.

Swan, Abraham. *The British Architect: or, the Builders Treasury of Stair-cases*. Philadelphia: R. Bell, 1775.

Swan, Abraham. *A Collection of Designs in Architecture*. 2 vols. London: Robert Sayer, 1757.

Sylvester, Nathaniel Bartlett. *History of Rensselaer Co., New York*. Philadelphia: Everts & Peck, 1880.

Troy City Directory. Various compilers and publishers, Troy, 1829- 1900.

Voss, Frederick S. et al. *John Frazee (1790–1852) Sculptor*. Washington: Smithsonian Institution and the Boston Athenaeum, 1986.

Waite, Diana S. *Ornamental Ironwork: Two Centuries of Craftsmanship in Albany and Troy, New York*. Albany: Mount Ida Press, 1990.

Wallace, Philip B. *Colonial Houses: Philadelphia, Pre-Revolutionary Period*, 1931. Reprint. New York: Bonanza, n.d.

Wallace, Philip B. *Colonial Ironwork in Old Philadelphia*, 1930. Reprint. New York: Bonanza, n.d.

Wealth and Biography of the Wealthy Citizens of New York City, sixth edition. New York: The Sun Office, 1845.

Weise, Arthur James. *History of the City of Troy*. Troy, New York: William H. Young, 1876.

Weise, Arthur James. *The Firemen and Fire Departments of Troy*. Albany, New York: Weed-Parsons Printing Co., 1895.

Weise, Arthur James. *Troy's One Hundred Years*. Troy, New York: William H. Young, 1891.

White, Norval, and Elliot Willensky. *AIA Guide to New York City*. Revised edition. New York: Collier Books, MacMillan Publishing Company, 1978.

Williams, Edwin, ed. *New-York As it Is in 1833*. New York: J. Disturnell, 1833.

Wolfe, Gerard R. *New York, A Guide to the Metropolis, Walking Tours of Architecture and History*. New York: New York University Press, 1975.

Woodworth, John. *Reminiscences of Troy, from Its Settlement in 1790 to 1807*. Second edition, with notes by Joel Munsell. Albany: J. Munsell, 1860.

Periodicals and Journals

Carter, Geoffrey. "Samuel Thomson: Prolific New York Builder." *Newsletter/Preservation League of New York State* 17:3 (Fall 1991), pp. 4–5.

Chittum, Samme. "Hidden Treasure: Historic Buildings Tucked inside Brooklyn Navy Yard." *Newsday* (New York) September 20, 1992.

"City of Troy." *The Boston News-Letter and City Record*, 2:6 (August 12, 1826), pp. 66–67.

Cummings, Abbott Lowell. "The Ohio State Capitol Competition." *Journal of the Society of Architectural Historians* 12 (May 1953), pp. 15–19.

"Martin E. Thompson and William Sydney Mount." *Preservation Notes* 4:3 (October 1968), pp. 3–5.

North, F. J. "Martin E. Thompson." *The Studio* 145 (March 1953), pp. 86–87.

"Obituary" [Martin E. Thompson], *The American Architect and Building News* 2:260 (August 11, 1877).

"Public Buildings." *New-York Mirror* 7:12 (September 26, 1829), pp. 89–90.

Romaine, Lawrence B. "Martin E. Thompson (c. 1786–1877): A Reconstruction of His Architectural Career from His Account book." *Bulletin of the New York Public Library* 66:5 (May 1962), pp. 281–89.

Ross, William. "Street Houses of the City of New York." *The Architectural Magazine*. (London) 2 (1835), pp. 490–93.

Schimmelman, Janice G. "Architectural Treatises and Building Handbooks Available in American Libraries and Bookstores through 1800." *The Proceedings of the American Antiquarian Society* 95: part 2 (October 1985), pp. 317–500.

Schuyler, Montgomery. "The Small City House in New York." *Architectural Record* 8:4 (1899), pp. 357–88.

"The New State Arsenal at New York City." *Gleason's Pictorial* 7 (September 2, 1854), p. 133.

"The Old Assay Office, New York City," *Architectural Record* 35: (June 1914), pp. 580.

White, Richard Grant. "Old New York and its Houses." *Century Magazine* 26:6 (October 1883), pp. 845–59.

Wodehouse, Lawrence. "Martin E. Thompson, Architect of the United States Branch Bank." *Antiques* 102:3, (September 1972), pp. 410–13.

Unpublished Papers and Dissertations

Ezequelle, Betty J. *Martin E. Thompson*. Master's thesis, Columbia University, n.d. [c. 1978].

Scott, N. M. *The New York Row House, 1800–1850*. Master's thesis, Columbia University, n.d.

Sharp, Lewis Inman. *The Old Merchant's House: An 1831/32 New-York Row House*. Master's thesis, University of Delaware, 1968.

Stillman, Damie. *Artistry and Skill in the Architecture of John McComb, Jr.* Master's thesis, University of Delaware, 1956.

Troy Public Library. *Marriage Notices Appearing in Troy Newspapers 1797–1860*. Typescript. Troy, New York: Troy Public Library, 1938.

Troy Public Library. *Obituary Notices Appearing in Troy Newspapers 1797–1860*. Typescript. Troy, New York: Troy Public Library, 1938.

Troy Public Library. *Vital Records Appearing in Troy Newspapers* Vol. 1, 1812–1834. Typescript. Troy, New York: Troy Public Library, 1980.

Manuscript Collections

PERSONAL PAPERS

George Hyde Clarke Family Papers. Department of Manuscripts and University Archives, Olin Library, Cornell University, Ithaca, New York.

A. J. Davis Papers. Avery Architectural Library, Columbia University, New York.

A. J. Davis Papers. New-York Historical Society, New York.

A. J. Davis Papers. New York Public Library, New York.

A. J. Davis Papers. Prints and Drawings Department, Metropolitan Museum of Art, New York.

Elizabeth Shields Eddy Reminiscence. Transcribed by Ruthanne Mills (Brod), 1969. Rensselaer County Historical Society, Troy, New York.

Gansevoort-Lansing Papers. New York Public Library, New York.

Hart Papers. Rensselaer County Historical Society, Troy, New York.

William Hindley Sketchbooks. Avery Architectural Library, Columbia University, New York.

Peter McNab Account Book. Original formerly in the collection of Dorothy Sutherland, Albany, New York; original now unlocated. Photocopies on deposit at the Albany Institute of History and Art, McKinney Library and the New York State Library, Manuscripts and Special Collections, Philip Hooker Research Materials (SC20924).

Martin E. Thompson Papers. Avery Architectural Library, Columbia University, New York. Collection includes his receipt book (a.k.a. Notebook, IPL no. 396106) and a number of drawings. (Note: not all of these drawings are by Thompson. Talbot Hamlin and Jane Davies have done some work toward attributing them.)

Samuel Thomson Papers. Private collection.

George Tibbits Papers, Rensselaer County Historical Society, Troy, New York.

George Tibbits Papers (13253) New York State Library, Manuscripts and Special Collections, Albany, New York.

Richard Upjohn Papers. New York Public Library, New York.

Thomas Kelah Wharton, Diary Vol. I, 1830–34, New York Public Library, New York.

PUBLIC PAPERS

Entry Documentation for Building and Maintenance of Government Facilities, 1785–1855, New York (State) Comptroller's Office (AO 825), New York State Archives, Albany, New York.

Historic American Buildings Survey Collection, Library of Congress, Washington, D.C. Report on the Hart house, 1934.

Sing-Sing Prison Records, New York State Archives, Albany, New York.

Eno Collection. New York Public Library, New York.

Stokes Collection. New York Public Library, New York.

Index of American Design. Avery Architectural Library, Columbia University, New York.

General Register, Archives of the General Society of Mechanics and Tradesmen, New York.

Deeds, New York Municipal Archives, New York.

Deeds, Rensselaer County Courthouse, Troy, New York.

Federal Census, 1800–1870.

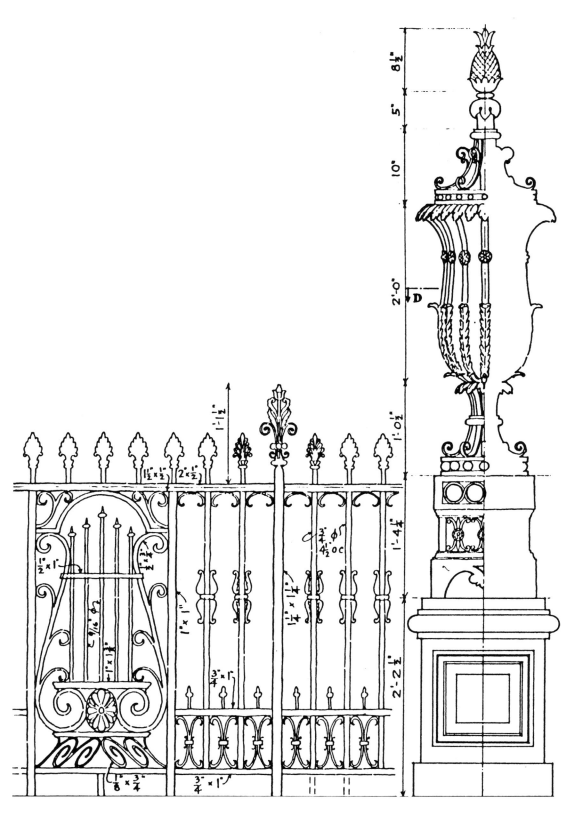

Detail, HABS Sheet 5

Comparative Views of 59 Second Street, 1892, 1934

The following eight pages reproduce photographs taken for the Harts, c. 1892,
and for Albert and Caroline Cluett, 1934.

121 59 Second Street, c. 1892.

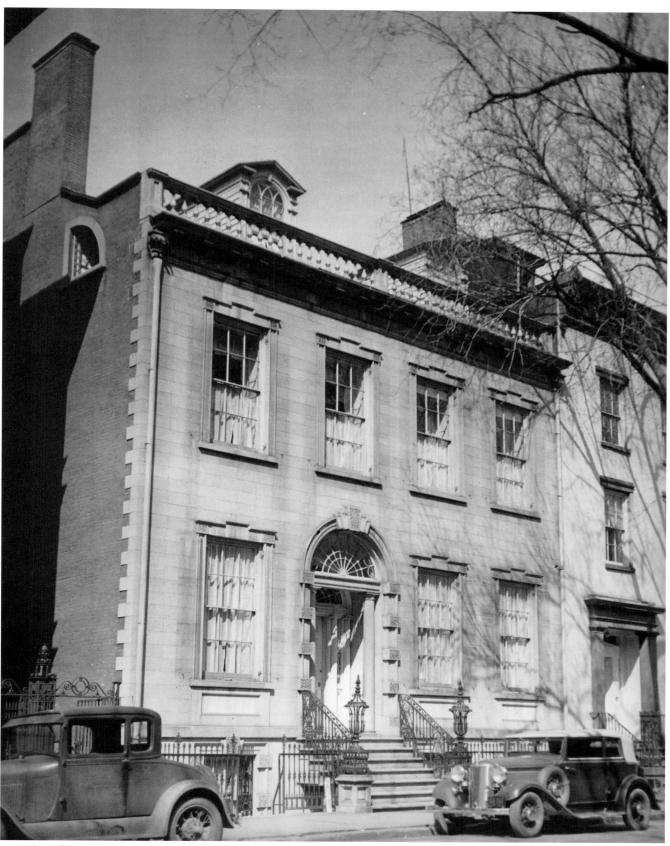

122 59 Second Street, Historic American Buildings Survey, 1934.

123 59 Second Street, staircase hall (102), c. 1892.

124 59 Second Street, staircase hall (102), 1934.

125 59 Second Street, front parlor (103) looking southwest, c. 1892.

126 59 Second Street, front parlor (103) looking southwest, 1934.

127 59 Second Street, front parlor (103) looking northwest, c. 1892.

128 59 Second Street, front parlor (103) looking northwest, 1934.

129 59 Second Street, dining room (106) looking west, c. 1892.

130 59 Second Street, dining room (106) looking west, 1934.

131 59 Second Street, front bedroom (204) looking southwest, c. 1892.

132 59 Second Street, front bedroom (204) looking southwest, 1934.

133 59 Second Street, showing original blinds and carriage step, c. 1900.

59 Second Street: An Architectural Description and Analysis

Douglas G. Bucher

THE EXTERIOR AND INTERIOR architectural assessment of 59 Second Street is based on an investigation carried out over many years beginning in 1975 and culminating in a much more intensive study commenced in 1995.

The goal of the investigation was to gain a thorough understanding of the evolution of this architecturally significant house and to produce a permanent record of the building as it now exists and as it existed during its ownership by the Harts and the Cluetts and the Rensselaer County Historical Society (RCHS). Throughout these descriptions the house is most often referred to as 59 Second Street which includes the residence, the carriage house, and the site. Occasionally, it is called the Hart-Cluett House, a reference to the three successive families which owned the property prior to 1953.

An important, sometimes difficult, part of the analysis was the attempt to date the architectural and decorative changes made to the house over the 173 years of its existence. The following periods of occupancy are used in the descriptions to provide general time frames for the changes:

1. Hart era 1827–1892, further defined as Richard Hart 1827–1843, Betsey Hart 1843–1886 and Sarah Wool Hart 1886–1892.
2. George and Amanda Cluett 1893–1910.
3. Albert and Caroline Cluett 1910–1953.
4. RCHS 1953–present

When possible, particularly for the period documented by the Hart Papers (c. 1840–1892) and work carried out by RCHS, specific dates for work carried out at the house, the site, and carriage house are provided. The use of "circa" with a date, for example circa 1836, indicates the work or event occurred about that time but the exact date or dates have not been determined.

This elevation by elevation, room by room, and surface by surface visual probe was complemented by information gleaned from several important collections housed at RCHS. These include a wonderful cache of photographs that record the exterior and interior of the house in circa 1892, 1904, and 1934, as well as illustrations and photographs of the various occupants, the neighborhood and Troy in general in the nineteenth and twentieth centuries. The 1892 and 1934 interior photographs are particularly exciting because they record the same views of the primary rooms as they appeared at the end of the Hart era and as occupied by Albert and Caroline Cluett. The quality of these early photographs permits an almost microscopic scrutiny of the interiors of the house.

Particularly important and useful in the understanding of the evolution of the house in the nineteenth century is the extraordinary collection of Hart financial records discovered in 1985 in ten wooden trunks housed at the Troy Savings Bank building only one block north of the Hart-Cluett House (called the Hart Papers in this study, see Figs. 134, 135). These documents record virtually all of the family financial transactions between the 1840s and 1892, including all work relating to the house and garden. A very complete inventory taken at the time of Betsey Hart's death in 1886 and included with these

134 Four of the wooden trunks that contained the Hart Papers.

135 A sampling of the Hart Papers prior to investigation.

documents complements the 1844 inventory recording the house after Richard Hart's demise in December 1843.

In addition to the detailed account of architectural, mechanical, and decorative changes made by the Harts, the papers also record the rich array of furnishings and other objects purchased by Betsey Hart in New York City and Troy for herself, the house, and her family. The chronological organization of the household information contained in the Hart Papers by Stacy Pomeroy Draper proved invaluable in the investigation of the building and resulted in a more complete understanding of the house as it was occupied by the Harts. The Hart Papers compliment and verify much of the information concerning the appearance of the house and the Hart family's lifestyle that is recorded in Elizabeth Shields Eddy's reminiscence of her stay in the house as a child in 1855. Additional useful information was provided by the set of seven drawings produced by the Historic American Buildings Survey (HABS) in 1934 to record the house as it then existed. Of particular importance is the layout of the kitchen, pantry, and bathroom that these plans provide. These drawings are reproduced in this study (Appendix IV) and served as the basis for the plans of the house as it exists today.

Although documentary information concerning the evolution of the house during the two periods of Cluett occupancy is lacking, a diary kept by Amanda Cluett did provide some sense of family life in the house in the early twentieth century. For Albert and Caroline Cluett's occupancy oral histories have proved very useful. For the most recent period beginning in January 1953, the records of the Rensselaer County Historical Society have provided information concerning changes and uses, particularly in the mid-1950s and 1960s when

H. Maxson Holloway, the first director of RCHS, initiated the first restoration and interpretation of the interior. Much of this work remains in place today and is significant as an example of mid-twentieth century restoration philosophy.

The assessment of 59 Second Street included an investigation of the systems historically used in the structure including plumbing, heating, gas, and electrical systems. There was also a service bell system that was originally manual but later was electrified. The house proved to be a textbook example of these "modern" conveniences as they evolved in an urban residence in the nineteenth and twentieth centuries. Beginning in the 1840s, the Hart-Cluett House had amenities such as piped water, a fully accessorized bathroom, central heating, gas lighting, and later electricity. The house was frequently updated to reflect technological advances, a process that continues today.

Complementing the architectural investigation of the original 1827 house and its additions is an analysis of the decoration and furnishing of the house as transformed by the Harts, Cluetts, and RCHS. This part of the study, included with the room descriptions, assembles information concerning the decoration, furnishings, and use of each room over time. An attempt was made through physical probing, including paint analysis, to uncover evidence for the work in the house recorded in the Hart Papers. Generally, Betsey Hart redecorated the interiors about every ten years with a major documented transformation occurring in circa 1849–50. These redecorations primarily involved repainting and the installation of new wallpaper, but sometimes included the purchase of new furniture, carpets, and curtains. This renewal of the interiors was continued by Sarah Wool Hart until 1892.

Primarily through photographic images of the interior it is possible to follow the decorative and furnishing patterns of the two Cluett families, particularly their interest in the "Colonial Revival." This aesthetic was favored by Albert and Caroline Cluett after 1910 and is best represented by the paneled wall treatments as well as the scenic wallpaper still in place in the entrance hall. The shorter duration of the two Cluett occupancies resulted in fewer changes to the interior decor between 1893 and 1953. The information included in this study concerning this important aspect of the house is only the beginning of a more complete Furnishing Plan Study that will be carried out in the near future as part of the restoration of the house.

Each portion of the exterior of 59 Second Street preserves, to a remarkable degree, original architectural fabric and conditions. The 1827 house retains the impressive entry sequence including the ironwork, marble architrave, and doorway that form the primary architectural feature of the façade. Although the rear additions are of much less artistic importance, they do retain all of their architectural integrity and preserve important information concerning the evolution of the house.

As part of the analysis of 59 Second Street the carriage house was also assessed. This remarkable structure, an original part of the complex as completed in 1827, is located at the rear west end of the large urban lot. Unlike the house, which is so well preserved, the carriage house has undergone extensive modification beginning in 1893 when the south bay of the building was demolished as a result of the division of the site. Changes were made by the two Cluett families to accommodate automobiles and after 1953 the carriage house-garage was significantly remodeled by RCHS to function as a meeting room and gallery.

The ground floor retains very little of its original nineteenth century character, but the spacious attic is completely intact including the impressive hoist used to lift carriages and sleighs for storage. The Hart Papers provide a detailed chronology of work undertaken at the carriage house in the nineteenth century. The papers also provide documentation for the now vanished washhouse that was located in the southwest corner of the original lot.

Although the following descriptions and analyses of the main house and carriage house attempt to be all-inclusive, it is likely that additional information will be revealed when further probes are undertaken during the restoration of the house scheduled to commence in the near future. These investigations will benefit from the removal of furnishings from the house, a condition that made the current assessment sometimes difficult and occasionally impossible. Of particular importance will be the investigation of Hart era surfaces hidden behind furnishings such as the parlor pier mirrors and under later finishes such as the Cluett era hardwood flooring.

As part of the work that will precede the restoration, much more intensive paint analysis will be carried out with particular emphasis on the discovery of wallpaper evidence as well as uncovering special finishes such as the faux graining known through photographs to exist on the second floor doors.

Any new information gained can only add to the already recognized architectural and historical significance of this remarkable house, the stylistic precursor to a large number of town houses constructed in New York City in the immediate years following 1827.

EXTERIOR

The Hart-Cluett House is located on a 45' wide and 130' deep urban lot on the west side of Second Street at number 59, north of Congress Street in downtown Troy, New York (Fig. 136). Today the house is flanked immediately to the north by a three-story brick house constructed in 1838 at 57 Second Street. Known today as the Carr Building, it is now part of the RCHS building complex. To the south, separated by a double walkway/passage is a freestanding four-story brick row house constructed in 1893 at 65 Second Street, now housing offices and apartments. This building occupies the site of the original Hart garden lot. Across the street to the east there are eight brick row houses of varying sizes and styles, the earliest date to the 1820s, prior to the construction of the Hart-Cluett House. Until relatively recently, several additional structures filled the now vacant sites on that side of the block.

136 59 Second Street, the east façade, 1972.

137 59 Second Street, exterior as completed in 1827, D. G. Bucher, c. 1999.

Second Street, which runs north-south, begins in south Troy and terminates at Monument Square one-and-a-half blocks north of the house. The two blocks between Congress Street and the Square were fashionable locations for the construction of town houses in the 1820s and 30s and the decision to build the house on this site is not surprising. The gleaming white marble of the new house was outstanding among the surrounding brick residences; only the nearby marble courthouse, constructed in circa 1828–1831, could compete with the visual prominence of the Hart's house at number 59.

Constructed as an urban dwelling and completed in 1827, at that time the house was freestanding and included its own yard or garden lot to the south (Fig. 137). A yard on the north side of the house separated it from the freestanding house at 53 Second Street, constructed for Jacob Merritt and Richard Hart's sister Mary in the early 1820s. By 1838, that site too featured a three-story brick house.

North of the Merritt house was the residence occupied by Richard and Betsey Hart until 1827. Nothing is known about that house which was replaced by a four-bay brick town house in the early 1830s which in turn was replaced by the Paine Mansion, constructed in the 1890s, now a fraternity house.

As the street evolved in the nineteenth century, spaces between the earliest houses were sold and additional houses were constructed resulting in the dense urban condition that now exists. This and the other blocks of Second Street to the north and south preserve a large collection of urban row houses of outstanding quality, representing a variety of styles; essentially a three-dimensional textbook of domestic and public architecture as it evolved in the nineteenth and early twentieth century.

The Hart-Cluett House has always been considered the most outstanding house in this neighborhood of architecturally important structures and as this study reveals, it has a much greater significance and influence than was initially assumed.

The house that William Howard had constructed as a gift for his daughter and son-in-law was superior in all aspects to the many town houses with similar details that followed it into the early 1830s. The 40' × 50' gable roofed two-story structure rests on a raised basement. The high roof ridge is parallel to Second Street. A 23' × 45' three-story and basement flat roofed rear addition extends from the west façade to a point 8' from the east face of the original carriage house. That imposing structure extends fully across the rear of the present site and separates the house from the alley. The three visible elevations of the original house completed in 1827 vary in scale and materials from the additions constructed in circa 1836 and 1893, thereby providing a clear visual separation between the original and later parts of the large structure.

An important visual feature of the overall appearance of the house and a significant maintenance consideration is the ancient elm tree that is located in the front of the house near the north edge of the property. This tree is one of two elms (the other is in front of number 57) that have shaded this side of Second Street since the nineteenth century.

EAST ELEVATION

The east façade, the primary elevation of the house, faces the street behind the original wrought and cast-iron fence that surrounds the deep areaway fronting the building. The entire four-bay wide façade from the base of the foundation to the top of the cornice is composed of finely cut and elegantly detailed pure white Westchester marble.

The marble foundation, which rises from the areaway, is laid up in eight stone courses which terminate in an 8" deep marble water table. The top of the water table is about 5' above the level of the sidewalk located in front of the areaway. The basement story includes three window openings, two to the north and a single opening south of the entrance stoop that projects from the façade

bridging over the areaway. These openings feature impressive architraves with vermiculated (wormlike) quoin blocks and three-part keystones and retain original eight-over-eight wood sash.

The retaining wall of the 3' deep areaway fronting the foundation is laid up in brownstone blocks and capped in white marble. The original wrought and cast-iron fence rises from this marble curb to a height of 3'6". The wrought-iron fence pales terminate in cast and wrought anthemion modeled in iron and brass. The primary ornaments of this elegant fence are the five large panels filled with an elegantly worked stylized lyre motif. A gate, at the south end of the fence provides access to the steps that descend into the slate paved areaway providing access to the basement doorway beneath the front stoop. The early twentieth century paneled door is approached by two original brownstone steps.

The main entrance is approached by a flight of seven white marble steps that rise to a recessed marble platform held within the body of the house. These steps are flanked by paneled marble pedestals that support the pair of elaborate wrought-iron basket-form newels,

138 59 Second Street, urn type newel at main entrance.

140 59 Second Street, detail of main entrance.

139 59 Second Street, the main entrance.

one of the outstanding components of the front façade (Fig. 138). These extraordinary sculptural creations may be the earliest examples of this newel type that formed the chief ornament of numerous New York City town house entrances in the late 1820s and early 1830s. Small applied cast-bronze elements decorate the cages which terminate at approximately 8'6" above the pavement in realistic cast-bronze and wrought-iron pineapples. The stair balustrade ascending behind each newel duplicates the detailing of the fence and includes the addition of a scroll work band beneath the handrail. The narrow handrail was originally finished with a polished sheet-brass cap of which only a fragment survives.

The main entrance is recessed approximately 4' into the body of the house. The arched white marble architrave is divided into sections by rectangular 9" × 3" blocks deeply carved with a vermiculated pattern and spaced about 19" apart. These blocks align with the stone coursing of the façade. The semicircular arch above the opening terminates in a five-part keystone whose center block features the vermiculated treatment. A large elegantly detailed glazed fanlight is held within this semicircular opening above a marble lintel which is supported by two 10' high white marble Tus-

can columns formed from single blocks of stone. The fanlight is arranged into nine radiating segments divided into sections by the four concentric semicircular bands. Small cast-lead ornaments decorate the wood and iron framework which supports the glass. The positioning of this fanlight, above an opening with no actual door, is one of the unique features of the Hart-Cluett House entrance (Fig. 139).

The inner doorway, set about 3'6" back from this open entrance, is constructed entirely in wood and includes pairs of tall slender Ionic columns which flank narrow sidelights filled with complex arrangements of glass set in wood and iron frames. This delicate tracery is ornamented with small cast-lead motifs. The columns support a molded wood lintel above which is positioned a large semicircular fanlight fitted with glazing, which duplicates the glazing pattern of the outer fanlight. The lintel incorporates rectangular blocks ornamented with carved wood raffle flowers above each column (Fig. 140).

The composition of the outer and inner architraves and doorways forms the primary architectural feature of the façade and the marble architrave is a stylistic element, probably first used here in Troy, that was to become very popular in New York City beginning in 1828. In that city the marble architrave would embrace the door and sidelights and the stoop would include a platform that projected out from the façade and over the areaway.

The continuous wall and curved ceiling surface in the recessed entry space is finished in plaster. The wall surfaces rise above a white marble base that duplicates the profile of the wooden baseboards in the interior of the house.

The original front door, 8' high by 3'4" wide, includes eight boldly detailed raised and recessed panels. Important early fittings remaining at this entrance include the brass eagle-form doorknocker and the brass bell pull. The outer door frame retains marks for the hinges that supported a louvered exterior door installed in the opening during the summer months. The Hart Papers make reference to this feature. In 1849, D. H. Wellington was paid for painting the front door and the front door blind with white paint. An interesting original construction detail of this area is the thin lead sheet set into the coursing of the marble stonework of the outer door architrave at 5'1" above the floor of the entry. This condition is not seen elsewhere in the building.

The four-bay wide, two-story façade includes three large window openings at the first floor and four openings at the second story. All of these openings, 4'5" wide by 9' tall, include molded marble architraves that feature a variation of the five-part lintel. The corner blocks include the vermiculated pattern and the center "tablet" is defined by a simple step-up of the top molding of the lintel. At first floor level the architraves rest on sills supported on projecting paneled aprons that are positioned on the water table, resulting in a very impressive overall effect at these openings, a unique feature of this façade. The tooling pattern of these panels produces a handsome effect.

The face of the marble blocks forming this façade are finished with fine vertical tooth-tooling. Other surfaces were honed and some of this original finish can be seen in the protected area beyond the outer entrance. The Harts remembered the marble as sparkling in the moonlight during construction. The long narrow blocks are laid up in 37 courses that extend from the watertable to the underside of the marble entablature. Each course is approximately 9⅜" high and great care was taken to ensure that this coursing aligned with the projecting details of the façade. The remarkably close tolerance of the joints of this stonework indicates that all of the fitting and much of the carving and finishing was done on site. Only the door and window surrounds were probably carved in New York City and then shipped via the Hudson River to Troy. Excavation at the rear of the house during the construction of the connecting passage in 1990 uncovered small fragments of the pure white Westchester marble resulting from on-site stone carving.

The seven window openings retain original wooden double-hung six-over-six sash with a total of twelve

14" × 24" panes of glass. The large scale of the windows becomes apparent when they are compared to the openings in the neighboring houses. Although the water tables of 59 and 57 Second Street align with each other the tops of the second-story windows at 59 extend well above the level of the sills of the third-story windows at 57.

The entablature, with its 1'6" deep overhanging cornice is formed entirely in the white Westchester marble. Seven finely carved blocks of stone form the entire cornice portion of the entablature. The underside of the cornice is ornamented by 18 simplified mutules. The gutter, recessed into the top surface of the cornice, was relined in terne-coated stainless steel in 1996.

A balustrade extends across the full width of the façade above the entablature. This wooden railing is divided into two sections by a paneled wood newel. The flanking end newels or pedestals are marble. The current balustrade, with its vasiform turned wood balusters, is a reconstruction of the original balustrade carried out in the 1960s and most recently repaired in 1996. Inspection of early photographs reveals that while there are currently 44 balusters originally there were a total of 56, resulting historically in a much denser appearance for this important feature.

In 1996, new terne-coated stainless steel rainwater leaders were installed in the locations of the original leaders visible in the circa 1892 photograph. When that photograph was taken the original large elaborately detailed leader heads were in place. They included a band of cast-lead acanthus leaves and a star and ball motif at the top of the funnel. At both ends of the façade the marble water table retains the original semicircular recess to accept the leader as it extends down the face of the foundation. The leaders end above the marble caps that finish the north and south ends of the areaway. The top surface of each marble cap includes a trough that directs the rainwater away from the face of the building.

The final feature of this façade is the pair of tall dormer windows that appear above the top edge of the balustrade. The arched double-hung sash in the window openings are flanked by paneled pilasters that support a partial pediment or fronton. The cheeks of the dormers are finished in horizontal clapboards that were restored in 1996. The form of these dormers originates in late eighteenth century design precedent.

Into the early twentieth century the first and second floor window openings featured pairs of original wooden blinds (Fig. 141). Each blind leaf included three

141 Detail, 59 Second Street, the marble steps were protected by wooden treads during the winter season, c. 1892.

panels of operable louvers. The original iron supports for these blinds remain in place and the blinds are now stored in the carriage house. There is no evidence that blinds or shutters were ever used at the basement windows.

142 Detail, 59 Second Street, south elevation, c. 1892.

SOUTH ELEVATION

The 95' long south side of the house is now largely obscured by its close proximity to the building at 65 Second Street. Prior to the sale of the garden site and the construction of that structure, this façade was a strong visual component of the house.

This elevation consists of three distinct sections, the original 1827 surface with its tall masked gable and two chimneys, and the two simply detailed additions that continue toward the west (Fig. 142). The original 50' deep 1827 section of the elevation includes two full stories and a half-story attic above a raised basement. The irregular fenestration of this elevation is related to the room arrangement within.

Above the 30" high marble foundation and water table this brick façade is laid up in American common bond that retains paint residue. Originally and throughout the nineteenth century this surface was covered in mastic (stucco) scored to imitate the marble blocks of the front façade. The blocks of the front façade return at the east corner forming quoins. The stuccoed surface was likely painted white to match the adjacent marble. Marble quoins were also formerly located at the west corner of the original house but were removed when the addition was constructed circa 1836.

There are two small basement windows in the foundation and they extend up above the level of the marble water table which is lower than the corresponding feature of the front façade. The east opening is original and includes a marble lintel. In the pavement below this opening an original semicircular well extends down into the ground providing light and air to the sub-basement window. A brownstone curb surrounds the well and an iron grate covers the opening. The second window in the foundation is an addition inserted when the rear wing was constructed circa 1836 and includes a brownstone lintel.

At first floor level the fenestration includes a large opening fitted with double-hung six-over-six sash and featuring a marble lintel and sill. This window was moved to this location from the rear west elevation of the original 1827 house when the addition was constructed circa 1836. The woodwork as well as the stone were probably salvaged from the earlier location.

The most prominent feature here is the shallow three-sided bay window that extends out into the side passage. This large wooden appendage replaced the original south entrance doorway and porch after the garden lot was sold in 1893. In later life Elizabeth Shields Eddy referred to this projection as "a silly little bird-cage of a bay." Obviously she was not happy with the changes made by the Cluetts.

The original porch in this location was two bays wide with three wooden Doric columns supporting a full cornice and low hipped roof. Steps descended to the yard from the west end of the porch. This important Hart era feature is recorded in the circa 1892 photograph which shows the porch fully enclosed by louvered panels (see Fig. 142). Elizabeth Shields Eddy referred to this as the south stoop. In 1849, D. H. Wellington was paid for "oaking" (faux painting) the south door.

The fenestration of the second floor includes the original window that opens to the interior main stairway as well as the opening to the west that included the marble sill and lintel that was moved to this location from the rear elevation circa 1836.

The primary architectural focus of this elevation in its original form was the third-story gable end. The pitched roof line was largely hidden by the brick parapet extending between the two chimneys and forming an impressive terminus to the top of the house. The original symmetrical gable fenestration with the centered roundheaded window flanked by two quarter-round windows was modified by the raising of the rear roof slope in circa 1910. At that time a full window opening was inserted at the west end of the elevation, replacing one of the quarter-round openings and a small opening was created immediately east of the central arched window. The parapet wall between the chimneys retains its original brownstone cap with a finely molded edge detail. The south elevations of the two additions are simply detailed with rows of comparatively small windows defining each of the three floors and basement.

The circa 1836 west addition is arranged in three bays (Fig. 143). The low foundation is a single course of

143 59 Second Street, showing the west addition (c. 1836), D. G. Bucher, 1999.

well-finished brownstone blocks above which the American bond brick wall rises to the roof line. This surface was originally painted white. The upper openings feature plain white marble lintels and sills and include original six-over-six sash. The exceptions are the two original basement window openings which have brownstone sills and lintels. The sash and frame, as well as the lintel and sill of the larger first floor opening, were removed to this location from the original rear façade of the 1827 house at the time of the construction of the addition. A significant original feature of this elevation is the low arched opening that formerly provided access to the passage or areaway under the wing. The brick lintel of the opening remains in place immediately below the large east first floor window and the bricks forming the east end of the arch spring from a white marble block that is part of the original water table of the west façade of the 1827 house. The opening was partially filled in with brick circa 1893 and includes a window opening which has a brownstone lintel. A description of the former opening, called "a broad, springing arched-way," is included in Elizabeth Shields Eddy's reminiscence of the house in 1855.

The unusually positioned window located between the second and third floor level at the east end of the façade was inserted there in 1893 as part of the renovations and expansion of the house carried out for George and Amanda Cluett. In the nineteenth century the windows in this portion of the rear wing featured pairs of louvered shutters.

The circa 1893 continuation of the rear wing follows the general form and detailing of the earlier addition. The low foundation is formed of a single course of cut bluestone with the American bond brick wall rising above to the level of the roof above the third floor. Fenestration consists of two windows at each level including the basement. All of the window openings above the basement have bluestone lintels and sills and original double-hung six-over-six sash.

The basement windows of the south elevation are protected by iron grilles probably installed for the George Cluetts. Two of the openings at the east and west ends of the foundation have fixed bars while the others are hinged to open outward.

The 4'10" wide walkway that extends the full length of the south elevation is finished in very hard yellow brick pavers set in cement. Separating this property from the adjoining building to the south is a tall

wrought and cast-iron fence set in a raised stone curb. These conditions date to work carried out in circa 1893 when the Hart property was divided and the house to the south was constructed for William Kemp. The nineteenth century garden walkway was in this same location. According to Elizabeth Shields Eddy it was a "path of flagstones, flanked by brick."

WEST ELEVATION

This elevation includes two wall surfaces, the narrow end of the rear addition and the visible portion of the original west wall of the 1827 house and the modifications made to it. Also forming a part of this elevation, is the wood and glass connecting passage constructed in 1990 to join 59 Second Street to the adjacent Carr Building.

The simply finished west brick elevation of the circa 1893 rear addition rises from a low single-course bluestone foundation. The primary feature is the covered wooden porch located at the north end of this elevation. The high platform is approached by five steps and two square wooden posts support a low shed roof. This porch has been repaired and possibly rebuilt since its original construction. The opening beneath the platform was until recently fitted with a pair of louvered doors. The first floor door opening is now filled with a paneled door installed in the 1960s, replacing a door with a glazed panel. The two first floor window openings have bluestone lintels and sills and retain original six-over-six sash. A single matching window is located at the second floor level directly above the first floor doorway. There is no fenestration in the third floor brick wall.

The west elevation of the original house presents a complex assembledge of original conditions and later modifications and additions (Fig. 144). As completed in 1827, this elevation related somewhat to the front of the house. An exposed basement extended from the base of the areaway to the marble water table. Above this line, the first and second floor brick wall extended up to some sort of entablature or cornice with the west slope of the original gable roof above. There were no dormers on this surface of the original slate-covered roof. The basement foundation, now fully enclosed within the circa 1836 extension of the house and the glass and wood passage constructed in 1990, is composed of a low base of tooled white marble blocks supporting a rubble stone wall finished in mastic and terminating in a mar-

144 59 Second Street, rear courtyard and west elevation, 2000.

ble water table. The rubble stone visible below the marble base was originally below grade, but was exposed when the passage was constructed. The marble architraves of the basement door and window openings include tooled marble quoins and marble lintels. Together these features form a very elegant base for the rear elevation. Unlike the front façade, the rear of the house was arranged in five bays above the four-bay basement story. At the first floor a narrow centrally positioned doorway, topped by a semicircular fanlight, was flanked by pairs of large scale windows matching those on the front elevation. The sills and the lintels of these openings (two survive) were finished in tooled white marble. The original semicircular marble lintel and fanlight from the dismantled central doorway survives in a later, hidden location above the interior door between Rooms 110 and 112. This important architectural feature was uncovered during a recent investigation of the interior.

The second floor originally included five window openings evenly spaced across the wall surface, but the second window from the south end of the elevation may have been false (a shallow recess in the masonry covered by closed blinds) to accommodate interior planning considerations and exterior symmetry. All of these first and second floor windows duplicated the scale of the openings in the front elevation. Today the pairs of windows at the north end of the first and second floor survive intact including the iron supports for exterior blinds. Several of the original rear windows and the doorway were removed when the rear addition was constructed in circa 1836, but the window sash and marble trim were reused in various locations at that time. The brick of this original façade was painted white to match the white marble of the front of the house and the painted mastic or stucco of the south elevation. Today the accumulated and very aged paint has a grey appearance.

The red brick third story is arranged in five bays which are fully visible across the top of this elevation. The windows, with stone sills and brick lintels, are of a much smaller scale but feature double-hung six-over-six sash. The brick has never been painted. This upper story dates to the expansion of the third floor attic area carried out for Albert and Caroline Cluett in 1910 or slightly later.

In 1990, the west elevation was again modified when the two-story wood and glass connector was constructed against the wall between the north wall of the rear addition and the south brick wall of the neighboring Carr Building. This new construction masks and protects the surviving original basement and first floor windows of the 1827 house. Excavation for this new structure revealed a large brick cistern located beneath the paving of the courtyard. This brick tank accepted water collected from the roof of the main house and rear wing. A large enclosed courtyard is formed by the original house, the rear addition, the carriage house, and the house to the north. The yellow brick paved surface is continuous around the house and probably dates to work undertaken circa 1893.

NORTH ELEVATION

This elevation includes two distinct sections, the circa 1836 addition and the extension constructed circa 1893. The earlier part of the façade abuts the rear wall of the 1827 house and consists of brick laid up above a low brownstone block foundation. The irregular fenestration includes original openings and openings made at the time of the extension of the wing. The small basement window opening has a tooled brownstone lintel and sill. Additional original window openings include the first floor opening that was converted into a doorway in 1990 and the second floor opening directly above it. Both openings made use of marble lintels and sills removed from the rear elevation of the 1827 house when the wing was constructed circa 1836.

The two later window openings (c. 1893) at the first and second floor level have bluestone lintels and sills, the material typically used in the later extended portion of the rear wing. An important feature of this façade is now enclosed within the connecting passage. The wide opening with a brick jack arch provides access to the passage beneath the wing. This opening was closed up with brick circa 1893 but was reopened in 1990. It corresponds to a similar opening formerly part of the south elevation. They provided access to the "area," a wide stone paved passage that extends beneath the dining room.

The configuration of the wall immediately below the roof line reflects the changes made to the pitch and level of the roof in the nineteenth century. At the west corner where the circa 1836 and 1893 additions meet at roof level, the end of the original rear brick parapet wall of the earlier part of the addition is visible.

The elevation of the 1893 addition toward the west is laid up in brick above a low bluestone block foundation. The four original window openings, one at each floor level, beginning at the basement, include bluestone lintels and sills and original sash.

The north elevation of the 1827 house, now largely hidden by the Carr Building constructed in 1838, is a plain brick wall that includes no windows or doorways. This blank surface was probably created in anticipation of eventual construction on the site to the north. This wall was not stuccoed like the south wall but it was painted white. The attic level gable end is still exposed and can be viewed from the roof of the Carr Building at 57 Second Street.

ROOF

The roofs that cover the original house and the rear extensions preserve a complex series of conditions. Current conditions reflect the restoration and rehabilitation work carried out in 1996.

On the east slope of the gable roof of the 1827 house

145   59 Second Street, slate roof during installation, 1996.

a standing seam metal roof, dating to circa 1893 or 1910, was removed and deteriorated sheathing boards were replaced. Unfading green slate was then installed over an adhered underlayment of EPDM, a synthetic rubber material used in roofing membranes (Fig. 145). Fragments of the original slate roof were uncovered during this work. The Hart Papers include many references for the repair of the slate roof on the house and carriage house in the nineteenth century. Slate was also restored to the two dormer window roofs where the original slate is visible in the circa 1892 exterior photograph.

A fully adhered EPDM surface was installed on the west slope of the main roof. This is the roof surface modified circa 1910 when full-sized rooms were created in the west half of the original 1827 attic space. The original gable roof rafters were raised upward to form the current roof surface and at that time a flat seam metal roof was installed. The original framing shows no evidence for dormers on the original west roof surface. The skylight is contemporary with that circa 1910 remodeling project and this feature was renewed in 1996.

As part of the work carried out in 1996 an EPDM membrane was also installed on the flat roof surface covering the rear additions. The conditions there preserve the remarkable history of the changes made to the roof that covers the rear part of the house. The attic areas above the two sections of the addition are accessible from the roof hatch in the northeast corner. This opening originates in the third floor stair hall (Room 311) of the wing. Intact in the attic space of the older addition are two earlier roof surfaces, one above the other, followed by the current roof structure that covers the entire rear wing. The original roof that covers the circa 1836 addition has a low pitch that slopes downward to the north and the surface retains the original covering of flat-seam terneplate.

In 1850, a new roof surface was constructed approximately 18" above the earlier surface and pitched down to the south. In that year Joseph C. Taylor was paid for installing 118 sheets of 20" × 14" tin. That surface also survives intact in the attic.

The extension of the rear wing circa 1893 resulted in the construction of a third roof structure (the current condition) that covered the entire rear wing. The recessed east portion of the roof located where the addition joins the original house is the result of conditions created when the attic of the original house was expanded in circa 1910. This trough-like space was created to accommodate three of the five new windows added to the rear of the original 1827 house at the third story.

A total of six brick chimneys extend above the roofs of the house. Four original massive tall brick chimneys are prominent features of the north and south gable walls of the original 1827 house. These chimneys served a total of eleven interior fireplaces. Each section of the rear wing includes a single brick chimney. The earlier chimney, located near the center of the current roof, is capped by a tall sheet metal ventilation hood dating to the early twentieth century.

146 59 Second Street, the main entrance, 1999.

INTERIOR

The interior of the large town house at 59 Second Street is arranged on three floors above a full basement and additionally includes a small cellar room beneath the basement and a small unfinished attic above the third floor of the original house.

The various rooms, halls, and other spaces are dispersed over three distinct parts of the house; the original structure completed in 1827, the "back building" from circa 1836, and the final addition from circa 1893. A connecting passage, constructed in 1990 to join 59 Second Street to the Carr Building next door at 57, forms a fourth space.

Similarly the interiors of the carriage house exist on three levels, the first floor, a partial cellar, and a full half-story or loft space.

The following descriptions of the interior spaces begin with the first floor entrance hall, proceed to the floors above and end with the description of the basement and cellar. This allows the reader to comprehend the house as if he were a visitor entering through the front door and walking through the labyrinth of spaces that form 59 Second Street (Fig. 146).

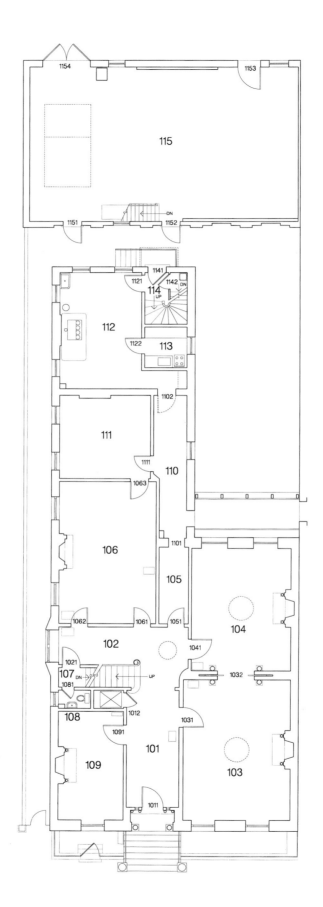

FIRST FLOOR PLAN

147 59 Second Street,
first floor plan, 1999.

0'   5'   10'   15'

FIRST FLOOR

The plan and architectural detailing and decoration of the first floor reflect the evolution and expansion of the house over 173 years under ownership of three families and the Rensselaer County Historical Society (RCHS). (Fig. 147)

The first floor plan is composed of the large rectangular mass (40' × 50') of the original house completed in 1827, the back building (24' × 25') added by Richard Hart in circa 1836, and the final rear expansion (21' × 25') constructed for George and Amanda Cluett in 1893 or slightly later. The Harts, Cluetts, and RCHS were also responsible for a series of architectural and decorative changes made to the interior as well as the insertion of mechanical systems and other amenities.

As completed in 1827, the first floor plan included four rooms, two halls, a passage, and a closet arranged behind the four-bay façade facing Second Street (Fig. 148).

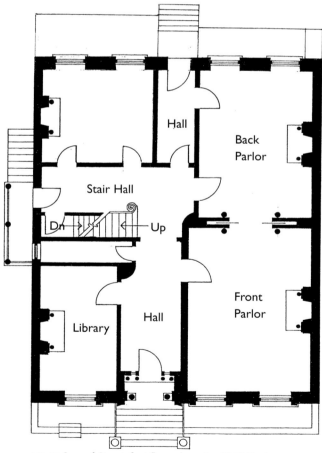

148 59 Second Street, first floor plan, 1827, D. G. Bucher, 1999.

An amply-sized hall (101) is entered from the recessed vestibule. Perpendicular to the west end of the hall is the stair hall (102) with the extraordinary curving staircase that rises upward to the third floor. This elegantly detailed staircase is one of the outstanding features of the house.

West of the stair hall a narrow passage (105) originally extended to the rear wall of the house where a doorway opened to the backyard.

The primary rooms of the house, the front (103) and back (104) parlors, are positioned along the north sides of the circulation spaces.

The two large parlors are joined by an impressively scaled opening fitted with a pair of sliding doors. This beautifully detailed opening is another of the outstanding features found in the house.

Immediately adjacent to and south of the entrance hall is a small room (109) that originally functioned as the library. The southwest corner was occupied by another small room (106) that probably functioned as the family dining room. That space, the adjacent back passage (105), and the back parlor all overlooked the rear yard and the handsome façade of the carriage house with served as the visual termination of the yard and garden.

The superb original architectural detailing surviving in these rooms is representative of the finest work produced during the first quarter of the nineteenth century, a period that ended in the last glorious flowering of the Federal style which was rapidly replaced by newly fashionable Grecian forms. Some of the finest surviving examples of ornamental plaster work and wood carving from this exuberant era are in the parlors.

A significant modification and enlargement of the first floor and the entire house was begun by Richard Hart about 1836 (Fig. 149). This work involved the addition of a three-story brick wing (called the back building) to the rear of the house. This new construction was probably carried out by John Colegrove, the builder of the original house. It included a significant enlargement of the southwest room, creating the present large dining room (106). Another room (111), which was later to function as Betsey Hart's bed chamber, filled the west end of the addition that also included a service stair hall (110). The original rear passage (105) was converted into a pantry for the storage of china and glassware, conveniently located next to the new dining room.

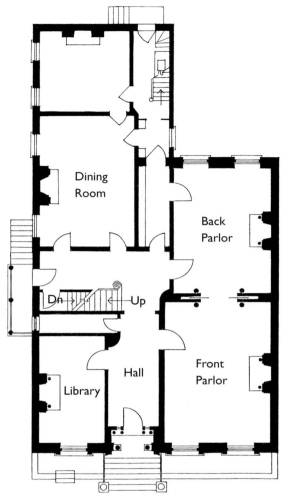

149 59 Second Street, first floor plan, c. 1836, D. G. Bucher, 1999.

Although Richard Hart's enlargement of the house occurred only about ten years after the initial construction, the rapid change in fashion is apparent in the detailing used in the dining room and adjoining spaces.

The boldly scaled but simply detailed marble mantel and cornice in the dining room reflect the new preference for the Greek Revival style but the retention of the original door and window architraves, and baseboard indicates a certain respect for the house created in 1827 and a economical reuse of existing materials. However, the detailing of the service stair and particularly the newel post, now positioned in the second floor back hall (212), are representative of the bolder Greek Revival architectural forms.

The first floor plan was further expanded after the purchase of the house by George and Amanda Cluett in 1893. In that year or soon after, the final extension of the rear wing was constructed and included a large new kitchen, pantry, and service stair at first floor level. In a gesture of respect for the existing house, the woodwork of the addition copied the Greek Revival detailing of the 1836 wing rather than a more current fashion. Only the appearance of the new service stair (114) reveals the late nineteenth century origin of the addition.

A subtle but significant change was made to the original house for George and Amanda Cluett. The carefully planned work involved the modification of the archway that separated the entrance hall (101) from the stair hall (102). The widening of the arch necessitated changes to the cloak closet (107) and the bottom risers of the main stair. The planning involved to accomplish this change indicates that an as yet unidentified architect was likely involved.

At the same time that the arch was modified and the rear wing expanded, hardwood floors were laid in the primary rooms throughout the house, and new bathrooms were introduced.

Albert and Caroline Cluett also made carefully planned changes to the house after they occupied the structure in 1910. The most significant modification on the first floor was the introduction of chair rails and panel moldings to the walls of the reception room (109), dining room (106), parlors (103, 104), and stairwell (102). It was at this time that the French scenic wallpaper was placed in the entry and stair halls.

In 1938, a small elevator connecting the first and second floors was installed in the north end of the original cloak closet (later a toilet room) and the remaining space became a lavatory entered from the landing of the basement stair (107).

Significant modifications were made to certain first floor rooms after the house was occupied by RCHS in 1953. The list of changes is long and includes the removal of Cluett-era cabinetry from the kitchen (112) and hall pantry (110) and the removal of the Hart-period service door connecting the dining room and hall pantry. In 1964, the doorway connecting the back parlor (104) to the rear hall (105) was removed. Fortunately, the mahogany door and the trim were retained to be installed in other locations.

The placement of large display cases in the 1960s in what was then called the Troy Room (111), resulted in the removal and loss of the Cluett-era mantelpiece from that important room. These and additional changes seem to have occurred under the guidance of RCHS Director H. Maxson Holloway.

Beginning in the early 1980s, efforts were made to restore the Cluett kitchen (112) and the bedroom (111) formerly occupied by Betsey Hart.

In 1990, the plan of the first floor was subtly but significantly modified by the creation of the glass enclosed external passage that connects 59 Second Street to the Carr Building at 57 Second Street next door. To accomplish this connection, an original window opening in the 1836 back building was converted into a doorway.

The following first floor room descriptions are based on a careful inspection of each space. Unfortunately, the rooms are fully furnished making inspection of certain surfaces impossible. Some probing into the physical fabric was undertaken but much more needs to occur to answer additional questions about the evolution and functioning of the spaces. A small hole was made in the north wall of the dining room to determine the type of lath used in its construction. The discovery of hand-split lath indicated that the partition was an original feature of the first floor plan and permitted an accurate reconstruction on paper of the 1827 plan.

Removal of the architrave corner blocks from the west doorway (D1102) in the service hall (110) revealed that they were probably part of the trim of the doorway (D1042) removed from the back parlor in 1964. The as yet uninvestigated surface of the original Hart-era flooring hidden by the Cluett period hardwood surfaces would answer many questions concerning changes made over the years. Evidence for the Hart-era pantry cabinetry in the passage (105), the location of the stove in the entrance hall (101), and the original configuration of the arch and cloak closet, all could be found on the original floor surface.

Similarly, evidence for the placement of pictures, mirrors, and other objects on the wall surfaces exists under the canvas wall covering installed for Albert and Caroline Cluett. Important evidence concerning the decor of the parlors is preserved behind the two pier mirrors in those rooms. These massive furnishings have remained in situ since their placement in the late 1840s.

101 Entrance Hall

The entrance hall is the primary formal access to the house and was used by the family and guests. The architectural character of the hall serves as an introduction to details found in the rooms beyond. In the four-bay house type the extra width of the building permits the placement of the staircase in another space beyond the entry hall thereby producing a greater sense of spaciousness in the entrance area.

The long rectangular hall (8'6" × 18'8") includes the main entrance centered in the east wall, a single doorway in the north partition, two doorways in the south partition, and a broad tall arched opening located at the west end of the space (Fig. 150).

Beyond the west opening, there is the perpendicular extension of the hall that includes the formal staircase that rises to the third floor.

The current appearance and plan of the hall results from modifications made for the two Cluett families in circa 1893 and again in 1910.

150 The entrance hall (101) looking west, 2000.

As originally completed and prior to 1893, the west end of the hall had a slightly different configuration. The current 7' wide elliptical arch was originally approximately 5'3" wide and included a semicircular top. The southwest closet space extended into the hall in that corner and the closet door opened into the closet space; swinging from the west jamb. These conditions are recorded in the circa 1892 photograph of the hall and evidence for the plan may exist on the original wide board flooring preserved beneath the Cluett-era floor surface (see Fig. 123). The arch and closet modifications were made for George Cluett after his purchase of the house in 1893. The incentive for this undertaking was probably related to the loss of natural light in the adjoining stair hall (102) due to the construction of the Kemp house next door in 1893 on the former site of the Hart garden. The impression of ample natural light in the hall in the mid-nineteenth century was recorded in Elizabeth Shields Eddy's reminiscence where she notes that the space was "flooded with light from the large South windows on the stairs." The construction of the Kemp house severely diminished the amount of daylight in the stair hall.

The broadening of the arch allowed natural light from the front entrance fanlight to penetrate into the stair hall.

This work included the reconstruction of the north end of the narrow closet (108) which originally extended slightly into the hall. Modifications to the south wall of the hall resulted in the reconstruction of a section of the cornice, including the southwest corner rosette and the replacement of part of the baseboard.

The modified archway is recorded in a photograph of the west end of the hall taken in 1904 (Fig. 151). At that time, the newly formed arch included an elaborate lattice-like panel insert at the top of the opening and a rod supporting a pair of velvet portieres. This seems to contradict the architectural reason for widening the arch; to permit more light penetration.

The Albert Cluetts modified the hall decor circa 1910. The lattice was removed from the archway and a classically detailed chair rail was installed on the walls. Above the new chair rail the wall surface was covered in a scenic wallpaper (*Eldorado*) originally produced by the French firm of Zuber et Cie in 1848–49. This later printing was produced using the original woodblocks. This is the most recent in a series of wallpaper treatments used by the Harts and Cluetts in the hall. Though

paper probably covered the walls beginning in 1827 the earliest record of this treatment is the "marble paper" supplied by the New York City firm Solomon and Hart in 1850. Repapering of the hall occurred in 1866 and 1880. This last Hart wall decor is recorded in a circa 1892 photograph (see Fig. 123).

Important documentary and visual information concerning the entrance hall is provided by the 1844 and 1886 inventories, Mrs. Eddy's reminiscence, the Hart Papers, and photographs dating to circa 1892, 1904, and 1934 (see Figs. 123, 151, 124).

This hall has functioned as the main entrance to the Rensselaer County Historical Society since that institution's occupancy of the structure in January 1953.

FLOOR

The floor is finished in narrow 2¼" wide strips of tongue-and-groove oak, laid east/west. This surface was installed by the George Cluett family. The original wide-board flooring survives under this surface and runs in an east/west direction. The original surface probably retains evidence for the former configuration of the west end of the hall. The oak flooring is a honey color, but Cluett-era photos record a darker finish.

During the Hart era the wide-board floor surface was at first fully covered by a painted floor cloth and later by wall-to-wall carpeting. The hardwood Cluett surface was partially covered by various oriental patterned rugs.

WALLS

All four walls are finished with plaster on wood lath. The plaster surfaces have always been covered in wallpaper. During the George Cluett era a picture molding was added to the walls below a deep frieze paper. The 3" wide wood chair rail, located at about 33¾" above the floor, was installed for the Albert Cluetts sometime after 1910. The south and west hall walls have undergone careful but significant modifications. As originally constructed for the Harts, the opening in the west partition was narrower than the current condition and included a half-round arch rather than the current elliptical arrangement. The opening was made wider for the George Cluetts in 1893 or slightly later. The newly formed arch included an elaborate lattice insert as recorded in a 1904 photograph. This feature was removed by the Albert Cluetts. The widening of the arch necessi-

151 The entrance hall (101), 1904.

tated modifications to the original south wall, the closet door, and the cornice directly above.

CEILING

The original plaster-on-lath ceiling is 13'7" above the floor. The southwest ceiling surface including the cornice next to the west end of the south wall was replaced when the archway and closet (now elevator) area was modified for the George Cluetts.

BASEBOARD

The original wood baseboard, approximately 11¾" high, is composed of a tall stepped fascia topped by a reverse ogee with astragal crownmold. Slightly different proportions exist on the section of baseboard located between the door that provides access to the elevator and the door to Room 109. This surface was installed when the archway and south wall were modified.

CORNICE

The original plaster cornice was run in place and includes four applied cast-plaster corner rosettes. The southwest corner rosette and short sections of cornice that extend from that corner are replacements dating to the modifications of the archway and south wall made after 1893.

DOORS

There are five original openings in the hall: the main entrance in the east wall (D1011); a single doorway in the north wall (D1031); two doorways in the south wall (D1091 and D1012), and a tall wide archway in the west wall (D1013). Each opening retains the original 5½" wide architrave composed of symmetrically molded trim with an applied triple reeded band and square corner blocks set with carved wood four-leaf rosettes (called raffle flowers by the nineteenth century wood carver, Henry Farnham). The same elegantly conceived trim is used throughout the original house in all of the primary rooms.

The front door architrave (D1011) includes an original molded plaster half-round arch that frames a large glazed fanlight. The opening to the stair hall (D1013) includes a molded wood elliptical arch with a key block ornamented with a carved wood acanthus leaf. The key block is an original feature but the flanking wood architrave moldings date to the modification and widening of the arch for the George Cluetts sometime after 1893.

D1011: This opening retains the original eight-panel, stile-and-rail door which is 3'4" wide × 7'11" high × 2" thick. The inside face has a faux mahogany grained finish. The exterior face is painted white.

Hardware: Original fittings include a pair of 5" high cast-iron butt hinges and a 6½" × 10" sheet-iron rim lock with original brass knobs and brass-edged keeper. A large brass escutcheon with drop cover is positioned on the outside face of the door. The original large brass key is preserved in RCHS

152 The original front door lock.

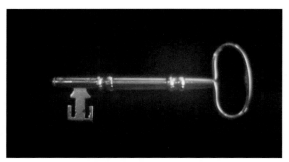

153 The original front door key.

collections. A small surface mounted Yale latch and lock cylinder was installed by RCHS. (Figs. 152, 153)

D1012: The opening is fitted with an original tall narrow eight-panel, stile-and-rail door which is 2'5" wide × 7'10" high. The hall face has a very fine faux mahogany grained finish. The original partition which included the closet door opening into which this door was positioned was located approximately 2'6" north of the current position. The modifications of the west archway resulted in the repositioning and reconstruction of the partition and door opening to this current position. In both instances, the door was hinged to the west joint and opened into the long narrow closet space. The modification of the north end of the closet to house a small elevator in 1938 resulted in a reworking of the door to swing outward into the hall. Evidence for these changes is preserved on the door jambs.

D1013: As originally constructed, the proportion of this 7' wide arched opening duplicated that of the main entrance (D1011). The width of the opening was increased and the rounded arch was made elliptical soon after the house was purchased by the George Cluetts in 1893. A 1904 photograph of the hall shows the upper part of the modified opening filled with a panel of ornamental wood lattice. This was probably removed sometime after the Albert Cluetts acquired the house in 1910.

WINDOWS

There are no conventional windows in the entrance hall but the front door (D1011) does include narrow flanking sidelights and a large semicircular fanlight; these permit natural light to enter the hall. Each sidelight includes a rectangular glazed panel divided into small geometric shapes by narrow iron, lead, and wood muntins. Within the deep recess of each sidelight is a single five-panel shutter which can be closed over the glass. The semicircular fanlight is divided into nine radiating segments which, in turn, are separated into four sections by concentric semicircles. On the exterior face applied cast-lead ornaments provide additional detail.

HEATING

Heated air enters the hall through a 16½" × 24" white enameled cast-iron Rococo pattern floor register installed in the 1850s. Prior to that the hall was heated by a stove which is listed in the 1844 inventory of household furnishings. The exact position for the stove and its method of exhaust have not been determined but it may have been a dumb stove which was joined to a stove positioned in the basement hallway (B1) directly below this space. Heated air from the basement stove would pass through the dumb stove and then be exhausted via a stove pipe that passed up through the house or to a nearby flue. Such a stove could be removed and stored elsewhere during warm months.

LIGHTING

Artificial lighting is provided by a two-branch silver-plated electric wall sconce fitted with two frosted and cut glass shades. This fixture was installed by the Albert Cluetts and replaced a two-branch gas bracket shown in the 1904 photograph. That fixture was probably installed by George Cluett, but it may possibly have dated to late in the Hart era. According to the summer 1960 RCHS newsletter the sconce was restored in that year. There is no evidence for the placement of a suspended lighting device; perhaps this hall shared light provided by the pendant fixture located in the adjoining stair hall (102).

The deep ledge above the front door and in front of the fanlight was a traditional location to place a small oil lamp at night. The ledge may have been used this way in the nineteenth century.

A double electrical switch is positioned on the east wall south of the entrance door. These switches control the wall bracket and the exterior light at the entrance.

EQUIPMENT

There are three motion sensors attached to the ceiling surface.

OTHER FEATURES

A small elevator is located in the space beyond door (D1012). This area was formerly the front half of a long narrow closet space (later a toilet room) that extended to the south wall of the house. The elevator, manufactured by the Inclinator Company of America, was originally installed in 1938. This work included the modification of the original closet door so that it would swing outward into the hall. At that time the elevator traveled from the first to second floor. In 1969, with funds from the Howard and Bush Foundation, RCHS

modified the elevator to serve the basement and third story. A small metal manufacturer's plate attached to the north wall of the cab identifies the elevator as an "Elevette" patented May 21, 1929.

FURNISHINGS AND FITTINGS

The furnishing and appearance of the hall is documented in the inventories dating to 1844 and 1886, as well as in the Hart family financial records (See Appendix II). Two photographs, a circa 1892 Hart-era view and a 1934 view, record a small portion of the entrance hall. A 1904 photograph, from the George Cluett era, records the north, south, and west walls of the hall which are decorated with flowers and vines for the debut of Beatrice Cluett.

As the primary entrance area of the house this hall was never extensively furnished. The decorative treatment of the wall and floor surfaces gave the space its overall character.

The "Hall" listed in the 1844 inventory probably included the space now referred to as the stair hall (102). Together, the spaces featured an oil cloth (floor cloth) on the floor, two tables (one with a cover), four chairs, and a stove. There were also two lamps. The appearance of the 1844 oil cloth is unknown but in 1847 a new floor cloth was installed; supplied by D. Powers and Company for $70.00. This is probably the "oil cloth in black and white squares" remembered by Elizabeth Shields Eddy.

The positioning of the stove included in the 1844 inventory has not been determined, but it is likely that it was placed near the north wall of the hall. Evidence for the stove's location may exist on the original wide board flooring still extant beneath the current Cluett-era surface.

Mrs. Eddy's reminiscence describes the ambiance of the hall in 1855, referring to the walls which looked like yellow marble, the white woodwork and polished mahogany doors, but makes no mention of specific furnishings.

Hall furnishings are however recorded in the inventory taken in 1886. As in the earlier inventory the adjoining stair hall (102) is included in the listing. Items that were probably located in the entrance hall include a carpet (wall-to-wall), a hat stand and mirror, an umbrella stand, one or two chairs, and an oil cloth in front of the entrance door. A photograph of the stair hall (102) taken circa 1892 shows a small portion of the southwest corner of the entry hall. It records the appearance of the wallpaper and wall-to-wall carpet. Documents indicate that the wall decor was supplied by Robert Graves and Company of New York City in 1880 and installed by A. A. Sandersen and Son.

After the sale of the house to the George Cluetts in 1893 architectural modifications were made to the hall and the decor and furnishings were changed. Though no inventory from this period exists, a photograph taken in 1904 records the west end of the entrance hall. The widened arch, with its inset lattice lunette, is visible as is the wallpaper and corresponding deep border paper; both in a bold Gothic heraldic motif. Framed prints decorate the north wall while a mirror and a stuffed deer's head are positioned on the south wall. A late nineteenth century spool-turned armchair and an antique Grecian sofa furnish the space. A pair of velvet portieres are suspended in the arch.

The stair hall (102) as decorated for the Albert Cluetts (after 1910) is recorded in a 1934 photograph. Only a small portion of the entrance hall (101) is visible. The hardwood floor installed for George Cluett can be seen under several small oriental rugs and the walls are covered in the scenic wallpaper installed circa 1910. The block printed paper, originally produced by Zuber et Cie, at Rixheim, Alsace, France in 1848–49, is titled "Eldorado." The paper was reprinted from the original blocks in the early twentieth century. It is that edition of "Eldorado" which is still in place on the hall walls.

FINISHES INVESTIGATION

Physical, documentary, and photographic evidence provide clues concerning the treatment of the surfaces in the hall over a span of approximately 173 years. The plaster walls have always been covered in wallpaper. The first documented treatment was installed in 1850 and consisted of 20 rolls of grey marble paper supplied by Solomon and Hart of New York City. After the paper was placed on the walls the surface was varnished. This treatment accounts for the description in the reminiscence of 1855 of "walls . . . papered or painted to look like pale, yellow marble."

The hall was again papered in 1866 when L. Marcotte and Company of New York City supplied 52 rolls of paper. W. W. Whitman was paid to install the wallpaper and border paper.

In 1880, Robert Graves and Company of New York City supplied 70 pieces of bronze paper, 82 yards of frieze, 54 yards of dado and 54 yards of border for

the hall. This elaborate decor, recorded in the late-nineteenth century photograph of the stair hall, was installed by A. A. Sandersen and Son (see Fig. 123). This aesthetic style decor remained in situ until the house was purchased and redecorated by the George Cluetts. A 1904 photograph records the paper installed for the Cluetts, probably in conjunction with the modifications made to the arched opening between the entrance hall and stair hall. The "Gothic" style paper and matching border paper appears also on the walls of the stair hall (102). The French scenic wallpaper currently in the hall was produced by Zuber et Cie from original blocks dating to 1848–49. Unfortunately, when the paper was reprinted in the early twentieth century, a poor quality high acid content wood pulp paper was used. At the time of its installation for the Albert Cluetts, the paper was varnished, probably to protect it and intensify the colors. This has resulted in an overall yellowing and deterioration of the paper. RCHS accession records describe the wallpaper (53:161) as "Scenic Hand Printed Wallpaper, Les Zones Terrestre" (Scenes of the World) but the paper now on the walls is *Eldorado* produced by Zuber et Cie in 1848–49. "Les Zones" was first produced in 1855. Since the two papers are similar in appearance, it is likely that the person who wrote the accession description misidentified the design.

The original hall woodwork is covered in approximately twelve painted finishes, all of which, except for the sixth layer, are yellowish white followed by the current white surface. The intermediate layer is a yellowish gold color that is found in a comparable layering relationship in other rooms of the house. The ceiling and cornice have always been finished in white paint but there is evidence of the use of tinted distemper paint on some of the molded detail. The pink paint currently found on the moldings was applied in the early 1980s based on an analysis of the surface. The application of this color may date to the painting of the ceiling by L. Cherest in 1873 or possibly the work carried out by A. A. Sandersen and Son in 1880.

102   Stair Hall

The stair hall is located at the west end of the entrance hall and forms the core of the original house. The primary feature, an impressive curved staircase, ascends in a continuous run from the first to the second floor and then continues in a second duplicate run to the third story (Fig. 154).

154 The staircase hall (102), 1976.

In plan, the rectangular hall (9'9" × 21'4") includes three doorways in the west partition, a single doorway in the north partition and a shallow bay window in the south wall. The east partition includes the tall wide arched opening to the entrance hall and a single doorway in the partition beneath the stair run. The staircase fills the south end of the hall and the wall surface follows the curve of the stairs between the first and the second floors. Centered in the curved wall surface is a large window opening that formerly allowed south light to flood the hall. The combination of curves found in this hall—the curved stairway, the arch, the two small fanlights, and the rounded surface of the north partition—combine to produce a unique and elegant space.

The stair hall retains most of its original architectural character but some significant modifications and additions were made by the Cluett families beginning at the end of the nineteenth century. The George Cluetts replaced the south entrance that provided access to the garden, with the shallow bay window extant today. At the same time, the arched opening in the east partition was made wider, allowing the bottom risers of

the stairway to wrap around the base of the arch and extend into the entrance hall. The original wide board floor surface was covered by the narrow board hardwood surface in place today. In 1910 or slightly later, the Albert Cluetts had installed a chair rail along with the scenic wallpaper that still ornaments the hall walls. Narrow moldings were placed on the wall surfaces along the stairway creating the appearance of large panels. A lattice panel, part of the expanded archway, was removed at this time.

The hall decor was modified many times for the Hart family as well as the Cluetts. Various documents as well as three photographs record many of these decorative changes.

Aside from changes in surface treatment, the earliest modification was the installation of the register grate in the floor near the southwest corner. This occurred in the 1850s and this fitting remains in use today.

During the Hart era, this space not only functioned as the stair hall, providing access to the upper floors as well as the basement, but also included a doorway to the exterior. A low door, in the south wall beneath the curved stair run, opened to a side porch and the garden beyond. These original features are recorded in the circa 1892 photographs of the stair hall and the exterior of the house. The six-panel door (shown in the photograph) appears to match the still extant door (D1021) that provides access to the basement stairway.

The flood of natural light from the south window as described by Elizabeth Shields Eddy was lost when the south half of the property was sold and a three-story town house was constructed in 1893 for William Kemp. This significant change in the ambience of the main hall and the stair hall was probably a primary factor in the decision to enlarge the archway in the east partition.

For RCHS, the stair hall continues to serve as a busy center of activity as it did for the Harts and Cluetts.

FLOOR

The floor is finished in narrow 2¼" wide strips of tongue-and-groove oak, laid east/west. This surface dates to the George Cluett era and covers the original wide board flooring.

The oak surface is now a honey color, but Cluett-era photos record a darker finish. During the Hart era the wide board floor surface was fully covered by a floor cloth and later by wall-to-wall carpeting. The hardwood Cluett surface was partially covered by various oriental patterned rugs.

WALLS

The north, east, and west partitions are finished in original plaster on wood lath. The south wall is of plaster applied to masonry below the stair run and plaster on wood lath forming the curved partition above the stair run. The south and east surfaces were modified for George Cluett after 1893. This work included the widening of the archway in the east partition resulting in modifications to that surface and the replacement of the south entrance door by a shallow projecting bay that includes two small square glazed windows and a low seat.

The original curved wall surface in the northeast corner results from the difference in size between the front (103) and back (104) parlors. The dead space behind this curved surface was later (circa 1850) used to house duct work for the gravity hot-air heating system. Modifications made to the wall surfaces for the Albert Cluetts included the installation of a wood chair rail at 33¾" above the floor and the placement of narrow moldings on certain wall surfaces to create a paneled effect. They exist above the arched opening in the east partition, on the wall surface below the stair run, and on the wall surface that follows the stair to the second floor.

A significant and unusual unique original detail survives high on the west wall. A small rectangular (plaster?) plaque with a molded edge is set into the plaster wall surface. Incised in the flat surface is the date "1827," the year that the Hart family occupied the house.

CEILING

The original plaster-on-lath ceiling is 13'7" above the floor. A continuous flowing plaster surface forms the underside of the stairs as it ascends to the second floor. The original circular plaster ceiling medallion is centered in the ceiling surface at the north end of the hall. The molded plaster ring includes a series of applied cast-plaster leaves. The center of this feature has always functioned as the point of suspension for the stair hall lighting devices.

BASEBOARD

The original wood baseboard, approximately 11¾" high, survives on the north, east, and west walls. The original base was removed from the south wall when the bay window was installed.

CORNICE

The original plaster cornice was run in place and is continuous around the stair hall. Only the outer cornice molding follows the plaster ceiling surface that forms the underside of the stair.

DOORS

There are six original door openings in the stair hall: three openings in the west partition (D1051, D1061, D1062); a single opening in the north partition (D1041); a broad arched opening at the foot of the stairway (D1013) and a small doorway below the stair (D1021). A seventh original opening was formerly centered in the south wall. This garden entrance was removed after the house was acquired by George Cluett. All of the openings retain the original symmetrically molded trim and raffle flower ornamented corner blocks. The elliptical top of the archway retains the original acanthus ornamental key block but the curved trim is a replacement dating to the widening of the opening.

Two of the doorways in the west partition include original glazed semicircular fanlights (D1015, D1061) and acanthus ornamental key blocks. The north fanlight (D1051) opens to the service hall (105) but the south light (D1061) which now is open to the dining room (106) was, until modified by RCHS, a false light that was covered on the dining room side by a plastered wall surface (Fig. 155). This condition is visible in the circa 1892 and 1934 photographs of the stair hall and the 1904 view of the dining room.

The architrave of door D1062 was modified by RCHS when the original southwest doorway in the back parlor (104) was removed. The acanthus ornamented center tablet from the top of the parlor door architrave was salvaged and installed in a corresponding position in the head of this door. Both Hart and Cluett photographs record door D1062 in its original condition.

D1021: This opening retains the original six-panel, stile-and-rail door. The hall face retains old, possible original, mahogany graining. The door swing was originally into the space beneath the stair. Modification of the swing, made by RCHS, necessitated the trimming of the south stile.

Hardware: Original fittings include a pair of 4" high cast-iron butt hinges, a small 4¾" × 5¾" rim lock, a small brass knob on the lock and a silvered

155 The doorway (D1061) into the dining room.

knob on the hall face. The shield-shaped brass (originally silvered) keyhole escutcheon was moved slightly when the door swing was changed. There are Hart-era mortised night bolts at the top and bottom of the door.

D1022: The former door and door opening to the garden no longer exist. A circa 1892 photograph, which shows the door in situ in the south wall, reveals that it was identical to the door (D1021) beneath the stairway. This missing door originally opened to the south porch and the garden beyond. Sections of the trim and the two corner blocks which now form the architrave of the bay window in this location were probably reused from the former door opening.

WINDOWS

The stair hall includes two window openings. The original opening, which is positioned above the curved run of the stair between the first and second floors, is recorded with the description of the second floor stair

hall (201). A shallow bay window is located in the south wall beneath the stair run. The horizontal window opening includes two fixed square sashes with single panes of glass. Beneath the projecting sill there is a horizontal molding and a wood wall surface. Below is a built-in window seat with a lift seat attached by three butt hinges. The storage compartment beneath the seat is lined with narrow beaded boards. The bay window and seat date to the George Cluett era.

In the 1934 photograph of the stair hall a portion of the west bay window sash is visible. The square glass area appears to be filled with an elaborate pattern of ovals and swags applied to the surface of the glass or formed in leaded glass. The inside vertical edges of the east sash retain possible evidence for the attachment of this ornament.

HEATING

Heated air enters the hall through a 16½" × 24½" white enameled cast-iron Rococo pattern floor register dating to the 1850s. It is positioned in the southwest corner and can be seen in the circa 1892 photograph of the hall.

LIGHTING

This hall has always been lit by various lighting devices suspended from the center of the plaster centerpiece at the north end of the space. The current fixture consists of a chain suspended electrified etched and cut glass inverted bell lantern. The fixture, which is possibly an antique from the 1830s, is shown in the 1934 photograph of the hall and was probably installed in the Albert Cluett era.

Hart-era documents record some of the fixtures used here beginning in 1850 when a gilt and stained glass gas lantern was installed. The earlier, pre-gas-era fixture may have been similar to the Cluett electrified fixture but would have held a candle or small oil lamp and been suspended by a counterweighted pulley so that the fixture could be lowered for lighting and cleaning.

The 1850 gas fixture was apparently replaced in 1866 by a pendant gas fixture and globe (shade) supplied by Ball, Black and Company of New York City. This is probably the fixture recorded in the circa 1892 photo of the stair hall. In that view the Neo-Grec–style fixture features a single cut and frosted glass shade of a type used after the mid-1870s. At that time the shade support ring size was increased from about 2½" to 4" or 5" in diameter.

EQUIPMENT

Security devices located in the stair hall include the activation panel for the ADT security system located next to the window seat and a smoke alarm affixed to the ceiling near the northeast corner.

STAIRCASE

The primary feature of the hall and one of the most significant original architectural features of the house is the dramatic curving staircase that extends in twenty-four risers to the second floor. From that point it continues in a similar manner to the third story (Fig. 156).

Beginning at the arched opening in the east partition, the stair rises in a straight run toward the south. Against the rounded south wall the stair continues in a full curve and then extends in a short straight run to the second floor. The straight treads are 12" deep and the risers are 7⅜" high. Scroll patterned string brackets are applied to the face of the open stringer. The bottom tread includes a scrolled end that supports the slender turned iron newel surrounded by five turned mahogany balusters. There are two balusters per tread at the

156 Original staircase to upper floors.

straight runs and a single baluster at the narrower ends of the treads of the curved run.

The delicately shaped mahogany handrail spirals above the newel and rises in a continuous run to the third story. The handrail is stabilized by a series of turned iron balusters that are positioned among the wood balusters and are visually indistinguishable from the wood members. The first iron baluster is located on the seventh tread and is mortised into the face of the stringer. Additional iron balusters are located on the fifteenth and twenty-third treads. When the archway was widened for George Cluett, the bottom two treads and risers were reworked by extending them to the east so that they now wrap around the base of the arch. Evidence for this modification is concealed under the stair carpet runner. This change is apparent in comparisons of the circa 1892 and 1934 photographs of the stair hall.

FURNISHINGS AND FITTINGS

The inventories of 1844 and 1886 and Hart family financial records provide considerable information about the furnishing and appearance of the stair hall. An important visual record is provided by the circa 1892, 1904, and 1934 photographs (see Figs. 123, 151, 124).

Only a few objects are included in the "Hall" listing of the 1844 document (see Appendix IIA). Of the items included probably one of the two lamps was located here as well as one of the tables (probably one end of the large three-part dining table). The floor was covered by an oil cloth. A stair carpet (runner) is noted later in the inventory. Some sense of the appearance of the stair hall and its furnishings in 1855 is provided by Elizabeth Shields Eddy's reminiscence that refers to the hall "flooded with light from the large South windows on the stairs." She goes on to note, "The walls . . . papered or painted to look like pale, yellow marble, and the floor . . . covered with oil cloth in black and white squares." She states that one of the semicircular ends of the three-part dining table was located between the two doors (D1061 and D1062) of the dining room.

The 1886 inventory records the contents of the entrance hall which includes the stair hall (102) as well as the front hall (101). Of the items listed, the carpet, a rug, stair carpet, and gas fixture were used in this hall (see Appendix IIB). These furnishings and fittings can be seen in the circa 1892 photograph of the stair hall.

The floor surface is covered by a small scale oriental

patterned carpet made up of 27" wide strips sewn together; probably a cut pile Wilton. A similar cut pile oriental patterned runner is positioned on the stairway. It is held in place by flat brass stair rods; possibly some of the 42 stair rods purchased in 1856 from Heartt and Company.

A small handwoven oriental rug (Bokhara), complete with fringe, is placed in front of the north door (D1061) to the dining room.

The Neo-Grec-style pendant gas fixture shown in the photograph may be the one purchased in 1866 from Ball, Black and Company of New York City. The single glass shade would date to the mid-1870s or later when the larger diameter gas shade supports replaced the small sized fittings.

A 1904 photograph, from the George Cluett era, records a small portion of the stair hall (see Fig. 151). A tall-case clock can be seen between two arched doors in the west wall and a runner can be seen on the stairway. Portieres were located in the archway and in the door openings to the dining room and the service hall.

The stair hall as transformed for the Albert Cluett family is recorded in a 1934 photograph (see Fig. 124). Within the architecturally modified space (widened arch and hardwood floors) are various furnishings and fittings. Oriental patterned rugs are placed on the hardwood floor and an oriental patterned runner covers the stairs. The runner is tacked in place without the use of stair carpet rods. A chain suspended electrified cut and etched glass lantern is positioned beneath the ceiling centerpiece. This fixture, which may be antique, remains in situ today.

Furnishings include a tall-case clock placed between the dining room door and the door to the service passage and a scroll arm Grecian sofa between the dining room doors. Both pieces were probably considered to be antiques when placed here by the Cluetts.

FINISHES INVESTIGATION

An understanding of the changing decor of the hall over time is provided by physical evidence as well as various documents and photographs. Analysis of plaster walls revealed that they have always been covered in wallpaper. The earliest documented treatment is the grey marble paper that was put up and varnished in 1850. This was the "pale yellow marble" surface that Elizabeth Shields Eddy remembered from 1855. At the same time, the ceiling was painted white.

In 1866, the hall was repapered in 52 rolls of paper supplied by L. Marcotte and Company of New York City. About the same time, 79 yards of border paper were purchased from W. W. Whitman for use in the hall.

An elaborate wall treatment was created in 1880 with paper supplied by Robert Graves and Company of New York City. Included in the purchase were 70 pieces of a bronze (metallic) patterned paper, 82 yards of frieze paper, 54 yards of dado paper and 54 yards of border (Fig. 157). The complex scheme is recorded in the circa 1892 photograph of the hall (Fig. 158). Paper was again applied to the walls after the archway was modified by the George Cluetts. The Gothic patterned paper can be seen in the 1904 photograph of the hall (Fig. 124).

The current wall treatment, a scenic paper first manufactured in 1848–49 by Zuber et Cie titled *Eldorado* was installed after Albert and Caroline Cluett occupied the house in 1910. The chair rail was installed at the same time.

The scenic wallpaper panel now positioned between the doors to the dining room (D1061 and D1062) and on the flanking wall surfaces, differs from the one shown in the 1934 photograph of the hall. The change was made at an undetermined time.

An article in the August 13, 1962 issue of the *Times Record* indicates that the scenic wallpaper, referred to as *Le Zone*, was cleaned along with other work and repairs to the house made in that year.

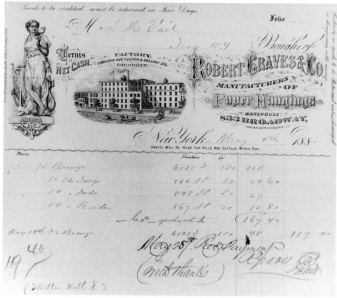

157 Robert Graves & Company wallpaper bill, 1880. This decor is recorded in the circa 1892 hall photograph.

158 The Robert Graves & Company wall decor, c. 1892.

The installation of the scenic panels currently on the west wall may have occurred at that time. Unused rolls of the paper are preserved in RCHS collections.

The newspaper article perpetuates the mistaken identification of the paper by referring to it as *Le Zone*. The actual title of the paper is *Eldorado*. This is confirmed by an inscription (Zuber et Cie 1849) worked into the block printed design and found on the section of paper that wraps around the curved wall surface at the north end of the hall. *Eldorado* was produced in 1848–49 while *Le Zone* dates to 1855.

103   Front Parlor

The front parlor is the largest room in the house (17'¼" × 23'10") and with the slightly smaller matching parlor immediately to the west, forms a suite of elegantly detailed formal rooms for the use of family and guests (Fig. 159).

In plan, the rectangular room includes a pair of tall window openings in the east wall, a single doorway in the south partition, a broad opening with sliding doors in the west partition, and a chimney breast and mantel centered on the north wall.

The superb woodwork and plaster work preserved in the two parlors exhibit the finest craftsmanship and design emanating from sources in New York City in the late Federal era. This architectural detailing may be the earliest example of a style that for a few brief years was fashionable in New York and other east coast locales. The woodwork with its boldly carved applied ornament, considered the last surviving evidence of the older Baroque tradition by architectural historian Talbot Hamlin, is represented in this parlor in its most refined form.

All of the superb original architectural treatment survives in this important room including the ornately detailed plaster work and wood trim. Features of note include the monumentally scaled architrave and pair of mahogany sliding doors in the west partition, the large plaster centerpiece partially recessed in the ceiling, and the handsome black Italian marble mantel. The now electrified gasolier, suspended in the center of the room, was installed for Betsey Hart in 1850 and is representative of the finest fixtures available at that time. Although the room was regularly redecorated by the Harts and Cluetts, it was not until 1910 that significant physical changes were made.

In 1910, the Albert Cluetts ended the long tradition of the use of wallpaper and installed a wall treatment consisting of painted canvas embellished with an arrangement of applied panels above a new chair rail. Prior to this change, the George Cluetts had installed a hardwood floor ending the necessity of fully covering the floor surface with wall-to-wall carpeting.

A remarkable body of documentation survives concerning the decoration and furnishing of the front parlor; beginning with the 1844 inventory, Hart Papers spanning some 50 years, a partial description of the room in 1855, the very detailed 1886 inventory as well as photographs from circa 1892, 1904, and 1934. The 1886 inventory is particularly effective when compared to items shown in the two circa 1892 photographs of the room (see Appendix II B and Figs. 125 & 127). The Hart Papers, which for the parlor begin in 1843 with a payment for tuning the piano, continue through the nineteenth century recording purchases of furniture and

159 The front parlor (103), 1976.

decorative arts as well as paint and wallpaper. The records end in 1891 with a payment for tinting the parlor ceiling and regilding the cornice.

After RCHS occupied the house, beginning in January 1953, modifications made in the parlor included removal of Cluett era built-in bookcases from the south wall, rehabilitation of the 1850 chandelier and the removal of the Hart-era drapery cornices (in 1960), and removal of the overmantel mirror. The drapery cornices (minus the pier glass top) were installed in the second floor rear bed chamber (205) and the mirror was placed above the mantel in the reception room (109).

In its current transformation, the front parlor exhibits architectural features from the Hart and Cluett eras as well as furnishings formerly belonging to these families.

FLOOR

The floor is finished in narrow 2¼" wide × ⅜" thick strips of tongue-and-groove oak, laid east/west and dating to the George Cluett era. This surface is shown with a dark finish in a 1904 photograph of the parlor. The original

wide board flooring (1⅜" thick) survives beneath this surface. The location of the Cluett bookcases can be discerned on the floor surface next to the south wall.

WALLS

All four walls are finished in original plaster on wood lath and at the chimney breast plaster on brick masonry. The lath is furred out from brick masonry at the north and east walls. These plaster surfaces have always been covered by wallpaper and are now covered in painted canvas. A 3" wide classically detailed wood chair rail is positioned at 31" above the floor. Above the rail, the canvas-covered walls are divided into simulated paneled surfaces by 1½" wide moldings. The moldings, the chair rail, and the canvas finish were installed by the Albert Cluetts.

Along the south wall, there is evidence for a pair of double built-in bookcases recorded in a 1934 photograph of the room. When the cases were removed by RCHS sometime after 1952, it was necessary to install additional chair rail molding and add to the panel moldings which were missing from these locations.

CEILING

The original plaster-on-lath ceiling is about 13'7" above the floor and the original large molded plaster centerpiece is positioned in its center (see Fig. 97). The circular medallion features a recessed center with a central rosette of applied cast-plaster acanthus leaves. The recess is surrounded by a lace-like filigree band and by concentric double rings in a reeded pattern entwined in a molded grapevine motif. This impressive ceiling ornament is approximately 5' in diameter. The design for a similarly detailed centerpiece is found in Plate 27 of Asher Benjamin's *The American Builder's Companion* published in 1806 (see Fig. 98).

BASEBOARD

The original wood baseboard, approximately 11¾" high, is composed of a tall (7") stepped fascia topped by a reverse ogee with astragal crownmold.

CORNICE

All four walls retain the original plaster cornice composed of a run-in-place ground and applied cast-plaster elements including egg-and-dart moldings, acanthus leaves, rosettes, and stylized flowers. A similar but later variation of this cornice exists in the parlors of the Seabury Tredwell House in New York City.

DOORS

There are two original openings in the parlor: a single doorway in the south partition (D1031) and the impressively scaled opening with a pair of sliding doors (D1032) centered in the west partition. Each opening retains the original architrave, door, and door hardware. The south doorway features the typical architrave used throughout the house including the symmetrically

160 Bold carving ornaments the center tablet of this door architrave in the front parlor (D1031).

molded trim (5½" wide) with tripartite reeding and corner blocks with applied carved wood raffle flowers. The trim rests on tall plinths with recessed panels set with a three-lobed motif. A unique feature of the parlor architraves is the rectangular center tablet with boldly carved acanthus appliqués (Fig. 160).

The grandly conceived architectural wooden architrave of the opening fitted with sliding doors (D1032) consists of a pair of tall fluted Ionic columns resting on paneled plinths and supporting an elaborate five-part lintel. Above the Ionic capitals, there are box-like elements ornamented by large carved raffle flowers and topped by an acanthus band. A similarly detailed rectangular center panel features a symmetrically-formed acanthus branch. Additional trailing vines flank this panel. An inner architrave, surrounding the door opening, features a series of small and large elongated rectangular panels. A jarring feature of this otherwise symmetrical arrangement of panels occurs at the head of the opening. There the small center panel is offset to the north of the center of the opening. This visual "mistake" in the fabrication of this impressive piece of carpentry supports the notion that this and other trim elements in the house were fabricated off site, probably in a New York City carpenter's or cabinet maker's shop (Fig. 161). Similarities to still-extant work in the Albany Academy (1816) produced by Henry Farnham make it likely that he developed the style and may have supplied the ornament and possibly the entire architrave from New York City where he worked after 1819.

The prefabricated architrave, shipped to the construction site for installation, would have been difficult to correct if a mistake in detailing was made. Curiously, the same problem occurs on the back parlor face of this architrave. Visually, the parlor architrave features the same components as a contemporary trabeated fireplace mantel piece, but on a much larger scale.

> D1031: This opening retains the original eight-panel, stile-and-rail mahogany door which is 3'3" wide × 7'10" high. The recessed panels are trimmed with a ¾" wide quirk ovolo molding.
>
> Hardware: Original fittings include a pair of 5½" × 5½" cast-iron butt hinges with silver-plated covers, a mortice lock with a 7⅞" × ⅞" silver-plated face, two 2⅛" diameter silvered brass knobs and roses and two silvered brass drop cover escutcheons. Although there are no markings on the hardware,

161 Door opening (D1032) joining the parlors.

it matches other original household hardware stamped "w pye n-york patent." (see Fig. 103)

D1032: A pair of impressively large eight-panel, stile-and-rail mahogany sliding doors are 3'6½" wide × 9'11' high × 1¾" thick. The doors slide on a brass floor track into pockets centered in the reveal of the opening. Their finish is in remarkable original condition since the doors were generally kept hidden within the wall pockets.

Hardware: Original fittings include a silvered brass edging on the south leaf, a 7⅝" silvered mortise latch, two pairs of silvered brass knobs and roses and silvered drop cover escutcheons. An iron stop is centered at the head of the opening.

WINDOWS

There are two original window openings symmetrically positioned in the east wall. The tall window recesses have architraves composed of the typical symmetrically molded trim and corner blocks with carved raffle flowers. The openings are fitted with original very large six-over-six double rope-hung sash which have ¹¹/₁₆" wide muntins and fourteen ¾" × 24" panes. Below the sills

there is a single-panel apron. The deep window recesses are fitted with pairs of two-tier paneled bifold shutters. The shutters retain original cast-iron hinges and brass latches (lower tier only). Seven of the separate sections have small brass knobs of recent origin (the eighth knob is missing). Each shutter pocket has two recessed panels.

HEATING

Heated air enters the room through a 16½" × 24" white enameled cast-iron Rococo pattern floor register positioned near the southwest corner. This feature probably dates to the 1850s, but is definitely post-1846 when a Fox and Company patent air furnace was installed in the house. Originally, the room was heated by the fireplace. The firebox was fitted with a coal grate but evidence for this object was lost when a new soapstone lining was installed in the fireplace after 1893.

LIGHTING

A lighting device has always been positioned at the center of the ceiling where the elaborate plaster centerpiece serves as the point of suspension (Fig. 162). The six-arm

162 This ornate gasolier, now electrified, has remained in the front parlor (103) since 1850.

ormolu brass electrified gasolier is elaborately detailed in Rococo scrolls and floral motifs and the six branches terminate in winged griffons. Six ornate chains provide additional embellishment above each arm.

This and a matching fixture in the back parlor (104) were purchased by Betsey Hart in New York City from Peirce and King in 1850. They were manufactured by Cornelius and Son of Philadelphia. Both fixtures may have been electrified after 1910 for the Albert Cluetts, although 1934 photographs record what appear to be large candles positioned in platelike holders installed in the position of the original gas burners. The current condition of the chandelier, including the awkward attachment to the ceiling, results from work carried out by RCHS after 1952.

The 1850 gas fixture replaced a chandelier, possibly of the argand burner type, that probably dated to the earliest years of the Hart occupancy and is included in the 1844 inventory.

FIREPLACE

A 6'7¾" wide × 10" deep plastered masonry chimney breast is centered on the north wall. The original black and gold Italian marble mantel is composed of a pair of smooth tapered columns topped by Ionic capitals supporting a deep lintel composed of paneled end blocks and a central paneled tablet. The mantel shelf, with a molded edge, is 4'6½" above the floor. The mantel is positioned against a background of white grey-veined marble. The firebox and hearth are formed of slabs of grey soapstone which date to the Cluett occupancy and replace the Hart-era materials.

The white marble surfaces flanking the mantel include holes at 27", 29", 30", and 33" above the floor, for the placement of two different sets of fire tool brackets. A circa 1892 Hart-era photograph records a pair of brass brackets with urn-like finials. A 1934 photograph illustrates a different pair of brackets which have ball finials. Currently, there are no brackets in these locations.

FURNISHINGS AND FITTINGS

The evolving decor of the front parlor is recorded in documents and photographs from the Hart and Cluett eras over a span of ninety years. Significant inventories survive from 1844 and 1886 and the reminiscence of 1855 provides important information concerning colors and textile types. Two remarkable sets of photographs dating to circa 1892 and 1934 record the very different treat-

ment of the parlor by the Harts and Cluetts. The Hart Papers provide an important record of the room's changing decor from 1843 to 1891, with insights into the evolution of American taste during the second half of the nineteenth century.

First decorated and furnished in 1827, likely with objects acquired beginning in 1816, the parlor included almost nothing from the early years when it was photographed circa 1892. The overmantel mirror provided by Matthew Marshall, New York City looking glass manufacturer, and an extraordinary pair of cut glass argand girandoles positioned on the mantel may date to the earliest years of the Hart marriage and appear to be the only early furnishings remaining in the room at that time.

The 1844 inventory combines the contents of the front and back parlors, but it is possible to extract some of the furnishings used in the front parlor from this extensive list. Likely furnishings used here include a sofa (possibly the circa 1816 sofa from Duncan Phyfe's shop which at one time belonged to the Griswold family, Hart descendants and which was sold at Christie's on January 24, 1987), a piano and stool, a center table, pier table, window seats, curtains and fixtures, and a chandelier. Additional objects from the list used in the parlor could include various chairs and lighting devices. Two mirrors, valued at $50.00, may have flanked the mantel in the north wall. The large circular convex mirror, now located in the dining room (106), may be one of a pair of mirrors used here. Stylistically dating to about the time of Richard and Betsey's marriage, this valuable object may have been an important part of the decoration of the parlor. In 1851, two oval mirrors in the then fashionable Rococo style were placed in this prominent position flanking the fireplace.

The chandelier, included in the 1844 document, was likely an argand (oil fueled) fixture of the most fashionable type.

The "lamp girandoles" included in the inventory may be the extraordinary cut glass argand lighting devices positioned on the mantel shelf in the circa 1892 photograph (see Fig. 127). These appear to be the only objects that may have remained in the parlor throughout the Hart occupancy.

Elizabeth Shields Eddy's reminiscence of the room as it appeared in 1855 refers to a long mirror (pier) between the windows and carved rosewood furniture covered in crimson satin or damask with curtains to match. In summer, the chairs and sofas were covered in red-striped white linen.

This description reflects a very different room from the one provided by furnishing lists in the 1844 inventory. Beginning in the late 1840s, Betsey Hart began to update the parlor to reflect the newly fashionable Rococo style. Many of these changes were recorded in the circa 1892 photograph.

A rosewood parlor suite (Fig. 163) was purchased in 1849 from the fashionable New York City cabinetmaker Charles A. Baudouine (see Figs. 41 & 42). In 1850, Peirce and King provided the elaborate ormolu gasolier. In the same year, A. T. Stewart and Company of New York supplied the satin damask curtains and fittings and Elijah Galusha provided impressive gilt cornices and a "glass top" that extended across the length of the east wall. At the same time, two matching oval mirrors were purchased from the same cabinetmaker. A large payment made to Galusha in 1847 may have included the two tall pier mirrors, one located here and one positioned in the back parlor. The 1850 "glass top" was made to fit on the top of the pier mirror frame purchased earlier. In 1858, the final touch to this fashionable Rococo decor was provided by the wall-to-wall Aubusson carpet purchased from Rinquet-LePrince and Marcotte of New York.

The very detailed 1886 inventory apparently records all of the furnishings found in the front parlor including the many small objects d'art scattered throughout the room (see Appendix IIB). This list, coupled with the circa 1892 photograph, provides a remarkable record of the room as it evolved during the last 40 years of the Hart family's occupancy. Mention of many of these items can be found in the surviving Hart financial records. Important decorations include an elaborate porcelain centerpiece and a pair of "Huntsmen" figures purchased from Allcock and Allen of New York in 1850 as well as two oil paintings. "Sunday Morning" was purchased in 1858 from Henry H. Leeds and Company of New York and a landscape by William E. Brown was purchased from Thomas A. Wilhurt of New York.

The circa 1892 photograph records the square piano purchased from I. W. Andrews in 1848 for $400.00 as well as the large overmantel mirror (now located in the back parlor) with the label of Mathew Marshall, 174 Fulton Street, New York.

Close inspection of the Hart photograph reveals the "blocks for sofa" (small blocks positioned behind the

163 Detail, the Baudouine suite in the front parlor (103), c. 1892.

rear legs of the sofa to prevent it from rubbing the wall-paper) provided by the Troy firm Green and Waterman in 1878.

Prominent in the photo is the treatment of the black marble mantel. The shelf is upholstered in a tufted and fringed lambrequin and the firebox opening is covered in a matching grate screen. These were provided by Green and Waterman in 1873.

Centered on the mantel shelf are small framed photographic copies of portraits of Richard and Betsey Hart. An engraved portrait of Betsey, late in her life, is framed and hung from the north column of the opening between the two parlors. The frame is draped with a withered vine forming a memorial to the departed mistress of the house.

A single photograph taken in 1904 records the front parlor as it appeared during the period that George and Amanda Cluett occupied the house (Fig. 164). Although furnishings have been removed and the room is

decorated with greenery and flowers for Beatrice Cluett's debut party, there is much evidence for the room's decor as developed for the Cluett family.

The hardwood flooring is partially covered by a large oriental rug. Important Hart-era furnishings remain in situ including the pier mirror, the elaborate Rococo style drapery cornice, and the gasolier installed in 1850.

A framed picture appears to be positioned above the mantel indicating that the Hart-era overmantel mirror has been moved; in fact, it was located in the reception room (109) at this time.

In 1934, a series of photographs were taken of the front and back parlors. Two of these views duplicate the front parlor views dating to circa 1892 which look toward the northwest and southwest (see Figs. 126 & 128).

The decor created by Albert and Caroline Cluett is very much the product of early twentieth century concepts of comfort and informality and includes an eclec-

164 The front parlor (103) viewed from the back parlor, 1904.

165 Front parlor (103) looking east, 1934.

tic array of new and antique furniture. A single color cut-pile rug covers most of the hardwood floor surface. The furniture, including a large sofa and baby grand piano, is placed about the large room in an informal manner. Included in the parlor are new pieces, generally comfortable chairs and a three-cushion sofa, as well as antique furnishings. The Hart-era gasolier remains in place but large out-of-scale, wax candles have replaced the gas fittings and glass shades used by the Harts and George Cluetts.

Above the black marble mantel there is a large gilt framed curved-top overmantel mirror. This may be the mantel glass purchased for the library (109) from Galusha in 1859 and possibly relocated here by the Albert Cluetts. A significant aspect of the parlor is provided by the pair of built-in and painted bookcases that are positioned against the south partition. The position of these cases can still be seen on the flooring along that wall. The installation of the bookcases may coincide with the placement of the panel moldings on the wall surfaces for the Albert Cluetts.

The 1934 parlor photograph looking toward the east wall reveals that the 1851 gilt drapery cornices and pier

mirror tops still dominate that end of the room. The pairs of drapery cloak pins that hold back the curtains in the photo may also survive from the Hart-era installation (Fig. 165).

The parlor walls retain evidence for the placement of objects on those surfaces. Single marks at about 9'3" above the floor can be seen centered in the north wall surfaces flanking the fireplace. These marks represent the placement of the two large oval mirrors provided by Galusha in 1851. One of these impressive objects remains in the RCHS collections and was a gift of Miss Juliette Shields in 1949 probably in anticipation of RCHS occupancy of the house. Measurements of the large eagle-topped convex mirror now located in the dining room (106) indicate that it and a possible long-lost mate (the two mirrors in the 1844 inventory) could also fit in the same location.

The chimney breast retains evidence for the attachment of the curved-top mirror used by the Albert Cluetts now located in the former library (109) and some markings for the height (83") of the large square Hart-era mantel mirror now located in the rear parlor (104). Evidence for the placement of all of the objects used here by the Harts and Cluetts survives under the canvas wall covering and behind the pier mirror.

Inspection of the tall pier mirror and the top surfaces of the window architraves that flank the mirror revealed evidence for the attachments of the Hart-era drapery cornices and mirror top (see Fig. 31). Small square holes, located above each architrave corner block formerly held the iron brackets that supported the cornices. The pier mirror is secured to the wall by two iron brackets that extend into the plaster wall surface and are fastened to the top of the frame by screws. A square mortise hole in the top of the mirror frame relates to a drapery treatment that predates the 1851 Galusha cornice.

The room today retains two important Hart-era furnishings that have always remained in situ; the pier mirror with its corresponding marble shelf and the ornate gasolier. It also now contains a number of objects returned by Hart and Cluett descendants.

FINISHES INVESTIGATION

The changing decor of the parlor is recorded by various documents, photographs, and physical evidence.

Analysis of the woodwork including the elaborate architrave centered in the west partition revealed that those surfaces have always been finished in a yellowish/white or white paint. There are approximately 10 layers of finishes. Elizabeth Shields Eddy recalled white woodwork and polished mahogany doors.

Hart family financial records contain numerous references to painting, but it has not been possible to determine specifically when the parlor woodwork was painted.

The plaster ceiling, cornice, and centerpiece have always been finished in white paint. An 1849 account refers to "whitening ceiling" by D. H. Wellington and the same painter was whitening the cornice in 1850. The circa 1892 parlor photograph reveals that the cornice and centerpiece had some details picked out in a dark finish. Samples from these surfaces revealed that the finish was gold leaf. This treatment was probably first applied by W. W. Whitman in 1872 when twenty-three books of gold leaf were used as part of the redecoration of the parlor. In 1891, Thomas Buckley of Albany was paid for tinting the parlor ceiling and regilding the cornice. These finishes are seen in the 1892 photograph.

The plaster wall surfaces were investigated for evidence of finishes. Until the Albert Cluett era, beginning in 1910, the wall surfaces were always covered in wallpa-

per. The Hart family records indicate that extensive use of wallpaper occurred throughout the house during the nineteenth century. The earliest documented use of this treatment in the parlor occurred in 1851 when eighteen pieces of paper and thirty yards of border paper, purchased from Solomon and Hart of New York, were installed by D. H. Wellington. This undertaking was part of an extensive redecoration of the front parlor which began 1849 when a suite of rosewood furniture was purchased from Charles Baudoine followed by the installation of the ormolu gasolier (1850) and the installation of the gilt drapery cornices and oval mirrors supplied by Elijah Galusha in 1851. If a large payment to Galusha in 1847 included the parlor pier mirrors, then the parlor redecoration actually began a few years earlier.

The parlor was again redecorated in 1872 under the guidance of L. Marcotte and Company of New York which supplied twenty-two rolls of pearl ground white and gold figured paper. W. W. Whitman installed this paper along with 234' of gold leafed molding. This is the decor recorded in the circa 1892 photographs (see Figs. 125 & 127). The glint of gold leaf can be seen on the narrow gessoed wood moldings that outline the wall surfaces above the base, beneath the cornice, and in the corners.

An investigation behind the upper end of the pier mirror revealed fragments of a late nineteenth century wallpaper on the east wall. The soiled white plaster wall surface retained paste residue and an embossed floral pattern paper featuring a yellow ground with pink flowers and mica highlights. This is probably the paper recorded in the 1904 photograph of the parlor as decorated for George and Amanda Cluett's daughter's debut (see Fig. 164). Further probing behind the mirror may reveal additional evidence concerning the earlier wall treatments.

The Albert Cluetts had the wallpaper removed from the parlor walls. The plaster surfaces were covered in painters' canvas, producing a stable surface for the application of paint. The wall surfaces were ornamented with narrow 1½" wide moldings forming a series of simulated panels above the chair rail installed at the same time. This treatment is illustrated in the series of parlor photographs taken in 1934 and survives in situ today (see Figs. 126 & 128).

The removal of the built-in bookcases, formerly positioned against the south partition, by RCHS necessitated the addition of moldings to the bottom portion of two of the wall panels.

104   Back Parlor

The back parlor is slightly smaller (16'1" × 21'1½") than the adjoining front parlor but duplicates the architectural details of the larger room. The Harts may have considered the front parlor as a formal space for guests while this room was used by the family for day-to-day activity (Figs. 166 & 167).

In plan, the rectangular room includes a pair of tall window openings in the west wall, a single doorway in the south partition, a broad opening with sliding doors in the east partition, and chimney breast and mantel centered on the north wall.

All of the superb original architectural details survive in the parlor with the exception of one of the original pair of symmetrically positioned doorways in the south partition. This southwest opening was removed in 1964 by RCHS. There is documentary evidence that the mahogany door was removed to the opening of what is now the RCHS main office (109) and that the ornamental corner blocks and center tablet from the architrave were incorporated into door trim in other rooms.

Elizabeth Shields Eddy indicates in her reminiscence of the house in 1855 that, "On the right, as you entered [the house], was the front parlor . . . , and back of that, with sliding doors between, which were never closed, the back parlor." For the Harts, both parlors were very much one space although the front room was more formally furnished than its counterpart at the back of the house.

During the Hart era the decor of the parlor evolved, and included changes in wallpaper as well as the carpet, furnishings, and the chandelier. However, it was the

Cluett families that made the first architectural changes in the room. Hardwood flooring was installed by the George Cluetts and the paneled wall treatment, which included the chair rail, was installed for the Albert Cluetts. Finally, in 1964, the above-mentioned doorway to the service hall (105) was removed by RCHS.

An important body of documentation survives detailing the decoration and furnishing of the back parlor. There are two Hart-era inventories (1844 and 1886), Elizabeth Shields Eddy's reminiscence of her childhood visit in 1855 as well as photographic images recording the room in circa 1892, 1904, and 1934.

It should be noted that Elizabeth Shields Eddy's description of the house has proved to be quite accurate based on confirming evidence in other documents including the extraordinary collection of Hart family financial records spanning the years between the 1840s and 1892.

The earliest reference to the back parlor in the documents occurs in 1850 when the Cornelius and Son gasolier was provided by Peirce and King and a rosewood etagere was purchased from Alexander Roux. Both of these furnishings are recorded in the 1886 inventory and the etagere is visible in the circa 1892 photograph. One of the last references is a July 1889 payment to Louis Muller for putting up the draperies and lace curtains, also illustrated in the Hart-era photograph. The 1934 photographs record the room as it was arranged for Albert and Caroline Cluett. The Historic American Buildings Survey (HABS) floor plans of the house, produced in the same year, indicate that the back parlor served as a library and the photographs show three large bookcases lining the walls of the room. These finely made cabinets remain in the RCHS collection.

166 Back parlor (104) looking west, 1976.

167 Back parlor (104), looking northeast, 1976.

After RCHS occupied the house, beginning in January 1953, the bookcases were eventually removed for use in the Society's library, formerly located in basement room B10. From 1963 to 1965 the library was housed in the southeast second floor bedroom (209). In 1965, it was relocated to the northeast basement room (B02). In 1969, it was placed in basement room B10. The bookcases may have been used in all of these locations. The Cluett panel moldings were removed from the walls in 1964 but the chair rail was retained. It was probably RCHS that wired the gasolier for electricity.

The current appearance of the back parlor generally dates from the 1964 restoration, and includes architectural features from the Hart and Cluett eras. It is furnished with important examples of the work of Elijah Galusha as well as the Hart overmantel mirror originally located in the front parlor.

FLOOR

The floor is finished in narrow 2¼" wide strips of tongue-and-groove oak, laid east/west and dating to the George Cluett era. Now a honey color, this surface has a dark finish in the 1904 photograph. The original wide-board floor surface exists under this surface.

WALLS

All four walls are finished in original plaster on wood lath except at the chimney breast which is of plaster applied to brick masonry. The lath is furred out from the brick walls enclosing the north and west sides of the room. Painted canvas now covers the plaster surfaces which formerly were covered in wallpaper.

A 3" wide classically detailed wood chair rail is positioned at 31" above the floor. There is evidence on the wall surfaces above the rails for the placement of narrow moldings formed into a series of large panels. These moldings were removed by RCHS. The chair rail and panel moldings were installed for Albert and Caroline Cluett in 1910 or slightly later.

The location for an original doorway, removed by RCHS in 1964, can be detected at the west end of the south partition. This doorway opened to the service hall (105). The chair rail along the south partition was installed by RCHS after the doorway was removed.

CEILING

The original plaster-on-lath ceiling is about 13'7" above the floor. The original large molded plaster centerpiece is positioned in the ceiling. The partially recessed medallion duplicates the centerpiece located in the front parlor.

BASEBOARD

The original wood baseboard, approximately 11¾" high, is composed of a tall (7") stepped fascia topped by a reverse ogee with astragal crownmold. A short section of reproduction base is installed in the location of the doorway removed by RCHS in 1964.

CORNICE

All four walls retain the original plaster cornice composed of a run-in-place ground and applied cast-plaster elements. All details duplicate those used in the front parlor.

DOORS

There are two original openings in the parlor: a single doorway in the south partition (D1041) and the large opening with a pair of sliding doors (D1032) centered in the east partition. Each opening retains its original architrave, door, and door hardware. A third original opening, removed by RCHS in 1964, was located in the south partition and matched doorway D1041 in detail. The door was hinged to the east joint and opened into the parlor. It provided access to the service hall (105).

The architraves of both extant openings match those found in the front parlor and feature the same boldly carved applied wood ornaments including raffle flowers and acanthus vines. The mantel-like architrave of the opening in the east partition duplicates the details found on the front parlor face of the opening. The irregular spacing of the small panels at the top of the opening is also duplicated, again indicating the probable off-site fabrication of this important piece of woodwork.

> D1041: This opening retains the original eight-panel, stile-and-rail mahogany door which is 3'3¾" wide × 7'10" high × 1⅝" thick. The recessed panels are trimmed with a ¾" wide quirk ovolo molding.
>
> Hardware: Original fittings include a pair of 5½" × 5½' cast-iron butt hinges with silver plated covers, a mortise lock with a 7⅝" × ⅞" silver plated face, two 2⅛" diameter silvered brass knobs and roses and two silvered drop cover escutcheons. These unmarked fittings match the marked William Pye

hardware used on the dining room doors. (see Fig. 103)

D1042: This door, architrave and opening were removed by RCHS. The center tablet from the architrave was installed on the hall (102) face of doorway D1062. The corner blocks were placed at opening D1102 in the back passage (110). The location of the doorway is visible in the south wall of the parlor and the north wall of the service hall (105). The modification was carried out by Wilson Large in November 1964. The mahogany door was installed in the opening to the library-reception room (109). The original door for that opening was removed by the George Cluetts and apparently lost.

D1032: The description of this important opening and pair of sliding (pocket) doors is included with the front parlor analysis.

WINDOWS

There are two original window openings symmetrically positioned in the west wall.

The tall window recesses have architraves composed of the typical symmetrically molded trim and corner blocks with carved raffle flowers. The openings are fitted with original six-over-six double rope-hung sash which have 11/16" wide muntins and fourteen ¾" × 24" panes. A single panel apron is located below the sill. Pairs of two-tier paneled bifold shutters are positioned in the pockets flanking the sash. The shutters retain original cast-iron hinges and brass latches (on the lower tier). Small brass knobs of recent origin are used to open the lower tier of shutters.

HEATING

Heated air enters the room through a 16½" × 24" white enameled cast-iron Rococo patterned floor register positioned in the southeast corner. This fitting dates to the 1850s. Originally, the parlor was heated by the fireplace which was fitted with a coal grate. Evidence for the grate was lost when a soapstone lining was installed after 1893.

LIGHTING

The impressive ceiling centerpiece has always been the location for a suspended lighting device. The six-arm ormolu brass electrified gasolier is identical to the fixture located in the front parlor. Both fixtures were supplied by Peirce and King in 1850 and were manufactured by Cornelius and Son of Philadelphia. Both chandeliers include an additional gas cock hidden within the fixture to which a table lamp can be attached by a hose. The 1850 fixture replaced the chandelier included in the 1844 inventory. That fixture was probably of the argand type and dated to circa 1827.

The 1934 photographs show the gasolier fitted with six large wax candles. Apparently, the fixture was not yet wired for electricity which may have been carried out after 1952 by RCHS.

EQUIPMENT

A servant's electric call button, set in a turned wood frame, is positioned on the south wall immediately east of Door D1041 at 50" above the floor. It probably dates to the George Cluett era or possibly 1890 when three battery powered electric bells were installed for Sarah Wool Hart.

FIREPLACE

A 6'7¾" wide × 10" deep plastered masonry chimney breast is centered on the north wall. The original black and gold Italian marble mantel is identical to the one located in the front parlor. The firebox and hearth are formed of slabs of grey soapstone which date to the Cluett eras. There is evidence on the back surface of the firebox that it held a fire and the 1934 photograph shows logs in the fireplace. The white marble surfaces flanking the mantel include two sets of holes for the placement of fire tool brackets. The 1934 photograph illustrates a bracket that matches the Cluett-era fitting used in the front parlor. Brackets of a different design were used by the Harts.

FURNISHINGS AND FITTINGS

Like the front parlor, the evolving decor of this room is recorded in documents and photographs from the Hart and Cluett eras. Significant inventories survive from 1844 and 1886 and the reminiscence of 1855 provides information concerning colors and textiles. Photographs from circa 1892, 1904, and 1934 record changes from the Hart era through the occupancy of Albert and Caroline Cluett (see Figs. 125, 127, 164, 126, 169).

The Hart Papers provide a detailed picture of the evolution of the back parlor's decor from the 1840s to 1891. The parlor was first decorated and furnished in 1827, probably with objects from the Harts' previous

168 Back parlor (104), as viewed from the front parlor, c. 1892.

residence at 49 Second Street. Some items likely dated to their marriage in 1816. Only a few possessions from the earliest years can be seen in the circa 1892 photographs.

The most significant documented early furnishing in the back parlor that may date to 1827 is the extraordinary drapery support pole visible in the circa 1892 photographs (Fig. 168). Consisting of a large central wreath positioned above the later (circa 1847) pier mirror, and including flanking tendril-like curved arms that reach to the north and south walls, this extravagant fitting supported voluminous drapery and heavy tassels and ropes.

In her 1855 reminiscence, Elizabeth Shields Eddy refers to the "large gilt wreath with curved arms extending over the windows . . . the draperies were hung in soft, graceful folds." She records the use of maroon velvet and dark red winter draperies in the back parlor. A window treatment of similar design is illustrated in the broadside advertisement issued by Joseph Meeks and Sons of New York City in 1833.

A payment made to Green and Waterman in 1883 for laundering two pairs of antique curtains may be a reference to the longevity of this window treatment. This elaborate drapery support or a duplicate may have

originally been placed in the front parlor only to be removed in 1851 when Elijah Galusha supplied newly stylish Rococo cornices for the front windows. The inclusion of a matching "glass top" (the unit placed above the pier mirror with the new cornices) was necessary due to the possible loss of the wreath and drapery that may have formerly concealed the unornamented mirror frame. Investigation of the top surface of the pier mirror in the front parlor revealed a mortise hole that does not relate to the installation of the Galusha "glass top" but may have held the support for the wreath. A similar hole exists in the top of the frame of the back parlor pier mirror. Both pier mirrors may date to a large payment made to Galusha in 1847. They were definitely installed in the two parlors sometime after the 1844 inventory was made and before 1851. The Rococo detailing of the shelves at the bottom of each mirror suggests a late 1840s date for these important furnishings.

Another early furnishing, visible in the circa 1892 photograph, is a fine French clock positioned under a glass dome on the mantel (Fig. 127). The gilt bronze timepiece is of classical form and includes a standing female figure. It stylistically dates to the early years of the nineteenth century and may well be one of the furnishings acquired at the time of Richard and Betsey's marriage in 1816.

The 1844 inventory includes a clock in one of the parlors and the 1886 document lists a gilt mantel clock in the back parlor, probably the object seen in the photograph. Rebecca Howard also owned a French clock (it was cleaned in 1857) but it was in the back bed chamber (206) in the 1886 inventory, the same time that the gilt mantel clock was located here.

A Grecian armchair with boldly scrolled arms is visible in the 1886 view. This circa 1830 chair is currently in the collections of RCHS (71:95.1.11) and was a gift from Ruth Hart Eddy, a Hart descendant. It may be the hair cloth arm chair reupholstered by Green and Waterman in 1889. The slip seat still features black hair cloth.

The 1844 inventory includes the contents of the front and back parlors in a single listing but it is possible to extract some of the items likely used here. These include a carpet (wall-to-wall), a pier table, a sideboard, curtains and fixtures, a chandelier, and a clock. Other furnishings from the long list might include the sofa or two couches, several of the chairs, and possibly the rocking chair. The pier table may be the marble top table shown in the dining room in the 1892 photograph. Its removal to that room may have occurred when the pier mirrors were installed in the late 1840s.

The 1886 inventory is very specific and includes some forty furnishings and objects in the back parlor (see Appendix II b). Permanent furnishings include the chandelier, carpet, pier mirror, and brocade curtains with lambrequins suspended from the impressive snake-like pole. There were several rosewood chairs and two sofas covered in plush and an oval rosewood center table. The rosewood etagere was positioned on the north wall to the left of the mantel. It was probably the very expensive richly carved and mirrored etagere purchased from Alexander Roux of New York in 1850.

The Neo-Grec-style gas chandelier, visible in the 1886 photograph, may be the six-light fixture with etched globes, purchased from Ball, Black and Company of New York in 1866. When this new fixture was installed, the 1850 Rococo style fixture was probably moved to the dining room where it was recorded in the 1892 photograph.

A small gas table lamp, visible in the photograph, is probably the "drop light" included in the inventory. There are two oil paintings noted in the inventory, and both are landscapes. One was positioned above the sofa on the south wall, the other above the mantel.

The inventory as well as visual evidence provided by the circa 1892 photograph indicates that the back parlor was less formal than the adjoining room. The collection of furnishings was more eclectic, including pieces both formal and informal, old and new. The back parlor was what we today would call the living room, the space most frequented by the family.

The only clue concerning the appearance of the back parlor as furnished by George and Amanda Cluett comes from the 1904 photograph that shows only a portion of the east wall of the room, but records the full length of the front parlor. Most of the furnishings are removed from the front room which is shown filled with flowers and greenery. The wall surface of the back space is covered in a boldly patterned abstract floral wallpaper. South of the columned opening in the east partition, there are two framed photographs; the larger image may be of George Cluett.

The 1934 photographs record the front and back parlors in great detail. The back space, noted as the library on the 1934 HABS drawings of the house, is dominated by three large mahogany glass-doored bookcases, one

169 The back parlor (104), looking northeast, 1934.

positioned against the south wall and a pair flanking the mantel (Fig. 169). These large case pieces remain in the RCHS collections. The room is comfortably outfitted with several pieces of upholstered seat furniture including a large three cushion sofa (its mate is located in the front parlor) and several lamps including a floor lamp. The Hart pier mirror remains in situ as does the 1850 gasolier which is shown with six large wax candles. The two rear windows include simple pairs of tied back curtains suspended from drapery cornices which may date to the nineteenth century. In 1960, these cornices were modified by Gunther's Frame and Art Shop of Troy to fit the windows in the former Cluett sitting room (111). A color slide shows these cornices in use in that space in 1961.

The RCHS has used the back parlor to display a significant collection of furniture produced by the outstanding Troy cabinetmaker, Elijah Galusha (1804–1871). The room retains the original Hart-era pier mirror as well as the 1850 gasolier. The large overmantel mirror, used by the Harts in the front parlor, is also located here. Dominating the room from its position on the south wall is the very large full-length portrait of Benjamin Marshall painted by Abel Buell Moore. This significant work was originally located at Troy's Marshall Infirmary and was placed here in November, 1964.

FINISH INVESTIGATION

The changing decor of the back parlor is recorded by various documents, photographs, and physical evidence. Analysis of the woodwork revealed that the surfaces have always been finished in a yellowish/white or white paint. There are approximately ten layers of finishes on the trim. Elizabeth Shields Eddy recalled white woodwork and polished mahogany doors.

The plaster ceiling, cornice and centerpiece retain evidence of the application of white paint and the Hart financial records include several references to "whitening" ceilings. In 1850, D. H. Wellington made use of lemon-colored paint, possibly on the ceiling or cornice of this room. The ceiling was again whitened in 1854. The gold leaf detailing visible on the cornice in the circa 1892 photos may have been applied by W. W. Whitman in 1872 when he used 23 books of leaf as part of the redecoration of the front parlor.

The plaster wall surfaces were investigated for evidence of finishes. The plaster surface under the painted canvas applied during the Albert Cluetts era is soiled but unpainted. The surface retains traces of paper and paste. Apparently, the walls have always been papered. A small fragment of a wood pulp paper retains traces of a gold or copper leaf finish. This is probably the boldly patterned paper installed for the George Cluetts and recorded in a 1904 photograph (see Fig. 164).

The circa 1892 photographs record the back parlor as seen through the opened sliding doors. The walls are papered in a light ground damask-like pattern of a repeating stylized floral motif. A narrow (approximately 6" deep) border appears as a dark band below the cornice. A very narrow molding may separate the border from the wallpaper. It has proven impossible to determine which of the accounts of wallpaper purchases and installation included in the Hart Papers relate to this room.

The Albert Cluetts had all traces of previous wallpaper removed and the plaster surfaces were covered with painters' canvas. This surface was then decorated with narrow 1½" wide moldings forming a series of simulated panels above a newly applied chair rail. This treatment is recorded in the 1934 photographs.

In 1964, the panel moldings were removed by RCHS but the Cluett chair rail was retained and all surfaces were painted white.

105 Service Hall (Former Pantry)

This long narrow 5' wide passage has functioned in various ways for the Harts, Cluetts, and RCHS. In plan, the

170 Looking west through the door opening (D1101) in the original back wall of the 1827 house.

rectangular space includes doorways filling the east and west walls and prior to 1964 a doorway in the north wall.

As originally completed in 1827, this area functioned as a passage or hall leading from the stair hall (102) to the back door and the rear yard beyond. The doorway in the west wall was originally an exterior door and included a semicircular fanlight at the top of the architrave (Fig. 170). The wood and glass fanlight and the external stone arch were removed to what was a new exterior doorway (D1102) in the rear wing constructed in circa 1836. The passage also provided access to the back parlor through the doorway formerly at the north wall. This was probably the service route from the basement kitchen to the Back Parlor that on occasion served as the formal dining room prior to the creation of the current dining room (106) in circa 1836.

The character of this passage changed after the first addition to the rear of the house was constructed for Richard Hart around 1836. This project included the enlargement of Room 106 to create a spacious formal dining room. The extension of this passage to the west (110) included a service door into the new dining space. Cabinetry and shelving were installed in this passage and it became the "dining room pantry where the dishes lived" recalled by Elizabeth Shields Eddy. Evidence for the shelving can be seen on the south wall. The 1886 inventory indicates that this space and possibly part of the adjoining area (110) was used for the storage of china and glassware.

The expansion of the rear wing for the George Cluetts in 1893 to include a new kitchen resulted in the removal of the shelving in this space. A vertical board wainscot was installed in place of the Hart-era cabinetry and new cabinets and shelves were installed in the adjoining space (110) from which the Hart-era service stair was removed. Although there are no photographs that record the area, the 1904 view of the entrance (101) indicates that a portiere was positioned in the east door opening (D1051).

The 1934 HABS floor plan, produced during the era of the Albert Cluetts, refers to this space as a passage. A mistake in the plan deletes the door to the back parlor but that original feature is recorded in the 1934 parlor photograph. Becky Cluett, Caroline Cluett's granddaughter, indicates that a small oval sink was located in the southwest corner. It was here that the children washed their hands prior to having dinner in the small dining room (111).

The parlor doorway was removed by Wilson Large in 1964. Since that time, the busy passage has functioned as a coat room and circulation space for museum visitors.

FLOOR

The floor is finished in 9" × 9" black and white rubber tiles laid in a checkerboard pattern. The tiles were supplied by Devane's Floor Coverings and the work was carried out by Wilson Large in 1959. The flooring condition under the tiles is unknown but may consist of Cluett-era narrow hardwood boards laid over the original wider boards of the Hart-era surface. There are cuts in some of the tiles next to the north wall that indicate the former position of the architrave of the doorway that until 1964 opened to the back parlor.

WALLS

All four walls are finished in original plaster on split wood lath. A section of the north wall is composed of sheet rock installed in the door opening, removed in 1964. A small probe in the south wall, on the dining room (106) side, confirmed that the wall is an original feature of the house and is constructed of plaster on split wood lath. A probe in the west wall, behind one of the architrave corner blocks, revealed the use of later sawn lath. This surface was modified when the rear wing was constructed for Richard Hart circa 1836.

Each wall features a 43" high vertical board wain-

scot. The south wall wainscot dates to the George Cluett era and matches material in the pantry passage (110) and rear kitchen (112). Hart-era cabinetry was probably removed when the wainscot was installed. Marks on the wainscot in the southwest corner may relate to a small oval sink formerly located here. The wainscot on the north wall is composed of boards with a different profile. This surface, which covers the former parlor door opening location, was installed by RCHS, possibly in 1964.

CEILING

The original plaster-on-lath ceiling is approximately 13'7" above the floor.

BASEBOARD

No original baseboard remains in this hall. The south, east, and west walls include a quarter round shoe molding at the base of the Cluett-era wainscot. The north wall features a plain 3½" high base and quarter round contemporary with the wainscot above it.

CORNICE

This space never included a cornice but there is evidence at about 11'3½" above the floor for the possible location of a picture molding, dating to late in the Hart occupancy or early Cluett era.

DOORS

There are two original door openings in the hall, a single doorway with a fanlight (D1051) in the east wall and a single opening (D1101) in the west wall. A third original doorway in the north partition was removed in 1964.

Both extant openings feature the typical architrave with raffle flower blocks. The east doorway (D108) includes an original semicircular fanlight. The architrave around the fanlight is of molded plaster and includes a wooden key block ornamented with a carved wood acanthus leaf. The semicircular sash is 2'11" wide and 17½" tall. The glazing is divided into five segments within two concentric half circles. The stair hall face includes applied swags and cast-lead ornaments.

The west door architrave (D1101) was modified when the addition was constructed in circa 1836. The opening originally included a fanlight similar to but slightly larger than the east fanlight. This feature is now positioned above the west door (D110) in the kitchen passage (110). Both of these openings were successively the rear exterior doorways of the house. Inspection of the corner blocks of the west door revealed that they may be from the architrave of the back parlor doorway removed in 1964.

> D1051: This opening retains the original eight-panel, stile-and-rail mahogany door. The recessed panels are trimmed with ¾" wide quirk ovolo moldings.

> Hardware: Original fittings include a pair of 4¾" high cast-iron butt hinges, a mortise lock with a silver-plated brass face plate marked "W PYE N-YORK PATENT," two silvered brass knobs, roses and drop cover escutcheons. The north door stile retains marks for a spring-type door closer dating to the later Hart era.

> D1101: The door from this opening is removed but hinge marks indicate that it opened into the rear hall (110). This opening in its original form functioned as the back door of the house and the door would have opened into this hall. There is no visible evidence for the earliest condition.

> D1042: The doorway was removed in 1964. The mahogany door is now located in the doorway to the former library/reception room (109).

WINDOWS

There are no external windows in the hall but an original fanlight exists above the east doorway. The west door originally included a fanlight that looked out to the yard and carriage house. In circa 1836, that fanlight was moved to its current location above doorway D1102.

HEATING

This hall has never been heated.

PLUMBING

According to Becky Cluett a small oval sink (lavatory) was located in the southwest corner.

LIGHTING

A fluorescent tube fixture installed by RCHS, is attached to the south wall. A Hart-era gas pipe protrudes from the west end of the north wall at 71" above the floor. This was the position for a gas bracket light. There is no evidence for the lighting used here by the Cluett families.

EQUIPMENT

An electric service bell push button, probably installed for the Albert Cluetts, is located above the dado next to the east door architrave.

OTHER FEATURES

The south wall includes a beaded edge wood rail with thirteen iron hooks for coats as well as a wood hat shelf above. An iron pipe is mounted below the shelf and extends the full length of the hall. These features were installed by RCHS so that the passage would function as a coat room. The bead edge rail may be a much earlier feature taken from the north wall when the doorway was removed in 1964. There are outlines for such a feature on that surface.

FURNISHINGS AND FITTINGS

The furnishings and fittings used here have evolved over time as the room's function has changed. Prior to the enlargement of the house by Richard Hart in circa 1836, this area served as a passage or hall with direct access to the rear yard through the west doorway. There were probably few if any furnishings here, but there may have been a wood coat hook rail attached to the north wall. Marks for this typical feature exist on that wall at about 72¼" above the floor. The beaded edge rail currently on the south wall may be from this position.

After Room 106 became the formal dining room (circa 1836), this space and its continuation in the new rear addition (110) functioned as pantries. The 1886 inventory refers to "Pantry No. 1 and No. 2." This may be the "No. 1" space that housed several large dinner sets as well as numerous other pieces and sets of china. It is possible that the "No. 1" and "No. 2" designations refer to cabinets rather than separate rooms and that both were located in this space.

There is extensive evidence on the south wall for the positions of shelving and cabinetry. The ⅞" thick shelves ran the full length of the wall and were positioned at 50½", 64½", 76½", 87¼" and 101½" above the floor. Elizabeth Shields Eddy indicated that the north door (D1051) in the west wall of the stair hall "led into the dining room pantry where the dishes lived . . . (and) the pantry also had a door that opened into the back parlor."

The Hart financial records refer to this and possibly the adjoining space (110) as the "Hall Pantry," "Pantry," and "China Pantry."

In 1856, William Crawthere laid oilcloth in the Hall Pantry. Many years later in 1890, a cupboard was made for the pantry by H. Cozzens, who had done work in the pantries throughout the 1880s.

The George Cluetts may have had the shelving removed from this space as part of the enlargement of the rear wing to include a modern kitchen (112). By the time the house was recorded by HABS in 1934, there were no cabinets or shelves here but such features are shown in the adjoining passage (110) which had included a Hart-era service stairway prior to the expansion. Becky Cluett remembers a small oval sink in the southwest corner and there are marks on the wainscot for such a feature.

RCHS uses this area for circulation as well as a coat room for museum visitors. RCHS records indicate that Wilson Large painted the passageway and laid the floor tiles in 1959.

106　Dining Room

The large first floor room known as the dining room has evolved in a manner different from the other original spaces (Fig. 171).

The rectangular room (15'9" × 23'5") includes two doorways in the east partition, a single doorway in the west partition, and on the south wall a centered chimney breast and mantel flanked by tall windows. This configuration dates to the circa 1836 construction of a rear wing, probably carried out by John Colegrove, the contractor who constructed the house in 1826–27. This addition made for Richard Hart included the enlargement of the predecessor to this room, and the addition of a service stair hall as well as the basement, first, second, and third floor rooms.

Upon completing the original portion of the house in 1827, the room in this location was much smaller than the current space. The earlier room, approximately 15' x15'9", encompassed the east two-thirds of the existing space.

In plan, that room included the two doorways still extant in the east partition, a chimney breast and fireplace centered on a much shorter south wall and one or, more likely, two windows in the west wall.

The original room's finishes probably matched those in the library-reception room (109), but the function of the room can only be speculated. Too small to serve as a formal dining room, it probably functioned

171 The dining room (106), 1976.

as the everyday family dining space with formal dining taking place in the much larger back parlor. According to the 1844 inventory, a sideboard was still located in the back parlor several years after Room 106 was enlarged and functioning as the dining room.

The existence of the two doorways in the east wall (one is the formal entrance and the other is located directly across from the basement stair leading to the kitchen) reinforces the notion that the original space was used for dining. Similarly, the back parlor originally included two entrances, the formal one opening from the stair hall and a second opening from the service hall.

The addition of the rear wing in circa 1836 resulted in an increase in the size of this room by about one-third. The extensive work included the movement of the chimney breast several feet to the west and the installation of a new "Greek Revival" style white marble mantel. The window openings, located in the original west wall, were moved to new locations flanking the fireplace. New doorways in the west and north partitions opened to the small west room (111) that later served as Betsey Hart's bed chamber and to a newly created hallway-pantry (110). The enlarged room included a new plaster cornice which was much bolder in form than the original feature. The two primary features, the marble mantelpiece and the plaster cornice, produced a room very representative of the Greek Revival style fashionable some ten years after completion of the original house.

Insight into the appearance and use of the enlarged room is provided by the Hart inventories, which refer to this as the dining room, Elizabeth Shields Eddy's description and photographs from circa 1892, 1904, and 1934 (see Figs. 129, 175, 130). The Hart family financial records also refer to this space, beginning with a redecoration by D. H. Wellington in 1850 and a final change in decor by Thomas Buckley in 1891 for Sarah Wool Hart.

A significant feature of the room in its current form is the small fanlight above the door (D1061) to the stair hall. This feature was walled over on the dining room side until sometime after 1952. Although there is no record of the type of material used to cover the opening, a 1904 photograph clearly shows the wall in place, complete with wallpaper and picture molding, above the door opening. A color slide, dating to the early years of the occupancy of the house by RCHS, also records the wall surface covering the fanlight. In that view, the

172 The dining room (106), looking northeast, c. 1960.

Cluett-era wall panel moldings are in place including one in the position of the fanlight (Fig. 172). Photographs of the stair hall side of the opening show the glazed fanlight but no vision of the room beyond. Upon completion of the house in 1827, the fanlight probably was open between the hall and the original southwest room. The enlargement of the room in circa 1836 probably included the covering of the glazed opening on the dining room side, possibly to accommodate the growing collection of family portraits displayed in the newly enlarged room. Elizabeth Shields Eddy noted that portraits of Betsey Hart and Rebecca Howard were positioned above the two doorways in the east wall in 1855.

By the time the room was inventoried in 1886 and photographed in 1892, the portraits were dispersed among the Hart family, but an investigation of the plaster wall surfaces now hidden behind the Cluett-era canvas covering could reveal the positions of the pictures.

Modifications made after the sale of the house to George and Amanda Cluett in 1893 include the installation of the hardwood flooring and the addition of a picture molding and new wallpaper and the placement of a new gasolier. These changes are recorded in a 1904 photograph (see Fig. 175).

About 1910, the Albert Cluetts considerably changed the ambiance of the room by modifying the traditional treatment of the walls; paper was replaced by a canvas covering that was painted after the installation of panel moldings and a chair rail. Additional moldings were added to increase the depth of the plaster cornice. The chandelier was removed and six silver-plated electric wall sconces were installed. Two photographs record the dining room in 1934, the year the house was documented in plans, sections, and details by HABS. The floor plan indicates that the door opening formerly located in the north partition, featured a swinging door. This condition is confirmed in one of the 1934 photos. Apparently, the Hart-era door was modified for one of the Cluett occupants to better function for serving from the Cluett-era first floor pantry (110) and kitchen (112).

After January 1953, RCHS removed the circa 1836 service door in the north partition and the panel moldings from the walls, the fanlight was uncovered above the east doorway, and an electrified antique gasolier

was suspended from the center of the ceiling (the Albert Cluetts had not used a chandelier). Currently, the dining room retains features and furnishings from all the periods of occupancy but does not actually portray any one era (Fig. 173).

FLOOR

The floor is finished in narrow 2¼" wide strips of tongue-and-groove oak, laid east/west. This surface was installed for the George Cluetts in 1893 or later. A 1904 photograph records a dark finish on this surface. The wide board surface beneath this flooring may date to 1827 or circa 1836 or be a combination of both periods.

WALLS

The walls are finished in plaster on wood lath. A portion of the south wall and the chimney breast consist of plaster on masonry. A probe into the east end of the north partition revealed that the plaster was applied to split wood lath; the condition throughout the original 1827 portion of the house. The west wall and the west third of the north wall surfaces are formed of sawn wood lath dating to the circa 1836 expansion of the

173 The dining room (106), looking east.

room. A 3" wide wood chair rail, matching the rails in the parlors and entrance hall, was added to the wall surfaces by the Albert Cluetts. At the same time (circa 1910) narrow moldings were applied to the wall surfaces above the rails forming the panel arrangement seen in 1934 photographs. This panel treatment was removed by RCHS after 1953.

CEILING

The plaster-on-lath ceiling is about 13'7" above the floor. The ceiling was partially or fully reconstructed when the room was enlarged in circa 1836. Only the east two-thirds of the surface represents the ceiling surface of the original room. If original wood lath remains, it should be of the split variety while the circa 1836 lath would be of the more uniform sawn type. There is no evidence that a ceiling centerpiece ever existed here.

As part of the 1891 redecoration of the room, a wood molding was applied to the ceiling surface forming a large rectangular panel. This condition is recorded in the circa 1892 photograph. The molding was removed when the room was redecorated for the George Cluetts.

BASEBOARD

The wood baseboard, approximately 12½" high, matches the profile used in the other primary first floor rooms. The sections of base at the east end of the room are original, but additions were made when the room was enlarged in circa 1836.

CORNICE

The boldly detailed plaster cornice was run in place and dates to the expansion of the room in circa 1836. The character of the original 1827 cornice is unknown, but it was probably similar to, or duplicated the cornice in the library-reception room (109). Photographs from the Hart and George Cluett eras reveal that the bottom stepped portion of the cornice was added by the Albert Cluetts, probably at the time the chair rail and wall moldings were installed. The original intent of the designer/fabricator of the circa 1836 cornice was for a wallpaper frieze or border to be positioned immediately beneath the molded plaster to provide visual support for this feature at the juncture of the wall and ceiling. In the final Hart redecoration of the room in 1891, the frieze paper was extended down to the level of the tops of the door casings, creating an exaggerated appearance popular at the end of the nineteenth century.

DOORS

There are three door openings in the room: two original openings in the east wall (D1061 and D1062) and a single later opening in the west wall (D1063). An additional later doorway was located in the north partition but was removed sometime after 1952. Each opening features the 5½" wide architrave composed of symmetrically molded trim resting on ornamental plinths and including square corner blocks featuring carved wood raffle flowers. The trim of the west opening (D1063) dates to circa 1836 and reproduces the original trim at the other openings.

Door D1061 includes a semicircular fanlight. This original feature was formerly only visible on the stair hall face of the doorway. The plaster wall surface covered the opening on the dining room side. This original condition is shown in the 1904 photograph of the room, and in a color slide possibly dating to the 1960s. The fanlight was exposed by RCHS at an undetermined date.

D1061: The original eight-panel, stile-and-rail mahogany door is hinged to the south jamb.

Hardware: Original fittings include a pair of 4⅝" high cast-iron butt hinges, a 7⅝" tall brass mortise lock stamped "W PYE N-YORK PATENT," silvered brass knobs and keyhole escutcheons.

D1062: The original eight-panel, stile-and-rail mahogany door is hinged to the north jamb.

Hardware: Original fittings include a pair of 4½" high cast-iron butt hinges, a 7⅝" tall brass mortise lock stamped "W PYE N-YORK PATENT," silvered brass knobs and keyhole escutcheons.

D1063: This circa 1836 eight-panel, stile-and-rail door is hinged to the south jamb. This door copies the detailing of the original doors. The dining room face has a faux mahogany grained finish.

Hardware: Original circa 1836 fittings include a pair of 4⅝" high cast-iron butt hinges, a brass faced mortise lock stamped "McKinney & Jones Troy 34", silvered brass knobs and keyhole escutcheons. The locksmiths William McKinney and Eber Jones of Troy were in partnership from 1835 to 1836.

D1064: This door was removed sometime after 1952, but photographs reveal that it matched door D1063. It was originally hinged to the east jamb and provided direct access to the pantry. During the Cluett era, it was converted into a swinging door, making it more convenient to serve food from the new first floor kitchen.

WINDOWS

There are two window openings in the south wall flanking the chimney breast. The openings date to the enlargement of the room circa 1836, but the sash and trim are salvaged from the original windows located in the west wall of the former smaller room. The tall windows have architraves composed of the typical symmetrically molded trim and corner blocks with raffle flowers. The openings are fitted with six-over-six double-hung sash. Below the sill there is a paneled apron. There are no interior shutters although it is likely that the long-gone original west windows did include built-in shutters like those in the back parlor (104).

HEATING

Heated air enters the room through a 16½" × 24½" white enameled cast-iron Rococo pattern floor register that dates to the 1850s. It is located in the southeast corner (Fig. 174). A smaller (probably slightly later) 14½" × 21" cast-iron floor register is located next to the north wall. The duct work no longer exists below this register.

Originally, the room was heated by the fireplace, possibly with a coal grate insert. Elizabeth Shields Eddy recalled that a stove, referred to as "The Seven Sisters," was positioned in front of the fireplace in 1855. This may be the Nott stove repaired by J. T. Davy in 1843.

174 The 1850s enameled iron floor register (Room 106).

LIGHTING

Artificial lighting is provided by a large electrified six-arm, ormolu and damascene Rococo style gasolier. This circa 1850 fixture was probably manufactured by Cornelius and Son of Philadelphia. It was installed here in 1962. The fixture was originally in the house at 18 Second Street, Troy, and was given to RCHS by Leland O. and John A. Palitsch.

This is the most recent of a series of fixtures placed here. Whether the original smaller 1827 room had a suspended lighting device is unknown and the 1844 inventory does not record a chandelier in the enlarged room. Generally, the absence of a centerpiece in a formal room indicates that it was not planned for a chandelier to be placed there.

In the later nineteenth century, Betsey Hart had the gasolier purchased for the back parlor in 1850 placed here.

Additional lighting is provided by six silver-plated double arm electric wall sconces. Pairs are symmetrically positioned on the south, east, and west walls. The south pair were originally positioned on the north wall but were moved sometime after 1952. These fixtures were installed by the Albert Cluetts and are recorded in the 1934 photos. There was no chandelier in the room at that time. The Albert Cluetts installed electrical outlets on the sides of the chimney breast so that electrical fixtures could be placed on the marble mantel.

FIREPLACE

A plastered masonry chimney breast, 6'2" wide × 8" deep, is centered on the south wall between the windows. A bold, simply detailed grey veined white marble mantel frames the soapstone lined firebox. The hearth matches the marble of the mantel. The chimney breast and the marble mantel date to the enlargement of the room in circa 1836. Prior to that work, the chimney breast was positioned about three feet further east, directly beneath the extant fireplace in the second floor bedroom (207) above. The original mantel probably matched the one still in place in the library-reception room (109). The soapstone firebox was installed for the George or Albert Cluetts. During the Hart era, a coal grate was probably positioned in the firebox and Elizabeth Shields Eddy recalls a stove in front of the fireplace in the 1850s.

A 1904 photograph records that George and Amanda Cluett had a wood and mirror glass multi-tiered shelf

175 The dining room (106), looking east, 1904.

unit placed on the mantel. In the photo, it is largely obscured by the floral arrangements that cover the fireplace and fill the room (Fig. 175).

FURNISHINGS AND FITTINGS

Although there is no documentation for the original smaller room in this location, it is likely that it functioned as the family dining room. In three-bay town houses the front basement room frequently served this use, but the four-bay plan allowed this function to move to the first floor. The original room, approximately 15' × 15'9", was too small for formal dining with guests. The enlarged and remodeled room, the second largest room in the house, definitely served as the Hart family's dining room both for informal and formal occasions. The dining room is recorded in the two nineteenth century inventories as well as in the Elizabeth Shields Eddy reminiscence and in photographs from circa 1892, 1904, and 1934. Furnishings noted in the 1844 inventory include a wall-to-wall carpet, a sideboard, a dining table, eight chairs, a child's high chair, as well as two pictures, a portrait, two alabaster jars, two candle-

sticks, and curtains. A shovel and tongs were placed by the fireplace. Some of these items can be identified in the circa 1892 photograph (Fig. 129). The chairs are from a set provided by Duncan Phyfe circa 1816; four are shown in the photo and three remain in the RCHS collections. Additional chairs from this set are now in the collection of the New-York Historical Society in New York City. The simple vernacular high chair is also visible in the Hart-era photo, as is the large marble-topped sideboard shown against the west wall. The curtains noted in the inventory are recorded in the photo suspended from elaborate and very architectural Gothic style cornices. The 1844 document makes no mention of a chandelier in the dining room and it is possible that there was no suspended lighting device in the room during the earliest years. Only a single portrait is recorded in 1844.

Mrs. Eddy's reminiscence of 1855 describes the room as it was approximately eleven years after the inventory was made. We are told that the dining table consisted of three sections; the two semicircular end sections were located in the library (109) and stair hall (102) while the center section was placed against the east wall of the dining room. The sideboard was positioned against the west wall. By then, there were seven family portraits in the room; Richard Hart (in old age) over the mantel, William Howard over the sideboard, grandfathers White and Philip Hart, and Richard Hart (as a young man) on the north wall and above the two doors in the east wall, Rebecca Howard and Betsey Hart. Investigation of the wall surfaces above these doors revealed the locations of the nails that supported these two important portraits about 15" below the cornice. The placement of the portrait above the northeast door (D1061) explains why the fanlight was not exposed in the dining room. This condition is recorded in the 1904 photograph of the room (Fig. 175) and in a much more recent, but undated color slide.

The 1886 inventory provides a full account of the furnishings in the dining room which is complimented by the visual evidence of the circa 1892 photograph. Early Hart furnishings listed in this inventory include the eight mahogany chairs by Phyfe, a child's chair (high chair), a cane seat chair, the sideboard and a marble-top table. This boldly detailed circa 1830 table is positioned against the north wall in the photo and might be one of the pier tables formerly located in the parlor as recorded in the 1844 inventory. The 1886 document also lists a mantel mirror (the three-part horizontal mirror seen in the photo) as well as a pier glass and mirror. This may refer to the large circular convex mirror which currently is positioned on the west wall of the room. In the nineteenth century, this important circa 1816 furnishing may have originally been placed, with a possible mate, in the front parlor. The purchase in 1850 of the two oval parlor mirrors may have resulted in the removal of one of the convex mirrors to the east wall of the dining room. The wall surface between the two east doorways needs to be investigated for evidence of the mirrors attachment to that surface. The caption of a photograph of the dining room that appeared in the March 30, 1963, issue of the *Times Record* notes that the convex mirror was in the house for 135 years.

Additional dining room furnishings include a mahogany sofa which the photograph reveals to be a circa 1830 Grecian sofa covered in black hair cloth. This may be the sofa that Elizabeth Shields Eddy describes in the library (109) in 1855 and which was repaired and reupholstered in 1880. The clock and vases recorded in the 1886 inventory and shown on the mantel in the photograph were purchased from Cox Brothers of New York in 1864 and described as a "bronze & marble mantel set clock 'Meditation' and vases to match."

Damask drapes and lace curtains are suspended from elaborate Gothic-style cornices. Investigation of the window architraves revealed the positions of the pairs of Hart-era drapery tieback pins at 4' above the floor.

The 1892 photograph records an important service device in the dining room. Immediately west of the now missing doorway to the pantry is a small circular object that may be a service bell. Three battery powered electric bells were installed in the house in 1890.

The inventories, Hart financial records, and the circa 1892 photograph provide clues concerning lighting in the dining room. The 1844 inventory makes no mention of a chandelier in this room.

In 1860, John Cox and Company of New York supplied a five-light bronze and fire-gilt sliding chandelier, possibly for this room. Sliding gasoliers were typically positioned above dining tables.

In 1866, a new six-light chandelier was installed in the back parlor and it may have resulted in the removal of the 1850 Cornelius and Son fixture from that space to the dining room where it is recorded in the circa 1892 photograph. Perhaps the sliding gasolier did not function properly, which was frequently the case with this type of fixture.

In 1871, G. V. S. Quackenbush supplied thirty-eight yards of Brussels carpet and border as well as a crumb cloth for the dining room. In 1888, the carpet was "made over" by Louis Muller. This oriental patterned wall-to-wall carpet is shown in the circa 1892 photograph.

The dining room as decorated and furnished for the George Cluetts is recorded in a 1904 photograph (Fig. 175). The removal of the rug for the debut party exposes the recently installed hardwood floor. A large multi-shelved and mirrored overmantel is positioned on the marble shelf and a gasolier, with a central light flanked by groups of gas candles, is suspended from the ceiling. A narrow picture rail molding is affixed to the wall surfaces about 10" above the door architraves. An imposing antique sideboard is positioned between the two doors in the east wall. This furnishing is part of the RCHS collections and is currently in the same location.

Two photographs from 1934 record the dining room as transformed for the Albert Cluetts (Figs. 49 & 130). The most dramatic change to the decor is the paneled wall treatment that included the addition of a molding than extends the cornice down onto the wall surface. There is no chandelier, but pairs of electric wall sconces are positioned on the north, east, and west surfaces. These fixtures remain in the room today.

Pairs of striped silk drapes hang in straight panels at the windows covering all of the woodwork. These drapes remain at the windows, although they have been modified to hang inside the architrave, possibly to show off the woodwork, and they are now tied back by cords looped over brass cloak pins.

As furnished by RCHS, the dining room reflects the occupancy of the Harts and Cluetts. The circular convex mirror may survive from the Hart era while other furnishings, including the George Cluett sideboard and Albert Cluett drapes, survive from the later occupancies. At the November 17, 1952, RCHS meeting held at the Troy Club, it was remarked that the Cluett House would soon be turned over to the organization and that the dining room furnishings would remain in place. RCHS modified the room by the removal of the paneled wall treatment although the chair rail was retained. Two of the wall sconces were moved to the south wall. In 1962, the elaborate circa 1850 gasolier from 18 Second Street was installed above the dining table.

FINISHES INVESTIGATION

The dining room decor can be partially reconstructed through evidence from the Hart financial records, the Hart and Cluett photographs as well as physical investigation.

There are approximately ten painted finishes on the woodwork. The room in its original smaller form had trim painted in the same yellowish/white used throughout the house. After the room was enlarged in circa 1836, the trim was painted in a yellow/beige color. Later repainting of the trim included yellowish/whites, ivory, and the most recent white finishes. The circa 1910 chair rail is finished in yellowish/white, ivory, and the current white.

The original doors in the east wall are of mahogany. The later west door is finished in faux graining to simulate mahogany.

The plaster wall surfaces have always been covered in wallpaper and after 1910, in painted canvas. The canvas surface, which originally was ornamental with applied panel moldings, is covered in four finishes: a pink/white, grey/white, yellowish/white, and the current white paint.

The earliest documented decoration of the dining room dates to 1850 when Solomon and Hart of New York City supplied twenty pieces of wallpaper and thirty-three yards of border. This decor was installed by D. H. Wellington who also used lemon (yellow) and white paint, probably on the ceiling.

In 1871, Marcotte and Company of New York, supplied twenty-two rolls of tan and gold figured paper for this room. The redecoration was carried out by W. W. Whitman who installed the wallpaper, border, and moldings as well as applied paint, frescoing (probably polychromed the cornice) and gold leaf.

The last Hart-era decoration was carried out in 1891 by Thomas Buckley of Albany. He tinted the cornice and applied paper to the walls and ceiling and installed 50' of ceiling molding and 50' of picture molding. The results of this work are recorded in the photograph taken in 1892 (Fig. 129). The ceiling is covered in two different paper patterns separated by the applied wood molding. A very deep frieze paper extends from the cornice to the picture molding positioned at the top of the door architraves.

The George Cluetts installed a much simpler treatment. The molding was removed from the ceiling and a new picture molding was placed a few inches above the height of the door architraves. The wall surfaces were covered in light color patterned paper.

In circa 1910 or later, the wallpaper was removed and the wall surfaces were covered in a painted canvas with applied panel moldings and a chair rail. Sometime after RCHS occupied the house, the panel moldings were removed from the wall surfaces but the chair rail remains in place. A small brass plaque affixed to the hallface of the north hall door is inscribed "The Albert E. Cluett, Senior Memorial Room, 1953."

107   Hall – Stair to Basement

This very small hall, really a landing, provides access to the basement stairway and to a small lavatory (108) that is located in what is part of the Hart-era cloak closet.

In plan, the space includes doorways in the east and west partitions and to the north the stairway descending to the basement. The original plan of this simply detailed space did not include the opening in the east partition and that condition is recorded in the 1934 HABS drawings. The doorway was created in 1938 when the north end of the adjoining original long narrow cloak closet was modified to include an elevator. No mention is made of this space in any of the Hart or

Cluett documents and it is not recorded in photographs. Currently, this is an active passage used by staff and visitors. During the Hart era, all of the food prepared in the kitchen would pass through this space and onto the dining room.

FLOOR

The surface is finished in narrow 2¼" wide strips of tongue-and-groove oak, laid east/west. This surface was probably installed for the George Cluetts over the original wide board opening.

WALLS

The walls are finished in original plaster on wood lath. There is evidence on the south wall for a 3" wide wood rail located at 67" above the floor. This surface probably included some sort of garment hook.

CEILING

The original surface is finished in plaster on wood lath. The surface follows the slope of the underside of the second floor stair.

BASEBOARD

The original 8½" high base includes a simple top bead.

CORNICE

There is no cornice.

DOORS

There are two doorways: an original opening (D1021) in the west partition and a much more recent opening (D1081) in the east partition. The west door was originally hinged to swing into this space as recorded in the 1934 HABS floor plan. The direction was changed by RCHS after 1952.

WINDOWS

There is no evidence that a window ever existed here but Elizabeth Shields Eddy states that there was a small internal window in the cloak closet (108) that looked onto the kitchen (basement) stairs. She may have mistaken the original window opening in the south wall of what is now the lavatory (108) for such an opening or perhaps there was a small opening that allowed borrowed natural light from room 108 to enter this space. It would have been destroyed when the lavatory door was installed in 1938.

HEATING

This space has never been heated.

LIGHTING

The electric wall sconce on the west partition was installed for RCHS. There is no visible evidence for earlier lighting devices.

FURNISHINGS AND FITTINGS

The small size of the space prohibits the placement of any furnishings but there is evidence on the south wall for the position of a garment hook nail, possibly an original feature.

108   Lavatory – Former Cloak Closet

This small lavatory-toilet room is for use by staff and visitors. In plan, the narrow room includes a single doorway in the west partition and a window in the south wall.

The room in its current form dates to work carried out for the Albert Cluetts in 1938. The installation of the small elevator at the time necessitated a reduction in the size of the long (10'10") narrow space that functioned as a toilet room and coat closet. That space is recorded by the 1934 HABS floor plan and included a window at the south end and a doorway (current door D1012) at the north end. For the Harts, the space functioned as a cloak closet and there is evidence on the east and west walls for the locations of garment hook rails. The original Hart-era space had been modified from its original form when George and Amanda Cluett had the entrance hall archway made wider. A toilet may have been introduced to the space at that time.

The only mention of this space occurs in Elizabeth Shields Eddy's reminiscence of 1855 where she refers to this area as the cloak closet. The current room retains features from the Hart and Cluett eras as well as from RCHS.

FLOOR

The surface is covered in sheet vinyl installed for RCHS. The conditions under this surface are unknown but it is likely that original wide board flooring remains as the base for later surfaces.

WALLS

The south, east, and west walls are formed of original plaster on wood lath. The north partition is of gypsum board installed in 1938 when the elevator shaft was created in the north end of the original space. There is a wood enclosed pipe chase (8" × 10") in the southeast corner.

CEILING

The current ceiling surface, formed of fiberboard with a 1" wide wood seam batten at its center, is located considerably below the original plaster-on-wood-lath surface. The lowered ceiling condition dates to work carried out in 1960 by RCHS.

BASEBOARD

The original 1827 plain 8½" high base with bead top survives on all four walls. The material used on the north wall installed in 1938 was probably salvaged from the elevator shaft location.

CORNICE

A narrow wood cove molding joins the wall and ceiling surfaces.

DOORS

The single opening in the west partition was created in 1938 when the room was diminished for the installation of the elevator. The plain 4½" wide trim features a raised edge band.

> D1081: The six-panel, stile-and-rail door dates to 1938.

> Hardware: Fittings include a pair of small 3½" high brass butt hinges with ball finials marked "Stanley," a 5¼" high brass mortise lock, small brass knobs and oval keyhole escutcheons. The door face includes an applied sign inscribed "Rest Room" and a small brass door knocker in the form of a devil with the inscription "Lincoln."

WINDOWS

A single original window opening is located in the south wall. The architrave is formed of a plain 4" wide board with a beaded edge. The opening is fitted with original four-over-four double-hung sash which have ⅝" wide muntins and 10" × 14" panes. A late nineteenth century brass thumb latch secures the sash. The deep 1¼" thick sill has a delicate double-beaded edge. A 3¾" × 22½" cut-out in the sill probably accommodated the tank of the toilet formerly positioned in front of the window and shown in the 1934 HABS floor plan. The window recess is fitted with pairs of paneled bifold shutters. These original features retain their small cast-iron butt hinges and a small iron latch hook.

HEATING

This space has never been heated.

LIGHTING

A single electric wall sconce with its original opal glass bowl-like shade is positioned on the east wall at about 69¼" above the floor. This fixture dates to circa 1910.

PLUMBING

Fixtures include a white ceramic tank toilet (marked Kohler—1973), installed for RCHS in the 1970s and a small white ceramic lavatory marked Kohler U.S.A. with chromed faucets and exposed piping. The lavatory may date to the work carried out in 1938. The 1934 HABS floor plan indicates that an earlier toilet was positioned in front of the window. A wood enclosed chase in the southeast corner houses piping that serves the third floor kitchenette (310) formerly a bathroom.

FURNISHINGS AND FITTINGS

A wall-mounted wood medicine cabinet with a beveled glass mirror is positioned in the east wall. It dates to the Albert Cluett era as does a white ceramic toilet paper holder attached to the west wall.

The east and west walls retain evidence for the locations of wood rails that held garment hooks. On the west wall the rail was positioned at 70" above the floor. On the east wall there are markings at 70" and 82" above the floor. The south end of the lower rail remains intact within the wood enclosed pipe chase. The rails were probably removed when the original cloak closet was modified by the addition of the elevator in 1938.

109　Office – Former Library – Reception Room

This space is the first room encountered upon entering through the front door and has served various functions for the four owners of the house.

This is one of the "extra" spaces gained in the four-bay town house plan. The rectangular room (10'10" × 18'2") includes a single doorway in the north partition and a single tall window opening in the east wall. A chimney breast and mantel are centered on the south wall. All of the original architectural character survives in this small but important space.

Family tradition and the two Hart-era household inventories of 1844 and 1886 indicate that this room served as the library and a family sitting room. Elizabeth Shields Eddy recalled playing in the room and being read to by her grandmother, Betsey Hart. The library function was defined by two tall bookcases that flanked the chimney breast.

The room is recorded in a 1904 photograph showing Beatrice Cluett sitting among the flower arrangements that filled the space for her debut party (Fig. 176). George and Amanda Cluett may have used this space as a reception room for visitors. Albert and Caroline Cluett certainly did and the room is so defined on the 1934 HABS floor plan.

The first modifications were made when the hardwood flooring was installed after the George Cluetts occupied the house in 1893. Additional changes, made by the Albert Cluetts, included the installation of a chair rail and panel moldings to the surface of the walls. The moldings were removed by RCHS but the chair rail remains.

From the earliest years of RCHS occupancy, this space has served as the main office for the organization.

FLOOR

The floor is finished in narrow 2" wide strips of tongue-and-groove oak, laid east/west. This surface, installed by the George Cluetts, had a dark finish as recorded in the 1904 photograph. The original wide board flooring exists under this surface.

WALLS

All four walls are finished in original plaster-on-split-wood lath. The chimney breast consists of plaster on

176 Reception room (109), with Beatrice Cluett, 1904.

brick masonry. In 1910 or slightly later, panel moldings were applied to the canvas-covered wall surfaces above a 3" deep wood chair rail positioned 34" above the floor. The moldings were removed after 1952 by RCHS but their positions can still be discerned on the wall surfaces.

CEILING

The original plaster-on-lath ceiling is about 13'7" above the floor. There is no evidence for a centerpiece on the ceiling surface.

BASEBOARD

The original wood baseboard, approximately 11¾" high, is composed of a tall stepped fascia topped by a reverse ogee with astragal crownmold.

CORNICE

The original plaster cornice was run in place and includes a shallow cove with a central bead.

DOORS

There is a single original door opening in the north partition (D109). The opening retains the original 5½" wide architrave composed of symmetrically molded trim with an applied triple reeded band and square corner blocks set with carved raffle flowers.

D1091: The original mahogany door, hinged to the east jamb, was removed during the George Cluett era, and the opening was fitted with a portiere. This condition is recorded in two of the 1904 photographs (Figs. 151 & 176). Apparently, the original door was lost. In 1964, Wilson Large installed the current door which he had removed from the rear opening (D1042) in the back parlor. The newly installed eight-panel, stile-and-rail mahogany door was hinged to the west jamb making it unnecessary to modify the hinge location on the former parlor door.

Hardware: Original fittings to the door include a pair of 5½" high cast-iron butt hinges with silver-plated covers, a 7⅞" high mortise lock with a silver-plated face, two 2⅛" diameter silvered brass knobs and roses and two silvered brass drop cover escutcheons. The hardware was supplied by William Pye of New York.

WINDOW

A single original window opening is located in the east wall. The tall window recess is framed by the typical architrave with raffle flower corner blocks. The original large six-over-six double-hung sash have ¹¹⁄₁₆" wide muntins and 14¾" × 24" glass panes. A single panel apron is located below the sill. The bottom sash rail is fitted with a pair of metal grips dating to the mid-twentieth century. The deep window recess is fitted with a pair of original two-tier paneled bifold shutters. The shutters retain original cast-iron hinges and a brass latch.

HEATING

A cast-iron steam radiator is located in the recess below the window. This unit was installed for the Albert Cluetts and was moved to this position in 1961 from an unknown third floor location. During the Hart period, a window seat was placed in the window recess. A small (8" × 19½") white enameled cast-iron register is located in the floor next to the northwest corner. This may be the register installed by Bussey and Magee in 1856. Until the late 1840s, the room was heated by the fireplace which probably included a coal grate.

LIGHTING

A large six-arm electrified gasolier is suspended from the ceiling. The ornate Rococo style fixture, finished in ormolu with damascened detailing, dates to about 1850. It was placed here in 1962 and was originally located at 18 Second Street. Its mate is located in the dining room.

The 1844 and 1886 inventories make no mention of a chandelier in this room and the absence of a ceiling centerpiece indicates that the use of such a fixture was not originally planned for this space. A late nineteenth century multi-armed gas chandelier is recorded in the 1904 photograph of this room (Fig. 176). The delicate "Adam" style fixture featured gas candles and was installed for the George Cluetts. It is not known if the Albert Cluetts placed a fixture in this room.

EQUIPMENT

A servant's electric call button is positioned next to the doorway 53" above the floor. It probably dates to the George and Amanda Cluett era or may be one of the three electric (battery operated) bells installed for Sarah Wool Hart in 1890. Apparatus introduced by

RCHS includes a wall mounted radio-intercom panel, installed in 1969 (removed in 1998) and the ADT security panel and alarm bell.

FIREPLACE

A 6'2" wide × 11" deep plastered masonry chimney breast is centered on the south wall. The original solid black and black gold veined Italian marble mantel is composed of plain columns with ionic capitals supporting a deep frieze and projecting shelf. The fire box and hearth are formed of slabs of soapstone which date to George or Albert Cluetts occupancy. Any evidence for a Hart-era coal grate was lost when the soapstone was installed. The original brass supports for the Hart-era fire tool brackets remain in situ on each side of the mantel.

FURNISHINGS AND FITTINGS

The evolving decor of this space is recorded by several Hart-era documents and in the only photograph of the room which dates to 1904 when the house was occupied by the George Cluetts (Fig. 176). The 1844 and 1886 Hart inventories refer to this room as the "Library."

In 1844, the room included a bookcase and books, a sofa, five chairs, a sewing chair, and work table as well as a table and cover, a carpet and rug (probably a hearth rug), and a looking glass. The two candlesticks listed were probably placed on the mantel and the chart was probably positioned on the wall.

Elizabeth Shields Eddy further defines the room's appearance. She notes that a coal grate was placed in the fireplace during the summer and that bookcases flanked the mantel. One of the semicircular ends of the dining table was placed against the west wall and an old mahogany haircloth sofa was set against the long north wall. This may be the circa 1830 sofa shown in the dining room in the 1892 photograph. A mahogany haircloth-covered window seat was positioned in the window recess. Near the window was a small library table and the chair used by her grandmother, Betsey Hart.

The 1886 inventory provides greater detail regarding the furnishing of the room, but by that time many of the earlier pieces had been replaced. Items of note in the 1886 document include a gilt cornice and blue lambrequin at the window covered by a pair of lace curtains and a shade. A sofa and chair were also upholstered in blue. The two bookcases are probably the pair of low mahogany bookcases inlaid with green marble purchased from L. Marcotte and Company in 1861 for $348.00. A pair of bookcases of this description are in the RCHS collection and are currently in use in the library located in the Carr Building. The mantel mirror may be the mantel glass purchased from Elijah Galusha in 1859. A clock was positioned on the fireplace mantel shelf.

Several framed engravings were placed on the walls including the well-known illustration of Washington Irving and his friends. Evidence for the positioning of these ornaments survives on the plaster wall surfaces now hidden behind the Cluett-era canvas covering. The family bible was also kept here according to the inventory. Hart family financial records refer to this room as the library and reception room.

The earliest recorded purchase was made in 1850 from Galusha who supplied a window cornice. In 1859, he supplied a mantel glass for this room. In 1887, Louis Muller laid matting in the library.

The 1904 photograph records the room as decorated and furnished for the George Cluetts. A prominent feature is the large overmantel mirror that was located in the front parlor (102) during the Hart era. This important early furnishing was placed by RCHS in the back parlor (104). The Cluett decor includes several framed paintings on the walls as well as what appears to be a large circular ceramic charger (bowl) on the north wall. The dark finished floor is partially covered by small oriental patterned rugs. An antique or reproduction Empire-style fall front desk is centered on the west wall. This decor with its eclectic array of furnishings represents typical late nineteenth century taste for a conservative upperclass household.

There is no record of the room's appearance during the occupancy of the house by Albert and Caroline Cluett who used this space as a reception room and library. The Hart overmantel mirror likely remained above the fireplace since it does not appear in the photographs of other important rooms. Its simple form would have complimented the panel moldings installed on the canvas-covered walls by the Albert Cluetts. It is not known if a chandelier was used here during that period.

For RCHS, this important room has served as the main office as well as the director's office for many years. Period furnishings from the collection as well as functional office furnishings are used here. The north wall includes security apparatus as well as a large bulletin board.

The large gilt framed overmantel mirror now used here was located in the Albert Cluetts front parlor, but it may be the mantel glass supplied for the library by Galusha in 1859. Investigation of the wall surface behind the canvas covering may help to determine if this mirror has a history of use in this room.

FINISHES INVESTIGATION

Information concerning the changing decor of this room is found in the Hart family financial records, evidence in the room and in the only illustration of the space, the 1904 photograph (Fig. 176).

Investigation of the wall surfaces revealed that the white plaster had always been covered in wallpaper prior to the installation of the painted canvas finish for the Albert Cluetts.

Elizabeth Shields Eddy recalled that the library walls "were just the color of Grandmother's [Betsey Hart] little baked custards." No evidence for a painted surface was found on the plaster, so this custard color must have related to one of the wallpapers used here. The Hart family financial records include numerous payments for the installation of wallpaper, but the specific locations for these papers are frequently not recorded.

In 1869, L. Marcotte and Company supplied seventeen rolls of gray flowered paper and ninety-nine yards of blue and gilt border paper, possibley for the library. The 1886 inventory confirms the use of the color blue for fabric in this room. W. W. Whitman's invoice for the installation of the Marcotte decor includes a reference to hanging (blue and gilt) borders, a popular wall treatment that makes use of paper borders to create a series of simulated panels on the wall surfaces. In 1870, Galusha upholstered a sofa and covered furniture in blue tufts, possibly for this room.

The room may have again been redecorated in 1887 when Thomas Buckley of Albany installed wallpaper and ceiling paper in the "Reception Room." This work included the removal of the old paper.

The only image of this room is the view dating to 1904 that includes Beatrice Cluett. The elaborate Cluett decor features a boldly patterned floral wallpaper and matching deep paper border. The plaster cornice appears to be polychromed and there is a picture rail positioned between the border and wallpaper.

The Cluett panel moldings, installed circa 1910, were removed by RCHS, possibly when the room was reno-

vated in 1969. In the late 1970s, the walls were painted in a yellow tint to simulate the "custard color" recalled by Elizabeth Shields Eddy.

110   Passage – Former Pantry

This narrow hall, like its continuation to the east (105), has functioned in various ways for the Harts, Cluetts, and RCHS

In plan, the long rectangular space 5'7" × 22'7" includes single door openings in the north, south, east, and west walls and a window opening in the north wall.

The passage, the adjoining bedroom (111) and the west end of the dining room (106) along with additional spaces in the basement and second and third floor form the west addition added to the original house for Richard Hart around 1836. The 1844 inventory refers to this structure as the "back building." An important part of this expansion was the creation of a service or back stair which was located in this space. The stair originally extended from the first floor to the third floor in three runs. A more compact stair at the back of the hall descended to the basement. The stair to the upper floors was positioned against the north wall, ascending from the east end of the passage. The surviving portions of the stairway at the second floor level reveal the character of this important feature. The stair was removed from this space at the time of the construction of the final portion of the rear wing for the George Cluetts in circa 1893. The turned newel post, from the base of the stair at first floor level, was salvaged and reinstalled at the remaining portion of the stair in the second floor hall (211). The small stair to the basement was removed at the same time. The slightly irregular plan of the passage, which features a greater width at the west end, resulted from the need for more space to accommodate the service stair.

As originally completed, the passage included only a single window opening in the north wall. That original opening was converted into a doorway when the passage connecting the house to the Carr Building, next door at 57 Second Street, was constructed in 1990. An additional window opening was inserted in the north wall after the service stair was removed circa 1893. A second doorway was originally located in the south partition. It opened into the dining room (106), but was removed by RCHS sometime after 1952. This important service doorway is recorded in the 1892 and 1934 photographs of the dining room (Figs. 129 & 130).

The west doorway (D1102), which now leads to the first floor kitchen added by the George Cluetts, was, prior to 1893, the rear exterior door. The fanlight above the door opening was originally located above the rear west door in the back wall of the 1827 house (D1101) (Fig. 177). This important feature was moved to this location in circa 1836 when the "back building" was constructed.

For the Hart family, this passage functioned as a pantry as well as a circulation space. Physical evidence in the basement passage (B09) and Hart financial records indicate that a pantry sink was located here. Plumbing evidence indicates that the sink was positioned next to the north wall immediately west of the existing window. The small "twisting stairway" remembered by Elizabeth Shields Eddy was located immediately to the west of the pantry sink. Physical evidence for the sink and the stair arrangement exists on the original floor surface now hidden by later finishes including the tile installed in 1959.

The 1886 inventory lists the contents of two pantries, "Pantry No. 1 and No. 2," but this may refer to storage cabinets rather than two separate spaces. The inventory also lists a separate space called the "back stairs to second story" which is this passage (110).

The transformation of the space into a cabinet-lined butler's pantry, after the acquisition of the house by George and Amanda Cluett in 1893, is recorded by the 1934 HABS floor plans and physical evidence preserved on the wall surfaces. The floor plan shows two long built-in cabinets flanking the window in the north wall and evidence on that wall surface indicates that shelves were positioned at about 66½" and 92½" above the

177 The doorway (D1102), and fanlight in the west wall (110).

floor. The 53" wide stainless steel sink and counter, now located in the kitchen pantry (113) was positioned beneath the window between the cabinets. This was the approximate location of the Hart-era pantry sink and the Cluett sink made use of the earlier drain pipe that can still be seen in the basement room (B09) directly below. Further evidence is probably hidden behind the wood dado installed in circa 1958 by RCHS when the Cluett pantry cabinets and sink were removed.

There is additional evidence for shelving on the narrow section of the south wall immediately west of the now removed doorway (D1064) to the dining room. This shelving and a related partition that appear to have extended across the width of the hall, in that location, date to the Hart era. Additional physical evidence for these conditions is probably hidden behind the Cluett-era dado that exists on the south wall.

The Report of the House Committee submitted on February 5, 1953, recommended that a gas stove and electric refrigerator be placed in the butler's pantry (this space) so that it could function as a kitchen for the proposed curator. There was no need to install a sink since one already existed here.

In circa 1958, the Cluett-era cabinetry was removed and the wall surfaces above the dado were covered in masonite peg board so that the passage could be used as a museum exhibition area. The northeast cabinet was installed against the west wall of the kitchen pantry (113). In 1994, the pegboard was removed so that the passage could be partially restored.

FLOOR

The floor is finished in 9" × 9" black and white rubber tiles laid in a checkerboard pattern. The tiles were supplied by Devane's Floor Coverings and the work was carried out by Wilson Large in 1959. Narrow Cluett-era hardwood flooring, running east/west exists beneath this surface. The original circa 1836 wide board flooring underneath probably retains evidence for the position of the original Hart-era service stair and pantry sink.

WALLS

The north, east, and west walls are finished in circa 1836 plaster on brick masonry. The south partition is of plaster on wood lath. The masonry east wall is the rear wall of the original 1827 house.

Each wall features a 42½" high vertical board wainscot. The earliest wainscot, on the south, east, and west walls with a short section at the east end of the

178 The 1827 west exterior doorway fanlight in its current location (D1102).

north wall, dates to the remodeling of the passage for the George Cluetts. The profile of the vertical boards matches that found in the nearby kitchen (112). The wainscot along the north wall differs in detail and was installed by RCHS after the removal of the pantry cabinets. Wainscot of a third type fills the location of the former doorway (D1064) to the dining room and dates to after 1952.

There is evidence on the north and south walls and on the ceiling for a thin partition that was parallel to the east wall about 5'7½" from that surface. This missing surface predates the wainscot installed for the George Cluetts and was probably inserted in the passage at a very early date to provide a separation from the service stair located at the west end of the space.

CEILING

The ceiling is formed of plain surfaces at two different heights. The original plaster-on-lath surface is located west of the point where the passage becomes wider. The east ceiling surface, about 10" higher, is now covered in fiberboard with joints covered by wood furring strips and was installed after 1952. The difference in ceiling heights roughly corresponds to the difference in the floor level of the wing at the second floor.

BASEBOARD

There is no baseboard, but a quarter-round shoe molding is positioned at the bottom of the wainscot and probably dates to the 1959 installation of the tile flooring. Any original circa 1836 base was removed when the wainscot was installed beginning in about 1893.

CORNICE

No cornice has ever existed in this passage. A narrow 1" deep wood cove mold is located at the edge of the fiberboard ceiling surface at the east end of the space and is contemporary with that finish.

DOORS

Currently, there are four door openings in the passage: single original openings in the south (D1111), east (D1101), and west (D1102) walls, and a recent opening (D1103) created by lengthening a window in the north wall. Another original opening (D1064) was formerly located in the south wall but was removed after 1952.

The south and east doorways (D1111, D1101) retain the original circa 1836 architraves typically used throughout the addition. The same trim was reproduced for the doorway created in the north wall in 1990. The west doorway (D1102) includes a 39½" wide semicircular fan-light set into the plastered brick wall with no trim. The fanlight sash was originally located above the original 1827 doorway located at the east end of the passage. That opening was the rear exterior doorway of the original house (Fig. 178).

The architrave of the west doorway is composed of old reused elements including corner blocks probably removed from the Back Parlor doorway (D1042) dismantled in 1964 and trim from an unidentified location. The north side of the architrave trim is more recent material dating to after 1952 when the pantry cabinets were removed.

D1101: The circa 1836 door is missing from the opening but there are marks for three 4" tall hinges on the north jamb; the door opened into the passage.

D1102: The circa 1836 door is missing from the opening but there are marks for two 4½" hinges on the south jamb; the door opened into the passage.

D1103: Prior to 1990, this doorway was a window opening. A door has never existed in the opening.

D1064: The circa 1836 door opening formerly located here included an eight-panel door hinged to the east jamb and opening into the dining room. The door was converted into a swinging door when the first floor kitchen (111) was created circa 1893.

WINDOWS

Prior to 1990, there were two window openings in the north wall: an original circa 1836 opening (now a doorway) and a later opening created after the removal of the service stairs in circa 1893. This later opening includes two-over-two double rope-hung sash with ¾" wide muntins. The trim duplicates the profile of the 1836 door trim. Below the sill, the missing apron is replaced by a simple board installed by RCHS after the removal of the Cluett-era pantry sink in this location.

HEATING

There is no evidence that this passage was ever heated.

LIGHTING

There are three ceiling-mounted fluorescent fixtures installed by RCHS. There is no evidence for Cluett-era lighting devices. A gas pipe (60" tall) is affixed to the west side of the architrave of door D1111. A gas bracket light was positioned at the top of the pipe. This was the light source for the Harts and possibly the George Cluetts.

PLUMBING

Physical evidence of piping in basement room (B09) beneath this passage and Hart family financial records indicated that a pantry sink was located here, probably against the north wall beneath the former stairway to the second floor. Evidence for this feature also may exist on the original floor surface. The Albert Cluetts had a stainless steel sink and counter installed against the north wall beneath the window. The 53" wide × 24" deep unit was moved to the kitchen pantry (113) in circa 1958. The wood enclosed pipe chase in the southeast corner conceals a cast-iron soil line and gas piping. The enclosure originally housed plumbing, installed during the Hart era, that served the former second floor bathroom (207).

EQUIPMENT

There is evidence on the wall surface above the now covered opening (D1064) to the dining room for an electric call bell, dating to the Cluett era.

FURNISHINGS AND FITTINGS

The character of this space has evolved as its function changed for the Harts, Cluetts, and RCHS. As created in circa 1836, this was essentially a passage and service stair hall with little or no furnishings. There is evidence on the narrow section of the south wall next to the plumbing chase (southeast corner) for a 2¾" wide wood rail that was positioned at about 78" above the floor. This original feature was partially or completely removed when the chase was constructed in the nineteenth century. The rail may have supported a shelf or held hooks. Evidence for additional original wood rails that supported shelving exists on the south wall immediately west of the former doorway to the dining room. The 3" deep rails were positioned at 48¾", 64½", 79½", 93½" and 106¾" above the floor and there may be additional marks for rails hidden behind the wood dado.

Evidence on the north and south walls and ceilings indicated that a thin partition, possibly formed of boards, was part of the shelving located here. Wall paint layering revealed that these fittings were original or very early features of the passage but were removed in the nineteenth century.

Evidence on the north wall, including wood nailers

set into the plaster surface, defined the position of the pantry cabinets installed for the George Cluetts and recorded on the 1934 HABS floor plan. Shelving flanked the window and was positioned at about 66½" and 92½" above the floor. The cabinets consisted of two tiers, the upper units were about 14" deep and the base cabinets were 21" deep. These important pantry fittings were removed in circa 1958 by RCHS. The northeast unit was placed in the kitchen pantry (113) as was the pantry sink.

The wall surfaces were covered in masonite pegboard so that the corridor could function as a display area for collections. This material was removed in the mid-1990s.

FINISHES INVESTIGATION

Analysis of the original (circa 1836) wood trim revealed that it was first finished in yellowish/white followed by faux wood graining, possibly imitating oak. This Hart-era treatment survived through the George Cluett era when the wood dado was installed. The dado surface was varnished to match the faux graining. Beginning with Albert and Caroline Cluett, the woodwork, including the dado, was painted white. Later the dado and pipe chase enclosure were painted in a light blue while the other trim was finished in white. This scheme was carried out by RCHS.

The plaster wall surfaces retain approximately eleven painted finishes. The first finish is a yellow/gold, later repainted in a similar color but with a glossy finish followed by an ivory color and a pink/beige. After the pantry cabinets were installed for the George Cluetts the walls were painted yellowish/white.

111   Bedroom – Sitting Room

This small but significant room is located immediately west of the dining room and is part of the expansion of the house undertaken by Richard Hart in circa 1836.

In plan, the 14'5" × 14'10" room includes single doorways in the north and east partitions, a pair of windows in the south wall and a shallow chimney breast on the west wall.

The construction of the rear addition to the house in circa 1836 included this room as well as the adjoining hall (110) and the enlarged dining room (106).

The architectural detailing of this room reflects the fashion of the 1830s Grecian style, but the baseboard

duplicates the tall formal base used in the original 1827 house. This may have occurred because it was necessary to fabricate the older style baseboard for the expansion of the adjoining dining room. It is also probable that John Colegrove, the builder of the original house, was responsible for this addition. He would have produced the original baseboard and likely retained the molding plane used in its production.

Although the original intended use of the room is unknown, by 1844 it was furnished as a bedroom, according to the inventory of that year. Elizabeth Shields Eddy confirms that this was her grandmother, Betsey Hart's bedroom and indicates that a tall-post bed was located here. Betsey may have occupied this room after the tragic death of her husband in 1843. However, the 1886 inventory refers to this space as Mrs. Hart's sitting room and no bedstead is included in the list of furnishings.

A small portion of the room is shown in the 1892 photograph of the dining room (Fig. 179). The few furnishings visible beyond the door in the photo can be

179 Looking into Room 111 from the dining room (106), c. 1892.

identified in the 1886 inventory. Also shown is an interesting wall-mounted steam radiator.

This space may have functioned as a sitting room for George and Amanda Cluett and it was probably after 1893 that the wood mantelpiece, which was located here until the 1960s, was installed. It would have replaced the Hart period mantel.

The 1934 HABS floor plan indicates that this was Albert and Caroline Cluett's sitting room but there is no visual record of the space as furnished by them (see Appendix IV). Becky Cluett, Caroline Cluett's granddaughter, indicates that this was the children's dining room. The room retained its domestic character for a period of time after RCHS occupied the house beginning in 1952. The Report of the House Committee submitted on February 5, 1953, referred to this space as the "small dining room" and it may have functioned as such for the Cluetts. The report recommended that it might function as a living/dining space for the proposed curator. One of the cupboards from the adjoining butler's pantry (110) was to be placed here. In 1963, the appearance of the room was radically altered by the removal of the mantel and the installation of large wood and glass display cases that covered the wall surfaces as well as the two windows. The cases were a gift from the estate of George S. McKearin. The room currently is furnished to reflect its use by Betsey Hart but the fireplace is not restored.

FLOOR

The floor is finished in narrow 2¼" wide stripes of tongue-and-groove oak, laid east/west over the original wide board surface. This hardwood surface was installed for George and Amanda Cluett. Oak infill boards are located in the position of the original fireplace hearth removed in the 1960s by RCHS.

WALLS

The south and west walls are finished in plaster on brick masonry and the north and east walls are of plaster on sawn wood lath. The original plastered brick chimney breast is positioned in the west wall.

CEILING

The original plaster-on-lath ceiling is about 9'9" above the floor.

BASEBOARD

The original 12" high baseboard is identical in profile to the base used in the 1827 portions of the house. The section positioned along the face of the chimney breast is a reproduction installed when the mantel was removed.

CORNICE

The delicately detailed run-in-place plaster cornice is an original feature.

DOORS

There are two original circa 1836 door openings: a single doorway in the north partition (D1111) and a single doorway in the east partition (D1063). Both retain the original 6¼" wide architraves typically used in the circa 1836 addition.

D1111: This opening retains the original circa 1836 six-panel, stile-and-rail painted wood door. The rectangular recessed panels are framed in molding of the same profile used on the architraves.

Hardware: Original fittings include a pair of 4⅛" high wide swing cast-iron butt hinges stamped with a partially decipherable (__?__ AR & Son), a 6½" high brass faced mortise lock stamped McKinney and Jones Troy, two cast-brass knobs and two brass drop-cover keyhole escutcheons. A mortised night bolt with brass turn latch is positioned above the knob. All of these fittings can be seen in the 1892 photograph that records the door as seen from the dining room.

D1063: The original circa 1836 eight-panel door opens into the dining room.

WINDOWS

There are two original circa 1836 window openings symmetrically positioned in the south wall. The architraves duplicate the trim used at the door openings and rest on unusually detailed sills featuring a convex molding sandwiched between two flat fascias. The openings are fitted with original six-over-six double-hung sash. The west edge of the sill of the west window has been cut off, possibly when the display cases were installed here in the 1960s. Hardware includes a cast-brass Hart-era fastener on the west sash and a Cluett-era fastener on the east sash.

HEATING

The room is currently heated by two cast-iron steam pipes, positioned next to the north partition, that service the radiator in second floor Room 212. A wall-mounted cast-iron pipe radiator is shown on the north partition in the 1892 photograph that records this room as seen through the door (D1063) to the dining room. Steam heating apparatus was first installed in the house in 1862 by Baker and Smith of New York City and this was probably one of the early fittings for that system. Similar radiators remain in place in basement rooms B02 and B06. The room originally included a fireplace which heated the room. This important feature was removed in the 1960s.

LIGHTING

Currently there is no fixed lighting in the room. A cover plate centered in the ceiling represents the position of an electric fixture and possibly an earlier gas fixture.

FIREPLACE

The room as completed circa 1836 included a fireplace centered in the west wall. This important feature is recorded in the 1934 HABS floor plan and in a color slide dating to the 1960s. The wood mantel shown in the slide appears to date to the George or Albert Cluett era and must have replaced the Hart-era feature. The firebox is now closed up and the hearth is removed.

FURNISHINGS AND FITTINGS

In the 1844 inventory, this space is furnished as a bedroom, possibly its original intended use. Referred to as the "Bedroom Below," it included a bedstead, wash stand, bookcase, eleven chairs (possibly for use in the adjoining dining room), and a dressing case. The windows featured curtains. Elizabeth Shields Eddy remembered this space as her grandmother, Betsey Hart's bedroom. It was furnished with a tall four-post bed, a bureau, washstand, and a sewing table. Th sewing table may be the Hart family furnishing currently displayed in the room and bequeathed by Elizabeth Shields Eddy's daughter, Ruth Hart Eddy, in 1957. Betsey Hart may have first occupied this bedroom after the tragic death of her husband, Richard Hart, in 1843.

In the 1886 inventory, the room is included as "Mrs. Hart's Sitting Room" and the long list of furnishings includes a sofa, wash stand, commode, bureau and glass, table and spread, easy chair, Shaker rocker, willow rocker, three chairs, a bookcase as well as a carpet, lambrequin on the mantel, mantel clock, and a pair of curtains and shades. No bedstead is listed, perhaps the tall-post bed had already been given to a family member.

The 1892 photograph of the Hart dining room provides a glimpse into this room through the doorway connecting the two spaces. Visible furnishings include the Shaker rocker, a bookcase with glazed, fabric-lined, doors and a circular table with cover. Behind the table is a small caned-back side chair.

The Albert Cluetts and possibly the George Cluetts, used this space as a sitting room (Fig. 180) and it is so identified on the 1934 HABS floor plan. It was during this period that the wood mantel, removed by RCHS, was installed in place of the Hart-era mantel piece. In 1953, the space is referred to as the "small dining room," a function confirmed by Becky Cluett, who indicates that the Cluett grandchildren ate here. A round table was placed in the center of the room. No photographs record the room during the Cluett eras.

A color slide taken in 1961 records the room as furnished by RCHS as a sitting room. The window cur-

180 The Cluett era mantel was in place in this 1961 photograph of Room 111.

tains are suspended from a pair of cornices that Albert and Caroline Cluett had used in the back parlor (104) and are shown there in a 1934 photograph. RCHS records indicate that these furnishings were cut down to 48" in length for director H. Maxson Halloway by Gunther's Frame Shop in June, 1960. This modification was probably made so that the cornices would fit the much smaller windows in this room.

In 1963, the space was transformed into a changing exhibit gallery, known as the Early Troy and Uncle Sam Room. Furnishings including the curtain cornices as well as the fireplace mantel were removed and large wood and glass display cases were installed, completely covering the wall surfaces including the two windows. The cases were a gift of the estate of George S. McKearin.

In the 1980s, the room was restored to reflect its use by Betsey Hart as a bedroom.

112   Cluett Kitchen

This ample room was constructed soon after George and Amanda Cluett purchased the house in 1893. It functioned as the household kitchen for them and later, the Albert Cluetts (Fig. 181).

In plan, the 15'5" × 19'10" space includes pairs of windows in the south and west walls, two doorways in the north wall and a doorway in the east wall of the short extension of the room to the northeast. A shallow chimney breast is centered in the south wall.

The kitchen was created in circa 1893 as part of the westward expansion of the circa 1836 rear wing. Besides this space, the addition included an adjoining pantry and service stairway as well as new rooms in the basement, second, and third floors.

The primary reason for this expansion was probably the desire to create a new "modern" kitchen on the first floor near the dining room. The original kitchen, in use for about sixty-six years, was located in the basement. All of the prepared food was brought up the narrow stairway located beneath the main stairway and carried through the formal stair hall (102) and into the dining room. By late-nineteenth century standards this was considered inconvenient and old fashioned. The new room, with its four large windows and wood wainscot, was considered a healthier location for food preparation. Hygiene and convenience were concerns in home planning at the end of the nineteenth century; the Cluetts were simply making the house up-to-date.

181 The kitchen (112) looking southeast.

The new room featured all of the necessary amenities of a modern kitchen including piped hot and cold water, a cooking range and an icebox, as well as light and ventilation. There were built-in cabinets and an ample food pantry was just beyond the door in the north partition. Additional pantry space was created in the passage (110) that formerly included the Hart-era service stairs.

Albert and Caroline Cluett possibly updated the kitchen by installing a new range, a refrigerator and placing linoleum on the wood floor surface. A January 1954 House Committee Report notes that the kitchen and pantry were redecorated. The cabinet positioned against the east wall was removed in 1958 so that the former kitchen could function as a workroom. The pantry (113) became a small kitchenette for use by RCHS.

The eventual renovation of the room by RCHS included the installation of masonite pegboard on the wall surfaces above the wainscot. This obscured all aspects of the original kitchen, creating a very institutional appearance.

In the 1980s, the room was restored to reflect its

appearance during the period that George and Amanda Cluett occupied the house.

The doorway in the east wall preserves an important feature behind the wall surface above the opening which was the west exterior doorway of the circa 1836 addition. Concealed behind the lath and plaster wall surface above the doorway is a fully intact fanlight complete with the exterior semicircular stone lintel formed of three white marble segments. This stonework and the fanlight sash were moved to this location in circa 1836 from their original position above the rear (west) door (D1101) of the original 1827 portion of the house. This important architectural feature was concealed when the kitchen addition was added to the rear wing in circa 1893 for George and Amanda Cluett.

FLOOR

The original flooring consists of narrow 2½" wide strips of tongue-and-groove hardwood laid east/west. The surface is now painted. The surface was most recently covered by linoleum in a spatter pattern possibly installed for the Albert Cluetts in the late 1940s.

WALLS

All the walls are finished in original plaster on wood lath. The shallow chimney breast centered in the south wall is of plaster on brick masonry. An original 42½" high vertical beaded board wainscot exists on all walls. The top of this surface is finished in a 5" deep rail which is ornamented with an incised double bead. The same wainscot is found in the adjoining passages (105 and 110). The brick surface concealed by the east plaster wall is the former exterior face of the rear wall of the circa 1836 wing.

CEILING

The original narrow tongue-and-groove beaded boards are laid east/west and are positioned at 9'4" above the floor.

BASEBOARD

The original 3" high plain base has a narrow beaded top.

CORNICE

All four walls include an original narrow quarter-round molding, at the meeting of the ceiling and wall surfaces.

DOORS

There are three original door openings in the kitchen: two openings in the north wall (D1121 and D1122) and an opening in the east wall (D1102). Each retains the original architrave composed of 5" wide trim that generally duplicates the circa 1836 trim found in the earlier part of the rear addition to the original house. The molding profile is slightly more rounded that the feature it copies.

D1121: This opening retains the original stile-and-rail door with six vertical panels. This door and others in this part of the rear wing duplicate the doors created in circa 1836. Like the trim molding, the panel molding is slightly more rounded than the original 1836 profile.

Hardware: Original fittings include three 3½" high cast-iron butt hinges, a 5½" high iron mortise lock and a pair of 2¼" diameter disk-shaped turned wood knobs affixed to iron shanks. The rectangular wood keyhole escutcheons are attached to the door with nails.

D1122: This original door duplicates door D1121.

Hardware: Original fittings include three 3½" high cast-iron butt hinges. The lock is missing and the mortise is filled in but the strike plate is in place on the east jamb. The knobs and roses are missing but the wood escutcheons survive on both door faces. A key-operated Yale latch is surface mounted on the pantry face of the door and was installed by RCHS.

D1102: The door is missing from the deep recess of this opening. Prior to the construction of kitchen addition in circa 1893 this was the west exterior doorway of the circa 1836 addition.

WINDOWS

There are four original window openings, two positioned in the west wall and two flanking the shallow chimney breast centered in the south wall. The architraves duplicate the profile of the door rim and rest on a bullnose sill and a shallow apron. The openings are fitted with original six-over-six double rope-hung sash with ⅝" wide muntins and 10" × 18" panes. The sash are secured by original decorative cast-iron fasteners.

The 1934 HABS floor plan does not record the two openings in the west wall, a mistake made by the delineator of the drawing.

HEATING

There is a single original cast-iron steam radiator positioned below the north window in the west wall. Two circular stove pipe openings exist in the upper surface of the chimney breast. They served the cooking ranges positioned next to the south wall.

LIGHTING

A chain-suspended incandescent fixture is positioned at the center of the ceiling. The fixture, installed by RCHS in the 1980s includes a pressed opal glass shade. The location of this fixture is the same as the Cluett-era electrical fixture and possibly an earlier gas pendant. A spotlight positioned above door D1102 was installed by RCHS.

PLUMBING

There is physical evidence for the location of original kitchen plumbing. The sink was positioned in the southwest corner and there is evidence for the piping in the floor surface. The original sink was placed against the window trim and there is a cutout on that surface indicating the height and position of the fixture at 43" and 50" above the floor. The floor surface next to the west edge of the chimney breast preserved the outline of the stand that supported the original hot water tank.

The current antique fixtures in these locations, an enameled iron sink and galvanized iron hot water tank on a stand, were placed here in the 1980s when the room was restored to its Cluett-era appearance.

An original wood pipe chase is located in the southeast corner. It encloses the soil line piping for the second floor bathroom (215) directly above.

EQUIPMENT

The antique Service Stewart cooking range was placed here in the 1980s. The types of ranges used by the two Cluett families is unknown, but their position is defined by the location of the stove pipe openings in the chimney breast and evidence on the flooring for a large sheet metal pad that was attached to that surface with tacks. The pad is now simulated in painted plywood.

It is possible that the George Cluetts had a coal-fired range and the Albert Cluetts used a gas range. The existence of two stove pipe openings indicates that two stoves may have been used here simultaneously, a practice not uncommon in the late nineteenth and early twentieth century.

FURNISHINGS AND FITTINGS

There is no written documentation or photographic evidence concerning the appearance and function of the kitchen. It is likely that the arrangement and furnishing of this important service space evolved over the fifty-nine years of its use by the two Cluett families.

Between 1893 and 1952 tremendous advances occurred in kitchen appliances and notions of convenience and hygiene.

The basic furnishings and fittings of this or any kitchen included a cooking range, sink, icebox or refrigerator and a hot water source as well as counters and cabinets. Investigation of the room and information provided by the 1934 HABS floor plan revealed the locations, if not the type, of most of these kitchen elements. The stove or stoves were located next to the south wall and the small utilitarian sink was tucked into the southwest corner. The water heater was conveniently positioned between these furnishings. A built-in cabinet was located against the east wall. There is physical evidence for this 20" deep × 132" long feature on the floor and wall surfaces and it is recorded in the HABS floor plan which shows a two-section cabinet divided into four units. This important kitchen feature was removed in 1958 when the room was used for museum purposes. There is additional evidence for built-in shelving on the north wall of the short extension of the kitchen space in the northeast corner next to the passage door. The wall surfaces retained evidence for bracket supported shelves on the north wall between the doorways and on the south wall between the chimney breast and the southeast window. The shelves currently in these locations were installed in the 1980s.

The location for the original icebox and the later refrigerator is not known but a position along the north wall is likely.

113   Kitchenette – Former Pantry

This small 6'11" × 7' pantry is part of the expansion of the rear wing undertaken for the George Cluetts.

In plan, the nearly square room includes a single doorway in the south wall and a window opening in the north wall.

The 1934 HABS floor plan indicates that there was shelving on the west wall and physical evidence reveals that this was open shelving. This probably served as the food pantry. Dishes and cookware were probably kept in other locations in the kitchen (112) and former pantry (110).

After 1952, the space was modified to function as a kitchenette for RCHS. A range was installed here and the original open shelving was replaced by a cabinet unit removed from the pantry located in the passage (110). The sink from that space was also installed here at the same time (Fig. 182).

182 The cabinets were removed from the former hall pantry (110) and placed here (113)after 1952.

FLOOR

The floor surface consists of linoleum installed by RCHS in the 1990s over original narrow 2½" wide strips of tongue-and-groove hardwood laid east/west. An earlier linoleum, installed late in the Cluett period or by RCHS, formerly covered the wood surface. The wood surface is exposed under the west cabinet.

WALLS

All four walls are finished in original plaster on wood lath. There is evidence on the north and south surfaces for the original pantry shelving that existed along the west wall.

CEILING

The original plaster-on-lath surface is 9'4" above the floor.

BASEBOARD

The original 7½" high base has an integral ogee crown. The quarter-round shoe molding is contemporary with the linoleum.

DOORS

The original door opening in the south wall (D1122) includes trim that copies the trim profile of the circa 1836 openings.

WINDOWS

The single original window opening in the north wall features the same trim as the door, but the applied molding is removed from the outer edge of the architrave. The sill is 48½" above the floor. The opening is fitted with original two-over-two double rope-hung sash secured by the original iron fastener. This window opening matches the extant opening in the north wall of the passage (110); both features date to circa 1893. The missing molding probably incorporated evidence for the original shelving positioned on the east wall.

HEATING

This small room was never heated.

LIGHTING

There are two fluorescent fixtures that were installed by RCHS. The ceiling-mounted fixture is connected to surface mounted armored cable. The fixture mounted under the shelf on the east wall is powered by lamp cord. There is no visible evidence for the lighting devices from the Cluett periods.

PLUMBING

A stainless steel sink and counter (24" × 53") with a 12" high back splash is positioned against the east wall. The sink was placed here by RCHS, but was originally located between the cupboards formerly located against the north wall of the former pantry (110). The paneled wood cabinet door, positioned below the sink counter, appears to date to the Hart era and may be from the cabinetry formerly in that same location (110).

EQUIPMENT

Appliances placed here by RCHS include a Hardwick four-burner gas range and a small refrigerator, marked Indesit, located under the east counter.

FURNISHINGS AND FITTINGS

The most important furnishing is the large two-tier double cabinet and counter that is positioned against the west wall. The unit includes a 21" deep base cabinet fitted with three tiers of drawers and slide trays positioned beneath the 34" high counter. The counter surface is covered in 9" × 9" black rubber tile, probably installed in 1959. The drawers retain original brass pulls. The 14" deep upper cabinet consists of two side-by-side shelving units fitted with pairs of glazed doors. The interior shelving is adjustable. Physical evidence for hinge positions indicates that the lower portions of the doors were cut off, creating the deep counter space. The unit is finished with a cornice.

The 6'3" wide by 8'5" tall cabinet originated from the former pantry (110) and was modified and moved here circa 1958 along with the sink from that space. There is evidence on the wall surfaces behind this cabinet for the original open pantry shelving shown on the 1934 HABS floor plan.

Two original open shelves are located on the east wall above the sink and stove. There is evidence for two additional shelves at 34" and 67" above the floor. A mark for the bullnose edge of one of the missing shelves is visible on the edge of the door architrave. A nickel-plated brass towel bar, dating to the Cluett era, is attached to the face of the door.

114   Back Stair Hall

The back stair hall is an important part of the rear addition added to the house by the George Cluetts.

The small hall includes door openings in the south, west, and north walls and an impressive curving stairway ascending to the second floor and filling the east end of the space.

An enclosed stair provides access to the basement. The Cluett addition to the Hart-era rear wing included several important spaces as well as this hall. The stairs replaced the Hart-era service stair that was located in the pantry/passage (110) (Fig. 183).

Significant modifications made by RCHS after 1952 include the replacement of the original exterior door with the six-paneled door now in place and relocation of the basement door to its current position.

The repositioning of the door resulted in the creation of a small separate space at the top of the basement stair and separated the utility sink from the stair hall and rear entrance. According to a August 13, 1962, *Times Record* article, the original back door included a window.

After the 1955–56 conversion of the carriage house for use as RCHS meeting hall, this small vestibule functioned as the busy connector between the house and the auditorium.

FLOOR

The floor is finished in narrow 2½" wide strips of tongue-and-groove hardwood, laid east/west and now painted. The area at the head of the basement stairway includes a spatter-pattern linoleum, possibly laid over plywood placed on the original narrow boards. The same linoleum exists in the pantry (112) and formerly was used in the kitchen (112).

WALLS

The walls are finished in plaster on wood lath. The partition that encloses the basement stairway is composed of 3½" wide vertical beaded board.

CEILING

The original ceiling, including the underside of the staircase, is finished in plaster on wood lath. A plywood surface, installed by RCHS, is located in the area of the basement stairway, separating that space from the hall proper.

183 The service staircase (114) installed circa 1893.

CORNICE

There is no cornice in this area.

BASEBOARD

An original base follows the run of the stairway to the second floor and a similar 7½" base is located in the area to the head of the basement stairway.

DOORS

There are three openings in the hall: the original doorway in the west wall (D1141) that opens to the exterior, the doorway to the basement stair (D1142), and the doorway (D1121) to the kitchen. The exterior doorway and the kitchen doorway feature the original architrave design, and the basement door is positioned in a wood frame created when the door was relocated after 1952.

> D1141: This six-panel door replaces the original door and was installed by RCHS in 1962.

> Hardware: Fittings contemporary with the door include three butt hinges, a mortise lock and knobs, a Yale dead bolt and a brass slide bolt.

D1142: The original six-panel door is 29½" wide. The door was originally positioned in the opening located at the head of the basement stairway; the door was hinged to open against the north wall. It was moved to this location sometime after 1952.

Hardware: Original fittings include two iron butt hinges, a mortise lock, wood knobs, and wood keyhole escutcheons.

WINDOWS

There are no window openings in this space but some natural light enters here from the window located in the west wall of the second floor hall.

HEATING

This space was never heated.

LIGHTING

An incandescent wall bracket is positioned on the north partition adjacent to the stairway and was installed by RCHS. A utility fixture with an exposed incandescent bulb is located on the south partition of the basement stairway. Originally, lighting was provided by a single gas light bracket located on the south wall at 61½" above the floor.

PLUMBING

An enameled iron utility sink, supported on an iron bracket, is located in the northwest corner at the head of the basement stairway. A lead drain pipe is positioned below the sink. This sink appears to date to the George Cluett era.

STAIRWAY

The original circa 1893 winding staircase ascends to the second floor and fills the east end of the hall. The seventeen risers are 7¾" high. The massive turned newel supports a round oak handrail which rises above tapered and turned balusters. This stairway replaced the Hart-era service stair formerly located in the passage/pantry (110) adjacent to the dining room.

FURNISHINGS AND FITTINGS

An original horizontal bead-edged board is located on the west wall at 64" above the floor. The 3⅝" wide rail supported hooks but only one remains in place.

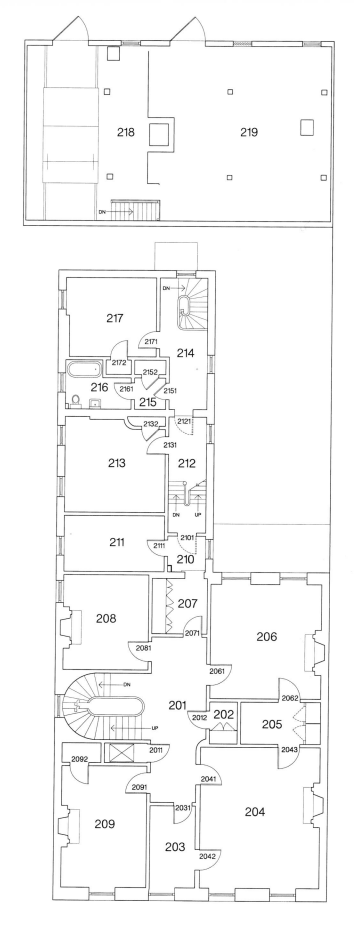

SECOND FLOOR PLAN

184 59 Second Street,
second floor plan, 1999.

0'   5'   10'   15'

SECOND FLOOR

The plan and detailing of the second floor preserve the influences of the Harts, Cluetts, and RCHS. The quality of the original architectural detailing extant here is equal to that of the primary first floor rooms, an indication of William Howard's desire for the very best workmanship throughout the house (Fig. 184). Only slight compromises exist; here the doors were grained to simulate the real mahogany of the first floor doors and the Pye hardware is of polished brass without the silver plating used on the first floor door fittings.

In plan, the second floor is composed of the original mass (40' × 50') of the 1827 house, a rear addition (24' × 25') added by Richard P. Hart and the final rear extension (21' × 25') constructed for George and Amanda Cluett after their purchase of the house in 1893.

Throughout the 173 years of occupancy and use, the second floor spaces have remained remarkably well-preserved. As completed in 1827, the second floor plan included four primary rooms arranged around an ample stair hall as well as three small spaces (probably dressing rooms) and several closets (Fig. 185).

The elegant curved staircase ascends to the second floor in an alcove-like area along the south side of the second floor hall (201). North of the hall, the primary bedrooms (204, 206) are arranged above the front and back parlors. These bedrooms are separated by an interconnecting dressing room (205) and a closet that opens directly on the hall. Smaller bedrooms are positioned in the southeast (209) and southwest corners (208). Additional dressing rooms (203 and 207) separated the bedrooms across the front and rear of the main block.

The halls, as well as the bedrooms and dressing rooms, feature the same elegant trim, including corner blocks with raffle flowers, found on the first floor. Each bedroom includes a finely detailed marble mantel.

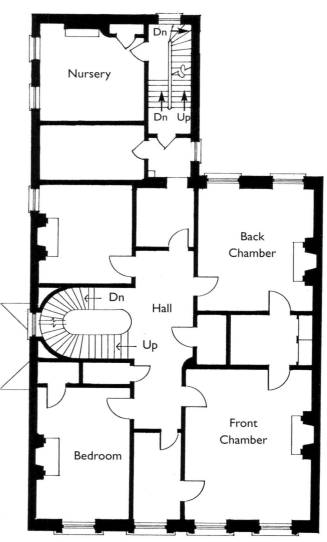

185 59 Second Street, second floor plan, 1827, D. G. Bucher, 1999.

186 59 Second Street, second floor plan, c. 1836, D. G. Bucher, 1999.

The most impressive original architectural statement is found in the curved sweep of the staircase as it continues to the third floor. An oval window positioned in the curved wall of the stairwell completes this elegant composition.

The second floor plan extends westward beyond the rear wall of the original house in a series of rooms and spaces added by the Harts and Cluetts. Richard Hart's circa 1836 addition included at second floor level, a small vestibule (210), service stair hall (212), a bedroom (213), and a storeroom (211). The connection to these new rooms was made through the original rear dressing room (207) which, by the 1840s, functioned as a bathroom (Fig. 186).

A service stair ascended from the first floor to the second and third level of the circa 1836 addition. The rooms of "the back building" were smaller in scale and simpler in character than the rooms in the original house and they reflected the change in taste from the Federal style to the Greek fashion of the 1830s. It is likely that this addition was constructed by John Colegrove, the builder of the original house. The smaller scale of the circa 1836 addition resulted in some unusual conditions.

As originally completed, Room 211 was peculiar in its proportions. The relatively large space had a ceiling height of about 6' and had no window. Obviously intended for storage, it was probably the "skirt room" included in the 1886 inventory. Later, after 1893, the Cluetts would dramatically remodel this space into a bathroom that replaced the awkwardly located Hart-era bathroom in Rooms 207 and 210.

A curious unfinished "space" exists between the floor of the hall (210, 212) and the ceiling of the first floor service hall (110) and it is accessible through a floor hatch in the landing area of hall 212. This space results from differences in ceiling heights of the original house and rear addition.

The final expansion of the second floor occurred when George and Amanda Cluett pushed the rear wing further west, to within a few feet of the original carriage house. In plan, this new addition was about equal in area to Richard Hart's circa 1836 construction.

At the second floor level, this addition included a service hall with a service stair (214), a servant's bedroom (217), and a bathroom (216). Although this new staircase stylistically relates to the end of the nineteenth century, the character of the other finishes generally duplicates the earlier detailing of the adjacent circa 1836 rooms.

Throughout the second floor, knowledge of the various room's functions and occupants comes from several sources. For the Hart period, the two inventories (1844 and 1886), and Elizabeth Shields Eddy's reminiscence provide clues concerning room usage. Only one Hart-era photograph records a second floor room, the northeast or front bedroom (204), traditionally the master bedroom. This room was occupied by Richard and Betsey Hart. Sometime after Richard's death in 1843, Betsey moved to the first floor room (111) next to the dining room.

There is considerably less information concerning the second floor rooms during the two periods of Cluett occupancy between 1893 and 1953. The 1934 HABS floor plan records the general function of each room including rooms in the rear wing which were occupied by servants.

Undoubtedly, the northeast room (204) was occupied by George and Amanda Cluett and after 1910, by Albert and Caroline Cluett. The southeast room (209) served as Caroline Cluett's sitting room according to oral tradition and it is labeled as such on the 1934 floor plan.

Modifications to the second floor during the Cluett eras included the installation of hardwood flooring, the insertion of built-in cabinets in Rooms 205 and 207, and dressing room 203 was converted into a bathroom relating to the master bedroom. In 1938, the hall closet was modified to house the elevator that connected the first and second floors.

After 1953, RCHS removed the plumbing fixtures from the Cluett bathrooms (203, 211) and replaced the toilet and lavatory in bathroom 216. Unfortunately, there is no visual record of the appearance of the missing fixtures or of the spaces as they were furnished and decorated for the Cluetts.

201   Stair Hall

The T-shaped second floor hall is the core around which all of the original bedrooms are positioned. The primary feature in the otherwise typical space is the dramatic sweep of the curved staircase as it rises in the stair alcove from the first to the third story. In plan, the hall includes eight doorways; three in the north wall, single doors in the east and west walls and three openings in the south wall. The wide stair alcove extends from the south side of the hall. A large window, in the curved south wall of the stairwell, originally provided ample natural light for this space, but the construction of the house to the south dramatically decreased this amenity.

A second window, oval in shape, is positioned in the curved wall of the stairwell at third floor level. This "internal" window receives natural light from a large curved-top window positioned in the south gable wall at third floor level. An accessible closet-like space exists between these two windows.

The stair hall retains all of its original architectural character, with only minimal changes made by the Cluetts. George and Amanda Cluett had the hardwood floor installed and panel moldings were placed on the curved walls of the stairway from first to second floor for Albert and Caroline Cluett (Fig. 187).

In 1938, the south closet located next to the stairway was modified to house a small elevator that extended from the first to second floor.

There is very little detailed documentation for the second floor hall, but the space is included in the Hart inventories and glimpses of the stair area are provided by two of the 1892 Hart-period photographs.

187 The stairway hall (201) looking southwest, 2000.

The hall continues to function as a primary second floor circulation area and it is minimally furnished following nineteenth century precedent.

FLOOR

The floor is finished in narrow 2¼" wide strips of tongue-and-groove oak, laid east/west over the original wide board flooring (7" to 8½" wide) which also runs east/west. The narrow board surface dates to the George Cluett era. Small portions of the original flooring can be seen along the edge of the stairwell and in closet 202.

WALLS

All wall surfaces are finished in original plaster on wood lath. Curved surfaces exist in the stair well and at the change in the wall plains of the north wall. At the meeting of the south wall of the hall and the walls of the stairwell there are original wood edge beads extending from the baseboard to the cornice. The stairwell walls include a chair rail that follows the stair run down to the first floor. The wall surfaces above the rail include applied wood panel moldings. These were installed for Albert and Caroline Cluett after 1910.

CEILING

The original plaster-on-lath ceiling is about 12'7" above the floor.

BASEBOARD

The original wood baseboard is composed of a full stepped fascia topped by a reverse ogee with astragal.

CORNICE

The original run-in-place molded plaster cornice exists throughout the space including the curved wall surfaces in the stairwell.

DOORS

There are eight original openings in this hall: single doorways in the east (D2031) and west (D2071) walls, three doorways in the north wall (D2041, D2012, D2051), and three in the south wall (D2091, D2011, D2081). Each opening retains the original architrave, door, and door hardware.

The symmetrically molded 5½" wide trim has a centered tripartite reeded band and corner blocks with applied carved wood raffle flowers. The trim is identical to the first floor trim (Fig. 188).

188 Hall closet door architrave (D2012) with raffle flower corner blocks.

D2011: The original eight-panel, stile-and-rail door is 32¾" wide × 95" high × 1¾" thick. The recessed panels are trimmed with a ¾" wide quirk ovolo molding. Originally, this door opened to a closet, but in 1938 an elevator was installed in the closet space.

Hardware: Original fittings include a pair of 4½" high cast-iron butt hinges, brass knob, and keyhole escutcheon. The knob is positioned at 36" above the floor, lower than on the other doors. A mortised night bolt with an oval brass turn button dates to the Hart era. Why this externally controlled latch was installed on what was originally a closet door is unknown.

D2012: The original eight-panel stile-and-rail door is 32¾" wide × 95" high × 1¾" thick and opens to a large closet.

Hardware: Original fittings include a pair of 4½" high cast-iron butt hinges, a 4" × 5½" iron box lock and brass knob, and escutcheon. The other doors open into the various rooms and are described with those spaces.

WINDOWS

An original window opening is centered in the south curved wall surface of the stairwell. The opening, set in a deep reveal, features an architrave that matches the typical door trim and includes the raffle flower corner blocks. The original six-over-six double rope-hung sash remains in place. The glass panes are 13" × 20". The reveal includes a pair of two-tier bifold paneled shutters. There are marks in the lower shutters for the locations of missing small knobs.

An additional opening, the oval "window" located in the curved wall of the third floor stair run, can be seen from this hall. A description of this important feature is included with the third floor hall (301) analysis.

HEATING

There is no evidence for heating devices in the hall, but warmed air from the floor registers in the first floor halls rises through the stairwell into this area.

LIGHTING

Lighting is provided by a chain-suspended electrified polished brass gasolier. The domed filigree brass shade is surrounded by three arms with pairs of "candle" brackets. In its original location, the fixture was suspended by a pipe rather than a chain. The circa 1880–90 fixture was placed here by RCHS circa 1960. It is unlikely that a gas fixture was suspended in this position here in the nineteenth century.

An electric wall sconce, with a frosted glass tulip-form shade, is positioned on the north wall between the doors to bedroom 205 and the hall closet. The fixture was installed by RCHS. Visible gas piping in the closet (202) indicates that a gas wall bracket light was originally in the same position. This was probably the only source of artificial light during the Hart period and probably for the George Cluetts. The 1953 House Committee report suggested that a "modern wall light" replace the gas fixture then in place.

EQUIPMENT

A wall-mounted intercom box, installed by RCHS in 1969, is positioned on the south wall next to the "elevator" door.

STAIRWAY

The original elegantly curved staircase to the third story is located in the south extension of the hall. The open-stringer stair ascends in twenty-two risers in two runs joined by a continuous curve. The mahogany handrail and turned balusters are continuous with the first to second floor run of the stair. The handrail is stabilized by five turned iron balusters included in the balustrade. They are faux painted to match the mahogany balusters.

OTHER FEATURES

In 1938, a small elevator was installed in the long narrow space that originally served as a closet and is shown as such on the 1934 HABS floor plan. The elevator originally traveled from the first to the second floor but in 1969, it was modified to include connection to the basement and third floor.

FURNISHINGS AND FITTINGS

The Hart inventories and a 1892 photograph provide information concerning the furnishing of the second floor hall. The 1844 inventory refers to a hall carpet, stair carpets, and a wardrobe that was probably located here. The 1886 document is more specific and includes a listing for the second story hall. Furnishings included a carpet, three chairs, and carpet on the stair to the third story. Both documents reveal that the hall was minimally furnished.

The only visual records of the hall are provided by two of the 1892 Hart-era photographs (see Fig. 123, 131). The view of the first floor stair hall (102) also shows the south window and curved wall surface of the stair as it ascends to the second floor. Natural light enters through the window which is uncurtained. The photograph of the north front bed chamber (204) provides a glimpse of the hall as seen through the opened bedroom door. The stair and wall treatment are shown but no furnishings are visible. References in the Hart financial records to the "hall" generally indicate the first floor hall and stair hall, but may also include this area. The marble paper purchased from Solomon and Hart in 1850 was probably used on the curved walls of the stairwell if not on the other walls of the second floor hall.

Some of the forty-two stair rods purchased from Heartt and Company in 1854, were used on the stairway extending from this space to the third floor hall.

The 1892 photographs indicate that the complex wallpaper decor purchased from Robert Graves and Company in 1880 was installed here as well as the first floor hall.

FINISHES INVESTIGATION

The hall walls are currently covered in a wallpaper titled "Diana" that reproduces an original early nineteenth century document from the Wayside Inn. The paper, manufactured by Katzenbach and Warren of New York City, was a gift from W. Phelps Warren in 1962.

The plaster wall surfaces have always been papered and fragments of earlier papers exist on the sides of the architraves of doorways D2031, D2081, and D2071.

202 Hall Closet

This large walk-in closet is an original feature of the second floor hall. In plan, the 4'2" × 7' room includes a single doorway in the south wall and a tall built-in cabinet filling the east end of the space. This may be the "Pantry" included in the 1844 and 1886 inventories. Another second floor space included in the 1886 document is referred to as the "Hall Closet" and it is likely that the space now occupied by the elevator is that closet.

There are several interesting features in this room. Sheet metal duct work for the original hot-air heating system is exposed next to the north wall near the floor. The ducts still serve the front and back bedrooms. Early gas piping is also visible. An impressive built-in cabinet was added to the space in the last quarter of the nineteenth century and the drawer pulls bear the patent date 1872.

This is one of the few places where the original Hart period floor surface is still visible and can be walked on.

FLOOR

The original 6" to 9" wide tongue-and-groove floorboards are laid east/west. The exposed surface is now painted red/brown but the surface covered by the later built-in cabinet is covered in a grey/white paint, the color in place when that feature was installed.

WALLS

All four walls are finished in original plaster on wood lath. The surface is painted.

CEILING

The original plaster on lath ceiling is about 12'7" above the floor.

BASEBOARD

The original 7½" high plain wood base includes a bead at the top edge. The base is continuous behind the later built-in cabinet.

CORNICE

There is no molding at the meeting of the walls and ceiling plains but a wood molding finishes the top of the cabinet where it meets the ceiling.

DOORS

The original door opening (D2012) includes a 3⅜" wide architrave with a Grecian ovolo and astragal molding at its outer edge. The door opens out into the hall.

WINDOWS

This interior space does not include a window.

HEATING

Residual heat enters this closet from the sheet metal ducts of the hot air system installed in 1846. An 8" diameter vertical duct rises out of the floor next to the north wall. It joins to a horizontal duct that extends to the east and west walls, supplying heated air to the two primary bedrooms (204 and 206).

LIGHTING

A porcelain socket, with pull cord and exposed incandescent bulb, is positioned above the door. This utility fixture probably dates to the Albert Cluett era. An exposed gas pipe, dating to the Hart period, is surface mounted on the north and west walls. It enters the space at the floor in the southwest corner and divides into two pipes. One pipe was connected to a wall bracket originally located in the adjoining hall (201), the other pipe extends to the north wall where a gas light bracket was originally positioned to light this closet. The pipe then extends through the north wall into the dressing room (205). A gas bracket was recently restored to that room approximately 67" above the floor.

OTHER FEATURES

The primary feature in the closet is the built-in storage cabinet that completely covers the east wall. The unit consists of two sections: a lower chest fitted with four tiers of drawers and an upper cabinet arranged in two tiers of cupboards with pairs of paneled doors and interior fixed shelves. A cornice molding completes the cabinet at the ceiling. The lower chest is built around the much earlier sheet metal duct so that the bottom drawers only fill half of the space. The ornate cast-iron drawer pulls are marked "Pat. Oct. 1 1872." The upper doors are secured by cast-iron spring latches. A brass hasp on the lower doors was probably installed by RCHS.

The patent date on the drawer pulls indicates that this cabinet was constructed sometime after 1872, but there is no record of this work in the Hart financial documents. Inspection of the floor surface beneath the bottom drawer revealed numerous cloves scattered on the surface.

FURNISHING AND FITTINGS

An important fitting, possibly contemporary with the cabinet, is the wood rail positioned on the north and west walls at 85" above the floor. The 3" wide beaded edge rail includes several 5" long turned wood garment pegs.

Two tiers of wood shelving are positioned against the west wall and was probably installed by RCHS. Marks for the location of clothes rod supports exist on the north wall and west side of the door architrave at 77½" above the floor. This feature was probably installed during the Cluett period.

The "Hall Pantry" included in the 1844 inventory was used for linen storage.

The 1886 inventory lists several items under the heading, "Second [story] Hall Closet" and "Pantry," so it is impossible to tell which of the objects were kept here. The diverse list includes a pair of steps (probably bed steps), a bureau, carpet, pair of vases, feather brush, and an oil painting.

FINISHES INVESTIGATION

The cabinet, which is now painted, was originally finished in varnish or shellac.

203   Hall Room - Former Cluett Bathroom

This small but prominently positioned room is located at the east end of the second floor hall. The rectangular 6'7" × 11'8" room includes single doorways in the north and west walls and a window in the east wall directly over the main entrance to the house.

The original architectural character of the room survives with only minor modifications made after 1893. During the Hart era, the room was referred to as the "Bedroom over Hall" in the 1844 inventory, the "Hall Room" in the Hart papers, and possibly as "Miss Hart's dressing room" in the 1886 inventory.

The direct connection between this room and the primary bedroom (204) makes it likely that its original intended function related to the bed chamber occupied by Richard and Betsey Hart. It may have functioned as a dressing room or perhaps a newborn child was placed here in close proximity to the parents. In large houses, small rooms such as this would change function depending on the needs of the family.

In later life, Sarah Wool Hart occupied the room to the south (209) as her bed chamber and probably used this space for a dressing room.

After the purchase of the house by George and Amanda Cluett in 1893, this may have become a bathroom. The only bathroom during the Hart period was located in Room 207, which also provided access to part of the rear addition.

For the Albert Cluetts, this room definitely served as a bathroom and is so recorded in the 1934 floor plan. Physical evidence indicates that the bathroom may have had a tall dado of unknown material, possibly tile. In 1953, the House Committee recommended that lockers be installed in this room for the use of the club groups meeting in the front bedroom (204).

The room was restored in 1967 under the direction of Mrs. Marcus L. (Dorothy) Filley in memory of RCHS director, H. Maxson Holloway. The work included the removal of the plumbing fixtures and the wall and floor finishes. The partially restored space was furnished and interpreted as a nineteenth century sewing room. A small brass plaque affixed to the hall face of the door is inscribed "The H. Maxson Holloway Memorial Room, Director 1957–1966, Given in his memory by members of the Rensselaer County Historical Society, 1967.

There is no visual record of this room in the nineteenth century or in its guise as a bathroom. Unfortunately, the Cluett bathroom fixtures were discarded and there is no record of the room's appearance other than clues provided by the 1934 floor plan.

FLOOR

The floor surface is finished in wall-to-wall cut pile carpet laid over plywood in 1967. The carpet was donated by Mr. and Mrs. Frederick Shear. The recent investigation revealed beige 9" × 9" composition tiles on the surface of the plywood. The tile and plywood finish was probably installed in the early years of the RCHS occu-

pancy of the house. The plywood appears to be laid over the original wide board flooring. There is no visible evidence for the bathroom floor finish.

WALLS

All four walls are finished in original plaster on wood lath. The lath is furred out from the brick masonry east wall. A 7" deep wood dado rail is positioned against the plaster surface at 63" above the floor. This Cluett-era finish is positioned above a gypsum board surface installed in 1967 after the removal of Cluett-era tile or an unidentified material. At that time, the dado rail was moved upward about 1". Marks for its earlier position can be seen on the door trim. The plaster and gypsum board surfaces are now covered in a flocked wallpaper installed in 1967.

CEILING

The original plaster on lath ceiling is about 12'7" above the floor.

BASEBOARD

The plain 7" tall base is contemporary with the installation of the gypsum board wall surface. The original wood baseboard, which would have matched the condition in the hall (201), was probably removed when the Cluetts converted the room into a bathroom.

CORNICE

The original run-in-place plaster cornice remains in situ on the ceiling.

DOORS

There are two original door openings: an opening to the hall in the west wall (D2031), and an opening to the northeast bedroom in the north wall (D2042). The openings feature the typical architrave which includes raffle flower corner blocks.

D2031: The opening retains the original eight-panel, stile-and-rail door which is 32½" wide × 95" high × 1¾" thick. The recessed panels are trimmed with a ¾" wide quirk ovolo molding.

Hardware: Original fittings include a pair of 4½" tall cast-iron butt hinges, a 7½" tall brass mortise lock stamped "W PYE N-YORK PATENT," brass knobs, roses, and keyhole escutcheons. A Cluett-period brass night bolt is positioned above the lock and the flat rectangular turn knob is located on the bathroom face of the door. There is a mark for a garment hook on the center stile between the two upper rectangular panels. The hook was probably contemporary with the Cluett bathroom.

D2042: This door opens into the adjoining bedroom. There is a mark on the upper center stile for the placement of a hook.

WINDOWS

The original window opening is positioned in the east wall tight into the southeast corner. This awkward placement allows the opening to be located directly above the first floor main entrance. The tall recess has the typical architrave, but with a single corner block. The top of the trim abuts the bottom edge of the plaster cornice. The opening is fitted with the original large six-over-six double rope-hung sash with 15" × 24" panes. A single panel apron is positioned below the sill. The deep recess is fitted with pairs of two-tier paneled bifold shutters. There are outlines for two small knobs that were formerly attached to the bottom shutters.

HEATING

A small seven-column cast-iron radiator is positioned in the window recess. A slab of white marble rests on the top of the radiator. This radiator likely dates to the George Cluett period when the room may have been converted into a bathroom. During the Hart era, the room was unheated.

LIGHTING

An electrified two-arm gas pendant is suspended from the ceiling. The 1870s Neo-Grec-style fixture makes use of the same components as the much larger gasolier located in bedroom 206. That fixture bears the mark of Archer and Pancoast of New York City. Both fixtures were donated by Mr. and Mrs. Lowell H. Bryce and the fixture was placed in this room in 1967. A Cluett electric fixture was in this location or approximately 12" to the west where there is evidence for a light fixture.

During the Hart period and for George and Amanda Cluett, lighting was provided by a gas light bracket positioned on the south wall at 86" above the floor. The antique gas bracket currently in that position was installed in 1967 and was donated by the Rensselaer County Junior Museum.

FURNISHINGS AND FITTINGS

Information concerning the use and furnishing of this small room is provided by the Hart inventories and financial records and the HABS floor plan produced in 1934. This is the "Bedroom over Hall" included in the 1844 inventory. Furnishings included a bureau, chair and carpet. The 1886 inventory may include the space as "Miss Hart's Dressing Room," which is furnished with a wardrobe and mirror. An annotated copy of the same inventory includes an added listing for a "Hall Bedroom" which would seem to be this space. At the time of the inventory that room was used for the storage of objects intended for family members. If this is the "Hall Bedroom," then "Miss Hart's Dressing Room" may be the southwest room (208) which otherwise is not mentioned in that document.

In 1889, a pair of lace curtains were installed in the "Hall Room" by Louis Muller. The room functioned as a bathroom for the Albert Cluetts and possibly earlier for the George Cluetts. The 1934 HABS floor plan illustrates a toilet, lavatory, and bathtub lined up against the south wall. As illustrated on the plan, the tub appears to be the free standing type set on legs or a full base. These fixtures were removed by 1967 when the room was restored to represent a nineteenth century sewing room. Becky Cluett, Caroline Cluett's granddaughter, indicates that a white marble sink was located on the north wall and the tub was next to the south wall near the window. This is contrary to what is recorded by the 1934 floor plan. An engraved brass plaque attached to the hall face of the door indicates that this is "The H. Maxson Holloway Memorial Room 1957–1966, Given in his memory by the members of the Rensselaer County Historical Society 1967."

FINISHES INVESTIGATION

The wall surfaces above and below the dado rail, are covered in a gold flocked wallpaper installed in 1967. This produced a condition that never existed for the Harts or Cluetts. The walls were always completely covered in wallpaper during the Hart period; there was no dado rail. With the introduction of the bathroom for the Cluetts, the lower wall surface, below the newly installed dado rail, was finished in tiles or an unidentified material.

The door is now painted uniformly but was originally finished in faux mahogany graining, as were all of the second floor doors in the original part of the house.

204   Front Bedroom, Hart-Cluett Bedroom

This is the largest bedroom and was traditionally occupied by the master and mistress of the house (Fig. 129). The rectangular 17'4" × 21'1" room includes two doorways symmetrically positioned in the south wall, a single doorway in the west wall and a pair of large windows in the east wall. The north wall includes a projecting chimney breast and fireplace. The room retains all of its original architectural character including door and window architraves ornamented with raffle flower corner blocks and a delicately molded plaster cornice. Changes made here after the Hart period include the installation of the hardwood floor surface and the use of soapstone for the fireplace hearth and firebox lining. In the Hart inventories and financial records, the space is referred to as the "Front Chamber" (1844), "North Front Room" (1886), and "Front Bedroom."

This room and the back bedroom (206) share and are connected by the small room (205) that separates the two spaces. The front bedroom has direct access to another small room (203) through a doorway in the south wall.

Two photographs record this bedroom: the Hart period view dating to 1892, and the 1934 image showing the room as it was furnished for Albert and Caroline Cluett (see Figs. 131, 132). In both photos, the bed is positioned between the two doorways in the south wall. The 1953 report of the House Committee recommends that this room be used for meetings of various clubs in the city. Lockers were to be installed in the adjoining room (203) to the south.

In 1957, the room was dedicated to Betsey Howard Hart and furnished with Hart family objects given to RCHS by Ruth Hart Eddy. A small brass plaque affixed to the hall face of the door is inscribed "The Betsey Howard Hart Memorial Room, Given by her great granddaughter, Miss Ruth Hart Eddy, 1957."

FLOOR

The floor is finished in narrow 2¼" wide strips of tongue-and-groove oak, laid east/west and including a border composed of three matching boards. This surface was installed for George and Amanda Cluett over the original wide board surface that also was laid in the east/west direction.

189 Front bedroom (204), 1976.

WALLS

All four walls are finished in original plaster on wood lath and on brick masonry at the chimney breast.

CEILING

The original plaster ceiling is about 12'7" above the floor.

BASEBOARD

The original 11½" high base matches the first floor condition.

CORNICE

The original plaster cornice consists of a series of moldings and coves run in place and matches the cornice in the back bedroom (206).

DOORS

There are three original door openings: a single doorway (D2043) in the west partition and two openings (D2041, D2042) in the south partition. Each opening retains the original architrave with raffle flower corner blocks and the original paneled door. All three doors open into this room.

D2041: The original eight-panel, stile-and-rail door is 37½" wide × 95" high × 1⅞" thick and the recessed panels are trimmed with a ¾" quirk ovolo molding. The door was originally grained to imitate mahogany.

Hardware: Original fittings include a pair of 4½" tall cast-iron butt hinges, a 7½" brass mortise lock stamped "W PYE N-YORK PATENT," brass knobs, rose, and brass keyhole escutcheons. A later brass mortised night bolt with flat oval turn knob, is positioned above the lock and dates to the Hart period. The 3½" face plate of this bolt is visible in the 1892 photograph of the room.

D2042: This original door duplicates the conditions of door D2041.

Hardware: The original door fittings match those on door D2041.

D2043: This original door generally duplicates the conditions of door D2041. There is evidence on the east face of the door for a 28" × 71" Cluett-era dressing mirror formerly attached to the surface.

Hardware: The original fittings match those on door D2041.

WINDOWS

Two original window openings are positioned in the east wall. The tall window recesses have architraves composed of the typical molded trim and raffle flower corner blocks. The architraves meet the bottom edge of the plaster cornice. The openings are fitted with original large six-over-six double rope-hung sash which have 15" × 24" panes. A single panel is positioned below the sill. The deep reveal is fitted with pairs of two-tier paneled bifold shutters. The fittings include original cast-iron hinges and brass latches. The small brass knobs were installed by RCHS.

HEATING

Heated air enters the room through an 11" × 16" white enameled cast-iron Rococo pattern wall register positioned above the baseboard of the west wall near the hall door. The original sheet metal duct is visible in the hall closet (202). This is part of the system installed in 1846 that included a Fox and Company patent air furnace. Prior to the installation of the furnace the room was heated by the fireplace that probably included a coal grate. The 1844 inventory indicates that the back bedroom (206) was heated by a stove and it is possible that one was used here also.

LIGHTING

Electric wall sconces, installed by RCHS, are positioned on the north and east wall at 96" above the floor. Gas pipes for two gas light brackets are located in the window trim flanking the central pier at about 59" above the floor. This gas lighting dates to the Hart period and the original or replacement fixtures were used by George and Amanda Cluett. The 1934 photograph shows two of the electric table lamps used by Albert and Caroline Cluett (Fig. 132).

EQUIPMENT

A mark on the west side of the chimney breast at 32½" above the floor is the likely location for a service bell lever. During the Hart period, a service bell system consisting of wires connecting bells and levers existed in the house, but little visible evidence for the system remains. Bell levers were typically placed on the side of a chimney breast. The bells were located in the basement, probably in the kitchen.

The 1934 Cluett-era photograph records the position and appearance of an electric service bell on the south wall near the east jamb of door D2041. There is currently a mark on the wall in this position at about 51" above the floor. The photo shows an electric cord extending from this location to the bed making it possible to summon a servant while remaining in bed.

FIREPLACE

The 80" wide by 10½" deep chimney breast is positioned slightly off center on the north wall. The original veined black marble mantel is composed of symmetrically molded pilasters supporting paneled tablets flanking a deep molded frieze. A square edged marble shelf is positioned above the architrave at 53½" above the floor. Flanking the mantel are original panels of white marble that extend to the edges of the chimney breast. Cluett-era soapstone lines the firebox and forms the hearth.

FURNISHINGS AND FITTINGS

This large second floor room functioned as a bed chamber for the Harts and Cluetts and its evolving decor is recorded in photographs from the Hart and Cluett periods as well as Hart-era financial records and inventories.

In the 1844 inventory, the "Front Chamber" included a bedstead, bureau, stand, four chairs and a psyche (cheval) glass. The floor was covered in carpet and two portraits graced the walls. The bedstead is probably the impressive sleigh bed recorded here in the 1892 photograph (Fig. 131). The bed and the elaborate canopy and drapery stylistically appear to date to the time that the Harts moved into the new house. A bed and canopy of similar design appeared in *The Practical Cabinet Maker Upholsterer and Complete Decorator*, published in London in 1826. An 1833 broadside advertisement issued by New York cabinet maker Joseph Meeks and Sons illustrates a bed and canopy of similar appearance. There are marks on the door architraves of the pair of doorways in the south wall for the ornamental brackets that held back the bed curtains that were suspended from the canopy. These brackets are recorded in the 1892 bedroom photograph.

The 1886 inventory includes a much more detailed list of furnishings used in this room. The mahogany (sleigh) bedstead and canopy were valued at $75.00. The inclusion of two pair of red curtains may indicate the color of the bed drapery and window curtains. The

long list of furnishings includes a bureau, commode, washstand, table and spread and a wardrobe and mirror. These last two furnishings can be seen in the 1892 photo. The wardrobe may be the "French wardrobe" supplied by Galusha in 1867 for $225.00. The inventory also lists a lounge, a large easy chair, two rockers, a sewing chair, and four mahogany chairs. The 1892 photo indicates that the four chairs may be part of the set of mahogany lyre-back dining room chairs supplied by Duncan Phyfe. A lambrequin covered the fireplace mantel shelf which included three candelabra, probably a set of girandoles. A large oil painting was also noted in the inventory.

The inventories are brought to life by the photograph of the room taken in 1892. The massive mahogany sleigh bed is shown projecting out into the room in the conventional manner of a bed with a head and foot board. Close inspection of the bed shown in the photo reveals that it was originally placed with one side against the south wall, filling the space between the doors. The exposed side featured details and carving not found on the side meant to face the wall. The elaborate curtains supported by the canopy were draped over the tall curving ends of the bed forming an impressive counterpoint to the marble mantel on the opposite wall. A set of bed steps is shown next to the bedstead and they may be the pair of steps that the inventory places in the "Hall Closet" or "Pantry" in 1886.

The oldest Hart furnishings shown in the photo include one of the lyre-back dining chairs and the two-branch centerpiece of the patinated bronze, ormolu, and crystal three-piece girandole set now displayed in the front parlor. These important Hart family heirlooms are marked Messenger and Phipson and may date to the 1816 marriage of Richard and Betsey. The photo records a light ground floral pattern wall-to-wall Brussels carpet on the floor.

The appearance of the room as furnished by George and Amanda Cluett is unknown, but a fine photograph taken in 1934 shows the bedroom as it was arranged for Albert and Caroline Cluett (see Fig. 132). The hardwood floor is almost entirely covered by a single color cut pile carpet. A massive tall post tester bedstead is located in the traditional position between the two south doorways. A tall drum-shaped marble topped commode stand is positioned next to the bed. A telephone is placed on the stand and an electric service bell wire is located in the wall next to the bed. A tall chest-on-chest fills the same position formerly occupied by the Hart mirrored door French wardrobe. These Cluett furnishings are in the collections of RCHS.

An engraved brass plaque on the hall door (D2041) indicates that this is "The Betsey Howard Hart Memorial Room, Given by her great grand daughter, Miss Ruth Hart Eddy [in] 1957." The 1957 Eddy bequest of Hart family heirlooms that were placed in this room included the tall post tester bedstead, a pedestal work table, and a mahogany card table. Additional objects included a three piece ormolu and crystal girandole set and a shell work "Temple of Fame" that was a school girl creation of Betsey Amelia Howard. This may be the "shell ornament" located in the back bedroom (206) in the 1886 inventory.

Stylistically, the tall post bed dates to the first decades of the nineteenth century and may be the bed acquired at the time of Richard and Betsey's marriage. If this is the case, then the mahogany sleigh bed replaced this piece about the time that the Harts moved into the house in 1827.

Prior to the removal of the furnishings from the Betsey Howard Hart bedroom in the mid-1990s, the room also included one of the pair of oval mirrors supplied by Galusha in 1851 for the front parlor.

FINISHES INVESTIGATION

Investigation of the plaster wall surfaces revealed that wallpaper was always used here until the redecoration of the room in 1957. At that time, paint was applied. The earliest documentation for the purchase of wallpaper may be the 16 pieces of chintz pattern paper and 30 yards of border paper supplied by Solomon and Hart of New York in 1852. In 1875, L. Cherest was paid for painting and decorating the front bedroom. This work probably involved the ceiling and cornice.

The wallpaper decor recorded in the 1892 photograph includes a small patterned flower and leaf motif paper below a very deep, boldly patterned floral frieze paper. A picture rail separates the two papers. This treatment was applied by Thomas Buckley of Albany who was responsible for the redecoration of several rooms in 1891 including this bedroom. The 1934 photograph records a pale colored diamond patterned paper on the walls. There is no border paper or picture rail.

The eight-panel doors, now painted white, were originally finished in faux mahogany, the condition shown in the 1892 photograph. The white finish was first applied for the Albert Cluetts.

205   Closet – Dressing Room

The space separating the front and back bedrooms includes this small room and the hall closet (202) immediately to the south. In plan, the rectangular 6' 11" × 11'5" room includes single doorways in the east and west partitions and a built-in double closet filling the north end of the space.

In 1844 and 1886, inventories refer to this as a closet but the size of the space and the direct connections to the two largest bedrooms indicates that it functioned as a dressing room. This space served as a dressing room for Albert and Caroline Cluett.

The space retains its original architectural character including the same woodwork used in the adjoining chambers. The pair of closets appear to be original features. The doors were removed by RCHS to make the display of collections more visible. A second pair of closets, positioned against the south wall, is recorded by the 1934 HABS floor plan. That feature was probably added to the space by either the George or Albert Cluetts and was removed by RCHS after 1953.

In the 1980s, the peg rail was restored to the walls at the south end of the space based on evidence found on the wall surfaces. A gas light bracket was installed on the Hart-era pipe that protruded from the wall at about 69" above the floor. Until the recent closing of the second floor to the public, this room was furnished as a dressing room.

FLOOR

The floor is finished in narrow 2¼" wide strips of tongue-and-groove oak, laid east/west and dating to the George Cluett period. The original wide board flooring laid east/west can still be seen in the north closet area. A change in the floor finish at the south end of the room may relate to the Cluett-era closets formerly located there.

WALLS

All four walls are finished in original plaster on wood lath. The built-in closet is constructed of wide wood planks forming the top and a partition between the units.

CEILING

The original plaster-on-lath ceiling is about 12'7" above the floor. The closet ceiling is formed of wood planks.

BASEBOARD

The original wood baseboard matches the base in the adjoining bedrooms (204 and 206). In the closet area the base consists of a plain board with a beaded top edge. The difference in the baseboard types indicates that the closet condition is original.

CORNICE

There is no cornice molding in this room.

DOORS

There are four door openings in this room: single doorways in the east (D2043) and west (D2062) partitions, and a pair of openings (D2051 and D2052) in the north closet partition. All the openings retain the original symmetrically molded trim with inset tripartite reeding and raffle flower corner blocks.

D2043, D2062: These doors open into the adjoining bedroom.

D2051, D2052: The doors are removed from the 29¾" × 95" openings. They were hinged to the east and west jambs. The doors are currently stored in the attic stair vestibule (307). The eight-panel doors have recessed panels on the outside face and flush panels on the inside face.

Hardware: Original fittings include the cast-iron butt hinges, iron rim locks (4¾" × 5½"), brass knobs, and keyhole escutcheons.

WINDOWS

This interior space does not include windows.

HEATING

This small room has never been heated.

LIGHTING

Incandescent spotlights, installed by RCHS, are positioned on the top surface of the built-in closet. There is no visible evidence for earlier electric lighting. A Hart-period gas pipe protrudes from the center of the south wall at 69" above the floor. The piping is exposed in the hall closet (202). In the 1980s, a gas light bracket was restored to this position.

CLOSET

A pair of built-in closets fill the north end of the room to a height of 8'6".

FURNISHINGS AND FITTINGS

The 1844 inventory indicates that carpet was used in this closet. The 1886 document notes that a chair and commode were located here, furnishings in character with the dressing room function.

According to the 1934 floor plan, there were double closets at either end (north and south) of the room. On the plan they are labeled "case." Evidence on the south partition for the gas light bracket and the peg rail indicates that the closets formerly located there were later insertions, made for George or Albert Cluett. The appearance of this closet feature is unknown and it was removed by RCHS sometime after 1953.

206   Back Bedroom – Carr Memorial Room

This room is identical in detail to the front bedroom (204) but is slightly smaller in size. The rectangular 16'1" × 17'2" room includes single doorways in the south and east walls and a pair of large windows in the west wall. A projecting chimney breast and fireplace are located slightly off center on the north wall. The room retains all of its original architectural character with the exception of the hardwood flooring which was installed for George and Amanda Cluett.

In the Hart family documents, this space is variously referred to as the "Back Chamber," "Back Bedroom," "Back Room—second story" and "Mrs. Howard's Room." This may also be the space referred to as the "Green Room" in some invoices. This room and the front bedroom (204) share and are connected by the small dressing room (205) that separates the two spaces.

In her 1855 reminiscence, Elizabeth Shields Eddy states that this was the room occupied by Rebecca Howard after she closed the Dey Street house and moved to Troy from New York City in 1845, after the death of her husband.

The furnishings and objects included in the 1886 inventory reflect this occupancy (1845–1870). The presence of the mahogany sofa and chairs indicate that Mrs. Howard used the room for more than just a place to sleep. The shell ornament listed in the inventory, a memento of her daughter's (Betsey) childhood, was probably one of only a few items moved from the Dey Street house. Sarah Wool Hart may have moved into this room after the death of her mother in 1886. The room continued to function as a bedroom for the two Cluett families but the actual occupants are unknown. According to oral tradition, this was a guest room.

If the 1953 suggestions of the House Committee were followed, this room functioned as an exhibition space for RCHS collections that previously were kept at the Troy Public Library. Until its recent closing, the back bedroom housed objects formerly belonging to General Joseph Bradford Carr and given to RCHS by his granddaughter, Mrs. Marjorie Carr Adams. A small brass plaque affixed to the hall face of the door is inscribed "The General and Mrs. Joseph Bradford Carr Memorial Room, Given in loving memory by their granddaughter, Marjorie Carr Adams, 1955."

FLOOR

The floor is finished in narrow 2¼" wide strips of tongue-and-groove oak, laid east/west. This surface, dating to the George Cluett period, is laid over the original wide board surface.

WALLS

All four walls are finished in original plaster on wood lath. The projecting chimney breast is finished in plaster on brick masonry. The plaster surfaces have always been covered in wallpaper.

CEILING

The original plaster-on-lath ceiling is about 12'7" above the floor.

BASEBOARD

The typical original wood baseboard, approximately 11¾" high, is composed of a tall stepped fascia topped by a reverse ogee with astragal.

CORNICE

The original run-in-place plaster cornice is identical to that in the front bedroom (204).

DOORS

There are two original openings in this room: the main access in the south wall (D2061) and an opening in the east wall (D2062). Both doorways retain the original 5½" wide architrave with the typical raffle flower corner blocks.

> D2061: The original eight-panel, stile-and-rail door is 37½" wide × 95" high × 1¾" thick.
>
> Hardware: Original fittings include a pair of 4½" high cast-iron butt hinges, brass faced mortise lock

marked "W PYE N-YORK PATENT," brass knobs, and drop cover keyhole escutcheons. A small brass mortised night bolt with a flat oval turn knob is positioned above the lock and dates to the Hart period.

> D2062: The original eight-panel stile-and-rail door is 38" wide × 95" high × 1¾" thick.
>
> Hardware: Original fittings include a pair of 4½" high cast iron butt hinges, brass faced mortise lock with the Pye marking and brass knobs and drop cover keyhole escutcheons.

WINDOWS

There are two original window openings in the west wall. The tall recessed openings are fitted with original six-over-six double rope-hung sash and a single-panel apron is positioned below each sill. Pairs of two-tier paneled bifold shutters are housed in the deep recesses. The shutters retain original cast iron hinges and brass latches.

HEATING

Heated air enters the room through a 11" × 16" Rococo pattern cast-iron wall register set in a narrow wood frame in the east wall above the baseboard. This important fitting dates to the early 1850s and is part of the hot air heating system installed beginning in 1846. The fireplace was the original heat source for this room and a coal grate was probably placed in the firebox. The 1844 inventory indicates that a stove was also used here; probably removed after the register was installed.

LIGHTING

During the earliest years, artificial lighting was provided by candles or oil lamps. The installation of a piped gas system provided the first permanent lighting. Two gas pipes protrude from the window trim at about 59" above the floor. This was the position for a pair of gas light brackets that flanked the wall pier between the windows.

The elaborate mid-1870s Neo-Grec-style electrified gas chandelier was manufactured by Archer and Pancoast of New York City. It was donated by Mr. and Mrs. Lowell H. Bryce in 1963. Fixtures of this scale were not typically used in bed chambers in the nineteenth century and there probably was never a ceiling fixture in this room prior to the installation of the chandelier.

FIREPLACE

The original 79" wide by 10¾" deep chimney breast is positioned slightly to the east of the center of the north wall. The original black and gold Italian marble mantel is composed of a molded architrave set on plain blocks and paneled corner blocks. The plain square-edged shelf is 53" above the floor. Panels of white marble flank the mantel. The firebox and hearth are finished in grey soapstone which dates to the Cluett era. There is evidence in the firebox for a fire. A manually operated service bell lever was probably positioned on the west face of the chimney breast at about 34" above the floor. The plaster wall surface under the wallpaper needs to be further investigated in this location.

FURNISHINGS AND FITTINGS

Information concerning the furnishing and decoration of the back chamber is included in the 1844 and 1886 Hart inventories, Elizabeth Shields Eddy's reminiscence, and Hart family financial records. The only known photographic evidence is provided by the 1934 photo of the front bedroom (204), which gives a glimpse of this room as seen through the opened doors of the closet (205) that separates the spaces.

In 1844, the back chamber included a bedstead, bureau, washstand, five chairs, and a single stand and cover. A carpet covered the floor and additional fittings included a stove, a lamp, and two pictures.

After the death of William Howard in 1845 and the closing of the Howard's Dey Street house in New York City, this room was occupied by Rebecca Howard. Elizabeth Shields Eddy recalled that in 1855 Grandmother Howard "had the West room over the back parlor. There was the big four-post bed with green moire curtains . . . below the windows . . . a beautiful little mahogany sewing table . . . and a long sofa between the window and the mantel piece . . . at the foot of her bed, a straight-backed rocking chair with a little, light table in front."

Work carried out in 1885 and 1888 by Louis Muller included putting up lace curtains and laying carpet in the "Green Room," probably a reference to this chamber.

The furnishings included in the 1886 inventory reflect Rebecca Howard's former occupancy of the bedroom (she passed away in 1870). Included in the room were a mahogany bedstead (at $70.00, valued more that the bedstead in the front bedroom), a bureau and mir-

ror, mahogany sofa and chairs, four mahogany chairs, a maple rocker, wash stand, towel rack, and a commode. A small stand is probably the sewing table mentioned by Elizabeth Shields Eddy. A carpet covered the floor and a pair of curtains and cornices as well as shades were featured at the windows. The mantel clock is probably the French clock cleaned in 1857 by James W. Cusack. An item of note that was kept in this room is the "shell ornament" included in the inventory. This important object was made by Betsey Howard (Hart) while in school and survives in the RCHS collections.

In 1889, Louis Muller was paid for putting up two pair of lace curtains in Miss Hart's room. There is only a single window in the room (209) she occupied in 1886. After that date, she may have moved into this space.

The room undoubtedly functioned as a bedroom for the two Cluett families. The 1934 HABS floor plan records this space as a bedroom and oral tradition indicates it was a guest room.

The glimpse of this space, as seen from the front bedroom in the 1934 photograph, records an oval mirror positioned between the two windows which feature tied-back curtains and a simple wood rocker is located near the fireplace.

The report submitted by the House Committee in February 1953 recommended that the southwest (208) and northwest (206) bedrooms be used as "museums" of the Society and that the display cases and property belonging to the Society then in the Troy Public Library be placed here as soon as possible.

The brass plaque affixed to the hall door indicates that this is "The General and Mrs. Joseph Bradford Carr Memorial Room—Given in loving memory by their granddaughter Mrs. Marjorie Carr Adams—1955." Many of the furnishings and other objects placed here formerly belonged to General Carr. Of particular interest is the tall post bedstead which bears a silver plaque inscribed "Aaron Burr's Bedstead Presented to General & Mrs. Joseph B. Carr by G. Hilton Scribner 1884."

FINISHES INVESTIGATION

References in the Hart financial records that may refer to finish work in this room include an 1852 payment made to D. H. Wellington for whitening (the ceiling) back chamber and an 1855 payment to the same mechanic for painting Mrs. Howard's Room. In 1875, L. Cherest was paid for painting and decorating the back bedroom—second floor. This work probably involved the use of some sort of polychrome scheme on the ceiling and cornice.

The plaster wall surfaces have always featured wallpaper; the current paper is a reproduction of an eighteenth-century paper from West Saint Mary's Manor in Maryland. It was manufactured by Katzenbach and Warren of New York City and given by W. Phelps Warren in 1958.

207   Passage – Linen Storage – Bath Room

In general relationships and location, this small room corresponds to the room (203) at the east end of the second floor hall. In plan, the 8'1" × 9'3" room includes single doorways in the east and west walls and an impressive display of built-in cabinets covering the south wall. Of the several second floor rooms in the original portion of the house, this space has the most complex history of modification and change in function. Unlike the other rooms, this space shows evidence of extensive remodeling.

As originally completed, the room featured single doorways in the south and east walls and a window in the west wall. In general appearance, it was much like the room (203) at the opposite end of the second floor hall and it probably functioned in a similar manner, serving as a bedroom and dressing room; the function changing as required by the family.

The Hart family financial records and the 1886 inventory indicate that a "bathing room" was located somewhere on the second floor; evidence indicates that this is that space. One of the rooms that functioned for the Cluetts as a bathroom (211) was for the Harts a space of very unusual character. That room had a ceiling height of only 6'1" and no window, making it unlikely that it was the Hart-period bathroom; an assumption made prior to the recent investigation of both spaces.

Possibly as early as the 1840s, Room 207 was used for bathing, although according to Elizabeth Shields Eddy's reminiscence this room was converted into a bathroom many years after 1855 when she stayed at the house. In 1849, the mason, E. A. Dunham, did work in the bathing room. Payments to William Barnes in 1872 for the installation of a bathtub and water closet likely refers to work carried out in this space. Evidence for these and other conditions would exist on the original floor-

ing concealed by the Cluett-era floor surface and there is physical evidence that plumbing entered the room through the west wall near the southwest corner. The 1886 inventory includes this space as well as an area called the "Bath Room Hall" which is the small vestibule (210) immediately to the west. The two rooms functioned as a single space since no door could be closed between them.

The enlargement of the rear wing for the George Cluetts included the extensive remodeling of Room 211, which along with Room 203 then became the primary second floor bathrooms. This space (207) then functioned as a hall, providing access to the new bathroom (211) and the service wing. In 1893, or slightly later, cabinets for the storage of linen were installed in this room. After 1953, the cabinets were used for the storage of RCHS library collections.

FLOOR

The floor is finished in narrow 2¼" wide strips of tongue-and-groove oak, laid east/west over the original wide board surface. This hardwood floor was installed for the George Cluetts. The original wide floorboards, which also run east/west, are exposed under the south cabinets.

WALLS

All four walls are finished in plaster on wood lath. Original conditions at the west wall were disturbed when the circa 1836 rear addition was constructed. At that time, a doorway was created in the approximate location of an original window opening. The work included the removal of the original lath and plaster wall surface and the reconstruction of a new surface about 11" further west. The removal of the window and related window recess and built-in shutters made the greater depth of the original west wall unnecessary. The vertical crack in the north wall, near the northwest corner, indicates the position of the room face of the original wall. A 49½" high vertical beaded board dado (3" wide boards) exists on the north, east, and west walls and may exist or have existed on the south wall now covered by the built-in cabinet. The dado boards extend down below the surface of the floor which was installed later. The dado may date to work carried out by H. Cozzens in 1891 for the bathroom.

CEILING

The original plaster-on-lath ceiling is about 12'7" above the floor. A narrow section next to the west wall was replaced when the wall was modified in circa 1836.

BASEBOARD

The original baseboard, which probably matched the base in the adjoining hall (201), was removed when the beaded board dado was installed. That surface is continuous to the floor.

CORNICE

The original run-in-place plaster cornice remains on the north, east and south walls, and is identical to the hall (201) feature. The section along the west wall was installed after the wall was modified in circa 1836. The cornice remains in place inside the later cabinet that conceals the south wall.

DOORS

There are two door openings in this room: the opening to the main hall (D2071) and the connection to the rear addition (D2072). The original opening in the east wall retains the typical 5½" wide trim with raffle flower corner blocks. The later west doorway features the typical trim used throughout the rear addition. A window was originally in this location.

There is evidence for another original door opening that was located in the south wall. That opening was closed when the built-in cabinets were installed against the south wall or earlier when the room was used as a bathroom.

D2071: The original eight-panel, stile-and-rail door is 32½" wide × 94½" high × 1⅞" thick.

Hardware: Original fittings include a pair of 4½" high cast-iron butt hinges, brass faced mortise lock marked "W PYE N-YORK PATENT," brass knobs, and drop cover keyhole escutcheons. A small brass mortised night bolt with a flat oval turn knob is positioned above the lock and operates from the hall door face. It dates to the Hart period.

D2072: This opening features a deep wood reveal that passes through the location of the original rear masonry wall of the 1827 house. No door was ever installed in this opening.

D2073: The door, trim and opening are removed, but the faint outline of this original feature can be seen on the north wall surface in Room 208.

WINDOWS

There is no window in this room but prior to the construction of the rear addition, a single window was located in the west wall. The absence of a door in the west doorway allows natural light from the window in the adjoining hall (210) to penetrate this dark room.

HEATING

This small room has never been heated but there is an 1872 reference to a 40-gallon French galvanized boiler for heating water for the bathroom. The location of this apparatus is unknown.

LIGHTING

A spun brass electric wall sconce (missing a glass shade) is positioned on the north wall at 74" above the floor. This fixture dates to the Albert Cluett era and may replace a gas fixture in the same location. The metal surface of the fixture is now painted.

PLUMBING

If this is the Hart-era bathing room, then a bath tub and a water closet were located here, probably along the south wall. Evidence for these fittings would exist on the original floor surface covered by the later Cluett flooring and cabinets. Physical evidence reveals that piping entered the room near the southwest corner. Early plumbing plans frequently included a tub, toilet and lavatory positioned next to each other in a built-in arrangement against a wall.

OTHER FEATURES

The primary feature of this small room is the impressive built-in cabinet that fills the south end of the space, completely covering the wall surface from floor to ceiling. The cabinet consists of two units; a lower chest of drawers 55½" high and an upper unit consisting of two tiers of cabinets with paneled doors. The chest is divided into two sections by a horizontal row of pull-out sliding trays. Below, there are a series of drawers (eight total) and two two-door cabinets. Above the sliding trays, there are two levels of large drawers (six total). Between the chest and the ceiling, there are two tiers of cabinets with paired doors (a total of twelve doors).

The hardware consists of simple grip-type brass drawer pulls and small brass spring latch door fasteners. There are three different types of latch knobs. The trays have brass pulls. Small stamped-iron name tag holders are attached to the six upper-tier drawers and five of the lower tier cabinet doors. Paper cards, inscribed to identify the contents of the unit, could be inserted in the holders.

All of the wood cabinetry is constructed using wire nails and the unit was probably installed for George and Amanda Cluett in 1893 or slightly later. The hardwood Cluett floor surface does not exist under the cabinet indicating that the two features are contemporary.

FURNISHINGS AND FITTINGS

Upon the completion of the house in 1827, this small space functioned as a bedroom or dressing room. A doorway in the south partition provided a direct connection to the southwest bedroom (208). It is likely that the use of this room varied in the earliest years of the Hart occupancy.

This is the space that began to function as a bathing room/bathroom, possibly as early as the 1840s. No mention is made of a bathroom in the 1844 inventory but a "Bath Room" and "Bath Room Hall" are included in the 1886 document.

Positioned in the former room were a chair, towel rack, rug and oil cloth as well as a lamp, dish, cup, and various utensils. An indication of the plumbing fixtures located here is provided by the Hart financial records. In 1872, William Barnes installed a bathtub and a Bartholomew (water) closet. In the same year, oil cloth was laid on the floor. H. Cozzens installed "245 feet" of lumber (probably wainscot) in the bathroom in 1891.

After the purchase of the house by George and Amanda Cluett in 1893, the bathroom function was moved to a nearby room (211) that was extensively remodeled to accommodated the new use. This room (207) then became a passage leading to the rear addition and the new bathroom. Cabinets were installed in the "passage" which then functioned as a linen storage area, convenient to the bedrooms and bathrooms.

For RCHS, this space has functioned as a store room as well as an access corridor to the rear wing where the caretaker's apartment and more recently the tenant's apartment was located. The area beyond this room now includes staff offices.

FINISHES INVESTIGATION

Investigation of the original wood door trim revealed that initially the woodwork was painted yellowish/white. This finish was repeated three times followed by an application of a faux wood graining. This finish may relate to the transformation of the space into a bathroom. The Hart financial records include numerous references to "graining" throughout the house beginning in the 1840s. This faux finish was later overpainted in numerous finishes of yellowish/white followed by more recent white paint.

The door was grained to imitate mahogany beginning in 1827, but was painted white after the Albert Cluetts acquired the house.

Indications of work carried out in the bathroom include payments made to L. Cherest in 1875 for painting and decorating and to A. A. Sandersen and Son in 1879 for painting and graining.

208   Southwest Bedroom

The southwest room is the smallest of the four original second floor bed chambers and is the one about which there is the least historical information. In plan, the 12'9" × 14'9" room includes a single doorway in the north wall and a projecting chimney breast and fireplace on the south wall. A window opening is located immediately west of the chimney breast. This arrangement dates to circa 1836 when the rear addition was constructed for Richard Hart. The original room plan featured a single window in the west wall. There was no opening in the south wall. There were two door openings in the north wall: one opening to the hall and another providing access to Room 207.

The circa 1836 addition had significant effect on this small room. The entire west wall, including the structural outside brick surface, was removed from first floor level to attic in this room and the dining room below. This also involved the removal of any window openings in these locations. A new and much lighter lath and plaster partition was constructed several inches west of the inside face of the original much thicker wall. This lightweight partition was necessary because it had to be supported on the floor structure that spanned over the newly enlarged dining room that was extended westward as part of the new rear addition. Trim from an original window opening in the west wall was salvaged and reused at the much smaller opening inserted in the south wall.

The second doorway in the north wall was removed when the cabinets were installed in Room 207 or possibly earlier when that space was converted into a bathroom.

This may be the space referred to as "Howard's Room" in the 1844 inventory. "Howard" is probably William Howard Hart (1820–1883), eldest son of Richard and Betsey Hart. He did not marry until 1847 and continued to reside at the house until that time. The function and occupant of this room after the departure of William Howard Hart is unknown. This may be the "Spare Room" mentioned in documents dating to the 1880s. For some undetermined reason, this room is not included in the 1886 inventory unless this is the space referred to as "Miss Hart's Dressing Room." There are no descriptions or photographs of this space.

It is likely that the room functioned as a bedroom for the two Cluett families that occupied the house from 1893 until 1953 and the HABS drawing includes this room as a bedroom. In Caroline Cluett's later years, a nurse stayed in this room. Beginning in 1963, this room housed a collection of Cluett furnishings. A small brass plaque affixed to the hall face of the door is inscribed "The Caroline Ide Cluett Memorial Room, 1963."

FLOOR

The floor is finished in narrow 2¼" wide strips of tongue-and-groove oak, laid east/west over the original wide board surface. This flooring was installed for the George Cluetts.

WALLS

The north, south, and east walls are finished in original plaster on wood lath. The west wall is composed of plaster on sawn wood lath and replaced the original wall which was removed when the rear wing was constructed circa 1836. The original west wall consisted of plaster on split lath furred out from the brick masonry of the back wall of the house. At the time of the expansion, the brick wall was removed at the first floor level (dining room) and here at the second floor level. The original west wall probably featured a single window opening.

CEILING

The original plaster-on-lath ceiling is about 12'7" above the floor.

BASEBOARD

The original wood baseboard, approximately 11¾" high, survives on the north, south, and east walls. The matching section along the west wall was installed when that wall was reconstructed in circa 1836. There are cut marks in the north baseboard in the location of the former doorway that connected to Room 207.

CORNICE

The original run-in-place plaster cornice matches the profile of the cornice in the southeast bedroom. The section along the west wall dates to the circa 1836 reconstruction of that surface.

DOORS

There is a single surviving original opening (D2081) in the north wall. Originally, a second opening was located in the west end of the same wall. It was removed when the cabinets were installed in Room 207 or possibly earlier. The remaining doorway features the original 5½" wide architrave with raffle flower corner blocks.

> D2081: The original eight-panel, stile-and-rail door is 35¼" wide × 94¾" high × 1¾" thick.
>
> Hardware: Original fittings include a pair of 4½" high cast-iron butt hinges, brass faced mortise lock with the Pye marking and brass knobs and drop cover keyhole escutcheons. A brass faced mortise night bolt is positioned above the lock and is operated with a small rectangular brass turn knob mounted on the hall face of the door. The curious placement of this Cluett-era bolt on the hall side of the door allows someone to lock a person in the bedroom with no way for that person to exit the room.

WINDOWS

There is a single window opening in the south wall that was installed when the rear addition was constructed in circa 1836. The architrave consists of the typical 5½" wide symmetrically molded trim with raffle flower corner blocks set on a sill composed of a convex molding sandwiched between two fascias. The trim above the sill is probably material reused from a window removed from the west wall. The opening is fitted with six-over-six double-hung sash dating to the circa 1836 remodeling. The shallow reveal does not include built-in shutters. Originally, there was one much larger window opening in the west wall that would have matched the conditions in the northwest (206) bedroom including the built-in shutters.

HEATING

There is no heating unit in this room but a steam pipe that services the radiator in third floor Room 302 is exposed in the northwest corner. Originally, the room was heated by the fireplace, possibly with a coal grate insert. The 1844 inventory indicates that a stove was located here.

LIGHTING

There is no fixed lighting in this room and no visible evidence for nineteenth century gas lighting.

FIREPLACE

The original 74½" wide × 10½" deep chimney breast is positioned slightly to the east of the center of the south wall. The original mottled dark grey marble mantel is composed of plain flat pilasters and a plain frieze supporting a projecting unmolded shelf positioned at 51½" above the floor. The firebox and hearth are finished in soapstone installed for the Cluetts. In the room as originally completed, there was no window next to the chimney breast.

FURNISHINGS AND FITTINGS

This room has always functioned as a bedroom. In the 1844 inventory the space referred to as "Howard's Room" is probably this bedroom. Included in the inventory listing are a bedstead, table, three chairs, and a washstand and dressing case. A carpet covers the floor and there are curtains at the single window. A stove is also located here. For some unknown reason, this room is not included in the 1886 inventory unless this is the space included as "Miss Hart's dressing room." References in the Hart financial records to a "spare bedroom" may be for this space. Louis Muller put up curtains here in 1884 and 1886.

Nothing is known about the room's use and occupancy during the two Cluett periods aside from the use of the space by a nurse who slept here in Caroline Cluett's later years. The night bolt, which locks from the hall side of the door, was installed during the Cluett era and allows someone or something to be locked in the room from the hall side of the door.

This is one of two second floor rooms that the 1953 Report of the House Committee recommends be used to display RCHS collections.

A small brass plaque attached to the outside face of the door is inscribed "The Caroline Ide Cluett Memorial Room 1963." The room was dedicated in October of that year and until recently displayed furnishings belonging to Albert and Caroline Cluett which were originally used in the front bedroom (204).

FINISHES INVESTIGATION

The plaster walls were covered in wallpaper in the nineteenth century and fragments of paper survive on the east side of the door architrave.

209   Southeast Bedroom

This is one of four original second floor bedrooms and the only one that includes a small adjoining closet; the other three chambers have related dressing rooms.

In plan, the 12'9" × 18'2" room includes single doorways in the north and west walls and a single window opening in the east wall. A projecting chimney breast is approximately centered on the south wall. This small but important room retains all of its original architectural character. Only minimal modifications were made by the two Cluett families. These include the installation of hardwood flooring and the introduction of soapstone to the fireplace (Fig. 190).

For the Harts, this probably always served as a bed chamber. It is included in the two family inventories as well as in financial records. In the 1844 document, it is referred to as the "Bedroom over Library." Sometimes called the "S. E. [Southeast] Room" in various invoices, by the time of the 1886 inventory this is Miss Hart's Room. At an undetermined time, Sarah Wool Hart occupied this room and used the small room immediately to the north (203) as a dressing room. She may have moved to another room (possibly the back bedroom—206) after the death of her mother in 1886. At that time, she may have used the southwest room (208) as a dressing room. How the room was used by George and Amanda Cluett remains unknown.

Sometime after 1910, Caroline Cluett arranged the room as her private sitting room and the 1934 HABS

190 Southeast bedroom (209) as furnished with objects that formerly belonged to Major General John Ellis Wool, 1976.

floor plan indicates this use. Oral tradition reveals that Mrs. Cluett had her breakfast here and it was in this room that she planned her daily chores including menus and shopping trips. She also saw her grandchildren here as well as close friends. Remarkably, the wallpaper used here during that period remains on the walls but was covered in paint sometime after the house was occupied by RCHS beginning in 1953.

In 1953, the House Committee recommended that this room and the adjoining bathroom (203) be made ready for use by a curator if the position was filled. Whether any work was undertaken here at that time is unknown. For a brief period, from January 1964 to the end of that year, this room housed the RCHS library. In December 1964, the room was opened as the General John Ellis Wool Memorial (Fig. 190) and a significant collection of furniture and other objects belonging to the General were displayed here. This important display was maintained until the recent closing of the second floor to the public. A small brass plaque affixed to the hall face of the door is inscribed "The General John Ellis Wool Memorial Room, Given in Memory by his great, great niece, Sarah Bleecker Griswold Tenney, 1964."

FLOOR

The floor is finished in narrow 2¼" wide strips of tongue-and-groove oak, laid east/west over the original wide board surface. The hardwood surface was installed for the George Cluetts.

WALLS

The walls are finished in original plaster on wood lath. The south and east surfaces are furred out from the exterior masonry walls. The chimney breast is of plaster on brick masonry.

CEILING

The original plaster on lath ceiling is about 12'7" above the floor.

BASEBOARD

The original wood baseboard, approximately 11¾" high, survives on all four walls.

CORNICE

The original run-in-place plaster cornice matches the profile of the cornice in bedroom 208. A later narrow wood picture molding, probably dating to the earliest

Cluett period or possibly late in the Hart ownership, is positioned along the bottom edge of the cornice.

DOORS

There are two original door openings: an opening in the north wall (D2091) to the hall and a closet door in the west wall (D2092). Both retain the original architraves with the raffle flower corner blocks.

D2091: The original eight-panel, stile-and-rail door is 37½" wide × 95" high × 1¾" thick.

Hardware: Original fittings include a pair of 4½" high cast iron wide swing butt hinges, brass faces mortise lock with the Pye marking and brass knobs and drop cover keyhole escutcheons. A brass mortise night bolt is positioned above the lock and is operated with a small oval brass turn knob mounted on the inside face of the door. This Hart period fitting is found on several other doors.

D2092: The original eight-panel, stile-and-rail door is 32½" wide × 95" high × 1¾" thick.

Hardware: The original hardware matches that extant on D2091 but the hinges are of the narrow variety.

WINDOWS

A single original window opening is located in the east wall. The architrave, complete with raffle flower corner blocks, extends up to the bottom edge of the cornice. The opening is fitted with original six-over-six double-hung sash above a single panel apron. The deep reveal includes pairs of two-tier paneled bi-fold shutters. The locations for small knobs on the lower tier are filled in by paint.

HEATING

A Hart-period cast-iron steam radiator is positioned against the east wall near the northeast corner. This may be one of the radiators installed in 1880 by the Troy Steam Heating Company. There is no evidence that the earlier hot air system was extended to this room. Originally, the room was heated by the fireplace, probably including a coal grate, but evidence for this condition was lost when the firebox was replaced in soapstone for the Cluetts.

LIGHTING

An electrified circa 1890 gas chandelier is suspended by a chain from the ceiling. The polished brass fixture features a central opal glass shade surrounded by four gas candle arms. The fixture was placed here in the 1960s. Originally, there was no suspended lighting device in this room. A Hart-era gas light bracket was positioned in the south side of the window architrave at about 53½" above the floor where the gas pipe is still visible. The gas pipe can be seen in the shutter pocket.

FIREPLACE

The original 74½" wide × 10½" deep masonry chimney breast projects from the south wall slightly east of center. The original mottled black/grey marble mantel is composed of plain flat pilasters and a plain frieze supporting a projecting unmolded shelf positioned 51" above the floor. The Cluett period soapstone lining and hearth replace the Hart-era finishes. The firebox shows evidence that the Cluetts had fires here.

CLOSET

The small rectangular closet space, accessed through the door next to the southwest corner of the room, is an original feature. The original 8" to 9½" wide tongue-and-groove floorboards are laid east/west. The surface is covered in brown paint.

All four walls are finished in original plaster on wood lath. The plaster-on-lath ceiling is concealed by a circa 1964 plywood panel inserted in the space at the level of the top shelf on the west and north walls. A plain low baseboard with a top bead is located at each wall.

The original 4¼" wide door architrave has a Grecian ovolo and astragal molding at its outer edge.

Conditions within the closet were modified by the Cluetts and RCHS. Two sections of an original wood garment rail exist on the south and west walls at 67½" above the floor. The 3" wide beaded edge rail that now includes six 2¾" turned wood pegs, was originally located at 85" above the floor where evidence is preserved in the wall surface. Shelving exists on the north, east, and west walls. Generally, the shelf conditions date to modifications and insertions made by the Cluetts and the Society. The top shelf on the north wall and the supports of the upper two shelves appear to be material from the Hart period. The plaster wall surfaces retain evidence for the positions of earlier rails and shelves.

An 8½" × 10½" wood enclosed plumbing chase is positioned in the southeast corner. This feature was installed to house the plumbing servicing the third floor bathroom (310) created for the Albert Cluetts.

FURNISHINGS AND FITTINGS

The furnishings used here varied depending on the function of the room. During the Hart period, this was probably always a bedroom. This is the "Bedroom over Library" included in the 1844 inventory. Furnishings included a bed, bureau, washstand, two stands (one with glass), and three chairs. The floor was covered by a carpet. The occupant of the room at this time is unknown.

The Hart financial records include references to several bedrooms including the "S.E. [Southeast] bedroom" and "Miss Hart's Room."

In the 1886 inventory, this space is referred to as "Miss Hart's Room" (Sarah Wool Hart). How long she occupied this room is unknown. Whether she continued to use this room until her death has not been determined. In 1886, the room included a walnut bedstead, a mahogany bureau, commode, washstand bookcase, rocker, three chairs, and a lounge with two pillows. A window seat was positioned in the window recess. Carpeting covered the floor and curtains and shades covered the window. The mantel was covered in a lambrequin and the clock was probably placed on the mantel shelf. The bed may be the walnut round corner bedstead provided by New York cabinetmakers Pottier and Stymus in 1861. The lounge was repaired by Louis Muller in 1884. A payment to Louis Muller in 1889 for two pairs of lace curtains for Miss Hart's Room may indicate that she had moved to another room, one with two windows rather than the one found in this space. Perhaps she moved into the room formerly occupied by her grandmother Rebecca Howard, a room probably kept intact by Betsey Hart after her mother's death in 1870. The function and appearance of this room during the occupancy of the house by George and Amanda Cluett is unknown.

At some point after 1910, this became Caroline Cluett's sitting room. Furnishings, according to oral tradition, included a large sofa against the north wall and a chaise in front of the window. A chest was located in the southeast corner and a desk or sewing table was next to the west wall. A round table, in the center of the room, and some occasional chairs were also included. Family paintings and photos were placed on the wall surface above the sofa.

The 1953 House Committee report recommended that this room and the adjoining bathroom (203) be made available for a resident curator, but whether this room was furnished for this use is unknown.

In January 1964, this room was opened for the first time as the RCHS library. The mahogany bookcases, used by the Albert Cluetts in the back parlor, were probably placed here. Furnishings and objects belonging to General John Ellis Wool, including an extraordinary sleigh bedstead, a small desk and a large chest, were placed here and the room was opened in December 1964 as a memorial to the General. The furnishings were formerly housed in the Wool residence at 75 first Street and are recorded there in a late nineteenth century photograph. A small brass plaque, attached to the hall face of the bedroom door (D2091) is inscribed "The General John Ellis Wool Memorial Room—Given in memory by his great great niece—Sarah Bleecker Griswold Tenney—1964."

FINISHES INVESTIGATION

The plaster walls have always been covered in wallpaper until the current paper was painted over sometime after 1953. There are two layers of green paint over the paper that was probably placed here for Caroline Cluett. The unpainted surface of the paper is preserved under the cover plate of the light switch. It appears to be a grey brick and mortar joint pattern covered in flowers.

In 1891, Thomas Buckley of Albany redecorated the "S.E. [Southeast] room," including tinting the ceiling and cornice, removing old paper and installing 15 pieces of paper 80 yards of frieze and 60 feet of picture molding. This is probably the molding that survives below the plaster cornice. A narrow fragment of the 1891 frieze paper may be preserved behind this molding.

210 Vestibule – Bathroom Hall

This small vestibule is located in the addition constructed circa 1836 at the rear of the original house. It provides the connection, at second floor level, between the two structures. In plan, the small square 4'7" × 4'9" room includes doorways in the south, east, and west walls and a window opening in the north wall. The low height of the ceiling places the window sill near the floor. To provide a functional ceiling height for this space an unusual condition was created at the third floor of the addition. The floor of the small room (312) directly above this area is positioned about 12" higher than the adjoining stair hall (311) floor surface, creating a step-up between the two spaces. This change in level is very apparent when one passes from this vestibule (210) into the adjoining stair hall (212) where the ceiling is only 6'1" above the floor.

No mention is made of this area in the 1844 inventories, but this is the "Bath Room Hall" included in the 1886 inventory. The absence of a door in the opening between the Hart bathroom (207) and this space indicates that they functioned together in the nineteenth century. It is probable that the door in the west wall (D2101) was kept locked during the Hart period. Differences in door molding profiles may indicate that this doorway did not exist until after 1893. Day-to-day access to the servants' rooms in the rear wing would be gained from the stairway that formerly ascended from the first floor service hall/pantry (110).

Prior to work carried out in 1893 or slightly later, the doorway in the south wall was much lower, approximately 6' in height, much like the small door (D3112) that opens to third floor room 312. During the Hart era the adjoining room to the south (211) had a much lower ceiling height. It was probably the "Skirt Room" included in the 1886 inventory.

George and Amanda Cluett had the bathroom relocated from Room 207 to the renovated and enlarged Room 211. This space (210) continued to have a relationship with the new bathroom, although it was now separated from that space by a door.

Sometime after RCHS occupied the house, beginning in 1953, the second floor rooms of the rear wing were made ready for a resident custodian. This space functioned as an entry vestibule to the custodian's apartment. To provide a separation between Room 207, used by RCHS for collections storage, and this vestibule, an accordion folding door was placed in the opening (D2072) between the spaces. This door was removed once the area was no longer used as an apartment.

The current use of the rooms in the rear wing for staff offices makes this small vestibule a busy passage.

FLOOR

The floor is finished in narrow 2¼" wide strips of tongue-and-groove oak, laid east/west. The surface, originally varnished, is now covered in paint. This flooring was installed for the George Cluetts and covers the original circa 1836 wide boards which are also laid east/west. That surface is exposed in the adjoining hall (212). The floor surface here is approximately 3" lower than the hardwood surface in the passage/linen storage room (207).

WALLS

The walls vary in finish: the south and west walls are of original plaster on a sawn wood lath and the north wall is of plaster on brick. The surface next to the door in the east wall is of narrow 3½" wide vertical beaded board laid over earlier plaster. A wood enclosed pipe chase is positioned in the southeast corner.

CEILING

The original circa 1836 plaster on sawn wood lath ceiling is approximately 85" above the floor.

BASEBOARD

The 11½" high base is almost identical to the baseboards in the original 1827 section of the house, but this material dates to circa 1836.

CORNICE

There is no cornice in this area.

DOORS

There are three door openings in this small area: an opening in the east wall (D2072) that has never held a door, an opening in the south wall (D2111) from which the door is removed and an opening in the west wall (D2101) with door removed.

All three openings have architraves composed of the same typical Greek revival trim profile (Grecian ovolo with fillet) used throughout the two periods of construction of the rear addition. Close inspection reveals slight variations in the profile which relate to the different periods of installation. The most recent trim is found on the door opening to Room 211 where the current size and detailing dates to the enlargement of the adjacent room carried out for George and Amanda Cluett. The same Cluett-era trim exists on the doorway in the west wall.

D2101: The paneled door is removed but was attached to the north jamb where there is evidence for two small hinges. The strike remains on the south jamb. This small hinge, secured by three screws, is the type used during the George Cluett period. This may indicate that the opening was created at that time.

D2072: The opening was created in circa 1836 and replaced a window opening in the same approximate position. A door has never existed in this opening.

D2111: The paneled door is removed but was attached to the west jamb, swinging into the adjoining room (211). Prior to the increase to the ceiling height of Room 211 in circa 1893, this door opening was no higher than about 6'. The door was probably similar to third floor door D3112.

WINDOWS

A single original window opening is positioned near the floor in the north wall. The trim matches the profile of the door trim. The opening is fitted with original six-over-six double-hung sash. The brass thumb latch was installed by RCHS. The low ceiling height results in the placement of this window much closer to the floor than normal practice. The natural light from this window provided illumination for the room that functioned as the Hart bathroom (207) and the windowless room with a low ceiling (211) located south of the vestibule prior to 1893.

HEATING

This small space has never been heated.

LIGHTING

There probably was no artificial lighting here until the installation of the incandescent wall sconce on the south wall by RCHS.

PLUMBING

The wood-enclosed pipe chase in the southeast corner conceals a cast-iron soil line drain pipe that serves the third floor bathroom (303).

FURNISHINGS AND FITTINGS

The 1844 inventory makes no mention of this space but in the 1886 document it is included as the "Bath Room Hall." A chair, carpet, and rug were located here and the inclusion of a stair carpet indicates that the compiler of the inventory looked into the adjoining stair hall (212). No mention is made of any window treatment.

The small shelf located in the southeast corner, at about 36½" above the floor, survives from the Hart period and was likely used to hold a lighting device.

211   Storeroom – Bathroom – Kitchen – Office

This room has undergone extensive remodeling since its completion in circa 1836. In plan, the rectangular (8'2" × 14'10") room includes a single doorway in the north wall and a single window opening in the south wall. The twentieth-century appearance and function of this room are very different from conditions during the Hart era. Originally, the space had a ceiling height of about 6'1", barely enough height to permit a person to stand up in the room. The doorway was lower, relating to the ceiling height, and there was no window opening in the south wall.

The low, dark space was undoubtedly used for storage. This unusual physical condition resulted from the expansion of the dining room on the first floor (that extension is directly below that space), and the position of the new third floor servants' rooms. This space is the "left over" area sandwiched between the first and third floor spaces.

The room is not mentioned in the 1844 inventory but it may be the "Skirt Room," a space used for storage, included in the 1886 inventory.

After the acquisition of the house by George and Amanda Cluett in 1893, this was one of the areas that was remodeled, probably in conjunction with the expansion of the rear wing to include a modern kitchen. The complicated project involved the restructuring of the ceiling at a greater height to create a more functional room. This increase in the ceiling height resulted in a decrease in the size of the room directly above (313). That space, originally a servant's room, was turned into a store room with a very low ceiling height and awkward access.

Along with an increase in ceiling height, a window was installed in the south wall and the doorway was increased in size. The new space was fitted-out as a bathroom, the largest in the house at that time. It essentially replaced the Hart-era bathroom formerly located in Room 207. The newly formed room included a wood wainscot as well as a toilet, lavatory, and bathtub. To reach this bathroom, family members passed through the linen storage area created in the former bathroom (207) and the small vestibule (210).

After the occupation of the house by the Society in 1953, this room was converted into a kitchen to be used by the resident caretaker who occupied an apartment created in the servants' area.

The room continued to function as an apartment kitchen for a succession of tenants who lived in the rear wing well into the 1980s.

The need for additional staff office space and storage areas resulted in the discontinuation of the tradition of a tenant's apartment in the rear wing in the late 1980s. The kitchen fixtures were removed from this room and it now functions as an office.

FLOOR

The floor is composed of a sandwich of surfaces and finishes dating to several periods beginning in circa 1836. The current surface is vinyl sheet flooring over underlayment. This surface was installed by Wilson Large in 1965. Underneath is an earlier finish consisting of 9" × 9" vinyl tiles (green with a red and white spatter pattern) laid over a hardwood floor which matches the surface in the adjoining vestibule (210). This tile was probably installed by RCHS when this space was converted into a kitchen for use by the caretaker. The hardwood surface dates to the bathroom function installed here after 1893. The original wide board flooring remains under all of these later surfaces.

The rectangular area of plywood infill next to the east wall may have contained a marble floor slab that was positioned beneath the Cluett-era lavatory formerly in that location.

WALLS

The north, east, and west wall surfaces are plaster on sawn wood lath while the south wall is finished in plaster on brick masonry. Generally, these surfaces date to circa 1836 although the plaster above six feet dates to the remodeling of the space after 1893. All four walls include a 48¼" high dado composed of molded vertical tongue-and-groove boards and a 5" tall cap rail with an inset bead ornament. The dado is contemporary with the conversion of the space for bathroom use after 1893.

CEILING

The ceiling is finished in square fiberboard acoustic tile installed by Wilson Large in 1965. The original plaster-on-lath surface, now hidden by the tiles, dates to the remodeling of the room for George and Amanda Cluett.

This work involved the construction of this ceiling several feet higher than the circa 1836 ceiling.

BASEBOARD

The plain 5½" high base is contemporary with the installation of the wood dado.

CORNICE

A narrow 1¼" wood strip is contemporary with the acoustical tile ceiling.

DOORS

In its current form, the doorway in the north wall (D2111) dates to the remodeling of the room after 1893. The trim closely duplicates the profile of the circa 1836 Grecian trim found in the rear wing. The door, which was hinged to the west jamb, is removed. The jamb leaves of two 3½" high cast-iron butt hinges remain in place as does the lock strike plate on the east jamb. The small size of the hinge is typical of work carried out in 1893. The original opening in this location was no more that 6' in height. The original door was similar to or may be the small third floor door (D3112) that opens to space 312 and is 58¼" high.

WINDOWS

The single window opening in the south wall includes trim that is identical to the door trim. The opening is fitted with six-over-six double-hung sash with 10" × 16" glass panes and ⅝" wide muntins. The bullnose sill sits above a plain apron. This window opening is contemporary with the creation of the bathroom. Prior to 1893, there was no window in the wall. This condition is apparent in the circa 1892 Hart period photograph that records the exterior south façade of the house (Fig. 121).

HEATING

A circa 1870s–80s cast-iron steam radiator is positioned against the west wall near the northwest corner. This may be one of the radiators supplied by the Troy Steam Heating Company in 1880 for an unidentified location, possibly the former bathroom (207). It was probably moved to this location after 1893. The "Skirt Room," originally located here, was likely unheated.

LIGHTING

The three-lamp fluorescent ceiling fixture and the incandescent wall lamp on the east wall were installed here when the room was remodeled as a kitchen by RCHS. There is no visible evidence for gas lighting.

PLUMBING

The plumbing history of this room spans three eras. Until recently, a cabinet-type kitchen sink was located against the east wall. The sink was installed when the space was remodeled by RCHS to serve as the caretaker's kitchen.

The 1934 HABS floor plan indicates that the bathroom, first created for the George Cluetts, included a lavatory and toilet against the east wall and a bathtub next to the west wall. The east wall wood dado retains evidence for the sink which was approximately 32" wide and was located about 5'9" from the north wall, the same location later occupied by the kitchen sink. The lavatory may have consisted of a marble counter and back splash fitted with a ceramic bowl. Beneath the counter, the floor included an inset marble pad. It cannot be determined if the Albert Cluetts replaced any of the bathroom fixtures. Prior to 1893, there was no plumbing in this space.

EQUIPMENT

A vertical gas supply line is located against the east wall near the northeast corner. This pipe serviced the post 1953 gas stove formerly in this location.

FURNISHINGS AND FITTINGS

As the function and form of this room changed so have the furnishings. The low ceiling height and absence of a window in the original room indicate that it was to be used for storage. Not mentioned in the 1844 inventory but included in the 1886 document as the "Skirt Room," it was apparently a store room. The few items found here at that time included a carpet (probably rolled up), a pail, and a jelly strainer. The designation "Skirt Room" likely refers to the use of the space as a closet for the large hoop skirts fashionable in the middle decades of the nineteenth century. A windowless room, conveniently located near the family bed chambers, would be the ideal place to store these and other clothing items. Family access to the room was through the bathroom, formerly located in Room 207.

After the purchase of the house by George and Amanda Cluett in 1893, the room was extensively remodeled to accommodate a modern bathroom. The new fittings included a toilet, lavatory, and bathtub.

Some or all of these plumbing fixtures were used by the Albert Cluetts after 1910 and fixtures are recorded in the room on the 1934 floor plan. There is no visual record of the appearance of the fixtures.

Sometime after 1953, the room was converted into a kitchen to be used by a live-in caretaker. A sink, stove, and refrigerator replaced the earlier plumbing fixtures. Recently, these kitchen fittings were removed so that the room could function as a staff office.

FINISHES INVESTIGATION

Throughout the various uses that occurred here, the plaster wall surfaces have always been painted. The wood dado, installed in 1893 or soon after, originally had a varnish or shellac finish but is now painted.

212   Stair Hall

The service stair hall extends along the north side of the rear addition constructed in circa 1836. In plan, the long rectangular (5'7" × 16'10") hall exists on two levels joined by a short flight of stairs. There are single doorways in the south, east and west walls and a window opening in the north wall. Generally, this arrangement of features dates to the remodeling of the hall that coincided with the expansion of the rear wing for George and Amanda Cluett. As completed for Richard Hart, the hall featured a window in the rear (west) wall and the stairway continued downward to the first floor service hall (110).

The difference in floor levels relates to the greater ceiling height of the first floor rooms in the original part of the house and the lower height of the ceilings in the rear wing. The stair and the upper landing in this hall provide a means to join the various levels.

The removal of the lower stair run in 1893 or slightly later was possible because a new stair was constructed at the far west end of the hall of the final addition to the rear of the house. Fortunately, when the Hart service stair was partially removed, the newel post and a short section of the handrail were salvaged and reinstalled at the remaining portion of the stair at this level.

During the two Cluett eras, this area was primarily the domain of the household servants. After 1953, this hall became part of an apartment, initially occupied by the resident caretaker and later a series of tenants. The hall now provides access to museum staff offices and is used minimally for storage.

FLOOR

The floor exists at two levels separated by the lower flight of the two-run stair way. The floor at the head of the stair, at the east end of the hall, is composed of original wide tongue-and-groove boards, laid east/west. Two centrally positioned boards can be removed providing access to the large "secret"crawl space beneath the floor (Fig. 191).

The floor at the west end of the hall consists of two areas. Three original wide (6" to 9") tongue-and-groove boards, laid east/west, remain in place along the south side of the hall. The additional narrower (6") boards that fill the north side of the hall, as well as the area under the lower stair run, were installed in the opening occupied by the portion of the stair that extended to the first floor and was removed in 1893. All of the hall flooring is painted.

WALLS

The north and west surfaces are of plaster on brick masonry and the south and east walls are of plaster on sawn wood lath.

CEILING

The original ceiling is finished in plaster on sawn wood lath. The underside of the stair run to the third floor is covered in gypsum board installed by contractor Jess Tuttle in the 1980s when work was done to stabilize the stair run to the third floor.

BASEBOARD

This circa 1836 baseboard duplicates the 11½" high base found in the primary rooms in the original 1827 house.

CORNICE

There is no cornice molding in this space.

DOORS

There are three door openings in this hall: original openings in the east wall (D2101) and south wall (D2131) and a later opening (D2121) in the west wall. The west opening was created when the rear wing was extended in 1893 or slightly later. Originally, a window may have been located here. All of the openings feature the typical 5" wide Greek revival trim which is used throughout the rear addition. Close inspection reveals that the profile varies slightly at the later west opening.

191 Opening in the floor surface (212).

D2121: The paneled door is removed from this opening. The north jamb retains three 3" cast-iron butt hinges and the lock strike survives in the south jamb. The deep wood-lined reveal passes through the brick wall that was formerly the rear wall of the circa 1836 addition.

WINDOWS

A single later window opening is positioned in the north wall. The trim matches the profile of the door trim and the sills and apron match conditions of the later window in Room 211. The opening is fitted with six-over-six double-hung sash with 10" × 16" glass panes. Prior to the Cluett expansion of the rear wing, there was probably a window opening in the west wall. The north opening was inserted as part of the expansion in 1893 or slightly later.

HEATING

This hall was never heated.

LIGHTING

There are two electric light fixtures in the hall. A brass wall sconce with an opal glass shade is positioned in the east wall and dates to the Albert Cluett period. A pull-down ceiling fixture is located near the window. This fixture dates to the 1960s. There is no visible evidence for gas lighting in the hall.

STAIRWAY

The original circa 1836 open riser stair exists in two runs at the east end of the hall. The stair ascends in six risers along the south wall to the upper floor level and then continues as a separate run along the north wall in ten risers to the third floor. The continuous mahogany handrail is oval in section and is supported by round tapered balusters, two per tread. The elegantly turned and tapered 43¼" high newel is positioned at the base of the stair (Fig. 192). Originally, the stair continued down to the first floor service hall (110). That run was positioned

192 This newel post was originally positioned at the foot of the staircase when it extended down to Room 110, prior to 1893 (212).

against the north wall and included approximately seventeen risers. When that portion of the stair was removed in 1893 or slightly later, the newel at the base of the stair at first floor level was salvaged and reused here. A short section of handrail above the newel was also reused. Inspection of this portion of the handrail revealed holes in the underside representing the original position of the balusters when the stair handrail was at the first floor.

FURNISHINGS AND FITTINGS

Neither of the Hart furnishings inventories make specific reference to this hall, but the 1886 document includes a stair carpet along with the list of items in the "Bath Room Hall" (210). That space is immediately adjacent to the stairway in this hall (212) and it is likely that the person producing the inventory saw the carpet through the doorway connecting the spaces. References in the Hart papers to work carried out in the "Back Hall" may include this space as well as the first floor hall directly below. None of the documents indicate that any furniture was kept here. Before the removal of the portion of the stair case that descended to the first floor, there was very little floor area here. After the removal of the stair and the placement of the window in the north wall, it is possible that the Cluetts placed some furnishings here.

During the period beginning after 1953, when the caretaker and later a tenant occupied this area, furniture was placed here and currently collection items are stored next to the stair.

213 Nursery – Bedroom – Living Room – Office

This room corresponds in size and general character to the first floor room (111) directly below, that was formerly occupied by Betsey Hart. In plan, the 14'5" × 14'10" room features a single doorway in the north wall and a pair of windows in the south wall. The west wall is composed of three surfaces: a shallow projecting central chimney breast flanked by the wall surface to the south and the projection of the closet that fills the northwest corner. This is the primary second floor room of the rear addition constructed in circa 1836 and the finishes indicate that it was a room of some importance.

Although there is no early documentation concerning the original function of this room, it is possible that the "Nursery" included in the 1844 inventory is this space. It is also possible that the nursery was located in the front basement room (B02), the location that was popular in New York City townhouses in the nineteenth century. The listing of the "Nursery" in the 1844 inventory document between the "Rooms in back building" and "Hall stove in Basement" makes either location possible.

The 1886 inventory includes this space as "Mrs. Hastings' Room." She served as the housekeeper for Sarah Wool Hart. Access to the room was from the service stair that originally ascended from the back hall (110), but was removed after 1893.

Servants probably occupied the room during the Cluett eras and after 1953, this space was included in the caretaker's apartment. More recently, the costume collection was kept here and currently the room functions as staff office space.

FLOOR

The original circa 1836 wide board (7" to 11") tongue-and-groove boards are laid east/west. The surface is now painted. A brick hearth, 14½" deep, is set into the floor surface and projects about 14½" from the west wall. Floorboards in the center of the room are cut to provide access to the wiring for an electric ceiling fixture formerly located in the room (111) below.

WALLS

The north, east, and west walls are of plaster on sawn wood lath. The south wall and projecting chimney breast in the west wall are of plaster on brick masonry.

CEILING

The ceiling is original plaster on sawn wood lath.

BASEBOARD

This 11" high baseboard duplicated the base used in the primary rooms of the 1827 house. There is no base on the face of the chimney breast. A small shoe molding dates to early in the Cluett occupancy.

CORNICE

A complex run-in-place plaster cornice extends around the room and across the chimney breast. This finish indicates the original importance of this room.

DOORS

There are two original door openings: the doorway (D2131) to the hall and the closet door (D2132). Both have the typical 6" side Greek Revival trim profile common to the circa 1836 rear wing.

D2131: The original door includes a symmetrical arrangement of six recessed vertical panels on both faces.

Hardware: Original fittings include two 4½" high cast-iron butt hinges, a 4" × 5¼" iron rim back marked "McKinney Troy," small brass knobs and an oval keyhole escutcheon. The original iron keeper has a brass strike edge.

D2132: The original closet door has the six recessed vertical panels on the room face and flush panels on the closet face.

Hardware: Original fittings include two 4¼" high cast-iron butt hinges and physical evidence for a small 3¼" × 4" plate latch, now missing and replaced by a narrow brass faced mortise lock with brown mineral knobs and two rectangular clipped corner iron keyhole escutcheons. These replacement fittings may date to late in the Hart period.

WINDOWS

There are two original window openings in the south wall with the typical Greek Revival trim. The openings retain original six-over-six double-hung sash.

HEATING

A circa 1870s–80s cast-iron steam radiator is positioned against the north wall near the northeast corner. This may be one of the radiators installed in 1880 by the Troy Steam Heating Company. The wide projecting chimney breast and the visible brick hearth indicate that a fireplace was originally positioned in the west walls, but there is no visible trace for the missing mantel. There is no baseboard on the face of the chimney breast. Evidence for a circular flue pipe opening in the face of the chimney breast indicates that a heating stove was used here, probably prior to the installation of the radiator.

LIGHTING

An electric three-bulb incandescent fixture with etched glass shade is centered on the ceiling. Hart-era gas pipes protrude from the wall surface between the two south windows. This was the location for gas light brackets.

PLUMBING

Exposed piping for the radiators located in Rooms 211 and 314 is situated near the northeast corner.

CLOSET

An original shallow closet is positioned in the northwest corner next to the chimney breast. The lath and plaster partition that encloses the closed curves at the south end to join the west wall. The closet interior includes a floor surface of painted linoleum covering the original wide boards and the walls are plastered. The plain 6½" high baseboard has a beaded top edge.

Fittings include three original wood shelves at the north end of the spaces and a beaded edge wood rail at about 72" above the floor on the west wall and on the curved wall surface. The rail supports iron garment hooks (late nineteenth century) of two different types.

FURNISHINGS AND FITTINGS

The furnishing of this large room changed as its function changed over time. This may be the "Nursery" noted in the 1844 inventory, but no specific list of items is included. A stove was probably used to heat the room at that time. In the 1886 inventory, this is the room occupied by Mrs. Hastings who, at one time, was the housekeeper.

The amply furnished room included a black walnut bed, three bureaus, a wash stand and towel rack, two chairs, a rocker and a child's chair. A small clock was likely positioned on the mantel and a carpet covered the floor. The rug may be a hearth rug or a bedside rug. Shades covered the windows.

Servants continued to occupy this room after 1893 and the 1934 HABS floor plan includes this space as a servant's bedroom, but there is no record of the furnishings used here. After 1953, this space served as the living room for the caretaker and later the tenant. Currently, the room is furnished as a double office.

214   Back Stair Hall

With the expansion of the rear addition in 1893 or slightly later, a new service stair was constructed in this location.

The stair hall is about 24' long and varies in width from 5'4" at the east end to 6'11" at the west end. The greater width accommodates the stairway in the northwest corner. In plan, the hall includes single window openings in the north and west walls and a doorway in the east wall as well as two door openings in the south wall. The doors, windows, and the trim of these openings duplicate in detail the features from the circa 1836 portion of the rear wing. The stairway is much heavier in detail than the feature it replaced and is characteristic of the late nineteenth century. Unlike the 1836 stair it replaced, this stair continues to the basement.

FLOOR

The original circa 1893 6" wide tongue-and-groove boards are laid east/west. Several layers of paint cover this surface.

WALLS

All of the surfaces are finished in original plaster on wood lath. At the change in plains of the south wall there is evidence for a now missing wood corner guard.

CEILING

This surface is approximately 9'5½" above the floor and is finished in plaster on wood lath.

BASEBOARD

The 7½" high wood base if finished with an integral ogee crown and fillet.

CORNICE

There is no cornice molding in this hall.

DOORS

There are three original openings: the doorway (D2121) that connects this hall to the earlier hall to the east, the doorway (D2151) which opens to the bathroom vestibule and the doorway (D2171) which opens to the back bedroom. All of these openings were created when the rear wing was extended in 1893. The architraves duplicate the trim profile found in the earlier (circa 1836) portion of the rear addition.

WINDOWS

There are two original window openings: one in the north wall and one in the west wall. Both feature the Greek Revival trim that duplicates the circa 1836 profile and include six-over-six double-hung sash. The north sash includes an original ornamental cast-iron fastener while the west sash is latched by a slightly later plain fastener.

HEATING

This hall was never heated. Two cast-iron heating pipes are exposed on either side of the doorway (D2171) in the south wall.

LIGHTING

A single incandescent fixture with a yellow glass shade is positioned in the ceiling above the stairway. The fixture dates to the late Albert Cluett era or soon after 1953. The original light source was a gas wall bracket positioned on the south wall just west of the doorway to the bathroom. Only the gas pipe remains in this position.

EQUIPMENT

A nonfunctional intercom unit is mounted on the wall immediately west of door D2171.

STAIRWAY

A stairway ascends in 17 risers from the first floor hall to this space. The open well is surrounded by an oak balustrade formed of turned balusters supporting a handrail that is circular in section. This stairway served as the replacement for the circa 1836 stair that was removed from Room 110 when the rear wing was extended in circa 1893.

FURNISHINGS AND FITTINGS

There is no documentation on the use of this hall other than as circulation space, but the size of the space and the two windows make it a pleasant space that may have been used by servants as a sitting area. At least one tenant of the rear addition apartment used this space as a library sitting area in the mid-1970s.

215 Bathroom Vestibule

This small (4'8" × 4'10") vestibule separates the stair hall from the servants' bathroom. In plan, the space includes doorways in the north, south, and west walls and a large closet fills the west end of the area. The vestibule retains all of its original architectural character from circa 1893.

FLOOR

The original circa 1893 narrow 2½" tongue-and-groove boards are laid east/west. This surface is painted.

WALLS

All wall surfaces are finished in original plaster on wood lath above a 49½" high vertical beaded board dado. The boards are 4" wide and have a triple bead on one edge.

CEILING

Original plaster on wood lath.

BASEBOARD

There is no baseboard; the dado boards extend to the floor.

CORNICE

There is no cornice molding.

DOORS

There are three original openings: the hall doorway (D2151), the closet door (D2152), and the opening (D2161) into the bathroom. The architraves and six-panel doors duplicate in detail the conditions of circa 1836, but close inspection of the profile reveals slight variations.

D2151: Original door with six vertical panels.

Hardware: Original fittings include a pair of 3½" high cast-iron butt hinges, mortise lock, turned wood knobs, iron shanks and roses, and rectangular wood keyhole escutcheons.

D2152: This door duplicates the details of D2151 with the exception of a missing knob rose on the hall face of the door.

WINDOWS

There is no window opening but the door (D2161) in the south wall includes a glazed opening.

HEATING

The space is heated by a single cast-iron steam radiator positioned next to the east wall. This may be one of the radiators supplied by the Troy Steam Heating Company in 1880. It was moved to this location when the rear wing was enlarged in circa 1893 (Fig. 193).

193 Steam radiator in use in since the 1880s (215).

LIGHTING

Artificial light is provided by a spun brass incandescent wall bracket with a frosted glass shade. This fixture was probably installed circa 1910. A gas pipe protruding from the east wall was the location for an original circa 1893 gas bracket light.

CLOSET

The west portion of this area incorporates an original closet. Finishes include wide floor boards (painted) and plaster-on-lath wall surfaces and ceiling. The baseboard matches the surface in the stair hall (214). An original bead-edge rail retains markings for missing garment hooks. Four shelves were inserted here later.

FURNISHINGS

It is unlikely that any furnishings were ever placed here. The closet was originally used by a household servant.

FINISHES INVESTIGATION

The same decorative floor paint treatment seen in the adjoining bathroom was also used here.

216   Bathroom

In plan, this small (7'4" × 10'2") L-shaped room includes a single doorway in the north wall and a single window in the south wall. The projection that forms the northwest corner of the room is the closet that is accessed from Room 217. This room is part of the addition constructed for George and Amanda Cluett in 1893 or soon after. It has always functioned as a toilet and lavatory room for the servants and possibly as a bathroom.

The 1934 HABS floor plan refers to this space as a bathroom and records a toilet and lavatory but no bathtub. The tub now located here probably dates to the Albert and Caroline Cluett period which began in 1910. It is similar to the still extant tub in the third floor bathroom (303) which was created after 1910 when the third floor/attic was enlarged. The current toilet and lavatory were installed in the 1960s, replacing the original fixtures.

An interesting decorative treatment that survives here is found on the floor surface. The unusual painted and stamped decoration probably dates to after 1910.

After RCHS occupied the house in 1953, this space served as the bathroom for the caretaker and later the tenants that lived in the rear wing apartment.

FLOOR

The original circa 1893 narrow 2½" wide tongue-and-groove boards are laid east/west. A white marble slab (27" × 56") is set into the floor surface along the east wall. The lavatory and toilet are set above this marble surface. A rectangular piece of plywood has recently replaced some of the flooring near the center of the room.

The original flooring and marble surface have been painted. From the 1960s and until recently, this surface was covered in linoleum.

WALLS

All the wall surfaces are finished in original plaster on wood lath above a 48½" high vertical board wood dado. The wide top rail features an inset horizontal bead motif. A narrow surface immediately east of the window opening is repaired by a sheet of fiberboard. The recessed bathtub area includes a simple dado rail placed at 23½" above the floor, the same height on the adjacent window sill.

CEILING

The ceiling is original plaster on wood lath at about 9'5½" above the floor.

BASEBOARD

An original plain 5½" splash board with a beveled top edge runs around the room.

CORNICE

There is no cornice molding.

DOORS

There is a single original opening in the north wall. The trim duplicates the profile common to the earlier, circa 1836, portion of the rear addition.

> D2161: This original door includes two vertical bottom panels and an upper glazed opening with four panes of frosted glass.

> Hardware: Original fittings include a pair of 3½" high cast-iron butt hinges, brass-faced mortise lock, turned wood knobs, and wood keyhole escutcheons.

WINDOWS

A single original window opening is positioned in the south wall. The architrave rests on a bull nose sill above a plain apron. The six-over-six double-hung sash have 10" × 16" glass panes. The sash are secured by an original cast-iron fastener.

LIGHTING

The wall-mounted incandescent fixture was installed in the 1960s. An earlier circa 1910 electric fixture was positioned in the ceiling above the lavatory. The original circa 1893 light source was a gas wall bracket positioned at 59½" above the floor between the lavatory and toilet.

PLUMBING

The bathroom includes a toilet, lavatory, and bathtub. The enameled iron tub is set on a raised iron base. This may be the original tub although the 1934 HABS floor plan does not record a tub in this location. There is also evidence on the floor surface for a dark green paint that

seems to be underneath the tub support base. The white ceramic toilet replaces the original fixture for which the outline is visible on the marble floor slab. The current toilet has a manufacturer's date stamp for 7/23/64. An outline on the wood dado indicates that the top of the tank of the original fixture was about 36½" above the floor. The original water intake pipe is still extant near the top of the dado. The pink/peach color enamel on iron lavatory was installed in the 1960s. The original fixture was approximately 25" wide.

A wood-enclosed pipe chase (5" x 9h") is positioned in the southeast corner. The cast-iron roof drain pipe is housed in this chase.

FURNISHINGS AND FITTINGS

This room has always functioned as a toilet and lavatory room. Original fixtures included a tank-type toilet and lavatory. These fixtures were replaced in the 1960s. The enameled iron bathtub was probably installed after 1910 and may replace an earlier circa 1893 tub. Evidence for an earlier condition may exist on the floor surface beneath the tub.

There are two towel bars; the earlier one is positioned on the west wall dado. Now painted, but possibly of nickel-plated brass, this fixture dates to one of the Cluett eras. The towel bar on the north dado dates to late in the Cluett occupancy or the later 1950s.

FINISHES INVESTIGATION

The narrow board floor surface retains an interesting painted finish consisting of a green background and an applied pattern "stamped" in white paint.

217 Bedroom – Office

This is the primary room of the expanded second floor of the rear wing constructed for George and Amanda Cluett in 1893 or slightly later.

In plan, the 12' × 15'5" room includes single doorways in the north and east walls and a window in the south wall. A shallow chimney breast projects from the east end of the south wall. Generally, the room's finishes duplicate the profiles and details used in the earlier, circa 1836, section of the rear wing.

Originally, a household servant occupied this room and the 1934 HABS floor plan refers to this as a "Servant's Bed Room."

This space continued to serve as a bedroom in the

1950s and into the 1980s when the second floor of the rear wing was arranged as a tenant's apartment. Currently, the room houses the office of the education director.

FLOOR

The original circa 1893 6" wide tongue-and-groove boards are laid east/west. The surface is painted. A 12" × 18" section of the flooring is cut near the closet door, probably for access to the electric wiring for the ceiling fixture in the kitchen directly below this room.

WALLS

The walls are finished in plaster on wood lath except at the shallow projection of the chimney breast which is of plaster on brick masonry.

CEILING

The plaster on wood lath surface is approximately 9'5½" above the floor.

BASEBOARD

The simple 7¾" tall base has an integral ogee crown and fillet.

CORNICE

A wood picture molding is positioned next to the ceiling.

DOORS

There are two original door openings: the opening (D2171) in the north wall to the hall and the closet door opening (D2172) in the east wall. Both openings feature the same 5" wide trim that duplicates the circa 1836 trim in the earlier part of the rear addition.

D2172: Original door with six vertical panels.

Hardware: Original fittings include three 3" high cast-iron butt hinges, brass-faced mortise lock, turned wood doorknobs, and wood keyhole escutcheons. The knob roses are missing.

D2172: Same conditions as door D2172, but here the butt hinges are 4" tall.

WINDOWS

Single original window opening in the south wall. The typical architrave rests on a bull nose sill above a plain apron. The six-over-six double-hung sash has 10" × 16" glass panes and is secured by an original decorative cast-iron fastener.

HEATING

A cast-iron steam radiator is positioned against the east wall near the northeast corner. The radiator is marked "Pat. Aug. 17, 1875." It may be one of the radiators supplied by the Troy Steam Heating Company in 1880 for some other location in the house and was relocated here after 1893.

LIGHTING

An incandescent wall sconce is positioned on the north wall next to the door. The fixture was installed after 1953. An original gas pipe protrudes from the north wall at about 60" above the floor. This was the location for a gas light bracket. The pipe includes a valve and nozzle for the attachment of a connecting hose for a gas table lamp or some sort of gas appliance such as a heater.

CLOSET

The room includes an original closet accessed through the door in the east wall. Original closet finishes include the same 6" flooring, plaster-on-lath walls and ceiling and plain trim at the door opening. Plain rails for garment hooks are located on the north, south, and east walls. Five iron hooks remain in situ, but there is evidence for additional hooks.

FURNISHINGS AND FITTINGS

The 1934 HABS floor plan indicates that this was a "Servant's Bed Room," but there is no documentation concerning the furnishing of the space. At the very least, it would have included a bed and chest and probably a chair and table. After 1953, this space functioned as the bedroom for the resident caretaker and later the tenant of the rental apartment. The room is currently furnished as an office.

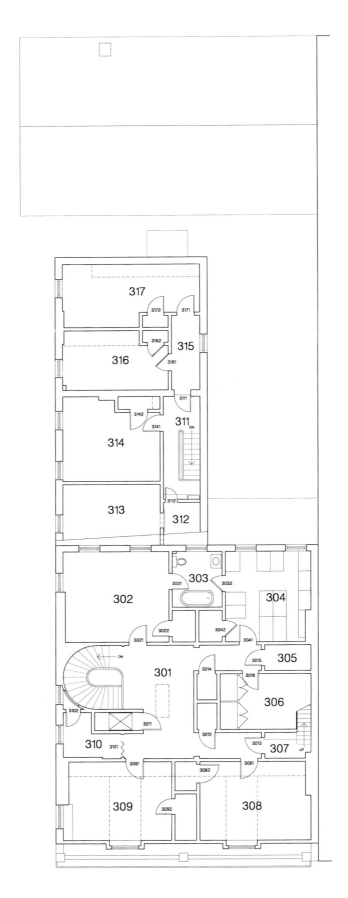

194 59 Second Street,
third floor plan, 1999.

THIRD FLOOR PLAN

0'   5'   10'   15'

THIRD FLOOR

The third floor is considerably modified from its original plan and appearance unlike the lower floors of the main house which generally retain their original architectural character (Fig. 194). Upon the completion of the house in 1827, the third story space was situated beneath the slopes of the gable roof which pitched to the east (front) and west (rear). Two dormer windows were positioned on the front slope; the rear had no dormers. The south gable elevation that faced the garden site included three third story window openings; a centrally positioned tall arched opening and two quarter-round openings near the east and west edges of the elevation. There were no openings in the north elevation which faced the adjoining property owned by Jacob Merritt.

The main stairway continues from the first floor to the level of the third floor in two dramatic curved runs forming one of the outstanding original features of the house. This arrangement is somewhat unusual. More typically, in a two story house with a third story space (attic) under the gable roof, the main stair will end at the second floor and a separate secondary stair (often enclosed) will continue to the upper floor.

The continuation of this elegantly detailed staircase to the attic story is yet another indication of the level of quality sought by William Howard for the house constructed for his daughter and son-in-law. This condition also indicates a certain degree of finish for the attic area as well as some other use besides a storage function.

Visible clues concerning the arrangement and function of the third floor in the earliest years of the Hart occupancy are minimal.

In plan, the third floor extended over the full area of the original house. The stair alcove was joined to the south side of a large central space or hall. A simple narrow stair, which ascended to the upper garret located beneath the ridge of the gable roof, was positioned at the north end of the central space. Two rooms, each with a dormer window, were positioned under the slope of the roof along the east side of the hall. Along the west side of the central space, an attic store room was positioned under the roof slope. There were no dormer windows in that area, but a quarter round window opening was positioned in the south masonry wall. A matching window was located in the southeast corner room.

All of these spaces were finished in plaster on split wood lath. The appearance of the door trim is unknown, but the baseboards were simple boards with a beaded top edge. Sections of original base were salvaged for reuse as scrap lumber when the rear (west) roof was raised after 1910 and can be seen in the garret space above the third floor.

The finest still-extant original features of the third floor exist in the stairwell alcove; they include the stair balustrade, the curved wall surface and related plaster cornice, and the large elegant oval "window" positioned in the curved wall surface.

This interior window opens to a small closet-like space which can be entered from room 310. That space includes the large arched window opening that is centered in the south gable wall of the house. Natural light from the gable opening penetrates into the stairwell through the interior oval window. The sash in the oval opening can be removed, possibly to allow air circulation through the stair well in the summer months.

The earliest functions of the third floor area remain unknown; no mention of these rooms is included in the 1844 inventory. In the 1886 document, references are made to the "Third Story Hall" which could be the large central area and the "Attic" which was probably the space west of the hall below the west slope of the gable roof.

Placement in the inventory just before the "Attic" listing of two rooms referred to as "Katie's Room" and "Alice's Room" makes it likely that they are the two east rooms with dormer windows. In the inventory contents listing, there was a shade for the dormer window in each room and a curtain for the quarter-round window in the southeast room.

Prior to the death of Betsey Hart, the third story of the main house was apparently occupied by household servants and also used for storage.

The construction of the "back building" in circa 1836 resulted in an additional third floor area that was at a lower elevation and unconnected to the areas just discussed. As originally completed, this compact addition included a narrow stair hall (315), two rooms (313, 314), and a large closet (312). Originally, both of these third floor rooms were entered from the stair hall (315). The larger room included two south facing windows while the smaller space (313) had only a single window.

The 1844 inventory records the contents of these spaces and other rooms in the rear addition under the general listing "Rooms in back building."

The 1886 inventory includes storerooms referred to as "#1" and "#2," which may refer to Rooms 313 and 314. After the purchase of the house by the Cluetts in 1893, Room 313 was extensively altered so that the room directly beneath it (211) could be enlarged to accommodate a bathroom. The alteration included the raising of the floor level in Room 313 to its current height, resulting in a space only minimally suited for storage.

After the modification of this third floor room, there is little evidence for additional significant changes to this portion of the rear wing.

The Cluett occupancy beginning in 1910 resulted in an extensive program of "improvements" to the third story of the original part of the house. The arrangement and finishes extant today resulted from a complete refurbishing of this part of the house by Albert and Caroline Cluett for the use of their children.

The rear (west) slope of the original gable roof was literally "raised-up" to create two full-sized rooms and a bathroom at the back of the third floor. The central hall was divided to create a smaller hall and several storage rooms and closets. A bathroom was created in the small space immediately east of the stair alcove and the two original east rooms with dormer windows were further separated by a pair of closets.

The result of this extensive undertaking was the creation of four large bedrooms (302, 304, 306, 309) and two full bathrooms (303, 310) as well as closets and storage rooms. The untouched original staircase still ascended in an amply sized central hall (301) that received additional natural light from a newly constructed skylight.

All of the original plain woodwork was replaced by skillful copies of the more elaborate original trim that ornamented the first and second floor openings. Rather than produce hand carved raffle flowers for the numerous new corner blocks, this detail was reproduced in cast plaster resulting in the identical appearance of each block. New doors were produced based on the paneled doors used in the rooms below.

It is likely that an architect was involved with this complex remodeling project, but no documents concerning the work seem to have survived.

The enlarged and remodeled third floor was occupied by Albert and Caroline Cluett's sons.

The third floor rooms of the original portion of the house were set aside in 1957 as an apartment for the first full-time RCHS director, H. Maxson Holloway. The still extant decor found in the various spaces survives from that occupancy. To provide a kitchen for the apartment, a Cluett-era bathroom (310) was remodeled. The next director, Archie Stobie, occupied the apartment with his family for a brief period.

For many years thereafter, the third floor rooms (including those in the rear wing) have functioned as collections storage areas while Room 302 has successively served as the office of the curator and registrar.

301   Stair Hall

This centrally positioned hall provides access to all of the rooms and smaller spaces that surround it. The rectangular hall includes the curved stair alcove which is positioned on the south side of the space and two narrow passages that extend the space to the north.

This third floor area includes several doors, a skylight, and the internal oval "window" in the stair alcove.

The central space includes single doorways in the east and west walls, wide openings in the south wall as well as the door to the elevator, and in the north wall openings to the two north corridors. The northwest corridor includes four doorways and the northeast corridor includes three doorways.

With the exception of the staircase and the detailing of the stair alcove, all of the features and finishes date to the remodeling carried out after 1910 for Albert and Caroline Cluett. The original configuration of the space is unknown, but it is possible that this central area extended completely or almost completely to the north wall of the house. Evidence for the original arrangement likely exists beneath the twentieth century surfaces, particularly the flooring. The most recent modification was the 1969 extension of the 1938 elevator to the third floor and into the hall.

The nineteenth century function of the original large space is unknown. The room in its current form is referred to as a stair hall on the 1934 HABS floor plan. In that plan, a conventional doorway in the south wall provides access to the bathroom located in Room 310. The current plan arrangement, including the projecting wall surface enclosing the elevator shaft and the wide opening to Room 310 (former kitchenette and bathroom), dates to work carried out in 1969. When the third floor served as the director's apartment, this large area may have functioned as the living and dining space. The hall now serves as an informal storage area for collections.

FLOOR

The floor is finished in narrow 2¼" wide strips of tongue-and-groove oak, laid north/south over the original wide board attic flooring. The hardwood surface is part of the remodeling carried out after 1910.

WALLS

The stair alcove retains original plaster on split wood lath wall surfaces. In the central space, the east and west walls include original structure, but the finished surface appears to be rock lath covered in a skim coat of plaster. This twentieth century material also forms the north wall and the walls of the two north corridors. The projection of the elevator shaft is of gypsum board dating to 1969.

The two projecting surfaces centered in the east and west walls cover original wood structural members that are visible in the attic space above this room.

CEILING

This surface dates to the post-1910 remodeling and is composed of rock lath covered in plaster. It replaces the original plaster-on-wood-lath surface. The ceiling is about 9'5" above the floor.

BASEBOARD

The 11¾" high molded wood baseboard copies the original base detail found in the first and second floor spaces. This baseboard is part of the twentieth century remodeling and replaces a simple plain base with a bead along the top. The east face of the elevator shaft projection features a plain low base.

CORNICE

The original complex run-in-place plaster cornice remains in the stair alcove. The cornice in the central area duplicates this feature, but appears to date to the post-1910 renovation.

DOORS

There are ten doorways and two wide openings in this space. The doors in five of the doorways open into the hall: doors D3011 and D3012 in the northwest corridor, doors D3013 and D3014 in the northeast corridor, and the elevator door D3015. There are two wide openings in the south wall; both include accordion folding doors installed in the 1960s. All of the openings feature the typical trim with raffle flower corner blocks. This trim

is a post-1910 copy of the first and second floor finishes; here the raffle flowers are of cast plaster rather than the carved wood of the originals.

D3011, D3012, D3013, D3014, D3015: These six-panel, stile-and-rail doors are identical in detailing, but vary slightly in width. They date to the post-1910 renovation and are similar to the original doors of the first and second floors.

Hardware: Original post-1910 fittings include three 4½" high brass plated iron butt hinges with ball finials, brass-faced mortise locks, brass knobs, and drop cover keyhole escutcheons. The door to the elevator (D3015) was, prior to 1969, positioned in the original opening to Room 310. That opening was modified when the elevator shaft was constructed. The other doors open into the various rooms and are described with those spaces.

WINDOWS

The large oval opening in the curved wall of the stairwell is an important original feature (Fig. 195). This

195 Original oval window opening and sash in the south wall of the stairwell (301).

interior opening is framed by molded wood trim that follows the oval curve as well as the curve of the wall. The curved rectangular sash is installed from the back side of the opening accessed in closet space 310A. The oval glazed portion of the sash includes wood muntins and applied cast-lead ornaments including a ribbon/bow motif at the center of the cross muntins. This impressive sash sits in the opening and is held in place by a few nails. Possibly it was removed in the summer so that the stairwell and related halls could be ventilated through the window in the south gable. The back side of this sash is covered in cotton sheeting, secured by tacks, so that the external window is not visible from the hall.

A large rectangular skylight is centered in the ceiling of the hall. An oval-shaped glazed opening, divided into segments by wood muntins, supports textured glass panels. This sash is divided into two sections and originally could be opened upward into the enclosed skylight shaft that extends up through the attic to the roof. This feature is part of the post-1910 renovation.

LIGHTING

There are two brass electric wall sconces with frosted glass tulip-form shades. These fixtures were installed when the director's apartment was created. A cover plate positioned on the underside of the skylight was the location of a suspended electrical fixture installed as part of the apartment renovation. The brass chandelier is now located in the entrance hall of the Carr Building, 57 Second Street.

STAIRWAY

The original stairway joins the third floor along the south side of the hall. In the stairwell, the wall surface forms a snake-like curve that follows the staircase down to the second floor. The continuous run of the mahogany handrail arrives at the third floor where it rests on a turned iron baluster and then curves to the east, continues in a straight run, and terminates in the east edge of the stair well opening.

The wide door opening to the stairwell is framed by the same corner block trim used at the door openings. The ceiling above the stairwell is slightly lower than the ceiling in the hall.

ELEVATOR

The 1938 elevator was extended to the third floor in 1969. This work included the removal of the door and doorway that opened to the space (310) that originally functioned as a bathroom, but was converted into a kitchenette in circa 1960. The door and trim were reused in the new gypsum board elevator enclosure to provide access to the elevator.

EQUIPMENT

A circa 1969 intercom box is attached to the west face of the elevator enclosure. A Cluett-era service push button is also installed in this wall surface and was moved here from some nearby location, probably in the original south wall.

FURNISHINGS AND FITTINGS

There are few clues concerning the possible function and furnishing of the various spaces that were originally located in the attic above the second floor. This central area and the possibly larger predecessor space always functioned as a circulation point. It is unlikely that there was much activity here since there was no separation of this space from the stairwell and therefore, the family bedroom spaces on the second floor. This may be the "Third Story Hall" included in the 1886 inventory. The only furnishings mentioned are a carpet and a chair. Since there was no skylight in the nineteenth century, this area was relatively dark. The 1934 HABS floor plan identifies this as the "Stair Hall" but provides no clues concerning either uses or furnishing.

H. Maxson Holloway, the first RCHS director, resided in the apartment created from these rooms beginning in circa 1957. He may have used this large central area as a living and dining room; the kitchen was in adjoining Room 310. The next director, Archie Stobie, resided here with his family for a few years beginning in 1967.

Currently, the space is amply filled with furniture and other collections items.

FINISHES INVESTIGATION

The plastered wall surface was originally painted; the wallpaper now in place was installed for H. Maxson Holloway sometime after 1957. When the elevator was extended to the third floor in 1969, the newly created wall surfaces were covered in matching wallpaper.

302   Sitting Room – Office

This room and the adjoining bathroom (303) and former bedroom (304) were created as part of the third floor remodeling carried out for Albert and Caroline Cluett after 1910. In plan, the room (14'4" × 16') includes a doorway in the east wall, two doorways in the north wall, and window openings in the south and west walls. A shallow chimney breast projects from the east end of the south wall. The two west windows look out over the roof of the rear addition.

Prior to the Cluett remodeling, this area and the two adjoining spaces (303 and 304) as well as the related closet areas, all formed a single long "attic" area located beneath the original west slope of the gable roof. The only window opening was the quarter-round opening formerly in the south gable wall. It matched the still extant window in Room 309. Physical evidence (visible in the attic structure above this room) indicates that the original attic space was fully finished in plaster. Access to the space was through a door positioned somewhere in the east wall. The attic was used for storage and is included in the 1886 inventory.

The extensive renovation of the third floor carried out after 1910 included the raising of the sloped roof along the back of the original house to create full-height rooms where formerly there was attic space. The original roof rafters that formed the sloping ceiling over the area were retained in place and simply raised up to a nearly horizontal position and a third story brick wall, complete with full sized windows, was built above the back wall of the house. This newly created room (302) was finished to match the detailing of the original second floor bedrooms.

The 1934 HABS floor plan indicates that this was a "Sitting Room," possibly related to the northwest bedroom (304) through a bathroom (303) separating the two spaces. Cluett family tradition indicates that the four Cluett boys used this as a bedroom. The function of this room during the era of H. Maxson Holloway and Archie Stobie is unknown. More recently, this was the curator's office and currently is used by the registrar.

FLOOR

The floor is made of narrow 2¼" wide strips of tongue-and-groove oak, laid north/south, possibly over original wide board flooring.

WALLS

The walls are finished in plaster applied to rock lath. The southeast chimney projection is finished in plaster on brick masonry with a small area to the west finished in plaster on rock lath.

CEILING

The 9'5" ceiling is finished in plaster on rock lath supported on framing contemporary with the post-1910 renovation.

BASEBOARD

The 11¾" high baseboard duplicates the baseboard type used in the original first and second floor rooms. A quarter-round shoe molding exists along the west wall.

CORNICE

A simple plaster cove, flanked by narrow moldings, extends around the room and dates to the post-1910 renovation.

DOORS

There are three door openings: the door (D3021) to the main hall, a closet door (D3022), and the bathroom door (D3031). The first two doors open into this room. The typical corner block architraves include raffle flowers of cast plaster.

D3021 and D3022: These six-panel, stile-and-rail doors are similar to the second floor bedroom doors. The closet door is slightly narrower than the other two doors.

Hardware: Original post-1910 fittings include three 4½" high brass-plated iron butt hinges with ball finials, brass-faced mortise locks marked with the numerals 9 and 20, brass knobs and drop cover keyhole escutcheons. A recent steel slide bolt is mounted to the hall face of door D3021.

WINDOWS

There are three window openings: two in the west wall and one in the south wall. The trim includes the raffle flower corner blocks. Each opening is fitted with six-over-six double-hung sash set above a 5½" deep molded wood sill. The glass panes are 11" × 16." Contemporary hardware includes brass sash fasteners and rectangular brass hand grips set in the bottom rails. The south opening is in the location of the original quarter-round window opening that was the only opening in the original attic located here. The 1934 HABS drawing shows a built-in seat beneath the south window, like the seat in Room 309, but there is no physical evidence that this feature existed here.

HEATING

A cast-iron steam radiator is located below the sill of the northwest window.

LIGHTING

The ceiling-mounted fluorescent fixture is operated by a pull cord and was installed by RCHS.

CLOSET

This closet was created as part of the renovation work carried out for Albert and Caroline Cluett. The finishes generally duplicate those used in the room. The baseboard is plain with an ogee crown molding. A garment hook rail is attached to the north, east, and west walls and includes a total of six brass-finished iron hooks. There is one original shelf and two later shelves installed above it.

FURNISHINGS AND FITTINGS

This area and the adjoining spaces (303 and 304) may be the "attic" included in the 1886 inventory. The items stored there included a feather bed and mattress, an iron bedstead, a bed, scrolls, frame, and chair. There were probably other items of such insignificant value that they were not listed.

It is not known how the current room, called a "Sitting Room" in 1934, was furnished by the Cluetts or how it functioned for H. Maxson Holloway and Archie Stobie. Currently, the space is filled with furniture and various collections items. An air conditioner is installed in the south window.

303   Bathroom – Collections Storage

In plan, this small bathroom is positioned between the two large west third floor rooms 302 and 304. The 6'11" × 9' space includes single doorways in the north and south walls and a window in the west wall. The room was created at the time the roof was raised and the back wall was extended sometime after 1910. It was used by the four Cluett boys who occupied the two adjoining rooms. This bathroom is remarkably intact with the exception of the toilet which replaced the original fixture sometime after 1962. The room is now used for storage and as the connecting passage to the northwest collections storeroom.

FLOOR

Recent indoor-outdoor carpet is laid over the same narrow hardwood flooring seen in the adjacent rooms. Probing may reveal evidence for Cluett-era linoleum under the carpet.

WALLS

The walls are finished in plaster on rock lath. A 53½" high dado covers the lower wall surface. This surface is composed of a stamped plywood-like material that simulates 3" × 6" horizontal tiles and is topped by a molded wood rail. An original wood enclosed pipe chase is located in the southwest corner.

CEILING

The ceiling is in plaster on rock lath.

BASEBOARD

The bottom of the simulated tile dado is finished in a plain 6" high splash board.

CORNICE

There is no molding at the top of the wall.

DOORS

There are two door openings: in the south wall (D3031) and the north wall (D3032). They feature the typical trim with raffle flower corner blocks.

> D3031 and D3032: Each opening has a six-panel, stile-and-rail door.

> Hardware: All of the original hardware has a polished nickel-plated finish. The mortise lock of D3032 is stamped with the numeral 4.

WINDOWS

The opening in the north wall features a six-over-six double-hung sash and the corner block trim rests on a simple bull nose sill. The sash retains the original fastener and hand grips.

HEATING

An original small cast-iron steam radiator is positioned below the window.

LIGHTING

The original pipe-suspended incandescent ceiling fixture is positioned above the lavatory. It retains the original ribbed opal glass shade. This fixture is operated by a pull chain.

PLUMBING

Original fixtures include the white enameled iron lavatory and a bathtub set on a ring base. Each fixture retains the nickel-plated brass fittings. The ceramic tank-type toilet is marked "C-Briggs 1-7 6-62" and replaced the original fixture. The pipe chase in the southwest corner houses the cast-iron roof drain pipe.

FURNISHINGS AND FITTINGS

Original Cluett bathroom fittings include a built-in wooden medicine cabinet fitted with a beveled glass mirror, five wall-mounted nickel-plated brass towel bars, and a toothbrush/glass holder. The bathtub retains the original nickel-plated brass shower curtain support rings and a soap dish attached to the east wall.

FINISHES INVESTIGATION

The yellow paint decor, applied to the walls and trim, included narrow wallpaper borders that outlined the door and window trim. This scheme was probably created when H. Maxson Holloway occupied the apartment.

304 Bedroom – Collections Storage

The former northwest bedroom is one of the full-sized rooms created when the rear roof slope was raised after 1910. The 13'11" × 4'4" room includes a single doorway in the east wall, two doorways in the south wall, and two window openings in the west wall. A shallow chimney breast projects from the east end of the north wall.

This room, along with the bathroom and Room 302, was originally a finished attic space located under the west slope of the former gable roof. All of the current visible finishes and details date to the extensive reconstruction of this part of the third floor carried out after 1910. The 1934 HABS floor plan indicates that this was a bedroom. According to family tradition, this room was a sitting room and gym space for the four Cluett boys. The use of the room immediately after 1953 is unknown, including the period when H. Maxson Holloway occupied the third floor apartment. The extensive built-in plywood collections storage bins were installed here during the directorship of Archie Stobie. The room serves as a storage area for small collections items.

FLOOR

Narrow 2¼" wide strips of tongue-and-groove oak are laid north/south, possibly over original wide board flooring.

WALLS

The walls are finished in plaster applied to rock lath. The northeast projection is finished in plaster on masonry.

CEILING

The 9'5" high ceiling is finished in plaster on rock lath.

BASEBOARD

The post-1910 11¾" baseboard duplicates the baseboard type used in the original first and second floor rooms.

CORNICE

A simple plaster cove, flanked by narrow moldings, extends around the room.

DOORS

There are three door openings: the door (D3041) to the hall, a closet door (D3042), and the bathroom door (D3032). The typical corner block architraves include raffle flowers of cast plaster.

> D3041 and D3042: Six-panel, stile-and-rail doors, the closet door is narrower and the hall door includes a large Cluett-era dressing mirror attached to the inside face.

> Hardware: Original fittings include 4½" high brass-plated iron butt hinges with ball finials, brass-faced mortise locks, and drop cover keyhole escutcheons.

WINDOWS

There are two window openings in the west wall constructed after 1910. Each opening is fitted with six-over-six double-hung sash with 11" × 16" glass panes. The trim includes the raffle flower corner blocks.

HEATING

A cast-iron steam radiator is located below the southwest window.

LIGHTING

The ceiling-mounted fluorescent fixture is operated by a pull cord and was installed by RCHS.

CLOSET

This closet was created as part of the renovation work carried out after 1910. The finishes generally duplicate those used in the room. The baseboard is plain with an ogee crown molding. A narrow raised platform at the rear of the closet (south) is finished in floorboards laid east/west.

FURNISHINGS AND FITTINGS

In the nineteenth century, the area of this room was included in the "attic." After the renovation carried out for Albert and Caroline Cluett, this room was used by the four boys as a sitting room and gym. The plywood shelving units which now fill the room were installed in the late 1960s when Archie Stobie was director and small collection items such as china, glassware, and metalwork are now stored here.

305 Closet

This large walk-in closet (4' × 7'8") is located at the north end of the narrow passage that extends from the central hall (301). It is one of the new spaces created after 1910, when the third floor was remodeled for Albert and Caroline Cluett. Small collection items are kept here.

Generally, the finishes duplicate those found in the hall and surrounding rooms. The baseboard is the basic type used in the other closets.

306 Storage Room – Textile Storage

The north end of the central portion of the third floor is occupied by this large storage room. In plan, the 9'11" × 11'8" space includes a single doorway in the west wall and a built-in closet which fills the south end of the room. The attic stairway, which ascends from hall 307 to the space beneath the roof, protrudes into the northeast corner of this room. The configuration and finishes found here seem to date to the reconstruction of the third floor carried out after 1910, although further probing into the finishes might reveal material from the George Cluett era or even earlier.

The 1934 floor plan refers to this as a "storage room altered" indicating that it was one of the third floor areas modified after 1910. The finishes in this room are of a slightly lesser quality than in the other third floor rooms. The ceiling plaster has a slightly rough surface and the attic stair structure is exposed in the northeast corner. The Cluetts used the room for the storage of household linens and clothing, and the space now houses textiles from the RCHS collection.

FLOOR

Narrow 2½" wide tongue-and-groove strips are laid north/south. These boards are different from those used in the adjoining rooms.

WALLS

The north and west walls are covered in 3½" wide strips of vertical beaded-board. The east wall features vertical beaded-board consisting of paired boards 3¼" wide. The north and west condition may predate the east surface. The south wall consists entirely of built-in cedar-lined closets dating to after circa 1910.

CEILING

The plaster ceiling surface has a slightly irregular finish. Along the west wall, the plaster surface abuts the wood board wall surface. Along the east wall, the plaster ceiling appears to extend over the top of the wall surface.

BASEBOARD

The plain low base found in the third floor closets is also used here.

CORNICE

There is no molding at the meeting of the walls and ceiling.

DOORS

The hall door opening (D3061) includes a six-panel, stile-and-rail door like the other third floor doors.

> Hardware: Original fittings include brass-finished butt hinges with ball finials, brass-faced mortise lock, and drop cover keyhole escutcheons.

WINDOWS

There are no window openings and there is no evidence that an opening ever existed in the north gable wall which was exposed on the outside prior to the construction of the house at 57 Second Street in 1838.

HEATING

This room was never heated.

LIGHTING

There is a single exposed incandescent bulb in the center of the ceiling.

STAIRWAY

The exposed undercarriage of the attic stairway that ascends from Room 307 is located in the northeast corner of the room, partially masked by a thin beaded-board partition. Eight risers extend into this room.

CLOSET

A pair of built-in closets entirely fill the south end of this storage room. The 2' deep closets are positioned side-by-side and separated by a board partition. The entire closet interior is lined in cedar boards. The two openings feature pairs of six-panel doors supported on pairs of butt hinges with ball finials. Each pair of doors can be secured by two bronze lever latches. There are adjustable cedar shelves in the interior.

FURNISHINGS AND FITTINGS

The exact arrangement and appearance of this room during the Cluett era is unknown. The pair of south closets were in place, but the wood shelving along the north wall appears to date to sometime after 1953. The large multi-drawer wood bureau set against the west wall is of twentieth century origin and was probably placed here by RCHS.

307   Attic Stair Hall

The steep narrow stair that ascends to the low attic space above the third floor is located in this small (4'2" × 7') vestibule-like room. Although this room appears to date to the post-1910 remodeling, the stair may survive from the Hart period. Certainly, the original stair was in this same location. The separation of this room from the attic above is provided by a hatch-like door that lowers to cover the stair opening in the attic floor. The 1934 HABS floor plan refers to this space as a closet. A minimum of collections items are currently kept here, including the two doors removed from the built-in closet in the second floor dressing room (205).

FLOOR

Narrow 2¼" wide strips of tongue-and-groove oak are laid north/south. A raised platform, finished in floorboards, is positioned next to the west wall.

WALLS

The walls are finished in plaster. The north surface is furred out from the masonry (brick) wall.

CEILING

The ceiling is finished in plaster, possibly on rock lath.

BASEBOARD

The simple low baseboard duplicates the finish found in the closets and in storage room 306.

CORNICE

There is no cornice.

DOORS

The single opening (D3014) in the south wall has a six-panel door. There was never a door in the opening into which the stairway ascends.

WINDOWS

There are no window openings in this space.

HEATING

This space was never heated.

LIGHTING

There is an exposed incandescent bulb ceiling-mounted fixture with pull cord.

STAIRWAY

The partially enclosed stair ascends through an opening in the west wall (Fig. 196). Five risers are visible in the hall; the remaining treads and risers are flanked by the two wall surfaces. The south wall is composed of vertical beaded boards, the same surface visible in Room 306. The north wall is finished in plaster. A board-and-batten hatchway door can be lowered to close the opening in the attic floor.

FURNISHINGS AND FITTINGS

The east and west wall surfaces include a wood rail that holds brass-finished garment hooks. A wood shelf, supported by an iron bracket, rests on the top of the west rail.

196 Original staircase ascending to the attic (307).

308   Bedroom – Collections Storage

This room and the southeast room (309) are original third floor spaces dating to the 1827 completion of the house. In plan, this 12'2" × 16'3" room includes a doorway in the west wall, a closet door in the south wall, and a single dormer window in the slope of the ceiling along the east side of the space. A partition, rather than closets, originally separated the two front rooms (308, 309). No mention of these rooms is found in the 1844 inventory, but these may be the spaces designated "Katie's Room" and "Alice's Room" in the 1886 inventory. Each of these servants' rooms included a window, the dormer windows extant today.

In its original condition, the room featured basic finishes including plastered walls and simple trim such as baseboards with a beaded top edge. The entrance into the room was probably in the same location as the current doorway.

After 1910, this room and its twin to the south were extensively modified including the insertion of a pair of closets between the two spaces. Elaborate trim that copied the conditions found in the first and second floor rooms replaced the original plain finishes.

The newly-finished room functioned as a bedroom and is noted as such on the 1934 floor plan. This room was included in the apartment occupied by director H. Maxson Holloway and later by Archie Stobie and his family. Since the 1970s, the room has functioned as a storeroom for furniture in the RCHS collections.

FLOOR

Narrow 2¼" strips of tongue-and-groove oak are laid north/south, possibly over original wide board flooring.

WALLS

The walls are finished in plaster applied to rock lath and the chimney breast is plaster on masonry. The east side of the room consists of a low knee wall of plaster on rock lath attached to original 1827 wood framing.

CEILING

The flat ceiling and the sloped surface beneath the roof are finished in plaster on rock lath.

BASEBOARD

The 11¾" high baseboard duplicates the base type used in the original first and second floor rooms.

CORNICE

The flat portion of the ceiling includes a simple plaster cove with a wood molding along the bottom edge.

DOORS

There are two door openings: the door (D3081) to the hall and the closet door (D3082). The typical corner block architraves include cast-plaster raffle flowers. A section of trim at the bottom of the south side of the architrave of doorway D3081 was cut out and replaced by a plain section of wood.

> D3081, D3082: Six-panel, stile-and-rail doors based on the original first and second floor doors.

> Hardware: Original post-1910 fittings on each door include three brass-finished iron butt hinges with ball finials, brass-faced mortise locks, and brass drop cover keyhole escutcheons.

WINDOWS

The east roof slope incorporates the narrow opening of the original 1827 dormer window. The recess is finished in plaster; the ceiling plane slopes slightly upward toward the east. The opening is fitted with the original arched-top double-hung sash. The semicircular-topped upper sash includes curved muntins forming pointed-arch tracery above three rectangular glass panes. The lower sash includes six (three-over-three) panes of glass. The brass recessed hand grips and fastener date to the post-1910 renovation. The sash is positioned above a deep wood sill above a molded wood apron.

HEATING

Probing of the north wall chimney breast may reveal the location for a stove pipe thimble, but no documents indicate that stoves were used on the third floor in the nineteenth century. A single low cast-iron steam radiator is positioned below the window. It was installed as part of the post-1910 renovation.

LIGHTING

A single stamped/turned brass electric wall sconce is positioned on the west wall near the doorway.

CLOSET

This post-1910 space includes the same finishes found in the room including the narrow board flooring and plaster wall and ceiling surfaces.

FURNISHINGS AND FITTINGS

No mention of this room is found in the 1844 inventory, but two servants rooms are noted in the 1886 document. This may be one of those spaces, which include a bed, bureau, washstand, chairs, a table, and a window shade. One of the rooms also had a curtain at the window.

The 1934 HABS floor plan includes this space as a bedroom, but how the Cluetts furnished the room is unknown. This may have served as a guest room when H. Maxson Holloway occupied the third floor apartment.

In the early 1970s, a deep plywood shelf was installed against the north and east walls to increase the area where collection items could be stored.

FINISHES INVESTIGATION

Wallpaper dating to the decoration of the room by H. Maxson Holloway remains on the west and north (chimney breast) walls.

309 Bedroom – Collections Storage

This is one of the two original third floor rooms (308, 309) that existed on the east side of the central hall. In plan, this 12'2" × 17'8" room includes a doorway in the west wall, a closet door in the north wall, and a single dormer window in the slope of the ceiling along the east side of the space. An original quarter-round window opening is a feature of the south wall, next to the projecting chimney breast.

Originally, there was no closet and only a partition separated the two front rooms (308, 309) and the trim finishes were very simple. The entrance into the room was probably in the same location as the current doorway.

This may be "Katie's Room" referred to in the 1886 inventory. In the room there was a shade and a curtain. The shade may have been placed at the dormer window while the curtain covered the quarter-round opening.

Modifications to the room after 1910 included the creation of the closet space and the installation of the elaborate corner block trim and related baseboard. The newly-finished room functioned as a bedroom, probably occupied by one of the Cluett children.

Later, the room was included in the apartment occupied by H. Maxson Holloway followed by Archie Stobie and his family.

Since the early 1970s, the room has functioned as a storeroom for furniture collections.

FLOOR

Narrow 2¼" wide strips of tongue-and-groove oak are laid north/south, possibly over original wide board flooring

WALLS

The walls are finished in plaster applied to rock lath with plaster on masonry at the chimney breast. The east side of the room consists of a low knee wall. In the mid-1980s, a small opening was cut in the knee wall revealing the "space" between that surface and the backside of the front wall of the house. Generally, the structural masonry outer wall at this level consists of thirteen brick courses which support a wood plate upon which rest the roof rafters. At a location beneath the dormer window, the masonry wall includes a large rough finished block of the white marble that forms the finished face of the front façade.

CEILING

The flat ceiling and the sloped surface are finished in plaster on rock lath.

BASEBOARD

The 11¾" high baseboard duplicates the base type used in the original first and second floor rooms.

CORNICE

The flat portion of the ceiling includes a simple plaster cove with a wood molding along the bottom edge.

DOORS

There are two door openings: the door (D3091) to the hall and the closet door (D3092). The typical corner block architraves include cast-plaster raffle flowers.

> D3091, D3092: Six-panel, stile-and-rail doors based on the original first and second floor doors. The closet door is shorter so that it fits the opening beneath the slope of the ceiling.

> Hardware: Original post-1910 fittings include brass-finished iron butt hinges with ball finials, brass-faced mortise locks, and drop cover keyhole escutcheons.

WINDOWS

The east roof slope incorporates the narrow openings of the original 1827 dormer window. The recess is finished in plaster. The opening is fitted with the original 1827 arched-top double-hung sash. This sash matches the sash in the other front room (308) dormer. The sash are positioned above a deep wood sill above a molded wood apron. The recessed brass hand grips and fastener date to the post-1910 renovation. The original quarter-round opening in the south wall is filled with a single wood casement sash which opens inward and is hinged to the west jamb. The glazing is arranged into five segments by wood muntins and additionally divided by two concentric circle segments. The trim is formed from the same molded wood trim used at the door opening, but the applied reeded insert was not installed. A low wood seat is built in beneath this window.

HEATING

Probing of the south wall chimney breast may reveal the location for a stove pipe thimble, but no documents indicate that a stove was used here. A single low cast-iron steam radiator is positioned below the dormer window.

LIGHTING

A stamped/turned brass electric wall sconce with an etched glass tulip-form shade is positioned in the west wall near the doorway.

CLOSET

This post-1910 space includes the same finishes found in the room, including the narrow board flooring and plaster wall and ceiling surfaces.

FURNISHINGS AND FITTINGS

This may be "Katie's Room" listed in the 1886 inventory. Furnishings included a bed, bureau, washstand, two tables, two chairs, a mirror, and a carpet. A shade and a curtain are also listed. How the Cluetts furnished this bedroom is unknown. This may have served as a guest room when H. Maxson Holloway occupied the third floor apartment. Beginning in the early 1970s furniture from the RCHS collection was stored here.

FINISHES INVESTIGATION

The wallpaper was installed by H. Maxson Holloway when he occupied the third floor apartment.

310   Bathroom – Kitchenette

Though small in size, this room has undergone a considerable amount of renovation since 1910. In plan, the room (7' × 9'3") includes a single doorway in the west wall, a wide opening in the north wall, and a single small window opening in the south wall. A projection (the elevator shaft) fills the northwest corner of the small room.

The appearance and arrangement of this room in the nineteenth century is unknown. It has not been determined if, in fact, this was a space separate from the central hall (301).

If this was originally a separate area, its plan was

simple. The rectangular closet-like room had a doorway in the north wall and a doorway in the west wall. The west door opened to the "space" between the south gable window and the interior oval window that overlooks the stairwell. There originally was no window in the south wall of this room; a condition clearly indicated in the 1892 photograph of the exterior of the house which so well illustrates the south elevation (see Fig. 121). There is no mention of this space in either of the Hart inventories or other family documents.

As part of the extensive renovation of the third floor for Albert and Caroline Cluett, this space was converted into a full bathroom, complete with toilet, lavatory, and bathtub. The positioning of these fixtures is recorded on the 1934 HABS floor plan. The window was inserted in the south wall as part of this work. In appearance, this bathroom was much like the still intact bathroom (303) located between the two west bedrooms.

This room was remodeled to function as a small kitchen when H. Maxson Holloway occupied the third floor.

In 1969, the space was modified when the 1938 elevator was extended to the third floor. The projection in the northwest corner was created to accommodate the new shaft. The doorway in the north wall was removed and the opening was enlarged to fill the remaining space. The actual door and trim were moved to their new location as the access to the elevator (D3015).

The room continued to serve as a kitchen when the apartment was occupied by Archie Stobie and his family. Since the removal of the apartment function from the third floor, this space has served as a work room and an informal collections storage area. The kitchen sink and stove were removed during the mid-1980s.

FLOOR

The floor surface is covered in circa 1960–1969 linoleum in a marble chip pattern. The plywood surface in the southeast corner represents the location of the kitchen sink.

WALLS

The walls are finished in plaster on rock lath above a 53½" high dado of a plywood material that simulates ceramic tile. A 2⅞" high molded wood cap finishes the top of the "tile" dado. The south face of the northwest corner projection retains evidence for the evolution of that surface which appears to be constructed of gypsum board. The plywood tile material is not found on the east face of the later projection.

CEILING

The ceiling is plaster on rock lath. The surface along the south wall slopes down above the window. The reason for this unusual configuration has not been determined.

BASEBOARD

The plain 5½" high base is part of the plywood tile dado installation. The section along the east face of the elevator enclosure is a later installation.

CORNICE

There is no cornice molding.

DOORS

There are two door openings: the wide opening (D3101) to the central hall and the door (D3102) to the closet area. Both openings include the typical trim with corner blocks. The wide north opening was modified in circa 1969 from the condition recorded by the 1934 HABS floor plan. The conventional door opening was widened to fill the entire remaining wall space. The trim was removed and reinstalled in a different manner. There are no corner blocks on the south face of the opening.

> D3101: The opening is fitted with a circa 1969 accordion folding door. The earlier north door (D3015) is now located in the opening to the elevator.

> D3102: Six-panel, stile-and-rail door dating to the post-1910 renovation.

> Hardware: The original mortise lock, knobs, and keyhole escutcheons are finished in polished nickel on the room side and plain brass on the closet side. This reflects the original bathroom function of this room.

WINDOWS

The small post-1910 window opening in the south wall is fitted with six-over-six double-hung sash. The glass panes are 9½" × 10" in size. The typical corner block trim rests on a plain sill with no apron. The hand grips and fastener have a polished nickel finish.

HEATING

Prior to the installation of the small cast-iron steam radiator after 1910, this room was not heated.

PLUMBING

The Cluett-era bathroom fixtures and the later kitchen sink are removed. The former lavatory and bathtub probably matched the fixtures in place in bathroom 303. The kitchen sink cabinet was positioned in the southeast corner where the plywood floor surface is exposed.

CLOSET

This original unusually configured space is located behind the curved wall of the main stair well. This is the area between the exterior south gable window and the "interior" oval stairwell window. The interior wood sash is composed of a rectangular curved frame that sets into the opening in the curved wall. It is secured in place by modern wire nails. The oval opening in the sash is glazed within the radiating pattern of the wood muntins. Modern white cotton fabric is tacked to the back side of the sash so that this space cannot be seen from the stairwell. It is likely that the sash was removable so that the stairwell could be ventilated via the south gable window. The operable sash in the south opening matches the sash in the dormer windows. This outside opening and sash can be seen in the circa 1892 photograph of the exterior of the house (Fig. 121).

FURNISHINGS AND FITTINGS

The nineteenth century function of this area is unknown. The post-1910 bathroom conversion included the installation of the built-in medicine cabinet in the east wall. The wood-framed cabinet includes a door set with a beveled glass mirror and includes nickel finished hinges and knob latch. The original interior glass shelves are replaced by wood shelves. Also surviving from the Cluett bathroom is a nickel-finished brass towel bar marked "Silver & Co. N.Y." A circa 1960s enameled steel wall cabinet with sliding doors remains on the east wall where it was positioned above the now missing kitchen sink cabinet.

FINISHES INVESTIGATION

The simulated tile dado was originally painted white. The plaster walls retain evidence for painted finishes covered by two layers of wallpaper, a red, white, and blue pattern followed by a yellow, red, and green flower pattern on a yellow ground paper. These papers date to the use of the room as a kitchen.

311   Stair Hall

This small stair hall is situated at the head of the service stair that originally began in the first floor hall pantry of the "back building" constructed circa 1836.

In plan, the rectangular (5'8" × 12'10") room includes doorways in the south, east, and west walls, and an open stairwell positioned next to the north wall. The low ceiling is approximately 7' above the floor and slopes downward to the north, following the slope of the original circa 1836 roof. In its original form, prior to the extension of the wing in 1893, there was a window in the west wall. A doorway is now in that location. The detailing of the small doorway in the east wall indicates that the opening may date to renovations by the Cluetts in circa 1893 to create a bathroom in second floor Room 211 (Fig. 197). Prior to that work, there was a second doorway in the south wall that opened to Room 313.

An important feature of this hall is the roof access ladder and ceiling hatch in the northeast corner. Origi-

197 Looking east to the doorway opening to Room 312.

nally, the hatch opened directly onto the roof surface, but later, for the Harts and Cluetts, two additional roof structures and surfaces were constructed resulting in two more access hatches above this opening.

This hall has always functioned as a circulation area and currently is also used for the storage of collections.

FLOOR

The original surface is finished in wide (8½" to 10") tongue-and-groove boards, laid east/west and now painted. The floor surface of Room 312 forms a raised platform, 12" above the floor, at the east end of the hall.

WALLS

The south, east, and west walls are of plaster on wood lath; the north wall is plaster on brick masonry. The original masonry of the west wall was partially or completely removed when the wing was extended in circa 1893.

CEILING

The original plaster-on-wood-lath ceiling surface follows the slope of the roof. At the center point, it is approximately 7' above the floor. The original roof access opening is finished with an edge bead and a later wood frame. A recent fiberboard panel covers the opening.

BASEBOARD

The same tall baseboard used in the first and second floor rooms is found here on all four wall surfaces.

CORNICE

There is no cornice molding.

DOORS

There are three doorways: the original opening (D3141) to Room 314, the doorway (D3111) to the rear addition, and the small door (D3112) to Room 312. All three openings feature the typical Greek Revival trim, which is used throughout the rear addition. Close inspection reveals that the profile varies slightly at the later west opening. Prior to circa 1893, there was a doorway in the east end of the south wall that matched doorway D3141. The door from that removed opening is now located in closet opening D3171 in Room 317.

D3111: This circa 1893 four-panel door copies the detailing of the original circa 1836 doors.

Hardware: Original fittings include a pair of 3" high cast-iron butt hinges, brass-faced mortise lock, wood knob and rose on the east face, wood rose and brown mineral knob on the west face, and rectangular wood keyhole escutcheons. The Yale latch was installed by RCHS.

D3112: Small circa 1893 four-panel door.

Hardware: Original fittings include a pair of 3" high cast-iron butt hinges, small brass-faced mortise latch (no key function), and turned wood knobs (roses missing). A small cast-iron (Corbin) rim lock with key is mounted on the outside face of the door.

WINDOWS

There are no window openings here, but prior to 1893 there was probably a window opening in the west wall.

HEATING

This hall was never heated.

LIGHTING

There is no visible evidence for a gas fixture. A utilitarian porcelain ceiling fixture with an exposed incandescent bulb dates to the Albert Cluett era.

STAIRWAY

The original stairway ascends against the north wall. The open stairwell is enclosed on the south and east sides by a mahogany balustrade composed of round tapered balusters supporting a handrail which is oval in section.

OTHER FEATURES

A built-in shelf-like ladder is situated on the east wall next to the northeast corner and provides access to the roof hatch.

FURNISHINGS AND FITTINGS

It is unlikely that any furnishings were placed here by the Harts or Cluetts. Currently, this hall is used for the storage of collection items.

312   Small Store Room

This small room is positioned about 12" above the floor surface of the adjoining hall.

In plan, the (5'8" × 6'5") space includes small doorways in the south and west walls. The current conditions date to modifications made in circa 1893 when Rooms 211 and 313 were remodeled.

Originally, this was a large walk-in closet that was entered from Room 313 when that space was still a full-height space. The opening in the south wall originally extended fully down to the level of the floor and included a door hinged to the west jamb. There was no opening in the west wall.

Currently, this room is used for minimal catch-all type storage.

FLOOR

The original surface is finished in the same wide tongue-and-groove boards seen in the stair hall; this surface is 12" above the hall floor. The flooring is removed in the southeast corner where plumbing pipe is located.

WALLS

The north and east walls are finished in plaster on brick masonry. The east brick surface is the original rear wall of the 1827 house and it retains evidence of a white paint finish. The south and west walls are of plaster on sawn wood lath. The surface below the south opening (D3121) is circa 1893 infill.

CEILING

The original sloped plaster on wood lath surface is approximately 6' above the floor.

BASEBOARD

The plain base includes a crown molding of the same profile used for the door trim.

CORNICE

There is no cornice molding.

DOORS

There are two door openings: a modified original opening (D3121) in the south wall and a later opening (D3112) in the west wall. Both have the typical Greek Revival trim used throughout the rear addition.

> D3121: Originally, this opening extended to the floor and included a door hinged to the west jamb and opening into this room. The shortened west jamb retains the mortise for the bottom 4½" high hinge

of the missing door. The structure of the wall's surface below this opening is a later insertion, filling the former doorway.

> D3112: This opening was created in circa 1893.

WINDOWS

This space has never included a window opening.

HEATING

This room was never heated.

LIGHTING

There is no evidence for any lighting.

PLUMBING

The cast-iron soil line in the southeast corner services the bathroom plumbing in Room 303 and the roof drain of the rear section of the raised roof of the 1827 house.

FURNISHINGS AND FITTINGS

No mention is made of this original closet in the Hart-era inventories. Original fittings include a beaded edge wood garment hook rail on the north wall and evidence for missing shelving on the east wall. There are later wood rails on the south and west walls and evidence for a rail on the east wall. The shelving and rail on the east wall were removed when the cast-iron pipe was installed after 1910.

FINISHES INVESTIGATION

The brick masonry of the east wall retains the original white painted finish of the rear of the 1827 house.

313 Store Room

This curiously configured space is the result of modifications made after the house was purchased by George and Amanda Cluett in 1893.

In plan, the (6'5" × 14'10") space includes a single low doorway in the north wall and a full-sized window in the south wall.

In its original circa 1836 form, this was a room similar to adjoining Room 314 and had the same ceiling height and floor level as that space. The room was entered from a doorway formerly located in the west end of the north wall. The extant opening (D3121) in the north wall extended down to the original floor level of room 312 and provided access to that space which served as a closet.

The original room was probably intended as a bedroom for a household servant, but by 1886 was used for storage. This may be "Store Room #1" or "Store Room #2" included in the inventory of that date.

The current unusual configuration is the result of extensive work carried out after the house was purchased by George and Amanda Cluett in 1893.

The installation of the bathroom in the room (211) directly below this space necessitated an increase in the original low ceiling height (6') of that area. This resulted in the raising of the floor level in this room. This is most apparent at the window in the south wall where the sill is now below the level of the floor.

The plan relationships of the second and third floor rooms immediately below and west of this space resulted in the creation of an enclosed "left over" area when the floor level was raised. This "space" is visible from an opening in the floor next to the northwest corner (Fig. 198).

The original floor surface exists in this now enclosed area, which extends below the west end of the room. The surface is approximately 3' below the current floor. The "space" also preserves the bottom half of the original west plaster wall as well as the baseboard along that surface.

The modification of this room included the removal of the original access door located in the north wall and opening from the stair hall (311). The door was reused in the closet created as part of the construction of Room 317.

Changes made to this room resulted in a space that was only minimally suited for storage.

FLOOR

Flooring consists of unfinished tongue-and-groove boards laid east/west. This surface dates to the circa 1893 modifications. A section of the original wide board flooring exists in the space visible from the opening in the northwest corner.

WALLS

Each wall preserves a different condition. The south wall is finished in original plaster on brick masonry. The west partition is of plaster on lath applied to a thin plank surface. Plaster on sawn wood lath forms the east wall which replaced the original rear brick wall of the 1827 house. The brick wall surface was removed in circa

198 The opening in the floor surface, northwest corner, Room 313.

1836 down to the level of the first floor; the masonry wall still exists as basement level. The north plaster on sawn wood lath wall consists of some original circa 1836 material and material installed when the floor level was modified and the doors were changed.

CEILING

The plaster on wood lath ceiling follows the slope of the original roof and is approximately 3'11" above the floor.

BASEBOARD

When the floor level was raised, no new baseboard was installed on the wall surfaces.

CORNICE

No cornice has ever existed in this room.

DOORS

There is a single small opening (D3121) in the north wall. Originally, this doorway extended down to the level of the floor of the closet (312). The jamb and trim are original material modified when the floor level was raised. The current west jamb retains a mortise for a 4½" high hinge. The original door into this room from the hall was located immediately west of the opening in the north wall. The door formerly located here is now in the closet opening in Room 317.

WINDOW

The original window opening in the south wall includes trim that matches the trim in Room 314. The opening is fitted with six-over-six double-hung sash with glass 10" × 16" panes. The sill is now situated below the level of the floor.

HEATING

The room in its current form is unheated, but prior to the raising of the floor a steam radiator, like the one in Room 314, may have been used here.

LIGHTING

There is no artificial lighting currently in the room, but prior to the raising of the floor a gas light bracket was probably located on one of the walls.

PLUMBING

A steam pipe from Room 208 enters this room through the east wall. A recently installed roof drain pipe is positioned next to the east wall extending downward from the ceiling and into the cast-iron drain line in Room 312.

OTHER FEATURES

A steel I beam is located at the top of the east wall, extending from the brick south wall to the surviving section of the brick east wall located in the adjoining room (312). This steel beam was installed after 1910 when the rear roof of the original 1827 house was lifted up to increase the size of the original attic space. A third story brick wall was constructed across the back of the original house. In this location, the brick wall is set on top of this beam.

FURNISHINGS AND FITTINGS

Although the original full-height room was likely intended for a servant, by the late nineteenth century, it was used as a storage room. This may be either "Store Room #1" or "Store Room #2" included in the 1886 inventory. After the room was modified circa 1893, it was only possible to use it for storage. Today the room is essentially empty.

314   Bedroom – Store Room

This is the larger of the two original circa 1836 third floor rooms and this space retains its original configuration.

In plan, the 12'10" × 14'10" room includes a single doorway in the north wall, a pair of windows in the south wall, and a broad closet projection at the north end of the west wall. A single door opens to the closet. All of these features survive from the original completion of the room.

The shallow chimney breast on the west wall includes an opening for a stove pipe indicating that this room was originally heated and was therefore an occupied space, probably a servant's bedroom. This room includes two windows, while the original smaller room to the east had only a single window. This space is labeled "Sitting Room" on the 1934 HABS floor plan.

Currently, paintings and other collection items are stored here.

FLOOR

The original surface is finished in 8½" wide tongue-and-groove boards, laid east/west. This surface is partially covered in a wood floorboard patterned linoleum and 9" × 9" tile patterned linoleum. Both date to after 1910.

WALLS

The south and west walls are finished in plaster on brick masonry. The north wall is of plaster on wood lath applied to framing, while the east partition is of plaster and lath on a thin wood plank surface. The closet projection in the northwest corner is finished in plaster on wood lath.

CEILING

The original plaster on wood lath surface follows the slope of the roof structure; at the south end of the room the surface is 8'1" above the floor and slopes to 7'1" at the north end.

BASEBOARD

The original 7½" high base is crowned by the same molding used at the door and window architraves.

CORNICE

There is no cornice, but a narrow 1½" tall picture molding is applied to the wall surface at about 1' below the ceiling. This finish dates to the George and Amanda Cluett era.

DOOR

There are two original door openings: D3141 in the north wall and D3142 to the closet. These four-panel, stile-and-rail doors have recessed panels on the room side and flush panels on the back face. The 5" wide trim includes the typical Greek Revival molding profile used throughout the circa 1836 addition.

D3141: The paneled surface faces into the room.

Hardware: Original fittings include two cast-iron butt hinges and an iron rim lock (4" × 6") with brass knobs. The lock is marked "McKinney, Troy, Manuf." A surface-applied Yale lock was installed by RCHS.

D3142: The paneled surface faces into the room.

Hardware: Original fittings include the cast-iron butt hinges and the small iron plate latch with brass knobs, and a late nineteenth century cast-iron rim lock (Fig. 199).

WINDOWS

There are two original window openings in the south wall; both have the typical 5" wide Greek Revival trim positioned above a 5" deep sill composed of a convex molding sandwiched between two fascias. The six-over-six double-hung sash includes 10" × 16" glass panes.

HEATING

Evidence for a circular stove pipe opening in the upper face of the chimney breast indicates that this room was heated by a stove in the nineteenth century. Currently, heat is supplied by a cast-iron steam radiator positioned next to the north wall. This is probably one of the radiators supplied in 1880 by the Troy Steam Heating Company.

LIGHTING

A gas pipe for a gas light wall bracket is positioned on the east wall and dates to the Hart era. Lighting is now provided by a utilitarian exposed bulb fixture positioned on the ceiling.

CLOSET

An original shallow closet projects into the room in the northwest corner. Interior finishes include wide board

199 Original plate latch on the closet door.

flooring, laid east/west, and plastered walls and ceiling. The baseboard matches the finish in the room. Nineteenth century fittings include wood shelving at the north and south ends of the space and wood garment hook rails on the north, south, and west walls. The north and south rails are original features.

FURNISHINGS AND FITTINGS

The two large windows, the closet, and evidence for a heating stove indicate that this room was originally intended for a household servant and was furnished as such. The 1886 inventory seems to indicate that by that time this room was used for storage and would be either "Store Room #1" or "Store Room #2" included in that document. The items in storage, such as bedsteads, bureaus, and chairs may well be the furniture used by the servants.

315 Hall

Access to the two third floor servants' bedrooms, located in the circa 1893 rear addition, is provided by this hallway. In plan, the long rectangular space includes single doorways in the south, east, and west walls and a window in the north wall.

This space and the adjoining rooms were added to the circa 1836 addition soon after the George Cluetts purchased the house in 1893. The doorway in the east wall was inserted in the location of a window that provided natural light to hall 311 prior to the construction of this addition.

Currently, the hall provides access to two collections storage rooms.

FLOOR

This surface consists of 6" wide tongue-and-groove prime boards, laid east/west and now painted red. The floor surface is about 4¼" lower than the floor in the adjoining earlier hall (311).

WALLS

All wall surfaces are of plaster on wood lath. The north surface is furred out from the exterior brick wall.

CEILING

This surface is finished in plaster on wood lath.

BASEBOARD

The 8" tall wood base includes an integral cyma reversa crown molding.

CORNICE

There is no cornice molding.

DOORS

There are three door openings: D3111 in the east wall, D3161 in the south wall, and D3171 in the west wall. All feature the same Greek Revival trim that generally copies the original circa 1836 trim used in the earlier part of the rear addition. The doors swing open into the adjoining spaces.

> D3171: This opening retains evidence on the jambs for a secondary door that was hinged to swing from the north jamb into this hall.

WINDOW

The single opening in the north wall includes the typical Greek Revival trim and six-over-six double-hung sash that are secured by a decorative cast-iron fastener. The bottom sash is now fixed in an open position to accommodate a circa 1960s air conditioner.

HEATING

A cast-iron steam radiator is positioned against the south wall.

LIGHTING

A gas pipe protrudes from the south wall at 62½" above the floor. A gas light wall bracket was located here. Illumination is now provided by a chain-suspended incandescent fixture with a frosted cut glass tulip form shade.

FURNISHINGS AND FITTINGS

This circulation hall was probably never furnished.

316 Bedroom – Painting and Sculpture Storage

This small servant's bedroom is one of two third floor rooms created when the rear wing was enlarged circa 1893. In plan, the rectangular room includes a single doorway in the north wall and a window in the south wall. A small closet projects from the northwest corner. In the 1930s, the Cluetts' cook used this space for her private sitting room.

Currently, paintings and sculpture from the collections are stored here.

FLOOR

Flooring consists of 6" wide tongue-and-groove pine boards, laid east/west and now painted.

WALLS

The walls are finished in plaster on sawn wood lath, except for the shallow chimney breast which is of plaster on brick. An original narrow wood picture rail molding is positioned on all the walls at about 10" below the ceiling.

CEILING

The ceiling is finished in plaster on wood lath. There are plywood repairs to the ceiling in the southeast corner.

BASEBOARD

The 8" tall wood base includes an integral cyma reversa crown molding.

CORNICE

There is no cornice.

DOORS

There are two door openings: D3161 in the north wall and the closet door D3162. Both openings feature trim that duplicates the circa 1836 profile found in the earlier half of the addition.

D3161: This four-panel, stile-and-rail door has recessed panels on the hall face and flush panels on the room side.

Hardware: Original fittings include two small cast-iron butt hinges, a brass-faced mortise lock and wood knobs, roses and keyhole escutcheons.

D3162: This four-paneled door is similar to the previous door, but dates to circa 1836. This may be the door used in the opening between Rooms 311 and 312 prior to the modifications made there in circa 1893.

Hardware: The original circa 1836 fittings remain including the pair of 3½" high cast-iron butt hinges and evidence for a 3" × 4" plate latch.

WINDOWS

The single opening in the south wall includes the typical Greek Revival style trim and six-over-six double-hung sash. The original fastener is broken and brass hand grips were recently installed on the bottom sash.

HEATING

A post-1893 cast-iron steam radiator is positioned against the west wall near the southwest corner.

LIGHTING

A gas pipe with a decorative stamped brass collar is positioned in the east wall at 59" above the floor. This was the location for a gas light bracket. A utilitarian electric fixture, with an exposed incandescent bulb, is located on the ceiling.

PLUMBING

A wood-enclosed pipe chase is located in the southeast corner.

CLOSET

An original 2'4" deep closet projects from the northwest corner. The internal finishes match those of the room.

FURNISHINGS AND FITTINGS

There is no record of the furnishings placed here for the use of the household servants and the Cluetts' cook. The 1934 floor plan refers to this space as a bedroom, but by the late 1930s this was a sitting room.

RCHS uses this room for the storage of collection objects, primarily paintings which are kept on a built-in wood rack that covers the west wall surface south of the closet. The radiator is concealed by this storage unit.

317 Bedroom – Painting Storage

Created as part of the circa 1893 expansion of the rear addition, this room was intended for the use of a household servant.

In plan, the 10' × 20'10" room includes two doors in the projection of the east wall (one to the hall and one to the closet) and a single window opening in the south wall. A shallow chimney breast projects from the southeast corner. The room generally remains as completed in circa 1893.

In the 1930s, the Cluetts' cook used this space as her bedroom with the adjoining room (316) serving as a sitting room.

Currently, paintings and other framed objects are stored here.

FLOOR

Flooring consists of 6" wide tongue-and-groove pine boards, laid east/west and now painted.

WALLS

The walls are finished in plaster on wood lath except at the shallow chimney breast, which is of plaster on brick. An original narrow wood picture rail molding is positioned on all walls at the level of the top of the door trim.

CEILING

This surface is finished in plaster on wood lath.

BASEBOARD

The 8" tall wood base includes an integral cyma reversa crown molding.

CORNICE

There is no cornice.

DOORS

There are two door openings: D3171 opens to the hall and D3172 which opens to the closet. The trim duplicates the profile of the circa 1836 architraves in the original part of the addition.

D3171: The original circa 1893 four-panel, stile-and-rail door is removed from the opening and is now stored in the adjoining hall (315).

Hardware: Original circa 1893 fittings include two 3" high cast-iron butt hinges, a brass-faced mortise lock, and wood knobs and roses.

D3172: This original circa 1836 four-panel door was formerly the access door to Room 313 prior to the extensive changes made to that space. This door corresponds to door D3141, which remains in its original position.

Hardware: Original fittings include two 3½" high cast-iron butt hinges and there is an outline for the original 4" × 6" rim lock and an oval keyhole escutcheon. The circa 1836 plate latch now in place originated on door D3162, which was also formerly located in Room 313.

WINDOWS

The original south window opening is fitted with six-over-six double-hung sash secured by a decorative cast-iron fastener.

HEATING

There is no accessible heat source in this room.

LIGHTING

A gas pipe with a decorative stamped brass collar is positioned in the west wall at 59½" above the floor. This was the location for a gas light bracket. The current lighting consists of four fluorescent ceiling-mounted fixtures installed by RCHS.

CLOSET

An original 2'4" deep closet projects from the east wall. The internal finishes match those of the room. The paneled door was the original access door to Room 313.

FURNISHINGS AND FITTINGS

There is no record of the furnishings placed here for the use of household servants or by the Cluetts' cook in the late 1930s. The built-in wood rack that extends along the west wall was installed by RCHS for the storage of paintings and other framed collections.

BASEMENT

The basement extends fully beneath the first floor of the house and the three primary divisions reflect the evolution of the house as constructed and expanded by the Harts and Cluetts (Fig. 200).

The basement plan is composed of the 40' × 50' rectangular block of the original house completed in 1827, the rear 24' × 25' Hart addition of circa 1836, and the final 21' × 25' extension of the rear wing added by George and Amanda Cluett after their purchase of the house in 1893.

All of the basement rooms have survived with a remarkable amount of original architectural character intact, particularly the original kitchen.

As completed in 1827, the basement included four rooms, a T-shaped hall, a pantry, and two large closets. The two primary rooms, one of which is the large kitchen, are located north of the wide central hall which extends from the front to the rear of the house (Fig. 201).

Two smaller rooms are situated south of the hall and are separated by the extension of the hall that includes the stairway to the first floor.

Access to the original part of the basement was from three locations: the staircase; the doorway at the east end of the hall that opens to an areaway beneath the marble front stoop of the main façade; and a second doorway, located at the west end of the hall, that originally opened to a paved exterior area and the yard beyond.

Approximately half of the height of the basement is positioned below the grade that surrounds the house and the front and rear (east and west) windows opened to wide areaways that were an integral part of the exterior architecture of the house.

An additional significant feature of the original 1827 plan includes a sub-basement room, today referred to as the wine cellar. This unique space is located beneath the south extension of the hall and the southwest room (B05) and is accessible by a narrow enclosed stairway located beneath the stair to the first floor.

The finishes of the original basement rooms are of good quality, much simpler than those of the first and second floors, but consistent with William Howard's apparent desire to construct an outstanding house. Two rooms include fireplace mantels of carved stone rather than of wood, which more typically was used in basement rooms.

In circa 1836, a rear addition was constructed for Richard Hart (Fig. 202). At basement level this expan-

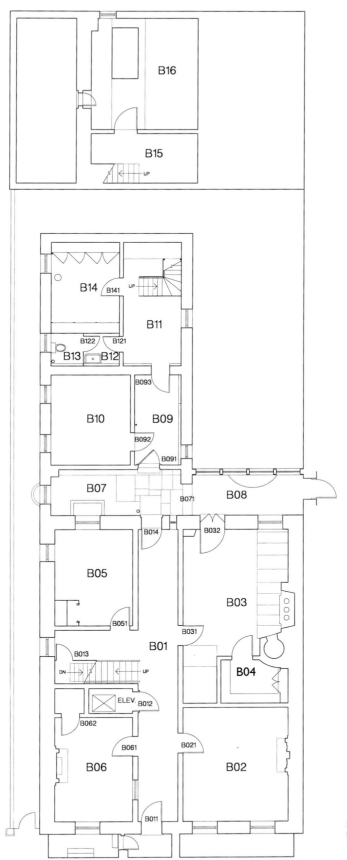

B16

B15

UP

B14   B141   UP

B11

B122   B121

B13   B12

B093

B10   B09

B092

B091

B07   B071   B08

B014   B032

B05   B03

B051   B031

B01   B04

B013

DN   UP

ELEV.   B012

B062

B061   B021

B06   B02

B011

200 59 Second Street,
basement plan, 2000.

BASEMENT FLOOR PLAN

0'   5'   10'   15'

sion was planned in a unique manner. The original paved outside areaway that extended across the rear of the house was incorporated into the expansion, resulting in a covered passage or "area" that extended under the dining room, but was open to the yards north and south of the new wing. Elizabeth Shields Eddy gives an excellent account of this part of the house in her reminiscence.

In her discussion of the garden, she writes "there was what always gave an air of mystery and romance to that yard—a broad, springing arched-way, running under part of the dining room, open at both ends and giving access by a flight of wide stone steps to what was known as the *area*, a wide, stone paved passage."

This passage remains intact, enclosed in the south end, forming Room B07 and now continuing into area B08 which was created in 1990. The circa 1836 addition also included an enclosed hall that featured a winding stair to the first floor and a large room that was used for the storage of coal.

The final enlargement of the basement is the extension of the rear wing added after the transfer of the

house to George and Amanda Cluett in 1893. Approximately the same size as the earlier addition, this area is divided into four spaces: a large room that includes a stairway to the first floor, and a small toilet room.

The original detailing in both the Hart and Cluett basement additions is of the most basic character. Until the house was occupied by RCHS, beginning in January 1953, all of the basement rooms remained very much in their original condition.

As early as November 1952, a "child's museum" was proposed for the basement and a year later the Junior League of Troy began planning to set one up. The new Junior Museum occupied basement rooms until December 1958.

In 1960, the Birchkill Arts and Craft Guild moved into the space vacated by the Junior Museum. Director H. Maxson Holloway initiated the restoration of the

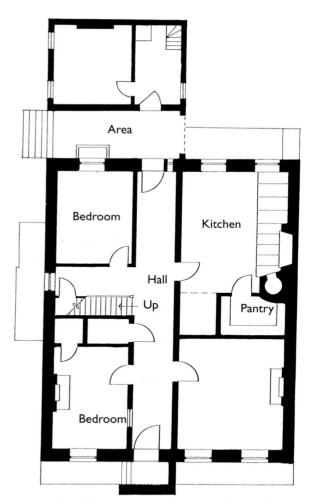

201 59 Second Street, basement plan, 1827, D. G. Bucher, 1999.

202 59 Second Street, basement plan, c. 1836, D.G. Bucher, 1999.

basement kitchen (B03) and cook's room (B05) in January 1965, and in 1966, the hall (B01) was converted into a Folk Crafts Hall.

Additional work occurred in the basement in 1969 with the creation of the laundry room in the passage (B07) followed by the installation of the RCHS library in the former coal room (B10).

In 1990, the basement plan was subtly modified and partially restored by the creation of the external passage (B08) that connects the Hart-Cluett house to the Carr Building. This new space is located in the areaway located along the back wall of the 1827 house, adjacent to the original kitchen.

More recently, the RCHS director's office was placed in the southeast room (B06).

B01   Hall

The original basement hall extends from the front to the rear of the 1827 house. Midway down the hall, there is a short extension to the south that includes the stairway to the first floor.

In plan, the T-shaped hall includes single doorways at each end of the main space as well as two doorways in the north wall. The south wall includes two doorways and the wide opening extension of the hall to the south (Fig. 203).

The short extension includes doors in the east and west walls and a small window in the south wall. The main feature of the extension is the staircase to the first floor and an enclosed stair that leads down to the wine cellar.

This hall remains remarkably intact; the only modifications result from twentieth century repairs or the insertion of plumbing, heating, or electrical systems which date to all the periods of occupancy.

This is a circulation space, one located at the center of below-stairs activity.

Both Hart inventories (1844 and 1886) refer to this as the "Basement Hall."

Albert and Caroline Cluett's grandchildren remember the hall as dark with low ceilings and pipes; the doors to the various rooms were kept closed.

With the transfer of the house to RCHS in January, 1953, much activity occurred in the rooms surrounding the hall.

This was part of the basement space occupied by the Junior Museum from 1954 to 1958.

203 Basement hall (B01), looking east, 1999.

In 1966, this space was converted into the Folk Crafts Hall.

Currently, the hall is used primarily for circulation with some display of collection items.

FLOOR

The floor surface is composed of various sections of flooring dating to different periods. In the main hall, original surfaces survive in the areas immediately east and west of the portion of the hall with the stairway. The 6" to 7" wide tongue-and-groove boards are laid east/west. Matching boards at the far west end of the hall are old replacements. H. Cozzens repaired floors in the basement in 1887 and 1890. The floor surfaces fronting the door to the kitchen and the surface in front of the east exterior door are recent replacements. The original flooring in the south extension of the hall features 8½" to 9" wide tongue-and-groove boards laid east/west. All of the flooring is painted.

WALLS

In the main hall, the north and south walls are of plaster on brick masonry while the east and west surface are of plaster on wood lath. In the south extension of the hall, the south and west walls are of plaster on wood lath and the east wall is of plaster on brick masonry. The surface below the stair is formed of wide bead-edged boards that enclose the stair to the sub-cellar. At the break in the south wall of the main hall for the opening to the stair hall extension, there are original wood corner beads. There are faint paint build-up outlines on the north and south walls for the locations of the nineteenth century ducts relating to the heating system.

CEILING

The original plaster on wood lath ceiling is about 8'2" above the floor.

BASEBOARD

The original 9¼" high wood base has an integral bead along the top edge. There are wood shoe moldings in various locations; the sloped molding dates to the nineteenth century, the quarter-round is more recent.

CORNICE

There is no cornice.

DOORS

The hall includes eight original door openings: D021, D031 in the north wall; D012, D061 in the south wall; D011 and D013 in the east and west walls; and D014, D051 in the south hall extension. Except for the doorway to the wine cellar (D014) and the west opening (D013), the 5" wide architraves have double fascia with a perimeter echinus molding and a bead around the opening. The trim of the west door is 3½" wide with a single fascia.

> D011: Original six-panel, stile-and-rail door with a four-light transom above the opening.

> Hardware: Original fittings include a pair of 4½" high cast-iron butt hinges and a 4¼" × 6½" iron rim lock and keeper. The Yale deadbolt may date to 1953, but the iron slide bolt is recent.

> D012: Original six-panel, stile-and-rail door, flush face on hall side. Plain wood boards added to the architrave so that door position could be moved outward when the elevator was installed in 1969.

Hardware: Circa 1969 fittings include a pair of butt hinges and a small reproduction iron rim lock.

> D013: This paneled and glazed door is not original to this opening. The upper section includes an opening filled with glass set in a pattern of wood muntins. When this door was installed, the opening was enlarged by removing the original transom which matched the conditions at the east doorway (D011). Stylistically, this door dates from the mid to late nineteenth century.

Hardware: Fittings include a pair of 4½" high cast-iron butt hinges and a 4¾" × 8" iron rim lock not original to the door. The Yale deadbolt is a recent installation.

> D014: This is the original vertical tongue-and-groove board door to the wine cellar.

Hardware: Original fittings include two small butt hinges and possibly the iron lift-latch. The iron rim lock and decorative keyhole escutcheon date to the mid-nineteenth century. There is evidence for a large, now missing, slide bolt.

WINDOWS

There are three original window openings. A narrow side light is positioned next to the west doorway (D013) in a deep wood-lined reveal. The opening is fitted with original two-over-two double-hung sash. Prior to circa 1836, this window opened directly to the exterior.

A small square opening is located high in the south wall of the stair hall. The trim is identical to the door trim. The three-over-three double-hung sash is set in a deep wood-lined reveal. In the nineteenth century, this window opened to the area beneath the former south porch.

A smaller interior window in the south wall opens to the southeast room (B06) and features the full double fascia trim.

HEATING

The 1844 inventory indicates that a stove was located here. The flue pipe passed through the north wall (between the two doorways) and into the kitchen where it entered the north wall chimney breast.

The installation of a Fox and Company Patent Air Furnace in the kitchen alcove in 1846 included the addition of hot-air ducts that connected to the floor registers in the first floor entrance hall (101–102), the dining room (106) and the library (109). This duct work was positioned against the ceiling of the basement hall.

The installation of the steam boiler in 1862 resulted in the placement of steam pipes next to the ceiling in this hall. The current arrangement of ducts and steam pipes is the result of modifications made during the Hart and Cluett eras. The fiberboard enclosure that conceals the ceiling mounted radiators next to the north wall, was installed by RCHS.

There is evidence at the west "sidelight" window and along the north wall for a cold air intake duct that extended from the window opening to the opening (now partially filled in) in the wall just east of the kitchen door (D031). The former opening connected to the boiler that was located in the kitchen alcove. In 1873, Gochoe & Tobin were paid for making lattice for the cold air box under the side (south) stoop. This may indicate that a similar outside air intake duct was located at the south window.

LIGHTING

During the Hart era and until circa 1910, gas lighting was the method of illumination in this somewhat dark hall, but no evidence for the fixtures (probably wall brackets) is evident. The current mixture of electrical fixtures, including the concealed lighting along the north wall, the four ceiling-mounted fluorescent fixtures and a spotlight, were installed by RCHS after 1953.

PLUMBING

Piping of various eras, including water, steam, and gas pipes are positioned next to the surface of the ceiling. A Hart-era cast-iron gas pipe is located above the transom of the east doorway (D011). In 1862, Daniel Southwick was paid for cleaning a gas pipe in the kitchen hall. The return pipe for the steam heating system is located beneath the floor and runs in an east/west direction.

EQUIPMENT

The current active gas meter is located at the east end of the hall in the northeast corner.

ELEVATOR

The 1938 Cluett elevator was modified in 1969 so that it could travel to the basement. It is housed in what was an original basement closet located just east of the stairway.

STAIRWAY

The original basement staircase is located against the east wall of the hall extension to the south (Fig. 204). The open stringer stair ascends in 13 risers to the first floor. The balustrade consists of a mahogany handrail (round in section) supported by a turned newel and balusters (two per tread). A much later (RCHS) handrail, mounted on decorative cast-iron brackets, is attached to the east wall. The very worn stair treads indicate that this was a very busy connection between the basement and first floor.

FURNISHINGS AND FITTINGS

The two Hart inventories (1844 and 1886) include this basement hall. A stove is located here in the earlier document. It was probably positioned near the north wall between the two doorways. The only items noted in the 1886 inventory are an oil cloth and a doormat.

An original 3" deep wood garment hook rail was located on the north and east walls between doors D011 and D021 at about 56½" above the floor.

A later wood rail was installed on the south wall immediately east of the door D061. It probably was added in the late nineteenth or early twentieth century and was removed after 1953.

204 Original staircase ascending to first floor (B01), 2000.

In 1966, this space was converted into the Folk Crafts Hall. About 1975, a wood mantel piece, incorporating a painting by the local nineteenth century artist Joseph Hidley, was installed against the north wall at the foot of the staircase. The original baseboard was cut and removed for this installation. In the mid-1980s, the mantel was removed and a new section of baseboard was inserted in the location.

FINISHES INVESTIGATION

All of the surfaces in the hall were investigated to determine the original and later finishes. The wood trim was originally finished in a very light cream/beige paint. A later layer of graining may date to the mid-nineteenth century. This finish was then covered by several re-paintings in yellowish white followed by a pink and a yellow color used during the Cluett eras. After 1953, a pale blue paint was applied followed by the more recent applications of white. All of the original paneled doors were first finished in the graining which survive on some basement doors.

The plaster walls were originally painted a pale cocoa brown. By 1855, the walls were covered in the same yellow "lemon" color used in the kitchen. Much more recently RCHS painted the walls white followed by the recent restoration of the yellow color.

Analysis of the ceiling surface revealed that the plaster was generally painted to match the walls. The earliest floor boards retain about eleven layers of painted finish, of which the earliest are a yellowish white, light tan, and a deep mustard gold. This last finish was covered in a dark brown followed by a deep red brown. Much more recently the floor has been painted grey.

B02   Basement Sitting Room – Toy Room

The second largest and best finished of the basement rooms is located at the front of the house directly beneath the front parlor.

The room includes a single doorway in the south wall and a pair of windows in the east wall. A very shallow chimney breast projects from the north wall and includes a simple, but elegant black marble mantel, the finest feature of this room. This room retains all of its original architectural character.

Front basement rooms in town houses, such as this space, are thought to have functioned as the informal dining room for the family in the early to mid-nineteenth century, although in this house, first floor room 106 (in its original form) may have served that purpose.

Regardless of the original intention, by 1844, this space may be the "Servants' Room under Hall" included in the Richard Hart inventory. This probably refers to a living or sitting room for the household servants.

The "Basement Sitting Room" included in the 1886 inventory is likely this space, again intended for the use of the servants rather than the family. The two pairs of curtains included in the inventory were placed at the two windows found here.

There is no indication for the use of this room when George and Amanda Cluett occupied the house, but oral tradition indicates that this was the playroom for Albert and Caroline Cluett's grandchildren. This was the only room the children had access to in the basement; the doors to all of the other spaces were kept closed.

In the earliest years of RCHS occupancy, beginning in 1953, this was probably one of the basement rooms used for art and ceramic classes.

In 1965, the library collection was installed here and in December 1968 the "Children's Room" was opened. This was intended to reflect the room's use by the Cluetts. Today, the space is referred to as the "Toy Room." A small brass plaque affixed to the hall face of the door is inscribed "Given in loving memory of Mark Britton Crawford by Mr. and Mrs. Harold B. Britton."

FLOOR

The original wide (8" to 10") tongue-and-groove boards are laid east/west and are now painted. The surface along the east wall is partially covered by three recent sheets of plywood, which are painted to match the floor boards.

WALLS

The south and west walls are finished in plaster on brick, while the north and east surfaces are of plaster on wood lath furred out from the masonry wall surfaces. The very shallow chimney breast projects about 1¼" from the north wall.

A 27" high dado composed of 3¾" wide vertical beaded boards covers the east wall to the height of the window sill. Probably not an original finish, it was added during the Hart occupancy.

CEILING

The original plaster on wood lath surface is about 8'2" above the floor.

BASEBOARD

The 9¼" high base has an integral bead along the top edge. The shoe molding is a recent addition.

CORNICE

A 6¼" wide run-in-place plaster cornice extends fully around the room. The profile of this feature dates it to after the original construction of the house, perhaps to about the mid-nineteenth century.

DOORS

There is an original door opening (D021) in the south wall. The original 5" wide trim has a double fascia with a perimeter echinus molding and a bead around the opening.

D021: The original six-panel, stile-and-rail door has recessed panels on the room face and flush panels facing the hall. The room face retains original graining.

Hardware: Original fittings include a pair of 4½" high cast-iron butt hinges, a 4⅛" × 7" iron rim lock with brass knobs and an oval brass keyhole escutcheon. These are marks for a post 1953 dead bolt, which is now removed and replaced by a recent slide bolt.

WINDOWS

Two original window openings are positioned in the east wall. Each opening has eight-over-eight double-hung sash set in a deep reveal that includes a pair of two-tier bifold paneled shutters. The deep wood sill has a bullnose front edge.

Hardware includes pairs of original brass bar latches for each pair of shutters and delicately detailed brass sash fasteners with acorn finials, which may be original. The sash are covered by recently installed interior plexi-glass storm sash.

HEATING

The room was originally heated by the fireplace with its original brass and iron coal grate. There is evidence in the face of the chimney breast for a stove pipe hole, indications that a stove was used here.

205 This wall radiator in Room B02 may date to 1862.

A Hart-era iron pipe steam radiator is mounted on two boards attached to the west wall. This is one of the earliest radiators remaining in use in the house and may be contemporary with the installation of the steam boiler in 1862 (Fig. 205).

LIGHTING

A Hart-era gas pipe enters the room above the north-east window and extends down to the north side of that opening where a gas light wall bracket was formerly located. Light is now provided by two ceiling-mounted fluorescent fixtures installed by RCHS.

FIREPLACE

The shallow chimney breast includes an original fire-place with a black marble mantel that includes fluted pilasters supporting a frieze with a central tablet and a projecting shelf. The firebox is concealed by an early, or possibly original, brass and iron coal grate set into a reduced soapstone-lined opening. This insertion rests on a narrow brick hearth.

FURNISHINGS AND FITTINGS

The finishes in this room including the marble mantel and the plaster cornice indicate that this may have been a well-furnished room. The 1844 inventory does not list the individual contents, but places a value of $5.00 on the furnishings.

There is a full description of the contents of the "Basement Sitting Room" in 1886, including a mahog-any sofa, two tables, a large rocker, and nine chairs. Other items included a mirror, two vases, and a clock, all of which may have been placed on or above the mantel. There were two pairs of curtains at the windows and a carpet on the floor.

A payment to H. Cozzens in 1884 for repairing a table and chair in the "Girls Sitting Room" probably refers to this space. In 1888, Louis Muller was paid for laying a carpet in the "Servants' Sitting Room."

According to oral tradition the Cluett toy room was furnished with cabinets that held the toys and a couple of stuffed chairs used when reading books. Since the opening of the "Children's Room" in December 1968, the room has displayed selections from the RCHS collection of toys, including a large early twentieth century dollhouse.

B03   Hart Kitchen

The original 1827 kitchen is the largest of the many rooms in the basement. In plan, the 15'11" × 20'8" room includes a small extension in the southeast corner. There is a single doorway in the south wall and a door to the pantry in the east wall. The west wall includes a single window and doorway, both of which opened to the exterior prior to the construction of the connector to the Carr Building in 1990. The primary feature of the kitchen is found on the north wall where the mass of the original cooking fireplace and oven form an impressive composition. This important room retains much of the ambience of the original kitchen, although some modifications were made by the Harts and Cluetts during the nineteenth century. Originally, there were two window openings in the west wall and access to the exterior of the house was through the door at the west end of the adjoining hall.

The southwest window was converted into a doorway when the back building was expanded for George and Amanda Cluett. The detailing of the modified opening and door reflects that era. Another significant modification occurred when the G. Fox & Company Patent Air Furnace was installed in the small space next to the pantry in 1846. How this space functioned prior to this undertaking remains unknown. It may have been part of the pantry or more likely a separate pantry entirely, although there is no clear evidence that a wall ever separated the space from the kitchen.

In 1827, the kitchen included such necessary features as a large deep fireplace used for cooking and an adjoining bake oven (Fig. 206). West of the fireplace, next

to the window there was a sink provided with water from a hand pump connected to the nearby exterior cistern. A pantry or pantries were located at the east end of the room. The room was well-finished with plaster walls and ceiling, and the floor was constructed of wood boards except for the area fronting the fireplace, oven, and sink which was of large slabs of stone. Two large windows in the west wall provided ample natural light and ventilation. The installation of the hot air furnace in 1846 certainly affected the kitchen's appearance and would have added considerable heat to an already amply heated room.

The two Hart inventories refer to this space as the kitchen and the 1886 document lists the many items kept here.

Hart family documents include numerous references to the kitchen spanning the years from 1848 to 1891. Of particular note is the evolution of cooking practices as documented by the purchase of several cooking ranges that were installed in the firebox. The first documented installation was for a "T Range" purchased in 1849 and, after two replacements, the final purchase in 1872 of a "Water Front French Range"; the Bramhall, Deane and Company range is still in place today. Possibly complementing the coal-fired ranges that were positioned in the fireplace was a gas stove in place here before 1873, when it was noted as being repaired. It was not unusual in the late nineteenth century to have both types of ranges, with their different cooking characteristics.

Also documented are various refrigerators beginning in 1851 and followed by replacements or additions in 1856 (a No. 4 P & B Refrigerator), 1865 and 1875 with the purchase of a No. 4 Palace Refrigerator. A plumber was necessary for the installation of this appliance. The placement of the refrigerator is unknown, although it is likely that it was well away from the heat of the stove and the furnace.

The sink is the additional necessity referenced in the documents. Extant at the earliest period, the first specific reference to the sink is 1873 when the faucets are repaired and the hot water line from the range was fixed. In 1881, the sink was relined in galvanized iron. The material of the sink is unknown.

Much earlier references to the water supply system include an 1843 pump bill and an 1849 invoice for repairing the cistern pump.

The brick cistern was discovered in 1990 when the

206 The basement kitchen (B03), 1976.

areaway west of the kitchen was further excavated for the construction of the connector to the Carr Building. It is likely that the kitchen sink was positioned on the stone floor surface adjacent to the west windows, a location very near the cistern.

Installation of the G. Fox & Company Patent Air Furnace in 1846 impacted the kitchen through its location in the east alcove area. The sheet metal exhaust duct from the furnace extended from the furnace across the ceiling to an opening in the chimney breast above the fireplace/range. The stone paving at the west end of the alcove was positioned in front of the furnace, which was located on the brick floor surface in the alcove (Fig. 207). Coal for the furnace and the cooking range was stored in Room B10 in the back building.

In 1862, Baker and Smith of New York City was paid for the installation of "steam apparatus" in this same location. Again, the new steam boiler was exhausted into the flue above the kitchen range. Both the original furnace and the later boiler would have added considerable heat to the kitchen in the winter months.

The remarkable preservation of this important room, including the range installed in 1872, is the result of the removal of the kitchen function from the base-

ment to the fine new first floor room (112) completed in circa 1893 for George and Amanda Cluett.

How the Cluetts used the former kitchen after 1893 is unknown; it probably became the laundry. The original washhouse was destroyed when the site was divided in 1893 and William Kemp built the house to the south. It is possible that the conversion of the west window into a doorway (D033) occurred at this time to provide access to the brick-paved drying yard where there is evidence for the placement of clotheslines. Albert and Caroline Cluett may have maintained the laundry here as well.

After 1953, this was one of the basement rooms used for painting and ceramic classes, and later by the Junior Museum followed by the Birchkill Arts and Crafts Guild.

In 1965, work was commenced to restore the kitchen to its Hart-era appearance and today the room continues to be one of the highlights of a tour of the house.

FLOOR

The floor surface consists of three areas: large slabs of brown sandstone are positioned side-by-side along the north wall and in front of the fireplace and oven. Smaller pieces of stone separate the large slabs from the

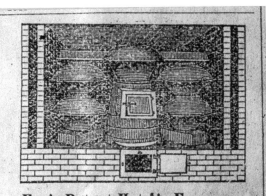

Fox's Patent Hot Air Furnace.

THIS FURNACE is a new article for heating Public Buildings, Factories, Dwelling Houses &c. The safety from fire, economy in fuel, and purity of air produced by it, combined with its durability, (being made of cast iron and brick), will on examination convince the most critical observer of its superiority over any other Furnace ever offered to the public. The subscribers having purchased of Jordan L. Mott, Esq., the right to use his patent in the construction of Furnaces with Rings, Rims, and Frames of Metal; and having adopted the use of Rings in the construction of the pot or fuel burner of the Furnace, consider it as one of the greatest improvements of the age, obviating the liability of cracking or burning out, as in Furnaces erected without Rings. This improvement alone is worth to the purchaser at least $15 per annum.

G. FOX & CO., New York.

The undersigned being Agent for the above Furnace, is prepared to furnish them at the manufacturers' prices. All persons wishing to warm buildings of any kind, are invited to call at Robinson, Corning & Akin's Stove Store, No. 311 River street, where I have one of the Furnaces ready for inspection; or, call on me at No. 88 Eighth street, where references and all necessary information will be given.

se15   H. T. CASWELL, Troy, N. Y.

207 1847 Troy newspaper advertisement for the Fox's Patent Hot Air Furnace.

wall. The three slabs at the west end are very worn and deteriorated, possibly due to the presence of water (sink) in this area. The majority of the current floor surface is finished in poured cement which was probably installed circa 1893 and replaced the wood flooring dating from the Hart era. That surface was similar to the condition in the adjoining pantry where the boards are laid on wood sleepers set directly on the ground.

The flooring in the southeast alcove consists of brick pavers (the location of the furnace and later boiler) and three brown sandstone slabs that extend out into the kitchen area. This stone surface served as the work area for stoking and cleaning the furnace and both the brick and stone date to the installation of the G. Fox & Company Patent Air Furnace in 1846 or the 1862 boiler.

WALLS

The south and east walls are finished in plaster on masonry as is the chimney breast and oven projection. The north wall and the upper portion of the west wall are of plaster on wood lath furred out from the masonry surfaces. The stepped-out lower surface of the west wall is plastered directly on the masonry.

CEILING

The plaster on wood lath ceiling is about 8'2" above the floor.

BASEBOARD

There is no baseboard except for a short 10½" tall section on the east wall. Additional base possibly was removed when the wood flooring was replaced by the cement surface.

CORNICE

There is no cornice, but an original continuous 5" deep board with bottom edge bead extends across the west wall immediately below the ceiling. This surface trims the top of the door and window openings. A similar board is located on the south wall.

DOORS

There are three door openings: D031 and D032 are original, while D033 is a later insertion. The two original openings have the same double fascia architrave used in the hall (B01). The opening (D033) in the west wall has the Greek Revival trim used in the back addition in circa 1836 and 1893, and the opening may date to the later period.

D031: Original six-panel, stile-and-rail door with the recessed panels facing into the kitchen and the flush panels facing into the hall.

Hardware: Original fittings include a pair of 4½" high cast-iron butt hinges (reset by RCHS) and a brass and iron Suffolk thumb latch. There is a ghost mark for a later small rim lock above the latch.

D032: The door and hardware match the conditions of door D031.

D033: This large door includes three vertical panels below an opening divided by muntins into nine sections, each glazed with a 11" × 18" pane. This door may date to circa 1893.

Hardware: Original fittings include three 4" high cast-iron butt hinges, a brass face mortise lock, hollow two-piece stamped iron knobs, and a brass keyhole escutcheon on the west face. Iron slide bolts are positioned at the top and bottom rails.

WINDOWS

There is a single original window opening in the west wall (a second opening was converted into a doorway). The opening has the original eight-over-eight double-hung sash set in a deep reveal that includes a pair of two-tier paneled bifold shutters. The trim matches that of the original doorways. The shutters have original brass latch bars and recent brass knobs. The sash is secured by an original or very early brass fastener with acorn finials. The glazed panel in the west door functions as a window.

HEATING

Originally, the kitchen relied on the fireplace and later the cooking range for heat. The installation of the furnace and later the steam boiler provided additional heat for this space. After 1893, a large wall-mounted cast-iron steam radiator was affixed to the south wall (now hidden by a large two-tier kitchen cabinet).

LIGHTING

There is no visible evidence for gas lighting that would have existed here during the Hart era. The current electric lighting, installed by RCHS, includes a series of incandescent bulbs concealed by a plywood soffit on the north, south, and west walls as well as bulbs lighting the fireplace/stove and the brick oven.

A small antique brass gas wall bracket is attached to the north wall and was installed by RCHS, but there is no original gas piping there.

PLUMBING

There is no evidence for the Hart-era kitchen sink or any plumbing fixtures from the Cluett eras. A 4" diameter iron pipe is visible in the cement floor surface beneath the west window opening. The pipe has a cap marked "RIGNALL." It is likely that the Hart and Cluett sink were in this location as the cistern is located nearby. By the late Hart era and certainly after 1893, the sink was connected to the city water system.

FIREPLACE

The primary original feature of the kitchen is the massive fireplace and bake oven that fills the northeast corner of the room. The chimney breast projects about 13" from the north wall. The fireplace opening (56½" × 72") is formed of well finished brown sandstone blocks (six courses high), which support a massive brown sandstone lintel.

The original firebox is of brick, but it is largely obscured by the later cooking range. The upper iron eye-hooks that supported two pot cranes are visible in the back corners of the firebox, the bottom hooks are hidden by the range. The cast-iron range, marked "Bramhall, Deane & Co. New York" was installed in 1872 (Fig. 208). It is 30" high and the cooking surface measures 27" × 54". The larger fireplace opening has brick infill on either side of the range.

A small opening in the stonework on the west side of the chimney breast is concealed by a fitted sheet metal cover with a small brass knob. This is an ash clean-out for the chimney. The oven proper is formed entirely in brick showing evidence of deterioration from the intensive heat produced during many years of use. A brick flue connects the oven to the chimney flue above the fireplace. Original sheet iron covers exist for the oven opening and the ash slot and a hinged sheet iron door covers the opening to the ash clean-out. The entire fireplace and oven assembly is in a remarkable state of preservation.

A small cupboard, located above the oven, is an additional original component of the fireplace/oven feature and a single panel wood door opens to the small space finished in plaster and with a brick floor.

208 Cast-iron range marked "Bramhall, Deane & Co. New York" in B03.

EQUIPMENT

A bifold plywood screen in the southwest corner covers mechanical equipment including the main electrical panel box, ADT apparatus, and the telephone connection. This condition was created by RCHS.

FURNISHINGS AND FITTINGS

This large important basement room functioned as the kitchen for some 66 years until the new kitchen space was constructed for George and Amanda Cluett. Both Hart inventories include the kitchen. The 1844 document simply notes that the kitchen furniture is valued at $40.00. The 1886 inventory provides much more detail, including a long list of cookware and dishes, as well as furniture such as four tables, four chairs, a clock, and two ice closets. The Hart financial records provide additional information about the appearance of the kitchen.

In 1857, and again in 1882, oil cloth was laid on the wood flooring.

William L. Adams was paid for repairing the kitchen clock in 1854 and H. Cozzens repaired tables and chairs in 1883 and 1884.

The house had a manual service bell system during the Hart era and the bell rack probably was located here, but no physical evidence for this important fitting has been found. The wood rails positioned next to the ceiling on the south and west walls may have supported the bells and/or other fittings.

Necessary kitchen appliances would include a cooking range, a refrigerator, and a sink. All were used here and are recorded in the Hart financial records. Several generations of coal-fired ranges were installed in the original cooking fireplace and sometime after the mid-nineteenth century a gas range was used as well. The final Hart-era refrigerator was installed in 1888 and an ice chest was purchased in 1889. The current copper sink and cast-iron pump are placed on a wood cabinet made up of vertical-beaded board. The antique sink and old pump were donated to RCHS in 1965. Although this sink was installed by RCHS as part of the restoration of the Hart kitchen in 1965, it is generally in the same location as the various earlier sinks.

FINISHES INVESTIGATION

The plaster wall surface retains about thirteen layers of painted finish. The earliest colors include a pale cocoa brown, which was also used in the hall (B01), followed by two finishes of a light beige and then three layers of a yellow/beige of which one is probably the "lemon color" applied in 1855.

Later finishes dating to the Cluett eras, include a pale yellowish pink and a light pink/beige which are the same colors used by the Cluetts in the first floor service hall (110).

The original woodwork was first painted in a very light cream/beige. This was later covered by a layer of wood graining. The Hart financial records reveal that the kitchen windows were grained in 1850.

The plaster ceiling retains evidence for finishes of white paint. In 1877, there is an invoice for scraping and painting the ceiling white.

The doors were originally grained and that surface can be seen on the pantry door and the hall door.

B04　Pantry

This small and well-preserved pantry is a significant adjunct to the original Hart kitchen. In plan, the room includes a single door in the west wall and original shelving arranged on the north, east, and south walls. The northwest corner consists of the curved mass of the brick oven which projects into the room. Radiant heat from the oven mass would have warmed this small room.

This was probably a dish and cookware pantry rather than a food pantry. The deep shelves have applied beads to support dishes and trays in an upright position against the wall. The 1886 inventory includes a lengthy list of cookware and dishes under the kitchen heading, but the items were likely kept here. The door to the pantry can be locked and the built-in cupboard at the north end of the room could be locked as well. There is no documentation for the use of this space by the two Cluett families (Fig. 209).

Since the restoration of this room and the kitchen beginning in 1965, dishware, pottery, and glassware from the collections have been displayed here.

FLOOR

The original floor surface consists of 6" to 10" wide tongue-and-groove pine boards laid east/west and now painted red. The original wooden kitchen floor would have matched this surface.

209 The pantry (B04), as viewed from the kitchen (B03).

WALLS

The south, east, and west walls are finished in plaster on brick and the north wall is of plaster on wood lath, which is furred out from the masonry foundation wall. The curved section of the west wall follows the profile of the kitchen oven. Original shelving and cabinetry cover the north, east, and south walls.

CEILING

The original plaster on wood lath surface is about 8'2" above the floor.

BASEBOARD

The plain 7¾" high base has an integral bead along the top edge.

CORNICE

There is no cornice molding.

DOORS

The original door opening, D032, has a single fascia architrave which is 3½" wide.

HEATING

The pantry was never heated, although when the brick oven was in use this space would receive some warmth.

LIGHTING

There is no visible evidence for Hart-era gas lighting, but a cover plate on the ceiling may represent the position of a post-1910 Cluett electrical fixture. The surface mounted incandescent fixture above the door was installed by RCHS.

FURNISHINGS AND FITTINGS

The primary feature of the pantry is the original built-in shelving and cabinet. The south and east walls are covered by three tiers of original 17" deep wood shelving. The 1¼" thick shelves have an edge bead detail.

An upper fourth-level shelf was installed as part of the 1965 restoration of the kitchen and pantry. The cabinet is constructed against the north wall and the shelves are concealed by a pair of paneled wood doors supported on small iron butt hinges. The west door leaf retains an original hand-wrought hook, but the corresponding eye is missing from its position on one of the shelves. The east leaf includes an open keyhole and evidence for a missing cabinet lock. Many of the kitchen items included in the 1886 inventory were stored in this cabinet on the shelves.

The curved wall surface includes two original 4" high wood rails for hooks. The current iron hooks in place there were installed circa 1965. The floor surface here may have been the area where the tin pails and wooden pails, noted in the 1886 inventory, were kept.

FINISHES INVESTIGATION

During the Hart era, the plaster wall surfaces in this room were painted to match those in the kitchen.

The wood cabinetry received about seven successive finishes in a light cream/beige, the same color used in the kitchen. This woodwork was never grained.

B05   Servant's Bedroom

The southwest room is the only basement room that has a sub-basement beneath it—the space that functioned as a wine cellar.

In plan, this room includes a single doorway in the east wall and window openings in the south and west walls. The closet that projects from the southeast corner masks a wood-enclosed air duct that is part of the Hart-era steam heating system.

All of the original features are intact here, but several additions were made by RCHS when the room was restored in the mid-1960s. These include the vertical board dado and the closet (Fig. 210).

This is the only basement room in the original part of the house that does not have a fireplace. It has been assumed that this was a servant's bedroom, but the absence of a heat source indicates that it may have originally been intended for storage. Certainly before the construction of the "back building" there was a lack of storage areas in the basement, particularly for food stuffs.

The introduction of the hot-air heating system in 1846 would have provided some heat for this room from the duct that serviced the dining room directly above. The use by a servant after this date is more likely. Two servants' rooms, "Miss Smith's" and "Miss Brown's," are included in the 1886 inventory and likely this is one of those spaces. By that date, the steam radiator housed in the wood duct in the southeast corner provided heat to this room. How the two Cluett families used this room remains unknown.

In 1965, RCHS began to restore this space as the cook's room from the Hart era. As part of that recreation a cast-iron heating stove was placed here with a sheet metal stove pipe extending to the south wall. In reality there is no flue outlet in the location where the pipe meets the wall.

FLOOR

The original 8" to 9" wide tongue-and-groove pine boards are laid east/west. The surface was refinished in 1965. The three narrower boards next to the north wall are replacements.

WALLS

The south, east, and west walls are finished in plaster on wood lath, furred out from the masonry of the south and west foundations. The north wall is of plaster on

210 Bedroom (B05) looking southwest, 1999.

brick. A 34" vertical beaded board dado covers the lower portion of each wall and the closet projection. This surface was installed as part of the 1965 cook's room project.

CEILING

The plaster on wood lath ceiling is about 8'2" above the floor. The textured finish was applied as part of the 1965 rehabilitation of the room.

BASEBOARD

The plain, tall wood base has an integral bead at the top edge. The beveled shoe molding may date to the Hart era and is found in other basement rooms.

CORNICE

There is no cornice.

DOORS

The original door opening (D051) in the east wall has 3¼" wide single fascia trim.

D051: The six-panel, stile-and-rail door has recessed panels on the west face and flush panels on the hall face. The door swing was changed in 1965; originally, it was hinged to the south jamb.

Hardware: Original fittings include a pair of 4" high cast-iron butt hinges, an iron rim lock now mounted upside down due to the door swing change, two brass knobs, and an oval brass keyhole escutcheon. There is evidence for a removed Yale-type bolt on the room face.

WINDOWS

There are two window openings: an original large opening in the west wall and a small later opening in the south wall. The original west opening has the same double fascia trim used in the hall. The eight-over-eight double-hung sash are set in a deep reveal, which includes pairs of two-tier bifold paneled shutters. The deep sill has a bullnose edge. The shutters retain the original brass bar latch, but the brass knobs date to about 1965. The sash is secured by the original or very early brass fastener with acorn finials. The later small opening in the south wall is framed in plain board trim and is filled with a six-light casement sash.

HEATING

There is no fireplace in this room. Further probing is needed to determine if a small circular patch in the plaster wall directly beneath the later south window opening might be the location of a chimney flue opening. This position aligns with the dining room chimney breast directly above. This may indicate that a stove was used here, although the current arrangement places the sheet metal flue pipe in the wrong location. The room now receives some heat from the steam radiator housed in the wood duct in the southeast corner. An insulated steam pipe is positioned near the ceiling next to the north wall. It is covered by a plywood valance and enclosure.

LIGHTING

There is no visible evidence for Hart-era gas lighting. The fluorescent fixture next to the north wall and the wall-mounted spotlight were installed by RCHS.

CLOSET

The closet is constructed of plywood and includes the application of the wood dado. This feature was added to the room as part of the work carried out in 1965. Inside the closet is a much earlier Hart-era wood-enclosed duct that is part of the heating system installed in 1862 or 1872. An access panel at the base of the duct includes an ornamental cast-iron hand grip.

FURNISHINGS AND FITTINGS

If one assumes that this is the more simply furnished of the two basement servants' rooms listed in the 1886 inventory, then Miss Brown's room included a bed, wardrobe, washstand, and three chairs. The floor included matting and two strips of carpet. A mirror was also used here.

B06   Servant's Bedroom – Gift Shop – Office

The southeast room is the better finished of the two rooms that were occupied by household servants. In plan, the rectangular room includes single doorways in the north and west walls and a window opening in the east wall. This window looks out into the areaway that extends across the front of the house. A shallow chimney breast is centered on the south wall and includes the finest feature of the room, a stone mantel with an iron and brass coal grate. An original closet is accessible from the door in the west wall.

During the Hart era, this was probably always occupied by a household servant. In the 1844 inventory this space is referred to as the "bedroom under library," and this may be "Miss Smith's Room" included in the 1886 inventory.

How this room was used by the Cluett families is unknown.

In 1965, when the RCHS library collection was installed in the northeast room (B02), this space was used as a study room with maps, photos, and prints.

In 1975, the gift shop was placed here and remained in this location until it was moved to the newly renovated first floor of the Carr Building in 1982.

Currently, this room serves as the office for the director of the RCHS.

FLOOR

The original wide board tongue-and-groove boards are laid east/west and are partially covered in old oilcloth painted grey. The east third of the floor surface is replaced by plywood installed by RCHS. The entire surface was recently covered in carpet.

WALLS

The south and east walls are finished in plaster on wood lath furred out from the masonry foundation walls. The north and west surfaces are of plaster applied to brick. All four walls include a 34" high vertical beaded board dado set on the original baseboard. This is the wainscoting for which Gochoe and Tobin were paid in 1870 for installation. At that time, this space was referred to as the "small room in cellar."

CEILING

The original plaster on wood lath surface is about 8'2" above the floor. The current painted textured surface is a recent application.

BASEBOARD

The original 9½" high base includes an integral bead along the top edge. The beveled shoe molding may date to the Hart era. The base along the east wall was replaced due to water damage.

CORNICE

There is no cornice.

DOORS

There are two original door openings: (D061) to the hall and (D062), which provides access to the closet. Both openings have the original 4¾" wide double fascia trim.

D061: The original six-panel, stile-and-rail door has flush panels on the hall face and recessed panels on the room side.

Hardware: Original fittings include a pair of 4" high cast-iron butt hinges, a 4½" × 7" iron rim lock, two small brass knobs, and an oval brass keyhole escutcheon. Recent applications include a Yale dead bolt and a small brass slide bolt.

D062: This original six-panel door duplicates the configuration and original hardware of D061 and the paneled side faces the room.

WINDOWS

The original east window opening has the typical double fascia trim. The eight-over-eight double-hung sash is flanked by pairs of two-tier bifold paneled shutters fitted in the deep reveals. The deep wood sill has an applied bullnose edge contemporary with the installation of the wainscot.

The small original interior opening in the north wall is framed by the same narrow echinus molding used on the door trim. The four-light casement sash retains part of the original latch, but the butt hinges are replacements.

HEATING

Four generations of heat sources are extant in this room. The room was originally heated by the fireplace and the slightly later coal grate insert. There was a stove flue pipe opening in the upper face of the chimney breast indicating that a stove was used here also. The wall-mounted cast-iron steam radiator is part of the installation of 1862 or 1872.

LIGHTING

There is no visible evidence for Hart-era gas lighting. The two fluorescent ceiling fixtures were installed by RCHS.

PLUMBING

The cast-iron soil pipe and the water pipes near the northeast corner extends from the former second floor bathroom (203) installed for the Cluetts. The city water supply enters the house in the southeast corner where the water meter is located.

FIREPLACE

The very shallow 1½" deep chimney breast includes a fireplace with the original mantelpiece and a coal grate insert. The stone mantel (now painted) is composed of fluted pilasters supporting a frieze with a central tablet. The stone hearth is covered in paint. The coal grate insert was placed in the firebox soon after the completion of the house in 1827 and consists of panels of soapstone which form a small mantel into which the ornate cast-iron and brass grate is set. The coal basket pivots for clean out.

CLOSET

The original walk-in closet is located through the door in the west wall. Finishes duplicate those extant in the adjoining room and the original floor boards are exposed; they average 7" to 9" in width. The electric hoist mechanism for the elevator is located in this closet. The electric panel box on the north wall is labeled "Inclinator Co. of America Harrisburg Pa 11/20/68."

FURNISHINGS AND FITTINGS

The 1844 inventory refers to this space as a bedroom and the contents are valued at $15.00, but the specific items are not listed.

Of the two basement servants' rooms included in the 1886 inventory, the one called "Miss Smith's Room," which seems to include better furnishings, is probably this space. Included in the room was a bed, a bureau and mirror, table, washstand, and four chairs. There were curtains at the window and a carpet and two rugs covered the floor.

The function of this room between 1893 and 1953 remains unknown.

After the occupancy of the house by RCHS beginning in 1953, this room was furnished for varying purposes including a gift shop and most recently as the director's office.

FINISHES INVESTIGATION

The inside face of the door to the hallway retains the original grained finish that simulates figured maple.

Fragments of wallpaper survive on the surface behind the wall-mounted radiator and therefore probably date to the Hart era.

B07   Area – Passage

This passage, referred to as the "area" in the Elizabeth Shields Eddy's reminiscence, is a space unique to this house.

In plan, the rectangular "area" includes doorways in the east and west walls and a wide opening in the north wall. Single windows are positioned in the south and east walls and a narrow sidelight is positioned next to the east doorway. An access stair to the wine cellar is positioned in the stone paving next to the east wall (Fig. 211).

The unique configuration of this passage is the result of the joining of an original condition, the 1827 rear areaway, with the "back building" added to the house circa 1836. At this location a passage was created that passed under the extension of the first floor dining room (106). This passage was open to the exterior at each end.

Elizabeth Shields Eddy referred to this as the wide stone paved passage that "gave an air of mystery and romance to that yard." (Fig. 212)

211 The passage (B07) looking south, 1982.

212 The "area" passage beneath the dining room, as it appeared in 1836, D. G. Bucher, 1999.

As completed circa 1836, the south end of the space included a broad flight of stone steps that ascended to the south yard. A shorter flight of steps at the north end provided access to the narrow areaway, which fronted the two kitchen windows.

The brownstone paving formed part of the original 1827 areaway located in front of the basement entrance. The east wall is the original exterior foundation wall of the west or rear face of the house. The marble water table, quoins, and lintels are an indication of the superb detailing and finishes that were used at the back of the house construction for Richard and Betsey Hart by William Howard.

The wide, steep stairway that ascends in front of the east wall beneath the window provides access to the sub-cellar or wine cellar. The items stored in that space were placed there through this access opening.

According to Elizabeth Shields Eddy, the door in the west wall opened to the back building where there was a cold storage room for apples and vegetables and a "twisting stairway leading up to the back hall (110) from which opened Grandmother's room."

During the Hart era, it is likely that the open north and south ends of this passage were temporarily closed during the cold months of the year with some sort of wood partition. No mention of the "area" is found in the Hart inventories.

With the purchase of the house in 1893 by the George Cluetts and the construction of the extension to the "back building," the character of the passage changed. The open ends were infilled with brick. The new south wall included a small window opening. This unique interior-exterior space became another basement room. How this enclosed space functioned is unknown; perhaps it simply served as a passage connecting the two parts of the basement.

In 1966, items were sought for display so that this space could be interpreted as a laundry room, but it is unlikely that such a function ever existed here.

FLOOR

The surface is formed of large, very worn, brown sandstone pavers which date to the original completion of the house in 1827. An opening to the wine cellar is incorporated into the floor surface next to the east wall.

WALLS

The walls vary in material and date of construction. The east wall, the original rear foundation of the house, is constructed of parged masonry with openings, water table, and foundation finished in cut and tooled white marble. The west wall is laid up in brick dating to circa 1836. The south wall (until 1990 the north wall also) is of brick infill dating to circa 1893. The brown sandstone piers at the north and south end of the west wall were part of the openings at each end of the nineteenth century "area."

CEILING

The ceiling is finished in wide tongue-and-groove boards laid east/west. The boards to the north are slightly narrower. A hinged plywood panel that separates the original surfaces conceals wiring and various conduits. It was installed by RCHS.

BASEBOARD

There is no baseboard in this former outdoor area.

CORNICE

There is no cornice.

DOORS

There are three openings: D013 in the east wall, D091 in the west wall, and the wide opening in the north wall.

D013: This is the original rear exterior doorway to the basement of the 1827 house. The deep wood reveal is positioned in an opening formed of dressed marble quoin blocks set upon the marble water table and foundation.

D091: This opening into the circa 1836 basement addition is of brick supporting a plain wood lintel. The wide opening in the north wall dates to circa 1836 and was restored in 1990. The opening is spanned by a flat brick arch.

WINDOWS

There are two window openings: the large east opening dates to 1827 and the smaller south opening was created circa 1893. An original narrow sidelight is positioned next to the east doorway.

The south opening has a plain wood lintel above the brick opening. The original six-light wood casement sash is now covered in plywood. The original exterior iron security bars are hinged and can be secured by a bar latch and padlock.

The door sidelight retains evidence for a hinged panel at the top half of the opening that would cover the air intake duct for the Hart-era furnace formerly located in the kitchen (B03).

HEATING

There is no heating device here, but a steam pipe is positioned next to the ceiling.

LIGHTING

The spotlight was installed in circa 1966.

PLUMBING

The large cast-iron drain pipe located next to the east doorway is marked "Monitor Iron Works."

OTHER FEATURE

An access opening to the wine cellar is located in the floor and wall surface beneath the window in the east wall. The narrow opening is covered by a hinged wood panel that conceals the steep flight of steps.

FURNISHINGS AND FITTINGS

Utilitarian items may have been placed here during the Hart era, but no mention is made of the space in the two inventories. How this area was used by the two Cluett families remains unknown.

In 1966, the space was refurnished by RCHS for interpretation as a laundry area, a function it most likely never served.

B08   Connector Passage

The interior passage was created by RCHS in 1990 when the connector was constructed joining 59 Second Street to the Carr Building next door to the north at 57 Second Street (Fig. 213).

Prior to that undertaking this was a narrow outdoor areaway immediately beyond the west wall of the Hart Kitchen. The conditions prior to the 1990 reconstruction were the result of work carried out when George and Amanda Cluett had the rear wing enlarged in circa 1893. That work included the installation of yellow brick pavers in the courtyard and the rebuilding of the original Hart-era areaway in poured concrete. An original feature that remained in situ during the Cluett reconstruction was the ash bin positioned at the far north end of the areaway. Formed of panels of slate, this was a feature dating to the original construction of the house.

213 The brick cistern exposed in the passage (B08).

The construction of the circa 1836 "back building" impacted this location. A short flight of masonry steps ascended from the enclosed area (B07) to the paved surface originally positioned just below the water table of the rear basement foundation. The kitchen window looked out onto this paved area. One of the two original kitchen windows was converted into a doorway circa 1893, the condition existing today. This provided direct access from the kitchen, probably used by the Cluetts as a laundry, to the paved courtyard where clotheslines were located.

The creation of the connector necessitated the enlargement of the areaway to create a passage to the basement of the Carr Building. During the excavation to enlarge the area, the Hart-era brick rainwater cistern was discovered approximately 5' west of the rear wall of the house.

This important original feature was incorporated into the new poured concrete wall that defines the west side of the connector and supports the wood and glass structure of the first floor connector. The new concrete floor surface ramps downward to the north to compensate for the difference in basement floor levels between 59 and 57 Second Street.

B09   Back Basement Hall

The "back building" constructed in circa 1836 included this hall as well as the adjoining room (B10) to the south and the passage known as the "area."

In plan, this space includes doorways in the south, east, and west walls and a small window in the north wall. Generally, the current condition dates to the work carried out circa 1893 when the back building was enlarged for George and Amanda Cluett.

As completed circa 1836, this room included a "twisting stairway" in the northwest corner. Elizabeth Shields Eddy remembered this as the cold storage room for apples and vegetables. The south door opened to the room where coal was stored. There was no doorway in the west wall. The floor was probably finished in brick pavers, now replaced by poured concrete.

The expansion of the wing for the Cluetts resulted in the removal of the winding stairway that ascended to the first floor service hall (110). A similar new stairway was constructed in hall B11, which was connected to this space by a new doorway opened in the west wall. This newly remodeled space essentially functioned as a passageway to the rear basement rooms.

In 1969, the RCHS library was installed in Room B10 and this space served as an adjunct storage area where metal filing cabinets held photographs and other library collections. With the removal of the library to the Carr Building this again became solely a hallway.

FLOOR

The floor is poured concrete dating to circa 1893 and now painted red. The original Hart-era surface was probably brick.

WALLS

The walls are finished in plaster on brick and rubble stone masonry. Along the north wall a shallow 4" deep brick ledge begins at about 48" above the floor and ascends diagonally and vertically to the ceiling. This condition may be a later insertion to reinforce the structure of the wall.

CEILING

The original surface is finished in plaster on wood lath which is now very deteriorated and largely covered in fiberboard secured by nails and installed after 1953.

BASEBOARD

There is no baseboard and the plaster wall surface extends to the cement floor.

CORNICE

There is no cornice.

DOORS

There are three door openings: D091 in the east wall, D092 in the south wall, and D093 in the west wall. The south and east openings retain the original plain circa 1836 trim with an inner bead.

D091: The original six-panel, stile-and-rail door has recessed panels on the area (B07) side and flush panels on the back hall (B09) side.

Hardware: Original fittings include a pair of 4" high cast-iron butt hinges and the iron latch bar for a lift latch. The brass Suffolk latch on the east face is a RCHS replacement. There is an outline for a missing Hart-era 2¾" × 4" rim lock and a surface-mounted slide bolt.

D092: Original door composed of wide vertical tongue-and-groove boards held by wide horizontal battens. The door originally opened into Room B10 and was hinged to the east jamb. The door was cut down to open outward, probably circa 1969.

Hardware: Original fittings include a pair of 4" high cast-iron butt hinges repositioned on the face of the door. The outline for the original Norfolk type thumb-latch is visible on the face of the door. The Yale bolt and small brass knob date to circa 1969.

D093: The door has been removed, but the single leaves of three 3" high butt hinges remain on the north jamb.

WINDOW

The original opening in the north wall has narrow plain 2⅞" wide trim set above a single bullnose sill. The twelve-light casement sash is hinged on two 3" tall butts and is secured by a small brass turn latch. The board below the sill is a recent addition.

HEATING

This space was never heated, but piping from the steam system passed through the space and the condensate return pipe is located next to the north wall along the floor.

LIGHTING

Two utilitarian fluorescent tube fixtures are attached to the ceiling and date to circa 1969.

PLUMBING

Important Hart-era features include a sheet metal (tin) shower head set in a wood frame in the southwest corner of the ceiling. This unique survivor is oval in shape (7¼" × 10" × 4¼" high) and includes a decorative scallop edging. A small sheet metal tube enters the back (south) face of the head and there is evidence for a rope activation cord in the wood frame (Fig. 214). The corresponding base of the shower "stall" was removed when the cement floor was installed. This shower was probably used by the male members of the Hart family or possibly the person that maintained the coal bin (Room B10).

The cast-iron drain pipe that is positioned next to the ceiling (originally secured by a hand-wrought hook) and extends down the south wall was connected to the pantry sink formerly located in first floor room 110. The Harts and the Cluetts had a sink in that location. A short section of Hart-era lead water pipe protrudes from the ceiling next to the iron drain pipe.

214 Nineteenth century sheet-metal shower head (B09).

EQUIPMENT

The end of a sheet metal speaking tube is positioned above the west doorway. The tube is continuous in the back stair hall (B11) and dates to the George Cluett era.

STAIRWAY

The "twisting stairway" referred to by Elizabeth Shields Eddy was most likely located in the northwest corner, but there is currently no visible evidence for this important feature. The framed opening for the stair must remain in the ceiling structure, but is now covered by the ceiling finishes.

FURNISHINGS AND FITTINGS

The Hart inventories make no specific reference to this space, but Elizabeth Shields Eddy indicates that apples and vegetables were kept here. This may indicate that shelving was located here. The original stairway would have filled much of the northwest corner and a shower stall was located in the southwest corner. How or if the stall was separated from the room remains unknown.

B10　Coal Bin – Library – Office

A small, simply detailed space, this room has experienced very divergent uses. In plan, the rectangular room includes a single doorway in the north wall and a pair of windows in the south wall. This is essentially the arrangement of the room as completed circa 1836 and it is probably the "coal cellar" referred to in the Hart financial records.

By the 1830s, if not earlier, large amounts of coal would be necessary to fuel the fireplace grates and heating stoves as well as the kitchen cooking stove.

The installation of the Fox & Company Patent Air Furnace in 1846 would have greatly increased the need for a conveniently located area for the storage of coal. Coal was carried up the stairs formerly located in the adjoining hall (B09) to the upper floors of the house.

The room was extensively renovated in 1966 so that the RCHS library could be installed here. The work included the raising of the floor level and the covering of all wall surfaces. The only surviving nineteenth century surface is the narrow board ceiling.

As part of the library installation the three bookcases used by Albert and Caroline Cluett in the back parlor (104) were placed here. In 1993, the library was moved to its current location in the Carr Building. This room now functions as an office.

FLOOR

The raised plywood floor surface is covered in carpet and dates to the 1966 renovation for the library. The original surface may be brick, but is currently not accessible.

WALLS

All wall surfaces are covered in vertical-groove plywood paneling. The original walls are of brick, possibly with a plaster finish.

CEILING

The original finish is of 4½" wide tongue-and-groove beaded boards laid east/west. Steam pipes which run along the north wall are enclosed in with plywood paneling and perforated masonite.

BASEBOARD

There is no baseboard.

CORNICE

A narrow furring strip is positioned at the top of the paneled wall surface.

DOORS

The original door opening is framed by a plain 4½" wide board with an inner beaded edge. The door remains in situ, but originally was hinged to the east jamb and opened into this room.

WINDOWS

Conditions at the two original window openings in the wall are covered by modern plywood paneling. The original sash is divided into twelve lights and is hinged at the top, opening inward. The east sash retains the original pair of cast-iron butt hinges and a small circular brass turn latch. The west sash is supported on recent brass-plated hinges.

HEATING

The room receives heat from the steam pipes that pass through the space along the north wall.

LIGHTING

The three fluorescent ceiling-mounted fixtures were installed in 1966.

FURNISHINGS AND FITTINGS

The Hart financial records record a payment to H. Cozzens in 1885 for "making coal cellar door." If the current door dates to this period, then the Norfolk latch, whose outline can be seen on the door, was probably reinstalled from an earlier door in the same location.

Evidence for other nineteenth century conditions is probably hidden behind the plywood paneled wall surface.

The built-in shelving along the south wall was installed in 1966.

B11   Back Stair Hall – Work Room

The addition to the house by George and Amanda Cluett included this hall and the adjacent south rooms. In plan, the rectangular space includes a single doorway in the east wall, two doorways in the south wall and a single window in the north wall. The primary feature is the enclosed staircase, located at the west end of the space, that ascends to the first floor back hall. Beyond the stair projection there is a narrow continuation of the hall used primarily for storage.

Generally, this hall retains all of its original features and character, but there is no documentation on how the space was used by either Cluett family. This area was renovated in 1969 in conjunction with the installation of the RCHS library in Room B10.

FLOOR

The poured cement floor, now painted red, is probably the original condition. At some time an asphalt coating was applied to the surface, possibly to alleviates a damp condition. A crude raised platform of random boards, predating the RCHS era, is positioned next to the west wall.

WALLS

All four wall surfaces are of brick that is now painted white. The east wall is the west foundation wall of the circa 1836 addition and the lower half is laid up in random stone, which is covered in cement parging. The west wall includes an opening for the steam pipe that extends from the boiler in the cellar of the carriage house into this basement. The stair to the first floor is enclosed by partitions constructed of vertical beaded boards.

CEILING

The ceiling is finished in plywood panels joined by narrow wood battens probably installed circa 1969 over the original plaster on wood lath surface. Numerous pipes and wires cover the ceiling surface.

BASEBOARD

There is no baseboard.

CORNICE

A narrow quarter-round wood molding is contemporary with the plywood ceiling.

DOORS

There are three original door openings: D093 in the east wall, and D121 and D141 in the south wall. The south doorways have plain 4" wide trim. The east opening is positioned in the brick foundation wall of the circa 1836 addition. The hinges remain in place for a missing door that enclosed the storage area beneath the stairway.

WINDOWS

The original six-light casement sash is positioned in the brick opening. The sash is hinged to the west jamb and opens into the room. There are original iron bars on the exterior of the opening.

HEATING

There is no heating unit here, but the insulated steam pipe that runs along the ceiling next to the south wall, provides heat to this hall.

LIGHTING

Fixtures installed by RCHS include a ceiling-mounted fluorescent unit, an exposed incandescent bulb, and a spotlight.

PLUMBING

Various water and drain pipes are located next to the ceiling, including lead piping that connects to the utility sink at the head of the stairway and the sink in the kitchenette (113).

STAIRWAY

The enclosed staircase to the first floor includes thirteen risers; four of the treads are winders. The wood handrail on the west wall was installed by RCHS.

EQUIPMENT

Sections of an original sheet metal speaking tube (contemporary with the construction of the Cluett addition) remain in place along the south and east walls. The tube is supported by small iron brackets. It originally extended into Room B09, but what two spaces it joined is undetermined.

FURNISHINGS AND FITTINGS

Four utilitarian wood shelves are installed in the angle of the stair enclosure. Two tiers of wood shelving supported on steel brackets are attached to the north and west walls and were installed circa 1969.

B12   **Utility Sink Room**

This small room functions as a vestibule for the toilet room and houses a utility sink. In plan, the space includes doorways in the north and south walls. The utility sink is located in the south east corner. Generally, the conditions here date to the expansion of the rear wing circa 1893.

FLOOR

The floor is poured cement now painted red.

WALLS

The east wall consists of brick laid above a stone foundation, the original rear foundation wall of the circa 1836 addition. The north wall is of brick and the south and west partitions are constructed of narrow vertical beaded board.

CEILING

The ceiling is plaster on wood lath.

BASEBOARD

There is no baseboard, but a narrow wood nailing strip extends along the bottom of the west partition.

CORNICE

A narrow nailing strip extends along the top of the west partition.

DOORS

There are two original door openings set in the board partitions with plain wood trim.

D121, D122: These stile-and-rail doors have six tall narrow vertical panels.

Hardware: Original fittings include pairs of 3" high cast-iron butt hinges and small iron rim locks marked "Corbin USA." There are brown mineral knobs.

HEATING

This space is unheated.

LIGHTING

A porcelain utility fixture with an exposed incandescent bulb is attached to the south partition.

PLUMBING

A large, white porcelain enamel cast-iron sink with an integral back splash is attached to the east wall. It may date to around 1915, the date found on the toilet in the adjoining room.

FURNISHINGS AND FITTINGS

The two brass-plated iron coat hooks on the west partition date to either of the Cluett eras.

B13   Toilet Room

In plan, this small room includes a single doorway in the north wall and a single small window in the south wall.

A toilet was always located here, but the current fixture was installed after 1915.

FLOOR

The floor is raised wood covered in linoleum installed by RCHS.

WALLS

The east wall is of brick laid up above a parged stone foundation and the south wall is of brick. The north and west partitions are constructed of narrow vertical beaded board.

CEILING

The ceiling is original plaster on wood lath. A recent section of gypsum board is nailed to the south edge of the surface.

BASEBOARD

A section of plain base is positioned along the east wall.

CORNICE

A narrow nailing strip extends along the top of the north and west partitions.

DOORS

There is no trim on the south face of the door opening.

WINDOWS

The original opening in the brick foundation wall is now filled by a sheet of plywood that conceals the original six-light sash, which is hinged to the east jamb.

HEATING

This space is unheated.

LIGHTING

A surface-mounted gas pipe on the east wall indicates that a gas light wall bracket was in place here during the earliest Cluett era. A white ceramic utility fixture with an exposed incandescent bulb is mounted on the north partition.

PLUMBING

A white ceramic tank toilet is positioned against the south wall. The tank lid is stamped "7 23 15" possibly the date July 23, 1915. A cast-iron drain pipe is located in the southeast corner.

FURNISHINGS AND FITTINGS

A recent wood shelf, supported on metal brackets, is attached to the west partition.

B14   Storage – Work Room

The large southwest room is one of the spaces created when the rear wing was expanded for George and Amanda Cluett.

In plan, the room includes a single doorway in the north wall and a small window in the south wall. Original built-in cabinets covered the west wall surface. How this room originally functioned is unknown. Its close proximity to the first floor kitchen, by way of the nearby stair, makes it probable that kitchen supplies were stored here. Until recently, this room was used by

RCHS as the exhibit preparation work shop. It currently is largely used for storage.

FLOOR

The floor is poured cement now painted red.

WALLS

The north, south, and west walls are of brick, which is now painted. The east partition is constructed of narrow vertical beaded boards.

CEILING

The ceiling is finished in gypsum board installed by RCHS. The original plaster ceiling remains in the west cupboard.

BASEBOARD

There is no baseboard.

CORNICE

There is no cornice.

DOORS

The original opening in the north brick wall has plain board trim.

D141: The stile-and-rail door has six narrow vertical panels.

Hardware: Original fittings include three 3" high cast-iron butt hinges and an iron keyhole cover on the outside face. The mortise lock and knobs are missing.

WINDOWS

The original six-light casement sash is positioned in the brick opening. It is attached to the west jamb by two small butt hinges. Original iron security bars are located on the exterior.

HEATING

The room is unheated except for an insulated steam pipe positioned near the ceiling. A flue opening in the south wall may indicate that a gas fired hot water heater was formerly located here.

LIGHTING

A single fluorescent fixture is attached to the ceiling.

PLUMBING

An electric "Energy Saver" hot water heater is located next to the south wall.

FURNISHINGS AND FITTINGS

An original cabinet unit is built in against the west wall. The shelves are concealed by four doors constructed of vertical beaded boards. The three upper shelves are original. The lower shelf and supports were installed by RCHS.

Hardware: The doors are supported on iron strap hinges and secured by ornamental cast-iron spring latches. A plain latch is located on the north door. Three of the doors have surface-mounted iron locks marked "WB."

Fittings installed by RCHS include the work surface and shelving along the east partition and the peg board attached to the south wall.

B15 Wine Cellar

The sub-basement wine cellar is one of the unique, but little-visited portions of the original house. This room is located beneath the south extension of the basement hall (B01) and the southwest servant's room (B05) (Fig. 215).

In plan, the rectangular space includes a single small window or ventilation opening in the south wall and an access opening and steps in the west wall. A stairway from the basement hall descends into the room along the east wall and an enclosed storage space is located beneath that stair.

215 The wine cellar (B15) looking northwest.

The most important feature is the original wooden cage-like enclosure that fills the northwest corner. Although currently in a very deteriorated state, it is evident that this enclosure included a lockable door and was fitted with shelving. Additional nineteenth century shelving was located along the south side of the room.

The "Wine Closets" included in the 1886 inventory probably refer to the storage enclosure in this room. The deteriorated conditions encountered here may indicate that this space was unused after the house was acquired by the Cluetts in 1893.

FLOOR

Red brick pavers laid in a herringbone pattern form the original floor surface.

WALLS

The walls are of rubble stone retaining a finish of whitewash. Brick frames the opening in the west wall and at the "window" opening. A wood plank wall encloses the space beneath the east stairway.

CEILING

The exposed floor joists, that are laid north/south, and underside of the basement floor boards form the ceiling. All of the wood retains multiple layers of whitewash.

DOORS

The original bulkhead-type "door" opening to the rear exterior of the original 1827 house is located in the west wall. A steep flight of brick and stone steps ascends within the opening. A two-part wood cover, fitted to the upper opening, can be secured in place by a wrought-iron hook.

The opening to the storage area beneath the east stairway is covered by a plank door with original hardware including two small cast-iron butt hinges, a small iron rim lock, and an iron hasp. The enclosed "cage" storage area included a door constructed of vertical spaced wood slats. The hinged door included a rim lock so that the contents of the "cage" were secure.

WINDOWS

The small opening in the south wall is located on the exterior at the bottom of a deep stone lined semicircular "well." The brick jambs supports a wood lintel; the sill has deteriorated beyond recognition. There is no surviving evidence for a sash.

HEATING

This space was never heated, but a pipe from the steam heating system passes through this area. The opening in the ceiling next to the south wall is an air intake for the steam radiator that provides heat by convection to the first floor stair hall and dining room.

LIGHTING

Lighting is provided by an incandescent spotlight that must be plugged into an outlet located in the basement hall.

PLUMBING

A large cast-iron drain line is located next to the ceiling along the north wall.

STAIRWAY

The original wood stairway ascends in ten risers to the basement hall along the east wall.

FURNISHINGS AND FITTINGS

The original secure storage area is located in the northwest corner. Formed of closely spaced vertical wood slats on the south and east sides, and the stone foundation walls to the north and west, this closet included three tiers of wood shelving arranged along the north, east, and west sides. Access was through a doorway centered in the south slat partition. The entire assembly was finished in whitewash. There is evidence next to the south wall for whitewashed supports that held two deep storage shelves. The closet space beneath the east stairway retains supports for two wood shelves.

The contents of the wine closets in 1886 included cases of champagne of various labels as well as bottles of wine and sherry with a total value of about $180.00.

CARRIAGE HOUSE

The story-and-a-half 45' long brick carriage house extends fully across the rear west end of the current lot at 59 Second Street. This was not always the situation; as originally completed, the carriage house was an additional 4'6" in length (see Fig. 63). Between 1827 and 1893 the Hart property extended 30' further south, incorporating the plot of land now occupied by the Kemp-Frear House at 65 Second Street. The carriage house was partially situated on that piece of the property, but that end of the building was demolished in 1893 when the neighboring house was constructed. A small, presumably simple, brick washhouse occupied the southwest corner of the original site abutting the south gable end of the carriage house or barn as it was sometimes called. Together these structures formed a barrier separating the house and garden from the alley to the west (Fig. 216).

The elegantly detailed east façade of the carriage house, prior to its modification in 1893, functioned as a beautiful backdrop for the garden that surrounded the Hart House to the south and west. The fine vista from the back parlor windows, which looked out on the garden and the carriage house beyond, was first marred by the construction of the "back building" or rear addition circa 1836. This necessary addition to the original house was built in a simple utilitarian manner with no architectural pretense. Unfortunately, this three-story box-like brick mass and its later extension obscured the beauty of the carriage house façade as viewed from the house.

The Hart Papers include many references to work carried out on the carriage house also referred to as the barn, stable, and coach house.

Unlike the house, this structure has undergone significant modifications since its completion which culminated in the extensive reworking of the first floor interior in 1955 to accommodate a much-needed meeting room and exhibition space for RCHS. That newly created space was first used in 1956 and continued to function for meetings and exhibits until the new meeting room opened in the Carr Building in 1982.

Both the exterior and interior of the carriage house were investigated as part of the overall assessment of 59 Second Street. Unfortunately, the extent of relatively recently installed interior finishes made it impossible to thoroughly analyze the surviving early surfaces. Original and early conditions were much more evident in the half-story or attic and in the cellar.

EXTERIOR

The primary façades face east and west and the upper half of the south gable end is visible above the brick garage at 65 Second Street. The north gable end is hidden by the large structure at 57 Second Street known as the Carr Building. The long rectangular 28' × 45' brick building is one-and-a-half stories high with a gable roof whose ridge runs in a north-south direction, parallel to the alley. Originally, all of the brick walls were painted white to match the house.

216 The east facade of the carriage house, north end, 1985.

EAST ELEVATION

This is the primary architecturally-detailed façade that was visible from the house. The original symmetrical arrangement of the elements of this elevation acted as the terminus of the yard, separating the house and yard from the noisy and active alley.

The current disposition of the five-bay façade dates to the diminishment of the carriage house in 1893. At that time, the sixth or southernmost bay, complete with blind arch, was removed. The façade is laid up in brick upon a very low cut brownstone foundation. The five remaining semicircular arches rise from six shallow 2' wide piers forming a blind arcade and the 6' wide arches spring from white marble blocks at the top of each pier.

Beginning at the north end the first two arches include false window recesses centered in the brick wall surface. These "openings" include marble sills and flat splayed brick lintels. The third arch, now at the center of the façade, features an original doorway fitted with a paneled door dating to the 1986 renovation. The fourth arch includes a window opening and six-over-six wooden sash contemporary with that renovation.

Prior to 1955, a doorway was located here. Originally, there was no opening in this bay. A paneled door in the fifth blind arch also dates to the 1986 renovation and replaces a flush door installed in 1955. Physical evidence in this arch indicates that originally and prior to 1955 this arch was fully open and probably included a pair of wide arched doors that opened into the building. The missing sixth arch possibly included a false window as found at the north end of the building.

The elevation of the attic or half-story above the arcade is ornamented with a series of three blind round openings or "bull's-eyes" and two rectangular white marble tablets with inverted corners. A fourth bull's-eye was positioned above the missing south arch. This façade terminates in a simple wood entablature which was originally topped by a wooden balustrade that matched the still extant feature that fronts the roof of the main façade of the house. A single baluster of this now missing and unrecorded feature is visible in the circa 1892 photograph of the exterior of the house. Several documents in the Hart Papers refer to work on the balustrade. In 1852, John B. Colegrove was paid for replacing 32 balustrade bannisters for the carriage house.

Sometime after 1893, the balustrade was removed and a massive built-in wooden gutter was installed on the roof surface. This replaced the original sheet metal–hung gutter, a condition that survived on the west alley façade. Because of severe deterioration and ongoing maintenance problems this built-in gutter was removed in the early 1980s and the hung gutter condition was recreated.

SOUTH ELEVATION

The brickwork of this elevation is visible above the roof line of the one-story garage at 65 Second Street. This surface was constructed in circa 1893 when the south bay of the carriage house was demolished and appears to include reused bricks, probably from the demolition.

WEST ELEVATION

This is the informal workaday façade of the carriage house that faces the alley. The 45' long story-and-a-half brick façade is arranged in five irregularly disposed bays of window openings and doorways. The wall rises from an approximately 10" high brownstone block base.

In 1893, this façade was decreased in length by about 4'6" when the south end of the Hart property was sold to William Kemp (Fig. 217). Original features include the three windows and the two hayloft doors that open from the attic story and the two windows, entrance doorway, and the wide opening at the south end of the first floor. The now-closed opening at the center of the façade was probably inserted when George and Amanda Cluett acquired their first automobile in the early twentieth century. It has not been determined if an earlier opening was located here.

The five original window openings have brownstone sills and flat splayed brick lintels. The north first floor sill was repaired in 1986. Two of the upper openings retain original three-over-six sash and the original vertical board hayloft doors are supported on long wrought-iron strap hinges. The third upper level opening is now fitted with an aluminum louver. The first floor north door and the pair of vertical board doors in the 8'5" south opening are 1986 replacements installed by RCHS. The wrought-iron Suffolk-type thumb latch on the north door is a reproduction. The two first floor window openings have recent six-over-six sash. There is no cornice below the edge of the gable roof. Original iron gutter brackets support a recently installed sheet metal gutter.

The location of the Cluett-era garage doorway is 12'6" wide and filled-in with red brick. The steel lintel above this opening remains in place but is covered by a board on this face. Original wood lintels remain at the other two first floor door openings, but the woodwork at the jambs was renewed in 1986. A small bricked-up circular opening for a stovepipe can be seen in the wall surface directly above the south window. The flue pipe for a nineteenth century heating stove exited the building in this location. A cellar window well extends out from the foundation into the alley. The concrete block lined well is of twentieth century origin, but may replace an earlier feature.

ROOF

The ridge of the gable roof is parallel to the alley. Originally, the roof was covered in slate to match the roof of the house and the Hart Papers include payments for repairs to this roof variously referred to as the stable roof or barn roof. The current asphalt shingle roof was installed in the early 1980s and replaced an earlier asphalt shingle roof installed by RCHS. An important, but now missing, feature of this roof was the cupola which is noted in the Hart Papers as being repaired in 1874. There is no visual record and little physical evidence for

217 West facade of the carriage house, after 1893, D. G. Bucher, 1999.

this long missing roof ornament. Its function was to ventilate the interior of the carriage house. In 1852, extensive repairs were carried out on this roof and at that time a tin ventilator was installed, but there is also no trace of this feature. A tall square brick chimney, near the west edge of the roof, exhausts the boiler in the cellar. The chimney was probably constructed when the Cluetts installed the earliest boiler in this location. Prior to 1893, the boiler was located in the basement of the house.

INTERIOR

The interior of the carriage house is arranged on three levels; a partial below-grade cellar, the first floor, and the half-story or attic above the main floor. As originally completed in 1827 the building extended about 4'6" further to the south, that portion of the structure was demolished in 1893 when the original Hart property was divided. The current south end wall was constructed at that time. The Hart Papers include numerous references to work carried out on this structure referred to as the coach house, stable, and barn. Many payments were made for repairs and renovations of the interior.

In 1955, extensive renovations were carried out by RCHS to convert the structure into a large auditorium-like hall for the meetings of the Society as well as a space for art exhibits. This project involved the removal of

virtually all of the historic Hart- and Cluett-era finishes and fittings, aside from the wall and ceiling surfaces, leaving only a shell of a space.

A low stage, complete with operable curtains, was installed at the north end of the large open room. Fortunately, the area above the first floor was untouched and is now the only part of the carriage house that retains the ambiance of the nineteenth century.

The meeting room function was transferred to the Carr Building after the initial renovation of that structure in 1982. In 1986, the first floor was again renovated in an attempt to regain some of the nineteenth century character of the space. The stage was removed and surfaces were uncovered that had been covered in pegboard in 1955. Most importantly, the stair to the attic was recreated in its original location. In 1955, a pull-down type stair was inserted in the opening, making access to that interesting space difficult. Unfortunately, it was determined that little evidence remained for the original configuration of the carriage house. The removal of the wood flooring in 1955 destroyed all evidence for the position of the horse stalls and other important spaces and features.

The walls did retain some evidence for earlier conditions, particularly a large area of faux grained vertical boards that survived at the north end of the east wall. This surface was carefully covered to protect it. For a brief period after this most recent renovation the carriage house served as an exhibit gallery for the display of the Society's small collection of horse drawn wheeled vehicles, a sleigh, and an early motor car. The collection of Troy-made cast-iron stoves was also displayed here.

FIRST FLOOR

The appearance and finishes of the first floor as they now exist are the result of the extensive remodeling carried out in 1955 and the renovation of that work undertaken in 1986. At the same time, the interior was investigated for evidence or surviving finishes dating to the Hart and Cluett eras.

The floor was finished in 9" × 9" vinyl tile over a thin concrete slab poured over corrugated sheet metal laid on the original wood floor joists. This surface was installed in 1955, at which time the nineteenth century floorboards were removed. The tile was removed in 1986. The Hart Papers indicate that the original floor was replaced by spruce plank in 1865–66. The floor hatch, located next to the wall between the two east doorways, is the original opening to the cellar but the cover is a replacement.

The walls are of painted brick covered in various locations by other materials. The south brick wall was constructed in 1893 when the building was shortened by 4'6". The vertical board surface covering the north end of the east wall was installed in 1986 to protect a Hart-era faux grained vertical board surface that had been covered by material installed in 1955. In 1852, D. H. Wellington was paid for graining and varnishing a closet in the barn, possibly in this location.

A similar surface installed in 1986 covers the location of the large opening in the center of the west wall that was probably created in the early twentieth century when George and Amanda Cluett acquired an automobile. A steel lintel forms the top of this former opening.

In 1955, all of the interior partitions that divided the large space according to function were removed. The wall surfaces and the ceiling surface provide some clues concerning the locations of these missing partitions.

References in the Hart Papers and other documents indicate that this building included an area for carriages and sleighs, a stable with horse stalls, a manure box, a cabinet for harnesses as well as at least one closet (possibly a small room). At one time the Harts kept a cow here. A stove was used to heat the building, but whether anyone lived in the carriage house has not been determined.

The ceiling is 9'10" above the current floor. The north two-thirds of the ceiling is finished in boards of varying widths and the termination of the boards at the south end of the space indicates the location of a nineteenth century partition; south of that line the framing is exposed. The large opening in the south end of the ceiling is an important surviving nineteenth century feature. In 1873, Gochoe and Tobin were paid for the installation of a carriage lift as well as a stairway to provide easy access to the second story where the lift mechanism was housed. The two large plank panels that cover the opening are partially hinged and also slide on tracks on the attic floor to provide access to the storage area.

A brick chimney mass projects from the west wall immediately north of the pair of exterior doors. This chimney serves the boiler located in the cellar and was probably constructed when the Cluetts had the first boiler placed here. The Hart-era stove used to heat this space had a flue pipe that passed directly through the west brick wall to the alley.

All of the doors in place today were installed by RCHS and the openings vary in age. The large opening at the south end of the west wall is original and retains its wood lintel. This was probably always the carriage entrance into the building. Whether a similar door was located where the Cluetts installed their garage door is difficult to determine. The small door opening at the south end of the east wall was, prior to 1955, a large arched opening probably fitted with a pair of doors. The north doorway in the west wall is the original single-door opening to the alley.

The south end of the board ceiling surface retains some exposed electrical wiring from the George Cluett era.

SECOND FLOOR — ATTIC

This floor extends fully over the first story and is positioned beneath the structure of the gable roof. The east and west brick walls extend up into the space approximately 6' and include in the west surface the original windows and two hay loft doors. There are no openings in the east wall or in the tall gable end walls. All of the brick wall surfaces remain unpainted, and it is evident that the south wall was rebuilt.

The roof framing divides the space into three bays with pairs of 7" × 8" wood posts defining each division (Fig. 218). These 9' × 7" high posts rest on wood plates

218 Carriage house attic (219) looking east, 2000.

laid over the floor joists that span from the east to the west walls. There is no support for these posts at the first floor level. This braced frame supports two massive 12" high purlins which in turn support the roof rafters.

The original wide plank tongue-and-groove flooring survives throughout the attic and is laid north/south. The primary feature in this surface is the large opening at the south end of the space that can be closed over by a large pair of sliding and hinged panels. A vertical board partition divides the space forming an enclosed room at the south, the location of the carriage lift. The lift mechanism is housed in a small recess that is part of this partition. The installation of the lift in 1873 also involved work in this south room, boards were attached to the roof framing to create a more finished space to protect the carriages and sleighs. When the floor panels are in an opened position, this space is visible from the first floor.

A nineteenth century wooden bin located next to the east wall is the area where the original exterior blinds from the house are stored.

CELLAR

This original below-grade space is located at the center of the building forming a partial cellar beneath the carriage house. Access is from an original stone and brick stairway that descends into the space against the east wall. The walls are laid up in rubble stone and the original room is divided into two spaces by a gypsum board partition installed in 1981. The floor is of poured concrete dating to the twentieth century; the original floor was probably brick. The ceiling is finished in gypsum board applied over the original wood floor joists that support the first floor. The joists support corrugated metal panels which in turn support the poured concrete floor installed in 1955.

An 1848 reference in the Hart Papers indicates that at that early date charcoal was stored here. At an undetermined date after 1893 a steam boiler, which provided heat for the house, was installed here. The main steam line and the return line pass through the east stone foundation wall. In 1981, a new boiler, convertible to gas or oil, was placed here and serves both the Hart-Cluett House and the Carr Building. The partition and the steel fire door were also installed at that time. The window opening in the west wall is fitted with a ventilation louver and the opening may be contemporary with the installation of the Cluett-era boiler.

Immediately south of this room there is an enclosed chamber that houses the oil tanks used to fuel an earlier boiler located here prior to 1981.

WASH HOUSE

There is little written information and no visual record of the Hart-era washhouse that occupied the southwest corner of the original south garden lot of 59 Second Street and was demolished in 1893. Elizabeth Shields Eddy indicates that at the west end of the yard there was "a low, white brick laundry called 'the wash house,' a three foot brick path . . . leading to the door." The Hart Papers include references to this small but important structure called the washhouse and laundry.

The interior included a boiler, stove, pump and sink as well as a cistern. After 1893, the Cluetts used the original Hart-era basement kitchen as a laundry and the north and south brick walls flanking the courtyard behind the main house retain the wood supports and iron hooks for the Cluett clotheslines.

ACKNOWLEDGMENTS

First and foremost I want to thank Breffny A. Walsh, RCHS Director (1970–1990), who enthusiastically encouraged me in my ever widening quest to uncover the story of the Marble House in Second Street. This quest was further encouraged by her successor, Anne W. Ackerson and the current Director, Donna Hassler, who recognized the merit of publishing the results of this twenty-five year endeavor.

A special thanks to all of the staff at RCHS, both past and current, and especially Kathryn Sheehan, Registrar, for her insights into the Cluett families and her patience in assembling the illustrations for publication.

I want to thank Dean Leith, past President of the Board of RCHS for his constant support and encouragement throughout the long process of research and writing.

To my firm, John G. Waite Associates Architects, and its predecessor firms, I owe a special debt of gratitude for patience and encouragement. Of the staff at John G. Waite Architects I want to thank Bill Palmer and Lee Pinckney for their contributions, as well as Grace Jukes and especially Donna Jackson-Spriggs for her patience in typing the complicated manuscript. I want to particularly thank Jack Waite whose enthusiasm for the Marble House and Troy in general was the inspiration for the thoroughness of this endeavor. To Diana Waite I am grateful for the discovery of John Colegrove, the original contractor for the house, and for her constant support.

The Turpin Bannister Chapter of the Society of Architectural Historians has for many years been the gracious host of several lectures about the house and its occupants, events that helped to organize my ideas about the Marble House.

Local institutions that played important roles include the Troy Public Library where much information was gleaned from old Troy newspapers, and the Troy Savings Bank, the long-time guardian of the Hart Papers.

I want to thank Joan K. Davidson for her support through Furthermore, the publication program of the J. M. Kaplan Fund, and Senate Majority Leader Joseph L. Bruno for the generous funding provided by the State of New York.

John Winthrop Aldrich, Deputy Commissioner for Historic Preservation, shares my enthusiasm for the house and Troy and graciously consented to write the Preface for the publication.

To my co-authors, Stacy Pomeroy Draper and Walter Richard Wheeler, I am particularly grateful, for without their efforts this document would not exist.

And finally, to Frederick D. Cawley, who edited the manuscript and made what was an overwhelming amount of information into a coherent document, a very special thank you.

DOUGLAS G. BUCHER

Raffle flower detail, pen and ink, c. 1964

59 Second Street, soiled marble wall surfaces surrounding the main entrance.

59 Second Street: Problems of Repair

Douglas G. Bucher and William P. Palmer

59 SECOND STREET has survived with nearly all of its original building fabric intact, despite having undergone two major expansions in the nineteenth century and renovations in the twentieth century. Although some original building elements were either removed or covered over at these times, most of the work that was undertaken dealt carefully with the original building. There seems to always have been a recognition of the significance and inherent quality of the original house.

The house and carriage house are generally in good condition, although they have received uneven levels of maintenance over the past fifty years. This is the case largely because of the soundly designed construction details, the use of high-quality materials, and the care that went into the original construction of the buildings. When the Rensselaer County Historical Society took possession of 59 Second Street in 1953, the conditions then reflected the extremely high level of maintenance and care bestowed on the buildings by the Harts and Cluetts over a 126-year period.

Although the fabric of the building is generally in good condition, there are serious concerns with the heating, plumbing, fire detection, and electrical systems, which are outdated and in a very deteriorated state. Leaks from the plumbing and heating systems over the past several years have caused significant damage to interior finishes.

Another concern involves rising damp and moisture penetration in the walls of the basement, possibly exacerbated by the installation of concrete floors in that area. Related to this water penetration are problems with the drainage system around the perimeter of the house. This is most apparent at the front of the house where the two rainwater leaders fail to carry water away from the foundation and areaway.

The long-term failure of the various roofs, which caused considerable damage to interior finishes, was until recently a major concern. In 1996, the condition was corrected by a major restoration campaign.

The following is an itemized listing of the problems in the house and carriage house, as well as the site.

HOUSE—EXTERIOR
East Façade

Although commonly called Tuckahoe, or Westchester, marble, the stone is actually a dolomitic limestone. The stone on the east facade of the house is generally in sound condition, with signs of deterioration common for a building of its age. Although carved elements of the marble cornice have deteriorated, tool marks are still evident on the faces of the ashlar blocks (Fig. 219).

Marble elements of the cornice that are protected from direct contact with rainwater have lost much of their detail because of the damaging effects of atmospheric pollutants. The long-term interaction between moist surfaces of the stone and sulfur dioxide in the atmosphere, in the presence of catalytically active materials from fly ash or automobile exhaust, has caused dark gypsum crusts to form (Fig. 220). When this crustal material is exposed to moisture, the sulfate can go into solution and lead to the chemical deterioration of mar-

220 Dark crusts under the cornice indicate that the Westchester marble is being converted to gypsum.

ble (conversion to gypsum). Crusts have also formed on the protected surfaces beneath window lintels and sills, however actual damage to these marble surfaces is minimal.

Atmospheric pollutants have also soiled the entire marble façade. The pure white marble now has a light grey appearance. In addition to an aesthetic concern, this soiling will promote the eventual deterioration of the marble surfaces. Rust stains have also formed on the marble adjacent to embedded iron shutter hold backs and on the lintel above the outer entrance.

Vertical and diagonal cracks appear in two marble window lintels and one sill, but there does not appear to be any stone displacement. Severe cracks, open joints, and marble stone displacement also appear on the north wall and south arch that support the entrance steps (Fig. 221).

Mortar joints in the marble masonry are generally sound, although a few joints have eroded. Some joints have been pointed with hard portland cement mortar that does not match the original color and ultimately may damage the adjacent soft stone.

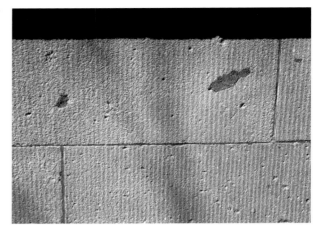
222 Patching material does not match marble surface.

Lead expansion shields for the attachment of a previously removed plaque remain embedded in the marble to the left of the main entrance. Past repairs to holes in the marble were noted, but the patching material does not match adjacent marble surfaces in color, texture or tooling (Fig. 222). Holes and chips in the surfaces of other stones also exist.

Carved surfaces on the capitals and bases of the two marble columns that flank the main entrance have deteriorated and lost their detail. There is slight separation between the inner face of the quoined architrave of the outer door opening and the marble façade indicating movement of that important feature. The top surfaces of the marble pedestals that support the urn newels flanking the entrance steps have cracked around the anchors for the metal bases (Fig. 223). Several pieces of marble are now missing.

The marble coping for the south window areaway opening has been displaced and the stucco surface of the window well walls is deteriorated (Fig. 224). At the north window areaway, mortar joints on the east brownstone wall have also deteriorated. Poor drainage of these areaways over many years has caused water to enter the foundation and damage interior building fabric in the basement. Both areaways sometimes contain an unsightly accumulation of debris and leaves that retain damaging moisture (see Figs. 221 & 224).

Water drainage along the east façade has been a long-term problem. Elm tree root systems have uplifted the sidewalk and caused it to pitch toward the building, rather than to the curb. Consequently, water runoff is directed to enter the window areaways. Due to condi-

221 Marble block displacement, cracks and open mortar joints below entrance steps. Debris interferes with drainage of window areaways.

223 Cracked marble on edge of urn pedestal.

225 Severe corrosion at base of iron railing.

224 Deteriorated stucco on wall of south window areaway.

226 Typical deteriorated paint on window sash and trim

tions at grade level, the rainwater leaders do not direct water away from the building.

Excessive paint build-up on the iron railings obscures the details. Numerous elements of the metalwork have badly rusted and a cast-iron anthemion finial is missing on the south segment of the railing. Severe corrosion occurs at the base of the railing where this condition has been exacerbated by the use of deicing salts on the sidewalk (Fig. 225). Although the iron urn newels were restored about twenty years ago, a number of copper leaves have been deformed or broken off by vandals.

Paint has peeled from most of the lower surfaces of window jambs, sash, and sills, thereby exposing the bare wood to decay. Remaining painted surfaces are severely alligatored and no longer protect the wood substrate (Fig. 226). Glazing compound is generally deteriorated or missing on all window muntins. Open joints between the wood jambs and surrounding masonry permit water infiltration.

Heavy accumulations of alligatored paint on the

227 Accumulated layers of paint obscure details on main entrance door and trim. Lead elements on fanlight are missing.

front entrance door and wood architrave obscure their details. Panel molding joints on the door are also open. Lead elements on the door fanlight and sidelights are missing (Fig. 227). In addition, the plaster of the recessed entrance walls has cracked.

South Elevation

The brickwork is generally sound over most of this façade, however mortar joints have severely eroded at the parapet level of the wall. Rainwater can enter the wall through these open joints and eventually cause serious damage to the masonry.

Two brownstone window lintels have partially de-laminated, since the stones were originally laid with vertically oriented bedding planes (Fig. 228). In normal construction practice, this problem is prevented by placing sedimentary stones with their bedding planes perpendicular to the direction of loading.

Mortar joints in the marble foundation stones are deteriorated.

The brick pavers of the walkway appear to be embedded in concrete with no apparent method for water drainage. Since the impervious brick pavement abuts the building face, water may be puddling along the base of the wall, allowing moisture to enter the masonry. This condition may be contributing significantly to the problem of moisture damage on the basement perimeter walls.

The brownstone rim of the light well for the wine cellar window is damaged and has settled, probably as a result of poor rainwater drainage (Fig. 229). This condition directs water into the light wall.

All wood elements of the bay window appear to be deteriorated. Wood joints in the base of the window are open and allow water to enter. The interior of the window base is moist and appears to have been damaged by wood attacking insects. This insect infestation may still be active (Fig. 230).

229 Settlement of light well rim at base of south façade.

230 Deteriorated wood base to bay window on south façade.

Wood windows on this façade show an overall lack of maintenance and their condition compares with those previously noted on the east façade.

West Elevation (Rear Addition)

Brick masonry on this façade is generally sound, with only a few open mortar joints noted.

A foundation sandstone block and adjacent brick-work located below the porch have been damaged. It appears that this damage may be caused by poor water

228 Deteriorated brownstone window lintel on the south elevation.

231 Damaged brownstone and brickwork at base of west façade beneath porch stair.

232 Damaged brick pavers in the courtyard.

drainage in this area and ponding against the wall, as well as the use of deicing salts (Fig. 231).

Wood elements and paint on the porch have been damaged by moisture and the lack of maintenance. Windows have not been maintained and exhibit the same problems as found on the south and east façades.

West Elevation (Original House)

Brick masonry of this façade is generally sound. Windows have not been maintained and exhibit the same problems as found on the other façades.

North Elevation (Rear Addition)

Foundation brownstones have delaminated due to the vertical orientation of their bedding planes. This condition has been exacerbated by the abutting surface of impervious brick pavers that hold moisture against the wall.

The brick masonry of the wall is generally in good condition. Problems include a few open mortar joints and some holes that had been drilled in the face of bricks. Bluestone window sills and lintels appear to be in good condition. Windows have not been maintained and their condition matches those located on the other building façades.

The brick pavers in the courtyard form a very uneven surface, with many damaged units (Fig. 232). The only provision for water drainage in this area is a surface drain located adjacent to the west porch, although there does not appear to be adequate pitch toward the drain.

North Elevation (Original House)

The exposed brick wall visible above the roof and parapet of the Carr Building has some open mortar joints.

HOUSE — INTERIOR

Utility Systems

The heating, electrical, fire detection, and plumbing systems are obsolete and expose the building to the possibility of water and fire damage.

Water leaks from deteriorating plumbing and heating equipment have caused significant damage to plaster walls and ceilings over the years. The existing mechanical system also does not provide much needed ventilation for the building. The electrical system has been modified in a piecemeal fashion over the years to accommodate changing requirements. Fire detection

233 The water pipes and drain lines were installed over a one hundred and fifty year period and have considerably deteriorated.

234 This jumble of electric and telephone wiring is in close proximity to the deteriorated plumbing lines.

235 The electric wiring is inadequate throughout the house.

and intrusion alarm systems have been temporarily upgraded in recent years, however components and wiring for obsolete systems still remain exposed (Figs. 233, 234, 235).

First Floor

The major building conservation problem on the first floor is the water damage to the windows, plaster walls, cornices and ceilings at the east end of the original house. This damage was caused by long-term roof leaks on the main roof that have been corrected by the installation of a new roof on the entire building in 1996.

Damage to other ceilings and wall surfaces on this floor have been caused by malfunctioning plumbing and heating systems.

Generally, all surfaces need cleaning, minor repairs, and painting.

Room 101

- Minor cracks and separation of the finish coat of plaster exist on the ceiling.
- Minor cracks exist on the plaster cornice and on the wall surface below the chair rail.
- Panel moldings on door D1011 are loose.
- Glazing compound is poorly installed and cracked on the leaded sidelights and interior fanlight over door D1011. A section of muntin is missing on the interior fanlight.
- Areas of oak strip flooring are loose and not firmly attached to the wood subfloor which is the original floor surface.
- The floor finish is worn.
- The wallpaper is very soiled and has rubbed and deteriorated areas.
- The twentieth century surface-mounted door lock is inappropriate.

Room 102

- The lower rail and left stile are damaged on the left sash of the window located on the south wall, adjacent to the basement stair.
- The oak strip flooring is loose and not firmly attached to the subfloor in some locations.
- One baluster is loose at the bottom of the main stair.
- The wiring of the suspended lantern fixture is deteriorated.
- The wallpaper is very soiled and has rubbed, torn, and deteriorated areas.

Room 103

- Moderate to severe water damage to the plaster ceiling exists on east side of the room, caused by long-term roof leaks (Fig. 236). Minor plaster cracks exist on west end of the ceiling.
- Paint on window sash and stops is severely deteriorated.
- Window pocket shutters are not operable.
- Plaster has been poorly patched around the chandelier stem at the center of the ceiling medallion.
- The wiring of the chandelier may be deteriorated.
- All painted surfaces are soiled and in need of re-painting.

236 Plaster on ceiling, cornice and walls in Room 103 damaged by long-term roof leaks.

Room 104

- Paint on window sash and stops is deteriorated.
- Window pocket shutters do not operate.
- Plaster has been poorly patched around the chandelier stem at the center of the ceiling medallion.
- The wiring of the chandelier may be deteriorated.

Room 105

- The floor is covered by historically inappropriate vinyl tiles.
- An historically important doorway is missing in the north wall.
- The shelf and coat hanger bar along the south wall is historically inappropriate.

Room 106

- Doors D1061 and D1062 bind at their thresholds.
- The floor finish is worn.
- Floor boards adjacent to doors D1061 and D1063 are loose.
- The plaster ceiling and cornice at the west end of the room are severely deteriorated due to roof drain leaks.
- The visibility of the fanlight above the door may not be historically appropriate depending on the interpretation of this room.

Room 107

- Minor plaster cracks exist on the ceiling and all walls.
- The floor finish is worn.

Room 108

- The ceiling is covered by homasote panels that may not be historically appropriate depending on the interpretation of the space.
- Floor is covered by historically inappropriate sheet vinyl.
- The mortise lock to door D1081 does not operate properly.

Room 109

- Minor plaster cracks exist on the ceiling and all walls.
- The floor finish is worn.
- The installation of mechanical equipment on the surface of the north wall has caused damage to that surface.

Room 110

- The floor is covered by historically inappropriate vinyl tiles.
- The west end of ceiling is covered by historically inappropriate homasote.
- Minor plaster cracks and separations of the plaster finish coat exist on the walls.

- A window counterweight rope is broken.
- A glass pane is broken in the fanlight over door D1102. The corner blocks on the architrave to this door are loose.
- The Cluett-era pantry cabinets and sink are removed from the north wall.

Room 111

- Major water damage to the plaster exists on the ceiling and the upper surface of the wall in the northeast corner of room. This damage was caused by leaks from a defective radiator in the room above (Fig. 237).
- Minor plaster cracks exist on the walls, ceiling, and cornice.

237 Plaster on ceiling, cornice and walls of Room 111 caused by water from leaking heating equipment in the room above.

Room 112

- Severe plaster cracks and separations of the plaster finish coat occur on the segment of west wall facing door D1102.
- Minor patches of flaking paint exist on the wood ceiling.
- Cluett-era cabinetry is missing from the east wall.

Room 113

- The floor is covered by historically inappropriate vinyl sheet flooring, depending on the interpretation of the room.
- Minor plaster cracks and separations of the plaster finish coat exist on the walls and the ceiling.
- The cabinet and sink were removed from Room 110.

Room 114

- Major separations of the plaster finish coat exist on all walls and the ceiling.
- The exterior door is historically inappropriate.

Second Floor

Severe water damage to plaster, windows, and floors along the east wall of the original house has been caused by long-term roof leaks and is similar to conditions found in the rooms below on the first floor.

Damage to plaster walls and ceilings in other areas of this floor have also been caused by malfunctioning plumbing and heating equipment.

Severe separations and losses of the plaster finish coat on walls and ceilings generally occur throughout the west addition. This problem does not appear to be caused by water infiltration, but may be due to the improper application of the finish coat of plaster.

Room 201

- Bifold shutters on the stairway window are not operable.
- The floor finish is worn.
- Strip floor boards have buckled adjacent to door D2071.
- The electrified gasolier and the electric wall bracket are historically inappropriate.

Room 202

- Built-in cabinet doors do not close properly.
- Minor cracks exist on the plaster ceiling.

Room 203

- Moderate to severe water damage exists on the plaster ceiling and cornice. This and other water damage in this room has been caused by a long-term roof leak.
- The window trim, bifold shutters and sash are damaged and deformed from water infiltration.
- The historically inappropriate plywood flooring at the east end of the room has been damaged by water infiltration.
- The position of the Cluett dado rail was modified.
- The electrified gasolier is historically inappropriate.

238 Plaster on ceiling, cornice and walls in Room 204 damaged by long-term roof leaks.

Room 204

- Severe water damage to the plaster exists on the east wall and on the ceiling and cornice at the east end of the room. This damage has been caused by a long-term roof leak (Fig. 238).
- Window trim and bifold shutters are damaged and deformed by water infiltration.
- The large oriental rug is stuck to the floor surface by the deteriorated carpet pad.
- The electrical lighting is historically inappropriate.

Room 205

- Minor plaster cracks exist on the ceiling.
- The closet doors have been removed.
- The electrical lighting mounted above the closets is a fire hazard and inappropriate.

Room 206

- Minor to moderate plaster cracks exist on the ceiling and cornice.
- Paint on the window trim and sash has deteriorated.
- Bifold window shutters do not operate properly.
- Historically, this room did not include a chandelier.

Room 207

- Major water damage to plaster exists on the walls, ceiling, and cornice. This damage was caused by leaking plumbing associated with the bathroom on the floor above and with a roof drain.
- A small section of the raffle flower on the architrave corner block is missing at door D2071.

Room 208

- Moderate plaster cracks exist on all walls, cornice and ceiling.

Room 209

- Severe water damage to plaster exists on east wall and on the ceiling and cornice at the east end of the room. This damage has been caused by a long-term roof leak.
- Window trim, sash, and bifold shutters have been damaged by water infiltration.
- Moderate plaster cracks exist on the north, west, and east walls, and on the west end of the ceiling and cornice.
- The electrified gasolier is historically inappropriate.

Room 210

- Severe separations of the plaster finish coat exist on all walls and the ceiling.
- An access opening in the wood strip floor in northeast corner has been patched with plywood.
- A window pane is broken.
- The pipe chase cover is deteriorated.
- The south and west openings are missing their doors.

Room 211

- The ceiling is covered by historically inappropriate adhered acoustic tiles. There is evidence of potential damage to the original plaster ceiling.
- The floor is covered by sheet vinyl.
- Minor plaster cracks with a moderate separation of the plaster finish coat exist on walls.
- Wood wainscot on the east wall is damaged.

Room 212

- The stair railing assembly is not secure.
- Severe separations of the plaster finish coat exist on all walls (Fig. 239).
- Wood floor boards are loose on the stair landing.
- A window pane is cracked.
- The electric ceiling light is historically inappropriate.

Room 213

- Moderate plaster cracks exist on the ceiling, cornice and all wall surfaces.
- Moderate separations of the plaster finish coat exist on the west wall.

239 Severe separation and losses of plaster finish coat in Room 212. This condition occurs on most plaster walls and ceilings in the west addition.

- The upper hinge to closet door (D2132) is not fastened to the frame.
- The electric ceiling fixture is historically inappropriate.

Room 214

- Severe separations of the plaster finish coat and plaster cracks exist on the ceiling and all walls.
- Paint on the window sash is deteriorated.

Room 215

- Moderate to severe separations of the plaster finish coat and plaster cracks exist on all walls and the ceiling.
- Closet door (D2152) does not close properly.

Room 216

- Moderate water damage to the plaster exists on the upper area of the south wall.
- Minor plaster cracks exist on the ceiling and walls.
- Wood or marble flooring beneath the sink and toilet has been replaced by historically inappropriate plywood.
- The lock mechanism to door D2161 does not operate properly.
- Two etched panes of glass are cracked on door D2161.

Room 217

- Moderate to severe separations of the plaster finish coat exist on all walls and the ceiling.

Third Floor

Plaster surfaces of walls and ceilings throughout this floor have been water damaged from long-term roof leaks. Finishes on windows are generally deteriorated and floor finishes are worn.

Room 301

- Severe water damage to the plaster ceiling and cornice exists at the west end of hall. This damage was likely caused by roof leaks. Moderate plaster cracks exist on other areas of the ceiling.
- The floor finish is worn.
- The folding door at the stairway opening is historically inappropriate.

Room 301A

- Minor screw holes from removed shelving exist on the plaster walls.

Room 302

- Extensive water damage to the plaster ceiling has been caused by roof leaks.
- Plaster walls and the cornice are moderately cracked.
- Paint on the window sills and sash is deteriorated.
- The floor finish is worn.

Room 303

- Severe plaster cracks exist on the ceiling and walls.
- Paint is peeling from the walls and ceiling.

Room 304

- Moderate plaster cracks exist on the cornice and ceiling.
- Minor separations of the plaster finish coat exist on the ceiling.
- Paint is deteriorated on the window sash.
- The floor finish is worn.
- Inappropriate plywood shelving fills the room.
- Ceiling-mounted electrical lighting is historically inappropriate.

Room 305

- Screw holes from removed shelving exist on the plaster walls.

Room 306

- The floor finish is worn.

Room 307

- Minor cracks exist on the plaster walls.

Room 308

- Ceiling plaster is water damaged from a long-term roof leak at the base of the dormer window above.

Room 309

- Minor plaster cracks exist on the ceiling and cornice.
- Paint is deteriorated on the south quarter window sash and sill.
- Plaster is water damaged on the east knee wall and an opening has been cut in that surface.

Room 310

- Minor plaster cracks exist on the ceiling and walls.
- The wainscot panel board adjacent to the radiator has been damaged by a malfunctioning air vent.
- The floor is covered by historically inappropriate sheet vinyl.
- Paint is severely deteriorated on the window sash.
- Paint is severely deteriorated on the sash of the arched window in the closet. One glass pane in this window is broken (Fig. 240).
- Door D3102 does not close properly.

240 Moisture damage to window in closet in Room 310.

Room 311

- Severe plaster cracks and separations of the plaster finish coat exist on the ceiling and all walls.
- The stair railing assembly is not secure.

Room 312

- A one-foot long section of floorboard is missing.
- Moderate plaster cracks exist on the walls and ceiling.
- The east masonry wall is deteriorated due to the installation of plumbing.

Room 313

- Moderate plaster cracks exist on the ceiling and all walls.
- The floorboard adjacent to door D3121 has been removed.

Room 314

- Moderate plaster cracks exist on the ceiling and all walls.
- The rim lock on door D3141 is loose.
- Paint is deteriorated on the window sash.
- The floor is covered by two sheets of linoleum.
- The rim latch on door D3142 is not operable.

Room 315

- Moderate plaster cracks exist on the ceiling and all walls.

Room 316

- Plaster damage and loss exist on the south wall.
- Ceiling plaster has been damaged by water at the south end of the room.
- Minor cracks exist on the other plaster walls.
- Paint on the window sash is deteriorated.

Room 317

- Moderate cracks exist on the plaster walls and ceiling.

Basement

The major building conservation problem in the basement is the serious deterioration of the perimeter wall surfaces that has been caused by the long-term migration of moisture through the foundation walls. Some surfaces appear to be more damaged than others but the general problem is pervasive. The bases of masonry bearing walls in the middle of the basement also exhibit some deterioration caused by rising damp. Poor site drainage and control of rainwater from the roof and in the window areaways over many years have contributed significantly to this problem.

Defective and obsolete heating systems have also deteriorated the building fabric, particularly the flooring and baseboards in the front hall.

Paint finishes throughout the basement are generally worn, dirty or peeling.

Room B01

- The baseboard is warped and detached along the south side of the wall, at the east end of hall.
- A two-foot section of baseboard is detached from the north wall, opposite the stair.
- The baseboard is loose along the north wall, at the west end of hall.
- Some floorboards are loose at the west end of hall.
- Minor plaster cracks and paint loss exist on the walls.
- Sections of the plaster ceiling are very deteriorated or missing and the wood lath is exposed.
- An historically inappropriate lighting valence exists along the north wall.
- Plaster is damaged on the south wall below the window, adjacent to the wine cellar entrance.
- The former furnace ventilation opening in the north wall needs to be properly restored.

Room B02

- Minor plaster cracks exist on the ceiling, cornice, and all walls.
- Paint and plaster have been damaged by the adjacent wall radiator in the southwest corner (Fig. 241). There is evidence of steam leaks on the radiator.
- Several elements of the black marble fireplace surround are cracked and displaced.
- Plywood patches on floor at east end of room indicate probable water damage to the floor surface beneath.
- Wood wainscot boards below windows are loose and deformed from water damage. This problem has been caused by poor water drainage in the window areaway over many years.
- Bifold window shutters do not operate freely.
- Paint on the window sashes is deteriorated.
- The latch mechanism to door B021 requires adjustment.

241 Plaster damaged by defective radiator in Room B02.

Room B03

- Moderate plaster cracks and paint loss exist on all walls.
- The base of the architrave to door B032 is deteriorated.
- The mortise lock to door B032 is inoperable.
- Plaster cracks and an historically inappropriate stipple finish exist on the ceiling.
- A major plaster loss and deterioration exist on the walls and ceiling in the southwest corner of the room and in the area of the removed hot-air furnace (Fig. 242).
- Historically inappropriate valence lighting exists around perimeter of the room.

242 Major plaster loss and damage on south wall of Room B03.

- Bifold window shutters are inoperable.
- An open joint exists between the window sill and frame.
- The latch to door B031 is inoperable and the door does not close properly.
- Inappropriate wiring and equipment exists in the southwest corner.

Room B04

- Minor plaster cracks exist on the walls and ceiling.
- Doors to the built-in cupboard do not close properly.

Room B05

- An historically inappropriate stipple finish exists on the plaster ceiling.
- Historically inappropriate valence lighting exists along the north wall.
- Minor separations of the plaster finish coat exist on all walls and the ceiling.
- Plaster is severely water-damaged below the window on the south wall.
- Bifold window shutters are not operable.
- Paint is deteriorated on the window sash and trim on the south wall.
- An historically inappropriate closet exists in the southeast corner.

Room B06

- Elements of the fireplace surround are severely deteriorated and displaced as a result of long-term moisture migration through the foundation wall.
- An historically inappropriate stipple finish exists on the plaster ceiling.
- Minor plaster cracks exist on the walls and ceiling.
- Woodwork and plaster are severely damaged adjacent to the wall-mounted radiator in the northeast corner. There is evidence of past leaks on this radiator.
- Bifold window shutters are not operable.
- Open joints exist between window sill and frame.
- Historically inappropriate wall-to-wall carpet covers the floor surface, which is damaged along the east wall.
- Stored items in the closet may interfere with the operation of the lift mechanism and pose a fire hazard.

Room B07

- The brownstone pier in the southwest corner and brickwork along the south wall are severely deteri-

243 Brownstone pier in Room B07 deteriorated by moisture migration.

orated as a result of long-term moisture migration through the foundation wall (Fig. 243).
- Access holes cut in the beaded-board ceiling to expose electrical equipment have not been covered.
- The hinged plywood board next to the ceiling is historically inappropriate.
- The wiring concealed by the ceiling panel is hazardous and inappropriate to this location.

Room B08

- Minor cracks exist in the stucco surface on the east wall.

Room B09

- Plaster is moderately to severely damaged on the north wall as a result of long-term moisture migration through the foundation wall (Fig. 244).

244 Plaster on walls of Room B09 damaged by moisture migration.

- Minor spalling due to moisture migration exists on the surface of the concrete floor.
- Major plaster deterioration on the ceiling has been temporarily stabilized by the attachment of a fiberboard covering.
- A nineteenth century iron pipe support hook has come loose from its position on the ceiling.
- The tin shower head needs conservation.

Room B10

- Since all walls are covered by recent furred-out plywood paneling, inspection of the underlying building fabric was not possible.
- A carpeted plywood floor has been installed on sleepers. The condition of the underlying floor is not known.
- The swing of the door has been modified.

Room B11

- Severe brick deterioration exists along lower sections of the north, south, and east walls as a result of long-term moisture migration. The most severe deterioration is located adjacent to the steam condensate return line located at the base of the north wall (Fig. 245).
- The original plaster ceiling has been replaced/reinforced with historically inappropriate ¼" plywood.
- Areas of the asphalt coating on the floor have been deteriorated by moisture migration.

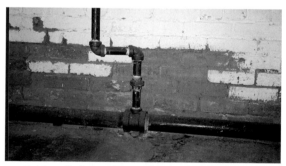

245 Brick walls damaged by moisture migration around condensate return line in Room B11.

Room B11A

- Moderate to severe deterioration of brickwork exists on the south, west and north walls as a result of long-term moisture migration.
- Historically inappropriate plywood covers the ceiling.

- This area has an accumulation of material that should be removed.

Room B12

- Minor plaster cracks exist on the ceiling.

Room B13

- Minor deterioration of brickwork exists on the foundation wall, caused by moisture migration.

Room B14

- Moderate deterioration to the brickwork occurs at the base of the north, south and west walls, caused by moisture migration.
- Minor spalling exists on concrete floor from moisture migration.

Wine Cellar

- The wood lintel and floor joist connections at the window opening on the south wall are severely deteriorated by moisture.
- Ends of joists pocketed in the north and south walls are deteriorated by moisture. The deteriorated joists are supported along both walls by shoring that was installed many years ago.
- Mortar in the masonry walls has deteriorated as a result of long-term moisture migration. There is no evidence of foundation stone displacement.
- Plaster is severely deteriorated on the south wall at top of stair to wine cellar, as a result of moisture migration.
- The wood storage bins are missing many elements and the slat door is removed.

CARRIAGE HOUSE — EXTERIOR

On the east façade, mortar joints in the brickwork have been repointed over the years with hard portland cement mortar. Cracks in the brickwork have also been repaired with this hard mortar mix. The appearance of this work is unsightly, since the pointing mortar does not match the original surrounding mortar in color, texture and joint profile.

In addition to this aesthetic concern, repointing with hard portland cement mortar can severely damage the masonry, since it is much harder than both the original lime-based mortar and the bricks themselves. Mortar in historic masonry walls must be flexible enough to accommodate the forces that are normally exerted within the walls caused by temperature changes, moisture migration and settlement. Accordingly, historic bricks bonded or pointed with hard portland cement mortar are likely to crack or split as temperatures increase and decrease. Likewise, changing temperatures can cause the bond between the mortar and brick to break. The resulting gaps allow water to penetrate the wall and cause further damage.

Moreover, the relatively impermeable portland cement mortar prevents moisture vapor from passing through the façade. Trapped moisture vapor will condense and freeze as temperatures drop, resulting in forces that may cause bricks to split.

Severe deterioration occurs on the sandstone foundation and brickwork along the base of the east wall of the Carriage House (Fig. 246). Stone surfaces have flaked off and bricks have disintegrated. This deterioration has been caused by the capillary movement of water through the masonry, and has been aggravated by the use of deicing salts on the adjacent brick paved walk. Contributing to this problem has also been the poor drainage of rainwater in this area of the courtyard. Efforts to patch damaged areas of the sandstone foundation with portland cement mortar have actually accelerated the deterioration process.

Although the cornice was repaired when the building was reroofed in the 1980s, a section of the soffit that abuts the Carr building appears to be damaged by water. This damage may be caused by roof leaks associated with ice dams forming at the roof eaves during the winter.

On the south façade, mortar joints in the brickwork are generally eroded. If water is allowed to penetrate the brickwork through these open joints, destabilization of the wall may occur. The most damaging action is caused by freezing water in the masonry that expands as it freezes and exerts forces within the wall.

On the west elevation, the sandstone sills of the windows have delaminated. A crack also exists in the brickwork over the north door. Water can enter the wall through this opening and eventually cause further damage. The corrugated leader on the south end of the façade is not securely fastened to the building. Generally, all of the woodwork will need to be painted in the near future.

CARRIAGE HOUSE — INTERIOR

First Floor

- Cracks exist on the concrete floor. These cracks are probably the result of normal shrinkage that occurred during the concrete curing process, rather than related to any structural problems. Structural concrete slabs are typically reinforced with a grid of welded wire fabric and then scored on the surface with control joints to resist shrinkage cracking.

Second Floor

- The wood plate over the southwest window has deteriorated from a roof leak.
- The end of the rafter over the southwest door has deteriorated (Fig. 247).
- The wood lintel over the southwest door is deformed and deteriorated. This lintel was also seriously dam-

246 Severe deterioration of brickwork and sandstone at base of east carriage house façade.

247 Carriage house roof rafter is deteriorated over southwest door. Lintel has been damaged by the installation of a modern lifting mechanism.

aged and weakened by the installation of the track for the modern hoist mechanism in recent times (Fig. 10).

- The wood plate and end of the rafter have deteriorated above the northwest window.
- On the west side of the building, the fifth rafter from the north has split at the bird's-mouth cut.
- A vertical crack exists in the brickwork on the east wall above the stairs.

- Generally, the floor framing is understructured for the weight of the roof framing system it supports.

Cellar

- Stone treads and brick risers are deteriorated from rising damp. This condition could pose a safety hazard.

59 Second Street: General Recommendations for Repair and Restoration

Douglas G. Bucher and William P. Palmer

THE PRINCIPAL GOAL of this historic structure report is to provide a framework for guiding the current, as well as the future, restoration efforts. The historic structure report process will help to ensure that the integrity of the building is not compromised and that its remaining historic fabric is preserved intact while necessary modifications are made to accommodate new heating, plumbing, electrical, and other systems. The twentieth century modifications that have compromised the historic character of the building should be reversed. Restoration work should be based on sound physical and documentary evidence, so that the work can be carried out in a manner that is historically accurate.

Approach to Restoration Work

The restoration of the house, carriage house, and site should be approached from a curatorial standpoint: the buildings should be treated with the same care that is given to a rare painting or valuable piece of furniture. Its restoration and long-term care should be entrusted only to building restoration specialists who have been trained in the conservation of historic building fabric. Trained craftsmen develop a sensitivity to historic materials and the ways in which they were used and combined. They understand that inappropriate, expedient solutions often cause greater problems and result in treatments that are irreversible. Trained craftsmen are willing to take the time to find the appropriate materials and solutions needed to do the work correctly. It is also important to realize that accurate restoration work often will be difficult and require extraordinary dedication to excellence. When compromises need to be made in the installation of mechanical systems, the highest priority should be given to the preservation of the building's historic fabric.

The installation of new utility systems has often been the most damaging renovation activity in historic buildings, partly because overly sophisticated systems designed to provide unnecessarily high levels of comfort for the occupants and collections were installed. Such systems often require large amounts of space for equipment in the building and cause the destruction of much original building fabric in order to conceal piping and ductwork.

In almost all cases, the introduction of a new heating and ventilating system will have some visual effect on the historic interiors. In order to minimize these effects, a new system should be designed to provide acceptable comfort levels, but should not be expected to provide the highest levels of heating and air conditioning that would be found in an entirely new structure. New utility systems should be designed by engineers who specialize in the insertion of modern systems in historic buildings. This design work should be directed by restoration architects to ensure that the integrity of the building is protected through the selection of the least intrusive systems. Original building fabric, even that which is normally concealed, should not be disturbed or removed for the installation of mechanical systems which have a life expectancy of little more than a generation. The systems must be skillfully designed so that they provide adequate levels of comfort while meeting these building conservation requirements.

The exposed pipes and radiators of the existing steam system are now part of the historic character of the building and although at the end of their usefulness they must be preserved. All of the utilities installed by the Harts and Cluetts have historical value and should be preserved when feasible and remain as in situ artifacts, albeit disconnected and unused. Concern for the preservation of all original building fabric should be extended to other sections of the building such as windows, doors and hardware, plaster walls and ceilings, and floorboards. Where windows need to be repaired in order to function properly, all original components should be preserved and stabilized, using consolidants where required. In the same manner, damaged original plaster should be patched. No entire wall or ceiling surfaces should be removed because it may be easier for workers to provide entirely new surfaces. Original wood trim should not be disturbed or removed. Where damage has occurred, the elements should be stabilized and repaired in situ.

59 Second Street retains many elements of the original construction and significant later nineteenth and twentieth century changes and additions. These elements must be carefully preserved during the restoration work.

Detailed recommendations concerning the restoration of the interior spaces will be developed in conjunction with the Furnishings Plan Study to be undertaken in the near future, as well as with the wealth of information presented in this monograph.

The basis of any interior restoration program is a determination of how the house and its site will be interpreted. At 59 Second Street, this must recognize the contributions of all of the owners, the Harts and Cluetts, as well as the presence of the Rensselaer County Historical Society after 1953.

The most challenging task will be the integration of all of these stories into the "Marble House in Second Street."

The following general recommendations are primarily concerned with the work that is necessary to insure the long-term preservation of the House and Carriage House.

HOUSE AND CARRIAGE HOUSE EXTERIOR

There is no evidence of significant structural problems on the exterior of either the house or carriage house that threaten public safety. Nevertheless, a significant number of important problems that threaten the physical integrity of the buildings must be corrected to prevent further deterioration of historic fabric and preserve the buildings for future generations.

SITE DRAINAGE

Certainly the most serious long-term threat to the Hart-Cluett House and carriage house continues to be the penetration of rainwater through the foundation walls around both buildings. To correct this problem, a comprehensive analysis of existing conditions must be undertaken which will involve a series of probes in the problem areas. After the causes are determined a series of strategies to control rainwater drainage from the roof and on the ground need to be developed.

On the east elevation of the house, the sidewalk around the base of the elm tree must be lowered to restore proper drainage of water away from the building and toward the curb. The extent of root penetration through the building's foundation wall and under the basement floor and window areaway must also be determined. It is possible that invasive roots may be interfering with the proper drainage of the areaways.

Window areaway drain lines should be examined to determine their condition and direction, if in fact they do exist. Preferably, they should be connected to the City's storm system. Likewise, the two rainwater leaders on the east façade should also be connected to drain lines below grade that lead to the storm system.

On the other three house façades and on the east carriage house façade, the full extent of damage caused by the impervious pavers must be examined. Physical probes through the paver surface must be done to determine the exact composition of the brick pavement system, the presence of an existing underground drainage system and the condition of the foundation wall below grade. Brick-paved surfaces should also be examined for surface puddling and drainage patterns during periods of rain. A new system of underground drainage may be necessary.

MASONRY

Marble elements on the east façade of the house must be cleaned to remove harmful soiling and return the color of the marble to as near its original appearance as possible. The selected cleaning method must remove soiling deposits without harming the composition or tooling of the stonework. Normally, marble masonry can be effectively cleaned using alkaline-based chemical products, especially formulated for use on marble. Field testing must be conducted first to determine the gentlest and most effective treatment.

Chips and holes in marble surfaces should be patched by using either "dutchman" or "plastic" repair techniques. Cracks in marble should be repaired using epoxy resin designed for this purpose.

Movement detected in the marble architrave of the outer main entrance should be further investigated and repaired as needed.

Displaced stonework at the east window areaways must be relaid and pointed.

Open joints in marble, sandstone or brickwork on all façades of the house and carriage house must be re-pointed with lime-rich mortar to match the original in composition, color, texture, hardness and profile. Deteriorated or hard portland cement mortar must also be removed from brickwork and then repointed.

Deteriorated or cracked bricks on the house and carriage house should be replaced with new bricks that match the originals in color, size, and texture. Damaged or delaminated faces of sandstone sills, lintels, and foundation stone should be redressed. Face bedded sandstone may need to be reinforced with threaded rods and injected epoxy resin. Crumbling sandstone sills on the carriage house may also be candidates for treatment with stone consolidants.

A decision must be made, based on the interpretation of the house as well as maintenance considerations, whether to paint the brick surfaces that were historically painted white.

METALWORK

All old layers of paint and rust should be removed from surfaces of the metal railings and south passage gates on the east façade of the house, followed by the application of a rust-inhibiting primer before repainting. Missing or badly damaged metal elements should be replicated using original construction materials and assembly techniques.

The urn newels may need to be reset in the marble pedestals in a manner that will prevent additional damage to the marble.

The sheet-brass caps should be restored to the tops of the front entrance handrails.

WINDOWS

Deteriorated paint should be removed from all wood frames and sash. Damaged or deteriorated wood elements must be renewed using dutchman repair techniques. All window glazing putty should be replaced. Prime and then paint all wood surfaces. Apply a sealant to prepared joints between wood window trim and masonry openings.

Wood elements of the bay window on the south façade may require complete replacement due to their advanced state of decay. This window should be inspected for active infestation by wood damaging insects.

EAST ENTRANCE

Paint build-up should be carefully removed from all wood surfaces of the door and architrave to restore the appearance of their ornamental details. Panel moldings on the doors should also be refastened. Missing lead elements on the fanlight sidelights should be replicated.

Cracked plaster surfaces on the sides of the recessed entry should be repaired.

WEST PORCH

The porch needs to be repaired and painted and the louvered doors should be repaired and reinstalled to the opening beneath the porch.

ROOF BALUSTRADE

The correct number of turned balusters should be restored to this important architectural feature.

SHUTTERS

The extant shutters should be repaired and painted and any necessary new shutters should be fabricated so that these important elements can be restored to the east façade.

SIDEWALK

The sidewalks in front of 59 Second Street and the Carr Building should be restored to slate.

SIGNAGE

The flag should be moved to a location at the Carr Building.

Except for the small bronze plaque that identifies the house and its date of completion all signage should be restricted to the Carr Building. This includes any signage that might appear on the iron fence at 59 Second Street.

CARRIAGE HOUSE

Consideration should be given to the recreation of the balustrade missing from the east façade of the carriage house and for the restoration of the arched opening and pair of large doors formerly at the south end of that façade.

The metal louver located in the second-floor window of the west façade should be removed and the correct sash restored.

HOUSE—INTERIOR

Utility Systems

Existing heating, plumbing, and electrical systems should be replaced by new equipment that is engineered to meet the specific needs of this house museum.

Historic components of the heating and plumbing systems, such as radiators, piping, lavatories, and water closets should be preserved when feasible and disconnected, drained of water and retained in place as important evidence of the building's evolution.

Electrical requirements for a house museum should be minimal. Disconnected historic wiring and fixtures should also remain in place, while historic fixtures that are to be reused should be carefully conserved and rewired.

Exposed components for the obsolete intrusion and fire detection system should be removed.

The feasibility of installing a sprinkler system should be investigated.

First Floor

Room 101

- Repair plaster cracks on ceiling, cornice, and walls.
- Repair loose panel moldings on door D101.
- Replace glazing compound on sidelights and fanlight over door D1011 and conserve any damaged original or old glass. Replace missing elements of fanlight.
- Repair loose wood strip floor boards.
- Conserve and refinish worn areas of wood floor.
- Clean and conserve wallpaper if it is to remain in situ.
- Rewire electric wall bracket if it is to remain in situ.

Room 102

- Repair damaged sash of south window.
- Tighten loose balusters on stair and repair handrail above newel post.
- Repair architrave of door D1062 when center block is reinstalled in Room 104.
- Repair loose wood strip floor boards and conserve and refinish worn areas.
- Clean and conserve wallpaper if it remains in situ.
- Rewire suspended electrical fixture.

Room 103

- Repair and replace damaged plaster on ceiling and cornice.

- Repair plaster cracks on ceiling.
- Repair deteriorated window elements.
- Repair and adjust bifold window shutters to operating condition.
- Replace plaster patching in ceiling medallion.
- Conserve and refinish worn floor surfaces.

Room 104

- Restore architrave and door to former opening in the south wall.
- Repair and adjust bifold window shutters to operating condition.
- Replace plaster patching in ceiling medallion.
- Repair south wall if Marshall portrait is removed.

Room 105

- Remove vinyl floor tiles and underlayment. Determine condition of wood strip floor beneath and repair or refinish as required.
- Restore door opening in the north wall.
- Remove post-1953 wood dado material.

Room 106

- Cover fanlight opening above door D1061.
- Adjust doors D1061 and D1062 to close properly without binding at threshold.
- Repair damaged wall, ceiling and cornice plaster.
- Repair loose wood strip floor boards.
- Conserve and restore finish on worn areas of wood flooring.
- Restore architrave and door to former opening in the north wall.

Room 107

- Repair plaster cracks on ceiling and walls.
- Restore finish on worn areas of wood flooring.

Room 108

- Inspect original plaster ceiling above suspended homasote surface and determine restoration needs.
- Remove modern sheet flooring and underlayment. Investigate condition and type of original floor beneath and determine restoration needs.
- Repair mortise door lock.

Room 109

- Remove mechanical equipment and bulletin board from the north wall.
- Repair plaster cracks on ceiling and walls.

- Restore finish on worn areas of flooring.
- Repair deteriorated window elements.
- Repair and adjust bifold window shutters to operating condition.
- May need to fabricate new mahogany door if the current door is restored to its correct location in Room 104.

Room 110

- Remove vinyl floor tiles and underlayment. Determine condition of wood floor beneath and repair or refinish as required.
- Remove homasote that covers the ceiling. Investigate condition of plaster ceiling to determine needed repairs.
- Repair plaster cracks. Remove loose areas of plaster finish coat and replace with new plaster.
- Replace window counterweight rope.
- Replace broken glass in fanlight over door D1102 and refasten corner blocks on architrave.
- Open and restore doorway in the south wall.
- Restore and reinstall Cluett-era pantry, cabinetry and sink.

Room 111

- Replace areas of water damaged plaster on ceiling and walls.
- Repair plaster cracks on walls, ceiling and cornice.
- Repair deteriorated window elements.
- Investigate possibility of restoring missing mantel to west wall.

Room 112

- Remove areas of loose plaster finish coat on walls and replace with new plaster.
- Remove loose paint from wood ceiling and restore finish.
- Reconstruct and restore cupboards along the east wall.

Room 113

- Remove vinyl sheet flooring and underlayment. Investigate condition of original floor beneath to determine restoration needs.
- Repair plaster cracks on the walls and ceiling.
- Remove areas of loose plaster finish coat on walls and ceiling and replace with new plaster.
- Remove cabinet and sink and restore to original location in Room 110.

- Reconstruct original pantry shelving on east and west walls.
- Remove inappropriate lighting.

Room 114

- Remove areas of loose plaster finish coat on walls and ceiling and replace with new plaster.
- Remove post-1953 exterior door and restore Cluett-era door.
- Restore basement door to original position at head of stairway.

Second Floor

Room 201

- Remove inappropriate wallpaper.
- Repair and adjust bifold shutters on window to operating condition.
- Restore finish on worn areas of wood flooring.
- Repair buckled wood strip floor boards.
- Remove inappropriate electrified gasolier and electrical wall bracket.
- Remove brass dedication plaque from various room doors.

Room 202

- Adjust built-in cabinet doors to close properly.
- Repair plaster cracks on ceiling.
- Remove post-1953 shelving from west wall.

Room 203

- Remove inappropriate wallpaper.
- Replace water-damaged areas of plaster on ceiling and cornice.
- Repair water-damaged window trim and restore bifold shutters to operating condition.
- Repair water-damaged original flooring.
- Restore dado rail to proper position if it is to remain in situ.
- Remove inappropriate electrified gasolier.
- Further explore room for evidence of Cluett-era bathroom fixtures.

Room 204

- Replace water-damaged areas of plaster ceiling, cornice and walls.

- Repair water-damaged window trim and restore bi-fold shutters to operating condition.
- Remove oriental rug now glued to flooring by deteriorated carpet pad.
- Conserve and restore floor finish.
- Remove inappropriate lighting.

Room 205

- Repair plaster cracks on ceiling.
- Reinstall two doors to closets.
- Remove inappropriate wallpaper.
- Remove dangerous electric lighting fixtures.

Room 206

- Repair plaster cracks on ceiling and cornice.
- Repair and adjust bifold shutters to operating condition.
- Remove inappropriate wallpaper.
- Remove electrified gasolier.

Room 207

- Replace water-damaged plaster on ceiling, cornice and walls.
- Restore damaged raffle flower on corner block of door architrave.
- Further explore room for evidence of Hart-era plumbing fixtures.

Room 208

- Repair plaster cracks on ceiling, cornice and walls.

Room 209

- Replace water-damaged areas and cracks in plaster on ceiling, cornice and walls.
- Repair water-damaged window trim and bifold shutters. Restore shutters to operating condition.
- Conserve and restore floor finish.

Room 210

- Remove areas of loose plaster finish coat on walls and ceiling, and replace with new plaster.
- Patch access hole in wood floor with similar material.
- Repair wood pipe chase cover.
- Repair broken window pane.
- Restore doors to openings in the south and west walls.

Room 211

- Remove acoustic tiles from ceiling. Investigate condition of plaster ceiling above to determine restoration needs.
- Remove sheet vinyl and underlayment to determine condition of flooring material beneath.
- Remove loose areas of plaster finish coat on walls and replace with new plaster.
- Repair plaster cracks on walls.
- Repair damaged wood wainscot boards.
- Further investigate locations for Cluett-era bathroom fixtures.
- Remove inappropriate lighting.

Room 212

- Tighten joints on stair railing assembly.
- Refasten loose floor boards.
- Remove loose areas of plaster finish coat on walls and replace with new plaster.
- Replace broken window pane.
- Remove inappropriate light fixture.
- Restore dado to west opening.

Room 213

- Remove loose areas of plaster finish coat on walls and replace with new plaster.
- Repair plaster cracks on the ceiling, cornice and walls.
- Refasten hinge on door D2132.
- Remove inappropriate light fixture.

Room 214

- Remove loose areas of plaster finish coat on walls and ceiling and replace with new plaster.

Room 215

- Remove loose areas of plaster finish coat on walls and ceiling and replace with new plaster.
- Repair plaster cracks on ceiling and walls.
- Adjust closet door D2152 to close properly.

Room 216

- Replace water-damaged plaster on walls.
- Repair plaster cracks on walls and ceiling.
- Repair latch mechanism to door D2161.
- Repair damaged floor surface and conserve decorative painted surface.

Room 217

- Remove loose areas of plaster finish coat on walls and ceiling and replace with new plaster.

Third Floor

Room 301

- Replace water-damaged plaster on the cornice and ceiling.
- Repair plaster cracks on ceiling.
- Refinish worn areas of the wood floor.
- Remove folding door at stairway opening.

Room 301A

- Patch holes in plaster walls.

Room 302

- Replace water-damaged plaster on the ceiling.
- Repair plaster cracks on the ceiling and cornice.
- Repair deteriorated window sash elements.
- Refinish worn areas of the wood floor.
- Remove inappropriate light fixture.

Room 303

- Repair plaster cracks on ceiling and walls and surfaces in southwest corner.
- Repair deteriorated window sash elements.
- Disconnect water supply to plumbing fixtures at basement level.

Room 304

- Repair plaster cracks on the cornice and ceiling.
- Remove loose areas of the plaster finish coat on the ceiling and replace with new plaster.
- Repair deteriorated window sash elements.
- Refinish worn areas of the wood floor.
- Remove inappropriate lighting.
- Remove plywood shelving units.

Room 305

- Patch holes in plaster walls.

Room 306

- Refinish worn areas of the wood floor.
- Remove inappropriate lighting.
- This room may become a connecting passage to the Carr Building, in which case a new doorway will be opened in the north wall.

Room 307

- Repair plaster cracks on the plaster walls.

Room 308

- Replace water-damaged plaster on the ceiling.

Room 309

- Repair plaster cracks on the ceiling and cornice.
- Replace water-damaged plaster on the east knee wall and convert temporary inspection access hole into permanent opening for future inspections.

Room 310

- Repair plaster cracks on the ceiling and cornice.
- Repair steam-damaged wainscot panel.
- Remove sheet vinyl flooring. Investigate condition of floor below to determine restoration needs.
- Repair deteriorated areas of arched window in closet and replace broken pane.
- Adjust door D3102 to close properly.

Room 311

- Repair plaster cracks and replace loose areas of plaster finish coat on the ceiling and all walls.
- Tighten joints on stair railing assembly.

Room 312

- Replace missing floorboard.
- Repair plaster cracks on ceiling and walls.
- Repair pipe penetration in east brick wall.

Room 313

- Repair plaster cracks on ceiling and all walls.
- Replace missing floorboard.
- Repair deteriorated window sash elements

Room 314

- Repair plaster cracks on ceiling and all walls.
- Tighten latch on door D3141.
- Repair latch on door D3142.
- Repair deteriorated window sash elements.

Room 315

- Repair plaster cracks on ceiling and all walls.
- Repair deteriorated window sash elements.

Room 316

- Repair or replace areas of damaged plaster on walls and ceiling.
- Repair cracked plaster on walls.

- Prepare and paint window sash and trim.

Room 317

- Repair plaster cracks on walls and ceiling.

Basement

Room B01

- Repair and reattach loose and deformed baseboards.
- Tighten loose floorboards.
- Repair or replace damaged plaster on walls including opening into Room B03.
- Repair or replace damaged plaster on ceiling, remove inappropriate repairs.
- Remove inappropriate lighting.

Room B02

- Repair plaster cracks on the walls and ceiling.
- Replace water-damaged plaster. Before this work begins the rainwater drainage problem at the east side of the building must be solved.
- Repair cracks on marble fireplace.
- Repair damaged floorboards and wainscot boards at east side of room.
- Repair and adjust bifold window shutters to operating condition.
- Remove inappropriate electric ceiling fixture.

Room B03

- Repair base of architrave to door B032
- Repair latches on doors B032 and B031.
- Remove stipple finish on ceiling and repaint.
- Repair plaster cracks on walls and ceiling.
- Replace areas of plaster loss and damage on the walls and ceiling.
- Repair bifold window shutters to operating condition.
- Repair open joints on window trim.
- Remove inappropriate lighting.
- Remove mechanical equipment and cover panel from southwest corner.

Room B04

- Repair plaster cracks.
- Adjust built-in cupboard doors.
- Remove post-1953 shelving.

Room B05

- Remove stipple finish from ceiling.
- Repair plaster cracks and replace deteriorated plaster on walls.
- Repair and adjust bifold window shutters to operating condition.
- Remove post-1953 closet in southwest corner.
- Remove surface that conceals the steam heating pipe.
- Remove inappropriate lighting.

Room B06

- Restore displaced and deteriorated elements of the fireplace surround.
- Remove stipple finish from ceiling.
- Repair or replace damaged woodwork and plaster in northeast corner.
- Repair cracked plaster on walls and ceiling.
- Repair and adjust bifold window shutters to operable condition.
- Repair open joints in window trim.
- Remove carpet and restore wood flooring.
- Remove stored items from the closet that contains the lift mechanism.

Room B07

- Remove wiring and conduit from ceiling.
- Cover open access holes in wood ceiling and remove hinged plywood panel.
- Remove loose surfaces of brick and repaint.
- The deteriorated brownstone pier may require stone consolidation treatment.

Room B08

- Repair cracks in the stucco wall surface.

Room B09

- Replace water-damaged plaster on walls.
- Restore or replace damaged plaster ceiling.
- Reinstall iron pipe support to ceiling.
- Carefully conserve the sheet metal shower head.

Room B10

- Remove modern wall paneling and flooring and inspect condition of original walls and floor beneath. Restore those surfaces.
- Rehang door in correct manner.

Room B11

- Remove plywood from ceiling and repair plaster.
- Repair deteriorated masonry wall surfaces after moisture problems are corrected.
- Carefully conserve fragments and evidence of speaking tube system.
- Remove inappropriate lighting.

Room B11A

- Remove plywood from ceiling and repair plaster.
- Repair west wall where steam pipes enter and exit the basement.
- Carefully maintain evidence of speaking tube system.

Room B12

- Repair plaster cracks on the ceiling.

Room B13

- Repair brick wall surface after moisture problems are corrected.

Room B14

- Repair brick wall surfaces after moisture problems are corrected.
- Remove any built-in post-1953 shelving and storage units.
- Remove inappropriate lighting.

Wine Cellar

- Replace or repair wood lintel over window and repair connections to floor joists.

- Repair deteriorated ends of joists and pocket into masonry walls, as originally constructed. Remove modern shoring.
- Repair and restore the wine storage cage including the reinstallation of the slat door.
- Repair and reinstall door to closet under the staircase.

CARRIAGE HOUSE — INTERIOR

First Floor

- Patch cracks in concrete floor.
- Restore original arched door openings in the east wall.
- Remove inappropriate lighting.
- Conserve grained wood paneling on the east wall.

Second Floor

- Reinforce sections of the deteriorated wood plate over west windows.
- Splice new ends on deteriorated rafters.
- Restore missing braces between posts and purlins.
- Remove modern lift mechanism at southwest door. Repair and reinforce damaged wood lintel.
- Remove fan and louvers from west window; restore sash to opening.

Cellar

- Repair and replace deteriorated stone treads and brick risers on stair.

APPENDICES

I: Genealogies

    A: HART FAMILY

    B: CLUETT FAMILY

II: Inventories

    A: RICHARD P. HART, 1844

    B: BETSEY A. HART, 1886

III: Life Chronology and Architectural Works
    of Martin Euclid Thompson

IV: Historic American Buildings Survey Drawings

59 Second Street Owners Genealogy

A. HART FAMILY GENEALOGY

Philip Hart   m.   **Susanna Akins**   **William Howard**   m.   **Rebecca French White**
(1748/9–1837)   (1759–?)   (1777–1845)   (1779–1870)
    10 children including   1 child (see Betsey Amelia Howard) below

Richard Philip Hart   m. 1800   1) Phebe Bloom
(1780–1843)   (died c. 1801)

        Phebe Bloom Hart
        (1800–1813)

            m. 1805   2) Delia Maria Dole

            m. 1816   **3) Betsey Amelia Howard**
                    (1798–1886)
            14 children, 1 died in infancy

        Mary Amelia Hart   m. 1837   Harrison Durkee
        (1816–1884)   (1812–1886)
                7 children

        Harriet Howard Hart   m. 1836   Ezra Thompson Doughty
        (1818–1870)   (died 1843)
                2 children

        Phebe Bloom Hart   m. 1838   David Thomas Vail
        (1819–1870)   (died 1882)
                4 children

        William Howard Hart   m. 1847   Mary Elizabeth Lane
        (1820–1883)   (1823–1899)
                no children

        Elizabeth Hart   m. 1843   John Augustus Griswold
        (1822–1891)   (1818–1872)
                7 children

A. HART FAMILY GENEALOGY *(continued)*

Jane Rebecca Hart   m. 1844   Samuel Gale Doughty
(1824–1861)   (died 1869)
                          5 children

Richard Philip Hart, Jr.   m. 1853   Maria Davis Tillman
(1826–1892)   (1829–1886)
                          6 children

Joseph Moss Hart   m. 1852   Georgiana Riddell
(1827–1885)   (no dates available)
                  2 children, died in infancy

Susan Hart   m. 1855   William Shields
(1829–1900)   (1826–1880)
                          2 children

Caroline Hart   m. 1851   Hamilton Leroy Shields
(1831–1899)   (died 1889)
                          8 children

Julia Ann Hart   m. 1856   William Fletcher Burden
(1833–1887)   (1830–1867)
                          5 children

Frances Hart   m. 1858   Samuel M. Vail
(1835–1921)   (died 1889)
                          3 children

Sarah Wool Hart
(1838–1892)

Austin Spencer Hart
(1841–1842)

B. CLUETT FAMILY GENEALOGY

William Cluett   m.   **Ann Bywater**
(1806–1890)   (1805–1876)
       7 children including

George Bywater Cluett m. (1863) **1)** Sarah Bontecou Golden
(1838–1912)   (1840–1864)
             1 child, died in infancy
        m. (1867) **2) Amanda Rockwell Fisher**
                   (1847–1918)
        8 children, 2 died in infancy

    Walter Herbert Cluett
    (1870–1942)

    Nellie Agnes Cluett
    (1871–1959)

    George Rockwell Cluett
    (1868–1868)

    Bessie Louise Cluett
    (1872–c. 1873)

    E. Harold Cluett
    (1874–1954)

    George Bywater Cluett, Jr
    (1876–1939)

    Alfonzo Rockwell Cluett
    (1877–1900)

    Beatrice Cluett
    (1886–1973)

Edmund Cluett m. **Mary Alice Stone**
(1840–1907)   (1847–1937)
      2 children including

Albert Edmund Cluett m. Caroline Ide
(1872–1949)   (1873–1963)
         4 children

    John Girvin Cluett
    (1906–1960)

    Edmund Cluett II
    (1908–1979)

    Albert E. Cluett, Jr.
    (1910–1960)

    Richard Ide Cluett
    (1914–1967)

APPENDIX II

A. LISTING FROM RICHARD P. HART INVENTORY LEDGER, 1844
HART PAPERS

NOTE: When Richard P. Hart died December 27, 1843, he left a large family with several minor children as well as his widow, Betsey. This inventory not only documents the contents of 59 Second Street, but also gives a good idea of the extent of his investments, land holdings and stocks. The printed page at front lists William Howard, Executor &c, with aid of Alanson Douglas and Amos S. Perry, Appraisers as doing the inventory, dated August 31st, 1844.

Bank Stock	# shares	$/share	Appr	par value	Appr
Troy City Bank, Troy	565	$50.	100%	28,250	$28,250.
Merchants & Mechanics, Troy	100	$50.	95%	5,000	5,000
Farmer's Bank, Troy	36	$40.	100%	1,440	1,440
Bank of Troy	760	$20.	100%	15,200	15,200
Howard Trust & Bkg Co.	334	$100	67%	33,400	22,378
Cash Deposited in HBT sub to 5%int				49,000	49,000
Adams Bank, N Adams (MA?)	30	$100	80%	3,000	2,400
Rochester City Bank	28	$100	100%	2,800	2,800
Bank of Vergennes (VT)	128	$50	100%	6,400	6,400
Union Bank, New York	400	$50	115.5%	20,000	20,000
Dutchess Co. Bank Po'keepsie	80	$50	50%	2,000	2,000
Clinton Co. Bank, Plattsbg	50	$100			Nothing
					$156,718.

Miscellaneous Stock	# shares	$/share	Appr	par value	Appr
Schy & Sar RR Co	118	$100	45%	$11,800	5,310
Utica & Schy do	25	$100	126%	2,500	3,150
Troy Turnpike & RR	10			1,684	Nothing
Sandlake & Nassau Turnpike	40	$20	20%	800	160
Watervliet Turnpike	61	$90	100%	5,490	6,100
Troy & Sandlake Tpk	140	$16	10%	2,240	2,464
Schagh & Lansbg Tpk	50	$25	50%	1,250	625
NY & Albany RR	35		75%	835	626.25
Rens & Sar Ins.	220	$11	100	2,420	2,420
Keesville Iron Manufg	300	$20	100	6,000	6,000
Steamer Jonas C. Heartt	1	$500	60%	500	300
Troy & NY SteamBt Assoc	128	$100	50%	12,800	6,400
Troy House Assoc.	6	$500	100	3,000	3,000
Ohio 6%State Stock		$5000	100%		5,000
Indiana 5% State stock		$8000	44%		3,520
Troy City 7% stock		$22000	100%		22,000
Southern Life & Trust Co.	20				nothing
Saratoga & Wash'n RRCo	20				do
Renn & Saratoga do	100				do
Pittstown Turnpike Co	5				do
Dutchess Whaling Co	56				do
Troy Library Assn	1				do
					$67,075.25

Mortgages & Bonds (43 items)

Value listed as $80,150.81

Bills Receivable (77 items)

Value listed as $103,572.87

Protested Bills (19 items)

Value listed as $1,787.25

Book Balances

Value listed as $140,877.78

Judgements

Value listed $7273.10

Total assets of Estate of Richard P. Hart $557,455.06

Liabilities against Estate of Richard P. Hart $ 36,241.47
Value listed as
Total Value of Estate of Richard P. Hart $521,213.59

Not included in the value of estate
Household Inventory
Value listed as $2,445.00

Inventory of Personal Property in the House of RP Hart, dec'd

	Appraisal
In Parlors	
Carpets $50. Druggets $5. Rugs $12.	$ 67
1 Sofa $30. 2 Couches $40. $1 Side Board $40	110
1 Piano, Cover & Stool $100 1 Table $10	110
1 Centre Table $20 1 Rocking Chair $10	30
2 Arm chairs $20 2 Window seats $10	30
10 Chairs $25 2 do $5	30
2 Pier Tables $30 Curtains & fixtures $30	60
2 4 light candelabras $6 1 6 light do $6	12
1 Astral lamp $1 2 Chandeliers $100	101
2 Nest Tables $5 1 Clock $30	35
2 Girandoles $15 3 Lamp Girondoles $30	45
1 Glass Girandole $10 1 Sett Waiters $5	15
2 Mirrors $50 4 Paintings $10	15
1 Fender $2 Shovel & Poker $1 Snuffer $1	4
In Hall	
Oil Cloth $20 Table & Cover $15 4 Chairs $4	39
2 Lamps $5 1 Stove $15 1 Table $20	40
Library	
Carpet $15 Table & Cover $10 Sofa $10	35
5 Chairs $5 1 Sewing Chair $5 Rug $1	11
Looking Glass $10 2 Candlesticks $2 Chart $1	13
Book case & Books $75 Work Table $5	80
Dining Room	
Carpet $15 Dining Table $25	40
Side Board & Furniture $50 8 Chairs $12	62
High Chair $1 Table & Cover $10 Portrait $20	31
2 Pictures $5 Shovel & Tongs $1 Curtains $10	16
2 Alabaster Jars $3 2 Candlesticks $2	5
Stair Carpets $10 Hall carpet $10	20
Wardrobe	5

Back Chamber

Bed, Bedding & Bedsteads $50 Carpets $10	60
Bureau $10 Dressing Case $10	20
Wash Stand & furniture $15 Stove $5	20
Lamp $2 Stand & Cover $3 2 figures $1	6
5 Chairs $7 3 Pictures $2	9

Carpet &c in Closet between Chambers	2

Continued
Brot forward

Front Chamber

Bedstead, Bed & Bedding $100 Carpet $20	120
4 Chairs $5 Dressing Case $30 Bureau $10	45
Stand $5 2 Candlesticks $10 Ornaments $10	25
2 Portraits $10 1 Psyche Glass $20	30

Bed Room over Hall

Carpet $2 Bureau $2 Chair $0	4

Bedroom over Library

Carpet $5 Bed & Beding [*sic*] $20 Bureau $5	30
Dressing Case $15 Washstand &c $4	19
3 Chairs $3 Stand $3 Stand with Glass $3	8

Howard's Room

Bedstead, Bed & Bedding $30 Dressing case $15	45
Stove $1 Washstand $3 Table $3	7
3 Chairs $3 Carpet $3 Curtains $1	7

Linen &c in Pantry in Hall 2d Story	100

Bed Room below

Carpet $5 Bedstead, bed & bedding $30	35
11 Chairs $11 Book Case $10 Dressing Case $15	36
Washstand $5 2 Candlesticks $5 2 Lamps $2 2 Curtains $2	14

Silver ware, Forks & Spoons, &c	250

Crockery, Glass & China Ware	100

Rooms in Back Building

Bed, Bedding &c $10 Carpet $2 Chair $1 Carpet $2	15
Table $1 Hall Carpet $1 Carpet $10 Bed &c $10 Table $1	23
Bureau $5 Dressing Case $5 Carpet $5 Bed &c $10	25
Table $3 Stand $1 Carpet $2 Bed &c $10 2 Chairs $2 Stand $1	19
Furniture in Nursery	25
Hall Stove in Basement $10 Kitchen Furniture $40	50
Furniture & Servant's Room under hall	5
Do in bedroom under library	15
Vegetables, Fruit, &c in cellar	10
Barouche, Sleigh, Harness, Cow	150
Saddle, Bridle & Stable Furniture	10
	$2,445.00

Alanson Douglas ⎫
A. S. Perry ⎬ Appraisers

B. DAY BOOK, ESTATE OF BETSEY A. HART DECD, SALE AT HOUSE DECR 16/86, HART PAPERS

N O T E : This ledger includes a handwritten household inventory of all spaces in 59 Second Street plus items kept at the "Office," probably in the Troy Savings Bank Music Hall Building. Values are given for items in one column with a second and third column which notes who in the family "bought" the items and what the price was. An additional inserted group of pages at the front of the ledger note by name who "bought" what items with some additional notes about location of items. It is possible to use the c. 1892 photographs of the interior of the house to identify many of the actual objects listed in the inventory.

    Finally, "WHD Com" is William Howard Doughty Committee which looked after Sarah Wool Hart's concerns. William Howard Doughty was Betsey Hart's grandson and helped take care of her business affairs after the death of her son, William Howard Hart. Many of the items listed were kept for Sarah W. Hart to use in 59 Second Street where she continued to live after her mother's death until her own death in 1892. Bills or other documentation exist for many of the items listed. More complete listings for Betsey Hart's estate exist in the Rensselaer County Surrogate Court papers.

Page 1 of inventory book
(Synopsis of value of property for each heir)

J.W. Griswold	196.	
Mrs. J. A. Griswold	381.05	
Mrs. S. M. Vail	108.50	
Miss Phebe Vail	55.30	
Mrs A. Vail	57.80	
WH Doughty for self	633.70	
Thomas Vail	221.	
Miss E. A. Durkee	195.50	
Mrs. Susan Shields	88.75	
Mrs. Eddy	40.50	
Mrs. H. L. Shields	68.10	
Mrs. Green	22.50	
Miss F. Vail	3.25	
Henry Burden	16.	2087.95
Mrs. Willard, carriage	350.	
sleigh	100	450.
		2537.95
S.W. H. Com		5282.17
		7820.12
DeFreest, Harness		40.
		7860.12
less for gold pencil not there		6.
		7854.12

The articles bought in by T. Vail, being all for other heirs & after charging such heirs respectively the bill to go out will be as follows

J.W. Griswold	190.
Mrs. Griswold	389.05
Mrs. S. M. Vail	217.50
Miss Phebe "	55.30
Mrs. A. "	71.80
WH. Doughty for self	723.70
Miss Durkee	195.50
Mrs Susan Shields	88.75

Mrs. Eddy	40.50		
Mrs. H. L. Shields	68.10		
Mrs. EM Green	22.50		
Miss F. Vail	3.25		
Henry Burden	16.		
Mrs. J (?) L. Willard	450.		
DeFreest	40.		
WHD Committee	5282.17	7854.12	

[PAGE 2]

Household Furniture etc in House 59 Second St

Front Parlor

1 Carpet Aubusson	50.	WHD Com	50.	
1 Piano & Stool	75.	"	75.	
1 Oval Mirror	25.	"	25.	
1 do	25.	"	25.	
1 Square Mirror mantel	40.	"	40.	Margin note: *10.00
1 Pier Mirror	50.	"	50.	
2 Rosewood Sofas	100.	"	100.	
3 " Arm chairs	75.	"	75.	
6 " Chairs	60.	"	60.	Margin note: 1 chair $3.00 silk _?_.
1 " Chair plush covered	3.50	"	3.50	
1 Carved Rosewood table	15.	"	15.	
4 Japanese lacquered tables	15.	"	15.	Margin note: x 7.00
1 Round table & Cover	32.	"	32.	Margin note: x 15.00
1 Oil painting (large)	100.	"	100.	
1 " (small)	20.	"	20.	Margin note: x 10.00
1 Table cover (on lacquer table)	5.	"	5.	
1 Porcelain Centre piece	40.	"	80.	Margin note: add $40
1 Embroidered table cover	75.	"	75.	
1 Porcelain & bronze card receiver	5.	"	5.	
1 Porcelain box (fancy)	5.	"	5.	
1 Pair Japanese bronze figures	100.	"	130.	Margin note: add $30

[PAGE 4]

Front Parlor (cont')	915.50		985.50	
1 Bronze Card receiver	5.	WHD Com	5.	
2 Pairs lace window curtains	30.	"	30.	
2 " brocade " "	50.	"	50.	
1 " Girandoles	40.	"	40.	
1 " bisque figures	50.	"	50.	Margin note: add $30
9 framed photographs & easel	—	"	1.00	Margin note: add $1.00
1 Mantel Lambrequin & Grate screen	25.	WHD Com	25.	
2 Gilt Cornices	—	"		
1 China Vase (trefoil)	4.	WHD Com	4.	
1 Maastricht Vase or bowl	5.	"	5.	
1 Tea pot	1.	"	1.00	
1 Small picture (silver bronze frame)	—	"		This line crossed out
1 China dish (flowers)	2.	"	2.	
1 Japanese Cylindrical vase	1.	WHD	—	This line crossed out
1 Gas Chandelier & globes	20.	WHD	20.	
1 Porcelain bowl (leaves)	1.	JWG	2.	Margin note: deduct 1.00
1 Photograph (Woodside)	—	—	—	

[PAGE 6]

Back Parlor	1149.50		1250.50	
1 Carpet	30.	WHD Com	30.	
1 Pair lace Curtains	7.	"	7.	
1 " brocade "	15.	"	15.	
1 " lambrequins & Cornices	—	"		
1 Pier Mirror	50.	"	50.	
2 Rugs	5.	"	5.	
5 Rosewood chairs (plush)	17.50	"	17.50	
1 " Chair (carved)	5.	"	5.	
1 " " small	3.50	"	3.50	
2 Sofas (plush)	40.	"	40.	
2 Mahogany arm chairs	20.	"	20.	
2 " Rockers	10.	"	10.	
1 Upholstered Chair	20.	"	20.	
1 Rosewood Oval table	15.	"	15.	
1 " Etagere	50.	"	50.	
1 Oil painting landscape	50.	"	50.	Margin note: *40.00*
1 " Small meadow	10.	"	10.	Margin note: *10.*
1 painting Water color	3.	"	3.	Margin note: *15.*
1 Pair large China Vases	20.	Mrs. SMV	25.	Margin note: *deduct 20.00*
1 Gilt Mantel Clock	50.	WHD Com	50.	
1 Turkish table cover	15.	"	15.	

[PAGE 8]

Back Parlor cont'

1 Chandelier	20.	WHD Com	20.	
1 Drop Light	5.	"	5.	
1 Porcelain, bud vase	1.	"	1.	
1 Majolica tray	2.	"	2.	
4 Photograph albums	—	"	.50	Margin note: *add 50¢*
1 Large Cup & Saucer	2.	"	2.	
1 Medallion Card Receiver	—	"		
1 Inkstand fruit	.50	"	.50	
	1616.00		1722.50	

[PAGE 10]

Library

1 Carpet	30.	Com	30.	
2 Book Cases	100.	"	100.	
1 Gilt Cornice	3.	"	3.	
1 Window Shade	1.	"	1.	
1 Window Seat & pillow	3.	"	3.	
1 Rug	2.	"	2.	
2 Ottomans	4.	"	4.	
1 Mahogany Arm chair	5.	"	5.	
1 Sofa blue	15.	"	15.	
1 Chair "	5.	"	5.	
1 Table walnut	15.	"	15.	
1 Blue Lambrequin	5.	"	5.	
1 Pair Lace Curtains	5.	"	5.	
1 " colored engravings large	10.	"	10.	

1 " " " Small	5.	"	5.	
1 gilt thermometer	.50	"	.50	
1 Pair portraits (Washington & wife)	5.	"	5.	
1 " " Lincoln & Grant	5.	"	5.	
1 Engraving (Irving & friends)	5.	"	5.	
6 Family Photographs	—	"	.50	Margin note: *add 50¢*
1 Mantel Clock & Ornaments	30.	"	30.	

[PAGE 12]

Library cont'

1 Bronze Vase	10.	Com	10.
1 blue Japanese Vase	1.	Com	1.
1 Family Bible	—	—	—
1 Mantle Mirror	40.	Com	40.
Quantity of printed Books (all at residence)	100.	not sold	
	2020.50		2027.50

[PAGE 14]

Entrance Hall

1 Carpet	25.	Com	25.
1 Hat Stand & Mirror	75.	"	75.
1 Umbrella "	2.	"	2.
1 Mahogany Chair	5.	"	5.
1 Chair	1.	"	1.
1 Long Rug	20.	"	20.
1 door oil cloth	—	"	—
3 door rugs small	1.50	"	1.50
1 Gass fixture	3.	"	3.
1 Stair carpet	10.	"	10.
	2163.00		2170.00

[PAGE 16]

Dining Room

1 Dining table & Spread	30.	Com	30.	
1 Carpet	40.	Com	40.	
1 Square Mahogany table	8.	Com	8.	
1 Marble top table	8.	Com	8.	
1 Pier mirror	40.	Com	40.	
1 Mantel mirror	15.	Com	15.	
1 Mahogany Sofa	20.	Com	20.	
8 Mahogany Chairs	40.	Com	40.	
1 Cane Seat chair	1.	Com	1.	
1 Child's chair	.75	Com	.75	
2 Pair damask curtains	5.	Com	5.	
2 " lace "	5.	Com	5.	
2 Window Shades	2.	Com	2.	
1 Gas Chandelier & Globes	20.	Com	20.	
1 Candelabrum	5.	Com	5.	
1 Nut tray (majolica)	.75	Com	.75	
1 fruit tray	.75	Com	.75	
1 Clock	20.	Mrs J.AG	30.	Margin note: *deduct 30*

| 2 Vases | | 5. | Com | 5. |
| | | 2429.15 | | 2446.25 |

[PAGE 18]

Silver

at house	oz.			
1 Sugar bowl	13¾	11.	sold with 1 other	
1 Cream Pitcher	8¾	7.	piece (see	500.
1 Slop bowl	14¼	11.40	below) to WH	
			Doughty individually	
1 Syrup Cup	10½	8.40	WHD Com	8.40
1 Butter dish	21½	17.20	WHD Com	26.
1 Sugar basket & Sifter	15	12.	WHD Com	30.
1 Round tray	29	23.20	Miss Vail	51.
1 Ice Cream Knife	4	3.20	Mr A Vail	3.50
1 Crumb Knife	4	3.20	WHD Com	3.20
8 Table Spoons	18¼	14.60	WHD Com	8.40
6 Desert Spoons	8	6.40	"	6.40
11 Tea Spoons	8¼	6.60	"	6.60
6 Coffee Spoons	2¾	2.20	"	2.20
3 Salt Spoons	½	.40	"	.40
1 Mustard Spoon	½	.40	"	.40
8 Forks large	18½	14.80	"	14.80
8 Forks breakfast	13	10.40	"	10.40
1 Ice Tongs	3½	2.80	"	2.80
1 Sugar "	2	1.60	"	1.60
1 Pie Knife	3½	2.80	"	2.80
1 Soup ladle	6	4.80	"	4.80
2 Gravy ladles	3½	2.60	"	2.60
		2429.25		2446.25

Margin note: *Howard set*

[PAGE 20]

Silver (contd)

at house cont.	oz.			
1 grape Scissors		5.	WHD Com	5.
6 fruit knives		3.	"	3.
2 Small forks	1¾	1.40	"	1.40
2 Napkin rings	1½	1.20	"	1.20
1 Butter knife	1¾	1.40	"	1.40
		179.00		698.30

at Office				
1 silver covered dish			WHD self	80.
1 " " "			Tom Vail	65.
1 " " " smaller			Mr JAG	80.
1 " " "	145¾	116.60	Miss Durkee	80.
1 Butter dish	21½	17.50	Mr. A. Vail	26.
1 Coffee Pot Large	23½	18.80	Sold with other 3 pieces of Howard Set	
			for $500. See above	
1 " " "H"			WHD Com	51.
1 Sugar Dish "H"		50.40		

1 Cream pitcher "H"				
1 Tete a tete set 3 pieces	25½	20.20	Mrs Susan Shields	30.
1 Coffee kettle	31¼	25.	Mrs. JAG	40.
1 Chafing dish	25	20.	WHD self	30.
1 Castor & cruetts	22½	18.	Mrs. JAG	25.
1 doz large forks	28	22.40	Mrs. JAG	30.
10/12 tea forks		6.	4 to WHD Com 2.	
			6 to JWG	5.
		2429.25		2446.25

[PAGE 22]

Silver contd

at Office contd

1 Cheese Scoop	2¾	2.20	JWG	3.
3 Ladles		.80	Miss Durkee	9.
1 Spoon holder				
1 Cover included in Hsd/Howard set		3.40	belonging to Howard set & sold to WHD see above	
10 large Forks "H"		18.60	4 WHD Com	4.20
			6 JWG	15.
10 Small "	16	12.80	9	
			1	
10 table spoons	23¼	18.60	4 WHD Com	6.20
			6 JWG	13.
9 Dessert Spoons	13¾	11.	6 Mr SMV	12.
Ink "H"			1 WHD Com	1.
			2 Ink "H" Mr. Eddy	7.50
2 Doz Tea "	19	15.20	1 doz Ink "H" JWG	14.
			1 " " " Mr. Eddy	13.
2 Preserve Spoons	4	3.20	Wm HL Shields	5.
2 Ladles	8¼	6.60	1 Tom Vail	6.
			1 Mr HLS	5.25
1 Gravy Spoon	2½	2.	Mrs Susan Shields	2
2 Pairs Sugar Tongs	2¾	2.20	1 WHD self	5.
			1 Mrs. S Shields	2.50
1 Sugar sifter	1¾	1.40	Mrs. Green	3.
2 Salt spoons	½	.40	Tom Vail	1.
1 Mustard spoon				
2½ doz coffee spoons	14	11.20	6 WHD Com	3.
			12 SMV13.	
			12 Henry Burden	16.
5 Napkin rings	3¾	3.	WHD Com	4.00
11 Nut picks	5¼	4.20	WHD Com	6.
		3039.95		3858.20

[PAGE 24]

Plated Ware

at House

1 Water Pitcher & tray	3.	WHD Com	3.
1 Ice Bowl	5.	"	5.
2 Trays, small & large	3.	"	3.

1 Tea pot Jap.	2.50	"	2.50	
3 Castors	5.	"	5.	
1 Soup Tureen & tray	3.	"	3.	
2 Decanters trays	3.	"	3.	
1 Coffee Urn	5.	"	5.	
1 Toast rack	3.	"	3.	
1 Pickle fork	.50	"	.50	
1 Cracker box	2.	"	2.	
1 Cider pitcher	2.	"	2.	
1 Coffee pot	2.	"	2.	
1 Cake tray	2.	"	2.	
2 Vegetable dishes (oval)	2.	"	2.	
2 " " (round)	2.	SMV $10 ea	20.	
2 Covers Melon shape	2.	WHD Com	2.	
2 Vegetable dishes & trays	2.			This line crossed out
1 Sauce boat	8.	"	8.	
1 Pudding dish	2.	"	2.	
12 Dinner knives	—	"	.10	
6 Dinner forks	—	"	.10	
	3095.95		3858.20	

[PAGE 26]

Plated Ware contd

at house contd

7 Tea knives	—	WHD Com	.10	
12 " "	—			Margin note: *not there*

at Office

1 doz steel knives	—	WHD Com	.10	
2 Decanter stands	—	SMV lot	1.50	
2 Snuffers & trays	—	1 set Mr. JAG	10.	
		1 " Mr. JWG	6.	
1 Extinguisher	—	Mr. JAG	.10	
1 Soup Tureen	15.	WHD Com	15.	
1 Cake basket	—	Miss Durkee	31.	
2 butter knives	.75	Mrs G	1.	
Egg spoons gilt	—	WHD Com	.02	
1 doz tea knives	6.	Mr. A Vail	6.50	

Sundry

in dining room

1 Tea pot agate	2.	Com	2.	
1 Egg set china	2.	"	2.	
1 Framed tile	.50	"	.50	
2 Common trays	.25	"	.25	
1 Large mirror trays				
2 Small or mats	2.50	"	2.50	
3 Carvers & forks	—	"	—	
8 Straw table mats	—	"	—	
1 Plated tray		Mrs. Green	10.	
1 " "		Tom Vail	7.	Margin note: *deduct $28.00*
1 " "		Miss Durkee	11.	

	3127.95		4049.97

[PAGE 28]

Dining Room contd

1 Sideboard	50.	Com	50.
	3177.95		4099.97

[PAGE 30]

Dining Room Pantries

1 Dinner set 154 pieces	15.	Tom Vail	90.	In pencil "Gilt & White"
1 Set figured 105 pieces	15.	see close		
1 Dinner set 196 pieces green & white	20.	Mrs. S. Shields	22.	No. pcs. crossed out
5 old Platters	1.50			
5 Fruit dishes	1.50			
15 Soup plates	1.50			
18 Jelly moulds	3.60	see close of inventory for items from		
12 Blue tea cups	1.20	this sold separately		
1 Bowl				
2 Pitchers	1.			
1 Tea Set 56 pces	5.			
86 pieces gilt & yellow	15.			
12 gilt band finger bowls	12.	Mr. J. Wool Griswold	20.	
11 Champagne glasses gilt band	6.	" " "	132. (?)	
12 Mugs & Saucers				
24 Cups & "				
24 Plates		See close of inventory		
1 China Dish		for items from this		
1 " Tea pot		sold separately		
12 Coffee cups & saucers				
2 Mugs				
17 tea cups & saucers				
1 Pitcher				
1 Bowl				
5 Plates				
13 "				
9 Saucer Plates				
1 Carved dish				
7 Fancy dishes				
6 plates				
7 Butter plates				
1 Dinner plate & dish				
	3179.95		4099.97	

[PAGE 32]

Dining Room Pantries, cont

brought up, see ante
3 Vegetable dishes
1 Ice cream set
1 Tea set
2 Salts
1 Old Soup dish

11 " blue dishes
6 " Soup "
33 " Common dishes
2 Egg dishes
2 Syrup cups   25.

Pantry No. 2

4 Tumblers
1 Measure glass
1 glass flower dish
1 bottle
4 Pitchers
6 Ice glasses
2 Coffee canisters
3 small plates
2 tea pots
8 Cups & Saucers
2 cream pitchers
2 pudding dishes
2 glass Jars
1 pie plate
1 tea cup
1 Coffee "
1 Soup dish
4 Tin cans
1 tray & stand   All these items noted: *See close of*
3 other pieces   10.   *inventory for items out of these,*
9 Sweet meat dishes   *bid separately*
1 Cheese cover
2 Covered dishes
7 Lamp chimneys
12 Fruit
35 Wine glasses
16 Finger bowls
1 Glass cup
2 Wine measures
3 Old Glasses
5 Egg glasses
                                       3311.25   4099.97

[PAGE 34]

Pantry No. 2 contd

up from ante
8 Cider glasses
1 Jelly glass
18 Lemonade glasses
2 Water Pitchers
1 Cream Pitcher
17 Tumblers
12 Kitchen articles
1 Jar
1 trap

1 Sugar box   15.

12 Platters
1 Milk Set
1 Dish
1 Ornament
1 Cup
1 Cracker pail
3 Glass pitchers
1 celery glass
18 Water glasses
4 Tumblers
2 Jelly tumblers
47 Whine glasses
8 Cider glasses
6 Egg glasses
5 Salts
3 Saucers
2 Preserve dishes
1 Cider bottle (decanter)

1	"		"
1 Decanter Quart cut			
1	"	"	"
1	"	"	"
1	"	Pint	"
1	"	"	"
1	" cracked "		"
1	"	"	"
1	"	"	"
2	"	water bottles	
2	"	"	

Note: *See close of inventory for items from this sold separately*

1 fruit dish 25.

                              3351.25   4231.97

[PAGE 36]

Wine Closets

10 Galls Sherry	30.	
2 " "	6.	
1 bot: Champagne	2.50	
4 " "	10.50	Margin Note: *Not Sold*
1 Case " Gold Lac	28.	
1 part Case " Mumm Pts	10.	
1 Lot Sherry various pkges	50.	
11 bot: Chateau Latour	25.	
4 " Claret	4.	
1 Case " Montty	6.	
6 Bot: V. Cliquiot	7.50	

                              3530.75   4231.97

[PAGE 38]

Mrs Hart's Sitting Room

1 Carpet	20.	Com	20.
1 Washstand & furniture	15.	Com	15.
1 Sofa	20.	Com	20.
1 Commode	2.50	Com	2.50

1 Bureau & Glass	20.	Com	20.	
1 Mahogany stand	7.	Com	7.	
1 Wall Cabinet & Contents	20.	Com	20.	
1 Table & Spread	15.	Com	15.	
1 Easy Chair	15.	Com	15.	
1 Shaker Rocker	5.	Com	5.	
1 Willow Rocker	2.50	Com	2.50	
3 Chairs & 2 Cushions	4.	Com	4.	
2 Pair Curtains	5.	Com	5.	
2 " Stuff "	20.	Com	20.	
2 " Shades	2.	Com	2.	
2 hand glasses	2.	"	2.	
1 Thermometer	.50	"	.50	
1 Work basket	2.50	"	2.50	
1 Lambrequin	—	"	—	
1 Mantel Clock	25.	T.Vail	25.	Margin note: *deduct 25.00*
2 China Vases	15.	Com	15.	
1 Pair gilt Candlesticks	2.	Mr JAG	7.	Margin note: *deduct 2.00*
1 fancy thermometer	.50	Com	.50	
	3530.75		4231.97	

[PAGE 40]

Mrs. Hart's Sitting Room contd

1 gilt bell	1.	Mrs. A Vail	1.	Margin note: *deduct 1.00*
1 Book Case	75.	Com	75.	
1 Engraving "farewell"	5.	Mr. JWG	13.	Margin note: *deduct 5.00*
1 " "Daniel & Lions"	5.	Mr. T. Vail	14.	Margin note: *deduct 5.00*
2 Small photographs	—	Com	.25	
1 Cardrack & cards	—	Com	.25	
	306.50		330.00	

Back Stairs to 2d Story

1 Carpet	2.	Com	2.	
	3839.25		4563.97	

[PAGE 42]

Second Story Hall

1 Carpet	15.	WHD Com	15.	
3 Chairs	1.50	"	1.50	

2d Hall Closet & Pantry

1 Carpet on 3d Story Stairs	10.	"	10.	
1 Pair Steps				
1 Feather brush				
1 Oil Painting	5.	"	5.	
1 Carpet	5.	WHD Com	5.	
1 Bureau	5.	WHD Com	5.	
1 Pair Vases	—	WHD Com	2.	Margin note: *add 2.00*
	3880.75		4607.47	

[PAGE 44]

Miss Hart's Room

				Margin note: *Hall bedroom*
1 Carpet	20.	WHD Com	20.	
1 Black Walnut Bedstead & bedding	47.	"	47.	
1 Lounge & 2 Pillows	15.	"	15.	
1 Commode	5.	"	5.	
1 Mahogany Bureau	15.	"		Margin note: *deduct 15/ belongs to Mrs Susan Shields*
1 Lambrequin	2.50	"	2.50	
2 Candelabra	2.	Miss Durkee	21.	Margin note: *deduct 2.00*
2 Vases	2.	WHD Com	2.	
1 Clock	3.	"	3.	
1 Washstand & furniture	7.	"	7.	
1 Bookcase	15.	"	15.	
1 Rocker	1.	"	1.	
3 Chairs	1.50	"	1.50	
1 Picture "Mother & children"	3.	Belongs to Mrs. Susan Shields		Deduct 3.00
2 Small engravings	1.	"	1.	
1 Window Seat & Cushions	5.	"	5.	
Curtains &Shade	18.	"	18.	
	4043.75		4771.47	

[PAGE 46]

North Front Room

				Margin note: *Surrendered to Susan Shields Deduct 30.*
1 Carpet	25.	WHD Com	25.	
1 Mahogany bedstead & bedding	50.	" "	50.	
1 Canopy	25.	" "	25.	
1 Stand & Glass	30.	JW Griswold	31.	
1 Commode	5.	Com	5.	
1 Bureau Mirror & furniture therefore	40.	WHD Com	40.	
1 Lounge & Cushion	10.	" "	10.	
1 Lambrequin	3.	" "	3.	
3 Candelabra Mantel	12.	" "	12.	
2 gilt Candlesticks	2.	Miss Durkee	11.	
2 Cologne bottles	.50	WHD Com	.50	
1 Washstand & furniture	17.	" "	17.	
1 Workbasket	5.	" "	5.	
1 Wardrobe & mirror	50.	" "	50.	
2 Table & spread	20.	" "	20.	
1 Pitcher & tray	1.	" "	1.	
1 Large Easy chair	5.	" "	5.	
1 Rocker	1.	" "	1.	
4 Mahogany chairs	20.	" "	20.	
2 Sewing chair	1.	" "	1.	
1 Willow rocker	1.	" "	1.	
1 Cane (child's) chair	.50	" "	.50	
	4043.75		4771.47	

[PAGE 48]

II Story
North Front Room contd

2 Pair Curtains & shades	10.	WHD Com	10.
2 " red Curtains	10.	" "	10.

1 Large Oil Painting	5.	" "	5.	
Small stand & basket	1.	" "	1.	
	4393.75		5131.47	

[PAGE 50]

II Story
Closet back of Front Room

1 Commode	1.	WHD Com	1.
1 Chair	1.	" "	1.
	4395.75		5133.47

[PAGE 52]

II Story
Back Room

1 Carpet	20.	WHD Com	20.	
1 Washstand & furniture	15.	" "	15.	
2 Large Vases	10.	" "	10.	
1 Towelrack	.50	" "	.50	
1 Mahogany Sofa & cushions	15.	" "	15.	
1 Rocker	1.	" "	1.	
4 Mahogany Chairs	16.	" "	16.	
1 Small Maple chair	1.	" "	1.	
1 Bureau & Mirror	50.	" "	50.	
1 Mahogany bedstead & bedding	70.	" "	70.	
1 Commode	5.	" "	5.	
2 Pairs Curtains & Cornices	10.	" "	10.	
2 Shades	2.	" "	2.	
Candlesticks	2.	Mrs. JAGriswold	9.	Margin note: *deduct $2*
1 Mantel Clock	10.	WHD Com	10.	
1 Shell ornament	—	" "	.50	Margin note: *add 50¢* (This piece is in RCHS Collection)
	4624.25		5369.47	

(p.54)

II Story
Miss Hart's Dressing Room

1 Wardrobe & Mirror	50.	WHD Com	50.
	4674.25		5424.47

[PAGE 56]

II Story
Bath Room

1 Rug	1.	Com	1.
1 Towelrack	.50	"	.50
1 Chair	.50	"	.50
1 Soapdish	—	"	.10
1 Cup	—	"	.10
Tin utensils	—	"	.10
Oil cloth	—	"	.10
	4676.25		5426.87

[PAGE 58]

II Story
Bath Room Hall

1 Carpet	3.	Com	3.
1 Rug	—	"	.10
1 Chair	1.	"	1.
1 Stair Carpet	2.	"	2.
	4682.25		5432.97

[PAGE 60]

II Story
Mrs. Hasting's Room (old)

1 Bureau (dressing)	10.	Mr. JWG	40.	Margin note: *deduct 10.00*
1 Walnut bed & bedding	20.	Com	20.	
1 Large Bureau	5.	"	5.	
1 Small "	30.	"	30.	
1 Washstand & furniture	5.	"	5.	
1 Towel Rack	.50	"	.50	
1 Centre table & Cover	3.	"	3.	
2 Chairs	1.	"	1.	
1 Rocker	.50	"	.50	
1 Child's Chair	.50	"	.50	
1 Carpet	7.	"	7.	
2 Shades	1.	"	1.	
1 Rug	1.	"	1.	
1 Inkstand	—	"	.10	
1 Small clock	2.50	"	2.50	
	4769.26		5550.07	

[PAGE 62]

III Story
Third Story Hall

1 Carpet	1.	Com	1.
1 Chair	1.	"	1.
	4770.25		5552.07

[PAGE 64]

II Story
Skirt Room

1 Carpet	2.	Com	2.
1 Chair	—	"	.10
	4773.25		5554.17

[PAGE 66]

II Story
Store Rooms 1 & 2

1 Carpet	3.	Com	3.	Note: these spaces probably on 3rd story of back wing
1 Rug	.25	"	.25	
1 Bureau	8.	"	8.	

1 Dressing table	5.	"	5.	
2 Common Stands	.50	"	.50	
8 Japanese trays	2.	"	2.	
3 Chairs	.50	"	.50	
7 Baskets	.50	"	.50	
1 Kettle (porcelain)	.75	"	.75	
1 " (brass)	.75	"	.75	
1 large platter cover	.25	"	.25	
3 Gal. bottle & preserving jars	—	"	.10	Margin note: *add 10¢*

No. 2

1 Bedstead & bedding	35.	"	35.	
2 Arm chairs (chintz)	2.	"	2.	
Coverings parlor furniture, screen	—	"	.10	Margin note: *add 10¢*
2 Chairs	.50	"	.50	
1 Stand	.50	"	.50	
1 Music Stand	.50	"	.50	
1 Carpet	.50	"	.50	
Warming pans & footstool	6.	See end	—	Margin note: *sold at end Less 6.00*
	4839.75		5614.87	

[PAGE 68]

Basement
Hall

Oil Cloth	—	Com	.10
Door mat	—	"	.10
	4839.7		5615.07

[PAGE 70]

Basement
Sitting Room

Mahogany Sofa & pillows	10.	JWG	10.
2 Tables & spread	15.	JWG	15.
1 Mirror	3.	Com	3.
1 Large Rocker	1.	"	1.
9 Chairs	4.50	"	4.50
2 Pairs Curtains	1.50	"	1.50
2 Vases	.25	"	.25
1 Clock	1.50	"	1.50
1 Carpet	15.	"	15.
	4891.50		5666.82

[PAGE 72]

"Miss Smith's" Room (Servant)

1 Bedstead & bedding	7.	Com	7.
1 Bureau & Mirror	5.	"	5.
1 Table & Spread	5.	JWG	5.
1 Washstand & furniture	1.	"	1.
4 Chairs (2 broken)	2.	"	2.
Carpet	15.	"	15.
Curtain	.50	"	.50

2 Rugs	—	"	.10	
	4927.00		5702.42	

[PAGE 74]

"Miss Brown's" Room (Servant)

1 Bed & Bedding	5.	Com	5.	
1 Wardrobe	3.	"	3.	
2 Table covers	4.	"	4.	
1 Washstand & furniture	1.	"	1.	
3 Chairs	.75	"	.75	
Matting	2.50	"	2.50	
2 Strips Carpet 1 mirror	—	"	.10	Margin note: *add 10¢*
1 Mirror	—	"	.10	Margin note: *add 10¢*
	4943.25		5718.87	

[PAGE 76]

Katie's Room (so called)

1 Bed & Bedding	5.	WHD	Com	5.	
1 Bureau	3.	"	"	3.	
1 Washstand & furniture	.50	"	"	.50	
1 Carpet	2.	"	"	2.	
2 Common tables	.50	"	"	.50	
1 Mirror	.50	"	"	.50	
2 Chairs (broken)	1.	"	"	1.	
Shade & Curtain	—	"	"	.10	Margin note: *add 10¢*
	4955.75			5731.47	

[PAGE 78]

"Alice's Room" so called

1 Bed & Bedding	5.	WHD	Com	5.	
1 Bureau & glass	8.	"	"	8.	
1 Washstand & furniture	.50	"	"	.50	
1 Carpet	5.	"	"	5.	
2 Painted table	.50	"	"	.50	
1 Window Shade	—	"	"	.10	Margin note: *add 10¢*
2 Chairs	.50	"	"	.50	
	4975.25			5751.07	

[PAGE 80]

Attic

1 Feather bed & mattress	13.	WHD	Com	13.	
1 Iron bedstead	3.50	WHD	"	3.50	
	4991.75			5767.57	

[PAGE 82]

Kitchen

3 Platters		Com
6 Small bowls		"
3 Large "		"

6 tea cups & Saucers	"
4 tumblers	"
6 dinner plates	"
6 tea spoons	"
6 table "	"
6 dinner knives	"
1 Bread knife	"
1 Salt glass	"
1 pepper box	"
1 Sugar bowl	"
4 Pitchers	"
1 Coffee pot	"
1 Tea pot	"
2 Collenders	"
2 Skimmers	"
2 Milk bowls	"
2 Ladles	"
7 Pots	"
7 Sauce Pans	"
1 tea kettle	"
3 Measures (pts)	"
5 Old Coffee pots	"
1 tin pail	"
1 freezer	"
9 baking tins	"
6 bread tins	"
2 Strainers	"
1 Scales	"
2 Jugs	"
1 Chopping bowl & knife	"
5 Deep dishes	"
1 Butter bowl	"
6 Cooking Spoons	"
2 Milk ladles	"
4 frying pans	"
12 muffin rings	"
2 dish pans	"
6 baking plates	"
4 Tables	"
4 Chairs	"
6 Small plates	"

	4991.75		5767.57

[PAGE 84]

Kitchen cont.

2 trays	Com
2 plate knives	"
1 Scissors	"
1 Clock	"
2 Coal hods	"
2 Ironing boards	"
1 Moulding board	"
1 Rolling pin	"
6 Jelly moulds	"

14 Jars		"	
1 Table		"	
2 Chopping bowls		"	
2 Ice closets		"	
4 Wooden pails		"	
	5011.75		5787.57

[PAGE 86]

Wood House

2 Step Ladders	2.	Com	2.
2 Coal hods	—	"	
50 feet hose & reel	2.50	"	
1 lawn mower	2.50	"	
2 ladders	1.	"	
Wheelbarrow	2.	"	
2 door mats	—	"	
	5021.75		5797.57

[PAGE 88]

Laundry

1 Stove	5.	Com	
1 Ironing table	1.50	"	
1 " board	.50	"	
2 horses	1.	"	
1 Block	.25	"	
1 Arm Chair	.25	"	
2 Coal hods	—	"	
8 flat irons & two rests	.80	"	
4 Wash tubs	2.	"	
4 brushes	1.	"	
3 Soap barrels	2.	"	
1 pounding barrel	.50	"	
2 tin boilers	—	"	
1 grind stone	—	"	
1 lawn sprinkler	—	"	
	5036.55		5812.37

[PAGE 90]

Stable

1 Carriage	200.	Mrs. Willard	350.	
1 Pair Steps	1.	" "	1.	
1 feed box	—	Com	.10	
1 Double Sleigh	50.	Mrs. Willard	100.	
1 Robe Box	5.	Com	5.	
House window awnings	2.50	Com	2.50	
1 Shovel	—	"	.10	
1 Rake	—	"	.10	
1 Double Phaeton	100.	"		Margin note: *not sold*
1 Harness	25.			Margin note: *Entered at end*
	5420.05		6271.17	

[PAGE 92]

Jewelry (at office)

1 Gold penholder & pencil	.50	Mrs A Vail	.25
1 pair seals	2.	Mrs. Capt Shields	.25
1 " ear rings (gold)	—	Mrs. Griswold	.25
1 pencil (gold)	1.50	Mrs. S. Shields	.25
1 " (small) gold	1.		6
4 Studs (gold & shell)	1.	Mrs. P Vail	.50
1 pair diamond lace pins	50.	1–Mrs. SM Vail	27.
		1–Mrs. Griswold	30.
1 Silver Spectacle case	5.	JWG	6.

Margin note: *deduct at close*

Supplementary

1 Gold watch	15.	Mrs. Griswold	15.
1 Enamel (green) brooch	—	Mrs P. Vail	.50
1 " & pearl (hair) "	1.	P Vail	.25
1 small " "	—	JWG	.50
1 Chain bracelet	—	Mrs. Eddy	.50
1 Topaz & pearl pin	—	Mrs A Vail	.50
1 Diamond brooch	1000.	Com	1000.
1 pr Plated candlesticks	8.	Com	8.
1 Bed in Attic	10.	Mrs. Griswold	10.
Scrolls "	.50	JWG	.50
Frame	2.	Mrs. Shields	2.
Chair	2.	Com	2.
(not in Peck's inventory			
	6519.55		7382.42

[PAGE 94]

Office Furniture

1 Steel Safe	300.
1 Large Desk	5.
1 High table	2.
1 table	2.
1 Cupboard	1.
1 Letter press	3.
Maps	—
1 Carpet	50.
Oil Cloth	5.
Wood & glass partition	—
	368.

Margin note: *not included in either appraisal footing(?) or sold footing(?)*

Life Chronology and Architectural Works of Martin Euclid Thompson

Walter Richard Wheeler

THIS CHRONOLOGY is based upon that produced by Betty J. Ezequelle for her article on Martin E. Thompson published in the *Macmillan Encyclopedia of Architects,* Vol. 4 (Adolf K. Placzek, ed. New York: The Free Press, 1982, pp. 207–08). Additional attributions come from the research of Lawrence B. Romaine, Jacob Landy, Roger Hale Newton, and Regina M. Kellerman. Many new commissions and biographical details were discovered in the process of gathering materials for the architectural history essay in this volume.

In form the chronology loosely follows that developed by Jane Davies for her list of the works of A. J. Davis, published in *Alexander Jackson Davis, American Architect 1803–1892* (Amelia Peck, ed. New York: Rizzoli, 1992). Major sources for attribution and understanding of particular projects are listed in parentheses. Notes citing exhibitions at the National Academy of Design can be referenced in the Exhibition List, published by the New-York Historical Society. Buildings known to be extant are so noted.

1785/6	Born, in Hudson County, New Jersey.
1816	First appears as a "carpenter" in the New York City *Directory.*
1822–	Member of the General Society of Mechanics and Tradesmen, New York.
c. 1822–26	Works in collaboration with Josiah R. Brady. Conjectural.
1822–24	Second Branch Bank of the United States (later Assay Office), Wall Street, New York. Drawings exhibited at the National Academy of Design in 1826. (Edmund March Blunt. *The Picture of New York.* New York: A. T. Goodrich, 1828, pp. 250–51.) Façade preserved at the Metropolitan Museum of Art, American Wing.
1823	First listed as an "architect and builder" in the New York City *Directory,* living at 17 Essex Street.
c. 1824	Tradesmen's Bank, 177 Chatham Street, New York. Attribution from obituary.
1824–27	The Merchants' Exchange, Wall Street, New York. Designed by Thompson with assistance from Josiah Brady. (Drawing "with the Original Cupola by J. R. Brady" exhibited by A. J. Davis at the

National Academy of Design in 1828. (*American Magazine of Useful & Entertaining Knowledge* 1: 8 [April 1835], pp. 339–40.)

c. 1825	The Phenix Bank, 24 Wall Street, New York. Alternate date for construction sometimes given as c. 1818. (Lithographic view exhibited at the National Academy of Design in 1828 by A. J. Davis.)
1825	Catherine Market, Catherine Street, New York. Possibly only renovations to an existing building.
1825	Thompson joins Board of Directors and is acting as "surveyor" for the Trader's Insurance Company, 31 Wall Street, New York.
1825–26	Second Unitarian Church, Mercer Street at Prince Street, New York. ("[T]he designs of the front entablature . . . drawn by J. [*sic*] G. Pearson," *The New-York Mirror* 7: 12 [26 September 1829], pp. 89–91.) Author's attribution; attributed to Brady by Jacob Landy.
1825	One of 30 founding members, with Ithiel Town, of the National Academy of Design. Thompson remains a member until his death in 1877.
1825–27	Richard P. and Betsey Howard Hart House, Troy, New York. Author's attribution. Extant.
1826	Thompson exhibits drawings for the Second Branch Bank of the United States at the National Academy of Design.
1826–27	A. J. Davis learning drafting under Brady, who is probably in partnership with Thompson during part of this time.
1826	Joseph Xifre house, 43 Harman Street, New York.
1826	Elisha W. King House at Pelham, New York.
1826	Thompson's partnership with Josiah R. Brady ends; partnership with Ithiel Town starts by December of that same year. Town & Thompson are listed at "32 Mechanics' Exchange" as "architects" in the 1827 *Directory.*
1827	Spring. A. J. Davis opens his own office on Wall Street, offering drafting services. Presumably provides drawings for Brady and Town & Thompson at this time.
1827–29	New York Institution for the Deaf and Dumb, Fourth Avenue at Fiftieth Street, New York. (Image in *New York Historical Collections.*)
1827	"New Boston" (Tremont) Theatre, Boston, Massachusetts (with Ithiel Town). (Drawings exhibited at the National Academy of Design in 1827.)

1827	Town & Thompson exhibit designs for "a church" and "a country seat" at the National Academy of Design.
c. 1827	LeGrand Cannon House, 19 Third Street, Troy, New York. Author's attribution.
1827	The Phoenix Bank, Hartford, Connecticut. Town & Thompson; probably designed by Ithiel Town.
1827–29	LeRoy Place, Bleecker Street, New York. Built by Isaac G. Pearson. Author's attribution.
1827–31	Rensselaer County Courthouse, Troy, New York. Author's attribution to Town & Thompson.
1827–28	Flushing Institute, Flushing, Long Island. By Town & Thompson. (Drawings exhibited at the National Academy of Design in 1827.)
1827–28	Spire for St. Mark's Church in the Bouwerie, New York. By Thompson while in partnership with Ithiel Town (*New-York Mirror* 5: 34 [1 March 1828], p. 271). Extant.
1827–29	Church of the Ascension, Canal Street, New York. (Drawings exhibited at the National Academy of Design in 1828.)
1827	Christ Church, Hartford, Connecticut. Probably largely by Ithiel Town. Attributed by Newton.
1827–29	Grammar School and houses on Murray, Barclay, Church and Chapel streets, for Columbia College, New York. Probably by Town & Thompson. (Some of the drawings for the project are signed by a pupil of Town & Thompson, Robert Cary Long, Jr., of Baltimore, and preserved at the Avery Architectural Library.) (*New-York Mirror* 6: 22 [6 December 1828], p. 169 and frontispiece.)
by 1828	Ithiel Town opens his architectural library to the public. It is housed in the office of Town & Thompson.
1828	Thompson is a founder and one of three vice presidents of the American Institute of the City of New York (*New York, As it Is in 1833*, p. 79).
1828	A. J. Davis has moved his office to 42 Merchants' Exchange building, the same site as the Town & Thompson office.
1828	"Hawkswood" Rodman's Neck, New York, overlooking the East River and Long Island Sound.
1828	"Design for a Villa for John Galt, Canada." (Drawings exhibited at the National Academy of Design in 1828.)
1828–29	"Additions" to New York City Hall (renovations to the former New York Institution for the Deaf and Dumb], to the rear of City Hall, New York. (Drawings exhibited at the National Academy of Design in 1829, now in the collections of the New-York Historical Society.)
1828	First Reformed Dutch Church, New Brunswick, New Jersey. (Alternate date of 1835 is sometimes given for its construction.)
1828	By the end of this year Thompson is working independently from Town.
c. 1828–29	Residence and lodges for Dr. David Hosack, Hyde Park, New York. (Drawings exhibited at the National Academy of Design in 1829.)
1829	By June. Town & Davis office opens at room next door to former Town & Thompson office in the Exchange (room 34), Davis replacing Thompson as Town's partner. Thompson moves to room 39.
1830	By June. Thompson, now at 183 Church Street, calling himself an *Architect & builder*.
1830	Thompson serves as one of two secretaries to the Workingmen's Convention in western New York (*Farmer's, Mechanic's and Workingman's Advocate* [Albany], 9 October 1830).
1830	Thompson exhibits two unidentified architectural designs at the National Academy of Design.
1830	Robert Ray house, 17 Broadway, New York. Destroyed 1845.
1831	Hall of Records (a.k.a. "Record Office"), remodeling of the old prison, City Hall Park, New York. (Drawings exhibited at the National Academy of Design in 1831; woodcut view drawn by Davis published in the *New-York Mirror* 9: 11 [17 September 1831], p. 81; a different view was published in *The Family Magazine* 2: 140 [1835]. Thompson's drawings for the project are at Avery Architectural Library, Columbia University.)
1831	Thompson exhibits "A Plan for a City Hall" at the National Academy of Design.
c. 1831–33	"The Row," Washington Square North, New York. Traditional attribution. It is probable that Samuel Thomson was the builder of at least some of these houses. Extant.
1832	May 10. Thomas Kelah Wharton (1814–1862) begins apprenticeship with Thompson, living with the latter's family at 24 Howard Street.
1832	Summer. Thompson contracts cholera. When he recovers in late July, he removes with his family to New Jersey.
1833	Thompson on board of directors of the Trader's Insurance Company; among the founders of the University of the City of New-York and on the board of directors for the New-York Institution for the Instruction of the Deaf and Dumb (*New York, As it Is in 1833*).
1833	New York State Prison, Sing-Sing, New York. Attribution from obituary. Betty J. Ezequelle suggests a design date of c. 1835 and that it was likely a design for the women's prison. Extant?
1833–41	United States Naval Hospital, Brooklyn Navy Yard, Brooklyn, New York. Extant.
c. 1833	St. Clement's Church, Amity Street near McDougal, New York. (Drawings exhibited at the National Academy of Design in 1833.)
1834–35	216–26 Thompson Street, New York. Attribution by Regina M. Kellerman based upon Thompson's Account Book and deeds.

1835	Commercial and Railroad Bank, Vicksburg, Mississippi.
1835	Steeple, First Dutch Reformed Church, New Brunswick, New Jersey (see 1828).
1835	Steeple, St. Mark's Church in the Bouwerie, New York, repairs (see 1828–29). Extant.
1835	Pulpit for the Ninth Street Church, New York.
1835	The Phenix Bank, Wall Street, New York (additions and/or alterations).
1835–37	St. James Roman Catholic Church, James Street, New York. Attribution by Jacob Landy.
1835–36	Spring Street Presbyterian Church, Spring Street, New York. Attribution by Jacob Landy.
1836	Baptist Church, Hudson, New York.
1836	Stores for Smith & Lowns, Beaver Street, New York.
1836	Stores for David Arthur, Beaver Street, New York.
1836	Stores for James Denniston, Beaver Street, New York.
1836	Stores for William Redmond, Beaver Street, New York.
1836–37	Park Place row for William Howard, Troy, New York. Author's attribution.
1836–37	James Colles house, Colles Avenue, Morristown, New Jersey.
1837	Wood house, James Colles estate, Colles Avenue, Morristown, New Jersey.
1837–39	163–165 Bleecker Street, New York, for Uriah and Montague Hendricks.
1837–38	James Lenox house "Netherwood," New Hamburg, New York.
1837–42	New York Institution for the Blind, Eighth and Ninth Avenue between Thirty-third and Thirty-fourth streets, New York. (Drawing of an "Architectural Elevation of Contemplated Institution for the Blind" exhibited by Thompson at the National Academy of Design in 1838.)
1838	Ohio State Capitol Competition, Second premium. Not built.
1839–40	David Austin house, Union Place, New York.
1839–40	228 Thompson Street, New York. Extant as the Grand Tocino Restaurant.
1839–40	Speculative houses, West Twelfth Street, New York.
1841	"Design for a State Arsenal." (Drawing at the New York State Archives, currently unlocated.) Probably that built and extant at Watervliet, New York.
1841	Stores at Murray Street and Park Place, New York.
1842–45	First Presbyterian Church (Dr. Paxton's), Fifth Avenue and at Twelfth Street, New York. Attribution from Thompson's obituary. Known to be by Joseph C. Wells. Extant. Alternately, the Scotch Presbyterian Church at Grand and Crosby streets, constructed in 1836, could have been meant.
c. 1842–43	The Block House (residence for commanding general of fort), Governor's Island, New York. Extant.
1844–53	Living on East Eleventh Street, New York.
1844	Ithiel Town dies.
1844	Conversion of Middle Dutch Church to Central Post Office, Nassau and Liberty streets, New York.
1845	Involved in selling/shipping of pickles through the Navy Yard.
1847–51	The Arsenal, Fifth Avenue at Sixty-fourth Street (within the present bounds of Central Park), New York. Extant.
1847–50	Serves as New York City Street Commissioner.
1850	3 Front Street, New York.
1850	17 Front Street, New York.
c. 1851	Store at 21 Park Place, New York.
c. 1851	Store 18 Murray Street, New York.
c. 1851	Store at New Street, New York.
1853–64	Living on West Twelfth Street, New York.
1853	Thompson re-erects the monument to the Great Fire of 1835, Wall Street, New York.
1853–54	Hanover Bank, 1 Hanover Square, between Pearl and Stone Streets, New York. Attributed in Thompson's obituary. Extant; presently known as India House.
c. 1864	Thompson moves to Glen Cove, Long Island, after the death of his wife Mary.
1877	Dies on 24 July.

Historic American Buildings Survey Drawings

In 1934, Albert and Caroline Cluett allowed architects from the Historic American Building Survey to document 59 Second Street. Seven sheets of drawings, two photographs and one data sheet were produced. The drawings which follow in this appendix have helped to provide much-needed information about the building during this period. While they do not answer all questions, and in fact have been found to contain some inaccuracies, they are the best evidence for changes that took place after Albert and Caroline Cluett moved into the building in 1910. The 1934 series of photographs (Figs. 126, 128, 130, 132) of the interior of 59 Second Street done by the Boice Studio of Troy for the Cluetts nicely compliment the HABS drawings.

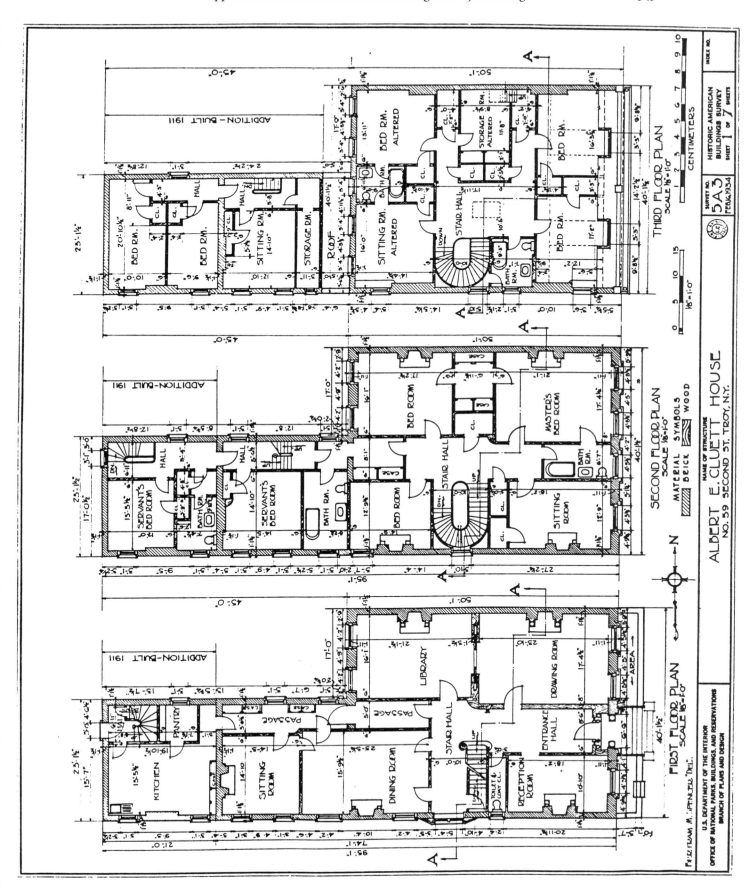

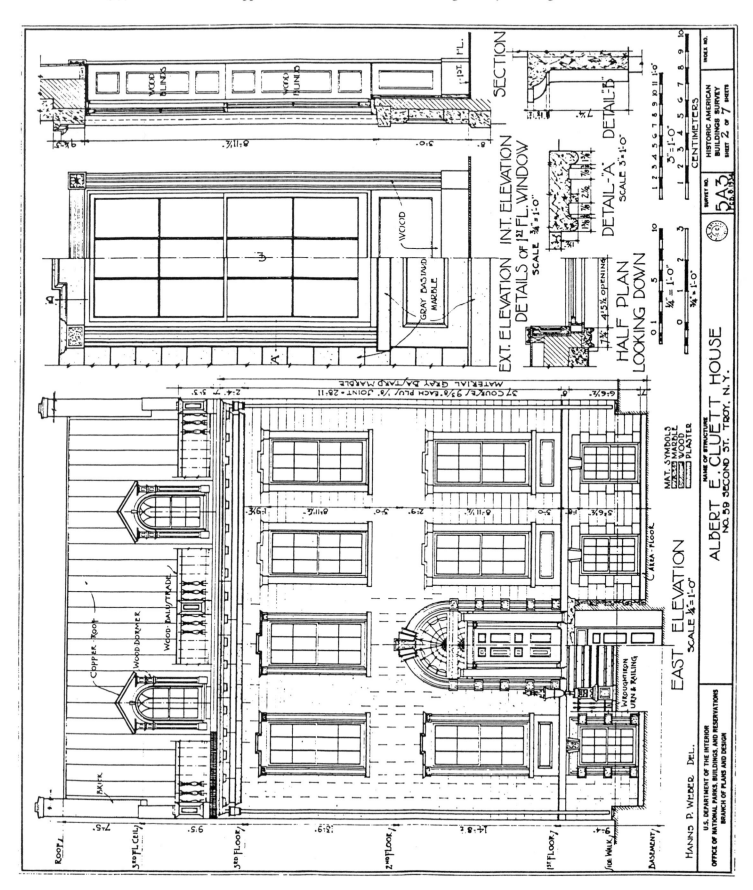

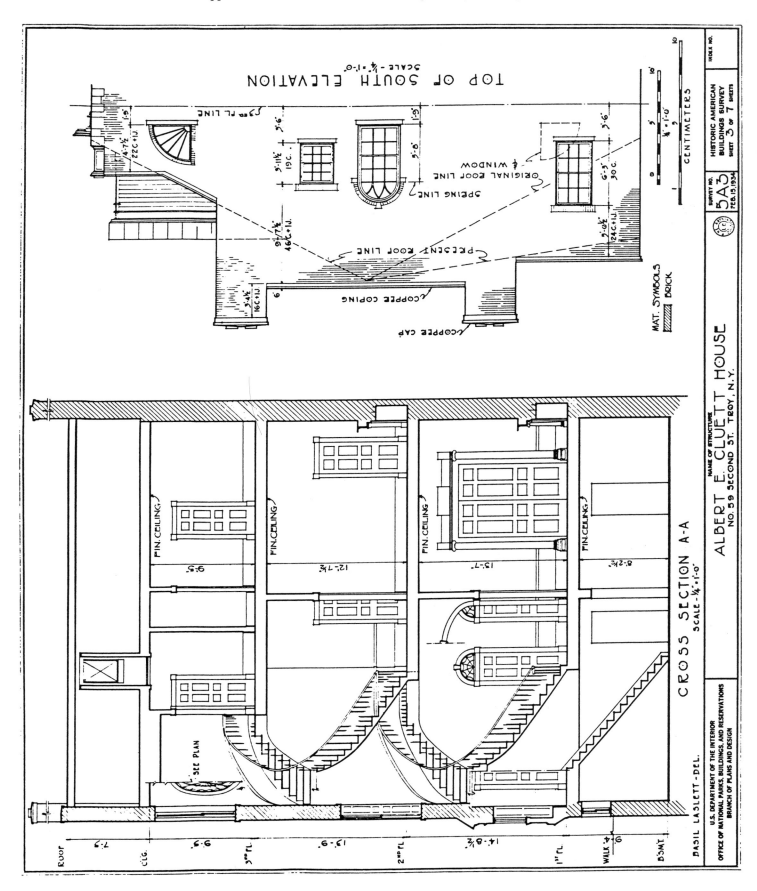

TOP OF SOUTH ELEVATION
SCALE ⅛" = 1'-0"

ORIGINAL ROOF LINE & WINDOW

SPRING LINE

PRESENT ROOF LINE

COPPER COPING

COPPER CAP

MAT. SYMBOLS ▨ BRICK

CENTIMETERS

CROSS SECTION A-A
SCALE ⅛" = 1'-0"

FIN. CEILING

BASIL LASLETT-DEL.

U.S. DEPARTMENT OF THE INTERIOR
OFFICE OF NATIONAL PARKS, BUILDINGS, AND RESERVATIONS
BRANCH OF PLANS AND DESIGN

ALBERT E. CLUETT HOUSE
NO. 59 SECOND ST. TROY, N.Y.

NAME OF STRUCTURE

SURVEY NO. 5A3
FEB. 15, 1934

HISTORIC AMERICAN
BUILDINGS SURVEY
SHEET 3 OF 7 SHEETS

INDEX NO.

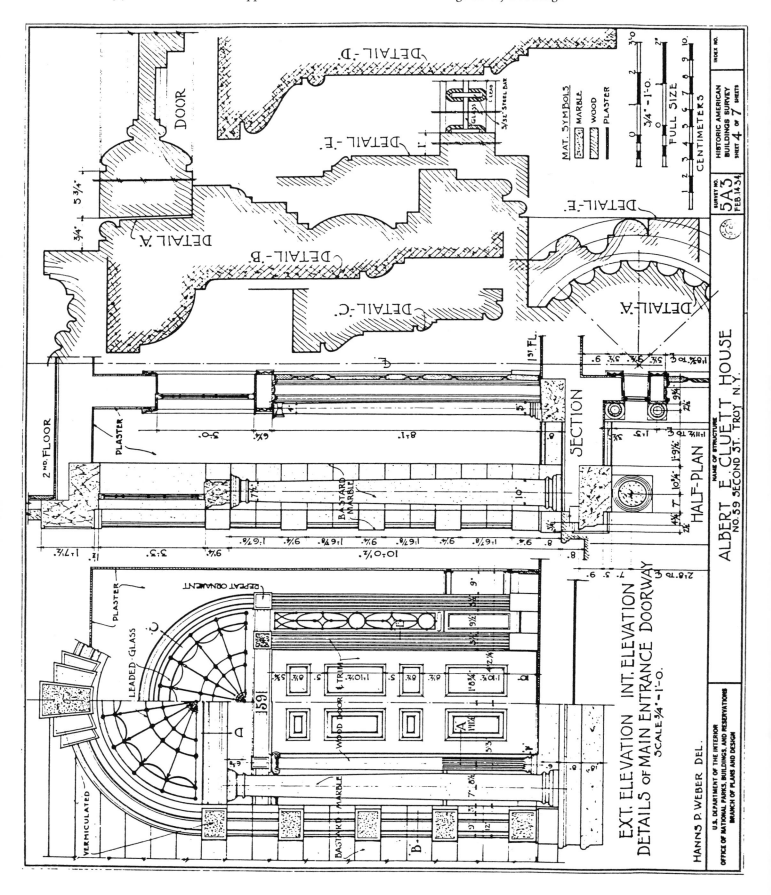

EXT. ELEVATION   INT. ELEVATION
DETAILS of MAIN ENTRANCE DOORWAY
SCALE ¾" = 1'-0.

ALBERT E. CLUETT HOUSE
NO. 59 SECOND ST. TROY N.Y.

HANNS P. WEBER DEL.

U.S. DEPARTMENT OF THE INTERIOR
OFFICE OF NATIONAL PARKS, BUILDINGS, AND RESERVATIONS
BRANCH OF PLANS AND DESIGN

HISTORIC AMERICAN
BUILDINGS SURVEY
SHEET 4 OF 7 SHEETS

SURVEY NO.
5A3
FEB. 14 34

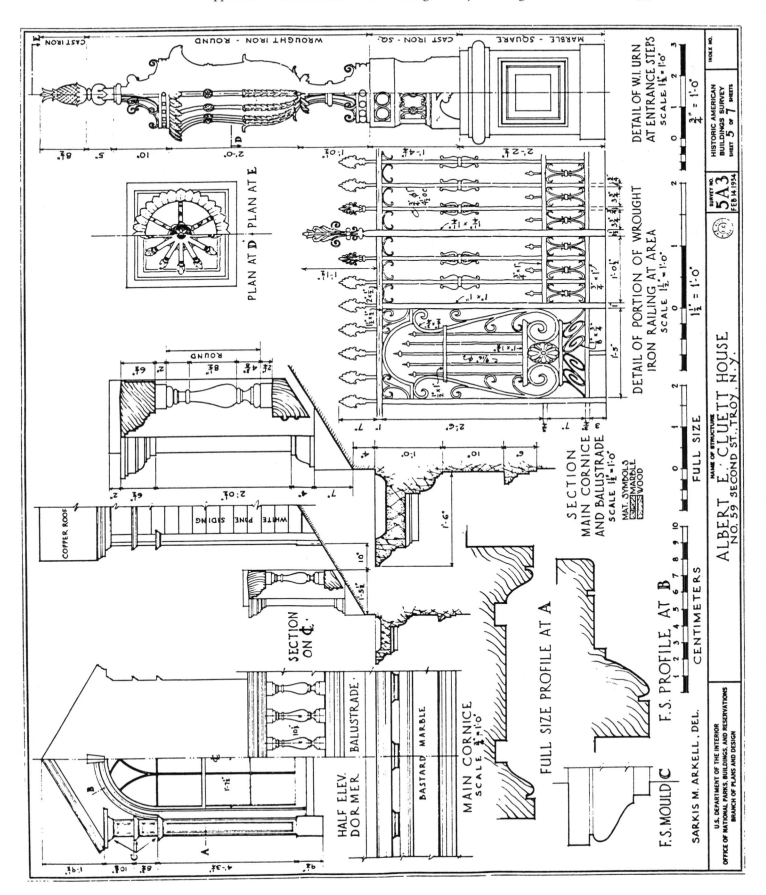

DETAIL OF W.I. URN
AT ENTRANCE STEPS
SCALE 1½" = 1'-0"

DETAIL OF PORTION OF WROUGHT
IRON RAILING AT AREA
SCALE 1½" = 1'-0"

SECTION
MAIN CORNICE
AND BALUSTRADE
SCALE 1½" = 1'-0"

MAT. SYMBOLS
MARBLE
WOOD

PLAN AT D   PLAN AT E

SECTION
ON ℄

HALF ELEV.
DORMER

BALUSTRADE

BASTARD MARBLE

MAIN CORNICE
SCALE ¾" = 1'-0"

FULL SIZE PROFILE AT A

F.S. PROFILE AT B

F.S. MOULD C

COPPER ROOF

WHITE PINE SIDING

FULL SIZE

CENTIMETERS
1 2 3 4 5 6 7 8 9 10

SARKIS M. ARKELL, DEL.

U.S. DEPARTMENT OF THE INTERIOR
OFFICE OF NATIONAL PARKS, BUILDINGS, AND RESERVATIONS
BRANCH OF PLANS AND DESIGN

NAME OF STRUCTURE
ALBERT E. CLUETT HOUSE
NO. 59 SECOND ST., TROY, N.Y.

SURVEY NO.
5A3
FEB 14 1934

HISTORIC AMERICAN
BUILDINGS SURVEY
SHEET 5 OF 7 SHEETS

INDEX NO.

CAST IRON   WROUGHT IRON - ROUND   CAST IRON - SQ.   MARBLE - SQUARE

ROUND

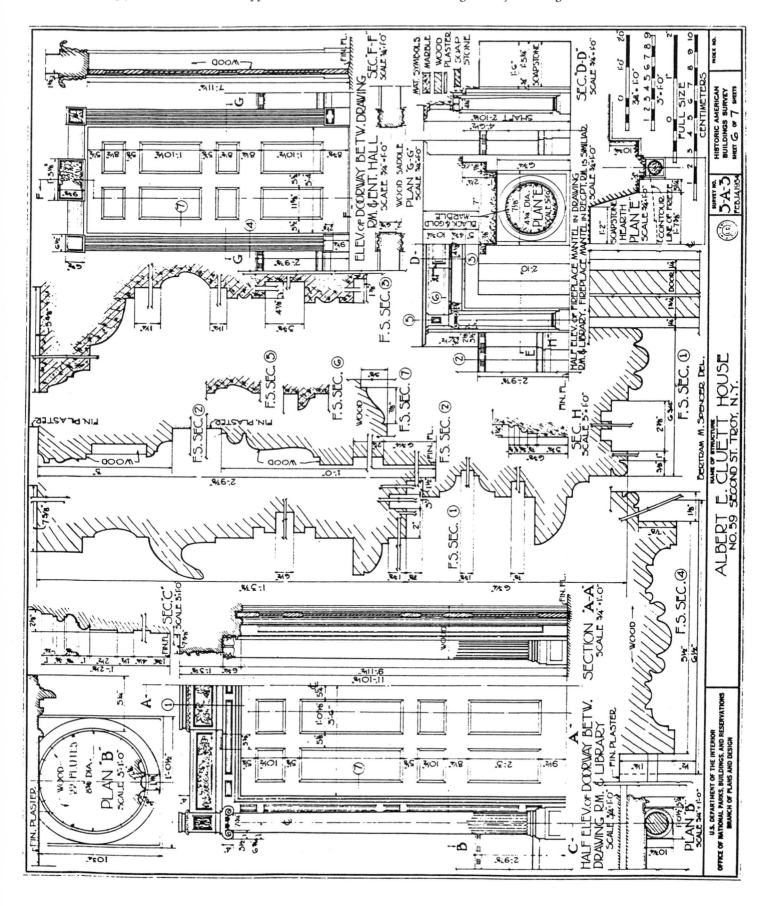

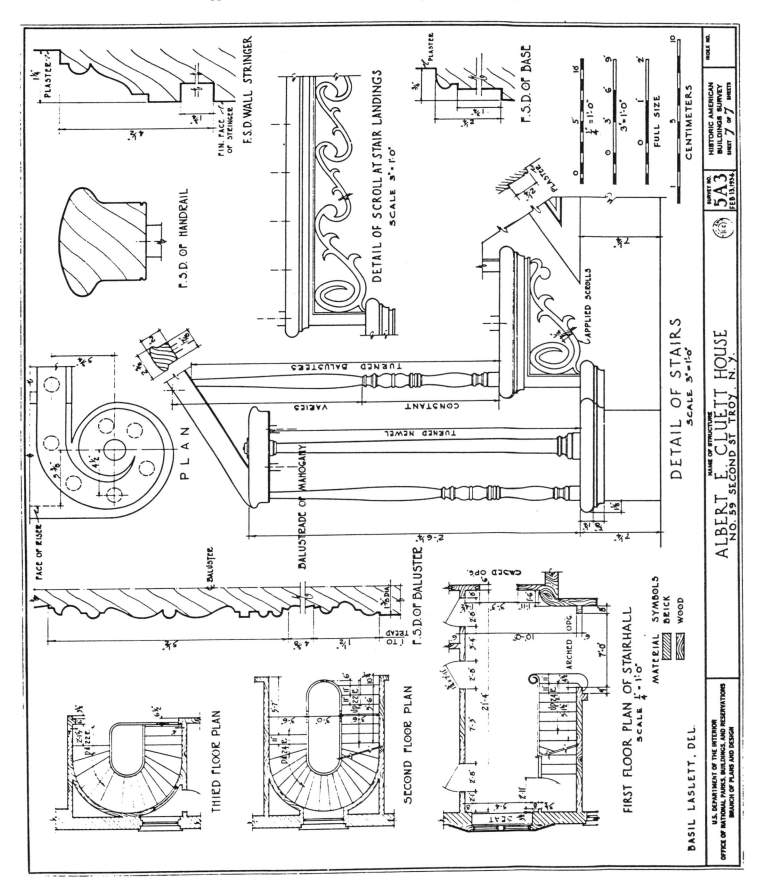

PHOTO CREDITS

Unless otherwise stated below, all images are from the collection of the Rensselaer County Historical Society, Troy, NY.

FIG#(s)	Credit
3, 5, 13, 14, 27, 29, 35, 36, 40, 45	Tom Killips photo.
10, 85	Edward Gale photo.
11	A. Cobden photo.
13, 14	Private collection.
18	New York State Library, Manuscripts & Special Collections, Albany, NY.
24	The George Bolster Collection, Historical Society of Saratoga Springs, NY.
27	Private Collection.
38, 41, 43, 46, 47, 51, 105, 118	S. P. Draper photo.
49	Boice Studio photo.
56	Collection of the New-York Historical Society.
57	The Metropolitan Museum of Art, Bequest of Susan Louise Thompson, 1959.59.68.
58, 64, 67, 69, 73, 82, 93	Avery Architectural and Fine Arts Library, Columbia University in the City of New York.
59	New York Public Library.
A.J. Davis quote (p. 94)	Alexander Jackson Davis Papers, Manuscript and Archives Division, New York Public Library, Astor, Lenox and Tilden Foundations.
60	Museum of the City of New York, NY, NY.
70, 72, 75, 108, 109, 110, 111, 112	W. R. Wheeler photo.
76	The Metropolitan Museum of Art, NY, NY.
78	James Irving photo.
79	Stephen Schreiber photo.
84, 90, 94, 100, 116	Library of Congress, Prints and Photographs Division, Historic America Building Survey, Washington, DC.
88, 95, 103, 140, 144, 145, 150, 152, 155–156, 170, 174, 177, 178, 181, 182, 183, 187–188, 191–193, 195–199, 203–205, 209–211, 213–215, 218	D. G. Bucher photo.
91	Frey photo.
101	Gansevoort–Lansing Collection, Manuscripts and Archives Division, New York Public Library, Astor, Lenox and Tilden Foundations.
113	Collection of Douglas G. Bucher.
117	The Merchant's House Museum, New York, NY.
220–247	John G. Waite Associates, Architects, PLLC Albany, NY.

COMPOSED IN ADOBE MINION TYPE

PRINTED AND BOUND BY THOMSON-SHORE, INC.

BOOK DESIGN BY CHRISTOPHER KUNTZE